Male Stickleback (*Gasterosteus aculeatus*) building a nest

J. R. NORMAN

A HISTORY OF
FISHES

SECOND EDITION BY

P. H. GREENWOOD D.Sc.

British Museum (Natural History)

ILLUSTRATIONS BY

W. P. C. TENISON

LONDON · ERNEST BENN LIMITED · 1963

Published by Ernest Benn Limited
Bouverie House · Fleet Street · London · EC4

First Edition 1931
Second Impression 1936
Third Impression 1947
Fourth Impression 1951
Fifth (Corrected) Impression 1958
Sixth (Corrected) Impression 1960
Second (Revised) Edition 1963

© *M. Norman and P. H. Greenwood 1963*

Printed in the Netherlands

A HISTORY OF
FISHES

TO
MY FRIEND AND COLLEAGUE
C. D. SHERBORN

PREFACE TO SECOND EDITION

DURING the thirty years since this book first appeared, the public for whom it was written has expanded almost as much as has our knowledge of the fishes themselves. In the same period the professional ichthyologist has become increasingly specialised in his interests and there is a real danger of communications between him and the public becoming even more tenuous. Norman's book is a valuable link across the gulf. The wide-ranging questions about fishes that Norman had to answer when he was a curator still flow into the Museum, but there is this difference in the situation: questioners can now be referred to 'A History of Fishes'. Norman's hope "that it will provide solutions to these (the varied questions) and other problems" (Preface to the Ist. Edition) has been fully realised.

Revising this book, which its author recognised as being planned on original lines, has not been easy for that very reason. The originality of Norman's approach lay in his treatment of fishes as living creatures and not merely as museum specimens. It is in our knowledge of fish biology that the greatest advances have been made since 1931. Thus, older ideas had to be corrected and brought into line with evidence from other fields of research, and the new ideas incorporated as well. But if these developments are to be fully appreciated the reader must still have the basic information on anatomy and physiology. My greatest battle has been to preserve the balance between these different aspects. In other fields too, especially that dealing with fossil fishes, great changes have taken place and this has led to disagreement amongst the authorities on the way the new findings should be interpreted; I have tried to include these facets as well. Naturally, the presentation of condensed information gives an impression of dogmatism, and many subjects must be presented in a dangerously oversimplified manner; I can only plead that lack of space has dictated these steps.

Like Norman, I have been concerned with the arrangement of the chapters, and particularly whether or not to start with a chapter on the principles of classification, from there leading on to an outline scheme of the way in which fishes are classified. Ultimately I decided to follow Norman and keep this chapter towards the end of the book; for those who would start with these subjects, then Chapter 18 is their Chapter I. For those who keep to the published order of chapters some explanation of the scientific names and classificatory groups used in the text may be helpful. Behind the common name of a fish, at least when it is first used in a chapter, the generic or specific name is given in italics; in other instances the order or family to which the fish belongs is used, these words being in Roman type. The family name is recognised by its ending in -*idae*, whilst the ordinal name ends in -*formes*, and that of the suborder in -*oidei*.

As in the first edition, the emphasis is put on the living fish, its feeding habits and food, its breeding habits, the way in which it swims, the manner in which it is adapted to meet the usual conditions of life, and those special adaptations shown by others which live in less ordinary environments. As far as possible these different aspects are treated together with the relevant anatomical and physiological background. However, complete descriptive integration of form and function is impossible in a book of this kind so some chapters must be more restricted in their content. Where possible cross-references are given in the text but the reader is still advised to use the index when tracking down the information wanted.

The originally double chapter on 'Fishes and Mankind' is here presented as a single unit. I have done this by cutting out most of the statistics relating to world fisheries. The figures are, I know, interesting but they are inevitably out of date even before publication. Furthermore, fishery statistics are nowadays more readily available through the numerous publications issued by the Food and Agricultural Organisation (F.A.O.) of the United Nations. Other deletions from this chapter are concerned with the culinary side of ichthyology, a subject adequately covered by books more likely to appeal to the housewife than will this volume.

As in earlier impressions the text figures are the work of Lt.Col. W. P. C. Tenison; I was extremely fortunate in being able to have the services of this artist, whose figures are now so widely known and reproduced. Most of the drawings illustrating the chapter on fossil fishes have been made anew for this second edition. I, like Norman before me must offer my sincere thanks to Lt.Col. Tenison for the skill and care he has shown in the preparation of the illustrations, both new and old.

A new feature of this edition is the inclusion of short bibliographies for each chapter. These are, of course, additional to the general reading list which follows the last chapter. The papers and books cited are ones which give a recent and synoptic treatment of the subject discussed. In most cases the literature given is readily available in or from libraries and museums.

I am greatly indebted to all those (and not least of all to J. R. Norman himself) who helped in the preparation of the first edition. In my case the debt is a double one. First because these people helped to produce a book which gave me my first broad insight into the subject which now so happily occupies my life, and also because their efforts have eased my task of revising this book.

Many of my colleagues in the Natural History Museum have assisted me with the preparation of this revised edition; I am particularly grateful to Dr. Ethelwynn Trewavas, Mr. N. B. Marshall, Mr. G. Palmer and Mr. A. C. Wheeler. Their views and advice have often been sought and have readily been given; naturally, I hold them in no way responsible for any errors I have made or allowed to be perpetuated. Finally I thank Mrs. Brenda Hudson who has spent many hours checking through the typescript and proofs.

LONDON, 1962   P. H. GREENWOOD

PREFACE TO FIRST EDITION

IN THE course of my work at the British Museum I am called upon from time to time to supply answers to all kinds of strange questions, some of them but remotely connected with fishes themselves. How fast does a fish swim? How many fishes are there in the sea? Why does a fish die when taken from the water? Where did fishes first come from? To what age does the average fish live? Can a fish think or feel pain? (A favourite query from the angler!) What is Rock Salmon? Are we depleting the stocks of fishes in the sea by over-fishing? It is in the hope that it will provide solutions to these and other problems that the present work has been written, and, believing that it has been planned on more or less original lines, I feel that no apology is needed for its publication. At the same time, it is hoped that it will serve as more than a mere book of reference—a storehouse of facts—and will prove of sufficient interest to provide general reading, not only for the student of fishes and the angler, but for all those who take an intelligent interest in wild life.

The customary method of dealing with any group of animals is to begin with a recognised scheme of classification, and to take up each of the smaller groups in turn, describing the main distinguishing features of some of the better-known members of each group, their mode of life, food, distribution, and so on. Sometimes one or two chapters devoted to the anatomy, development, etc., of the animals precede the more general part, but, as a rule, these subjects are omitted altogether or dismissed in a few lines. In the following pages I have tried to give some idea of the story of fish life in all its varied aspects, to show how the fishes "live and move and have their being." In one chapter the manner in which they swim is considered; in another their food; in another their breeding habits, their development, and so on. Many different kinds of fishes are mentioned in illustration of one point or another, and some inevitably figure in more than one chapter. Special stress has been laid throughout on the evolutionary aspect of fish life, the fishes themselves being regarded, not as museum specimens or corpses on the fishmonger's slab, but as living organisms which have been modified in a multitude of different ways in accordance with the nature of their surroundings, in order to fit them for the particular conditions under which they are compelled to live. The importance of the part played by the "struggle for existence" in moulding the bodies of fishes will be apparent, and I have endeavoured to show how many of the remarkable modifications of the various organs which go to make up the body of a fish, although sometimes meaningless at first sight, may be readily interpreted in terms of environment, animate or inanimate.

The relation of fishes to the life of mankind has not been neglected, and chapters dealing with the fisheries, fishing methods, fishery research and so on have also been included. The enormous development of our own sea fisheries towards the close of the last century led to a great interest being taken in the habits, and particularly in the feeding and spawning habits, of the edible species. Much important research has been carried out on these problems during recent years, but the results are mostly buried away in scientific journals not readily accessible to the public, who remain largely in ignorance of the work which is being continuously done in order to maintain or improve the harvest of the sea.

In preparing this work I have drawn on my knowledge of the vast literature of the various branches of the science of ichthyology, and have consequently consulted a large number of works of a technical nature, some of them in foreign languages, not available to the general reader. It would, of course, be of little value to include a bibliography of such works here, but a short list of the more important and accessible books of reference on fishes and kindred subjects in the English tongue is appended for the convenience of those who may wish to pursue the subject further.

The use of technicalities has been avoided as far as possible, and scientific terms have been included only where their omission would be at the expense of clarity. It has seemed to me convenient, however, to refer to each fish by its scientific name (usually only the generic name, but occasionally the specific name as well) in addition to that by which it is popularly known, except in the case of lesser-known species for which there are no vernacular appellations. In the legends below the figures the name of the species is nearly always given in full.

Regarding the illustrations, the figures in the text are, with very few exceptions, new, and have all been drawn specially for this work by my friend Lieut.-Col. W. P. C. Tenison. I take this opportunity of offering him my sincere thanks, not only for the great care that he has taken in their preparation, but also for the kindly interest he has shown in the book since its inception. We have been content to make the drawings as simple as possible, believing that it is better to show the salient and characteristic features of the fishes rather than to produce an artistic effect. Those illustrations copied from other works are duly acknowledged in their place, and I am especially indebted to Mr. Arthur Hutton, Professor F. B. Sumner, and to Professor Johannes Schmidt, for permission to reproduce the photographs appearing in plates I, II and IV respectively.

It only remains for me to tender my grateful thanks to my colleague Mr. M. Burton for the trouble he has taken in reading through the greater part of the manuscript, and for many helpful suggestions and criticisms; to Dr. E. I. White, for reading and criticising Chapter XVII; to Dr. E. S. Russell, O.B.E., for performing a like service in connection with parts of Chapters XIX and XX; and to Mrs. Tenison for assistance in the task of passing the proofs for press. Finally, I find it impossible to allow this opportunity to pass without recording the great debt which I owe to Dr. C. Tate Regan, F.R.S., the Director of the British Museum (Natural History); his very great knowledge of matters ichthyological has always been at my disposal, and the many valuable hints and suggestions that he has given me from time to time since my appointment to the museum have proved of the greatest assistance to me in my work there, and without them it is certain that the writing of this book would have proved a very difficult task.

LONDON, 1931   J. R. NORMAN

CONTENTS

PREFACE TO SECOND EDITION   VII

PREFACE TO FIRST EDITION   XI

1	INTRODUCTORY	1
2	FORM AND LOCOMOTION	7
3	FINS	27
4	SKIN, SCALES AND SPINES	52
5	RESPIRATION	69
6	MOUTH AND JAWS	88
7	TEETH AND FOOD	102
8	INTERNAL ORGANS	119
9	NERVOUS SYSTEM, SENSE ORGANS AND SENSES	136
10	VENOM, ELECTRICITY, LIGHT AND SOUND	160
11	COLORATION	176
12	CONDITIONS OF LIFE	194
13	BREEDING	213
14	PAIRING, COURTSHIP AND PARENTAL CARE	227
15	DEVELOPMENT	246
16	DISTRIBUTION	266
17	FOSSILS AND PEDIGREES	293
18	CLASSIFICATION	318
19	FISHES AND MANKIND	334
20	MYTHS AND LEGENDS	361

LIST OF BOOKS   371

INDEX   373

LIST OF PLATES

Male Stickleback (*Gasterosteus aculeatus*) building a nest   *Frontispiece*
     Photograph by Geoffrey Kinns

I   Scales of the Salmon (*Salmo salar*)   *facing page*   68
      By permission of Mr. J. A. Hutton

II   (A–B) Colour changes in a Mediterranean Flat-
      fish (*Bothus podas*)   *between pages* 186–7
      By permission of Professor F. B. Sumner

III   Cocoon of African Lung-fish (*Protopterus annectens*)
      embedded in mud   *facing page*   206
      Photograph by Mr. W. H. T. Tams

IV   Stages in the metamorphosis of the larval
      European Eel (*Anguilla anguilla*)   262
      By permission of Dr. Johannes Schmidt

V   Stages in the metamorphosis of the Plaice
      (*Pleuronectes platessa*)   264
      Photograph by Mr. H. H. Goodchild

VI   Slab of chalk (Sussex) with remains of *Hoplopteryx*
      superbus   296

VII   (a) A downpour of fishes in Scandinavia; (b)
      Fishing with the Remora; (c) The great Sea
      Serpent   364

LIST OF ILLUSTRATIONS

Page

1 CETACEAN AND FISH COMPARED
A. Common Dolphin (*Delphinus delphis*); B. Mackerel Shark
(*Isurus oxyrhynchus*). Both much reduced — 2

2 PECTORAL LIMB OF CETACEAN AND FISH COMPARED
A. Skeleton of paddle of Common Dolphin (*Delphinus
delphis*); B. Pectoral girdle and fin of a Bony fish. Both
greatly reduced — 3

3 ANIMALS OF FISH-LIKE FORM
Upper: An Ichthyosaur, an extinct reptile. Lower: Dolphin,
a mammal. Both much reduced — 4

4 A SWIFT PELAGIC FISH
Oceanic Bonito (*Katsuwonus pelamis*) x $^1/_8$ — 7

5 DIFFERENCES IN FORM
A. Mackerel (*Scomber scombrus*) x $^1/_4$; B. Trunkfish (*Tetrosomus
gibbosus*) x $^1/_4$; C. Sunfish (*Mola mola*) x $^1/_{25}$; D. Globefish
(*Chilomycterus antennatus*) x $^1/_4$; E. Seahorse (*Hippocampus* sp.)
x $^1/_2$; F. Common Eel (*Anguilla anguilla*) x $^1/_8$ — 8

6 SWORD-FISHES
A. Sail-fish (*Istiophorus americanus*); B. Spear-fish (*Makaira
audax*); C. Sword-fish (*Xiphias gladius*) — 9

7 TOPOGRAPHY OF FINS — 10

8 FLATTENED FISHES
A. Female Thornback Ray (*Raia clavata*) x $^1/_{12}$; B. Flounder
(*Platichthys flesus*) x $^1/_6$; C. Angelfish (*Pterophyllum scalare*) x $^1/_4$;
D. Oarfish or Ribbonfish (*Regalecus glesne*) x ca $^1/_{25}$ — 11

9 BODY MOVEMENTS OF A SWIMMING FISH (After Gray) — 16

10 BODY MOVEMENTS OF FISHES USED IN SWIMMING
Shark (above); Eel (below). After Marey — 18

11 FIN MOVEMENTS USED BY FISHES IN SWIMMING
A. Bow-fin (*Amia calva*) x $^1/_{10}$; B. Electric Eel (*Electrophorus
electricus*) x $^1/_8$; C. File-fish (*Monacanthus* sp.) x $^1/_4$; D. Ray
(*Raia* sp.) x $^1/_8$. (After Breder) — 20

12 A FISH WHICH SWIMS UPRIGHT
A small shoal of Shrimpfishes (*Aeoliscus strigatus*) x $^1/_2$
(After Willey) — 23

13 A FISH WHICH SWIMS UPSIDE DOWN
Cat fish (*Synodontis batensoda*) x $^1/_2$ — 24

14 FISHES THAT LEAP
A. Devilfish (*Manta birostris*) x ca $^1/_{50}$; B. Tarpon (*Megalops
atlanticus*) x ca $^1/_{25}$; C. Salmon (*Salmo salar*) x $^1/_{12}$; D. Grey
Mullet (*Mugil* sp.) x $^1/_{10}$ — 24

Page

15   STRUCTURE OF DORSAL AND ANAL FINS
      A. First dorsal fin of Mackerel Shark (*Isurus oxyrhynchus*),
      dissected to show cartilaginous supports; B. Anal fin of
      Chinese Sturgeon (*Psephurus gladius*), similarly dissected;
      C. Skeleton of dorsal and anal fins, and portion of vertebral
      column of Gar Pike (*Lepisosteus platystomus*).   *b*., basal
      cartilages; *f.r.*, fin-rays; *i. sp.*, interspinous bones; *r*., radial
      cartilages.   28

16   STRUCTURE OF PECTORAL FINS
      A. *Cladoselache fyleri.* (After Dean); B. *Pleuracanthus decheni.*
      (After Fritsch); C. Australian Lung-fish (*Neoceratodus
      forsteri*); D. Cod (*Gadus morhua*)   30

17   STRUCTURE OF CAUDAL FINS
      A. Sturgeon (*Acipenser* sp.); B. Ten-pounder (*Elops saurus*);
      C. Haddock (*Melanogrammus aeglifinus*); Sun-fish (*Mola mola*)   32

18   DORSAL AND ANAL FINS
      a. Sea Lamprey (*Petromyzon marinus*) x ¹/₁₀; *b*. Cod (*Gadus
      morhua*) x ¹/₁₀; *c*. Bow-fin (*Amia calva*) x ¹/₈; *d*. Wels or
      Sheat-fish (*Silurus glanis*) x ¹/₁₂; *e*. Sea Perch or Grouper
      (*Epinephelus* sp.) x ¹/₁₀; *f*. Stickleback (*Gasterosteus aculeatus*)
      x ¹/₂; *g*. Cardinal-fish (*Apogon frenatus*) x ¹/₄; *h*. Moorish Idol
      (*Zanclus canescens*) x ¹/₄; *j*. Sail-bearer (*Velifer* sp.) x ¹/₅;
      k. Flat-fish (*Engyprosopon grandisquama*) x ¹/₃; *m*. Bichir
      (*Polypterus bichir*) x ¹/₈   35

19   LOCKING FIN-SPINES
      A. Shoulder girdle and pectoral fin spines of a South American
      Catfish (*Doras* sp), ventral view, x ²/₃; B. Dorsal fin-spines
      and associated bones of a Triggerfish (*Balistes* sp.), lateral
      view, x ²/₃   37

20   A MODIFIED DORSAL FIN
      Remora or Sucking-fish (*Remora remora*), x ¹/₆   40

21   CERATIOID ANGLER-FISHES
      A. *Linophryne arborifer*, x ¹/₂; B. *Melanocetus johnsoni*, x ¹/₂;
      C. *Lasiognathus saccostoma*, x 1   41

22   CAUDAL FINS
      A. Fox-shark or Thresher (*Alopias vulpes*), x ¹/₂₅; B. Sting Ray
      (*Dasyatis lata*), ¹/₂₅; C. Frilled Shark (*Chlamydoselachus
      anguineus*), x ¹/₁₀; D. Allis Shad (*Alosa alosa*), x ¹/₄; E. Pipe-fish
      (*Microphis boaja*), x ¹/₃; F. Mailed Cat-fish (*Loricaria apelto-
      gaster*), x ¹/₄; G. Snipe Eel (*Nemichthys scolopaceus*), x ¹/₅;
      H. Black-fish (*Dallia pectoralis*), x ²/₅   42

23   SHAPES OF CAUDAL FIN
      A. Lunate or crescentic; B. forked; C. emarginate; D. truncate;
      E. rounded; F. pointed; G. double emarginate   44

24   PECTORAL FINS
      a. Eagle Ray (*Myliobatis freminvillii*), x ¹/₂₀; *b*. Spotted
      Dog-fish (*Scyliorhinus canicula*), x ¹/₈; *c*. Tunny (*Thunnus*

Page

thynnus), x $^1/_{30}$; *d*. Thread-fin (*Polynemus paradiseus*), x $^1/_8$; *e*. Fresh-water Sun-fish (*Lepomis megalotis*), x $^1/_4$; *f*. Mud-skipper (*Periophthalmus koelreuteri*), x $^1/_4$; *g*. Scorpion-fish (*Pterois volitans*), x $^1/_{10}$; *h*. Cirrhitid (*Paracirrhites forsteri*), x $^1/_5$; *j*. Flying-fish (*Exocoetus volitans*), x $^1/_8$; *k*. South American Cat-fish (*Doras* sp.), x$^1/_3$; *m*. Gurnard (*Trigla* sp.), x $^1/_{10}$ 45

25   FISHES WITH VENTRAL SUCKERS
A. Lump-sucker (*Cyclopterus lumpus*), x $^1/_4$; B. Cling-fish (*Lepadogaster gouani*), x $^1/_3$; C. Bornean Sucker (*Gastromyzon borneensis*), x $^1/_3$; D. Lower surface of Black Goby (*Gobius niger*), x $^1/_2$ 50

26   DERMAL DENTICLES
a. Isolated denticles of the Spotted Dog-fish (*Scyliorhinus canicula*); greatly enlarged; *b*. Diagrammatic cross-section of a denticle of a Selachian, showing the enamel covering and the central pulp cavity; greatly enlarged; *c*. Portion of skin with dermal denticles of the Bramble Shark (*Echinorhinus spinosus*), x $^1/_2$; *d*. "Buckler" of Thornback Ray (*Raia clavata*), lateral and dorsal view, x $^3/_4$; *e*. Tail-spine of Sting Ray (*Dasyatis* sp.), x $^1/_3$ 53

27   DEVELOPMENT OF DENTICLES AND SCALES
A. Semidiagrammatic section through the skin of an embryo Shark (After Gegenbaur); B. Diagrammatic longitudinal section through the skin of a Bony Fish to show position of scales (After Boas). *d*. Dermis; *e*. Epidermis   54

28   Saw-fish (*Pristis zijsron*), x $^1/_{20}$ 55

29   SCALES
a. Portion of skin and isolated scales of the Gar Pike (*Lepisosteus* sp.), x about 1; *b*. The same of the Bichir (*Polypterus bichir*), x $^1/_2$; *c*. Isolated scute of large Sturgeon (*Acipenser* sp.), x $^1/_6$; *d*. Cycloid scale of Tarpon (*Megalops atlanticus*), x $^1/_4$; *e*. Ctenoid scale of Soldier-fish (*Holocentrus ascensionis*), x 8   56

30   SCALES
A. Palaeoniscoid scale; B. Cosmoid scale. *Bo*., bone base; *Co*., Cosmine layer; *Ga*., Ganoine in A., enamel in B; *Ip*., Isopedine layer; *Sb*., layer of spongy bone. (After Goodrich)   57

31   FISHES WITH TUBERCLES
A. Diamond Flounder (*Platichthys stellatus*), x $^1/_4$; B. Black Sea Turbot (*Scophthalmus maeoticus*), x $^1/_8$; C. Japanese Flounder (*Kareius bicoloratus*), x $^1/_4$; D. Bat-fish. (*Ogcocephalus vespertilio*), x $^1/_4$ 60

32   FISHES WITH SCUTES
A. Sturgeon (*Acipenser sturio*), x $^1/_8$; B. Pampano or Carangid (*Caranx* sp.), x $^1/_4$; C. Unicorn-fish (*Naso brevirostris*), x $^1/_8$; D. South American Cat-fish (*Megalodoras irwini*), x $^1/_4$; E. Three-spined Stickleback (*Gasterosteus aculeatus*), x $^1/_2$ 61

33 ARMOURED FISHES
A. Hassar or Cascadura (*Hoplosternum littorale*), x ¹/₄;
B. Pogge or Armoured Bullhead (*Agonus cataphractus*), x ¹/₄;
c. Mailed Cat-fish (*Plecostomus garmani*), x ¹/₈; D. Trigger-fish
(*Balistes carolinensis*), x ¹/₄; E. Pine-cone Fish (*Monocentrus
japonicus*), x ¹/₄; F. Trunk-fish (*Lactophrys trigonus*), x ¹/₄;
G. Porcupine-fish (*Diodon hystrix*), x ¹/₈; H. Shrimp-fish or
Needle-fish (*Aeoliscus strigatus*), x ¹/₂   63

34 Carp (*Cyprinus carpio*), x ¹/₆. To show arrangement of scales   65

35 LATERAL LINES
a. Parrot-fish (*Scarus* sp.), x ¹/₈; b. Greenling (*Hexagrammos
stelleri*), x ¹/₂; c. Bream (*Abramis brama*), x ¹/₄; d. Viviparous
Perch (*Hysterocarpus traski*), x ¹/₄; e. American Flounder
(*Paralichthys dentatus*), x ¹/₈; f. Tongue Sole (*Cynoglossus
versicolor*), x ¹/₄   66

36 GILLS OF SHARK AND BONY FISH COMPARED
A. Dissection of head of Spotted Dog-fish (*Scyliorhinus* sp.)
seen from below x ¹/₂; B. The same of Salmon (*Salmo salar*),
x ¹/₂; g.a., gill-arch; g.c., external gill-cleft; g.f., gill-filaments;
g.o., external opening of gill chamber; ph., pharyngeal
opening; sp., spiracle   71

37 EXTERNAL GILL OPENINGS
A. Spotted Dog-fish (*Scyliorhinus* sp.), x ¹/₄; B.1, B.2. Thornback Ray (*Raia clavata*), x ¹/₆; c. Rabbit-fish (*Chimaera
monstrosa*), x ¹/₅; D. Trout (*Salmo trutta*), x ¹/₄; g.c., external
gill-clefts of Selachians; g.o.p., external opening gill chamber
in Chimaeras and Bony Fishes; n., nostril; sp., spiracle   73

38 GILLS OF CYCLOSTOMES
Dissection of anterior part of Hag-fish (*Myxine glutinosa*), x 1   74

39 CROSS-SECTIONS OF GILL ARCHES IN DIFFERENT FISHES
A. Typical Selachian; B. Chimaera; c. Sturgeon (*Acipenser*);
D, E. Bony Fishes. Gill-arch (dots); interbranchial septum
(white); gill-filaments (cross lines). (After Boas)   75

40 GILL RAKERS
A. Gill-arch of Allis Shad (*Alosa alosa*); B. The same of
Twaite Shad (*Alosa fallax*); c. The same of Perch (*Perca
fluviatilis*); D. Isolated gill-rakers of Basking Shark (*Cetorhinus
maximus*). All about ²/₃   76

41 EXTERNAL GILLS
A.1. Young South American Lung-fish (*Lepidosiren paradoxa*),
30 days after hatching, x 3; A.2. The same 40 days after
hatching, x 2; B. Young Bichir (*Polypterus* sp.), x 1¹/₂   77

42 ACCESSORY BREATHING ORGANS
A. Dissection of head of Climbing Perch (*Anabas testudinosus*);
B. The same of an Indian Cat-fish (*Heteropneustes fossilis*);
c. The same of an African Cat-fish (*Clarias lazera*). All about
natural size.   81

Page

43 FISHES THAT CAN LIVE OUT OF WATER
A. Snake-head (*Ophiocephalus striatus*), x ¹/₃; B. Cuchia (*Amphipnous cuchia*), x ¹/₈; *g.op.*, opening to gill chamber 83

44 SWIMBLADDER AND LUNG
A series of diagrams showing the relation of the swimbladder or lung to the oesophagus in different fishes, as seen in cross-section (left-hand column) and from the side. (After Dean) 85

45 INFERIOR AND SUCTORIAL MOUTHS
A. Opened mouth of the Sea Lamprey (*Petromyzon marinus*), x ¹/₃; B. Lower surface of head of Spotted Dog-fish (*Scyliorhinus canicula*), x ¹/₃; C. The same of Sturgeon (*Acipenser rubicundus*), x ¹/₃; D. The same of Mailed Cat-fish (*Plecostomus plecostomus*), x ¹/₃ 89

46 CARTILAGINOUS AND BONY JAWS
A. Lateral view of skull of Spotted Dog-fish (*Scyliorhinus* sp.), x ¹/₃; B. The same of Ten-pounder (*Elops saurus*), x ¹/₂; C. Lower surface of skull of Pike (*Esox lucius*), x ¹/₄; *br.1.*, first branchial arch; *hym.*, hyomandibula; *l.jaw.*, lower jaw; *mk.*, Meckel's cartilage; *mx.*, maxillary; *pal.*, palatine; *pmx.*, premaxillary; *ptq.*, pterygoquadrate; *smx.*, supramaxillary 91

47 DIFFERENT KINDS OF MOUTHS
A. Head of Elephant Mormyrid (*Gnathonemus elephas*), x ¹/₂; B. Of Gar-fish (*Tylosurus* sp)., x ¹/₄; C. Of Half-beak (*Hyporhampus unifasciatus*), x ¹/₂; D. Of Thick-lipped Mojarra (*Cichlasoma lobochilus*), x ¹/₂; E. Of Star-Gazer (*Uranoscopus oligolepis*), x ¹/₄; F. Butterfly-fish (*Chelmon longirostris*), x ¹/₂; G. Of Spoonbill or Paddle-fish (*Polyodon spathula*), x ¹/₄ 94

48 Long-nosed Gar Pike (*Lepisosteus osseus*), x ¹/₈ 96

49 A. Head of Flute-mouth or Tobacco-pipe Fish (*Fistularia tabacaria*), x ¹/₆; B. Head of John Dory (*Zeus faber*), with the mouth retracted and protruded, x ¹/₃; C. Skull of Large-mouthed Wrasse (*Epibulus insidiator*), with the jaws retracted and protruded, x ¹/₃; D. *Saccopharynx*; skull and vertebral column showing the changes taking place when the mouth is opened (right). x ¹/₃. (After Tchernavin, simplified; not all bones are shown.) 99

50 A. Cross-section through the lower jaw of an embryo Dog-fish (*Scyliorhinus* sp.), showing the gradual transition from dermal denticles (*d*) on the outer surface to teeth (*t*) on the inner surface. The dotted area in the centre represents the cartilage of the lower jaw. Greatly enlarged. (After Gegenbaur); B. Cross-section through the lower jaw of Sand Shark (*Carcharias taurus*), showing succession of teeth, x ¹/₂ 103

51 TEETH OF SHARKS AND RAYS
A. Inner view of lower jaw in White Cheeked Shark (*Eulamia dussumieri*), x ¹/₄; B. Lower jaw of Nurse Shark (*Gingly-*

Page

mostoma sp.), x ¹/₄; c. Jaws of Guitar-fish (*Rhina ancyclostoma*),
x ¹/₆; D. Jaws of Eagle Ray (*Myliobatis aquila*), x ¹/₄   104

52   SHARK TEETH
a. Tooth of Great White Shark (*Carcharodon carcharias*), x ¹/₃;
b. Of Tiger Shark (*Galeocerdo cuvieri*), x ²/₃; *c*. Of Comb-
toothed Shark (*Hexanchus griseus*), x ²/₃; *d*. Of Sand Shark
(*Carcharias taurus*), x ²/₃   105

53   ELFIN AND PORT JACKSON SHARKS
A. Elfin or Goblin Shark (*Mitsukurina owstoni*), x ¹/₃₀;
(*a*, isolated teeth of same); B. Port Jackson Shark (*Heterodontus phillippi*), x ¹/₂₀; (*b*, lower jaw of same)   106

54   PHARYNGEAL TEETH
A. Ventral view of skull and dorsal view of hyo-branchial
skeleton and lower jaw of Wrasse (*Labrus* sp.), showing
position of pharyngeal bones, x ¹/₂; B. Vertical section of
skull of Bow-fin (*Amia calva*), showing position of pharyngeals,
x ¹/₄; c. Lower pharyngeals of Carp (*Cyprinus carpio*), x ¹/₂,
p. pharyngeal bones   110

55   CARNIVOROUS FISHES
a. Cynodon scomberoides, x ¹/₈; *b. Chauliodus sloanei*, x ¹/₅;
c. Blue-fish (*Pomatomus saltatrix*), x ¹/₈; *d.* Barracuda (*Sphyraena barracuda*), x ¹/₅   111

56   JAWS AND TEETH
A. Skull of Rabbit-fish (*Chimaera monstrosa*), x ¹/₃; B. Jaws of
Parrot-fish (*Pseudoscarus* sp.), x ¹/₄; c. Skull of Caribe or
Piraya (*Serrasalmus* sp.), x ¹/₄; D. Head of Grey Mullet
(*Mugil* sp.), x ¹/₂; E. Head of Wide-mouth (*Haplostomias
tentaculatus*), x ¹/₂; F. Head of Lancet-fish (*Alepisaurus ferox*),
x ¹/₄   112

57   Archer-fish (*Toxotes jaculator*), x ¹/₃   115

58   Skeleton of the Nile Perch (*Lates niloticus*), x ¹/₈   121

59   VERTEBRAE
A. Cross-section through one of the vertebrae of Comb-
toothed Shark (*Heptranchias perlo*), x ¹/₄; B.1. Lateral view
of an abdominal vertebra of Cod (*Gadus morhua*), x ¹/₃;
B.2. Caudal vertebra of same, x ¹/₃   123

60   MODIFICATIONS OF VERTEBRAL COLUMN
A. Three vertebrae from the tail of Sail-fish (*Istiophorus*), x ¹/₈;
B. First eight vertebrae of *Stylephorus chordatus*, x 3. (After
Regan); c. Anterior part of vertebral column and spinal cord
(above) of *Eustomias brevibarbatus*, (After Regan and Trewa-
vas); D. Skull and first vertebra of *Chauliodus sloanei*, (After
Regan and Trewavas)   125

61   INTERNAL ORGANS
Dissection of a Perch (*Perca fluviatilis*), showing the principal
internal organs, x ¹/₃   127

Page

62 Large intestine of a Ray (*Raia* sp.) opened to show the spiral valve, x ²/₃   129

63 Vascular system of a fish. (After Grote, Vogt and Hofer). Arteries—white; veins—black   130

64 Brains: A. Dorsal surface of the brain of a Ray (*Raia* sp.), x ½; B. The same of a Cod (*Gadus morhua*), x ½   137

65 NOSTRILS AND OLFACTORY ORGANS
    A. Sea Lamprey (*Petromyzon marinus*), x ⅛; A.I. Upper view of head of same; B. Head of Herring (*Clupea harengus*), x ½; B.I. Front part of head dissected to show olfactory organ. (After Derscheid); C. *Linophryne macrorhinus* (unattached male larva), x about 2; *n.* nostril   141

66 BARBELS
    A. Head of Sciaenid or Drum (*Pogonias fasciatus*), x ½; B. Head of African Cat-fish (*Clarias lazera*), x ½; C. Head of Red Mullet (*Mullus surmuletus*), x ½; D. head of Cod (*Gadus morhua*), x ¼   142

67 BARBELS IN OCEANIC FISHES
    A. *Eustomias bituberatus*, x ¾; B. Head of *Eustomias tenisoni*, x 1½; C. Head of *Eustomias silvescens*, x 1¾; D. Head of *Photonectes intermedius*, x 2; E. Head of *Chirostomias pliopterus*, x 1¾; (After Regan and Trewavas)   143

68 Section (vertical) through the eye of a Bony Fish; semi-diagrammatic. (After Wall)   145

69 EYES
    A. Head of Hammer-headed Shark (*Sphyrna zygaena*), x 1/₁₀; B. *Gigantura chuni*, x ½; C. *Idiacanthus fasciola*, x ½; D. Four-eyed Fish (*Anableps tetrophthalmus*), x ½; E. *Opisthoproctus soleatus*, x ⅓   146

70 AUDITORY ORGAN OF A FISH
    a. Otolith (Sagitta) of Cod (*Gadus morhua*), x ²/₃; *b.* The same of Meagre (*Sciaena aquila*), x ²/₃   150

71 Section of the skull of Carp (*Cyprinus carpio*), showing the Weberian mechanism, x ½. I–IV. Weberian ossicles   152

72 LATERAL LINE
    a. Portion of lateral line of Frilled Shark (*Chlamydoselachus anguineus*), much enlarged; *b.* Scales of the Bow-fin (*Amia calva*), showing apertures of lateral line tubules; *c.* Lateral line scale of Bow-fin (*Amia calva*), greatly enlarged; *d.* Vertical longitudinal section through lateral line of Perch (*Perca fluviatilis*), much enlarged and diagrammatic; *e.* Lateral line scales of Osteoglossid (*Clupisudis niloticus*), x ½. (*a, b,* and *c* after Bashford Dean.)   153

73 Male Rabbit-fish (*Chimaera monstrosa*), x ⅛; *a.* Front view; *b.* Upper part of head   155

Page

74 A. *Melamphaes beanii*, x ¹/₂; B. Kentucky Blind-fish (*Amblyopsis spelaea*), x ¹/₂   156

75 POISONOUS FISHES
A, A'. Greater Weever (*Trachinus draco*), x ¹/₈; B. Stone-fish (*Synanceia verrucosa*), x ¹/₄   161

76 POISON GLANDS
A. Dorsal fin spine of Weever (After Hasler). A'. Opercular spine of Greater Weever (*Trachinus draco*) and its poison gland. (After Parker); B. A dorsal spine with poison sacs of Stone-fish (*Synanceia verrucosa*). (After Hasler)   162

77 A. Spiny Dog-fish (*Squalus acanthias*), x ¹/₁₀; B. Electric Cat-fish (*Malapterurus electricus*), x ¹/₄; C. Electric Eel (*Electrophorus electricus*), x ¹/₁₅   163

78 Electric Ray (*Torpedo*) dissected to show one of the major electric organs with the associated nerve supply. The prismatic areas on the surface of the organ indicate the vertical columns of electric plates, of which there may be 500,000 in each organ. (After Gegenbaur.) *e.o.*, electric organ   166

79 LUMINOUS FISH
A. Grenadier or Rat-tail (*Malacocephalus laevis*), x ¹/₄   169

80 LUMINOUS ORGANS
A. Lanternfish (*Diaphus metopoclampus*), x 1; B. *Ipnops murrayi*, x ¹/₂; C. *Anomalops katoptron*, x ¹/₂ (in the upper figure the luminous organ is retracted and therefore invisible)   170

81 SOUND PRODUCING ORGANS
A. Elastic spring mechanism of a South American Cat-fish (*Pseudauchenipterus nodosus*), showing the oval bony plates (*e.s.*) in which the bony springs terminate; *ca.* x ¹/₂, (After Bridge and Haddon); B. Swimbladder of a Sciaenid (*Micropogon undulatus*), showing the musculo-tendinous extensions (*m*) from the muscles of the body-wall, which partially invest the surface of the bladder, x *ca.* ¹/₂. (After Sörensen)   173

82 COLORATION IN PELAGIC AND BOTTOM-LIVING SHARKS
A. Sandbar Shark (*Carcharinus milberti*) x ¹/₂₅; B. Carpet Shark (*Orectolobus barbatus*), x ¹/₁₅   178

83 COLOUR PATTERNS IN TROPICAL MARINE FISHES
A. Muraena or Moray (*Gymnothorax petelli*), x ¹/₈; B. Bat-fish (*Platax orbicularis*), x ¹/₈; C. Butterfly-fish (*Pomacanthodes semicirculatus*), x ¹/₂; D. Butterfly-fish (*Chaetodon unimaculatus*), x ¹/₄; E. Sea Perch (*Grammistes sexlineatus*), x about ¹/₂   180

84 Tail of a Butterfly-fish (*Pomacanthodes semicirculatus*), with marking resembling Arabic characters   181

85 Frog-fish (*Histrio histrio*) in Sargasso weed x ¹/₂   182

86 Sea Dragon (*Phycodurus eques*), x ¹/₂   183

87 *Monocirrhus polyacanthus*, x 1   183

Page

88 Filefish (*Alutera scriptus*) among Eel-grass. (After Beebe) 184

89 Anglerfish (*Lophius piscatorius*), x ¹/₈ 188

90 The colour elements in the skin from the upper side of a freshly killed Flounder, seen by transmitted light 190

91 OCEANIC FISHES
A. "Great Swallower" (*Chiasmodus niger*), x ¹/₂; B. *Borophryne apogon*, x ¹/₂; C. "Gulper" (*Eurypharynx pelecanoides*), x 1; D. Hatchet-fish (*Argyropelecus* sp.), x ¹/₂; E. "Widemouth" (*Malacosteus indicus*), x ¹/₂; F. *Paraliparis* sp., x ¹/₂; G. "Gulper" (*Saccopharynx ampullaceus*), x ³/₄ 195

92 BLIND FISHES
A. Cuban Blind-fish (*Stygicola dentatus*), x about 1; B. Californian Blind Goby (*Typhlogobius californiensis*), x 1 197

93 A, B. "Capitane" (*Astroblepus chotae*), x about ¹/₂; C. Section of a pot-hole 22 feet deep in Santa Rita Creek, Colombia, showing the fishes ascending the rocky walls. (After Johnson) 201

94 A. Frost-fish (*Lepidopus caudatus*), x about ¹/₂₀; B. Tile-fish (*Lopholatilus chamaeleonticeps*), x about ¹/₂₀; C. Pilot-fish (*Naucrates ductor*), x about ¹/₂₀ 205

95 *Carapus acus* and Holothurians, x about ¹/₃. (After Emery) 209

96 Candiru (*Vandellia cirrhosa*), x 1¹/₂; v. Lower view of head, x 3 211

97 Reproductive and excretory organs of a typical Bony Fish (female); A. With oviducts continuous with the ovaries; B. With oviducts separated from the ovaries. (After Rey) 214

98 Heads of male breeding Salmon. A. Atlantic Salmon (*Salmo salar*), x ¹/₄; B. Pacific Sockeye Salmon (*Oncorhynchus nerka*), x ¹/₆ 217

99 Heads of Common Eel (*Anguilla anguilla*), x ¹/₃; A. Yellow eel; B. Silver eel; C. Mature eel 222

100 Breeding-grounds and distribution of the European Freshwater Eel (*Anguilla anguilla*) and the American Eel (*Anguilla rostrata*). The continuous curved dotted lines show the limits of occurrence of the larvae (the European species represented thus – – – – –, the American species thus . . . . .). In the case of the European Eel, that marked 10 embraces an area that must include the actual spawning places of the species, for within it larvae less than 10 millimetres in length have been captured in large numbers, but never outside it. The numbers on the other curves denote the length of the larvae in millimetres captured therein. The adults of the European species occur in the countries outlined with short horizontal lines, those of the American species in the regions shown by dots outside the coast line. (Based on Schmidt's data; see text) 223

101 Thornback Ray (*Raia clavata*), x ¹/₈. Ventral views of male and femal 228

Page

102 Sexual differences in Toothcarps (Cyprinodonts). A. Male and female Gambusia (*Gambusia* sp.), x 1; B. Male and female *Aphyosemion* sp., x 1   229

103 SECONDARY SEXUAL CHARACTERS
A. Male and female of the Common Dragonet (*Callionymus lyra*); B. Female, and head of male of *Bothus podas*; C. Male, and heads of male and female of Mailed Cat-fish (*Xenocara occidentalis*). All x *ca.* 1/3   231

104 Siamese Fighting-fish (*Betta splendens*), x 1¼. (From a photograph)   233

105 Male and female Bitterling (*Rhodeus amarus*) with freshwater Pond Mussel, x 2/3. The female is about to deposit eggs. (From a photograph)   239

106 Gunnel or Butterfish (*Pholis gunnellus*) with a mass of spawn, x 1/2   241

107 Breeding habits or the Florida Pipe-fish (*Syngnathus floridae*). *a.* Position of fishes during transfer of eggs; *b.* Attitude assumed by male while moving eggs backward in the pouch; *c.* Position of male during period of rest following several egg transfers, x *ca.* 1/4. (After Gudger); *d.* Portion of pouch opened to show eggs   242

108 A ceratioid Angler-fish (*Photocorynus spiniceps*): female with parasitic male, x 1½ (Male x 3)   244

109 Development of egg of Flounder (*Platichthys flesus*). Greatly enlarged. (After Johnstone.)   247

110 EGGS AND EGG-CAPSULES
A. Egg-capsule of Spotted Dog-fish (*Scyliorhinus* sp.), x 1/2; B. Of Port Jackson Shark (*Heterodontus phillippi*), x 1/2; C. Of Ray (*Raia* sp.), x 1/2; D. Of Chimaera (*Chimaera phantasma*), x 1/2; E. Eggs of Californian Hag-fish (*Polistotrema stouti*), x *ca* 5; E'. Animal pole of a single egg, greatly enlarged; F. Egg of Garfish (*Belone belone*), x *ca* 2½; G. Eggs of Black Goby (*Gobius niger*), x *ca* 10   248

111 DEVELOPMENT OF SHARK AND BONY FISH
A. Three stages in the development of the Spiny Dogfish (*Squalus acanthias*). I and II nat. size, III *ca* x 1/2 (I after Balfour). B. Three stages in the development of Salmon. I and II Alevins, nat. size; III Parr, x 1/2   253

112 Viviparous Blenny or Eel Pout (*Zoarces viviparus*), x 3/8   254

113 Two views of the head of the larval Lamprey or Pride, x 4   257

114 LARVAL FISHES
A. *Argyropelecus* sp. x 4. (After Brauer); B. Eel leptocephalus x 1½ (after Roule); C. *Idiacanthus* sp., x 2½. (After Regan); D. Anglerfish (*Lophius piscatorius*) x 2½ (After Tåning); E. Sunfish (*Masturus lanceolatus*) x 2½, (After Schmidt); F. Truncated Sunfish (*Ranzania laevis*), x 8. (After Schmidt)   259

Page

115 DEVELOPMENT OF SAILFISH AND DEALFISH
A. Three stages in the development of a Sailfish (*Istiophorus* sp.) (After Günther) I. 9 mm. x 3^1/$_2$; II. 14 mm. x 3^1/$_2$; III. 60 mm. nat. size. A full grown specimen is shown in Fig. 6A; B. Three stages in the development of the Dealfish (*Trachypterus arcticus*) (After Emery and Smitt) I. 16 mm. x 1^1/$_4$; II. 100 mm. x ^{1}/$_4$; III. 1,000 mm. x ^{1}/$_{10}$ 261

116 Land distribution in Eocene times. (After Gregory)   267

117 Distribution of the genera *Sardina* and *Sardinops*. The mean annual surface isotherms of 6°, 12°, and 20° C. are shown   272

118 LIVING LUNGFISHES AND THEIR DISTRIBUTION
A. African Lungfish (*Protopterus aethiopicus*), x about ^{1}/$_8$; B. South American Lungfish (*Lepidosiren paradoxa*) a breeding male with vascularized pelvic fins, x *ca* ^{1}/$_8$; C. Australian Lungfish (*Neoceratodus forsteri*), x *ca* ^{1}/$_{10}$. In the map the black area marked A represents the distribution of the genus *Protopterus*, that marked B of *Lepidosiren*, and that marked C of *Neoceratodus*; the area of C if shown to scale, would be little more than a pin-prick   282

119 OSTEOGLOSSIDS (OSTEOGLOSSIDAE) AND THEIR DISTRIBUTION
A. *Clupisudis niloticus*, x ^{1}/$_8$; B. *Osteoglossum bicirrhosum*, x ^{1}/$_4$; C. *Arapaima gigas*, x ^{1}/$_{15}$; D. *Scleropages leichardti*, x ^{1}/$_4$. In the map the black area marked A represents the distribution of the genus *Clupisudis*, that marked B and C, of *Osteoglossum* and *Arapaima*, and that marked D of *Scleropages*   283

120 Sketch maps showing the distribution of four major families of freshwater fishes. (After Regan)   285

121 Restoration of the Pleistocene geography of the British Isles, showing the coast-line coincident with the 80 fathom contour. (After Jukes-Browne.)   290

122 Geological time-scale (after de Beer; from various sources)   295

123 RESTORATIONS OF SILURIAN AND DEVONIAN CYCLOSTOMI   299
A. An Anaspid (Cephalaspidomorphi), *Pharyngolepis oblongus*, lateral view, x 1; B. A Drepanaspid (Pteraspidomorphi), *Drepanaspis gemuendensis*, dorsal view, x ^{1}/$_5$; C. An Osteostracian (Cephalaspidomorphi), "*Cephalaspis*" *lyelli*, dorsal view, x ^{1}/$_2$. (A after Stensiö; B after Stensiö and Obrutscher; C after Traquir)

124 Head of *Rhyncholepis* compared with that of a Lamprey (*Lampetra*); *n*., nostril; *p*., pineal organ. (After Kiaer)   300

125 *Jamoytius kerwoodi*, x *ca* ^{3}/$_4$. *b.a.*, branchial apparatus (or apertures); *e.*, eye; *l.f.f.*, lateral fin-fold; *m.*, mouth; *No.*, notochord. (Simplified after White and Ritchie)   300

126 A Pteraspid (*Pteraspis rostrata*), x *ca* ^{1}/$_3$. (After White)   301

127 VARIOUS PLACODERMS (SUBCLASSES ANTIARCHI AND ARTHRODIRI).
A. *Coccosteus*, an Arthrodire, x ^{1}/$_6$; B. *Rhamphodopsis*, a

Page

Ptyctodont Arthrodire, x ¹/₃; c. *Gemuendina*, a ray-like Arthrodire, x *ca* ¹/₇; D. *Bothriolepsis*, an Antiarch, x ¹/₇; E. *Pterichthyodes*, an Antiarch, x ¹/₃. (A, B, and E after Stensiö; c, after Broili; D, modified after Patten) 303

128 *Pleuracanthus sessilis*, a Protoselachian (order Pleuracanthiformes), x *ca* ¹/₇. (After Jaekel) 304

129 TEETH OF SOME EXTINCT BRADYODONTI
A. *Agassizodus* sp.; B. *Helicoprion bessonowi*; c. *Janassa bituminosa*. (From Moy-Thomas). All reduced 305

130 PALAEONISCIFORM FISHES
A. An upper Devonian Palaeoniscid, *Cheirolepis canadensis* (Suborder Palaeoniscoidei) x ¹/₄. (After Lehman). B. A Triassic Platysomoid, *Platysomus superbus* (Suborder Platysomoidei) x *ca* ¹/₃. (After Moy-Thomas and Bradley Dyne) 307

131 HOLOSTEAN FISHES
A. *Lepidotus notopterus* (Order Semionotiformes), from the upper Jurassic (After Thiollière and Saint-Seine), x *ca* ¹/₇. B. Dentition of *Lepidotus mantelli*; B¹, three teeth enlarged. c. *Eugnathus orthostomus* (Order Amiiformes) from the lower Lias (After Woodward), x ¹/₈. The scales have been largely omitted in figure c 308

132 CROSSOPTERYGIAN FISHES
A. *Holoptychius*, an upper Devonian Porolepiform. x ¹/₈. B. *Eusthenopteron*, an upper Devonian Osteolepiform, x ¹/₆. (Both after Jarvik) 311

133 *Undina penicillata* (x ¹/₄), an upper Jurassic Coelacanth. The large, ossified "swimbladder" is clearly visible below the vertebral column; also note the well defined epichordal lobe of the tail fin, *a*, the gular plates which lie between the halves of the lower jaw. 312

134 COELACANTHS
A. *Latimeria chalumnae*, the only species of extant Coelacanth, x ¹/₁₂. B, the axial skeleton of *L. chalumnae*; note the nature of the fin supports and the large notochord quite unconstricted by vertebral centra. c, part of the skeleton of a Jurassic Coelacanth (*Laugia*) x *ca* ¹/₂; in this genus the pelvic fins are anterior in position and associated with the pectoral girdle. In other respects, however, the axial skeleton agrees closely with that of *Latimeria*. (All after Jarvik) 313

135 Upper and lower jaws of the Australian Lungfish, (*Neoceratodus forsteri*) to show the tooth plates and nostrils; x ¹/₂ 315

136 FOSSIL LUNGFISHES (DIPNEUSTI)
A. *Dipterus* (Devonian) x ¹/₆. B. *Phaneropleuron* (Upper Devonian) x ¹/₅ (Both from Jarvik) 316

137 Diagrams of portions of supposed phyletic trees. (For explanation see text) 319

Page

138 The systematic position of the Herring, illustrating the main divisions used in a classification   323

139 TRAWLS
A. Otter Trawl, viewed from above; B. Beam trawl, viewed from above and an oblique side view of the mouth   339

140 SEINE NET
Diagrams illustrating the stages in laying and hauling a beach-operated seine   340

141 A. Steam drifter fishing. B. Trawler fishing with an Otter Trawl (astern) and with net hauled into the ship's side. This drawing combines two phases (fishing and bringing in the gear) of one operation   342

142 "BOMBAY DUCK"
The Bummalow (*Harpodon nehereus*) which is dried and salted to produce "Bombay Duck"   345

143 Sea Lice (*Lepeophtheirus salmonis*) on Salmon. *a.* Single specimen. x 3   355

144 Gill Maggots (*Salmincola salmonea*) on gills of Salmon. *a.* Single specimen, x 3   356

145 DOMESTICATED FISHES
A. Veil-tailed variety of Goldfish (*Carassius auratus*); B. Telescopic-eyed variety; C. Lion-headed variety. All x *ca* 1/3; D. Mirror or King Carp, a cultivated mutant form of the Common Carp. x *ca* 1/6   358

146 THE LARGEST FISH
Whale Shark (*Rhincodon typicus*), x *ca* 1/140. (After Gudger)   362

147 ONE OF THE SMALLEST FISHES
Mistichthys luzonensis, x 4. (After H. M. Smith)   362

148 "CRUCIFIX FISH"
Upper and lower views of the skull from a marine Catfish (*Arius* sp.) x 1/3   368

CHAPTER I

INTRODUCTORY

'These (the fishes) were made out of the most entirely ignorant and senseless beings, whom the transformers did not think any longer worthy of pure respiration, because they possessed a soul which was made impure by all sorts of transgression; and instead of allowing them to respire the subtle and pure element of air, they thrust them into the water, and gave them a deep and muddy medium of respiration; and hence arose the race of fishes and oysters, and other aquatic animals, which have received the most remote habitations as a punishment for their extreme ignorance.'　　　　　　　　　　PLATO

IT IS OF primary importance in a work of this nature to make it clear from the outset exactly what is meant by a fish, for in everyday speech the word 'fish' is often used to include any animal living in the water, a definition which appears in all the older dictionaries. Although convenient, this can hardly be described as scientifically accurate, including, as it does, such diverse organisms as whales, seals, salmon, oysters, cuttle-fishes, star-fishes, jelly-fishes, and sponges, creatures that differ from each other even more widely than do reptiles from birds or birds from mammals. The aquatic animals just mentioned, however, all fall naturally into two main categories in respect of one important feature—those with a vertebral column or backbone and those with none. Man has a backbone, and so have all the mammals, birds, reptiles, amphibians, and fishes; all the others have no backbone. The backboned animals or vertebrates are better known to most people than the majority of the lower animals; indeed, with the exception of a few like the oyster and lobster which are eaten as delicacies, the invertebrate animals are regarded for the most part with luke-warm interest, in some cases with actual disgust. This attitude is partly explained by the generally larger size of the vertebrates, by the greater ease with which they can be observed and studied, and by the beauty of many birds and mammals. It has been further fostered by the editors of popular works on natural history, who devote three-quarters of the available pages to the mammals and birds, crowding the unfortunate lower animals—every bit as interesting and quite often of extreme beauty—into a few short chapters.

A fish, therefore, is a vertebrate, and one specially adapted for a purely aquatic life. But this definition is still inadequate, for all the vertebrates living in the water are not fishes. What of the

I

whales, seals, otters, newts, and frogs? Take for example, the perennial argument as to whether or not a whale is a fish. Here there is the same fish-like body, the fin-like fore limbs or paddles, and often a fin in the middle of the back [Fig. 1]. Nevertheless, a whale is not a fish, but a mammal. A close examination of its skin reveals the presence of a few vestigial hairs in the region of the muzzle, the structure of the paddle is quite unlike that of the fish's

Fig. 1   CETACEAN AND FISH COMPARED
A. Common Dolphin (*Delphinus delphis*); B. Mackerel Shark (*Isurus oxyrhynchus*). Both much reduced.

fin [Fig. 2], being in all its essential parts just like that of the human hand, and the so-called dorsal fin is nothing more than a ridge of fatty tissue. Furthermore, although a whale is able to remain under water for considerable periods of time, it is forced to come to the surface at intervals to empty its lungs of air and to inhale a fresh supply—the familiar process of spouting or blowing. Whales also bring forth their young alive and, most important, suckle them just like any other mammal. In short, a whale is a mammal which has exchanged a terrestrial life for one passed entirely in water, a change which has led to the fore limbs being converted into paddles for swimming, while the hind limbs have completely disappeared. The seals give us some idea of one way in which this change has come about, representing, as it were, a stage between a typical walking mammal and a specialised swimming one. A seal is amphibious; that is to say, it is at home on land or in the water; but the hind limbs have lost a great deal of their power of supporting the body on *terra firma*, and the fore limbs are more paddle-like, the shape of the body is tapering and fish-like, and the external ears have more or less disappeared.

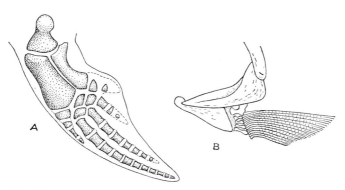

Fig. 2   PECTORAL LIMB OF CETACEAN AND FISH COMPARED
A. Skeleton of paddle of Common Dolphin (*Delphinus delphis*); B. Pectoral girdle and fin of a Bony Fish. Both greatly reduced.

The form of the tail provides a rough-and-ready means of distinguishing at a glance any whale or dolphin (Cetacea) from a large fish such as a shark; in the Cetaceans the flukes or lobes of the tail are horizontal, in the fishes they are vertical [Fig. 1]. It is of some interest to note that Aristotle (384–322 B.C.) was well aware of the differences between fishes and aquatic mammals, whereas many of the writers in historical times classed them all together as fishes. The distinctions between the two groups do not appear to have been generally understood until the later part of the seventeenth century, and ignorance as to the real nature of the Cetaceans must often have led our pious ancestors to break Lent, since they enjoyed steaks and cutlets of whale, porpoise, or seal on fast days under the fond delusion that they were consuming fish!

The Ichthyosaurs, a group of extinct aquatic reptiles, exhibit the same general fish-like form and paddle-like limbs, but these have clearly been acquired independently, as in the whales, as a result of the adoption of a life in the water [Fig. 3].

To summarize, a fish may be loosely defined as a vertebrate adapted for a purely aquatic life, propelling and balancing itself by means of fins, and obtaining oxygen from the water for breathing purposes by means of gills Fishes, thus defined, were formerly regarded as representing a single group of the great sub-kingdom of vertebrates, a group equivalent to the birds (Aves) or the reptiles (Reptilia); but a more thorough knowledge of their anatomy and evolutionary history has led to a different conclusion. The Lampreys and their allies (Cyclostomes), with their pouch-like gills, and mouths devoid of biting jaws, resemble some of the true fishes to a certain superficial extent in outward form, in habits, and in their

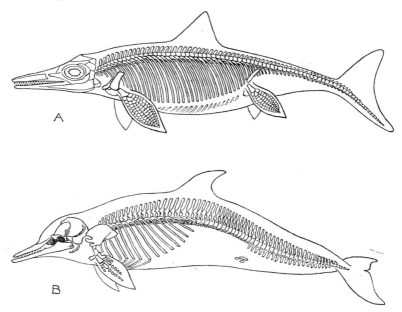

Fig. 3   ANIMALS OF FISH-LIKE FORM
Upper: An Ichthyosaur, an extinct reptile. Lower: Dolphin, a mammal.
Both much reduced.

general manner of breathing, and may well be regarded as 'fishes' in the popular sense. Actually, the two groups of animals are separated by characters just as fundamental as those which divide all the other fishes from the Amphibians, and the Cyclostomes must, therefore, rank as a separate group (*cf.* p. 297). The same is true to a lesser extent of the Selachians, a group including the sharks, rays, and Chimaeras, which have been separated from the Bony Fishes for a very long period of the earth's history (*cf.* p. 304). In speaking of fishes, therefore, it must be remembered that we are referring to three very distinct vertebrate groups, here considered together merely for the sake of convenience.

Certainly in number of individuals, and probably also in number of species, fishes are at the present time superior to mammals, birds, reptiles, or amphibians. Recollecting that three-quarters of the earth's surface is covered by the seas, and that many of the fresh waters of the land teem with fish life, this superiority of numbers is easier to understand. The surfaces of the great oceans, their middle layers, the abyssal depths and shore regions; the estuaries, rivers, swiftly flowing brooks, turbulent mountain torrents and placid lakes and ponds; each of these possesses its peculiar forms of fish life, variously adapted to the prevailing circumstances. There are probably more than 25,000 different species of fish in existence today, and many more new forms are discovered every year. Aristotle seems to have been familiar with only about 118 species, all of them found in the Aegean Sea. Pliny (*circa* A.D. 200), whose list included as many as 176 species, triumphantly exclaims: 'In the sea and the ocean, vast as it is, there exists, by Hercules! nothing that is unknown to us, and a truly marvellous feat it is that we are best acquainted with those things which Nature has concealed in the deep.' *Sancta simplicitas*! Regarding the number of individuals of any particular species, it is well nigh impossible to give an adequate idea of their abundance. It has been estimated that nearly 400 million cod and more than 3 thousand million herring are caught each year in the Atlantic and adjacent seas alone, and these numbers must represent but a minute proportion of the individuals in existence at a given time.

The particular branch of zoology which deals with the structure of fishes, both external and internal, their mode of life, their distribution in space and time, etc., is known as 'ichthyology' a word derived from the Greek *ichthys*, a fish, and *logos*, a discourse. The scope of ichthyology is enormous, and it is impossible to deal adequately with its many branches in the compass of a single volume. The anatomist, investigating and comparing the internal structure of the various kinds of fishes; the embryologist, concerned with the development of the individual from the egg to the adult; the systematist or taxonomist, classifying the fishes, and arranging them in larger or smaller groups according to their differences and resemblances; the physiologist, studying living activities and the function of organs and tissues; and the ecologist observing the relation of living fishes to their environment; each of these is continually adding his quota to our knowledge of fishes. The story of fish life does not begin and end with the fishes living at the present time. It began long before man made his appearance on this planet, and when there were no reptiles or amphibians, no birds, and no mammals. For facts concerning the past history of fishes we are indebted both to the geologist, who studies the formation of the rocks wherein the records lie buried, and to the palæontologist, who studies and describes the fossilized remains which may be found there. As will be shown later on, the geological record is necessarily fragmentary and very imperfect, but it has already provided a mass of evidence which has confirmed or modified the conclusions drawn from the study of anatomy, embryology, etc. Nor is this all. The body of a fish, as well as its inanimate environment, is continually subject to physical and chemical laws, so that, in order to arrive at a full understanding of fish life, it is necessary to go beyond the realms of natural history and draw upon the researches of the chemist, physicist, meteorologist, and even the mathematician.

The history of ichthyology, like that of zoology, may be said to have begun with Aristotle, who recorded many observations concerning the fishes of Greece. His information on their structure, habits, migrations, spawning seasons, etc., is, so far as it has been tested, extraordinarily accurate, but his ideas of species were exceedingly vague, being simply those of the local fishermen from whom he obtained the names of his specimens. As Günther has observed: 'It is less surprising that Aristotle should have found so many truths as that none of his followers should have added to them.' Pliny, Aelianus, Athenæus, and others certainly recorded some original observations, but the majority of scholars from the time of Aristotle until some eighteen centuries later were content to copy from his works, merely adding a number of fabulous stories and myths. In the sixteenth and seventeenth centuries the publication of the mighty works of Belon (1518–64), Rondelet (1507–57), Salviani (1513–72), Ray and Willughby (1686) and others, gave a fresh impetus to the study of fishes. From this time onwards the progress of ichthyology was rapid and continuous, and its history includes the names of Linnæus, Risso, Rafinesque, Bloch, Lacépède, and Cuvier, men whose pioneer work, often carried out in the face of great difficulties, with few specimens and inadequate apparatus and instruments, has laid the foundations on which modern ichthyologists are still building.

CHAPTER 2

FORM AND LOCOMOTION

OF THE MANY and varied forms of animal life found in the
sea and in fresh water few are more perfectly adapted for
life in a liquid medium than are the fishes. Many invertebrates spend the greater part of their lives attached
to or crawling sluggishly over a small area of the sea bottom;
others float more or less passively at the surface or in the middle
layers of the water, their movements largely dependent on the
action of the tides and currents. Squids and Cuttle-fishes alone
approach the fishes in speed and grace of form, but lack their
agility in the water, and are generally far inferior to them in their
mastery of the medium.

Water is a comparatively dense substance, and in order to attain
the most efficient movement with the greatest economy of energy
a certain form of body is essential. The shape of the body, therefore,
is not an arbitrary one, but conforms to a number of definite
mechanical principles. The mechanical conditions which led man
to construct his submarine to a certain pattern, in order to have a
vessel that would move freely in all directions under water, are
precisely the same as those which have determined the shape of the
fish's body, so that it is not surprising to find that the form of the
man-made submarine corresponds closely with that of the animate
fish. These mechanical principles cannot be dealt with here, since

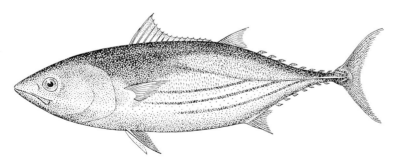

Fig. 4 A SWIFT PELAGIC FISH
Oceanic Bonito (*Katsuwonus pelamis*) x ¹/₈

7

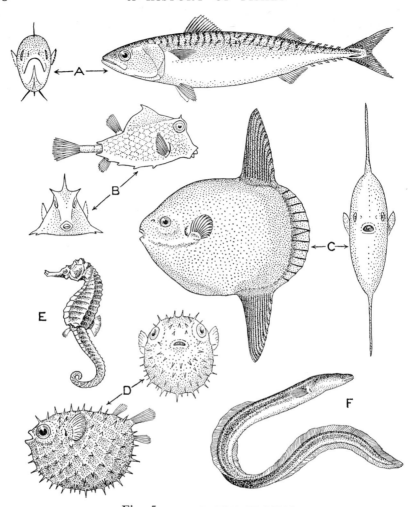

Fig. 5   DIFFERENCES IN FORM
A. Mackerel (*Scomber scombrus*) x ¹/₄; B. Trunkfish (*Tetrosomus gibbosus*)
x ¹/₄; C. Sunfish (*Mola mola*) x ¹/₂₅; D. Globefish (*Chilomycterus antennatus*)
x ¹/₄; E. Seahorse (*Hippocampus* sp.) x ¹/₂. F. Common Eel (*Anguilla
anguilla*) x ¹/₈

a study of this subject would involve many theoretical problems,
the proper understanding of which entails some knowledge of
higher mathematics. It must suffice to point out that the fine form
of a typical swift-swimming fish such as the Mackerel (*Scomber*)
[Fig. 5A] or Bonito (*Katsuwonus*) [Fig. 4] is one that is admirably

adapted from a mechanical point of view for cleaving the water, and is that which is clearly best suited for progression in that medium. The shape of the body of a Mackerel is fusiform; that is, it is shaped somewhat like a cigar, circular or elliptical in cross-section and thicker in front than behind. Every line of its smooth, rounded contour is suggestive of swift motion, there being an almost complete absence of irregularities or projections which might offer resistance to the water. There is no distinct neck as in the land vertebrates, the head merging insensibly into the trunk and the trunk into the tail, the boundaries between these regions of the body being denoted by the gill-opening and the origin of the anal fin respectively. Viewed from the front, the outline of the fish appears as a perfect ellipse of comparatively small size [Fig. 5A]. The beautifully moulded, bullet-shaped head, with its pointed snout forming an efficient entering angle, the firm, smooth eyes, so situated that their surfaces are level with the adjoining surfaces of the head and the closely fitting gill-covers, are all features aiding rapid progression. The small scales with which the body is covered offer practically no resistance to forward motion since they present a comparatively smooth surface. Finally, the smooth hollow curves of the hinder end of the body, extending from the region of greatest thickness backwards to the tail, are admirably adapted to reduce turbulence in the water displaced during forward motion.

The fins, which form so characteristic a part of the fish, may briefly be considered here. The fins are of two kinds, median or unpaired, and paired. The median fins consist of a *dorsal* in the middle line of the back, an *anal* on the belly behind the vent, and a *caudal* or tail-fin at the hinder end of the fish, which plays an important part in forward movements [Fig. 7]. In the fast-swimming Mackerel the dorsal and anal fins form sharp, thin keels, and, although these appear prominent when viewed from the side they are much less so in the front aspect of the fish [Fig. 5A]. The paired fins are of two kinds only, the *pectorals* and *pelvics*, corresponding to the fore and hind limbs of land vertebrates. The role of these fins in movement will be described on a later page (p. 32).

So much for the form of a typical pelagic fish. Departures from this ideal body-shape are both numerous and varied, but it must be remembered that many shapes which at first sight appear to be anything but streamlined prove to be well adapted to the particular habits of their possessors. One fact is quite obvious: any radical departure from the ideal form must inevitably lead to a loss in swimming efficiency, or, at least, to a marked restriction of speed, and this becomes more and more evident the further the fish departs from the typical shape. A fish like the Mackerel depends on speed, not only to obtain its food, but as a means of escape from enemies, and any marked restriction of its activities would leave it liable to

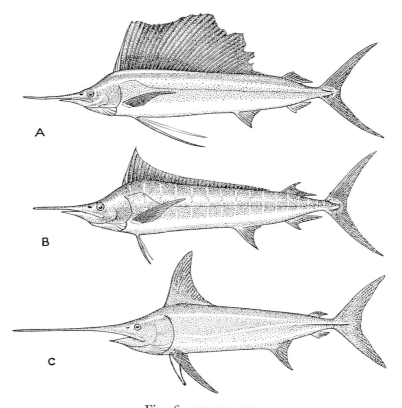

Fig. 6   SWORD-FISHES
A. Sail-fish (*Istiophorus americanus*); B. Spear-fish (*Makaira audax*);
C. Sword-fish (*Xiphias gladius*)

the danger of extinction. It is only where speed ceases to be of primary importance in the life of the species, and is replaced by some other compensating factor such as heavy armour, that a fish is able to dispense with the fusiform shape and survive in the struggle for existence.

Three examples selected from amongst the Sharks and Rays will serve to illustrate this point. The Blue Sharks and their allies (*Carcharinus*) possess slender, perfectly streamlined bodies, conical heads, pointed snouts, and powerful muscular tails [Figs. 1B; 82A]; the Carpet Sharks (*Orectolobus*) have stout thick-set bodies, considerably flattened from above downwards, massive heads, broadly rounded snouts, wide mouths, much reduced tails and comparatively small dorsal fins [Fig. 82B]; the Rays (Raiidae) have very broad,

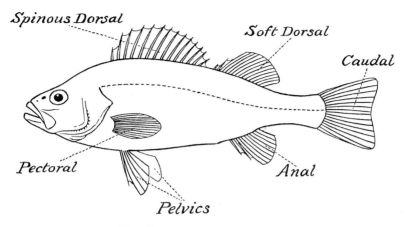

Spinous Dorsal *Soft Dorsal* *Caudal* *Pectoral* *Anal* *Pelvics*

Fig. 7   TOPOGRAPHY OF FINS

flat bodies, the head, trunk and enormously expanded pectoral fins
being united to form a circular or quadrangular disc, from which
the feeble tail with its tiny dorsal fins projects as a slender appendage
[Figs. 8A; 101].   The Blue Shark is an inhabitant of the open sea,
feeding almost exclusively on other fishes; it is essentially a strong,
speedy fish, every line of its body adapted for rapid progress in
pursuit of prey.   The Carpet Shark, on the other hand, relies on
cunning rather than speed to obtain a meal, lying in wait on the
sea floor until the prey comes within reach of its jaws.   The loss of
swimming power is here compensated for by the remarkable manner
in which the Shark resembles its surroundings, its appearance when
at rest being that of a weed-covered rock (*cf.* p. 178).   The uniform
steely blue coloration of the Blue Shark is replaced by a beautiful
variegated pattern which harmonises closely with the sea bottom.
The Ray, another sluggish, ground-living fish, also depends to a
large extent on its general resemblance to the surroundings to
escape observation by enemies.   Its flattened form is admirably
adapted for this particular mode of life, but, as will be seen later, an
unusual method of locomotion enables this fish to move with much
greater rapidity than would seem possible from its appearance.
Some still more specialised members of this order have acquired
other protective devices in addition to their coloration.   For
example, the Torpedo or Cramp-fish (*Torpedo*) has powerful
electric organs [Fig. 78], and the Sting-ray (*Dasyatis*) has one or
more strong, saw-edged and poisonous spines on its tail [Figs.
22B; 26E].
   A body flattened from above downward is generally spoken of as

'depressed,' while that which is flattened from side to side is 'compressed.' Among Bony Fishes the former type is rare, but the well-known Angler-fish or Fishing-frog (*Lophius*), in which mimetic resemblance and cunning in obtaining a meal have been brought to a pitch of perfection [Fig. 89], and the little Bat-fish (*Ogcocephalus*), with the upper surface of its body protected by a covering of hard bony warts [Fig. 31D], provide excellent examples. The laterally compressed body, on the other hand, unknown in Selachians, is common in Bony Fishes. Often the body is shortened as well, and, flexibility being no longer an absolute necessity, many of these forms have developed heavy protective armour of some kind. The brilliant little Butterfly-fishes (Chaetodontidae) of tropical coral reefs are excessively quick in their movements, in spite of their short, deep, flattened bodies, and they rely largely on their agility to escape being eaten, coupled with the fact that their deep bodies and strong, spiny fins make them awkward mouthfuls to swallow [Fig. 83c & D]. The beautiful Angel-fish (*Pterophyllum*) of the rivers of South America, a familiar object in aquaria, has a very much

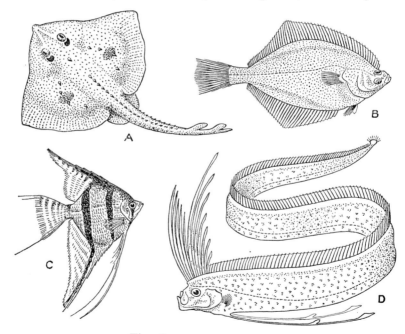

Fig. 8   FLATTENED FISHES
A. Female Thornback Ray (*Raia clavata*) x $\frac{1}{12}$; B. Flounder (*Platichthys flesus*) x $\frac{1}{6}$; C. Angelfish (*Pterophyllum scalare*) x $\frac{1}{4}$; D. Oarfish or Ribbon-fish (*Regalecus glesne*) x ca $\frac{1}{25}$

compressed and almost circular body, and the large fins have some of the rays drawn out into lengthy filaments [Fig. 8c]. It is a very slow swimmer, spending most of its time suspended almost motionless in mid-water, and relies on its disruptive coloration to escape detection. The Flat-fishes (Pleuronectiformes), a group which includes such well-known edible forms as the Halibut, Turbot, Plaice, and Sole, all have very flattened bodies, and, like the Rays, spend much of their time on the sea floor, where their mottled coloration harmonises with the ground on which they lie. [Figs. 8b; 31a–c]. The Plaice and the Skate are often lumped together as 'Flat-fishes,' but it is obvious that the resemblance is purely superficial. Both fishes have taken to a life on the bottom, where a flattened body is a decided advantage, but the Skate has become flattened from above downwards, whereas the Plaice is compressed from side to side. In other words, the colourless lower surface of the skate which rests on the bottom is the true lower or *ventral* side, whereas in the true Flat-fishes this surface represents the right or left side.

The Globe-fishes or Puffers (Tetraodontidae) and their relatives the Porcupine-fishes (Diodontidae) provide examples of fishes with shortened, rounded bodies, in which the consequent loss of swimming power is compensated for by the development of armour in the form of spines or small prickles (*cf*. p. 64 and Figs. 33g & 5d). In addition to their spiny covering, these fishes possess the power of swallowing water or air thereby inflating the body like a balloon. When thus inflated they float passively with the currents, more often than not upside down. If taken from the water a Puffer will generally inflate at once, but if slow to begin it can be persuaded to swell up by gentle tickling. When inflated, and with the spines erected, the fish is adequately protected against most predatory enemies, who would find it difficult to bite, much less to swallow. Observations made by Dr. Beebe, however, indicate that such protection is not always complete. He watched a number of little Porcupine-fishes, and saw that when they were threatened by a large Gar-fish, four feet in length, they bunched together for protection, giving the appearance of one large, round and prickly fish; occasionally, however, a single individual would become detached from the mass, whereupon it was promptly seized and devoured. The allied Trunk-fishes (Ostraciontidae) are also slow-swimming creatures, living at or near the bottom of the sea, and rely for protection on their armour, which here takes the form of a rigid bony case. [Figs. 5b; 33f]. Also related to the Porcupine-fishes and Puffers are the large and grotesque Sun-fishes (Molidae), of which there are three genera, all widely distributed in warm seas. The Round-tailed Sun-fish (*Mola*) has a deep, circular and somewhat compressed body looking as though the tail end had been amputated just behind the high dorsal and anal fins [Fig. 5c], a feature to which the popular name of 'Head-fish' refers. Such a body is probably well adapted for more or less passive drifting in ocean currents. The Round-tailed Sun-fish reaches a length of eight feet or more and a weight estimated at more than a ton. It is a sluggish fish, often observed basking or swimming lazily at the surface of the sea. Underlying the skin, which is very tough and leathery, is a layer of hard, gristly material some two or three inches thick—ample compensation for any loss of locomotive power!

At the other extreme are fishes with long bodies, which may be rounded as in the Eels (Anguilliformes) or very much compressed, as in the Ribbon-fishes (Trachypteridae) and Cutlass-fishes (Trichiuridae). From their shape one would hardly expect such fishes to be other than slow swimmers, but, as will be shown below, the adoption of a particular method of locomotion gives them a greater speed than the short-bodied forms mentioned above. The peculiar shape of the Eel's body [Fig. 5f] is almost certainly associated with its habit of living in soft river bottoms, wriggling in and out of the mud, creeping through reeds, or insinuating itself into holes and crevices as do its relatives in the coral reefs. Some of the Eels carry the elongation of the body to such an extreme that they have the appearance of a piece of slender whipcord, and the fins are often much reduced. Such a filiform type of body is characteristic of the curious Snipe-eels (Nemichthyidae), oceanic forms which sometimes descend to considerable depths [Fig. 22g]. When seen swimming at or near the surface, these Eels are not infrequently mistaken for snakes. It may be noted here that similarity in eel-like form is not necessarily indicative of close relationship, but may be the result of convergent evolution. The so-called Synbranchoid Eels [Fig. 43b], for example, are not closely related to the true Eels, and the same type of body in the two groups has evolved in response to the demands of similar environments.

In the Sea Horses (*Hippocampus*) the form of the body is unique, the head being bent at right angles to the trunk in a manner suggestive of a horse, and the trunk itself is definitely curved [Fig. 5e]. The tail is also unique in that it is prehensile and can be used by the fish to anchor it to moving or fixed objects. The body is protected by a series of bony, ring-like plates, and in some species the spines or membranous processes with which these are ornamented serve to break up the outline and so render the fish inconspicuous when swaying to and fro among aquatic vegetation. The Sea Horses are defenceless creatures, and depend largely on this mimetic resemblance to escape from predatory fishes.

The locomotion of fishes provides the biologist and physicist with a number of interesting problems, and has also attracted the attention of the marine engineer, some of whose mechanical inventions owe their inception, at least in part, to observations made upon living animals. Although actual swimming forms the main subject for consideration in this chapter, it must be remembered that this is by no means the only method in use, and 'walking' or creeping over the sea floor, skipping about on sand or mud, burrowing, wriggling on dry land, leaping and flying, are also indulged in by some fishes. These are however, rather in the nature of specialised developments, and, since they are often accompanied by a modification of certain organs may be conveniently considered in later pages. Flying, for example, which involves the modification of the pectoral fins, is discussed in the chapter devoted to fins.

The various vertebrates here grouped together as fishes include a very diverse assemblage of forms, but there is, nevertheless, a basic similarity in their swimming movements, however different these may appear to be at first sight. The earliest vertebrates probably swam by means of simple rhythmic contractions of the trunk and tail muscles producing certain definite contortions of the body; by the pressure of different parts of the body in succession against the surrounding water the animal was driven forward. Most fishes have retained the primitive arrangement of the great body muscles, the myomeres, as they are called (*cf.* p. 125), which form a series of blocks or segments, arranged in pairs one behind the other and separated by partitions. In this respect fishes differ from all land vertebrates, in which the main muscle masses are more or less concentrated on the fore and hind limbs, these being the normal organs of locomotion, whereas the corresponding pectoral and pelvic fins of fishes more often than not perform quite different functions, such as balancing and steering. We have already noticed the essential similarity in the shape of the body in the Cetaceans and fishes, but, owing to its different ancestry, the arrangement of the body muscles in a whale is quite unlike that found in a fish, and the swimming movements themselves are in a different plane, being up and down instead of from side to side. Two primary methods are employed by fishes to produce forward movements while suspended in a fluid medium: (1) body movements due to alternate expansion and contraction of the myomeres and (2) movements of the appendages (fins); a third method is by the action of jets of water expelled from the gill-openings during the process of respiration.

The first method is the most common and of the greatest importance, the others being, for the most part, auxiliary to it. It must be borne in mind, however, that in the majority of fishes the three are inter-related, and may all be used at different times, or even at the same time. Locomotion solely by means of fin movements, for example, may be employed when slow progress only is wanted, but, should danger threaten or prey appear in sight, body movements quickly come into play, and at the same time the increased rate of breathing assists in the general strengthening of the forward thrust. The Trout (*Salmo trutta*) uses body movements for forward progression, and will serve as an excellent example of the first method of swimming. When the Trout wishes to move forward the first action which takes place is the contraction of the first few myomeres at the front end of the body on one side

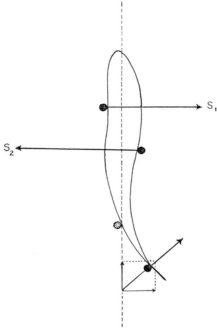

Fig. 9   BODY MOVEMENTS OF A SWIMMING FISH (After Gray).

only, resulting in the throwing of the head sharply to one side. The successive segments then alternately contract and relax from the head towards the tail, and the curve or flexure of the body is passed backwards [Fig. 9], so that at any one moment the body is thrown into a gentle 'S'-shaped curve.

The accompanying illustrations of a swimming fish give a good idea of the manner in which the body is undulated, and show how the flexure may be traced backwards from the head towards the tail [Figs. 9 & 10].

The actual forward thrust is effected by the pressure of the fish's tail against the surrounding water. In order to use its tail in this way the front end of the fish must be braced against the water. From the figure [Fig. 9] it will be seen that during any one cycle three points of the body are braced against the resistant medium. The reaction from the most posterior point is the propulsive one, whilst those from the two anterior points (S_1 & S_2) are at right angles to the fishes body and do not exert any force along the path of movement. These are the chief bracing points and are those which prevent undue oscillation from the forward path. To understand the action of these body movements on the surrounding medium it will be convenient to study an elongated type of fish such as the Eel (*Anguilla*), and compare its locomotor methods with those of the Trout. [Fig. 10, lower line compared with Fig. 9]. The movement is again initiated by the contraction of the first few myomeres on one side. The anterior part of the body is thus thrown into a curve, and this curve is passed backwards in a series of waves by the alternate contraction and relaxation of the serial muscle segments. The movement is mechanically the same as that of a long rope held at one end and given a smart jerk with the hand at right angles to its axis. This results in a wave passing down the rope, the curves gradually decreasing in size and eventually dying out because the initial action of the hand was the sole agent of propulsion. But, in the living fish each successive muscle segment gives an added impetus to the wave, and, so soon as the first wave has started backwards, a second follows, but on the opposite side, and so on. Here the forward thrust is attained almost entirely by the pressure of the fish's body against the water contained in the spaces between the curves. With this elongate form the fish gains much greater pressure areas from its sides than does the Trout, but, at the same time, it naturally loses the important terminal effect of the tail-fin. Indeed, we find that in all eel-like fishes the caudal fin is either very much reduced or wanting altogether. In most Eels the anterior part of the body is cylindrical in cross-section, whereas the hinder part is distinctly compressed; this feature has a mechanical advantage, since a blade-like structure which presents its surface more effectively to the water naturally provides a greater amount of thrust than a rounded one. Mechanically, this part of the Eel's body functions like the expanded caudal fin of other fishes. The elongate Ribbon-fishes (*Regalecus*), and other fishes with long bodies greatly flattened from side to side [Fig. 8D], undulate them into curves which are even more ample than those of the Eel, the extreme ribbon shape making this excessive bending comparatively easy to perform. It is of interest to note here that fishes with rounded, elongate bodies can move over rough surfaces out of water by applying the same locomotor forces normally used in swimming. Indeed, even a Trout can move across a board which is liberally provided with pegs against which the fish can exert a backward force. Thus it will be seen that movement in a fish is based on the same physical principles as all other types of locomotion. Namely, the exertion of a force against the surroundings which in turn apply an equal but directionally opposite force against the body which then moves in that direction.

If the locomotion of the Eel be regarded as one extreme type of body movement, that of the Trunk-fish (*Ostracion*) undoubtedly represents the opposite extreme, the Mackerel, Trout and other

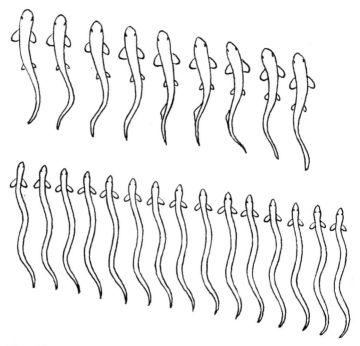

Fig. 10   BODY MOVEMENTS OF FISHES USED IN SWIMMING
Shark (above); Eel (below). After Marey

fishes being intermediate between the two types. In the Trunk-fish [Figs. 5B; 33F], with its head and body enclosed in a hard and inflexible bony case, from which the fleshy tail with a large fan-like caudal fin at the extremity projects freely backwards, undulations of the body are clearly impossible. Normally, the dorsal and anal fins form the chief propelling agents, but where greater speed is required the fish swings the tail vigorously from side to side, the movements being brought about by the alternate contraction of the muscles on either side of the fleshy part of the tail. A Trunk-fish swimming in this way may be likened to a small boat propelled by means of a single oar sculled from the stern, but the hydrodynamic principles involved are somewhat more complex because of the tail fin's greater flexibility.

The three types of body movements here described, and exemplified by the Eel, Trout, and Trunk-fish respectively, are arbitrarily chosen examples. Among fishes we find such a complete gradation from one extreme to the other that it is not easy to say where one begins and the other ends. The extremes are methods employed by comparatively slow-swimming forms, mostly living close to the shore, whereas those of the Mackerel and Trout are of the highest efficiency and pre-eminently suited for high speed. With the sole exception of fishes such as the Sea Horses, in which the locomotor emphasis is placed entirely on the fins, all existing forms fall somewhere within the series described above.

Turning to the second of the primary methods of locomotion, (by the action of fins) it may be noted that movements essentially the same as those of the body may be localised in one or more of the fins [Fig. 11], and the same kind of series occurs, ranging from a serpentine, undulating motion like that of the Eel to a fan-like waggle which recalls the tail movements of the Trunk-fish. It has been remarked that the caudal fin is operated primarily by the action of the muscles of the body and tail, but many fishes are capable of moving slowly forward by means of wave-like movements of the fin itself, the waves travelling at right angles to the longitudinal axis of the body. In most fishes the shape of the fins, and more especially that of the caudal, provides a very good index of speed and agility, the same type of fin occurring in quite unrelated groups of fishes whose swimming habits are similar. It is impossible to enter into the mechanical possibilities of the different shapes of caudal fin, but it may be said that as a general rule fishes with large tails, the hinder margins of which are square-cut (truncate) or rounded, are comparatively slow swimmers, and, although able to accomplish sudden short bursts of speed, they are incapable of swimming for long periods at a high speed, as are those species provided with deeply forked or lunate tails [Fig. 23A,B]. Such fishes have the upper and lower lobes of the fin long and pointed, and the fleshy part of the tail, known as the caudal peduncle, is nearly always very narrow and not infrequently strengthened by one or two fleshy keels on either side as in the 'Sword-fishes' [Fig. 6]. The Bonito (*Katsuwonus*), reckoned to be among the swiftest of all fishes, provides an excellent example of this type of caudal fin— crescent-shaped, without flesh, almost without scales, composed of bundles of rays, flexible, yet as hard as ivory [Fig. 4].

The other median fins, the dorsal and anal, may also be used by certain fishes as propulsive organs, especially in those forms whose bodies have radically departed from the streamline shape. The fins may act in conjunction with the caudal fin or as a substitute for it.

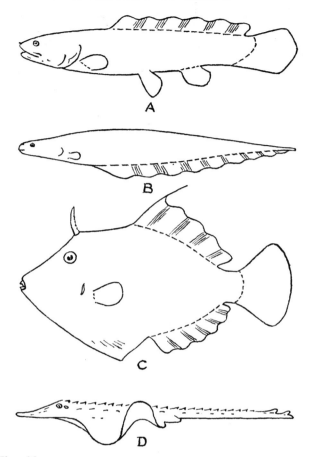

Fig. 11   FIN MOVEMENTS USED BY FISHES IN SWIMMING
A. Bow-fin (*Amia calva*) x ¹/₁₀; B. Electric Eel (*Electrophorus electricus*) x ¹/₈;
C. File-fish (*Monacanthus* sp.) x ¹/₄; D. Ray (*Raia* sp.) x ¹/₈. (After Breder).

By appropriate use of the muscles controlling the fin-rays (*cf.* p. 29)
a series of wavelike movements can be produced in the fin, similar
to those seen in the body of the Eel. In the Bow-fin (*Amia*) of
North America, for example, undulating movements of the long
dorsal fin are often used to propel the body slowly forward [Fig. 11A],
and the Electric Eel (*Electrophorus*), in which the dorsal fin is
wanting, employs the long anal fin in a similar way [Fig. 11B].
The File-fish or Leather-jacket (*Monacanthus*) has both dorsal and
anal fins placed a little obliquely, and makes use of both simul-

taneously for forward progression [Fig. 11c]. Other fishes, such as
the Globe-fishes or Puffers (Tetraodontidae) and Porcupine-fishes
(Diodontidae), move by flapping the short dorsal and anal fins in
a fan-like manner. The Sea Horse (*Hippocampus*), which charac-
teristically swims in an upright position, glides slowly through the
water by means of rapid wave-like movements passing along the
dorsal fin, which has the appearance of a tiny propeller revolving
in the middle of the fish's back [Fig. 5E]. The related Pipe-fishes
(Syngnathidae) swim in a similar way, but their bodies being
elongate and more flexible they are able to make more rapid
progress at times by throwing the body into S-shaped curves
[Fig. 22E]. Flat-fishes, when moving about on the sea floor, often
make use of the long dorsal and anal fins which fringe the upper and
lower edges of the body [Fig. 8B] to obtain a grip of the ground,
and by undulating these fins are able to progress at a fair speed.

We must now consider the part played by the paired fins in
locomotion. The pelvics may be dismissed at once, as these merely
assist in maintaining stability, and rarely, if ever, serve as organs of
propulsion. The pectorals, on the other hand, are often used for
locomotor purposes, particularly in those fishes of slow or moderate
speed. In slow-moving fishes these fins are generally spatulate in
shape, and may produce forward movements of the body by a
simple synchronised flapping, as in some of the Wrasses (Labridae).
In others, of which the File-fish (*Monacanthus*) and the Porcupine-
fish (*Diodon*) are good examples, wave-like motion similar to that
described in connection with the caudal fin, is employed. This type
of motion is particularly well-marked in the Rays (*Raia*) and their
allies, in which the pectoral fins are very much enlarged and
constitute practically the sole organs of locomotion. It will be
noticed, however, that the waves travel in a vertical plane instead
of a horizontal one—up and down instead of from side to side
[Fig. 11D]. In a few species, notably among the Damsel-fishes
(Pomacentridae), the pectoral fins seem to be operated after the
manner of oars, being brought forward almost edgewise and pulled
back broadside on. In fishes of high speed the shape of the fins is
generally long and falcate (i.e. sickle-shaped), and these are
probably used mainly for changing course, and for braking, but
scarcely ever for propulsion [Fig. 4]. Turning when in motion
would appear to be effected largely by appropriate movements of
the fins, and particularly of the pectorals and pelvics, but body
movements also play their part. Stops are nearly always made by
using the pectorals in the manner of brakes, but some forms pull
up by reversing their primary locomotor apparatus.

Finally, there remains the third factor in locomotion, namely,
the jets of water from the gill-openings during respiration. These
exhalations may play some part in driving the body forward, but

the effect varies with different fishes, being of greater importance to some and of little or none to others. A particularly powerful jet is usually expelled when a fish commences any swimming movement, thus giving an added impetus to the initial muscular efforts of the body in getting under way. Unless a fish is actually resting on the bottom, it is by no means as easy as it would appear to remain stationary in the water. Breathing cannot be suspended for a moment, and although this respiration may be comparatively slow as compared with that taking place when the fish is swimming, the exhalant jets of water are of sufficient strength to move the body forward, and some sort of action is necessary to counteract their force. Observation of a fish resting in mid-water in an aquarium shows that the pectoral fins are in more or less constant motion backing water, to counteract the forward thrust produced by the respiratory jets.

The speed attained by fishes has always been a subject of much speculation. Despite modern methods of research there is still little information on the speeds of different species. Gray is of the opinion that the maximum speed larger fishes (such as Salmon) could maintain for about twenty seconds would be 10 m.p.h. To keep up a speed of 5 m.p.h. a nine-inch trout would have to exert a backward thrust of about a half to a third of its own weight. It has been estimated that salmon can maintain a speed of 8 m.p.h.

That the 'swords' of swordfishes have been found deeply embedded in the timbers of ships is sometimes cited as evidence for the great speed attained by these species. However, this is susceptible to another interpretation. To quote Professor Gray . . . 'A little reflection will show, however, that the energy set free when the swordfish strikes the side of the dinghy, does not come from the movements of the fish's tail but from what is called the kinetic energy stored in the animal's whole body. If a fish, weighing 600 lb. and travelling at 10 m.p.h. runs into the side of a boat and is thereby brought to rest in a distance of 3 ft., the average force applied to the boat is about one third of a ton, and the whole of this force is applied over an area—the tip of the sword—of about one square inch. The blow would be the same as the blow of a sledge hammer weighing 10 lb. and meeting the boat at a speed of about 80 m.p.h. And, if a swordfish of 600 lb. travelling at 10 m.p.h. meets, end-on, a wooden ship travelling at 10 m.p.h. in the opposite direction, the average force applied at the point of the sword is about $4\frac{1}{2}$ tons.'

Practically all fishes adopt a horizontal position when swimming, but one or two species depart from this normal attitude. The vertical position of the Sea Horse (*Hippocampus*) has been already mentioned. The little Shrimp or Needle-fishes (Centriscidae) are curious creatures, with a long compressed body encased in a thin bony cuirass with a knife-like lower edge. One species found in the Indian Ocean lives in small shoals of about half a dozen individuals, and swims about in a vertical position with the long tube-like snout pointing upwards [Fig. 12]. On occasions, however, it has been observed to move in the normal horizontal attitude, and even vertically, but *head down*! A Cat-fish from the Nile and other

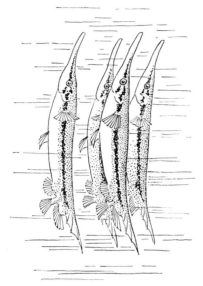

Fig. 12 A FISH WHICH SWIMS UPRIGHT
A small shoal of Shrimpfishes (*Aeoliscus strigatus*) x ¹/₂. (After Willey)

African rivers (*Synodontis batensoda*) has adopted the remarkable habit of floating or swimming leisurely at the surface of the water *with the belly upwards* [Fig. 13]. This habit, (also seen in other species of the genus) must have been well known to the ancient Egyptians, as it is frequently depicted in their sculptures and wall paintings in this anomalous position.

Among methods of locomotion other than swimming, leaping and burrowing may be considered briefly here, as they result from body rather than fin-movements. A fish may leap out of the water for one of several reasons, but usually to escape from an enemy, or to clear some obstacle. The strength and agility displayed by the Salmon (*Salmo*) [Fig. 14c] in leaping falls in its journey to the spawning ground is well known, and it has been observed to make repeated efforts to clear an obstacle which was too high for it, and to fall back at last through sheer exhaustion. It is this habit which

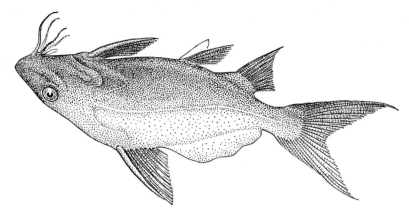

Fig. 13 A FISH WHICH SWIMS UPSIDE DOWN
Cat fish (*Synodontis batensoda*) x ¹/₂

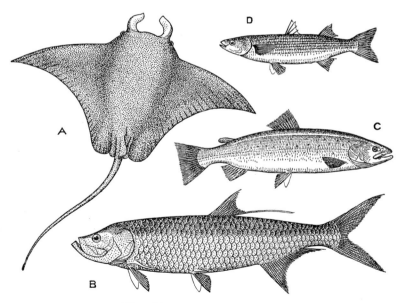

Fig. 14 FISHES THAT LEAP
A. Devilfish (*Manta birostris*) x *ca* ¹/₅₀; B. Tarpon (*Megalops atlanticus*)
x *ca* ¹/₂₀; C. Salmon (*Salmo salar*) x ¹/₁₂; D. Grey Mullet (*Mugil* sp.) x ¹/₁₀

has given the Salmon its name, the Latin *Salmo* being from the same root as *salire*, to leap.

The Tarpon (*Megalops*), a favourite with American sea-anglers, is another fish famed for its leaping powers, and its indulgence in this habit makes it necessary to employ some skill and perseverance in its capture [Fig. 14B]. Opinions differ as to the height to which these fishes are able to jump, but it is generally agreed that seven or eight feet probably represents the Tarpon's limit, while the Salmon is only able to better this by one or two feet. How are the jumps accomplished? Generally by the fish swimming rapidly upwards *through* the surface of the water into the air, giving a sharp flick with its tail as it leaves the liquid medium. All the active propulsion is provided by the muscular actions of the body while in the water, but the passing into the relatively less dense air accelerates the speed considerably and makes powerful leaps possible with a fairly slight muscular effort. Both Tarpon and Salmon hold the body in a curve while out of the water, and naturally fall to the concave side. Others, like the Grey Mullet (*Mugil*), keep the body rigidly in a straight line, so that the course in the air is determined solely by such external factors as the velocity of the wind, the angle of its direction to the fish, and so on.

The giant Devil-fish or Manta-ray (*Manta*), figuring in so many romances of tropical seas, is another fish which can leave the water on occasion and sail through the air to a height of more than five feet from the surface of the water. A full-grown specimen is somewhere in the neighbourhood of twenty feet long, and weighs more than 1000 lb., so that its sudden jump from the sea is an awe-inspiring sight. The noise made by its body as it returns to the water resembles the discharge of a cannon, being audible at a distance of a mile or more. The strength of this fish is prodigious, and when harpooned it will drag a boat through the water at great speed, so that it is sometimes necessary to cut the line at once to avoid disaster.

The habit of burrowing is generally associated with the eel-like type of body, but some of the Wrasses (Labridae) and the little Mud Minnow (*Umbra*) of North America and Central Europe are proficient burrowers. The latter is said to be perfectly at home in the mud, and one author claims that it can 'pass through soft mud with as much ease as other fishes do through clear waters.' The method of burrowing is quite simple, the fish merely employing active swimming movements with the snout pointed into the sand or mud. This is continued until a sufficient portion of the body is covered to enable its surface to obtain an effective grip, when progress is more rapid. Bottom-living forms like the Rays and Flat-fishes, instead of actually burrowing in the sea floor, wriggle their flattened bodies and throw sand over the upper surface until they are completely covered.

REFERENCES

BAINBRIDGE, R. (1961). Problems of fish locomotion. *Symp. zool. Soc Lond.*, No. 5.

GRAY, J. (1953). *How Animals Move*. Cambridge University Press.

GRAY, J. (1953). The locomotion of fishes: in, *Essays in Marine Biology*. Oliver and Boyd, Edinburgh and London.

HARRIS, J. E. (1953). Fin pattern and mode of life in fishes: in, *Essays in Marine Biology*. Oliver and Boyd.

WATTS, E. H. (1961). The relationship of fish locomotion to the design of ships. *Symp. zool. Soc. Lond.*, No. 5.

CHAPTER 3

FINS

THE NATURE and functions of the fins were indicated in the preceeding chapter (*cf.* p. 19). Briefly, fins are of two kinds: (1) median or unpaired, sometimes described as vertical fins; and (2) paired fins. The median fins include a *dorsal* in the middle line of the back, an *anal* along the belly behind the vent, and a *caudal* at the hinder end of the fish. The paired fins are of two kinds only, *pectorals* and *pelvics*, corresponding respectively to the fore and hind limbs of land vertebrates [Fig. 7]. The pectorals, sometimes referred to as the breast-fins, are always placed close behind the head, but the position of the pelvics varies in different groups of fishes.

Before considering the structure of the fins, it will be as well to discuss the manner in which they have arisen in the course of evolution. It is generally agreed that the earliest fish-like vertebrates possessed no true fins, but swam entirely by undulations of the body, and the fins were probably first developed as stabilising keels to counteract the tendency of the body to roll over sideways when in motion.

During the embryonic or larval stages of almost any fish the development of definitive median fins is preceded by a continuous fold of tissue extending along the back, round the tail and forward along the belly. Later in development this fold is strengthened by a series of parallel cartilaginous rods set at right angles to the body. Still later in ontogeny each rod splits into at least two portions. The lower pieces, known as basals, are situated within the body whilst the upper pieces or radials lie in the fin-fold. This condition is found in the living Lampreys and their allies (Cyclostomes) and is presumed to be the primitive condition of the median fin, such as might have occurred in the ancestors of all the modern fishes. From this condition the distinct dorsal, anal and caudal fins of higher fishes might well have evolved by the concentration of the radials into certain areas, coupled with the atrophy of the fold in the spaces between the fins. This, in fact, is what we can observe during the development of most living fishes.

The origin of paired fins is less clear, but the palaeontological evidence suggest that, like the median fins, the precursor of the

paired structures was a fin-fold, in this case running down each side
of the body from behind the gill openings to above the vent. The
only direct fossil evidence for such a fold is provided by *Jamoytius
kerwoodi* from the Upper Silurian of Lanarkshire. [See fig. 125].
Careful interpretation of other fossil Cyclostomes suggests that in
certain species there was a lateral fin-fold without much muscle
development and strengthened by scales and spines. Palaeontological evidence from other primitive fishes also lends weight to
the lateral fin-fold theory. For example, in the Acanthodians
(Lower Devonian) there is a ventro-lateral series of spines running
from behind the head to the anal fin; these could well have been
local strengthenings in a continuous fold of skin. The pectoral fin
of certain Placoderms (Devonian) shows undoubted evidence of its
origin by the concentration of radial elements, thus suggesting an
origin like that of the median fins.

In short, the available evidence from fossils, comparative anatomy
and embryology strongly hints at a 'fin-fold' origin for both median
and paired fins.

The condition of the continuous median fin in living Agnatha or
Cyclostomes was referred to above. Turning next to the Sharks we
find that, besides the demarcation of definite anal and dorsal fins,
the supporting radials are further subdivided than in Cyclostomes
and that the fins receive additional support from the presence of
numerous horny rays (ceratotrichia) situated beyond the radials.

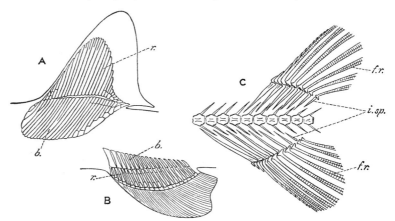

Fig. 15   STRUCTURE OF DORSAL AND ANAL FINS
A. First dorsal fin of Mackerel Shark (*Isurus oxyrhynchus*), dissected to
show cartilaginous supports; B. Anal fin of Chinese Sturgeon (*Psephurus
gladius*), similarly dissected; c. Skeleton of dorsal and anal fins, and
portion of vertebral column of Gar Pike (*Lepisosteus platystomus*). *b.*, basal
cartilages; *f.r.*, fin-rays; *i.s.p.*, interspinous bones; *r.*, radial cartilages.

In these fishes the ceratotrichia, as well as the cartilaginous radials, are completely covered by the skin and muscles associated with the fins, and are not visible externally.

Among the living Bony Fishes, the Sturgeons possess fins of a distinctly primitive type. The dorsal and anal are each provided with a fleshy lobe at the base, composed of fin muscles surrounding a series of rodlike structures (basals) within the body and radials in the muscular lobe [Fig. 15B]. The structure is strongly reminiscent of a shark's fin but the outer part of the fin is supported not by horny rays but by bony fin rays, actually modified scales, called lepidotrichia. This substitution of bony rays for horny ones obviously gives additional strength to the fin and in order to retain the necessary flexibility the rays are segmented into a number of sections.

In all the higher Bony Fishes the lobe at the fin base disappears, and the radials are reduced to mere nodules of bone or cartilage sunk within the body muscles but still articulating with the lepidotrichia which now form the sole external support for the fin. The basals persist as a series of rod-like structures, the interspinous bones, alternating with the neural and haemal spines of the vertebrae. It may be noted here that in the Lung-fishes (Dipneusti) and the Sturgeons, the fin rays are more numerous than the supporting radials. This must be considered a primitive character since it is the condition found amongst those early Bony Fishes which we know only as fossils. In later members of these orders we find a one-to-one relationship between rays and radials, just as in all the other living Bony Fishes (except, of course, the living Crossopterygian *Latimeria*, see p. 313).

The supporting skeleton of the caudal or tail fin [Fig. 17] is of a somewhat different nature to that of the dorsal and anal fins. It involves special modifications of the hinder end of the vertebral column. The caudal fins of adult fishes may be grouped into three principal forms, known as protocercal ('first tail'), heterocercal ('unequal tail') and homocercal ('equal tail').

The protocercal tail is probably the most primitive type. Here the hinder end of the notochord (*q.v.*) or the vertebral column is straight and divides the fin into two equal lobes. Around this central axis are arranged a series of rods which support the fin membrane. Although characteristic of many early fishes it is doubtful whether any forms living today have a primarily protocercal tail. The possible exception is *Latimeria* where the little epichordal lobe of the fin (probably the true caudal fin) has just this structure. The caudal of living fishes does, however, pass through a protocercal phase early in its embryonic development.

The heterocercal tail, characteristic of adult Selachians and certain primitive Bony Fishes, is best studied in such forms as the

Dog-fish (*Scyliorhinus*) or the Sturgeon. Here, the hinder end of the vertebral column is bent upwards and continues almost to the tip of the fin. The two lobes of the fin, although retaining their continuity around the tip of the column, are differentiated into a small upper lobe and a much larger lower lobe. The latter has its origin entirely from the lower side of the upturned vertebral column. Thus, both externally and internally the lobes of the caudal are asymmetrical.

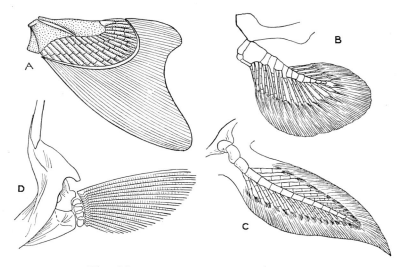

Fig. 16   STRUCTURE OF PECTORAL FINS
A. *Cladoselache fyleri*. (After Dean); B. *Pleuracanthus decheni*. (After Fritsch); C. Australian Lung-fish (*Neoceratodus forsteri*); D. Cod (*Gadus morhua*).

The homocercal fin, characteristic of most higher Bony Fishes, is superficially symmetrical; a prolongation of the body axis would seem to divide the fin into equal sized and continuous upper and lower lobes. Dissection, however, shows that this superficial appearance is misleading. Indeed the homocercal fin is nothing more than an extremely abbreviated heterocercal fin. The hinder end of the vertebral column, as before, turns upwards but unlike the heterocercal condition it does not reach the hindermost limit of the fin and the upper lobe is proportionally even smaller than in the heterocercal tail. Indeed, almost the entire fin is derived from the lower lobe, the upper lobe merely contributing a few small, unbranched rays to the upper, anterior margin of the fin. The great majority of lepidotrichia in the caudal articulate with the greatly expanded haemal arches (hypurals) of the last few vertebrae.

The transition from heterocercy to homocercy is found in numerous fossil Bony Fishes and can be seen in the living representatives of primitive groups, the Holosteans (*Amia* and *Lepisosteus*) and Brachiopterygians (*Polypterus*).

There remain a number of living fishes whose caudal fins cannot be classified in any of the three groups mentioned above, and for which special names have been coined. In many fishes (e.g. Rattails [Macrouridae], Eels [Anguilliformes], and some Blennies [Blennidae]) the tail is tapering and symmetrical, a so-called isocercal or leptocercal tail. Developmentally, this type of tail is brought about by the reduction in size of the lower caudal lobe and an elongation of the dorsal and anal fins until a continuous finfold is re-established. The true nature is, however, revealed by the internal asymmetry of the skeletal elements, at least in the young stages where the tip of the notochord is bent sharply upwards and hypurals are present. An internally symmetrical tail is found in the Cods (Gadiformes); here the true caudal is reduced and certain dorsal and anal fin elements have fused with it. Again, in the larva, the tail is fundamentally asymmetrical. The tail fin of modern Lung-fishes (Dipneusti) is still more difficult to interpret because we can gain no clues from embryology; at no stage is there any evidence of heterocercy. Yet, it is difficult to believe that this is a true protocercal tail because all the known ancestral Lung-fishes possessed clearly heterocercal tails. Perhaps the modern Lung-fish caudal fin is a pseudocaudal formed by the backward growth of dorsal and anal elements. Finally, mention must be made of a peculiar 'inverted' heterocercal tail, the so-called hypocercal form which is only known from certain early Agnatha. In this case the vertebral axis is turned sharply downwards and the lobe is developed from its upper surface, the lower lobe being greatly reduced.

From an evolutionary viewpoint, the heterocercal tail (and its modification, the hypocercal tail) is the most primitive, always assuming of course, that the even earlier fishes or fish-like vertebrates possessed a protocercal tail. Certainly the homocercal tail is a relatively recent acquisition.

The evolution, particularly the functional evolution, of paired fins has brought about even greater modification to the primitive parallel arrangement of the supporting basals and radials and their muscles, than was the case in the median fins. A detailed account cannot be given here and reference should be made to the more recent text books of ichthyology and comparative anatomy (see p. 370). In brief, the trend has been towards concentration of certain skeletal supporting elements, the development of a flexible fin web and a reduction in the area of attachment to the body so that greater mobility was achieved. Naturally, these changes have been effected in a number of ways some of which are shown in Fig. 16.

Since fin evolution and function are closely related we may now briefly consider the function other than propulsion of the various fins. In any moving body two major and conflicting problems must be resolved. One is the need for stability and the other for manoeuverability. The fin system of fishes provides a neat compromise.

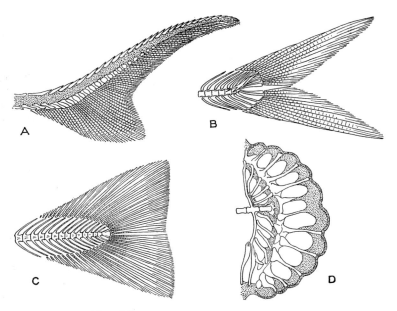

Fig. 17   STRUCTURE OF CAUDAL FINS
A. Sturgeon (*Acipenser* sp.); B. Ten-pounder (*Elops saurus*); C. Haddock (*Melanogrammus aeglifinus*); D. Sun-fish (*Mola mola*)

The median fins serve to control movement in the longitudinal and vertical axes of movement, namely rolling and yawing, whilst the paired fins are effective mainly in the transverse axis to control pitching and the horizontal direction of the body during forward swimming. From the outset, a distinction must be made between fin function in Sharks and Bony Fishes. In the former there is no swimbladder and consequently the body is heavier than water. The 'lift' provided by the hydrodynamic properties of a heterocercal tail helps to overcome this problem, but, it also tends to pitch the anterior part of the body downwards. The large, horizontally placed and relatively inflexible pectoral fins of a shark serve to counteract this pitching function and at the same time give additional lift. These fins also act as hydroplanes to give the body upward or downward direction in forward motion. They cannot serve as brakes because they are capable of only restricted flexure in the vertical plane. As a result, a shark cannot 'brake' and must turn if it is to avoid collision. Another characteristic of Sharks, relating to their lack of a swimbladder and consequent density (see p. 133), is that in order to keep off the bottom they must keep moving. The pectoral fins in Rays, of course, have taken on a totally different primary function, that of propulsion, but they must still serve for giving vertical direction to the swimming fish. The role of pelvic fins in Selachians is rather obscure and it is suggested that their principal function is as intromittent organs in copulation.

The functional pectoral-caudal fin interrelationship in the many fossil Cyclostomes and Placoderms was undoubtedly like that of the Sharks.

In Bony Fishes, the situation was dramatically altered with the evolution of a swimbladder which effectively reduced the density of the fish to that of the water. Problems of lift were thus greatly reduced and the paired fins freed for use in manoeuvering. As in Sharks, the pectorals still play a major part in controlling upward and downward movements but are relatively unimportant in the maintenance of a horizontal cruising plane. Their other and new function is that of brakes for which their large area and vertical or near vertical insertion is well suited. The pelvics act as counters to the pitching and lifting forces produced by the pectorals when braking and are also used to produce a rolling motion.

The spatial relationships, size and shape of the fins all show a remarkable correlation with the size, shape and centre of gravity of the fish's body, coupled with its way of life. A clear example, in fact, of the complicated but inescapable interrelationships which go to make up evolution.

Some of the modifications which the fins have undergone may now be considered.

In the Sharks (Pleurotremata) the dorsal fins retain their primary function of acting as stabilising keels, but in the Rays (Hypotremata), fishes adapted for a life on the sea floor, the need for such keels has disappeared and the dorsal fins are progressively reduced [Fig. 8A], until in the more specialised forms such as the Sting Rays (Dasyatidae) and Eagle Rays (Myliobatidae) they are altogether wanting [Figs. 8A; 22B; 24A]. In some of the Sharks, notably in the Bull-headed Sharks (Heterodontidae) of the Pacific and the so-called Squalid Sharks (Squalidae), each of the two dorsal fins is preceded by a stout, sharp spine [Figs. 53B; 77A]. The origin of these spines is somewhat obscure, but they are believed to be formed from the fusion of some of the denticles covering the front

parts of the fins (*cf.* p. 52). Such spines provide formidable defensive weapons, especially when associated with poison glands, as in our own Spiny Dog-fish (*Squalus*) (*cf.* p. 160).

Many of the Sharks now extinct possessed similar spines, and, not infrequently, where the remainder of the fish's body has been destroyed, these spines are the only record left. Many have been discovered in Devonian and Carboniferous strata, some saw-edged, some smooth, some straight, some curved, and some with elaborate sculpturing. The owners of some of these spines may never be discovered, but must have been of gigantic build, for a fin-spine found in the Carboniferous limestone of Bristol measured no less than three feet in length.

Among Bony Fishes the dorsal fin exhibits great diversity both in size and form, and is sometimes modified for the performance of special functions. It is rarely absent, but in the group of South American freshwater fishes known as Gymnotids, to which the Electric Eel (*Electrophorus*) belongs, it is either absent or reduced to a mere fleshy filament [Fig. 77c]. In the more primitive Bony Fishes the fin (or fins) is supported entirely by flexible and articulated rays, those at the front end generally being simple, while the majority are branched at their tips. Such fishes were grouped together by the older naturalists as Malacopterygians (soft fins) to distinguish them from the Acanthopterygians (spiny fins), in which the rays supporting the front parts of the dorsal and anal fins, as well as the outer rays of the pelvics, are converted into stiff-pointed spines. Occasionally these spines are slender and flexible, but they may always be distinguished from true soft rays by the absence of joints or branches.

In all Eels (Anguilliformes) the dorsal and anal fins are united with the caudal when this is present, and in the Morays or Muraenas (Muraenidae) the skin covering the fins is so thick that no trace of the rays is visible externally [Fig. 83a]. A peculiar conger-like Eel from the West Indies (*Acanthenchelys*) is worthy of mention, because, although the greater part of the dorsal fin is supported by soft rays in the usual manner, in a small section near the tail these have been converted into stiff spines. Examples of spines following soft rays are very rare indeed, but the Viviparous Blenny or Eel Pout (*Zoarces*) of British shores provides another case. The elongate dorsal fin occurs again in the Ribbon-fishes (Trachypteridae), which swim by means of wave-like movements of the body, aided by similar undulations of the fin. In the Oar-fish (*Regalecus*), a large oceanic species attaining a length of more than twenty feet, this fin extends along the entire upper edge of the compressed body, and the first few rays are prolonged into rather long filaments, each of which ends in a membranous flap [Fig. 8d]. The fins are bright scarlet in colour, and the general appearance of the head is not

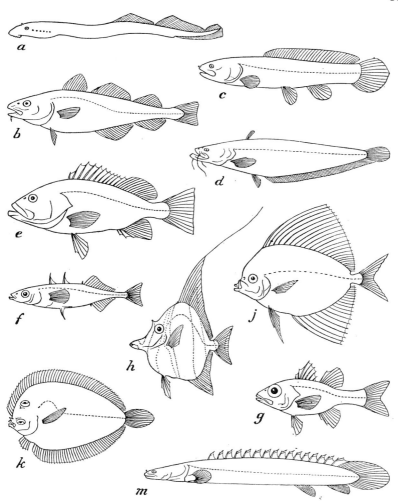

Fig. 18 DORSAL AND ANAL FINS

a. Sea Lamprey (*Petromyzon marinus*) x ¹/₁₀; *b.* Cod (*Gadus morhua*) x ¹/₁₀; *c.* Bow-fin (*Amia calva*) x ¹/₈; *d.* Wels or Sheat-fish (*Silurus glanis*) x ¹/₁₂; *e.* Sea Perch or Grouper (*Epinephelus* sp.) x ¹/₁₀; *f.* Stickleback (*Gasterosteus aculeatus*)x ¹/₂; *g.* Cardinal-fish (*Apogon frenatus*) x ¹/₄; *h.* Moorish Idol (*Zanclus canescens*) x ¹/₅; *j.* Sail-bearer (*Velifer* sp.) x ¹/₅; *k.* Flat-fish (*Engyprosopon grandisquama*) x ¹/₃; *m.* Bichir (*Polypterus bichir*) x ¹/₈

unlike that of a horse (*cf.* p. 365). In the closely related Deal-fish (*Trachypterus*) the form of the dorsal fin in the young fish is remarkable, the first six or so rays being produced into fine filaments more than four times as long as the fish itself. These streamers are ornamented with little membranous tags placed at intervals along their length [Fig. 115b]. Another member of the same order, known as *Velifer*, derives its name from the relatively huge size of both dorsal and anal fins [Fig. 18*j*].

In the majority of soft-finned fishes the dorsal fin is short and composed mainly of branched rays, only the first few being simple (as in the Herring [*Clupea*], and the Carp [*Cyprinus*], [Figs. 22d; 34]). Two extreme sizes of single dorsal fin are encountered in the Feather-back (*Notopterus*) or the Wels (*Silurus*), with a tiny flag-like fin in the middle of the back [Fig. 18*d*], and one of the fancy varieties of the Gold-fish (*Carassius*), in which it takes the form of a huge sail-like structure. In some fishes allied to the Carp, one of the simple rays of the fin is stiff and spinous, and not infrequently saw-edged behind, but no true spinous fin is developed. In the Cat-fishes, a strong spine resulting from the modification of one or more soft rays, nearly always precedes the remainder of the fin. It is often serrated on one or both of its edges, or is provided with formidable barbs, forming a powerful defensive weapon capable of inflicting a nasty wound [Figs. 32d; 24*k*]. Sometimes this spine is articulated with its basal support by means of an elaborate joint, enabling the fish to keep it erect when alarmed. When thus fixed, the spine cannot be involuntarily depressed without breaking it, but a rotary movement upwards and towards the body serves to release the catch and the fin can be lowered.

A curious modification of the dorsal fin is found in the Tarpon (*Megalops*), as well as in some of the members of the Herring family (Clupeidae), the last ray being drawn out into a long filament which is concave on its hinder edge and tapers to a fine point [Fig. 14b].

Among those soft-rayed fishes with more than one dorsal fin, mention may be made of the Gadids, which belong to the order of fishes known as Gadiformes, a group including such well-known food-fishes as the Cod, Pollack, Whiting, Haddock, Hake, and Ling. In the first four of these fishes there are three dorsal fins [Fig. 18b]; in the others only two. The little Rocklings (*Motella*), members of the same order, have a series of free rays just in front of the ordinary dorsal fin, and these may be continuously and rapidly vibrated for long periods. The function of such rays appears to be associated with sensory organs for locating and detecting food.

Among the spiny-rayed fishes, the rays at the anterior end of the dorsal fin may be transformed into spines as in the Sea Perch (*Epinephelus*) [Fig. 18*e*] or Fresh-water Sun-fish (*Lepomis*) [Fig. 24*e*],

or the spinous portion may be separated off as a distinct fin, as in
the Mackerel (*Scomber*) [Fig. 5A] or Cardinal-fish (*Apogon*) [Fig. 18g].
The evolution of spinous rays added a new function to the fins,
that of defence. Spines vary greatly in different fishes, both in
height and thickness, and may even be soft and flexible as in some of

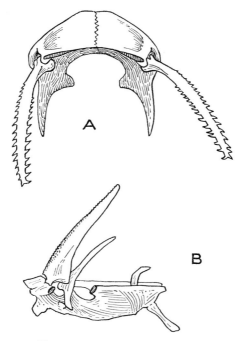

Fig. 19   LOCKING FIN-SPINES
A. Shoulder girdle and pectoral fin spines of a South American Catfish
(*Doras* sp.), ventral view, x ²/₃; B. Dorsal fin-spines and associated bones
of a Triggerfish (*Balistes* sp.), lateral view, x ²/₃

the Gobies and Blennies [Fig. 24f]. The Flat-fishes (Pleuronectiformes) provide an example of the secondary transformation of
spines into soft rays. It is known that these fishes have evolved from
spiny-rayed forms not unlike the Sea Perches, but have become
greatly modified for a life on the sea bottom. In a primitive form
from tropical seas (*Psettodes*) the dorsal fin commences well behind
the head, and the front part is still supported by stiff spines, but in
all other Flat-fishes the fin has extended forward on to the head,
and the spines have been reconverted into flexible articulated rays,
thus allowing the wave-like movements essential for swimming

(*cf.* p. 21). Some of the more specialised Soles (*Synaptura*), and the Tongue-soles (*Cynoglossus*), have both dorsal and anal fins united with the much reduced caudal, so that the three, together with the pelvic fin, form a complete fringe round the body.

In many of the Sea Perches and their allies the spines are unequal in size and strength, a somewhat delicate spine alternating with a stout one. In the Pine-cone Fish (*Monocentrus*) of Japan the spines are particularly formidable and are curiously arranged, being alternately directed to the right or left, none of them being truly vertical as in other fishes [Fig. 33E]. The closely related Soldier-fishes (*Holocentrus*) of the coral reefs of tropical seas derive their name from the stout and sharply pointed spines with which the fins are provided. In a few fishes, notably in the Weever (*Trachinus*) [Fig. 75] and in the Poison-fish (*Synanceia*) [Fig. 75], the spines of the dorsal fin are associated with poison glands, thus adding greatly to their efficiency as defensive weapons (*cf.* p. 161).

The Salmon provides an example of yet another type of dorsal fin. In addition to the rayed dorsal there is a second fin in the form of a small flap without any supporting structures, composed entirely of fatty tissue and covered with skin [Fig. 14c]. This is known as the adipose fin, and is found in all the members of the Salmon family, as well as in many Characins, and in the majority of Cat-fishes. In some of the latter the adipose fin is comparatively large [Fig. 13], and in certain species may develop a few soft rays. It is of interest to note that in the Mailed Cat-fishes (Loricariidae) this fin is a triangular flap of skin, the front edge of which is supported by a stout, movable spine [Figs. 22F; 33c], but in some related naked forms (*Astroblepus*) from mountain streams the spine has disappeared and the adipose fin has reacquired the typical Cat-fish form.

The position of the dorsal fin or fins also exhibits a fair amount of variation in different fishes. In the Gar Pikes (*Lepisosteus*, super-order Holostei) of North America [Fig. 48], and in the quite unrelated Pike (*Esox*, superorder Teleostei), both dorsal and anal fins are placed well back towards the hinder end of the fish; in the Herring (*Clupea*) and Carp (*Cyprinus*) the dorsal occupies a position more or less in the middle of the back [Fig. 34]; and in some of the Cat-fishes the rayed fin is considerably nearer to the head than to the tail [Fig. 18*d*]. During growth the vertical fins tend to undergo some change in form, those of young fishes being generally higher than those of adults. The position may also alter during the life of the individual fish, as in the Herring. In the larval stages the dorsal at first lies close to the tail, but its relative position shifts forward as growth proceeds. In the grotesque Shrimp-fish (*Aeoliscus*) the arrangement of the vertical fins is unique. The thin, bony cuirass encasing the body ends behind in a long, stout spine, and the two dorsal fins, crowded together at the hinder end of the fish, are placed below the spine, the second actually pointing *downwards*. The tail has been deflected at an obtuse angle from the trunk, and terminates in a small caudal fin, also pointing downwards [Figs. 12; 33H].

In the majority of fishes the dorsal and anal fins are capable of being erected or depressed at will, the separate spines or soft-rays being provided with special muscles for this purpose. When the fish is moving at any speed, the fins are always lowered, and in a fast-swimming form such as the Mackerel (*Scomber*) both the dorsal and anal can be folded away into grooves in the body, thus helping to maintain a streamline form. In the allied Sail-fish (*Istiophorus*) the spinous dorsal fin is of enormous size, but the whole structure can be tucked away into a deep groove when not required [Fig. 6A]. After a rapid burst of speed, most fishes erect the dorsal and anal fins to their fullest extent, in order to prevent undue rolling and yawing.

Among other fishes with more or less modified dorsal fins, the Trigger-fishes and Bichirs are worthy of mention. The Trigger-fishes (Balistidae) owe their name to the structure of the spinous dorsal, this being supported by three spines, the first very strong and hollowed out behind to receive a bony knob at the base of the second; by this mechanism the first spine remains immovably erect until the second, which acts as a trigger, is depressed, [Fig. 19B]. In the Bichirs (*Polypterus*, subclass Brachiopterygii), the anterior part of the dorsal fin takes the form of a number of separate, flag-like finlets, each consisting of a stout spine supporting a sail-like membranous flap [Fig. 18m], hence the name *Polypterus* (many fins).

In Mackerel (*Scomber*), Tunny (*Thunnus*), Bonito (*Katsuwonus*), and allied forms the soft dorsal fin is followed by a row of separate finlets, each of which is made up of a single much branched ray [Figs. 4; 5A]. Their function is obscure.

The Remoras or Sucking-fishes (Echeneidae) are characterized by the possession of an oval adhesive disc of complicated structure placed on the broad and flat upper surface of the head. It is provided with a varying number of transverse plates with free hinder edges, the whole being surrounded by a membranous border [Fig. 20]. By means of this disc the fish can attach itself to any flat surface, a slight erection of the plates creating a series of suction chambers. The adhesion is so strong that a Remora can only be dislodged with difficulty, unless it is slid forward or sideways. Some naturalists state that when attached these fishes seem to become quite insensitive, and show no sign of life however roughly treated. Remoras are in the habit of attaching themselves to Sharks, Whales, Porpoises, Turtles, and even occasionally to ships (*cf.* p. 364),

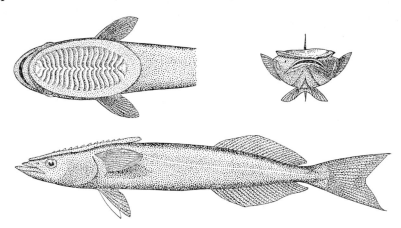

Fig. 20   A MODIFIED DORSAL FIN
Remora or Sucking-fish (*Remora remora*), x ¹/₆

and in this way not only gain protection, but are carried about without effort. The point of special interest about the sucker is that it is nothing more than a very much modified spinous dorsal fin, whose rays are divided into two halves, bent outwards in opposite directions, and have been transformed into the transverse plates.

Another remarkable modification is found in the Angler-fishes (Lophiiformes), in which the first ray of the spinous dorsal fin is placed on the snout and transformed into a line and bait. In the Common Angler or Fishing-frog (*Lophius*), for example, this ray is quite flexible and bears a membranous flag-like appendage at its tip, its function being to attract small fishes when waved about in the water in front of the Angler's formidable jaws [Fig. 89]. In the related Frog-fish (*Histrio*) and Bat-fish (*Ogcocephalus*) [Fig. 85] the line and bait is much reduced in size, and is sometimes represented merely by a short tentacle lodged in a cavity above the mouth. Among the Ceratioids, deep water oceanic Angler-fishes spending their lives in a region of more or less perpetual darkness, the bait generally takes the form of a luminous bulb of varying size which acts as a lamp to attract other fishes to destruction [Fig. 21]. In one species (*Lasiognathus saccostoma*) the basal part of the dorsal fin-ray is converted into a stout rod, followed by a slender line which is provided, not only with the usual luminous bulb, but also with a series of curved but non-functional horny hooks—a complete angler indeed [Fig.21c].

Another extraordinary angling device is found in *Ceratias holboelli*. The basal bone to which the rod (fin ray) and luminous 'bait' are attached lies horizontally in a groove running along the fish's back

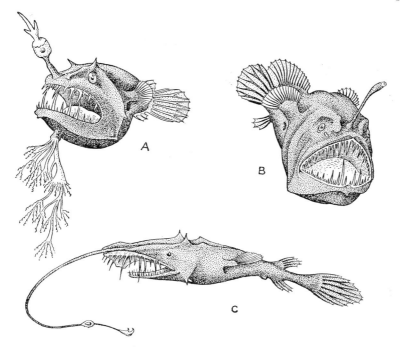

Fig. 21   CERATIOID ANGLER-FISHES
A. *Linophryne arborifer*, x ¹/₂; B. *Melanocetus johnsoni*, x ¹/₂; C. *Lasiognathus saccostoma*, x 1.

and head. To this bone are attached muscles which allow it to be protruded forward over the head or retracted, when it sticks out over the dorsal fin. Marshall has reconstructed the way in which this fish angles. 'When the fish is angling, the basal bone and rod are extended forwards so that the flashing, twitching bait is well beyond the mouth. On getting a 'touch' the retractor muscles of the basal bone move the bait closer and closer to the mouth; and if the prey is following, the rod is swung back when the basal bone comes to a stop, the large jaws open and the victim is engulfed. All this to move a light lure and attract food, but food means survival and survival may mean that the fish eventually contributes to the reproduction of its kind'.

The anal fin, placed on the lower edge of the body between the tail and the vent, may be briefly dismissed. Like the dorsal it exhibits some variation both in size and form in different fishes. In the Gymnotids, Eels, and other forms in which it functions as a locomotor organ, the anal fin is very long [Figs. 5F; 11B]; in other

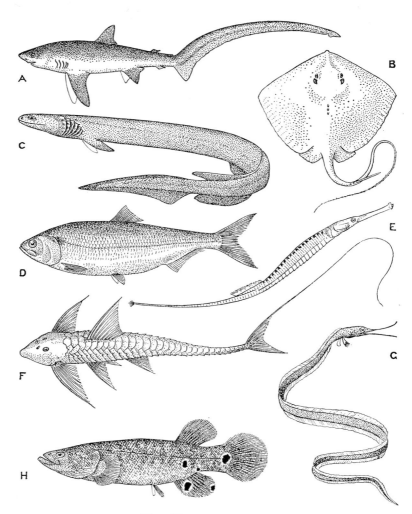

Fig. 22 CAUDAL FINS

A. Fox-shark or Thresher (*Alopias vulpes*), x ¹/₂₅; B. Sting Ray (*Dasyatis lata*), x ¹/₂₅; C. Frilled Shark (*Chlamydoselachus anguineus*), x ¹/₁₀; D. Allis Shad (*Alosa alosa*), x ¹/₄; E. Pipe-fish (*Microphis boaja*), x ¹/₃; F. Mailed Cat-fish (*Loricaria apeltogaster*), x ¹/₄; G. Snipe Eel (*Nemichthys scolopaceus*), x ¹/₅; H. Black-fish (*Dallia pectoralis*), x ²/₅.

fishes, where it acts mainly as a balancing keel, it is considerably shorter [Fig. 18]; in the Ribbon-fishes (*Trachypterus, Regalecus*) it is absent altogether [Fig. 8D]. It may be supported entirely by soft rays, or the first few rays may be converted into stiff spines, often of some size [Fig. 18*e, g*]. In some fishes, of which the John Dory (*Zeus*) and the Horse Mackerel (*Trachurus*) may be mentioned, the spinous portion is separated off from the remainder as a distinct fin [Fig. 32B]. In the Cod (*Gadus*) and related species the anal fin is divided into two portions, each composed entirely of soft rays [Fig. 18*b*]. In many of the South American Cyprinodonts, tiny fishes inhabiting fresh and brackish waters, the males are much smaller than the females, and the anal fin is specially modified to form an organ of elaborate structure used in copulation (*cf.* p. 228).

The last of the median fins, the caudal, has already been mentioned in discussing the tail itself, and little need be added here. Like the dorsal and anal, it is composed of both simple and branched rays supporting a thin membrane; true spines are never developed in this fin, but rudimentary or procurrent rays resembling spines may be found at the base of the lobes [Fig. 74A]. The Sea Horse (*Hippocampus*), which is unique in using the tail as a prehensile organ, shares with some of the Eels (Anguilliformes) and a few other fishes the distinction of being without a caudal fin [Fig. 5E]. The caudal fin of Sharks varies somewhat in form, but is rarely outwardly symmetrical, and the supporting rays are never visible externally. The function of the curious notch found in the upper lobe of the tail-fins of these fishes has never been satisfactorily explained. The Thresher or Fox Shark (*Alopias*) is outstanding for the great length of the upper lobe, which forms half the entire length of the fish [Fig. 22A]. This Shark is said to swim round a shoal of fishes, splashing the water with its tail, and thus driving them into a compact mass, where they form an easy prey. Among the bottom-living Rays (Raiidae) the caudal fin tends to be much reduced in size, whilst in the more specialised Sting Rays (Dasyatidae) and their allies it is wanting altogether, the long whiplike tail simply tapering to a fine point [Fig. 22B].

Among Bony Fishes with outwardly symmetrical tails, the shape and size of the caudal fin exhibits a good deal of variation [Fig. 23]. Six main types of fin may be recognised, described respectively as lunate or crescentic (Tunny), forked (Herring, Mackerel), emarginate (Trout, Carp, Perch), truncate (Flounder), rounded (Turbot and Lemon Sole) and pointed (Goby). The shape of the fin generally provides a good index of speed and agility. As a general rule, fishes with lunate or deeply forked caudals are capable of sustained swimming at high speed, whereas those with squarish or rounded caudals, although capable of sudden, short bursts of speed, are on the whole comparatively slow swimmers.

The Deal-fish (*Trachypterus*) and Sun-fish (*Mola*) may be selected as examples of fishes with unusual caudal fins. In the former this fin is unique in being directed upwards at right angles to the long axis of the body. In the young fish the rays of the lower lobe are prolonged into lengthy filaments like those of the dorsal and anal fins, but these become progressively shorter as growth proceeds and

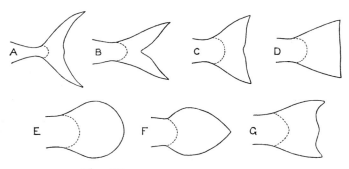

Fig. 23   SHAPES OF CAUDAL FIN
A. Lunate or crescentic; B. forked; C. emarginate; D. truncate; E. rounded; F. pointed; G. double emarginate.

finally the lower lobe of the fin disappears [Fig. 115B]. It will be recalled that in the Sun-fishes the body ends abruptly behind the short, high dorsal and anal fins, and is margined by a low, rounded caudal with a slightly wavy edge [Figs. 5c; 11D]. The supporting elements are derived from dorsal and ventral interspinous bones. The term '*gephyrocercal*' (bridge tail) is applied to a tail fin of this type. It represents a very specialized condition and is otherwise only found in the unrelated Pearl-fishes (*Carapus*).

So much for the median or unpaired fins. The paired fins, corresponding respectively to the arms and legs of the land vertebrates, are absent in the Lampreys and Hag-fishes (Cyclostomes), but, with few exceptions, one or both pairs are developed in other fishes.

The pectoral fins vary very little in position, being situated just behind the gill-opening or openings, and placed near the lower edge of the body in some fishes and higher up on the sides in others. The pectorals of the Sharks are considerably larger than those of the generality of Bony Fishes, [Fig. 24b]. A Shark seems to be quite incapable of making a sudden stop, and never uses the pectorals as brakes, being compelled to swerve to one side of any obstacle in its path. The enormous, flattened, lobe-like pectoral fins of the Rays and their relations (Hypotremata) joined to the sides of the head and body and forming the principal organs of locomotion, have

Fig. 24 PECTORAL FINS

a. Eagle Ray (*Myliobatis freminvillii*), x ¹/₂₀; b. Spotted Dog-fish (*Scylio-rhinus canicula*), x ¹/₈; c. Tunny (*Thunnus thynnus*), x ¹/₃₀; d. Thread-fin (*Polynemus paradiseus*), x ¹/₈; e. Fresh-water Sun-fish (*Lepomis megalotis*), x ¹/₄; f. Mud-skipper (*Periophthalmus koelreuteri*), x¹/₄; g. Scorpion-fish (*Pterois volitans*), x ¹/₁₀; h. Cirrhitid (*Paracirrhites fosteri*), x ¹/₅; j. Flying-fish (*Exocoetus volitans*), x ¹/₈; k. South American Cat-fish (*Doras* sp.), x ¹/₃; m. Gurnard (*Trigla* sp.), x ¹/₁₀

been described already [Fig. 24a]. They may also be used for steering, especially in those forms in which the tail is reduced to a mere filament. As in the case of the median fins, the paired fins of the Selachians are completely covered by skin and muscles, no trace of the rays being visible externally.

In the Bony Fishes these fins are nearly always relatively small, paddle-shaped organs, and only that part of the fin which is supported by the fin-rays is visible without dissection. These rays may be simple or branched, and in some of the Cat-fishes there is a stout spine along the outer edge of the fin, which may be saw-edged along one or both of its margins and attached to the body by an elaborate joint [Figs. 19A; 24k]. In the Mad Toms or Stone Cats (*Noturus, Schilbeodes*) of the United States, each of the spines is provided with a special poison gland at the base. Some Cat-fishes (*Doras* and *Clarias*) use the spines of the pectorals for progression overland, [Fig. 24k].

The shape of the pectorals varies to some extent. Fishes of moderate or slow speed, which may use these fins for propulsion or for backing water, have broad, rounded or spatulate pectorals [Fig. 24e]. In speedy fishes, on the other hand, where they are employed in executing wheeling or turning movements, the fins are always longer and frequently sickle-shaped (falcate) [Fig. 24c]. The peculiar leaf-like paired fins of the Australian Lung-fish (*Neoceratodus*) have been described on another page [Figs. 16c; 118c]. In the other Lung-fishes from Africa (*Protopterus*) and South America (*Lepidosiren*), the central lobe is long and narrow, the marginal fringe reduced or entirely suppressed, and the fins take the form of long, tapering filaments [Fig. 118A, B].

Rarely are the pectoral fins wanting, although they may be much reduced in size and efficiency. In some of the Pipe-fishes, however, and in certain of the Eels, they are absent. As in the case of the dorsal and anal, the pectorals have become variously modified in certain fishes for the performance of new functions, and the more interesting of these adaptations may now be examined.

The Flying-fishes (Exocoetidae) have greatly enlarged pectorals, [Fig. 24j], and use them to make flights through the air. In order properly to understand these flights, it is necessary to look at some more generalised members of the same order, the Skippers (*Scombresox*), Gar-fishes (*Belone*), and Half-beaks (*Hemirhamphus*). These fishes, especially the Half-beaks, are adept at leaping or 'skittering' over the surface of the sea. But the pectoral fins, being comparatively small, are only able to raise the head and forepart of the body out of the water, the tail remaining submerged and vibrating rapidly. There can be little doubt that the prolonged aerial excursions of the Flying-fishes are improvements upon the spasmodic jumps of the Gar-fishes and their allies. Flight is undertaken primarily in order to escape from enemies, or when the fishes are alarmed by approaching ships, but sometimes it occurs without any apparent cause. The actual flight seems to be carried out as follows: the fish increases its speed, rushing along near the surface of the water with its tail moving rapidly from side to side; it then makes a sudden leap out of the sea and is borne along through the air with the pectoral fins outstretched and practically motionless. The chief motive power of this soaring flight is supplied by the tail, there being no flapping of the 'wings' as in birds or bats; the pectoral fins act merely as aerofoils which enable to fish to *glide* through the air. The flight appears to be checked by the decreasing velocity of the fish, which returns to the water tail first, although it may plunge head foremost into the water without any visible attempt to check its speed. It is estimated that longer flights are from 200 to 400 metres in length, and the average speed under favourable conditions from 10 to 20 metres a second. The fish seems to be quite incapable of steering itself in the air, but during flight the elongate lower lobe of the caudal may become re-immersed in the water, and by a vigorous flip of the tail the fish can change its direction to the right or left, at the same time gaining increased speed. Likewise, the flight can be prolonged by the same means. As a rule the flights are close to the surface of the sea, but the fishes are not infrequently carried upwards to a height of 15 or 20 feet by a current of air, and in this way often land on the decks of ships. In the Flying Gurnards (Dactylopteridae), although the pectoral fins are even more enlarged than in the true flying fishes, the flight is more clumsy and less successful.

Among other fishes capable of short and generally erratic flights, the little Chisel-jaw (*Pantodon*) of African rivers and swamps, and some peculiar deep-bodied Characin fishes from South America (Gasteropelecidae) may be mentioned. The latter are known to rapidly beat the pectorals when in flight and to beat these fins against the surface of the water during the initial taxiing run. *Pantodon* can also 'flap' its pectorals but it is not known whether this motion is carried out when the fish is air-borne. Perhaps the powerful downward thrust is used for vertical take-off.

In the Sea Toads (Chaunacidae) and Frog-fishes (Antennariidae) the pectoral fins take the form of 'arms', ending in 'many fingered' 'hands,' by means of which they are able to crawl slowly about on the sea floor or to hang on to rocks or weeds [Fig. 85]. In the related Bat-fishes (*Ogcocephalus*) the 'arms' are even more muscular [Fig. 31D].

The small Mud-skipper (*Periophthalmus*), found on the coasts of tropical Africa, is renowned for its habit of leaving the water and moving about on the sand or mud in search of food. Of all fishes, this is the most amphibious. The pectoral fins of *Periophthalmus* are highly modified in connection with these habits [Fig. 24*f*]. The membranous part of the fin is carried at the end of a muscular stalk or arm and can be moved sideways as well as fore and aft. The usual movement on land has been well described as 'crutching', because of its resemblance to the movements of a man on crutches. The fish moves by swinging the pectorals forwards whilst the weight of the body is supported on the pelvic fins. Then, by pressing downwards and backwards with the pectorals the body is both lifted and drawn forwards until, at the end of the stroke, it falls forwards and rests on the pelvics. A more rapid movement, involving jumps of up to two feet is brought about by curling the body to one side and then suddenly straightening it. The caudal fin acts as a fulcrum and the fish is shot forwards. The agility of *Periophthalmus* is not confined to its terrestial excursions. The fish can skitter at speed across the water surface in a series of jumps as well as swim in a normal submerged fashion.

In certain fishes some or all of the rays of the pectoral fins may be drawn out into delicate filaments which carry tactile and gustatory organs. In the Thread-fins (*Polynemus*), for example, some four to eight of the lower rays are detached from the rest of the fin, and take the form of hair-like structures which may be longer than the fish itself [Fig. 24*d*].

In the Perch-like Cirrhitids or Firm-fins (Cirrhitidae), of which the Australian Trumpeter (*Latris*) is perhaps best known, the lower rays of the pectorals are simple, thickened, free at their tips, and sometimes more or less prolonged; here, again, they act as sensory organs, and probably aid the fishes in their search for food [Fig. 24*h*].

The Gurnards (*Trigla*) and Sea Robins (*Prionotus*) have two or three lower pectoral rays detached from the remainder and modified to form stout finger-like appendages [Fig. 24*m*]. These are well supplied with sense-cells and are used both in the search for food, and as limbs, forward movement being produced by placing the tips of the rays in contact with the sand and pushing backwards. In the Flying Gurnard (*Dactylopterus*) the upper wing-like portion of the pectoral is used for gliding, and the lower part, as well as the long thin pelvic fin, for creeping about on the sea floor. According to Dr. Beebe, the pelvic fins work alternately in a leg-like manner.

Coming, finally, to the pelvic or ventral fins, corresponding to the hind limbs of land vertebrates, it may be noted that, unlike the pectorals, their position varies considerably in the different groups of fishes, a fact of some importance in classification. In all the Selachians, and in the more primitive kinds of Bony Fishes, such as the Herring (*Clupea*), Salmon (*Salmo*), and Carp (*Cyprinus*), the pelvics are placed in the middle of the belly between the pectorals and the anal, and are said to be *abdominal* in position [Fig. 14B, C]. In other more evolved Bony Fishes, of which the Perch (*Perca*),

Bass (*Morone*), and Mackerel (*Scomber*) will serve as examples, they are *thoracic* in position; that is to say, they lie farther forward in the region of the chest and more or less below the pectorals [Figs. 5A; 24c, e]. In others, again, such as the Cods (Gadidae) and certain of the Blennies (Blennioidei), the pelvics are described as *jugular* in position, and actually lie in front of the pectorals in the region of the throat [Fig. 18b].

A number of Bony Fishes, and particularly those forms which spend most of their time in burrowing, pelvic fins are either very much reduced in size or are wanting altogether. All the living members of the order of Eels (Anguilliformes) are without pelvics, but these have undoubtedly been derived from fishes which possessed a full set of fins, confirmation of this view being provided by a fossil Eel (*Urenchelys*) from the Chalk of Mount Lebanon which shows distinct traces of both paired fins as well as a separate caudal fin. Pelvics are absent in all the Pipe-fishes (Syngnathidae), Synbranchoid Eels (Synbranchiformes), Gymnotids (Gymnotiformes), Globe-fishes (Tetraodontidae) and Porcupine-fishes (Diodontidae), and are also suppressed in many of the Blennies and Cusk-eels (Blennioidei, Ophidioidei). Even when developed, the pelvics may be reduced to mere filaments, as in some Cods (Gadidae), and in the Oar-fish (*Regalecus*), where they are represented by a pair of long rays, each expanded into a blade-like structure at the tip [Fig. 8D]. In the Sticklebacks (*Gasterosteus*) each pelvic is composed of a sharply pointed spine and one soft ray [Fig. 18f]; in the Pine-cone Fish (*Monocentrus*) [Fig. 33E] and in some Trigger-fishes, etc. it is reduced to a spine alone [Fig. 33D]. In certain species of Filefishes (Monacanthidae) the pelvic bone with its spine is freely movable, and is connected with the body by a wide flap of skin [Fig. 11c]; this is said to be used by the fish for fixing itself into crevices in the rocks or coral reefs.

It is very rarely that the pelvic fins have any propulsive function; they mainly function as accessory manoeuvring organs and as counters to the pitching force which results from the braking action of the pectoral fins. During rapid swimming they are generally drawn in close to the body. As in the case of the pectorals, some or all of the rays may be drawn out into lengthy filaments, as in the Dwarf Cod-fish (*Bregmaceros*) and Gourami (*Osphronemus*).

The most widespread modification of the pelvics is to form a sucking disc which enables the fish to cling to rocks, stones, and other fixed objects. The little Bornean Sucker (*Gastromyzon*), found only in the mountain torrents of Borneo (*cf.* p. 200), has the whole of the lower surface of the body modified to form a large sucker, in which the long and horizontally placed pectoral and pelvic fins play an important part [Fig. 25c]. The Gobies (Gobioidei), a large and varied suborder of fishes, mostly of small size, found mainly among the rocks between tide-marks, have the pelvic fins united to form a rather deep cup-like sucker [Fig. 25D]. In the Lump-sucker (*Cyclopterus*) and Sea-snail (*Liparis*) a somewhat similar sucking disc is developed, but the pelvics have been so much modified as to have completely lost their fin-like appearance [Fig. 25A]. The suction produced is very powerful, and some difficulty is experienced in removing a fish from an object to which it has attached itself. The Cling-fishes (Gobiesocidae) are curious little creatures found

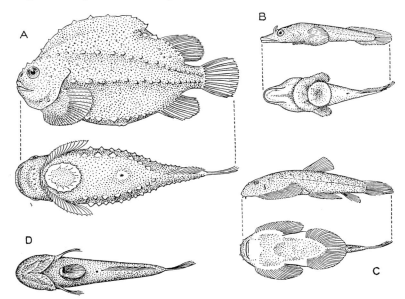

Fig. 25   FISHES WITH VENTRAL SUCKERS

A. Lump-sucker (*Cyclopterus lumpus*), x ¹/₄; B. Cling-fish (*Lepadogaster gouani*), x ¹/₃; C. Bornean Sucker (*Gastromyzon borneensis*), x ¹/₃; D. Lower surface of Black Goby (*Gobius niger*), x ¹/₂

between tide-marks among loose stones and shells, to which they adhere firmly by means of their suction discs. The disc is relatively large and of a complicated structure; it is composed largely of pads of thickened skin, but the widely separated pelvic fins and even the much modified bones of the pectoral girdle may contribute to its formation [Fig. 25B].

Among the Flat-fishes, the asymmetry so characteristic of the group extends to the pelvic fins in a large number of species. In the Scald-fish (*Arnoglossus*), for example, the pelvic of the left side, that is of the upper or coloured side, is large and placed along the lower margin of the body like a fringe, whereas that of the lower side is quite small and placed at some distance from the edge. In some specialised Australian Flat-fishes (*Rhombosolea*) the pelvic fin of the blind side, in this case the left side, has disappeared altogether, and the other elongate fin has become joined to the anal, thus completing a more or less continuous fin round the edge of the fish's body.

In all living Sharks and Rays the hinder parts of the pelvic fins in the male are modified to form elaborate organs known as 'claspers' or mixopterygia, which not only serve to grasp the female during copulation, but also assist in the process of fertilisation (*cf.* p. 227).

REFERENCES

HARRIS, J. E. (1953). Fin pattern and mode of life in fishes: in, *Essays in Marine Biology*. Oliver and Boyd, Edinburgh and London.

WESTOL, S. T. (1958). The lateral fin-fold theory and the pectoral fins of Ostracoderms and early fishes: in, *Studies on Fossil Vertebrates*. Athlone Press, University of London.

CHAPTER 4

SKIN, SCALES AND SPINES

THE SKIN of a fish, like that of any other vertebrate, is composed of two layers, a thin outer epidermis and an inner dermis. The epidermis is made up of several layers of simple cells, of which the outer are constantly worn away by wear and tear, and replaced by new ones developed at its base. The dermis has a more complicated structure, being made up of a thick layer of connective tissue, with which are mingled muscle fibres, clusters of fine blood-vessels, and nerves. The inherent slipperiness of a fish's body is due to the presence of a slimy mucus which is constantly secreted in large quantities by special cells and glands situated in the epidermis. The slime excreted varies greatly both in quantity, and probably also in chemical composition, in different species. In some of the Lampreys the glands are especially numerous, while a single Hag-fish (*Myxine*) placed in a bucket of water will soon convert the fluid into a thick mass of whitish jelly.

In addition to the skin, there is generally an outer covering of scales of one kind or another, generally spoken of as the exoskeleton, to distinguish it from the endoskeleton (skull, backbone, etc.). When scales are present the skin itself is nearly always thin and delicate, but in those fishes without scales, plates or spines it is strengthened in some way. Thus, in the naked Cat-fishes (Siluroidei) it is thick and leathery, and in the Sun-fish (*Mola*) the tough roughened skin is further reinforced by an underlying layer of cartilaginous material two or three inches in thickness. The curious Horse-fish (*Agriopus*) of South Africa is probably unique in being able to cast off its skin, at least in patches. The form of the scales, spines, or other related structures varies considerably in the different groups of fishes, and provides an important character for their classification.

In the Cyclostomes scales are altogether wanting, but a study of their extinct ancestors suggests that this is a feature of degeneration rather than a primitive character.

The dermal denticles of Sharks and Rays, sometimes known as odontoids or placoid scales are quite unlike the scales of Bony Fishes and will be described first. The surface of a shark's body is generally rough to the touch, due to the presence of innumerable tooth-like structures arranged in regular oblique rows, covering the whole of the head, body, and part of the fins. Each of these denticles consists of two portions, a bone-like base which is embedded in the skin and therefore invisible during life, and a superficial enamel-covered spine projecting freely outwards and backwards [Fig. 26*a*, *b*]. The fine structure and properties of this so-called enamel differ from the enamel of mammalian teeth; it is often

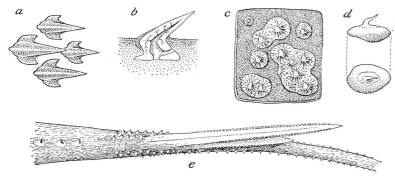

Fig. 26 DERMAL DENTICLES

a. Isolated denticles of the Spotted Dog-fish (*Scyliorhinus canicula*); greatly enlarged; *b.* Diagrammatic cross-section of a denticle of a Selachian, showing the enamel covering and the central pulp cavity; greatly enlarged; *c.* Portion of skin with dermal denticles of the Bramble Shark (*Echinorhinus spinosus*), x 1/2; *d.* "Buckler" of Thornback Ray (*Raia clavata*), lateral and dorsal view, x 3/4; *e.* Tail-spine of Sting Ray (*Dasyatis* sp.), x 1/3

referred to as vitrodentine. It is possible that this outer layer is formed from a tissue which does not occur in higher animals (Kerr, 1955). Such denticles provide the familiar 'shagreen,' and the proved durability of shark-leather is largely due to the re-inforcement provided by these structures (*cf.* p. 346).

In embryonic development the denticles make their appearance as minute conical or papilliform bodies within the skin; certain cells in the outer, epidermal layer of each cone give rise to a coat of hard enamel-like substance; the dermal portion gives rise to dentine or ivory with a central pulp cavity containing the blood-vessels and nerve [Fig. 27A]. The base of the cone spreads out to form the basal plate, in the centre of which is a hole for the passage of the blood-vessels and nerve.

Unlike the scales of Bony Fishes, the placoid scales of Sharks do not increase in size as the fish grows. Instead, new scales are added between the existing ones. This process goes on the whole time so that at any one moment there will be a number of newly erupted scales as well as some in the process of disintegration. These may easily be recognised by their lack of colour and general resemblance to grains of sugar.

The arrangement of the denticles already described is that found in the familiar Dog-fishes (*Scyliorhinus*, *Squalus*, *Mustelus*), as well as in most other Sharks, but the denticles themselves present considerable differences in form and size, being sometimes flat,

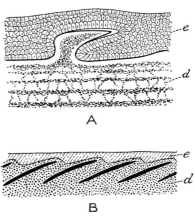

Fig. 27   DEVELOPMENT OF DENTICLES AND SCALES
A. Semi-diagrammatic section through the skin of an embryo Shark (After Gegenbaur); B. Diagrammatic longitudinal section through the skin of a Bony Fish to show position of scales (After Boas). *d*. Dermis; *e*. Epidermis.

sometimes spine-like, and sometimes taking the form of rounded knobs. In the Bramble Shark (*Echinorhinus*), however, they are distributed irregularly over the body, and appear as large rounded tubercles of varying size, each surmounted by a tuft of fine spines [Fig. 26c]. In the Rays (*Raia*) the denticles are generally scattered sparsely and unevenly over the upper surface of the head, body and pectoral fins; they are usually most prominent along the middle line of the back and on the upper part of the tail, and may be sharply pointed, flattened, or reduced to mere knobs [Figs. 26e; 101]. In the Thornback Ray (*Raia clavata*) the greatly enlarged denticles are known as 'bucklers' [Fig. 26d], and in other species of the same genus each principal spine has smaller accessory spines developed round its base. In the Torpedoes (Torpedinidae), on the other hand, and in some of the Sting Rays (Dasyatidae) and Eagle Rays (Myliobatidae), the denticles are absent and the skin is smooth.

Outstanding in the range of dermal armature is the tail-spine or 'sting' of the Sting Rays and related forms, which in these fishes takes the place of the dorsal fins. Its origin is somewhat obscure, but it may have arisen through the enlargement or fusion of certain denticles in the tail region. It is generally serrated along both margins, and may be as much as from eight to fifteen inches in length, providing a formidable weapon which, when the tail is lashed from side to side or curled round the intended prey, inflicts jagged wounds. The 'stings' are shed from time to time, and replaced by new ones growing from underneath; sometimes two or three may be present in one fish at the same time [Fig. 26e].

In the Saw-fishes (Pristidae), large, ray-like fishes found in all warm seas, the snout is produced to form a long flat blade, armed on either margin with a series of strong tooth-like structures

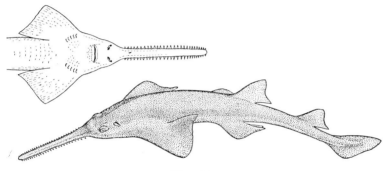

Fig. 28
Saw-fish (*Pristis zijsron*), x ¹/₂₀

[Fig. 28]. These are in fact enlarged teeth and are firmly implanted in sockets in the cartilage of the rostrum. Saw-fishes grow to a large size, specimens twenty feet in length being quite common, and 'saws' six feet in length and a foot across the base are by no means rare.

It is of interest to note that in the Chimaeras and their allies (Holocephali), although the skin is naked in the adult, small patches of denticles, essentially similar in structure to those of the Sharks and Rays, still remain on the claspers [Fig. 73], and in the young there may be a double row of denticles along the back.

The scales of all the Bony Fishes differ from the denticles of the Selachians, not only in their structure, but also in being derived entirely from the dermal layer of the skin [Fig. 27B]. Since the epidermis plays no part in their development, enamel no longer enters into their make-up. There are, of course exceptions. Denticles exactly like those of sharks are found on the body armour of certain South American cat-fishes (e.g. *Plectostomus, Callichthys* and

Loricaria) and on the sword of sword-fishes (*Xiphias* and *Istiophorus*).

Far greater diversity of scale structure is found amongst the Bony Fishes, particularly when the long extinct fossil forms are taken into account.

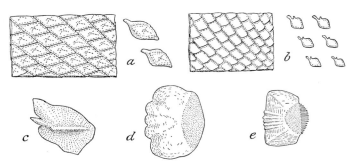

Fig. 29   SCALES

a. Portion of skin and isolated scales of the Gar Pike (*Lepisosteus* sp.), x about 1; *b*. The same of the Bichir (*Polypterus bichir*), x ¹/₂; *c*. Isolated scute of large Sturgeon (*Acipenser* sp.), x ¹/₆; *d*. Cycloid scale of Tarpon (*Megalops atlanticus*), x ¹/₄; *e*. Ctenoid scale of Soldier-fish (*Holocentrus ascensionis*), x 8.

The thin bony scales of the Teleostei represent one extreme whilst the thick, many-layered scales of most extinct Crossopterygii and Dipneusti represent the other. In the Crossopterygians the scale is composed of four distinct layers, [Fig. 30B], a basal one of dense bone (isopedine layer), a layer of spongy bone with numerous interconnecting canals, a layer of dentine-like tissue (cosmine layer) and finally a thin superficial layer of clear enamel. Such scales are called cosmoid and occur only in the Crossopterygii (including the one surviving species *Latimeria chalumnae*) and the fossil Lung-fishes (Dipneusti). The scales of living Lung-fishes differ greatly from the cosmoid type.

A modified form of cosmoid scale is found in the extinct members of the superorder Chondrostei. This is the so-called palaeoniscoid scale [Fig. 30A]. In these, the cosmine layer is greatly reduced in thickness, but the bone layer corresponding to the isopedine is thicker. The upper surface is covered not by a thin enamel coat but by a thick sheet of an enamel-like substance called ganoine. Ganoine resembles enamel in being a very hard tissue composed almost entirely of mineral matter. It differs from enamel in several ways. The living Chondrosteans, the Sturgeons and Spoon-bills (Acipenseriformes), have lost most of their scales, and those that persist are reduced to a bony plate.

A modified palaeoniscoid scale occurs in the superorder Holostei, another group which is best known from extinct forms. This type of scale (lepisostoid) is formed from only two layers, the ganoine and isopedine layers. No trace of a cosmine layer can be detected. Of the living Holosteans, the Gar-pikes (*Lepisosteus* sp.) retain a scale type not greatly different from that of the fossils, but in the Bowfin (*Amia calva*) the scales are reduced to thin bony discs.

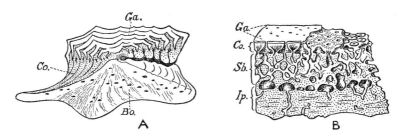

Fig. 30 SCALES

A. Palaeoniscoid scale. B. Cosmoid scale. *Bo.*, bone base; *Co.*, Cosmine layer; *Ga.*, Ganoine in A., enamel in B.; *Ip.*, Isopedine layer; *Sb.*, layer of spongy bone. (After Goodrich)

Another living fish with 'archaic' scales is *Polypterus*, the Bichir of Africa (and the related genus *Calamoichthys*), now referred to the subclass Brachiopterygii. The affinities of these two genera seem to lie with palaeoniscoid fishes and indeed some authors have placed them in that group. Their scale structure certainly suggests some such relationship. It is of the generalized palaeoniscoid type, with a cosmine layer, a basal isopedine layer and a superficial cover of ganoine.

From our knowledge of living forms with 'primitive' scales it seems probable that the scales of the extinct forms were covered by a layer of dermis as well as by the epidermis.

In most of the extinct Crossopterygii, Dipneusti, Chondrostei and Holostei the body was virtually encased in a thick armour of scales. The scales of *Polypterus* and *Lepisosteus* incorporate a system of fibres which link each scale row into a single unit; the different rows also have fibrous links but here the union is more flexible. Body flexibility in these forms must have been severely limited, the fishes relying for protection on their armour and not on speedy swimming. Likewise, none could be considered a swift-moving predator. They doubtless hunted by stealth or, as we suspect in many cases, fed on relatively slow-moving or sedentary prey.

Full body flexibility was only attained by the evolution of a scale type such as we find in the living Teleosts and some of the advanced Holostei (for example the Herring-like Leptolepids). Here the scale is reduced to two extremely thin plates, one calcified and one fibrous.

The typical scaly covering in a modern Bony Fish may best be studied in such fishes as the Carp (*Cyprinus*) or the Perch (*Perca*). In the Carp [Fig. 34] the whole body with the exception of the head and fins is protected by a number of regularly arranged, thin, flexible cycloid scales, overlapping one another like the tiles on the roof of a house. Each scale, which is shaped roughly like the human finger-nail, has the front end inserted deep into a pouch in the dermal layer of the skin, the hinder portion being quite free. The overlapping (imbrication) of the scales is, from a mechanical point of view, important, and may be explained in the following manner. The muscles attached to the dermis tend to exert a somewhat unequal pull, and, therefore, to depress the scale areas, particularly at their front margins; in this way the growing scale is forced to lie obliquely, and at a later stage its hinder end appears through the skin [Fig. 27B]. This free portion is covered by thin epidermal and dermal membranes. In the Perch the scales are very much smaller, but have exactly the same arrangement. A closer study of a scale under low magnification shows that its hinder end is provided with a row of small tooth-like spines instead of being smooth as in the Carp [Fig. 29*d*, *e*]. Such a scale is known as ctenoid (comb-like).

The arrangement of scales just described may be taken as typical of most Bony Fishes, but a large number of deviations from this occur, either in the direction of degeneration or of further specialisation. Cycloid (smooth) and ctenoid (spinate) scales are not so widely different as would appear from the above descriptions, as the one type is linked with the other by an almost complete series of intermediate stages. For example, the posterior edge of a cycloid scale may be wavy (crenulated), or the spines of a ctenoid scale may be soft and scarcely noticeable, in which case the scale is spoken of as ciliated. In some fishes the spines may extend on to the hinder free portion of the scale, giving it a roughened appearance. As a general rule, fishes with soft-rayed fins (e.g. Herring, Salmon, Roach) have cycloid scales, whereas the scales are ctenoid in the majority of spiny rayed fishes (e.g. Perch, Bass), but exceptions to this rule are numerous. Both types of scale may be developed on different parts of the body in the same fish. Thus in many of the Sea Perches (*Epinephelus*) the scales above the lateral line are mostly ctenoid and those below it cycloid, and in the Dab (*Limanda*) the ctenoid scales occur on the upper or coloured side, those on the blind or white side being quite smooth.

The scales exhibit great diversity in shape in the different species, ranging from the roughly circular to the long oval. They also vary greatly in size. In the Tarpon (*Megalops*), for example, each scale is more than two inches in diameter [Fig. 29*d*], whilst those of the

Mahseer (*Barbus*), the famous game-fish of the rivers of India, are even larger, each being about the same size as the human palm. At the other extreme we have the minute cycloid scales of the Tunny (*Thunnus*) and Mackerel (*Scomber*), and the microscopic scales of the Common Eel (*Anguilla*).

In Clupeid fishes (Herring, Sprat, Pilchard, Shad, etc.), the outer epidermal covering is very thin indeed, and the scales, which are placed in shallow pockets, appear to be lying on the surface of the body. Such scales are termed deciduous, because of the ease with which they are rubbed off when the fish is handled. In other fishes, of which the Plaice (*Pleuronectes*) will serve as an example, they are more or less deeply embedded in the skin. They are often also reduced in size, and instead of overlapping, remain quite separate from each other. The Common Eel (*Anguilla*) has a very slimy skin, which is, to all appearances, quite naked, but if a piece be examined under a microscope the presence of numerous, minute and deeply embedded scales is revealed.

The ancient Hebrews, misled by the naked appearance of the Eel's skin, included this species among the fishes forbidden to them by Moses. These strict laws, forbidding as they did many plentiful and tasty species, naturally became gradually modified; fish with 'at least two scales and one fin' were soon permitted, and, finally, any part of any fish on which traces of scales were visible.

The Dab (*Limanda*), with ctenoid scales on the upper surface and cycloid scales below, has already been described. Other Flat-fishes have smooth scales on the middle of the upper side whilst those on the head and near the edges of the body are spinate. In the Flounder (*Platichthys flesus*) most of the scales on the head, in the region of the lateral line, and also a series along the bases of the dorsal and anal fins, are represented by little thorny tubercles, generally stronger on the coloured side of the fish [Fig. 8B]; the remainder of the body is covered with embedded cycloid scales, but in an allied species, the Diamond Flounder of the Pacific coasts of North America, these have been almost entirely suppressed, and the entire head and body is armed with irregularly scattered spiny tubercles [Fig. 31A]. In another related form from Japan (*Platichthys bicoloratus*) the tubercles are aggregated into clusters, and take the form of bony patches of varying size [Fig. 31C]. In another group of Flat-fishes the closely related Turbot (*Scophthalmus maximus*) and Brill (*S. rhombus*) have quite different forms of scaly covering. The body of the Brill is armed with small cycloid scales, which are more or less overlapping, whereas the Turbot has a naked skin, but the coloured side bears a number of small, scattered, bony tubercles. The Black Sea Turbot (*S. maeoticus*), a distinct species, has very much larger tubercles, developed on both the lower and upper surfaces [Fig. 31B]. In many of the more specialised Flat-fishes

(Soles, Tongue Soles, etc.) some of those on the under side of the head become transformed into tiny membranous filaments, which are very sensitive and act as organs of touch.

Among other fishes with armature, mention may be made of the Lump-sucker (*Cyclopterus*), whose thick skin is studded with bony warts, some of which are enlarged to form a series of cone-like projections along the back and three rows on either side of the body [Fig. 25A].

Two domesticated varieties of the Common Carp (*Cyprinus carpio*) produced by fish culturists may be briefly described, since both these artifical forms exhibit modifications of the normal scaling. In the Mirror Carp (King Carp) there are one or two series of enlarged scales along the middle of each side, and generally some smaller scales near the bases of the fins; all these are more or less widely separated and the rest of the body is naked [Fig. 145D]. The Leather Carp has a thick, roughened skin, which is entirely devoid of scales.

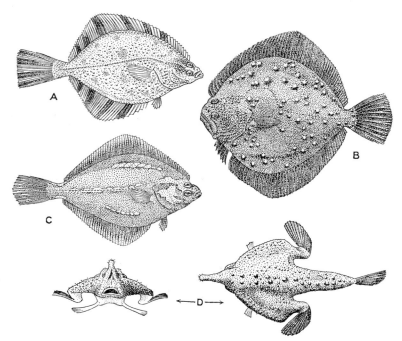

Fig. 31   FISHES WITH TUBERCLES
A. Diamond Flounder (*Platichthys stellatus*), x ¹/₄; B. Black Sea Turbot (*Scophthalmus maeoticus*), x ¹/₈; C. Japanese Flounder (*Platichthys bicoloratus*), x ¹/₄; D. Bat-fish. (*Ogcocephalus vespertilio*), x ¹/₄

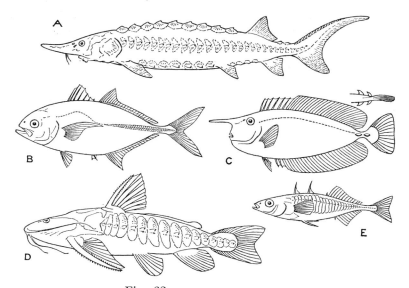

Fig. 32 FISHES WITH SCUTES

A. Sturgeon (*Acipenser sturio*), x ¹/₈; B. Pampano or Carangid (*Caranx* sp.), x ¹/₄; C. Unicorn-fish (*Naso brevirostris*), x ¹/₈; D. South American Cat-fish (*Megalodoras irwini*), x ¹/₃; E. Three-spined Stickleback (*Gasterosteus aculeatus*), x ¹/₂.

Among other instances of specialisation may be mentioned the the presence of scutes along the middle of each side in the region of the lateral line. These may result from the modification of ordinary scales or may develop as entirely new structures. In the Scad or Horse Mackerel (*Trachurus*), a member of a large group of fishes known as Pampanos or Carangids (Carangidae), the lateral line is armed with a row of numerous keeled shields, which in the tail region are armed with sharp, knife-like spines [Fig. 32B]. Somewhat similar spinous structures in this region occur in many of the Gurnards (*Trigla*). The members of a family of Cat-fishes found in the rivers of South America (Doradidae) possess a row of strong, bony scutes along the middle of either side, each scute is armed with a sharp spine bearing a superficial resemblance to the bucklers of the Sturgeons [Fig. 32D].

Scales are wanting in the little 'Tiddler' or Three-spined Stickle-back (*Gasterosteus*), but there is a series of large bony plates along each side, which in some specimens extends from the head to the tail, but in others is reduced to two or three plates behind the gill-opening [Fig. 32E]. The Stickleback is equally at home in salt or in fresh water, and there is a definite connection between the salinity of the water and the development of the plates. As far as the British Isles are concerned, individuals from inland waters nearly always exhibit the reduced number of plates, whereas examples from the sea are fully armed, intermediate types occurring in estuarine waters. Individuals from still more southerly localities may lack plates altogether.

It has been seen that the past history of fishes reveals a story of heavily armoured primitive forms followed by a definite decrease in armour. Those Bony Fishes which have readopted a coat of mail (although of a totally different structure) may now be considered. As a general rule, these are sluggish creatures, which have sacrificed speed and agility and have come to depend on their armour for protection from their enemies. The South American Cat-fishes, known as Hassars or Cascaduras (*Hoplosternum*), have the body completely encased in mail, made up of a double row of broad overlapping bony shields on each side. The arrangement of the shields is metameric, there being one pair to each vertebra or muscle segment. Allied to the Hassars are the Mailed Cat-fishes or Loricariids (Loricariidae), a large and varied family confined to the rivers of Central and South America. The body is protected above and on the sides by series of bony plates [Fig. 33c], the chest and abdomen being either naked or covered with much smaller plates. The plates on the sides have a metameric arrangement, and may be more or less sharply keeled or variously armed with small spines set in sockets. These smaller spines are of special interest, since they are formed of dentine capped with enamel; thus, they are essentially similar in structure to the dermal denticles of the Selachians. The Mailed Cat-fishes are sluggish creatures, spending most of their time attached to stones or other objects at the bottom of a stream, and the bony armour provides them with an efficient protection against enemies. In some very closely related fishes from the mountain streams of the Andes (*Astroblepus*), where the absence of carnivorous fishes places less premium on armour, the scutes have disappeared and the skin is naked [Fig. 93]. Among other Bony Fishes with a more or less complete body cuirass of bony shields, the Sea Robins of deep water (*Peristedion*), and the curious little Pogge or Bullhead (*Agonus*) found round British coasts [Fig. 33b], may be mentioned.

Among the members of the large and diverse order of fishes known as Tube-mouths (Aulostomiformes) there occur several interesting modifications of the scaly covering. The Snipe-fishes (*Macrorhamphosus*), for example, have each scale composed of a rhomboidal bony basal plate which is produced into a curved and backwardly directed spine, containing a definite pulp-cavity, reminiscent of that of the Selachian denticle. In the remarkable Shrimp-fishes (Centriscidae) the whole head and body is strongly compressed,

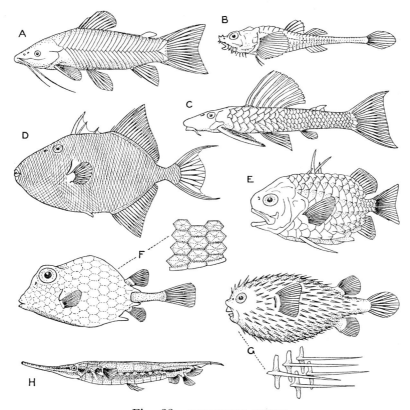

Fig. 33 ARMOURED FISHES

A. Hassar or Cascadura (*Hoplosternum littorale*), x ¹/₄; B. Pogge or Armoured Bullhead (*Agonus cataphractus*), x ¹/₄; C. Mailed Cat-fish (*Plecostomus garmani*), x ¹/₈; D. Trigger-fish (*Balistes carolinensis*), x ¹/₄; E. Pine-cone Fish (*Monocentrus japonicus*), x ¹/₄; F. Trunk-fish (*Lactophrys trigonus*), x ¹/₄; G. Porcupine-fish (*Diodon hystrix*), x ¹/₈; H. Shrimp-fish or needle-fish (*Aeoliscus strigatus*), x¹/₂

and is completely encased in a transparent bony cuirass with a knife-like lower edge. This is made up of a number of thin plates, fused with the underlying ribs in much the same way as the carapace of a tortoise [Fig. 33H]. In the Pipe-fishes (Syngnathiformes) the scales are replaced by a series of jointed bone-like rings, encircling the body from behind the head to the tip of the tail. Similar rings surround the prehensile tail of the Sea Horse (*Hippocampus*), but in the immobile trunk region they take the form of plates which are roughly cruciform in shape, and are interlaced with one another to form a complete outer skeleton. The edges of these plates are not infrequently produced into pointed spines or rounded knobs [Fig. 5E].

The bottom-living Bat-fishes (*Ogcocephalus*) have the upper surface of the body studded with spines or tubercles, not unlike the scales of the Snipe-fishes in structure, but lacking the pulp cavity, the projecting spine being solid [Fig. 31D]. Similar tubercles are sometimes found in the deep-sea Angler-fishes or Ceratioids, but these fishes mostly have a naked skin. In the Trigger-fishes (*Balistes*) the rough scales covering the body are like those of the Bat-fishes, the basal plate often being rhomboid in shape, with the outer surface roughened or armed with one or more small spines [Fig. 33D]. In the File-fishes (*Monacanthus*) the spines are more numerous, and are set so close together as to give the skin the appearance of velvet. In the allied Trunk-fishes (Box-fishes, Coffer-fishes, Cuckolds) a complete and solid coat of mail again occurs. The scales are represented by large six-sided bony plates, united with one another to form a strong box, from one end of which projects the mouth and from the other the naked tail. This box may be three, four, or even five-sided, and one or more of its edges may be armed with strong spines [Figs. 5B; 33F]. A West Indian species (*Lactophrys tricornis*), has two long spines projecting forward from the forehead, and is appropriately named the Cow-fish. The little Pine-cone fish (*Monocentrus*), although belonging to a totally different order of fishes, is another form in which the thick scales unite to enclose the body in a box [Fig. 33E].

The Surgeon-fishes (Teuthidae) of tropical seas derive their name from the presence of a lancet-like spine on either side of the caudal peduncle. Usually the spine is retracted into a sheath in the skin, but it can be quickly turned outwards and forms an effective weapon when the fish lashes its tail from side to side.

The scales of the Puffers or Globe-fishes (Tetraodontidae) are replaced by small, movable spines, which stand erect when the body is inflated with air. The related Porcupine-fishes (Diodontidae) have an even stronger protection, the roots of the long, stout spines coming into contact with one another and providing a more or less continuous coat of mail. In some species these spines are two-rooted and movable, so that they can be laid back flat or erected at will; in other forms the spines are three-rooted and fixed [Fig. 33G].

With few exceptions, the scales of Bony Fishes have a regular arrangement, and within certain limits both scale size and disposition is constant for any given species. For this reason, a count of the number of scales is often of some importance in identifying any particular fish. Generally, the scales are arranged in obliquely transverse series, and the number of these series is counted along the middle of the side from behind the gill-opening to the base of the caudal fin. To estimate the number of scales across the body (i.e. the number of longitudinal rows) the scales are usually counted in one of the transverse series, as a rule that which runs from the commencement of the dorsal fin downwards and forwards to the lateral line, and from thence downwards and backwards to the pelvic fin [Fig. 34]. Thus the scale formula for a particular species may be written: $44\text{–}47\ \frac{6\text{–}7}{9\text{–}10}$. This means that there are from 44 to 47 scales in a longitudinal series from the head to the tail *i.e.* the number of transverse rows, 6 or 7 between the origin of the dorsal fin and the lateral line, and 9 or 10 between the latter and the base of the pelvic fin *i.e.* the number of longitudinally arranged rows.

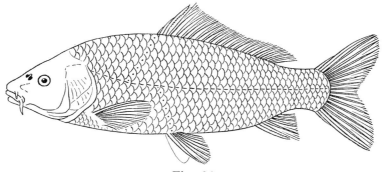

Fig. 34
Carp (*Cyprinus carpio*), x ¹/₆. To show arrangement of scales

Mention may be made here of the so-called hybrid between the Pilchard (*Sardina*) and the Herring (*Clupea*), 'specimens' of which turn up from time to time. At first sight this fish appears to have about 30 rows of scales along one side of the body, and more than 50 on the other. This is not, of course, a genuine hybrid, and the explanation of the abnormality is that the scales of the Pilchard are unequal in size, the oblique rows being alternately of larger and smaller scales, the latter being quite concealed by the former in normal fish. In the so-called hybrid all the scales of one side of the body are equal in size and regularly arranged, while those of the other are large and small as usual.

In many Bony Fishes there is an enlarged and somewhat modified scale in the angle where the anterior edge of the pectoral fin joins the body, and often a similar axillary or accessory scale occurs in the outer angle of the pelvic fin. It usually takes the form of a pointed dagger-like process, sometimes stiff and hard, sometimes soft and flexible. As a rule, axillary scales are present in the more generalised forms, but are lacking in the more specialised fishes. Again, they are often well developed in actively swimming forms, and absent or much reduced in those living at or near the bottom. This suggests that these scales are in some way connected with swimming. In the Salmon and Trout the axillary scale is surrounded by fatty tissue, and is supported at its base by a splint of bone connected with the outermost ray of the pelvic fin.

The lateral line, a conspicuous feature of most Bony Fishes, will be dealt with in detail in the chapter devoted to sense organs (*cf.* p. 152), and it will suffice to point out here that it consists of continuous grooves or canals in the head and body containing special sensory organs; at intervals these grooves communicate with the exterior through pores or by little tubes which run outwards through the scales [Fig. 72]. It is these pores or modified tube-bearing scales which form the characteristic external line, generally running from behind the head to the base of the caudal fin, and not infrequently continued on to the fin itself. The lateral line of the body may run more or less straight along the side as in the Trout (*Salmo*) or Carp (*Cyprinus*); it may be curved upwards to

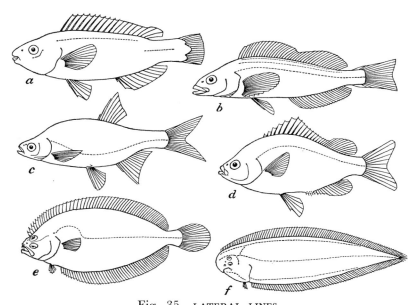

Fig. 35   LATERAL LINES

a. Parrot-fish (*Scarus* sp.), x $^1/_8$; *b.* Greenling (*Hexagrammos stelleri*), x $^1/_2$; *c.* Bream (*Abramis brama*), x $^1/_4$; *d.* Viviparous Perch (*Hysterocarpus traski*), x $^1/_4$; *e.* American Flounder (*Paralichthys dentatus*), x $^1/_8$; *f.* Tongue Sole (*Cynoglossus sp.*), x $^1/_4$.

follow the line of the back as in the Perch (*Perca*), or downwards and parallel with the line of the belly as in the Roach (*Rutilus*) or Bream (*Abramis*). In the Parrot-fishes (Scaridae) and others [Fig. 35*a*] it is discontinuous, the upper portion ending abruptly below the soft dorsal fin, and the lower portion commencing below it and running backwards to the tail in the usual manner. In the Greenlings (Hexagrammidae) of the North Pacific [Fig. 35*b*] there may be several lines on each side of the upper part of the body. Tongue Soles (Cynoglossidae) may have one, two or three lateral lines on the upper surface of the body and one, two or none on the lower side [Fig. 35*f*]. In many fishes, notably in the Flat-fishes, the line runs straight from the tail to the tip of the pectoral fin, and then forms a more or less well-defined arch above the fin itself. [Fig. 35*e*]. In certain groups (Gobies, Cyprinodonts) the superficial manifestations of the lateral line are entirely wanting. In the Sharks it is represented by a simple groove protected by overlapping denticles.

It is sometimes of considerable importance to be able to determine the age of a particular fish, especially of those fishes of commercial importance. This can be carried out, in some fishes at least, by what is known as scale-reading. The discovery, made several years ago by H. W. Johnston, that every Salmon carries its own life-history clearly written on each one of its scales, has proved to be of incalculable value to fishery biologists, and this method of age-determination has since been applied to a number of other species, generally with success.

It has already been shown how the scale of a typical Bony Fish develops in the dermis and gradually grows until it comes to overlap the one lying immediately behind it (p. 58). This growth goes on throughout life, but seems to be retarded as the fish becomes really old. As mentioned above, the definitive number of scales of any species remains constant throughout the life of the fish, so that as the fish grows the scales must inevitably increase more or less proportionally in size. Now, if the scales of a Salmon be examined under a lowpower microscope or hand lens, it will be observed that the surface is marked by a number of rings arranged concentrically. Some of these rings are seen to be well separated, others closer together, recalling the rings of growth exhibited in a cross-section of a tree trunk. They represent the new material manufactured by the dermis, and added to the scale from time to time. But since a Salmon grows unequally at different seasons of the year, this irregular growth is duly reflected in the scales. In spring and summer, when food is plentiful and the fish grows rapidly, the scales increase in size by the addition of a large number of rings well separated from each other; when growth slows down in autumn or almost ceases in winter the rings added become fewer in number and much closer together. This check in growth once a year enables us to determine the age of any fish by counting the number of winter 'zones'; that is to say, of areas of close rings.

A glance at the accompanying figures of Salmon scales [Pl. I] will give an idea of the manner in which this method is applied. The first represents the scale of a 5 lb. Grilse, caught in the River Wye in July when returning from the sea to spawn. The centre of the scale [Fig. A] shows clearly the two years spent in the river from the time of hatching until it descended to the sea as a Smolt, i.e. the two years' Parr life. This is followed by a number of well-separated rings representing the first summer in the sea, after which is a winter zone, followed in turn by an area representing half a second summer in the sea. It may thus be deduced that the age of this fish when caught was three and a half years. The second [Fig. B] was taken from a large spring fish of 22 lb. weight, caught in April, and shows two years' river life and three years' sea life. At the end of a winter's growth an irregular scar will often be seen running right round the scale. This is known to scale-readers as the 'spawning mark,' and is due to part of the scale being resorbed during the physiological hiatus which accompanies spawning. At the same time certain skull bones are partly resorbed whilst others are greatly enlarged. If the fish survives spawning, scale growth again becomes regular and the junction between the eroded area and the new scale material is irregular. Scale reading for age determination is not applicable to most tropical freshwater fishes. In these, growth is generally regular except during spawning periods. A 'spawning mark' therefore occurs but is due, not to scale resorption, but to a slight growth check.

From time to time the scales of a fish wear off or are otherwise dislodged, a not infrequent occurrence in such forms as the Salmon (*Salmo*) and Herring (*Clupea*). When this happens, new scales, known as replacement scales, are formed to take the place of those lost. Naturally these are of no value for scale-reading purposes, the concentric rings in the centre of the scale being absent.

REFERENCES

JARVIK, E. (1959). *Théories de l'Évolution des Vertébrés* Masson et Cie, Paris.

KERR, T. (1952). The scales of primitive living Actinopterygians *Proc. zool. Soc. Lond.*, **122**, 155–178.

KERR, T. (1955). The scales of modern lungfish. *Proc. zool. Soc. Lond.*, **125**, 335–345.

MENZIES, W. J. M. (1931). *The Salmon.* Wm. Blackwood, Edinburgh and London.

PLATE I

SCALES OF THE SALMON (*Salmo Solar*)

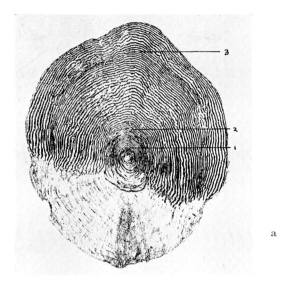

a

A. Scale from grilse caught in the River Wye, July 14th, 1909, 5 lbs., male, 24 inches long, showing 2 years in river and $1\frac{1}{2}$ years in sea. x about 12

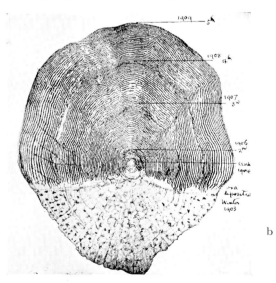

b

B. Scale for large spring fish, April 7th, 1909; 22 lbs., male, $38\frac{1}{2}$ inches long, showing 2 years' river and 3 years' sea life. x about 11

CHAPTER 5

RESPIRATION

RESPIRATION MAY BE defined as a physiological process through which oxygen is taken up by the blood and at the same time a waste product of metabolism, carbon dioxide, is given off. Fish blood, like our own, consists of a fluid (the plasma) in which float millions of red and white blood cells or corpuscles. The red corpuscles contain a remarkable substance known as haemoglobin [1]) which has the ability to take up oxygen under certain conditions and, under other conditions, to release it to the body cells, receiving in exchange carbon-dioxide.

This exchange of gases is essentially the same in a fish as in any higher vertebrate, the only difference in the respiratory process being in the organs through which it is effected, namely gills in fishes and lungs in other vertebrates. Even amongst fishes, however, there are some in which a lung-like structure has evolved and in which gills play a subsidiary role. But, be it lungs or gills, the physiological processes are similar, for in a lung the gaseous exchange can only take place after the oxygen from the air has been dissolved in the fluid which lines the fine cavities of the lung.

The supreme importance of oxygenated water to a fish is easily demonstrated, for if a fish is placed in a vessel containing water from which the oxygen has been removed, it rapidly succumbs. Likewise, if fishes are kept in a sealed container they will die once they have used up the oxygen originally contained in the water. The exact amount of oxygen consumed by a fish will depend on various factors such as the fish's activity and the inherent requirements of the particular species.

Water, as a medium, is less suitable for respiration than is air. For instance it is about 1,000 times more dense and therefore more energy must be expended in passing it over the respiratory surfaces. Furthermore, any given volume of air will contain more oxygen than the same volume of water under similar physical conditions. Yet fishes are particularly well adapted for respiration in water and, in fact, are able to utilize up to 80 % of the oxygen contained in the water passing across the gills, whereas man is only able to use about

[1]) Haemoglobin is absent from the blood cells of Antarctic fishes placed in the Chaenichthyidae; larval eels (*leptocephali*) lack haemoglobin but this develops as the larvae mature.

25 % of the oxygen inhaled by the lungs. Two factors seem to be primarily responsible for the fishes' efficiency. One is the structure of the gills and the arrangement of blood circulation through them; the other is the fact that there is a continuous flow of water across the gills at all stages of respiration.

A proper understanding of gill function is impossible without some account of their anatomy. The gills of any fish will serve as an example, since the fundamental structure is identical in both Selachians and Bony Fishes. If one lifts the gill-cover of a Herring, the gills are seen as a series of filaments attached to the curved gill arch. Each arch (there are four on either side) carries a double row of filaments which, in life, stand apart from one another like the arms of a narrow V. The naked eye shows only the individual filaments but under high magnification each filament is seen to be thrown into a large number of small folds (secondary folds) on both of its surfaces. These folds greatly increase the area of gill surface exposed to the water, thereby increasing the area over which gas exchange can take place. The actual area varies in different species and is positively related to their levels of activity. Active species like the Mackerel may have as much as 1,000 square millimetres per gram of body weight; in other words, an area equivalent to about ten times the external surface of the body.

The fine structure of the secondary folds allows the blood to come into very intimate contact with the water; indeed the two fluids are separated only by a very thin membrane through which the oxygen and carbon dioxide may readily pass. The folds are well supplied with blood, the flow of which is so directed that the blood and water streams pass one another in opposite directions. This arrangement of 'counter currents' is found in many parts of the animal body where an efficient exchange of dissolved substances is required between two fluids.

In the gills, the counter currents ensure that blood which is leaving the gills almost fully oxygenated meets water entering with its full oxygen content, while blood deficient in oxygen and entering the gills meets water from which much of the oxygen has already been extracted. In this way there is always a greater amount of oxygen in the water than in the blood it meets so that oxygen continues to pass into the blood throughout its passage through the gills. The efficiency of the counter current system is shown by the fact that the uptake of oxygen through the gills falls from 50 % to 9 % if the direction of water flow is experimentally reversed.

The principles of respiration are essentially the same in all fishes but there is a marked difference in the gross form of the gills in the Selachians, Cyclostomes and Bony Fishes. It will be convenient to describe, first of all, the conditions found in the Selachians and then to compare them with those existing in the other groups.

In a typical Shark the side walls of the pharynx, that is to say, of that portion of the alimentary canal at the back of the mouth and immediately in front of the commencement of the narrow gullet, are perforated by a series of narrow vertical openings [Fig. 36A: *ph*]. Each pharyngeal opening leads into a flattened pouch, which in turn communicates with the exterior by a comparatively narrow slit, the external gill-cleft, lying on the side of the head between the eye and the pectoral fin [Fig. 36A *g.cl.*]. As a rule these clefts are not very long, but in the huge Basking Shark (*Cetorhinus*) they extend from the upper to the lower surfaces of the body. They are normally five in number (excluding a small circular opening known as the spiracle, which may lie in front of the first gill-cleft), but in the Frilled Shark (*Chlamydoselachus*) [Fig. 22C], the Comb-toothed or Cow Sharks (Hexanchidae), and one of the Saw Sharks (*Pliotrema*), there may be as many as six or seven. In the Frilled Shark each of the partitions between the successive clefts is produced backwards as a curious fold of skin covering the cleft immediately behind [Fig. 22C].

The partitions, or interbranchial septa, between the separate

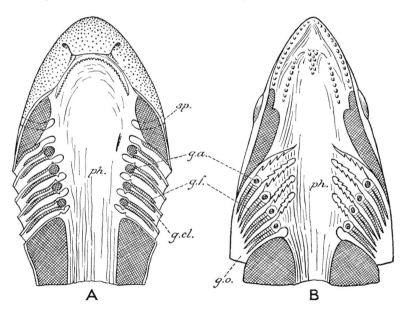

Fig. 36 GILLS OF SHARK AND BONY FISH COMPARED
A. Dissection of head of Spotted Dog-fish (*Scyliorhinus* sp.) seen from below x ¹/₂; B. The same of Salmon (*Salmo salar*), x ¹/₂; *g.a.*, gill-arch; *g.cl.*, external gill-cleft; *g.f.*, gill filaments; *g.o.*, external opening of gill chamber; *ph.*, pharynx; *sp.*, spiracle

gill-pouches are fairly thick, and are reinforced by sheets of tough fibre-like substance. Further support is provided by a series of cartilaginous bars known as the gill-arches, which lie at the inner edges of the septa and between the pharyngeal openings [Fig. 36A *g.a.*]. Each arch has the form of a half-hoop, and is broken up into several segments movably connected with one another, the lowest of which is nearly always joined by a coupling piece with its fellow of the opposite side [*cf.* Fig. 46A]. In this way, the inside of the pharynx is supported by a series of encircling jointed girders, the outer convex faces of which are fringed by a number of slender rods of cartilage, which project outwards into the septa and help to strengthen them. All the parts of the gill-arches are provided with their special muscles, which by their appropriate contraction bring the hoops closer together or move them wider apart, and thus diminish or enlarge the size of the intervening openings.

The opposing walls of each gill-pouch bear a number of branchial lamellae or gill filaments [Fig. 36, *g.f.*], whose free edges project into the cavity of the pouch. These are richly supplied with fine blood-vessles, and present the appearance of a series of thin red straps or plates, a feature from which the earlier name of Elasmo-branchs (strap gills) given to the Selachians was derived. Reference to the accompanying diagram will show how the gills are arranged in a typical Selachian [Fig. 36A]. It will be observed that the anterior wall of the first pouch has its row of filaments, but the posterior wall of the last pouch is not provided with these structures.

Mention may be made here of the organ known as the spiracle, which is the vestige of a gill-cleft, and, indeed, in the early embryonic stages of a Shark differs little from the clefts that lie behind it, although it subsequently degenerates. Even in the adult, however, the spiracle frequently retains a number of branchial lamellae. The spiracle varies greatly in size in the different families, being small or absent in some of the larger Sharks, and comparatively large in the Torpedoes, Rays, and Sting Rays, where it has acquired a special function to be described later on [Figs. 36A; 37A, B: *sp.*].

The living Cyclostomes (Lampreys and Hag-fishes), exhibit a type of respiratory organ which, although in some respects more primitive than that of the Selachians, presents several special and peculiar features. The respiratory lamellae are lodged in a series of muscular pouches, well separated from each other. In the Lamprey (*Petromyzon*) there are seven on either side, each of which opens directly to the exterior by a small rounded opening on the outside of the head. Internally each communicates by a similar orifice, not directly into the pharynx as in the Selachians, but with a special canal. This canal ends blindly behind, but in front opens near the mouth. There are, thus, seven external openings and one internal opening. In the Hag-fish (*Myxine*) each pouch opens

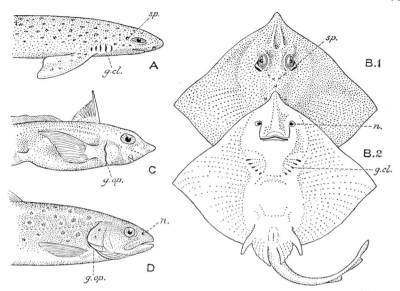

Fig. 37 EXTERNAL GILL OPENINGS
A. Spotted Dog-fish (*Scyliorhinus* sp.), x ¹/₃; B.1, B.2. Thornback Ray (*Raia clavata*), x ¹/₆; C. Rabbit-fish (*Chimaera monstrosa*), x ¹/₅; D. Trout (*Salmo trutta*), x ¹/₅. *g.cl.*, external gill-clefts of Selachians; *g.op.*, external opening of gill chamber in Chimaeras and Bony Fishes; *n.*, nostril; *sp.*, *spiracle*

directly into the pharynx, but on the outside it is drawn out into a tubular canal running posteriorly. Further back all the canals unite and open together by a single external aperture [Fig. 38]. The gill-pouches are large in the Lamprey, and are supported by an elaborate cartilaginous structure, the branchial basket, which in the Hag-fish is greatly reduced. In many respects this basket presents a superficial resemblance to the gill-arches of the Selachians, but it lies outside the gill-pouches instead of between them and the pharynx.

The general appearance of the gills in a Bony Fish such as the Salmon (*Salmo salar*) must be familiar to everybody, and may be readily seen by lifting up the bony plate lying on either side of the head behind the eye. How do these gills differ from those already described? In the first place, although the same internal pharyngeal openings (*ph.*) are present, these do not open separately to the exterior, but into a common branchial chamber [Fig. 36B], the outer wall of which is provided by a movable flap known as the gill-cover or operculum [Fig. 58]. The operculum is supported by a series of broad, flat scale-like bones, with or without the addition of a number of slender bony rods below, the branchiostegal rays. The hinder and lower edges of the operculum are nearly always free, so that the external opening is comparatively spacious, but sometimes these margins become more or less joined to the body of the fish and the outer opening is correspondingly reduced to a narrow slit or even to a minute upwardly directed pore. The same hoop-like gill-arches support the walls of the pharynx between the internal openings as in the Selachians, but are here composed of bone instead of cartilage. The extensive interbranchial septa

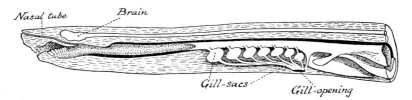

Fig. 38   GILLS OF CYCLOSTOMES
Dissection of anterior part of Hag-fish (*Myxine glutinosa*), x 1

of the Shark have been reduced to minute proportions, and the delicate red filaments form a double row of lamellae attached by their bases to the convex outer edge of each gill-arch [Fig. 39]. The half gill formed by the filaments on the anterior wall of the first cleft in the Selachians (the hyoidean hemibranch) has either disappeared or is represented by a mere rudiment as in the Gar Pike, and the fifth (last) branchial arch is gill-less [Fig. 36B]. The spiracle is generally wanting, at least in the adult fish.

The gill filaments belonging to the spiracular gill, on the other hand, persist in many Bony Fishes as a small, gland-like structure the pseudobranch. The pseudobranch, although sometimes deeply embedded in the tissues of the pharynx, always retains the fine structure of gill tissue. In some fishes, for example the Salmon, the pseudobranch is superficial and looks like a small tuft of gill lying in the angle between the upper filaments of the first gill arch and the operculum.

Certain Selachians, namely the Chimaeras and their allies (Holocephali), present a type of gill arrangement roughly midway between that of a Shark on the one hand and a Bony Fish on the other. The gills lie in a common branchial chamber, bordered on the outside by a skinny flap, simulating the operculum of Bony Fishes, and opening to the exterior by a single slit-like aperture [Fig. 37C]. The interbranchial septa are somewhat shorter than those of a Shark, so that the filaments project a little beyond their outer margins.

Passing to some of the more primitive Bony Fishes (e.g. Sturgeons), we find the septa become progressively shorter, until the condition described in the Salmon is finally attained [Fig. 39].

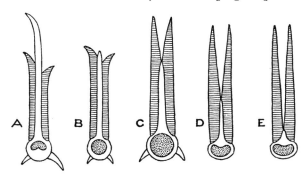

Fig. 39 CROSS-SECTIONS OF GILL-ARCHES IN DIFFERENT FISHES
A. Typical Selachian; B. Chimaera; C. Sturgeon (*Acipenser*); D, E. Bony Fishes. Gill-arch (dots); interbranchial septum (white); gill filaments (cross lines). (After Boas)

The type of gill structure described here is that found in almost all Bony Fishes, but in the Sea Horses and Pipe-fishes (Syngnathiformes), sometimes spoken of as Lophobranchs (tuft-gills), the filaments are reduced to small rosette-like tufts attached to quite rudimentary arches.

All the respiratory organs so far described have been internal, but in the young of certain fishes external gills are developed. These are of two types, true external gills which are distinct from the internal ones, and secondly, prolongations of the internal gill filaments which come to lie outside the body. The latter are more common. In embryo Selachians, for example, the long filaments serve as respiratory organs in those species which lay horny egg-capsules through which the sea water circulates. In the live-bearing Sharks, on the other hand, the filaments are probably more important as structures through which the uterine 'milk' is absorbed by the developing embryo (see p. 252). Similar absorbtive external gills are found in many live-bearing Bony Fishes (see p. 254). The external gills in the young of oviparous Bony Fishes (e.g. *Gymnarchus* [Mormyriformes] and *Clupisudis* [Osteoglossoidei]) are simply respiratory in function.

True external gills [Fig. 41] occur in the young of *Polypterus* (Brachiopterygii) and in Lung-fishes (Dipneusti) of the family Lepidosirenidae (*Lepidosiren* of South America and *Protopterus* of

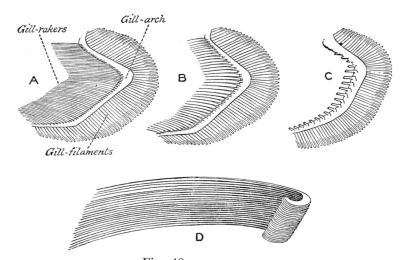

Fig. 40 GILL-RAKERS

A. Gill-arch of Allis Shad (*Alosa alosa*); B. The same of Twaite Shad (*Alosa fallax*); C. The same of Perch (*Perca fluviatilis*); D. Isolated gill-rakers of Basking Shark (*Cetorhinus maximus*). All about $^2/_3$.

Africa). External gills do not develop in the Australian Lung fish *Neoceratodus* which is placed in a separate family, the Ceratodidae. Young *Polypterus* have a leaf-like gill projecting backwards from each side of the head, above the ordinary gill-openings. In larval *Protopterus* and *Lepidosiren* there are four similar but smaller external gills on each side. The external gills are gradually reduced as growth proceeds and finally disappear, but in certain species of *Protopterus* non-functional vestiges can be seen in the adult.

One of the peculiarities of a fish's respiratory system is the fact that it can maintain a constant flow of water over its gills. A superficial examination of a fish breathing gives a false impression of discontinuous flow: the mouth opens, water is drawn in and after a short interval is expelled from under the gill-cover and the cycle is then repeated. But recent research has shown that there is really a continuous pressure gradient between the mouth cavity and the cavity formed between the gills and operculum, so that water will flow continuously across the gill surfaces. In physical terms this involves the function of two pumps slightly out of phase with one another. The pumps are the mouth and opercular cavities, and the pumping action is due to changes in their volumes brought about by the action of certain muscles. There are, of course, numerous slight modifications to this basic system, modifications usually associated with the different habits of the various species. For example, in some fast swimmers like the Mackerel and Tunny neither pump functions when the fish is swimming and they rely on the water forced through the slightly open mouth by their passage through the sea. In the case of the Mackerel the oxygen requirements are so high that the fish is obliged to swim continuously if sufficient water is to pass over the gills. In yet other species (e.g. Leopard sharks, see Hughes) pumping movements are absent during swimming but start once the fish comes to rest.

A fish can modify its breathing rate to suit its oxygen requirements and the basic rate varies from species to species according to their habits. If the water is deficient in oxygen the respiratory rate increases, as it will do if the fish is excited or very active. Temperature will also affect respiratory rates, but probably because of its effects on the solubility of oxygen.

Most fishes breathe in the manner described, but there are some which, owing to their peculiar mode of life, have been obliged to modify this process in accordance with their change in habits. The Lamprey (*Petromyzon*), for example, has adopted a parasitic habit, and spends a good deal of its time attached to other fishes by means of its sucker-like mouth. It is quite obvious that while in this position it would be impossible for the animal to inhale water through the mouth without losing its hold. Thus, water is often taken into and expelled from the branchial sacs by their external openings, through the alternate expansion and contraction of the muscular walls.

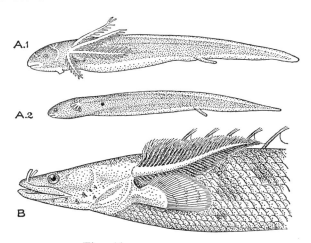

Fig. 41 EXTERNAL GILLS
A.1. Young South American Lung-fish (*Lepidosiren paradoxa*), 30 days after hatching, x 3; A.2. The same 40 days after hatching, x 2; B. Young Bichir (*Polypterus* sp.), x 1¹/₂

A Skate (*Raia*) is essentially adapted for a life on the sea floor, and it is of interest to note that the method of breathing has also been modified for this end. While swimming or crawling about it is able to breathe in the normal manner, but when resting on the bottom there is a grave danger of taking in sand with the stream of water and thus clogging up the delicate gill filaments. In all the members of this group of Selachians the mouth and external gill-openings are on the under side of the head, but the spiracle remains on the upper surface, and is represented by a comparatively large opening situated immediately behind the eye and provided with a movable valve [Fig. 37B.1]. To avoid the danger of introducing foreign particles into the gills, the Skate inhales water by way of the spiracles, expelling it through the gill-openings in the usual manner.

The respiratory modifications found in fishes normally inhabiting rapid streams or mountain torrents, where they are in the habit of fixing themselves to stones and other objects to avoid being swept away by the current of water, are dealt with in a subsequent chapter (*cf.* p. 202).

In addition to their respiratory function the gills play an important part in the excretion of certain waste products and in the mainte-nance of the fish's salt balance (see p. 132). Both marine and freshwater Bony Fishes secrete some nitrogenous waste products through the gills, in the form of ammonia and urea. It has been estimated that in the Carp (*Cyprinus*) and the Goldfish (*Carassius*) six to ten times as much nitrogenous matter is excreted through the gills than by the kidneys. Certain cells in the gill filaments are able either to take up or excrete chlorides. The importance of this mechanism for maintaining the salt balance of the body need not be stressed (see p. 132), and it is not surprising to find that 'chloride' cells are particularly well developed in fishes with a wide salinity tolerance.

In those fishes whose food consists of minute creatures swimming about in the water there is obviously a danger of some of these escaping by way of the pharyngeal openings and perhaps clogging or injuring the delicate filaments. This danger is lessened by special structures known as gill-rakers which take the form of a double row of stiff appendages on the inner margin of each hoop-like gill-arch [Fig. 40]. These rakers, by projecting across the pharyn-geal openings, serve to strain the water which is to bathe the gills, and to prevent any solid particles from passing over with it. Generally the front row of rakers on each arch interlocks with the hinder row on the adjoining arch, and the two together form an effective sieve. In the Pike (*Esox*), feeding almost entirely on other fishes, the gill-rakers are represented merely by bony knobs, which may serve to block the passage of larger food particles. In the Herring-like fishes (Clupeidae), on the other hand, the food consists of plankton, and the rakers are very numerous and take the form of long, slender, and close-set bristles. In many filter-feeders the mechanism is made even more perfect, each primary gill-raker giving off secondary and tertiary branches, the whole apparatus having the appearance of the finest gauze. The form and number of the gill-rakers may differ considerably even in two closely related species, but this difference may generally be correlated with a difference in the normal diet. The two species of Shad (*Alosa*) found in our own seas and rivers provide an excellent example: the Allis Shad (*A. alosa*), having about eighty rakers on the lower limb of each arch in the adult fish, whereas the Twaite Shad (*A. fallax*) has only thirty [Fig. 40A, B]. The Allis Shad feeds largely on small crustaceans, although it takes a certain number of larval fishes. The Twaite Shad does not eat crustaceans to nearly the same extent, but is much more destructive to the young fry of other fishes.

As a general rule, gill-rakers are wanting in the Sharks, many of which feed on other fishes, but the huge Basking Shark (*Cetorhinus*) and Whale Shark (*Rhincodon*) are both provided with many close-set, flattened and tapering gill-rakers, each perhaps four or five inches long [Fig. 40D]. In appearance they recall the baleen plates of the Whalebone Whales, which have exactly the same function, namely to act as a filter to strain off minute forms of animal life. When feeding, the Basking Shark merely opens its mouth and takes in a mass of water containing myriads of the minute crustaceans forming its usual food. The water rushes out over the gills, and the animals are left sticking to the inner walls of the throat and to the filtering mechanism, where they can be conveniently swallowed. Recent research seems to indicate that the gill-rakers of the Basking Shark (which are modified dermal denticles) are shed during the winter months and that new rakers replace them by early spring.

The vast majority of fishes cannot live out of water for any length of time. As a general rule, fishes with wide external gill-openings die more rapidly than those in which the apertures are reduced. A fish suffocates when it is removed from water, a paradoxical statement when one remembers that air contains more oxygen than water. However, when a fish is in air the gill filaments and secondary folds are not supported and they collapse, thus drastically reducing the respiratory surface over which gas exchange can take place. Also, without a film of water around the secondary folds, gas exchange cannot take place. Those fishes which do survive out of water have a gill structure which enables them to keep sufficient moisture trapped between the filaments to prevent both the collapse of the folds and the drying-out of the gill surface. Thus is partially explained the resistance of fishes with small openings to the gill chamber. Other factors involve the detailed structure of the gills themselves which are then less likely to collapse when the support of the water is withdrawn. Still further compensating factors may be involved. The Eel's resistance to 'drowning' in air is well known, and Eels often make considerable journeys through damp grass. In this case, the fish actually respires through its skin, which must of course be kept moist. Cutaneous respiration is important in many Amphibians (Frogs and Newts) but is denied to most fishes because of their covering of large scales. However, many embryo and larval fishes breathe in this way until the gills are fully developed. Indeed, in some larval fishes the continuous median fin fold is extremely well supplied with superficial blood vessels and acts as a gill; in others (the Sturgeon and many Cat-fishes) the opercular fold is heavily vascularized and serves the same purpose.

The remarkable little Mudskipper (*Periophthalmus*) of tropical countries spends a great part of its time 'walking' or skipping about amongst the roots of mangrove trees at low tide. While out of the water, the branchial chamber is filled with water and thus the gills may be used for respiration. Supplementing these is the highly vascularized skin of the mouth and pharynx through which some gas exchange takes place. The importance of keeping these various structures moist is seen by the fact that the fish must frequently recharge its branchial chamber with water, dipping its head into small pools at fairly frequent intervals and always after snapping at its prey when feeding out of water. The old idea that Mudskippers breathed through their tails finds no support in recent research on the respiratory methods of these fishes.

Another unusual method of breathing is adopted by some of the Loaches (Cobitidae) and the Mailed Cat-fishes (Loricariidae), which at times use the intestine for this purpose. The Giant Loach (*Cobitis*) of Europe, known in Germany as the 'Wetterfisch' (weather fish) on account of its supposed susceptibility to atmospheric changes, has been specially studied, and the process of breathing found to take place in the following manner. The fish rises to the surface, and by thrusting its mouth above the water, swallows a certain amount of air, which is passed down into the intestine. There is a bulge in the intestine just behind the stomach which serves as a reservoir; the fine blood-vessels lining the walls of this chamber extract the oxygen from the air. The remaining gases are finally voided through the vent.

It is well known that when the oxygen content of the water is greatly reduced, a fish is obliged to ascend to the surface to avoid suffocation. The habit of seeking oxygen by swallowing bubbles of air is found in many different kinds of Bony Fishes, but in certain forms living in shallow ponds and streams which dry up periodi-cally, or in pools rendered foul by decaying vegetation, this gulping of air becomes a necessity if the fishes are to survive at all. As a result, it is found that the intensification of the air-breathing habit over a very long period of time has led to the development of special accessory breathing organs in addition to the gills, thus enabling the fishes to survive for a comparatively long time out of water. These organs take the form of reservoirs for the storage of air. Anatomically these pouches are outgrowths from the pharynx itself or from the branchial chamber, and contain certain special structures richly supplied with blood-vessels through which the gas exchange is effected.

The so-called Labyrinth Fishes (Anabantoidei) of the fresh waters of tropical Asia and Africa derive their name from the possession of a labyrinth-like accessory breathing organ on either side of the head. This group of fishes includes a number of species familiar in aquaria, such as the Climbing Perch (*Anabas*), Gourami (*Osphronemus*), Paradise-fish (*Macropodus*), Fighting-fish (*Betta*), and so on, but it will only be necessary to mention the accessory breathing organs of the first of these.

The Climbing Perch (*Anabas*) was first made known in a memoir printed in 1797 by one Daldorf, a lieutenant in the service of the Danish East India Company at Tranquebar. The fish derives its

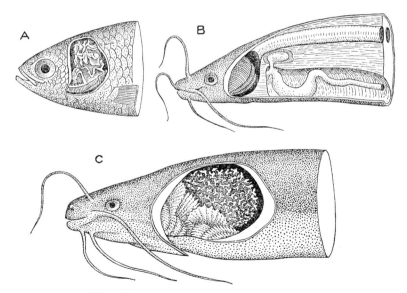

Fig. 42 ACCESSORY BREATHING ORGANS
A. Dissection of head of Climbing Perch (*Anabas testudinosus*); B. The same of an Indian Cat-fish (*Heteropneustes fossilis*); C. The same of an African Cat-fish (*Clarias lazera*). All about natural size.

name from a legend current in the East that it climbs palm trees and sucks their juice, and Daldorf stated that he had taken one in a slit in the bark of a palm which grew near a pond. The researches of an Indian naturalist, Dr. Das, have shown that, although the stories of the Climbing Perch being found in trees are quite well founded, the explanation of the facts is an erroneous one. The fish is in the habit of migrating from pond to pond, and during its overland travels it is not infrequently seized by crows or kites, and deposited high up in the forks of branches of the trees. Hence the origin of the story of its tree-climbing activities! The method of progression adopted on land is of interest, the gill-covers as well as the fins assisting in locomotion. The gill-covers are alternately spread out and fixed firmly to the ground by the sharp spines with which they are armed, while a vigorous push is given by the pectoral fins and the tail. When in the water, the Climbing Perch frequently comes to the surface to breathe air, and so vital has this method of respiration become to the fish that it will suffocate even in water saturated with oxygen if deprived of access to atmospheric air. The ease with which these fishes are able to survive out of water is taken advantage of by the natives of India and the Malay Peninsula, who carry them about alive for days on end in moistened clay pots, thus ensuring a regular supply of fresh fish. The jars must, of course, be kept tightly covered, or the intended meal will climb out and walk away!

The air swallowed is taken into two chambers situated one on each side above the gills, forming outgrowths from the ordinary branchial chambers. Each contains a rosette-like structure, made up of a number of concentrically arranged, shell-like plates with wavy edges, richly supplied with fine blood-vessels and covered with a gill-like epithelium. Each air reservoir communicates not only with the branchial chamber, but also with the pharynx, the entrance from the throat being controlled by a valve. Air enters by this aperture and passes out through the external gill-opening [Fig. 42A].

The related Snake-heads (Ophiocephalidae), long, cylindrical fishes with slightly flattened and somewhat serpent-like heads [Fig. 43A] inhabit rivers and ponds as well as stagnant pools in the marshes. The larger species grow to a length of three or four feet. Their habit of 'walking' over land by the aid of rowing movements of the pectoral fins is well known, and Snake-heads are sometimes exhibited as curiosities by Indian jugglers. They are extremely tenacious of life, and were carried alive by the Chinese to San Francisco and to Hawaii, where they are now naturalised and known as 'China-fishes'. They are able to survive prolonged drought, burying themselves in the mud and remaining in a torpid state during hot, dry weather. The various species differ in the

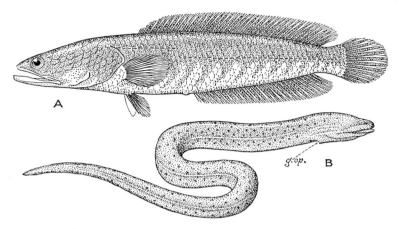

Fig. 43 FISHES THAT CAN LIVE OUT OF WATER
A. Snake-head (*Ophiocephalus striatus*), x ¹/₃; B. Cuchia (*Amphipnous cuchia*),
x ¹/₆. *g.op.*, opening to gill chamber

extent to which they have developed the air-breathing habit, as well
as in their power of living out of water. The accessory respiratory
organs are of a much simpler character than those of the Climbing
Perch, consisting of a pair of cavities lined with a thickened and
puckered membrane supplied with blood-vessels, and do not contain
any special structures. These lung-like reservoirs are not developments of the branchial chamber, but are pouches of the pharynx.

Other fishes provided with accessory breathing organs are certain
Cat-fishes of the rivers and swamps of Africa and Asia. In some
of these (*Clarias*; *Heterobranchus*) the organs take the form of elaborate
tree-like structures, growing from the upper ends of the gill-arches
and contained in a pair of air-chambers situated above the gills
[Fig. 42c]. Another Cat-fish (*Heteropneustes*) has organs of a simpler
nature, but the air-chambers bear a marked resemblance to lungs,
extending backwards as far as the tail as long tubular sacs growing
out from the branchial cavity, and situated close to the backbone
[Fig. 42B]. The epithelium lining the cavities in these fishes, and the
'trees' in *Clarias* and *Heterobranchus*, is especially interesting because
its fine structure is exactly like that of a gill filament.

The Cuchia (*Amphipnous*; Synbranchiformes) which grows to a
length of about two feet, bears a superficial resemblance to some
of the Eels [Fig. 43B], with which order it may be related. It is an
inhabitant of the fresh and brackish waters of India and Burma,
and spends much of its time in the grass on the banks of ponds.
The air-breathing organs consist of a pair of sacs growing out from
the pharynx above the gills. This curious fish seems to have lost

practically all its power of aquatic respiration, for when in the water it is forced to come to the surface at frequent intervals to gulp air. The true gills are very much reduced, being represented by a few rudimentary filaments attached to the second of the three remaining gill-arches.

It will be seen that air-breathing and the evolution of accessory respiratory organs are most highly developed in freshwater fishes. In fact the only marine species in which such organs are developed are those inhabiting intertidal regions where some degree of enforced aerial existence may be imposed by the tides. In certain layers of the sea, particularly below the warm surface layer, there are levels at which the oxygen content falls rapidly. It may even be difficult to find any trace of the gas. Nevertheless fishes do live in these zones but it is not known how they manage to adapt themselves to the oxygen lack. One authority suggests that the fishes remain inactive and virtually dormant during the day, only becoming active when they move into the well-oxygenated surface layers at night. Below the deoxygenated level, the oxygen content of the water rises again so that the abyssal fishes are not faced with the same respiratory problems as affect those fishes living at lesser depths.

The accessory respiratory organs just described are not the only structures used for air-breathing among fishes, and before concluding this chapter some more lung-like organs must be considered. The swimbladder must be a familiar object to those who have had occasion to examine the inside of a fish. Situated within the body cavity, and immediately below the backbone, it generally has the appearance of a long, cylindrical bag with glistening silvery walls. It is very variable both in size and form in different fishes, and may be present in one species and entirely absent in a closely related form. That it normally contains gas may be readily demonstrated by puncturing it with a needle, when the walls promptly collapse. There is no other single organ in any group of vertebrates which performs such a variety of functions as does the swimbladder of Bony Fishes. In the majority it serves as a hydrostatic organ or float, enabling its possessor to remain suspended at any depth without having to swim in order to do so (*cf.* p. 133). In others it is an organ for the production of sound (*cf.* p. 173), and in others, again, it is connected with the sense of hearing (*cf.* p. 152). For the present it must suffice to consider its relation to air-breathing and its connection with the lungs of higher vertebrates.

Like the lungs in Mammals, the swimbladder is intimately associated with the alimentary canal, and a study of the development of this organ shows that it begins as a minute pouch budded off from the gullet. This gets larger and larger, until it is finally separated off from the gullet, remaining connected only by a narrow tube known as the pneumatic duct. In some fishes this duct remains open throughout life, but in others it closes up or disappears altogether. When open it nearly always leads into the pharynx by a small aperture in the roof, but in the Lung-fishes (Dipneusti) and Bichirs (Brachiopterygii), in which the swimbladder is a true breathing organ, the opening is a small slit, the glottis, with well-defined lips, situated in the floor of the gullet [Fig. 44]. The lungs of higher vertebrates arise in exactly the same way, as an outgrowth from the gullet, and the glottis occupies the same position as in the Lung-fishes. Furthermore, whereas in the generality of fishes the swimbladder is a simple sac filled with a mixture of gases, in the Bow-fin (*Amia*) and Gar Pike (*Lepisosteus*), two other air-breathing forms, and to a more marked extent in the Lung-fishes, the inner walls are richly supplied with blood-vessels, and the surface area is

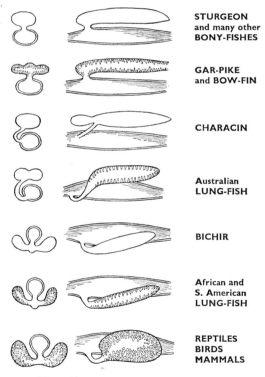

STURGEON
and many other
BONY-FISHES

GAR-PIKE
and BOW-FIN

CHARACIN

Australian
LUNG-FISH

BICHIR

African and
S. American
LUNG-FISH

REPTILES
BIRDS
MAMMALS

Fig. 44 SWIMBLADDER AND LUNG
A series of diagrams showing the relation of the swimbladder or lung to the oesophagus in different fishes, as seen in cross-section (left-hand column) and from the side. (After Dean)

greatly increased by being produced into recesses or alveoli, each of which is further subdivided much in the same way as in a true lung [Fig. 44]. Another important point is the fact that, whereas in nearly all fishes the bladder is a single structure, in the Bow-fin, Gar Pike, Bichir and some Lung-fishes it shows varying degrees of division, giving rise in the latter, to a structure resembling the paired lungs of higher vertebrates. In the Bichirs, for example, it is divided into two unequal parts, a long right-hand portion and a much shorter left-hand one; the two unite in front and open by a single aperture in the floor of the gullet. The swimbladder of the African (*Protopterus*) and South American (*Lepidosiren*) Lung-fishes is divided into two except for a small portion in front, and thus has the form of a pair of lungs. Finally, it may be noticed that the arrangement of the vessels taking the blood to and from the bladder in the Lung-fishes is very similar to that of the vessels connected with the lungs in Amphibians.

We must now consider the relationship, if any, existing between the hydrostatic type of swimbladder and the respiratory type. Many theories have been advanced but all are weakened by the lack of any fossil evidence. We can only argue from the evidence of comparative anatomy and embryology, and often this is contradictory.

Perhaps the most satisfactory conclusion is that the hydrostatic swimbladder and the respiratory one both had their origin from originally paired respiratory pouches which, in the course of evolution, gradually fused to form the structure we now find in the typical non-respiratory bladder. *Polypterus*, *Protopterus* and *Lepidosiren* retain the fairly primitive condition both with regard to function and the paired nature of the respiratory structures. It is not unreasonable to suppose that the swimbladder of the hydrostatic type evolved independently; certainly none of the species with highly modified respiratory bladders (*Polypterus*, *Amia*, *Lepisosteus* and the Lung-fishes) can be considered as lying on or very near the direct line of Teleost evolution. There are, of course, some Teleosts with respiratory and single swimbladders (e.g. *Pantodon* and *Clupisudis* [Osteoglossidae], and some Characins [Characidae]). But, it is not surprising that an organ once respiratory should retain these potentialities and it is perhaps suggestive that the fishes mentioned above are all considered to be primitive members of the Teleosts.

Since we have no knowledge of the swimbladder in those Crossopterygii which were probably ancestral to the Amphibia, it is impossible to give any certain views on the relationship of the lungs in higher vertebrates with those of fishes.

REFERENCES

CARTER, G. S. (1957). Air breathing: in *The Physiology of Fishes*, **1**. Academic Press, New York.

DAS, B. K. (1927). The bionomics of certain air-breathing fishes of India, together with an account of the development of their air-breathing organs. *Phil. Trans. Roy. Soc. Lond.* (B), **216**, 183–219.

FRY, F. E. J. (1957). The aquatic respiration of fish: in, *The Physiology of Fishes*, **1**. Academic Press, New York.

GREENWOOD, P. H. and OLIVA, O. (1959). Does a lungfish breathe through its nose? *Discovery*. Jan., 18–19.

HUGHES, G. M. (1961). How a fish extracts oxygen from water. *New Scientist*, 247, August; 346–348.

CHAPTER 6

MOUTHS AND JAWS

THE IMPORTANCE of food in the daily life of a fish is obvious, and is reflected in the form of the mouth, jaws, teeth, and so on. These structures present more diverse modifications than any other organ of the body. As will be explained in the present chapter, such modifications are more or less intimately associated with the mode or conditions of life, the manner of obtaining food, and the nature of the diet itself.

The Cyclostomes (Lampreys and Hag-fishes) differ from all other fishes in having a rounded, funnel-like mouth placed at the end of the head, which, although supported by special cartilages, is entirely devoid of true biting jaws. The mouth of the Lamprey (*Petromyzon*) acts as a sucker, by means of which it attaches itself to other fishes, feeding on them by sucking their blood and rasping off their flesh with the horny teeth on the muscular piston-like tongue [Fig. 45A]. At one time the absence of jaws was regarded as the result of degeneration associated with the adoption of semi-parasitic habits. But a detailed examination of some very ancient extinct forms now known to be ancestral to the modern Cyclostomes has shown that these also lacked true jaws (*cf.* p. 297). The Lamprey is able to strike its suctorial mouth against the skin of its prey, and becomes so firmly attached that it is rare indeed for the victim to shake off its persecutor before dying from loss of blood and tissues. The amazing strength of the sucker may be tested by allowing a Lamprey in an aquarium to attach itself to the hand or arm, and it will be found almost impossible to detach the fish without lifting it from the water. While engaged in feeding the Lamprey is carried about by its victim, and it is by no means uncommon for one of these pests to steal a ride on a Salmon or other fish when it wishes to ascend a river for spawning purposes. The sucking mouth is also used to anchor it to stones on the river bed, and it is of interest to note that the name Lamprey refers to this habit, being derived from the mediaeval Latin *Lampreda*, a corruption of the older *Lampetra*, from *lambere*, to lick, and *petra*, a stone. In the Hag-fishes (Myxinidae) there is no distinct funnel, and the almost terminal mouth is surrounded by short barbels or tentacles.

Among extant Sharks the mouth is nearly always crescentic in shape, and placed on the under side of the head [Fig. 45B], but in the primitive Frilled Shark (*Chlamydoselachus*) the wide mouth occupies a completely terminal position [Fig. 22c]. In other Sharks the position of the mouth seems to have been brought about by the forward prolongation of the front part of the head above the jaws to

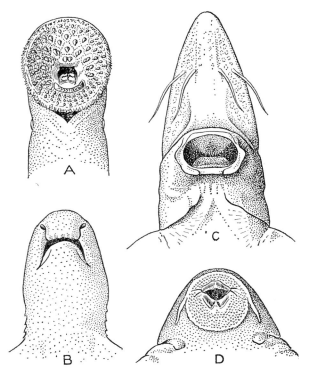

Fig. 45 INFERIOR AND SUCTORIAL MOUTHS
A. Opened mouth of the Sea Lamprey (*Petromyzon marinus*), x $^1/_3$;
B. Lower surface of head of Spotted Dog-fish (*Scyliorhinus canicula*), x $^1/_3$;
C. The same of Sturgeon (*Acipenser rubicundus*), x $^1/_3$; D. The same of Mailed Cat-fish (*Plecostomus plecostomus*), x $^1/_3$

form a snout or rostrum, a process associated with the evolution of a streamlined body-form. From the position of the mouth it is commonly assumed that a Shark is obliged to turn over on to its side or back in order to engulf its food. This, however, is by no means always so, and, although it may turn over when taking food at the surface, as in the case of a lump of meat thrown overboard from a ship, it has frequently been observed to maintain its normal position when seizing living prey, and to push the snout out of the water in order to bring the jaws into play.

In the sluggish, ground-living Rays (Hypotremata) the mouth is nearly always well under the head, and generally takes the form of a straight slit [Figs. 37B; 101]. Although for the most part a rather inactive creature, a Ray (*Raia*) will display great activity when a small fish or crustacean comes within its reach. Owing to the position of the mouth it is unable at once to seize its prey, but darts rapidly over it, covers it with its body and enlarged pectoral fins, and devours it at leisure. The large Rays known as Sea Devils (Mobulidae) differ from the remainder in living more or less in the open sea, and the mouth, in some of them at least, lies nearly at the end of the head. These fishes are remarkable in having the front parts of the pectoral fins prolonged forward to form a pair of fleshy appendages having the appearance of horns [Fig. 14A]. They are known as the cephalic fins. These structures are used, both by the smaller Devil fish (*Mobula*) and the larger Sea Devil (*Manta*), to form a kind of scoop through which the prey (small fishes and crustacea) are funnelled into the mouth.

Except in the Lampreys and their allies, the mouth of a fish is always supported internally by structures known as jaws. In order to understand the origin of these jaws it is necessary to consider again the half-hoops of cartilage (branchial arches) which in the Selachians lie in the side walls of the pharynx between the internal openings (*cf.* p. 72). There is little doubt that the earliest fish-like vertebrates possessed a series of these arches, all of them connected with gills, and that during later evolution the first two pairs became specially modified [Fig. 46A]. The first pair was transformed into biting jaws, consisting of an upper portion known as the pterygo-quadrate cartilage (*ptq.*), and a lower portion known as Meckel's cartilage (*mk.*). In some Sharks living to-day this first or mandibular arch still exhibits traces of its original character, and may lie in front of a gill-cleft and be associated with vestigial gills; in the remainder it has lost all trace of its branchial origin, and only the manner of its development provides a clue as to how it came into being. The second or hyoid arch has been much less modified, and is not very unlike the branchial arches which lie behind it. One of its functions is to provide a support for the 'tongue', but in most fishes it has acquired the secondary task of suspending the mandibular arch from the cranium. [Fig. 46A].

Examination of the skull of the Spotted Dog-fish (*Scyliorhinus*) shows that each half of the upper jaw is connected with its fellow in front below the cranium, and that the two halves of the lower jaw are similarly bound together. Further, the upper jaw is attached to the cranium by a muscular ligament at about the middle of its length, and the hinder ends of both jaws are slung from the back part of the cranium by the intervention of one of the segments of the second arch, namely, the hyomandibula cartilage (so called hyostylic suspension) [Fig. 46A]. In the Comb-toothed Sharks (Hexanchidae) the mode of suspension is somewhat different, the upper jaw being not only joined to the cranium by a process at the middle of its length, but also by another direct articulation with that part of the cranium which lies behind the eye-socket or orbit.

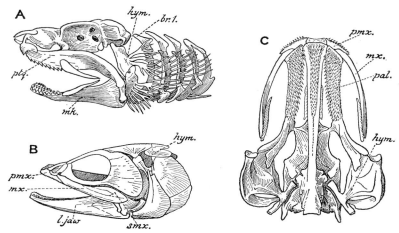

Fig. 46 CARTILAGINOUS AND BONY JAWS

A. Lateral view of skull of Spotted Dog-fish (*Scyliorhinus* sp.), x ¹/₃; B. The same of Ten-pounder (*Elops saurus*), x ¹/₂; C. Lower surface of skull of Pike (*Exos lucius*), x ¹/₄;

*br.*l., first branchial arch; *hym.*, hyomandibula; *l.jaw.*, lower jaw; *mk.*, Meckel's cartilage; *mx.*, maxillary; *pal.*, palatine; *pmx.*, premaxillary; *ptq.*, pterygo-quadrate; *smx.*, supramaxillary

Being relieved from taking part in the suspension of the jaws, the hyomandibula cartilage is here reduced to a relatively slender rod and below is connected with the remainder of the hyoid arch (amphistylic suspension). Yet another type of suspension is found in the Bull-headed Sharks (Heterodontidae); the jaws are slung from the cranium by the hyomandibula, but the upper jaw fits into a deep groove in the cranium and is firmly attached to it by strong ligaments. This condition may be considered as intermediate between the amphi- and hyostylic types of jaw suspension. In Chimaeras (Holocephali) and the Lungfishes (Dipneusti) this condition is carried still further, the upper jaw being completely fused with the cranium, and the supporting element of the hyoid arch is reduced to a mere vestige (autostylic suspension) [Fig. 56A].

In Bony Fishes the primary upper and lower jaws have become so much modified as to be scarcely recognisable in the adult fish, but the early development of the mandibular and hyoid arches throws considerable light on the manner in which the changes have taken place. During ontogeny the skull develops as a simple cartilaginous box, with a series of visceral arches all more or less similar in form. As growth proceeds, the first pair of these arches takes on the form of the jaws as seen in the adult Dog-fish, and these are suspended from the cranium through the intervention of the hyomandibula. Soon afterwards the cartilages are replaced by bones, these being of two kinds, cartilage bones which are preformed in cartilage, and dermal bones which arise as entirely new structures by the development of bone in the dermal layer of the skin. It will be unnecessary to deal with the disposition and manner of development of the several bones here, nor are their technical names of great importance; for such details reference must be made to any good text-book of zoology. The chief point of interest lies in the later history of the bones developed in connection with the primitive upper jaw or pterygo-quadrate cartilage. These never function as an upper jaw, but, together with certain dermal bones developing in the skin of that region, form a bony roof to the mouth, losing practically every trace of their original nature. These palatine and pterygoid bones are articulated with the cranium in front, and behind are generally suspended by the hyomandibula bone, the condition being essentially the same as in the Dog-fish. The primitive lower jaw or Meckel's cartilage becomes entirely invested or surrounded by bones, but retains its mobility as well as its original function. To replace the primary upper jaw an entirely new structure has arisen in Bony Fishes. It is made up of two dermal bones on each side known as the premaxilla and maxilla. The latter is sometimes provided with one or two small bones attached to its upper edge, the supramaxillaries. In the more generalised fishes the premaxillae are much shorter than the maxillae which are provided with teeth and form part of the border of the mouth [Fig. 46B]. In many forms, however, the premaxillae nearly or quite exclude the toothless maxillae from the gape, and the latter merely act as a lever for the protrusion of the former [Fig. 58]. The two premaxillae generally meet in the middle line, but in some species (e.g. the Pike) they are well separated [Fig. 46C], and in the Eels (Anguilliformes) they are altogether wanting.

In many Bony Fishes the mouth is placed at the end of the head, and the upper and lower jaws are equal in length, but this is by no means always the case, and considerable variations both in size and position are found in certain fishes. In some the mouth lies on the under side of the head, as in the Sharks, its inferior position usually being due to the forward prolongation of the forepart of the head to form a rostrum. In the Sturgeons (*Acipenser*), for example, the snout is particularly massive, varying in shape and length in the different species, and is provided with a transverse row of sensory barbels on its lower surface [Fig. 45c]. The mouth itself is small and circular, completely devoid of teeth in the adult fish, and is capable of being protruded to a remarkable extent. The Sturgeon feeds largely on small invertebrates, rooting up the mud or sand with its snout, and finally sucking them up by means of its funnel-like mouth. The related Paddle-fish or Spoonbill (*Polyodon*), found only in the rivers of the southern states of North America, has a comparatively wide mouth armed with small teeth. The rostrum, forming no less than one-fourth of the entire length of the fish, is a thin, flat, spoon-shaped blade, the outer surface of which is well supplied with sense organs [Fig. 47G]. This fish lives entirely on the minute organisms contained in mud, the snout being used for stirring purposes, whilst the food is strained from the water by the exceptionally long and close-set gill-rakers.

A semicircular mouth placed on the under side of the head, is characteristic of a large number of fishes habitually living in mountain streams or torrents (*cf.* p. 200). In many Indian and African species of Cyprinidae (Carps) the jaws are much strength-ened, and their edges have become sharp and cutting. One fish, which feeds on very fine weeds stripped from the rocks and stones of the river-bed, has the jaws provided with a strong horny cutting edge. In many of the Cat-fishes (Siluroidei) the mouth, together with the much modified lips, forms a broad, flat sucker by means of which the fish is able to cling to stones when resting. In the Mailed Cat-fishes (Loricariidae) of South America the sucker-like form of the mouth is well shown, the lips being greatly enlarged, reflected outwards, spread in circular form round the mouth, and often fringed with membranous tentacles of various sizes [Fig. 45D]. The mouth itself is provided with small, weak jaws, and armed with feeble teeth, the food consisting of algae and small animals.

Except in those species in which they are adapted for taking part in the formation of a sucking apparatus, the lips of fishes do not exhibit many striking modifications. However, it seems likely that the lips are often well-supplied with sense organs and are sometimes thickened into folds, thus increasing the surface area. In the Wrasses (Labridae) the lips are particularly thick, a feature from which the German name of *Lippenfische* is derived. In certain species of African Cichlids (Cichlidae) the central portions of both upper and lower lips are prolonged to form freely projecting fleshy lobes [Fig. 47D]. It is of interest to note that this peculiar modification, which may be connected with the method of feeding, has arisen quite independently several times. Each of the large African lakes,

Victoria, Nyasa, and Tanganyika, contains some hundred or more species of Cichlids which are found nowhere else, and each lake boasts of species with modified lips. The same feature occurs again in the Thick-lipped Mojarra (*Cichlasoma*) of Lake Nicaragua in Central America. There can be little doubt that similar conditions in each case, or perhaps the adoption of similar feeding habits, has independently brought about the development of the same peculiarity in but distantly related fishes.

In Weever-fishes (*Trachinus*) and Star-gazers (*Uranoscopus*) the jaws are directed obliquely or even vertically upwards, so that the opening of the mouth is more or less on the upper surface of the head. The Weevers are fairly active fishes, but spend a good deal of time buried in the sand with only the head exposed, from which position they are able to pounce on the small fishes and crustaceans

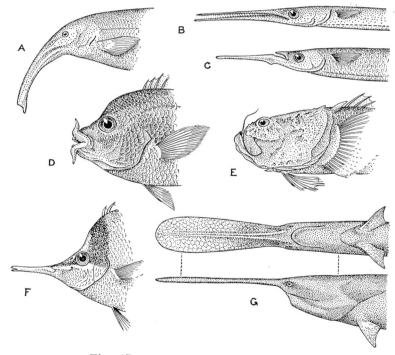

Fig. 47　DIFFERENT KINDS OF MOUTHS

A. Head of Elephant Mormyrid (*Gnathonemus elephas*), x ¹/₂; B. Of Gar-fish (*Tylosurus* sp.), x ¹/₄; C. Of Half-beak (*Hyporhamphus unifasciatus*), x ¹/₂; D. Of Thick-lipped Mojarra (*Cichlasoma lobochilus*), x ¹/₂; E. Of Star-Gazer (*Uranoscopus oligolepis*), x ¹/₃; F. Of Butterfly-fish (*Chelmon longirostris*), x ¹/₂; G. Of Spoonbill or Paddle-fish (*Polyodon spathula*), x ¹/₄

forming the bulk of their food [Fig. 75A]. It has been suggested that the brilliantly lustrous and mobile eyes of this fish serve to lure the intended meal within reach of its jaws. The Star-gazers [Fig. 47E] are less active fishes, with stout, clumsy bodies and large box-shaped heads flat on the upper surface and bounded in front by the almost vertical jaws. They lack the ability to chase and seize the small fishes on which they feed, and, therefore, resort to cunning to obtain a meal. A Mediterranean species buries itself deeply, until only the small, mobile eyes are projecting, and the upper part of the mouth-opening appears as a cleft in the sand. When thus hidden and immobile, the Star-gazer is difficult to see, having the general appearance of a brownish grey stone almost concealed by sand. Its presence is only betrayed by the slight movements connected with respiration. At times it protrudes from its mouth a little red filament, a membranous process of the lower breathing valve. This is made to move about on the sand, crawling, wriggling, contracting and expanding—in short, imitating the movements of a small worm. There can be little doubt that this serves as a bait to lure small fishes within reach of the concealed jaws of the Star-gazer. The deception is facilitated by the poor light of the shallow waters in which it usually lives. Another species from the coast of West Africa uses a broad membranous flap, gleaming white in colour, for the same purpose.

In most predaceous fishes with large mouths the bony jaws are strong structures, but in many deep-sea forms, and particularly among the members of the suborder known as 'Wide-mouths' (Stomiatoidei), they are relatively feeble and even somewhat flexible [Fig. 91], although armed with large, pointed teeth. It is not unusual to find a specimen which has swallowed another fish several times its own bulk. Such a meal is made possible by the mobility of the lower jaw, the two halves of which are very loosely bound together, and can be readily pulled apart in order to enlarge the gape. The Great Swallower (*Chiasmodus*), a curious deep-sea fish remotely related to the Perches, is another form with a capacity for dealing with out-sized meals. Here again the jaws are flexible and distensible [Fig. 91A]. Indeed, the action of swallowing is carried out, not, as is usual with fishes, by means of the muscles surrounding the gullet, but by the action of the jaws as in snakes. Actually, they do not so much swallow the victim, as draw themselves over it. In the rare Gulpers (Saccopharyngiformes) of the oceanic depths, the mouth is enormous [Fig. 49D] and both mouth-cavity and throat are capable of immense distension; the deep-sea Angler-fishes or Ceratioids possess similarly expansible maws.

In the Gar Pike (*Lepisosteus*; Holostei) of North America, and in such unrelated Teleostei as the marine Gar-fishes (Belonidae) and Sauries (Scombresocidae), both jaws are prolonged to form a more or less lengthy 'beak', armed with sharp, unequal teeth. This is another example of convergent evolution, for in spite of the similarity of their jaws the two groups of fishes are quite unrelated. The Gar Pikes [Fig. 48] are more or less solitary feeders, and subsist largely on a diet of freshwater crayfishes and small fishes of all kinds. The Alligator Gar Pike (*L. tristoechus*), abundant in the rivers around the Gulf of Mexico, and attaining a length of twenty feet or more, is very destructive to food fishes, and causes a great deal of damage to the nets of fishermen. It is not even good eating itself, the flesh being rank and tough, and, it is said, unfit even for dogs. If a Long-nosed Gar Pike (*L. osseus*) is observed on the feed, it will be seen to move slowly in the direction of a group of prey fishes, looking for all the world like a drifting log of wood. Placing itself in a suitable position, and carefully sighting its victim, the Gar

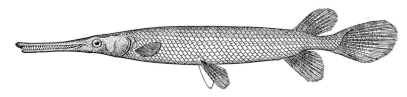

Fig. 48
Long-nosed Gar Pike (*Lepisosteus osseus*), x ¹/₈

gives a sudden, convulsive, sideways jerk of its head, at the same time endeavouring to grip the prey between its jaws. Many preliminary manoeuvres and tentative snaps are made before the body of the little fish is finally transfixed by the teeth. When this is accomplished the victim is gradually worked round into a convenient position, and unless it has again escaped during this process, is finally swallowed, generally head first.

The Gar-fishes [Fig. 47B] and Sauries, on the other hand, are equally voracious, but feed in large shoals, pursuing and capturing their prey whilst skimming along at the surface of the water, frequently transfixing the eyes or bodies of smaller fishes with their ram-like 'beaks'. Small fishes form the main item in their diet, but almost any animal substance is eaten. Some of the larger species of Gar-fish, perhaps five or six feet in length, may even be dangerous to man.

In the curious Half-beaks (Hemirhamphidae), related to the Gar-fishes and found in all tropical seas, only the lower jaw is produced, and forms a long, spear-like projection [Fig. 47C]. The teeth are minute and the diet is purely a vegetable one, consisting largely of green algae.

It is of interest to note that in the young both of Gar-fishes and Half-beaks the jaws are of equal length and not drawn out. But in the growing Gar-fish the jaws begin to lengthen, and for a time the lower jaw is longer than the upper, and the little fish resembles a Half-beak. The upper jaw soon increases further in length, however, and in the adult fish is longer than the lower (*cf.* p. 262).

In the grotesque Snipe Eels (Nemichthyidae) both the jaws are prolonged and the tips not infrequently curved in opposite directions, the one upwards, the other downwards [Fig. 32G]. These fishes feed on small Crustacea.

The Sword-fishes (Xiphiidae), Spear-fishes, and Sail-fishes (Istiophoridae) have only the upper jaw prolonged, forming in the first named a long, flattened, sword-like weapon, and in the others a rounded, tapering spear of varying length [Fig. 6]. The teeth in the jaws are small and numerous, extending forward on to the lower surface of the sword. The Common Sword-fish (*Xiphias*) is widely distributed in all warm seas, and grows to a length of fifteen to twenty feet. Its food seems to consist largely of fishes, and it is said to split large forms like the Bonito and Albacore with the sword, or to strike with lateral movements among a shoal of small fishes, afterwards devouring the stunned and wounded victims. It has, however, been suggested that the sword did not evolve as a weapon, but merely represents an extreme case of streamlining, the pointed rostrum acting as an efficient cutwater.

Many are the tales told of ships damaged or even sunk by the attacks of these fishes, but in most stories no attempt has been made to discriminate between Sword-fishes, Spear-fishes, and Sail-fishes, all of which have similar habits. There can be no doubt that they sometimes succeed in piercing the bottom of a boat, and, being unable to withdraw the sword by reversing it is snapped off in the struggles to escape. The museum of the College of Surgeons possesses a section from the bow of a whaler in which is impaled a sword a foot in length and five inches in circumference, which had penetrated through thirteen and a half inches of wood; in another specimen of ship's timber in the British Museum the transfixed sword has been thrust through no less than twenty-two inches. Another case on record concerns the ship *Dreadnought*, which suddenly sprang a leak on its voyage from Ceylon to London. On examination it was found that a hole about an inch in diameter had been neatly punched in the copper sheathing of the vessel. When a claim was duly made, the insurance company denied their liability, holding that the damage had been caused by some agent other than a fish, but when the case was taken to court the jury returned a verdict that the damage had been brought about 'by contact with some substance other than water', and added a rider that is was probably caused by a Sword-fish. It is open to grave doubt, however, whether these attacks on ships are deliberate, although it is freely stated that, since Sword-fishes have been described as attacking Whales in company with Killers, the fish merely mistakes the ship for a Whale. It seems more probable that the occurrences are no more premeditated than, say, a head-on collision between two motor-cars, and may be due to similar causes, namely, an inability to brake or alter course in time (see page 22).

In some fishes the anterior part of the head is drawn out, but the mouth itself remains small and is placed at the extremity of a long, tube-like beak. Among the Mormyrids (Mormyridae) of the fresh waters of Africa, for example, a number of diverse modifications of the snout are encountered. In many Elephant Mormyrids this takes the form of a curved, trunk-like structure, at the tip of which is the tiny mouth armed with few but relatively large teeth [Fig. 47A]. This remarkable appendage is inserted between stones or into the mud in search of insect larvae and small crustaceans which form the principal food. These fishes live mostly in more or less muddy water, and the eyes are small and often much degenerated. In some related genera the lower lip is provided with a fleshy mental appendage, which may be globular or viliform in shape; this is sensitive, and acts as an organ of touch and taste aiding in the search for food thus compensating for the poor vision. Similar modifications of the snout and jaws are found among the Gymnotids of South America. Many species of Butterfly-fishes (Chaetodontidae), nearly all inhabitants of coral reefs have the mouth placed at the end of a straight, tubular snout, and this is used for poking into crevices and holes in the coral in search of prey [Fig. 47F].

The members of the large and varied order of Tube-mouths all have the snout prolonged to form a rigid tube-like 'beak' with a small mouth at its extremity [Fig. 49A]. The jaws are short, and to achieve articulation with the hinder part of the skull in the usual manner, the articulatory part of the mandible (the quadrate bone) is drawn out into a long, rod-like structure. The Trumpet-fishes (Fistulariidae) and their allies have some minute teeth in the mouth, but these are wanting in all the other members of the order. The Pipe-fishes (Syngnathidae) live almost entirely on small crustaceans, and when searching for food they swim about slowly in a most curious manner, holding the body now in a vertical and now in a horizontal position, indulging in wriggles and contortions of every conceivable kind. The head is in constant movement, the long snout being poked into clumps of vegetation or into any other place where prey is likely to be encountered. The actual manner of feeding is remarkable, the tube-like 'beak' acting as a syringe, the prey being drawn in rapidly by sudden inhalent respiratory movements. The Sea Horses (*Hippocampus*) have a similar diet, which seems to be obtained in a like manner. The fish will approach

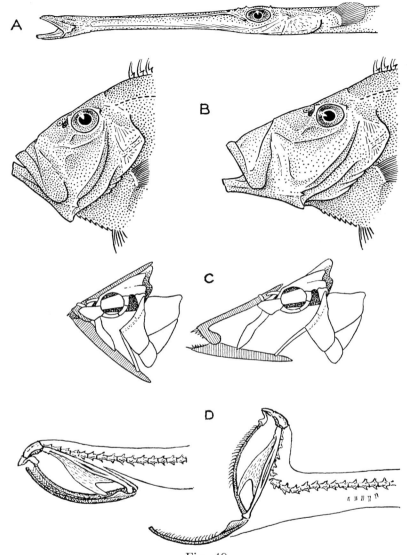

Fig. 49

A. Head of Flute-mouth or Tobacco-pipe Fish (*Fistularia tabacaria*),
x ¹/₆; B. Head of John Dory (*Zeus faber*), with the mouth retracted and
protruded, x ¹/₃; C. Skull of Large-mouthed Wrasse (*Epibulus insidiator*),
with the jaws retracted and protruded, x ¹/₃; D. *Saccopharynx*; skull
and vertebral column showing the changes taking place when the mouth
is opened (right), x ¹/₃; After Tchernavin; simplified, not all bones
are shown.

a small crustacean in a leisurely manner, peer at it for a second or two, and then, having placed its snout in a convenient position, suddenly engulf the meal.

In a number of fishes the mouth is described as protractile; that is to say, it can be protruded and withdrawn at will. In the Sturgeon (*Acipenser*) the funnel-like mouth is thrust downward by a forward swing of the suspensory bones of the hyoid arch, but in most other fishes the protrusion is accomplished by the premaxillaries of the upper jaw sliding forward on certain bones in the front part of the skull, the small maxillaries acting as levers. In many members of the Carp family (Cyprinidae) the mouth is especially protractile, and in the Bream (*Abramis*), for example, forms a sort of tube when protruded. The John Dory (Zeidae), with its large and very protractile mouth and mournful expression, has an interesting method of hunting the small fishes on which it feeds. Its deep and clumsy body is unsuited for chasing prey, but when swimming upright in mid-water its excessive thinness makes it quite inconspicuous, and when placed end-on towards the victim it is almost invisible and excites no alarm. In this way it is able to approach gradually until within striking distance, when the jaws are shot forward with great rapidity [Fig. 49B]. Among the Wrasses, one tropical form, *Epibulus*, has the mouth even more protrusible than that of the John Dory. In the latter only the upper jaw is thrust forward, but in *Epibulus* the lower jaw is also protruded, the bone to which it is articulated being long and movable, a condition quite unlike that of the other Wrasses in which it is quite short and firmly fixed. [Fig. 49C].

The order of fishes (Lampridiformes), including the Opah (*Lampris*), Deal-fish (*Trachypterus*), and Ribbon-fish (*Regalecus*) contains some strange and very diverse forms, but all agree in the mechanism of the jaws. In other fishes with protractile mouths only the lower end of the maxillary bone moves forward when the mouth is opened, the other end being fixed, but in the members of this group the maxillary of each side is thrust forward as a whole, the movement of the lower jaw pulling it away from the head.

Some particularly strange jaw and feeding mechanisms are to be found amongst deep-sea fishes of the suborder Stomatoidei. In all, however, the effect is similar, namely to gain the widest possible distension of the mouth and to protect the delicate gills and heart from possible damage by the struggling prey. An example may be drawn from *Chauliodus sloani*, whose anatomy was so beautifully elucidated by Tchernavin.

When about to attack, the head is thrown back until the snout has moved through almost a right angle from its position of rest. The anterior part of the vertebral column in *Chauliodus* is peculiar in that the vertebrae are without centra, thus giving this otherwise rigid structure a great degree of suppleness, without which the head could not be pulled upwards. At the same time as the head is thrown back, the lower jaw is pulled downward and the skeletal elements supporting the gills and surrounding the heart are pulled downwards and backwards out of the path which the food will follow. By such extreme means these fishes are able to swallow prey as large as or even larger than themselves, an important factor to animals living in an environment where food is not abundant and energy cannot be wasted in its pursuit. It must be emphasised, however, that the feeding mechanism seen in *Chauliodus* is only an exaggeration of that which is found in less modified forms like the Salmon.

Among the Flat-fishes the characteristic asymmetry is extended to the mouth and jaws in many forms. In *Psettodes*, the most primitive member of the group, the jaws are more or less of the same size, and the teeth almost equally developed on the coloured and on the blind side. The same condition is found in the Halibut (*Hippoglossus*) and in certain other species, which are in the habit of leaving the bottom and swimming strongly in active pursuit of other fishes. In other forms, however, of which the Plaice (*Pleuro-nectes*) and the Dab (*Limanda*) will serve as examples, the mouth is much twisted, being more developed and armed with a greater number of teeth on the lower or blind side. This modification is connected with different habits, these fishes being less active, keeping constantly at or near the bottom, and feeding mainly on Molluscs and other ground living invertebrates. In the Soles (Soleidae) and Tongue Soles (Cynoglossidae), which are even more specialised, the jaws and teeth are extremely feeble on the upper side of the fish, and the mouth is twisted almost completely on to the under surface. The Sole (*Solea*) is a retiring fish, burrowing into the sand and seldom moving, except at night. A study of the early development of these fishes reveals that they begin life with normal symmetrical mouths, but that soon after the larva is hatched the jaws become twisted towards the future blind side.

REFERENCES

TCHERNAVIN, V. (1938). Note on the chondocranium and branchial skeleton of *Salmo*. *Proc. zool. Soc. Lond.*, **108**, 347–364.

TCHERNAVIN, V. (1938). The absorption of bones in the skull of Salmon during their migration to rivers. *Fisheries, Scotland, Salmon Fish.*, No. 6.

TCHERNAVIN, V. (1948). On the mechanical working of the head of bony fishes. *Proc. zool. Soc. Lond.*, **118**, 129–148.

TCHERNAVIN, V. (1953). *The feeding mechanisms of a deep sea fish*, Chauliodus sloani *Schneider*. British Museum (Nat. Hist.) London.

CHAPTER 7

TEETH AND FOOD

THE MOUTHS of Cyclostomes are armed with horny, tooth-like structures, but are devoid of true teeth. The inner surface of the funnel-shaped mouth of the Lamprey (*Petromyzon*) is studded with conical yellow 'teeth,' and at its centre, placed above and below, are two horny plates with jagged edges, formed by the enlargement and fusion of several smaller 'teeth' [Fig. 45A]. Similar plates are found on the muscular protrusible tongue, which works like a piston and rasps off the flesh from the fishes on which the Lamprey preys. In the Hag-fishes (Myxinidae) the tongue is very powerful, and, apart from a single 'tooth' on the roof of the mouth, the comb-like lingual plates represent the only dental armature. When worn out, the 'teeth' of the Cyclostomes are replaced by new ones developing beneath those actually in use.

True teeth are found in the Selachians, and their similarity to placoid scales has already been mentioned (p. 53). The resemblance extends both to their structure and to their mode of development. From an evolutionary viewpoint, a shark's teeth may merely represent placoid scales which have become modified in shape and position, and to a certain extent in development, to fulfil another function.

As in the placoid scale, each tooth consists of a central mass of a bone-like substance, dentine, covered by an outer layer of enamel. The dentine is pierced by a pulp cavity containing cells, blood vessels and nerves.

The teeth are not directly attached to the jaw but are linked basally by a fibrous membrane and further steadied by the gum tissue. Sharks do not keep the same set of teeth throughout life. Instead there is a constant replacement, the older, functional teeth, gradually being replaced by younger teeth. The replacement teeth develop continuously and lie in a row behind each functional tooth so that the succession is linear and not vertical as in Mammals (and for that matter, most Bony Fishes). If we examine the jaws of a shark, we find that there are several rows of teeth lying roughly one behind the other and showing a gradual decrease in developmental perfection the lower they are in the row. [Figs. 50B; 51A–C). Usually there is but one row of erect, functional teeth and these are situated at the edge of the jaw. It seems that several factors are responsible for the forward progression of each tooth in a row, including the decay of the functional tooth. Perhaps the most important part, however, is played by the gradual increase in the pressure exerted by the cells which surround each developing tooth and lie between the bases of the more fully developed ones. The loose fibrous basal connections of the teeth in a row both ensure that

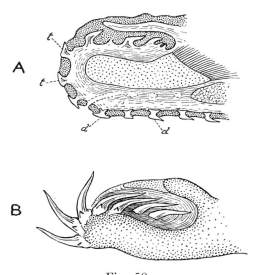

Fig. 50

A. Cross-section through the lower jaw of an embryo Dog-fish (*Scylio-rhinus* sp.), showing the gradual transition from dermal denticles (*d*) on the outer surface to teeth (*t*) on the inner surface. The dotted area in the centre represents the cartilage of the lower jaw. Greatly enlarged. (After Gegenbaur); B. Cross-section through the lower jaw of Sand Shark (*Carcharias taurus*), showing succession of teeth, x $\frac{1}{2}$

it moves as a unit, and help to direct the movement. The pressure developed on the functional teeth when the fish bites is another factor which helps to loosen these teeth. The developing teeth are protected by a thin membrane under which they lie until required to fill a gap in the functional row.

In certain sharks (e.g. the Dogfish *Mustelus*) and in most Rays, several rows of teeth are in use at once, but replacement takes place in the same manner as described above.

In size and form the teeth of Sharks exhibit great diversity, ranging from long, slender, awl-like structures to large, flat, triangular teeth [Fig. 52]. Not infrequently the teeth of the upper

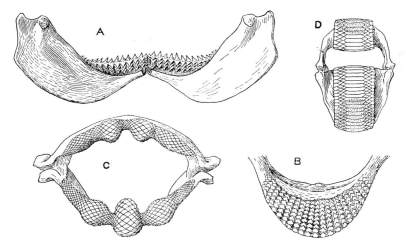

Fig. 51   TEETH OF SHARKS AND RAYS
A. Inner view of lower jaw in White Cheeked Shark (*Eulamia dussumieri*),
x ¹/₄; B. Lower jaw of Nurse Shark (*Ginglymostoma* sp.), x ¹/₄ C. Jaws of
Guitar-fish (*Rhina ancyclostoma*), x ¹/₆; D. Jaws of Eagle Ray (*Myliobatis
aquila*), x ¹/₄

jaw are quite unlike those of the lower, and different types of teeth
may occur in the same jaw. In the primitive Comb-toothed Sharks
(Hexanchidae) the teeth of the upper jaw are mostly provided with
a large central cusp or point with several smaller cusps on either
side. In the lower jaw each tooth consists of several pointed cusps,
graduated in size, all inclined in the same direction, and supported
on a long basal plate [Fig. 52c].

The teeth of the Great White Shark or Maneater (*Carcharodon*),
one of the most formidable of all the Sharks, are very powerful,
flattened, triangular in shape, and with the edges finely serrated
[Fig. 52a]. This Shark grows to a length of about thirty feet, but,
judging from the large size of some fossil teeth of a similar kind
predatory sharks of truly colossal size must have inhabited the seas
in past times. A tooth six inches in length must have belonged to
a Shark at least ninety feet long. The Tiger Shark (*Galeocerdo*),
another large species found in nearly all warm seas, has teeth of a
very peculiar shape, each one being flat and sickle-shaped, with a
fluted edge suggesting that of a patent bread-knife, and with a
triangular point at the summit which projects obliquely outward
[Fig. 52b].

So characteristic is the form of the teeth in many Sharks that it
is often possible to identify a species from one or two teeth alone,

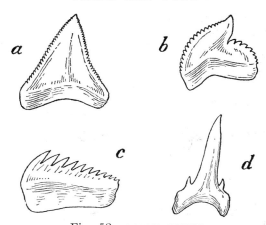

Fig. 52 SHARK TEETH

a. Tooth of Great White Shark (*Carcharodon carcharias*), x ¹/₃; *b.* Of Tiger Shark (*Galeocerdo cuvieri*), x ²/₃; *c.* Of Comb-toothed Shark (*Hexanchus griseus*), x ²/₃; *d.* Of Sand Shark (*Carcharias taurus*), x ²/₃

and in the case of many extinct forms these are the only parts of the fish which remain, all the rest of the skeleton having disappeared. Further, in those species in which the dentition is of more than one type, it is possible to state whether a certain fossil tooth belonged to the upper or the lower jaw, and whether it occurred in the front or at the side of the jaw. The curious Elfin or Goblin Sharks (Scapanorhynchidae) were first known from some teeth occurring in Upper Cretaceous strata, but a living specimen of this supposedly extinct family was found off the coast of Japan in 1898. It is remarkable for the long, blade-like snout, separated from the jaws by a deep cleft, and the teeth are of a characteristic pattern [Fig. 53A, *a*]. The known distribution of the species was further extended in an interesting manner. A 'break' occurred in one of the deep-sea telegraph cables lying at a depth of 750 fathoms in the Indian Ocean, and on its being brought to the surface the damage was found to have been caused by a fish which had left one of its teeth embedded in the cable; this tooth, which had broken off short, was identified as belonging to an Elfin Shark.

All the Sharks so far mentioned are active predatory forms and although they feed mainly on other fishes, the diet is sometimes more mixed. Porpoises, water birds, turtles, pieces of other sharks, crabs, and fishes of all kinds have been taken from the stomachs of Tiger Sharks, and a Man-eater (*Carcharadon*) has been recorded as having a good-sized Sea Lion in its stomach. The Hammer-headed Shark (*Sphyrna*), which seems to feed almost entirely on other fishes, includes the Sting Ray (*Dasyatis*) in its diet.

A specimen which had been feeding on these Rays was afterwards captured, and in addition to the half-digested remains in the stomach, no less than fifty 'stings' (the serrated tail-spines) were found embedded in different parts of the Shark's anatomy particularly in the region of the mouth and pharynx.

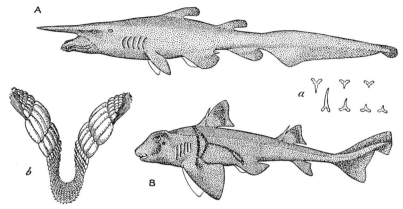

Fig. 53   ELFIN AND PORT JACKSON SHARKS
A. Elfin or Goblin Shark (*Mitsukurina owstoni*), x ¹/₃₀;
(*a*, isolated teeth of same); B. Port Jackson Shark (*Heterodontus phillippi*),
x ¹/₂₀; (*b*, lower jaw of same)

Most Sharks appear to chase and seize their prey as occasion offers, and in a more or less haphazard manner, but some may employ more systematic methods. The Sand Shark (*Carcharias taurus*), for example, a species common on the Atlantic coast of North America has been described as operating in shoals, forcing a school of Blue-fishes into a solid mass in shallow water, before rushing in and seizing the prey. The Thresher or Fox Shark (*Alopias*) feeds largely on Herrings, Pilchards and Mackerel. It swims round and round a shoal of these fishes, thrashing the water with its long tail [Fig. 22A] thus driving the prospective victims into a compact mass, where they form an easy prey.

Views on the man-eating habits of Sharks have changed considerably since the earlier edition of this book was published. There is now no doubt that Sharks will and do attack man, often with fatal results. Much research on this subject remains to be done but a general picture has been developed.

Some twelve species of Sharks are known to attack man; these belong to four families and include the White Shark (*Carcharodon carcharias*), the Mako (*Isurus oxyrinchus*), the Tiger Shark (*Galeocerdo cuvieri*), the Lake Nicaragua Shark (*Carcharinus nicaraguensis*), the Sand Shark (*Carcharias taurus*) and species of Hammerhead sharks.

Sharks usually attack singly, but mob feeding may occur when, as after an aircraft crashes or a ship is sunk, bodies and blood suddenly appear in the water. Frequently, a shark will single out an individual from amongst a crowd of bathers and will press home its attacks on that person, disregarding all others, even those in the immediate area.

Reputed methods of scaring off a shark are varied and of variable efficacy; a man-eating shark is unpredictable in its reactions. Thus, generalizations on shark attacks must be treated with caution. However, certain common features have been noted in well-documented cases: attacks are most frequent in tropical and subtropical seas; most take place when the water temperature is above 70° F (but attacks have taken place when the temperature was around 60° F); murky water is more dangerous than clear water; and the peak hours for attacks are between 15.00 and 16.00.

Most of the damage done by a shark's bite is to the soft tissues of the body, and mainly to the buttocks and legs. But there are records of limbs, especially arms, being amputated.

Being such large and reputedly fierce creatures it is not surprising that a number of seemingly 'tall' stories have grown up about Sharks. One of the more incredible tales was, however, vouched for by reliable authorities:

"In the eighteenth century an American privateer was chased by a British man-of-war in the Caribbean Sea, and finding escape impossible, the Yankee skipper threw his ship's papers overboard. The privateer was captured and taken into Port Royal, Jamaica, and the Captain was there placed on trial for his life (Mr. Cundall says 'for violation of the Navigation Laws'). As there was no documentary evidence against him he was about to be discharged when another British vessel arrived in port. The Captain of this cruiser reported that when off the coast of Haiti a shark had been captured, and that when opened the privateer's papers had been found in the stomach. The papers thus marvellously recovered were taken into court, and solely on the evidence which they afforded the Captain and crew of the privateer were condemned. The original papers were preserved and placed on exhibition in the Institute of Jamaica in Kingston, where the 'shark's papers,' as they were called, have always been an object of great interest. (Signed) A. Hyatt Verrill, New York, Nov. 20, 1915."

In the Nurse Sharks (*Ginglymostoma*) and the Hounds (*Mustelus*), which include in their diet a large percentage of molluscs and crustaceans as well as smaller fishes, there is a different kind of dentition. The teeth are small, pointed or flattened, and adapted for grinding and crushing rather than for cutting. They are arranged in pavement fashion, and all or most of the rows are in use at the same time [Fig. 51B]. These are comparatively sluggish

Sharks, feeding for the most part at or near the bottom of the sea. The Port Jackson Shark (*Heterodontus*), a member of the family of Bull-headed Sharks [Fig. 53B, *b*], has a remarkable dentition, and provides an example of a form with more than one type of tooth in the same jaw. The teeth in the front of the jaws are like small cones, but farther back these gradually pass into teeth which have the form of 'pads' or nodules of varying size. As might be supposed, this curious dentition is used for grinding and crushing purposes, the food consisting almost entirely of molluscs.

In the Guitar-fishes (Rhinobatidae), Saw-fishes (Pristidae), Rays (Raiidae), Sting Rays (Dasyatidae), and their allies, the teeth are nearly always small, blunt, and arranged in pavement fashion with several rows in use at once. Being bottom-feeders the food generally includes a high percentage of molluscs, crustaceans, and other armoured creatures like the sea-urchins, so that the dentition is of the crushing and grinding type. In one of the Guitar-fishes, known as *Rhina*, the tooth-covered jaws present a curious shape, the upper jaw being alternately hollowed and swollen, and the lower being provided with corresponding bumps and depressions to fit into the upper jaw [Fig. 51c]. In an allied form (*Rhynchobatus*) the jaws are much less wavy in outline, a single swelling in the lower jaw fitting into an indentation in the upper, whilst in the more typical Guitar-fishes (*Rhinobatus*) the mouth forms a straight horizontal slit. In some of the Rays and Skates, of which the common Thornback Ray (*Raia clavata*) will serve as an example, the teeth are actually different in the two sexes, those of the male being pointed and those of the female flat.

The dentition of the Eagle Ray (*Myliobatis*) is very specialised, the teeth being quite flat and arranged like paving stones in the form of a mosaic work, those in the centre of the jaws having the form of long hexagonal bars, and those at the sides being much smaller but also six-sided [Fig. 51D]. In the large Spotted Eagle Ray (*Aetobatis*) these side teeth are absent and the dentition in each jaw consists of a single row of long bars arranged one behind the other from before backwards in each jaw. The food seems to consist almost entirely of oysters and clams, and the crushing power of the jaws is truly remarkable. One author writes 'I have found in these Rays, clams which with their shells on must have weighed more than three pounds, and to crack which a pressure of perhaps a thousand pounds would be required.' In the Sea Devils (Mobulidae), on the other hand, with their fish diet, the teeth are very small, numerous flat tubercles.

The Chimaeras (Holocephali), although allied to the Sharks and Rays, present a totally different dentition, both in the form of the teeth and the nature of their fine structure. The jaws are armed with three pairs of large flat plates, two above and one below, studded with hardened points or 'tritors' [Fig. 56A]. In one or two species these points are absent, and the tooth plates bear a marked resemblance to the horny 'beaks" of turtles. With such a specialised dentition one might reasonably expect the food to be of a very definite nature, but actually the diet is a very mixed one and includes seaweeds, fishes, worms, echinoderms, molluscs, and crustaceans. Chimaeras are themselves preyed upon by other fishes, and have been found in the stomachs of Greenland Sharks; the young are eaten in large numbers by the Cod and its allies.

In the Selachians teeth are developed only in the jaws, but in the Bony Fishes they may be present on the tongue, on the roof of the mouth, in the throat and even on the outside of the head. The arrangement may be quite irregular, or they may be placed in one or more regular rows parallel with the edges of the jaws, or in rather broad bands or patches [Fig. 46c]. All the teeth are, as a rule, more firmly attached than those of the Selachians, although in certain fishes some or all of them are freely movable even though attached to the underlying bone. Very rarely, as in certain Characins (Characidae, etc.), and in the File-fish (*Monacanthus*) and Trigger-fish (*Balistes*), they are implanted in sockets in the bone. The succession is much more irregular, new teeth being formed at the bases of the old ones or in the spaces between them. In size and form they present an extraordinary diversity, the type of dentition being intimately associated with the nature of the food.

The teeth on the tongue (lingual teeth) are borne by the lower elements of the hyoid arch, whilst those inside the mouth are connected with the bones of the primitive upper jaw (i.e. the paired palatines and pterygoids) and with certain other bones developed beneath the floor of the cranium [Fig. 46c]. The pharyngeal or gill-teeth in the throat are connected with the inner margins of the branchial arches. As a rule, the lower ones are borne on a pair of bones known as the lower pharyngeals, lying behind and parallel with the lower limbs of the last arch, and representing the remains of a once complete branchial arch [Fig. 54]. The upper pharyngeals are toothed bones representing the upper elements of the preceding arches. In a number of Bony Fishes the lower pharyngeals are united to form a single plate-like bone, often of characteristic form.

A large number of Bony Fishes are piscivorous (fish-eaters); the teeth of such fishes are generally strong, and may be acutely pointed as in the Cod (*Gadus*), Perch (*Perca*), and Bass (*Morone*), serving mainly to seize the prey.

The Pike (*Esox*) has a large mouth which fairly bristles with teeth, those on the premaxillaries being small, while those on the sides of the lower jaw are strong and erect, being used for seizing the victims; those on the roof of the mouth are slender and pointed,

arranged in three parallel bands, and instead of being firmly
joined to the bones are attached by fibrous or elastic ligaments
[Fig. 46c]. These teeth on the palate are directed backwards
towards the gullet, and can be depressed in order to facilitate the

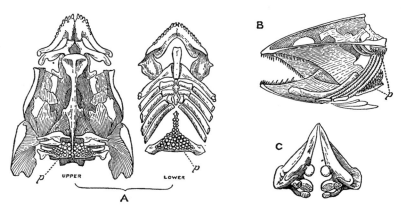

Fig. 54   PHARYNGEAL TEETH

A. Ventral view of skull and dorsal view of hyo-branchial skeleton and
lower jaw of Wrasse (*Labrus* sp.), showing position of pharyngeal bones,
x 1/2; B. Vertical section of skull of Bow-fin (*Amia calva*), showing position
of pharyngeals, x 1/4; C. Lower pharyngeals of Carp (*Cyprinus carpio*), x1/2.
p. pharyngeal bones

entrance of the prey; at the same time, however, as they cannot be
pressed in the opposite direction, they effectively prevent any
chance of escape.   Similar depressible teeth are found in the
Angler-fish or Fishing Frog (*Lophius*), and in many of the deep-sea
forms, such as the Ceratioid Anglers, Wide-mouths (Stomiatoidei),
Gulpers (Saccopharyngiformes), etc., which sometimes seize and
swallow fishes larger than themselves [Figs. 21; 91].   The Pike is
renowned for its rapacious habits.   Fishes are its normal diet, and
these are seized crosswise and swallowed head first.   Its method of
feeding is to lurk within a clump of vegetation, or to lie motionless
in the water.   As soon as a victim comes within reach it is over-
whelmed with a sudden rush and disappears in a smother of foam.
Water-birds, frogs, and voles are also devoured, and instances are
on record of human beings being attacked by hungry Pike.   Cases
of cannibalism in Pike are by no means rare.
    Another fish which is renowned for its ferocity is the Caribe or
Piraya (*Serrasalmus*) of the rivers of South America, an ugly-looking
creature with a deep, blunt head and short powerful jaws, armed
with sharp cutting teeth [Fig. 56c].   They are encountered in
swarms, and their usual diet consists of smaller fishes, but any

animal unlucky enough to fall into the water where they abound is immediately attacked and cut to pieces in an incredibly short time, the smell of blood attracting them in their hundreds. Human beings bathing or wading in the rivers have been attacked and

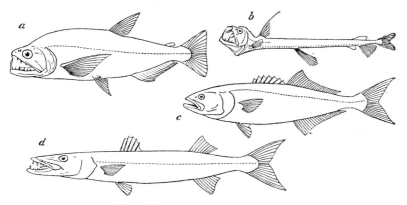

Fig. 55 CARNIVOROUS FISHES
a. Cynodon scomberoides, x ¹/₈; *b. Chauliodus sloanei*, x ¹/₅; *c.* Blue-fish (*Pomatomus saltatrix*), x ¹/₈; *d.* Barracuda (*Sphyraena barracuda*), x ¹/₅

severely bitten by Pirayas and a case is on record in which a man and his horse who fell into the water were subsequently discovered with all the flesh neatly picked off the bones, although the man's clothes were undamaged. Pirayas do not attain any great size, the largest scarcely exceeding a length of two feet, but their lack of inches is amply made up for by their voracity, fearlessness, and numbers.

For sheer ferocity the Blue-fish (*Pomatomus*), a silvery blue-backed fish, not unlike the Bass in appearance, is probably unique [Fig. 55c]. This species is found in the warmer parts of the Atlantic, swimming in large companies near the surface, and reaches a weight of fifteen pounds. Professor Baird writes of this species 'The Blue-fish has been well likened to an animated chopping machine, the business of which is to cut to pieces and otherwise destroy as many fish as possible in a given space of time . . . Going in large schools in pursuit of fish not much inferior to themselves in size, they move along like a pack of hungry wolves, destroying everything before them. Their trail is marked by fragments of fish and by the stain of blood in the sea, as, where the fish is too large to be swallowed entire, the hinder portion will be bitten off and the anterior part allowed to float away or sink.' It has been estimated that as many as one thousand million Blue-fishes occur annually in the summer season on the Atlantic coasts of the United States, and, allowing

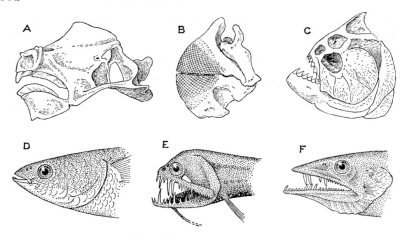

Fig. 56   JAWS AND TEETH
A. Skull of Rabbit-fish (*Chimaera monstrosa*), x $^1/_3$; B. Jaws of Parrot-fish
(*Pseudoscarus* sp.), x $^1/_4$; C. Skull of Caribe or Piraya (*Serrasalmus* sp.),
x $^1/_4$; D. Head of Grey Mullet (*Mugil* sp.), x $^1/_2$; E. Head of Wide-mouth
(*Haplostomias tentaculatus*), x $^1/_2$; F. Head of Lancet-fish (*Alepisaurus
ferox*), x $^1/_4$

a ration of ten fish per day to each Blue-fish, no less than
10,000,000,000 fish are thus destroyed each day, whilst about
1,200,000,000,000 are accounted for in a season lasting only
one hundred and twenty days. This estimate applies only to adult
fish, and if we take into account the young Blue-fishes, which are
equally destructive, the total will be very much greater. They seem
to pay particular attention to the Menhaden (*Brevoortia*), sometimes
driving shoals of them to the shore where they may be seen piled
up in rows.

Among other predatory fishes may be mentioned the Lancet-fish
(*Alepisaurus*), found in the depths of the oceans, a swift scaleless
fish with powerful jaws armed with knife-like teeth [Fig. 56F]. A
specimen has been described from the stomach of which was taken
'several octopods, crustaceans, ascidians, a young *Brama*, twelve
young Boar-fishes (*Capros*), a Horse Mackerel, and one young of its
own species.' In spite of its small size, the ubiquitous Stickleback
(*Gasterosteus*) is remarkably bold and greedy, being especially
destructive to the spawn and young fry of other fishes.

Other fish-eaters, such as the well-known Barracudas (*Sphyraena*),
have the powerful jaws armed with flattened, sharp-edged, dagger-
like teeth [Fig. 55*d*]. These fishes are found in nearly all tropical
and subtropical seas, and the larger species grow to a length of eight
feet and attain a weight of about one hundred pounds. In form

the Barracuda bears a marked likeness to the Pike, but this resemblance is purely superficial. Large individuals seem to be solitary in their habits, although the young congregate in shoals. The large species found in the West Indies, known as the Picuda or Becune, is much more feared by the inhabitants than any Shark, since it is not only extremely ferocious, but also utterly fearless.

Sir Hans Sloane (1707) observed that the Barracuda feeds on 'Blacks, Dogs, and Horses, rather than on White men, when it can come at them in the water.' Père Labat (1742) records that it prefers a negro to a white man, and further, that it will sooner attack an Englishman than a Frenchman! His explanation, however, that the hearty, meat-eating habits of the Englishman as compared to the daintier feeding of the Frenchman produces a stronger exhalation in the water to attract the nostrils of the Barracuda, savours more of national prejudice than of scientific accuracy.

In many Bony Fishes the teeth at the front end of the jaws are much larger than those at the sides, forming strong fangs or canine teeth, the usual purpose of which is to seize the prey. Occasionally, one or more canine-like teeth are found on the sides of the jaws, or, as in certain of the Wrasses (Labridae), at the two angles of the mouth. Some Gobies (Gobiidae) and Blennies (Blenniidae) have a pair of very long and curved canines in the lower jaw, situated inside the mouth and behind the ordinary teeth. In the formidable-looking, deep-sea fish *Chauliodus* all the teeth take the form of long-curved fangs, but the pair at the front of the lower jaw are extraordinarily long. The accompanying figures illustrate the way in which, when the mouth is closed, these fangs slip up the side of the snout, outside the jaws. The teeth of *Chauliodus* are slightly barbed at their tips, but in many deep-sea fishes, as well as in certain of the Sea Perches (Serranidae) and Flat-fishes (Pleuronectiformes), the barbs are strongly developed and the teeth are definitely arrow-headed. *Cynodon* a freshwater fish from the rivers of South America has a pair of very formidable canines at the front of the lower jaw, but instead of slipping outside the jaws when the mouth is shut these are received into special deep sockets in the palate [Fig. 55a]. Little is known of the feeding habits of this fish, but it is clear that in order to bring the canine teeth into play it must open the mouth to an extraordinary extent.

So much for the fish-eaters. In fishes with a more mixed diet, including all kinds of invertebrate animals (molluscs, crustaceans, worms, etc.), and in the vegetarians, the teeth may be chisel-like (incisors), blunt and crushing, slender and brush-like, small and jagged, or absent altogether, according to the nature of the food. This diversity in dentition is found, not only in the jaws, but also in the pharyngeal teeth and in those on the roof of the mouth.

The Flounder, for example, has the lower pharyngeals united to form a triangular plate, and the associated teeth are mostly in the form of bluntly pointed cones, the teeth in the jaws also being conical. The Plaice (*Pleuronectes*), on the other hand, has most of the pharyngeal teeth in the form of blunt crushing molars whilst the jaw teeth are chisel-like. A study of the food of the two fishes shows that the Plaice includes a much higher percentage of molluscs in its diet, and the crushing pharyngeal teeth are admirably suited for such food. Many of the Sea Breams (Sparidae) live on a similar diet, and the teeth are pointed in the front of the jaws and molar-like on the sides, being adapted respectively to break and grind up the shells of its prey. The Wolf-fish (*Anarrhichas*) has a group of long curved canines anteriorly in each jaw, and in the hinder part of the lower jaw a double row of rounded molars: the roof of the mouth is provided with three double rows of teeth, the middle ones flat and those at the sides pointed. Among the Cichlids (Cichlidae) of the Great Lakes of Africa all kinds of dentitions have been evolved in the course of time: the vegetarians have bands of small, notched teeth in the jaws, sometimes with an outer series of chisel-like incisors for cutting weeds or scraping algae from rocks, the fish-eaters have the large mouth armed with strong, pointed teeth, and those which live largely on molluscs have strong, blunt, pharyngeal teeth. In others the lateral teeth of the jaws are modified so that the fish may pull the snail from its shell before swallowing it; here the pharyngeal teeth are relatively fine. The dentition of some species is greatly reduced and deeply embedded in the gums, whilst the mouth is widely distensible. These species feed almost entirely on the eggs and young of other species, which they somehow contrive to extract from the mouth of the parent (see p. 238).

Many fishes include in their diet large numbers of larval aquatic insects, and flies, gnats, and the like, flying near the surface of the water are also seized and devoured, some fishes displaying great agility in leaping out of the water and securing the prey at a single snap. The Archer-fishes (*Toxotes*), found on the coasts and in the rivers from India to the Pacific, derive their name from the curious manner in which they obtain the insects on which they feed [Fig. 57]. Observing a fly hovering near the surface or settled on weeds or grass, the Archer slowly approaches, and, taking aim, squirts a drop or two of water from its mouth at the victim, which falls in the water and is soon secured. Their aim is said to be very accurate even at a distance of three feet, but recent experiments suggest that the results may be more haphazard and due to 'massed firepower' rather than individual 'sharp-shooting'.

Many fish, of which the familiar Herring (*Clupea*) is an example, are plankton feeders; that is to say, they live exclusively on the swarms of microscopic organisms, both animal and vegetable, swimming or floating at or near the surface of the sea and constituting what is known as the plankton (*cf.* p. 349). Like all other animals fishes are ultimately dependent on the material and energy supplied by plants. These plants in their turn are dependent on the rays of the sun to turn non-living materials into living

Fig. 57
Archer-fish (*Toxotes jaculator*), x ¹/₂

substances. For example, the little crustaceans known as Copepods feed on the microscopic plants called Diatoms, the plankton-feeding fish devour the Copepods, and are themselves eaten by other fishes. That the plankton provides a sufficiency of nourishment is shown by the fact that the huge Basking Shark (*Cetorhinus*) is able to subsist exclusively on such a diet (*cf.* p. 361). Diatoms likewise form an important part of the food of bottom-living animals such as molluscs, echinoderms, and worms, so that fishes feeding on these invertebrates are again dependent in the long run upon the vegetable kingdom. As might be expected from the nature of the food, the teeth of the Herring are small and feeble, and the food is strained from the water by the filtering mechanism provided by the slender gill-rakers (*cf.* p. 78). The Hickory Shad (*Dorosoma*) of America, a member of the same family, feeds mainly on mud, and the mouth is small and quite toothless. The Grey Mullets (*Mugil*) may eat small molluscs, or scrape the green weeds from the surfaces of stones or the wooden piles of piers and harbours, but their diet consists largely of decomposed animal and vegetable matter contained in mud. The numerous gill-rakers provide a sieve-like apparatus, and the dentition is represented merely by a fringe of minute bristle-like teeth [Fig. 56D].

In most of the Wrasses (Labridae) the jaws are armed with strong conical teeth, and the lower pharyngeals are joined together to form a plate of characteristic shape studded with blunt teeth [Fig. 54A], a dentition well adapted for dealing with crabs and molluscs. The allied Parrot-fishes or Parrot Wrasses (Scaridae) have the pharyngeal teeth forming a flat pavement, the convex surface of the upper plate fitting closely into the concave surface of the lower. In the jaws successive rows of tiny teeth develop, but these are fused together to form sharp-edged plates set in the short jaws, the whole apparatus recalling the beak of the parrot [Fig. 56B]. Some of these fishes are vegetarian, biting off pieces of seaweed with the 'beaks' and grinding them up between the pharyngeal plates, but others break off lumps of coral in order to obtain the soft coral polyps and other small animals which live in the coral. The common Mediterranean species, the famous *Scarus* so much esteemed by the ancient Greeks and Romans, is almost entirely a vegetable feeder, and the sliding movements of the pharyngeals when engaged in crushing pieces of weed led classical writers like Aristotle and Pliny to affirm that this fish 'chewed the cud.'

A similar but even more complete fusion of the teeth in the jaws is found among members of the order Tetraodontiformes. In the Globe-fishes or Puffers (Tetraodontidae) the teeth unite to form two sharp-edged plates in each jaw, and in the Porcupine-fishes (Diodontidae) feeding mainly on hard corals and molluscs, the teeth are joined to form a single plate in each jaw, sharp at the edge, but with a broad, crushing surface within. The small mouth of the huge oceanic Sun-fish (*Mola*) is armed with a similar beak-like dentition, but here the diet consists largely of other fishes. In the Trigger-fish (*Balistes*), belonging to the order Perciformes, each jaw is provided with eight strong, chisel-like teeth, which are used to bore holes in the shells of oysters, mussels, etc., in order to get at the soft parts. Curiously enough, the related File-fish or Leather Jacket (*Monacanthus*) has a somewhat similar set of teeth, although its diet is said to be a vegetable one.

Members of the family Cyprinidae (order Cypriniformes or Ostariophysi) which includes such well-known forms as the Carp, Gold-fish, Tench, Roach, Dace, Barbel, Bream and Minnow, have toothless mouths, but the pharyngeal teeth are well developed and highly specialised. These are the leather-mouthed fishes of Izaak Walton. 'By a leather-mouth,' he writes, 'I mean such as have their teeth in the throat, as the chub or cheven, and so the barbel, the gudgeon, the carp and divers others have.' The teeth are carried on a pair of strong, sickle-shaped lower pharyngeal bones [Fig. 54c]. and, instead of meeting the upper pharyngeals as in other fishes, they bite against a horny pad at the base of the skull. The teeth are arranged in one, two or three rows, the principal row containing four to seven teeth, the others one to three. The form of the individual teeth varies greatly in the different species, being pointed, hooked at the tips, serrated, spoon-shaped or molar-like. As a general rule the carnivorous species have hooked or pointed teeth, the vegetarians grinding molars. Sometimes the diet is a mixed one, and the Carp (*Cyprinus*), although mainly a vegetable feeder, will also eat worms, shrimps, insects, and smaller fishes, and it is said that the Barbel (*Barbus*) will not refuse any sort of animal or vegetable substance. Not a few species subsist largely on a diet of mud, from which they are able to extract sufficient nutriment in the form of decaying animal and plant matter. The manner in which they take in a mouthful of mud, extract the nutriment by a churning movement of the jaws, and finally eject the residue, is remarkable, and must be familiar to all who have observed Gold-fishes feeding in an aquarium.

In a group of marine fishes known as Stromateoidei or Butter-fishes, whose food seems to consist mainly of polyps, crustaceans, etc., the teeth in the jaws are minute, but the gullet has a remarkable structure, forming a pouch with thick muscular walls on which a number of little teeth are developed. The related Square-tail (*Tetragonurus*), living almost entirely on jelly-fishes, has a similar muscular gullet, but, this is devoid of teeth.

Before concluding this chapter it may be of interest to mention a few remarkable 'meals' which have come to light from time to time. Some years ago a number of X-ray photographs of fresh-water Eels (*Anguilla*) were taken, and among the curious objects seen in the stomachs were bones of water birds and voles, pieces of wood and metal, a steel spring, and a piece of lead pencil. The Wels or Glanis (*Silurus*) of Europe normally feeds on fishes, frogs, and crustaceans, but they are said to drag down and devour birds swimming at the surface. The Cod (*Gadus*) is another mixed feeder, and among the strange objects which have been taken from the stomach may be mentioned a bunch of keys dropped overboard from a trawler, a hare, a partridge, a black guillemot, a long piece of tallow candle, and, so it is said, from a specimen captured in 1626 and sent to the Vice-Chancellor of Cambridge, 'a work in three treatises.' Many of the deep-sea Angler-fishes (Ceratioidei) habitually seize and devour fishes larger than themselves, and this habit sometimes leads to the death of both victim and captor. Specimens have been found floating helplessly at the surface of the sea, each of which had neatly coiled away in its stomach a fish more than twice its own size.

The Common Angler (*Lophius*) does not rely entirely on its angling for food, but sometimes approaches water birds from below and drags them down.

REFERENCES

COPPLESON, V. (1959). *Shark Attack*. Angus and Robertson, Sydney.

HALSTEAD, B. W. (1959). *Dangerous Marine Animals*. Cornell, Maritime Press, Maryland.

HERALD, E. S. (1956). How accurate is the Archer fish? *Pacific Discovery*, **12**, 12–13.

TCHERNAVIN, V. (1953). *The feeding mechanisms of a deep sea fish*, Chauliodus sloani *Schneider*. British Museum (Nat. Hist.) London.

CHAPTER 8

INTERNAL ORGANS

THE PARTS of a fish so far described have been mostly those which can be seen without any detailed dissection. In the present chapter the true internal anatomy, including the skeleton, digestive system, circulatory system and so on, will be studied. Space will permit of only a brief survey of the more important of these internal organs, detailed descriptions of which will be found in the text-books mentioned in the bibliography.

The skeleton, whether composed of cartilage or bone, may be regarded as a local strengthening developed in certain regions of the connective tissue (itself forming a scaffolding pervading the whole body), which has been developed in order to give a general support to the body, to provide a protection for the delicate brain and spinal cord, and to furnish an attachment for the muscles. The skeleton of a fish is a complicated structure, and is often referred to as the endoskeleton in order to distinguish it from the superficial or exoskeleton of scales or scutes. Three main regions of the skeleton may be recognised: skull, vertebral column, and fin-skeleton. The last has been dealt with in a previous chapter (*cf.* pp. 28–30). The skull itself is made up of two distinct parts: the neurocranium, enclosing the brain and sense organs; and the visceral arches, including the upper and lower jaws as well as the series of segmented arches supporting the gills. The visceral arches have been discussed in the chapters devoted to the jaws and gills (*cf.* p. 90) and only the cranium need be described here.

To obtain a clear understanding of the general ground plan of a fish's cranium it is advisable to study it in its least specialized form, and for this purpose the skull of the common Spotted Dog-fish (*Scyliorhinus*) is both suitable and easily obtainable. It may be objected that the skull of the Lamprey (*Petromyzon*) is more primitive, but, although this is true of many features, there are others in which it has attained a marked degree of specialisation along lines peculiar to this class of fish-like vertebrates. In order to reveal the skull of the Dog-fish it is necessary to cut away the skin and muscles of the head, and in so doing it is quite easy to cut into and damage the underlying neurocranium. This fact should serve to fix in the mind one of the most important features of the Selachian skull, namely, that it is composed, not of bone, but of a much softer substance called cartilage. In all living Selachians the entire skeleton is cartilaginous, and this provides one of the principal characters separating them from the Bony Fishes. In some Sharks and Rays the cartilage is strengthened by the addition of calcareous salts but true bone is never developed.

The neurocranium of the Dog-fish [Fig. 46A] is a somewhat flattened oblong box, with more or less complete floor, roof, and lateral walls, but open in front and behind. Through the posterior aperture the spinal cord emerges from the brain, and on the cartilages forming the lower edge of this opening are two prominences or condyles by means of which the cranium is articulated to the first segment of the backbone. Within the trough-like cranium lies the brain, and the various nerves as well as the associated blood-vessels pass outwards through a number of holes or foramina in its floor and walls. On the outside of the box are two pairs of prominences, hollow capsules attached to the cranium: the pair at the front end are open below and lodge the delicate organs of smell, and the other pair at the hinder end enclose the organs of hearing. Between them, on either side in the centre of the cranium, is a cavernous recess known as the orbit in which lie the eyes. So much for the neurocranium of the Dog-fish.

In the Bony Fishes there is a much more complex neurocranium, in which true bones have to a greater or lesser extent replaced the cartilage, although in some of the more generalised forms large areas of the softer substance still remain. In the Sturgeon (*Acipenser*), for example, the head is covered with a dense bony armour made up of a large number of separate and symmetrically arranged plates, but below these is a cartilaginous cranium not very unlike that of the Dog-fish. In the Bichir (*Polypterus*), another primitive form, there is still more bony matter in the skull, for, in addition to the investing armour on the surface (which contains many fewer elements than that of the Sturgeon) some of the cartilages of the cranium itself have been replaced by bone. In the more highly evolved Bony Fishes the amount of cartilage in the cranium of the adult fish becomes less and less, until finally it is entirely absent as in the great majority of the members of this class living to-day.

As previously explained (*cf.* p. 92) the bones are of two distinct kinds, each with a different mode of origin, but they are so welded together to form a compact whole that in the adult fish it is often impossible to decide to which category a particular element belongs. Firstly, there are cartilage bones, so called because the bony tissue develops in the cartilage itself and eventually replaces it. Secondly, there are dermal or membrane bones, not preceded by cartilage, but developing as new structures in the thin membranes of certain regions of the head and forming an investing sheath

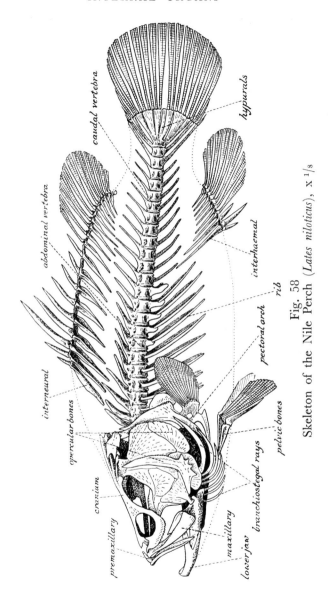

Fig. 58

Skeleton of the Nile Perch (*Lates niloticus*), x ⅛

on the outer surface of the neurocranium. The bones of the roof, most of those on the floor, as well as those supporting the gill-covers, are of this nature [Figs. 46B, C; 58].

The development of the neurocranium in a fish such as the Salmon may be briefly described. The first trace of the skull as seen in the unhatched embryo takes the form of two pairs of cartilaginous plates lying below the brain, known as the trabeculae and parachordals. Later, centres of cartilage start to grow in the regions of the organs connected with the senses of smell and hearing, the cartilages in the floor grow up the sides and meet above the brain, and later still, the capsules round the sense organs fuse with the remainder of the cranium. At this stage, which may occur as late as the second week after hatching, the cranium is still entirely cartilaginous, and is not very unlike that of the adult Dog-fish. Soon afterwards, dermal and cartilage bones begin to develop, much of the cartilage disappears, and the skull gradually assumes the adult form. It is of interest to note that the dermal bones have become so much an essential part of the cranium that no cartilage develops in the regions which they will finally occupy, and during the early stages of development the brain is protected merely by connective tissue in these regions.

The series of cartilages or bones constituting the axis of the body, and which give protection to the delicate spinal cord and certain blood-vessels running from head to tail, is known as the vertebral column or backbone [Fig. 58]. The separate elements are spoken of as vertebrae. In the developing embryo of any fish the first part of the skeleton to make its appearance is not the proper backbone but an unjointed rod of turgid tissue, the notochord, running along the axis of the body and ending in front between the rudiments of the cartilages forming the floor of the cranium. The ancestors of the fishes probably retained this simple axial rod throughout life, but with the ever-growing need for some protection for the spinal cord, as well as for a centre for the attachment of body muscles, the vertebral column was developed round it. During the development of the individual fish the different vertebrae arise as rings of cartilage which grow round the notochord and gradually constrict it. Later on, additional pieces of cartilage grow up to surround the spinal cord, and others are developed below as a protection for the main artery and vein. In all the higher fishes the notochord disappears altogether in the adult stage but it persists in the Crossopterygii and Dipneusti.

In the Lamprey (*Petromyzon*) the vertebral column is very simple, the notochord persisting in the adult, merely supporting a series of isolated cartilages on either side of the spinal cord. In the Selachians it is more complicated, but is still composed entirely of cartilage. Each vertebra is a complex structure made up of a number of pieces firmly joined together. The names of all these elements need not be mentioned here, and it will suffice to point out that the body of each vertebra, the centrum, takes the form of a ring of cartilage, which is hollow in front and behind like a dice-box; on its upper and lower edges this bears an arch of cartilage, the upper or neural arch protecting the spinal cord, and the lower or haemal arch performing a like service for an artery and a vein [Fig. 59A, B.2]. The lower arches are of two kinds,

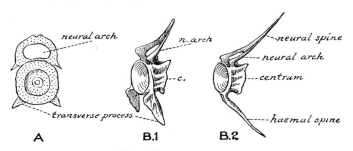

Fig. 59 VERTEBRAE

A. Cross-section through one of the vertebrae of Comb-toothed Shark (*Heptranchias perlo*), x $^1/_4$; B.1. Lateral view of an abdominal vertebra of Cod (*Gadus morhua*), x $^1/_3$; B.2. Caudal vertebra of same, x $^1/_3$

those in the tail region (i.e. of the caudal vertebrae) being complete and meeting below to form a tunnel, whilst those in the trunk region (i.e. of the abdominal vertebrae) project sideways as short processes to which are attached slender ribs, running outwards in the walls of the body and ending in the partitions between the segments of the body muscles. In some of the more primitive Bony Fishes, such as the Sturgeons (Acipenseridae) and Lung-fishes (Dipneusti), the vertebrae are still incomplete and are composed largely of cartilage; the unconstricted notochord persists between the vertebral elements. Two pairs of additional elements not found in the Selachians occur in Bony Fishes: the supraneurals, united to form neural spines, and the infrahaemals, united in the tail region to form haemal spines, but in the trunk region taking the form of what are known as pleural ribs. In most of the higher Bony Fishes the vertebrae are more or less completely ossified, and have the same essential form throughout the class [Fig. 59]. The Gar Pike (*Lepisosteus*) is unique in the form of its vertebrae, each centrum being convex in front and concave behind. In the remaining Bony Fishes the centra almost invariably have concave surfaces at both ends, although in the Eels (Anguilliformes) they may be flat or even convex in front. In a number of fishes the articulation between two vertebrae is made more effective by the development of little bony processes on the sides of the neural arches or the centra; these project backwards in one vertebra and meet a similar process projecting forwards in the next.

There are one or two remarkable adaptations of the vertebral column which are worthy of consideration.   In the deep-sea *Chauliodus*, for example, which throws the head back when striking at its prey (*cf.* p. 100), the first vertebra immediately behind the skull is enormously enlarged, being several times larger than any of those following. This serves to take the strain when the head is suddenly jerked back, and at the same time provides additional surface for the attachment of the muscles moving the head [Fig. 60D]. In some of the members of the genus *Eustomias*, oceanic fishes of the suborder of Wide-mouths (Stomiatoidei), the anterior part of the vertebral column is incompletely ossified and with the notochord is bent to form one or two distinct loops. The first vertebra is normal, but this is followed by six or seven without centra and made up of isolated bony elements. This curious modification is undoubtedly related to the violent movements of the head involved in protruding the jaws and in swallowing large prey, the incompletely ossified and bent anterior portion giving flexibility and acting as a shock absorber [Fig. 60c]. It has been suggested that the opening out and closing up of the bends, and the corresponding movements of the jaws, may assist in swallowing prey. In *Stylephorus*, another oceanic form with protractile jaws, a similar strain due to the backward jerk of the head is provided for by a complicated system of interlocking among the first few vertebrae by means of special bony processes [Fig. 60B]. Finally, in the Sword-fishes (Xiphiidae) and Spear-fishes (Istiophoridae), the vertebrae are tightly interlocked by horizontally arranged projections (zygapophyses) so that the vertebral column forms a rigid foundation for the powerfully developed tail muscles which, in these fishes, provide the main propulsive effort [Fig. 60A].

The changes undergone by the first two or three vertebrae in the Cyprinoids (Carp and Characins) and Siluroids (Cat-fishes) in connection with the so-called Weberian mechanism will be fully described in the next chapter.

Before leaving the skeleton, attention may be drawn to the curious bright green colour of the bones in the Gar-fishes (Belonidae), Skippers (Scombresocidae) and allied forms. This is unique among fishes, and remains even after cooking. There is a strong prejudice against eating these fishes on this account, but the colouring is not due to any harmful substance and the flesh is wholesome and nutritious.

The tissue clothing the skeleton, generally known as the meat or flesh, is made up of muscles, and provides the greater part of the bulk of the body. In the higher vertebrates the muscular system is a complicated one, but in the fishes the arrangement is comparatively simple. The most important muscles are the great lateral bands running along the body in the trunk and tail—the muscles concerned with swimming. In the ancestors of the fishes these muscles may have formed continuous bands running from the head to the tail, but in all living forms they are divided transversely into a series of segments, corresponding in number to the vertebrae, each of which usually has roughly the shape of an S. On either

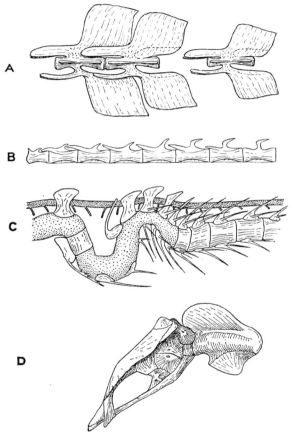

Fig. 60 MODIFICATIONS OF VERTEBRAL COLUMN

A. Three vertebrae from the tail of Sail-fish (*Istiophorus*), x ¹/₈; B. First eight vertebrae of *Stylephorus chordatus*, x 3. (After Regan); C. Anterior part of vertebral column and spinal cord (above) of *Eustomias brevibarbatus*, (After Regan and Trewavas); D. Skull and first vertebra of *Chauliodus sloani*, (After Regan and Trewavas)

side each of these segments or myotomes is further divided into an upper and lower half by a groove running along the length of the fish.   If the skin is removed from the side of a fish a number of parallel white stripes of zigzag form may be seen, representing the edges of the thin partitions (myocommata) between the successive myotomes.   In the neighbourhood of the fins the segments are variously modified for their special duties, and in the head there is a more complicated system of muscles, each with its own particular task: one set to move the eyes, another the gill-arches, another the jaws, and so on.

As a general rule, the muscles of a fish are white or pinkish in colour, but in the members of the group which includes the Tunnies (*Thunnus*) and Mackerels (*Scomber*) they appear deep red. The characteristic colour of the flesh of the Salmon (*Salmo*), a beautiful orange-red, is due to the presence of certain oils.   When a Salmon runs up the river after a season of abundant feeding in the sea the flesh is firm and red, and there is a good store of fat in the tissues, but as the time for breeding approaches the fat is expended on the development of the gonads and the flesh becomes pale and watery.   Not only the colour but also the taste of the flesh varies to some extent in different fishes.   The flavour of a fish is due to the presence of some peculiar chemical substance in the muscles which gives it its characteristic flavour.   There is, for example, an immense difference in the flavour of a Plaice (*Pleuronectes*) and a Sole (*Solea*), the latter being regarded by many epicures as the most tasty of all fishes.   The explanation of this difference in flavour is interesting.   In the Plaice, as in most other fishes, the chemical substance is present in the flesh when the fish is alive, but unless it is eaten soon after capture this soon fades away and the flesh becomes comparatively tasteless.   In the Sole, on the other hand, the characteristic flavour is only developed two or three days after death in consequence of the formation of a chemical substance by the process of decomposition: thus, it forms a tasty dish even when brought long distances.

After the muscles the alimentary canal or food channel may be considered, that lengthy tube which commences at the mouth and ends at the vent or anus.   The alimentary system also includes the mouth, jaws, and teeth, which have already been described, and such glands as the liver, pancreas, and spleen [Fig. 61].   The alimentary canal is found in its simplest and most primitive condition in the Lampreys and Hag-fishes (Cyclostomes), where it forms a straight tube running from mouth to vent, with the different regions scarcely indicated.   In the Selachians and in the vast majority of Bony Fishes the pharynx is followed in succession by an oesophagus, a stomach, an intestine, and a rectum. Commencing with the mouth, it may be noted that there is never a protrusible

tongue in fishes; further, although the mouth and intestine both
secrete a more or less copious supply of mucus to lubricate the food
mass and assist its passage, there are no salivary glands in the mouth
as in the higher vertebrates. As the food leaves the mouth it passes
along the pharynx, the walls of which are perforated by the gill
clefts, and enters the oesophagus from whence it passes on to the

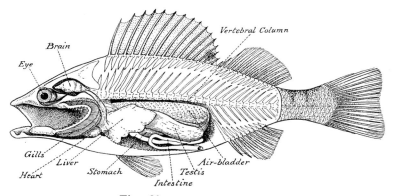

Fig. 61   INTERNAL ORGANS
Dissection of a Perch (*Perca fluviatilis*), showing the principal internal
organs, x $^1/_3$

stomach, where the processes of digestion commence. Generally,
a slight constriction in the tube marks the boundary between the
oesophagus and stomach, but in some fishes only the change in
the character of the cells lining the walls serves to indicate where
one begins and the other ends, the presence of gastric glands in the
walls of the stomach providing the most definite clue. The stomach
is generally somewhat larger than the oesophagus or the succeeding
intestine, and may be U-shaped, with the concave part of the U
directed towards the mouth, or may take the form of a blind sac with
the openings for entrance and exit close together at the front end.
Attached near the exit of the stomach may be seen in many Bony
Fishes a number of blind tube-like sacs, the pyloric caeca (from the
Greek *pyloros*, a gate-keeper, and the Latin *caecus*, blind). These may
be very numerous as in the Salmon (*Salmo*), few in number, or absent
altogether, and they also exhibit considerable variation in length
and breadth. No pyloric caeca occur in the Cat-fishes (Siluroidei),
Pikes (Esocidae), Wrasses (Labridae), Pipe-fishes (Syngnathidae),
and others; the Sand Eel (*Ammodytes*) is said to possess a single one,
the Turbot (*Scophthalmus*) two, other Flat-fishes three or a few more;
in the Whiting (*Micromesistius*) over one hundred have been
counted, and in the Mackerel (*Scomber*) nearly two hundred. Their

function is not yet properly understood, although they are believed to increase the area of intestine through which the products of digestion are absorbed into the blood. Pyloric caeca are not found in any of the higher vertebrates.

The walls of the stomach, although provided with a strong coat of muscles, are not, as a rule particularly thick, but in certain Bony Fishes these are specially modified to deal with a particular diet. In many of the lakes of Ireland there is to be found a form of Trout, known locally as the Gillaroo, which lives largely on shell-fish, and has a remarkably thick-walled and muscular stomach. In the Grey Mullets (Mugilidae) and in the Hickory Shad (*Dorosoma*) of America, fishes which feed largely on decomposing vegetable and organic matter mixed with mud, a gizzard like that of a fowl is developed. In the Mullets the walls are so thickened that the cavity inside is reduced to a mere crack, and is lined by a thick horny covering.

Finally, it may be noted that the stomach is absent in certain groups of fishes, *eg.* in the Carp family.

Passing from the stomach, the food, which is now more or less fluid, enters the intestine, the commencement of which is marked by the presence of a ring-like thickening (pyloric sphincter) of the inner surface of the canal, and by the entrance of the ducts leading from the liver and pancreas [Fig. 61]. The function of this part of the alimentary tract is connected with the completion of digestion and the absorption of food into the blood, the essential process of assimilation. The length of the intestine in a particular fish is thus closely connected with the nature of its normal diet. In the Sharks and Rays, and in many of the Bony Fishes feeding mainly on other fishes, the intestine is straight, or at the most is thrown into one or two simple loops, but in the vegetarians and mud-eaters it is exceedingly long and variously coiled and looped, so as to pack the maximum of absorptive surface into the minimum of space. In the Grey Mullets (Mugilidae), for example, it is very lengthy and closely coiled; in the Stone Roller (*Campostoma*), a member of the family of North American Suckers (Catostomidae), it is wound round and round the swimbladder, and in the Mailed Cat-fishes (Loricariidae) of South America it is disposed in numerous spiral coils like the spring of a watch. Mention may be made here of two important glands pouring their juices into that part of the intestine which lies immediately behind the stomach. These are the liver, a large irregular mass of tissue varying much in size and colour in different fishes, and generally provided with a gall-bladder as in higher vertebrates, and the pancreas, a more diffuse gland, a part of which is generally embedded in the substance of the liver [Fig. 61]. Sometimes the products of liver and pancreas are carried to the intestine by a common duct. Another dark red gland, the spleen, is found attached to the stomach in practically all fishes.

The large intestine, the last part of the alimentary canal, may be recognised by its straight course to the vent or sometimes by an increase in calibre. In the Sharks and Rays this develops a curious internal structure known as the spiral valve [Fig. 62].

Fig. 62
Large intestine of a Ray
(*Raia* sp.) opened to show
the spiral valve, x ²/₃

It occurs in its simplest form in the Lampreys, but attains maximum development in the Selachians, where it may be very complicated and exhibit a good deal of variation in the different species. In one Shark the spiral valve has as many as forty turns, whilst in some of the Hammer-heads (*Sphyrna*) it has the appearance of a scroll. The peculiar and characteristic shape of the fossilised faeces ('coprolites'), thought to have been excreted by extinct shark-like fishes, indicate that these forms also possessed a spiral valve. The function of this structure is to increase the area of absorptive surface, an end which is accomplished in the Bony Fishes by an increase in the length of the intestine. A somewhat simpler velve is found in the Sturgeons (*Acipenser*), Bichirs (*Polyp-terus*), Lung-fishes (Dipneusti), Bow-fin (*Amia*), and other primitive forms, but disappears in all the higher Bony Fishes.

In the Selachians and Lung-fishes the rectum opens into a cloaca, which also receives the ducts from the kidneys and reproductive organs, but in all the remaining Bony Fishes it opens to the exterior by the vent or anus, lying in front of the urinary and reproductive openings. The cloaca is invariably situated near the junction between the trunk and tail regions of the body: the vent, on the other hand, varies considerably in position in different fishes, and may occupy almost any position from the primitive one at the hinder end of the trunk to one between or even in front of the pectoral fins. In the Electric Eel (*Electrophorus*) and other Gymnotid fishes the vent is actually to be found in the throat.

Space will not permit a description of the elaborate and delicate structure of the lining membrane of the different parts of the alimentary canal, but it may be pointed out that this, for the most part, functions either to prepare the food for absorption into the blood or to carry out the absorptive process itself. Like any other animal, the fish, in order to live, has to convert the food into energy, and after the food is broken down and liquified in the stomach and intestines the nutritious part is taken up by the walls of the canal, whence it passes into the blood. The elaborate intercommunicating system of arteries and veins, by means of which the nourishment is carried to the cells in every part of the body, is known as the vascular system, and its principal features may now be described.

The essential organ of this system is the heart, in fishes a stout muscular pump of comparatively simple design and small size, situated in a chamber known as the pericardium, which generally lies below the pharynx and immediately behind the gills [Figs.

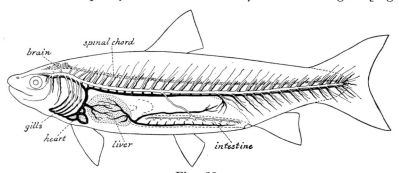

Fig. 63

Vascular system of a fish. (After Grote, Vogt and Hofer). Arteries— white; veins—black.

61, 63], although in some of the Eels (Anguilliformes) it is placed some way behind the head. The heart consists of four parts: a chamber or sinus venosus into which the veins open; an auricle or atrium; a deep red, thick-walled ventricle, the rhythmical contractions of which serve to drive the blood round the body; and a bulb at the base of the main artery carrying the blood to the gills. In the Selachians and more primitive Bony Fishes this bulb is muscular, provided with special valves, and pulsates like the ventricle, but in all higher forms these structures degenerate and the walls are incapable of contraction. It is of special interest to note that in the air-breathing Lung-fishes the auricle and ventricle are functionally divided into two by the development of a partition, thus foreshadowing the four-chambered heart of the higher vertebrates. From the ventricle the blood passes through the bulb into the great ventral aorta, from both sides of which branches carry it to the fine vessels in the gills, where the respiratory exchange of gases takes place (*cf.* p. 69). After losing its carbon-dioxide and receiving its charge of oxygen the blood, instead of returning to the heart, is again received into a main artery—the dorsal aorta— giving off various branches which divide again and again into smaller and smaller vessels, by means of which the oxygenated blood is carried to the remotest parts of the body [Fig. 63]. The blood gives up its oxygen to the oxygen deficient cells, receives their waste products, and then returns to the heart through the veins. All the main veins with the exception of those from the liver, unite into two large vessels running across the body, and these meet together as they open into the sinus of the heart. The details of the circulation vary somewhat in the different groups of fishes, but the essential features are as described above.

The amount of blood present in the body of a fish is a good deal less than in the higher vertebrates; and its flow through the arteries and veins is a sluggish one. Further, except in forms such as the Tunny (*Thunnus*), Albacore (*Germo*), and Sword-fish (*Xiphias*), remarkable for their great muscular activity, in which it is abundant and comparatively warm, the temperature of the blood is but little higher than that of the surrounding water. In addition to the blood-vessels, there is also the fine network of tubes known as the lymphatic system, widely distributed in the connective tissue of different parts of the body, collecting the blood plasma which oozes through the fine capillaries for the nourishment of the tissues, and carrying it back to the veins. In some fishes lymph hearts are present where the larger lymph vessels open into the veins, and the Common Eel (*Anguilla*), for example, has such a pulsating organ in its tail.

Among the remaining organs occupying the interior of the body-cavity are the kidneys, reproductive organs, swimbladder, and such ductless glands as the thyroid, thymus, and suprarenal bodies. The kidneys are generally long, thin glands, dark red in colour, situated immediately below the vertebral column. Their purpose is to extract certain impurities from the blood, poisonous by-products formed by the processes of combustion constantly taking place in living tissues. These, in the form of urine are excreted to the exterior by means of urinary ducts. Closely associated with excretion is the maintenance of the body's salt and water balance. The discussion which follows relates to Bony Fishes (particularly Teleosts); Selachians and Cyclostomes present somewhat different problems and solutions.

Most fishes are restricted to either salt or fresh water, that is to say they have a limited salinity tolerance (so called stenohaline species). The blood and body tissues of a freshwater fish have a higher salt content than the surrounding water. Thus, by osmosis occuring across permeable surfaces, like the gills, the fish tends to take in water and lose some salts the whole time. Therefore, if it is not to become water-logged the excess water must be excreted. Also, there must be the maximum control over possible further losses of salts. The kidneys play a vital role in both functions, their structure being well adapted for retaining body salts but removing excess water from the blood passing through them. Needless to say, a freshwater fish does not drink. Conditions are reversed in marine fishes. Here the salt concentration in the blood and tissues is less than that of the sea and consequently there is a tendency for the animal to lose water and gain salts. To combat this continuous process of dehydration the fish must drink large quantities of water. But, by the very act of drinking sea-water it is also taking in more salts which must eventually be removed from the body if the balance is to be maintained. Again it is the kidneys which play the principal part, but these organs are assisted by special salt secreting cells in the gills and possibly other parts of the body. Because of its need to conserve water and excrete excess salts, the urine of a marine fish is very concentrated and produced in small quantities. The urine of freshwater species, on the other hand, is very dilute and produced in copious quantities.

The salinity tolerance of different species shows considerable variation, some (the so called euryhaline species) being able to pass from salt to fresh water with ease. These fishes (of which the Three Spined Stickleback, Grey Mullet and Flounder are well-known examples) are able to carry out relatively rapid physiological adjustments to the whole excretory system. The centre of control for these changes is still unknown; it may be effected through the nervous system or through hormones.

Fishes, like the Salmon, which leave the sea to spawn in fresh water (anadromous species) or those like the Eel which live in fresh water as adults but spawn in the sea (catadromous species) do not necessarily have a wide salinity tolerance since the ability to adapt from one medium to the other is confined to certain phases in their life histories. In both types the change, once made, is not readily reversed.

The reproductive organs are of two kinds, ovaries in the female, testes in the male, or, as they are familiarly called, hard and soft roes [Figs. 61; 97]. These will be considered in greater detail in the chapter devoted to breeding (*cf.* p. 213).

It has previously been pointed out that the swimbladder is an organ which has been adapted to perform several different functions; its function as a lung has already been considered, (p. 84) whilst its connection with hearing and sound production has still to be discussed (p. 152). Probably its original function was as a respiratory organ but in the majority of Bony Fishes the swimbladder has taken on the role of a float or hydrostatic organ. Such an organ enables the fish to remain poised at any depth without rising or falling. This equilibrium is achieved by making the density of the fish about equal to that of the surrounding water. Since the density of a body is its mass per unit volume, the bladder is clearly connected with controlled variation in the latter factor. Calculations show that if a fish is to be in hydrostatic equilibrium, its swimbladder should occupy about 7 % of its body volume in freshwater species and about 5 % in marine species. These figures accord well with the actual average volumes measured, viz. about 8.5 % in freshwater species and about 5 % for marine species.

The swimbladder develops as an outgrowth of the alimentary canal. The duct connecting the bladder and foregut may persist throughout life (physostomatous condition) or it becomes closed early in life (physoclistous condition). In freshwaters there are more physostomes than physoclists, while in the sea, the latter predominate.

The walls of the swimbladder are richly supplied with blood vessels. In physoclists there are concentrations of blood vessels in a particular area, the so called red body or gas gland situated anteriorly in the ventral part of the bladder. It is through this gland that gases are actively secreted into the swimbladder. Another remarkable structure in physoclists is the oval, a thin area of highly vascularized wall in the upper, posterior part of the bladder. The oval can be shut off from the cavity of the bladder by a strong circular muscle. The oval functions to remove gas from the bladder. Neither structure is developed in physostome fishes because in these the bladder is filled, through the open duct, by the fish swallowing air at the surface; bubbles of excess gas are expelled through the same channel.

The control of the volume of gas in the swimbladder is essential if it is to function as a hydrostatic organ. When a fish swims downwards the external pressure is increased and the gas in the bladder is compressed; thus the volume of the bladder decreases and the fish's density is increased. Under these conditions if the volume of the swimbladder is not increased, the fish will continue to sink unless it expends considerable energy in swimming to keep at its level. When a fish rises, the pressure is reduced, the volume of the bladder increases and the physical effects are the reverse of those described above. These pressure changes do not affect shallow water species or most freshwater fishes to the same extent as deep-sea fishes, particularly those which make regular vertical migrations of several hundred feet in search of food. The power of changing the volume of gas is limited, however, and the process of secretion or absorption is by no means always a rapid one in fishes without an open duct. For this reason a sudden rise or fall is dangerous to the fish, and if it ascends suddenly from a considerable depth to the surface it may be quite incapable of descending again. Sometimes when deep-water fishes are brought to the surface by the trawl or dredge, so great is the expansion of the contained gases brought about by the rapid change in external pressure that the swimbladder is forced out through the gullet and projects from the mouth. Aristotle was aware of this phenomenon but not its cause, for he writes that 'very often the Synodon and the Channa cast up their stomachs (!) while chasing smaller fishes; for, be it remembered, fishes have their stomachs close to the mouth, and are not furnished with a gullet.'

The gases contained in the swimbladder are similar to those in the air, namely, oxygen, carbon-dioxide and nitrogen, but the proportions of the gases often differ considerably. The amount of oxygen is generally greater in marine than in freshwater fishes and is greatest (84 %) in certain deep-sea fishes. Conversely, in deep-living freshwater species the amount of nitrogen may be as high as 94 %.

The swimbladder is absent in Sharks and Rays, and it is not present in all Bony Fishes. It is not unusual to find considerable variations in swimbladder development amongst related species with different habits or habitats. There is generally a clear cut adaptive correlation between the degree of swimbladder development and the fish's way of life. For example, in bottom living species (both freshwater and marine) a hydrostatic bladder is of less functional value and is often absent or greatly reduced, as it is (and for the same reasons) in fishes living in fast flowing streams where movement is restricted to short, bottom-hugging dashes from rock to rock. Perhaps one of the most interesting correlations is that found in certain bathypelagic species (i.e. fishes living at depths between one hundred and two thousand metres and not confined to the bottom). Many bathypelagic fishes living at depths down to 1000 metres have well-developed swimbladders. Since these fishes make extensive vertical migrations, the gas secreting and resorbing mechanism of the bladder must be highly efficient. At least half the species living at depths *below* 2000 metres are also provided with well developed swimbladders. In very distinct contrast are the species whose usual life-zone is centred between 1000 and 2000 metres, for in these fishes the swimbladder is absent or reduced to a fat invested string of tissue. What is the reason for this degeneration? Clearly pressure is not a deciding factor because many of the even deeper-living species have fully functional swimbladders. Recent research suggests that the reason is one of biological economy associated with the poor food supply in the intermediate zone, an economy which is also reflected in the relatively poor development of many other organs and tissues. It must, of course, be realised that the regression of these tissues is also correlated with the loss of a swimbladder since the density of the fish must not become too greatly removed from one approaching that of the water, or the fish would, so to speak, be weighted down.

REFERENCES

BARRINGTON, E. J. W. (1957). The alimentary canal and digestion: in, *The Physiology of Fishes*, **1**, Academic Press, New York.

BLACK, V. S. (1957). Excretion and osmoregulation: in, *The Physiology of Fishes*, **1**. Academic Press, New York.

JONES, H. F. R. (1957). The Swimbladder: in, *The Physiology of Fishes*, **1**. Academic Press, New York.

MARSHALL, N. B. (1954). *A spects of Deep Sea Biology*, Hutchinsons, London.

MARSHALL, N. B. (1960). Swimbladder structure of deepsea fishes in relation to their systematics and biology. *Discovery Reports*, **31**, 1–122.

CHAPTER 9

NERVOUS SYSTEM,
SENSE ORGANS AND SENSES

THE PRINCIPAL ORGANS of a fish's body have now been briefly described, and it remains to consider the nervous system, the elaborate organisation of brain, nerves, and sense organs, unifying and co-ordinating the complex activities of the body, and placing the various parts in communication with one another and with the outside world. This has been compared to a telephone system with the central exchange represented by the brain. Although this analogy is in many respects a good one, it must not be pushed too far, for as will be shown in the following pages, there are a number of important differences between the two organisations.

As in higher vertebrates, the nervous system may be divided into brain, spinal cord, and nerves. In the newly formed embryo the first two are indistinguishable, and together form a simple tube, the medullary canal, lying along the upper surface of the body. That part of the tube which is to form the spinal cord soon becomes more solid through the thickening of its walls, but a minute central canal persists throughout life as a vestige of the original cavity. The anterior end of the tube in the head region enlarges to form the brain, and at the same time two transverse constrictions divide this into three hollow chambers or primary vesicles, known respectively as the fore-, mid-, and hind-brain. As development proceeds, certain parts of the walls of the vesicles become variously thickened, and others give rise to hollow outgrowths, which may be either median or paired. In this way the elaborate brain of the adult fish comes into being, the original three chambers continuing to exist as a series of linked spaces or ventricles.

It will be unnecessary to describe the brain of a fish in any detail, but a brief outline of its more important features and their functions may be given. At the extreme front is a pair of hollow chambers, the olfactory lobes, the inner cavities of which are in communication with the parts of the brain lying immediately behind. These lobes, centres of the sense of smell, are large in the Cyclostomes, relatively enormous in the Sharks and Rays [Fig. 64A] but in the majority of Bony Fishes tend to be reduced in size, and may be placed at the end of lengthy stalks [Fig. 64B]. In the Cyclostomes, Selachians and certain of the more primitive Bony Fishes including the Lung-fishes, the olfactory lobes are followed by another pair of outgrowths, the cerebral hemispheres, which may be completely differentiated into two lobes, or may coalesce to form a single cerebrum [Fig. 64A]. In the Cyclostomes these hemispheres are

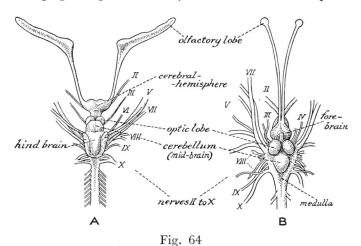

Fig. 64

Brains: A. Dorsal surface of the brain of a Ray (*Raia* sp.), x ¹/₂; B. The same of a Cod (*Gadus morhua*), x ¹/₂

very small, forming mere appendages of the olfactory lobes. They are rarely developed in Bony Fishes, but, instead, a bulging chamber with a non-nervous roof grows forward from the forebrain, and from its sides the olfactory lobes are formed. In higher vertebrates the cerebrum or cortex is the centre of the more complex mental processes, such as thought and reason, but in most fishes it seems to be mainly associated with the sense of smell, although it may also serve as a correlation centre for nervous impulses (messages) received from different parts of the body. Starting with fishes, and passing upwards through the amphibians and reptiles to the birds and mammals, this region of the brain becomes progressively larger, until in man it forms a very large and important part and its microscopic structure and organization becomes increasingly complicated.

Other important parts derived from the primary forebrain are the optic vesicles, which arise from the sides and later become transformed into parts of the eyes and their associated nerves, and the pineal body or gland, arising from the roof, which will be considered further in connection with the eyes. From the floor of the forebrain a hollow outgrowth, the infundibulum, develops, to which is attached the pituitary body or gland, whose secretion plays a vital part in the regulation of body activities. The remaining structures, which arise inside the original forebrain, are of minor importance and need not be detailed here.

The roof of the midbrain bulges out to form a pair of optic lobes [Fig. 64], which may or may not be connected with the main central cavity. They vary greatly in size in different fishes, and may cover the forebrain and press against the cerebral hemispheres. In some of the Lung-fishes (Dipneusti) the two are united to form a single oval body. As their name implies, the optic lobes are associated with visual sensations.

Experimental work associated with anatomical studies suggests that the midbrain is an important correlation centre for sorting out incoming sensory messages, particularly those connected with body posture and movement, and linking these to the appropriate motor responses. The midbrain also seems to be concerned with learning. In fact it plays a similar role to that of the cortex (the highly developed and organised forebrain) in higher animals. These functions are, of course, in addition to its primary connection with the eyes and thus with sight.

The principal part formed from the original hindbrain is a large single lobe, the cerebellum [Fig. 64], lying behind the optic lobes. Below this is the medulla oblongata, the cavity of which communicates with the cerebellum above and with the central canal of the spinal cord behind. In the Lampreys (Petromyzonidae) the cerebellum is very small, in the Hag-fishes (Myxinidae) it is absent altogether; in the Selachians and Bony Fishes it is very large, sometimes almost covering the optic lobes.

There is still much to be learned about the function of the hindbrain, particularly the cerebellum. Recent research suggests that the cerebellum is principally concerned with the maintenance of body posture. In the Mormyrid fishes, where the cerebellum is so greatly enlarged, there is probably some connection with the reception and interpretation of impulses from the fish's electrical field (see page 167).

The hindermost section of the brain, the medulla oblongata, is clearly derived from the spinal cord. It is the centre from which arise the fifth to tenth cranial nerves (see below) and it is thus associated with both sensory and motor nerve impulses from widely different parts of the body. It also serves as a relay station between the spinal nerves and correlation centres in other parts of the brain.

The brain never entirely fills the cavity of the neurocranium, the space between it and the membrane lining the inner surface of the cavity being filled with a sort of gelatinous tissue. In a young fish the brain is very much larger in proportion to the size of the body than in an adult. Its size also exhibits considerable variation in different fishes, although on the whole it may be regarded as relatively small. The brain of the Burbot (*Lota*) has been estimated to be $1/720$ of the weight of the entire fish, that of the Pike (*Esox*) $1/1305$ whilst in some of the Sharks it is relatively still smaller. It is a remarkable fact that the Mormyrids of tropical Africa have a brain which is a good deal larger in proportion to the size of the body than in any other fish, that of *Mormyrus*, for example, being between $1/52$ and $1/82$ of the weight of the entire fish, or twenty-five times greater than that of the Pike.

There is little more to add concerning the spinal cord, which is very uniform in structure throughout the Selachians and Bony Fishes. It usually extends the whole length of the body, but is much shorter in some of the Globe-fishes (Tetraodontiformes) and their allies. In the huge Sun-fish (*Mola*) it is remarkably reduced, being actually shorter than the brain: in a specimen two and a half metres long and weighing about a ton and a half the cord was only fifteen millimetres in length.

Structurally, a nerve is not the simple thread that appears to the naked eye; it is made up of an enormous number of very fine fibres lying together side by side like the separate wires of a telephone cable. Each of these fibres may be of considerable length and is about one-tenth of the thickness of a human hair. Actually, they are nothing more than fine processes drawn out from star-shaped nerve cells situated in the brain or spinal cord, the tissue of these organs being made up entirely of cells of this nature.

Most nerves contain fibres of two kinds, one carrying messages or nervous impulses outwards, the other inwards. The first or motor fibres carry impulses to the various muscles, causing them to contract; to the glands, causing them to secrete their special products; or to the stomach and intestines. The sensory fibres, on the other hand, carry nervous impulses to the brain or spinal cord from the sense organs, conveying warning of cold, hunger, pain, fear, and the like. As soon as these messages, which generally follow some change in the conditions of the outside world, are received, motor impulses are promptly sent back along the nerves, and by an appropriate contraction or relaxation of certain muscles, matters are quickly adjusted. The manner in which the various actions of the body are co-ordinated by the central nervous system will be dealt with in due course, and for the present it must suffice to point out that every muscle-fibre is supplied by its own nerve-fibre, one end of which forms a nerve cell in the brain or spinal cord and the other terminates in a cluster of fine branches spread out over the surface of the muscle-fibre. Every muscle is in turn made up of a large number of separate fibres, and is served by its own nerve, which controls its every action. When it is considered that to perform the simplest movement, the waving of a fin or the opening of the mouth, the co-ordinated action of a whole group of muscles is required, some idea will be gained of the vast number of nervous impulses continually going backwards and forwards from sense organs to brain and spinal cord, and from the brain and spinal cord to the muscles and glands.

The nerves may be divided into two categories, spinal and cranial, the former having their origin in the spinal cord, the latter in the brain. The spinal nerves are metamerically arranged, that is to say, their number is the same as that of the vertebrae, through or between which they pass out. The cranial nerves consist of ten pairs, which may be briefly described [Fig. 64]. The first or olfactory nerve is a purely sensory one connecting the nasal organ with the olfactory lobe. The second or optic nerve (II) is likewise sensory, and supplies the eye. In the Cyclostomes each optic nerve runs from the optic lobe direct to the eye of the same side; in the Selachians the two nerves are fused together to form an optic chiasma; and in the Bony Fishes the two cross each other below the brain immediately after leaving the optic lobes, the nerve from the left lobe going to the right eye and *vice versa*. The third, fourth, and sixth are principally motor nerves, and their function is to supply the muscles which move the eyes. The third or oculomotor (III) starts from the lower surface of the brain, the fourth or trochlear from the groove between the optic lobes and the cerebellum, but the sixth or abducens (VI), like the remainder of the cranial nerves, has its origin in the medulla oblongata. The fifth or trigeminal nerve (V), and the seventh or facial (VII), are mixed nerves, being partly sensory and partly motor. Both have branches which are widely distributed over the snout and jaws. The eighth or auditory (VIII) is another sensory nerve and supplies the inner ear. The ninth or glossopharyngeal (IX) is mixed, and has a branch which forks over the first gill-cleft and another long one running forward to the region of the palate. Finally, the tenth or vagus (X), another mixed nerve, is a complicated one, which not only gives off forked branches to the remaining gill-openings, but the main stem passes along the alimentary canal and sends nerves to its muscles and to those of the heart, whilst another stem, which separates from the nerve soon after it leaves the brain, supplies the whole of the sensory system of the lateral line (see page 152).

In their general plan the sense organs of a fish are not unlike those of higher vertebrates, but whereas certain senses of special importance to an animal living in a liquid medium are greatly accentuated, others are less developed.

The sense of smell resides in the olfactory organs, but, unlike the higher vertebrates, the nostrils or nasal openings are never used for breathing purposes. Typically, each olfactory organ consists of a somewhat deep pit lined with special sensitive tissue, and in order to provide the maximum of sensitive surface, the lining is generally puckered up into a series of ridges which may be parallel to each other or arranged in radiating fashion like a rosette [Fig. 65B']. The Cyclostomes are unique in possessing a single nostril on the upper surface of the head [Fig. 65A, A'], which in the Lampreys (Petromyzonidae) leads into a blind nasal sac, but in

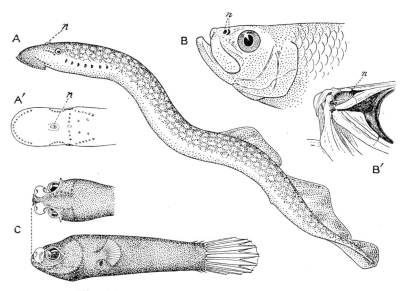

Fig. 65   NOSTRILS AND OLFACTORY ORGANS
A. Sea Lamprey (*Petromyzon marinus*), x 1/8; A'. Upper view of head of same; B. Head of Herring (*Clupea harengus*), x 1/2; B'. Front part of head dissected to show olfactory organ. (After Derscheid); C. *Linophryne macrorhinus* (unattached male larva), x about 2.; *n*. nostril

the Hag-fishes (Myxinidae) actually communicates with the buccal cavity. In the Sharks and Rays the olfactory organs are invariably large, and, like the mouth, are placed on the lower surface of the head [Figs. 36A; 45B]. The single opening of each organ is guarded by valvular flaps, provided with their own cartilages and moved by special muscles. In certain Sharks and Dogfishes deep oro-nasal grooves connect each organ with the angle of the mouth on the same side. In Bony Fishes these grooves are wanting, but in the Lung-fishes (Dipneusti) short canals link the olfactory pits with the mouth. The position of the nostrils varies considerably in different fishes; in some the anterior nostril is widely separated from the posterior, in others the two are almost in contact. Occasionally, as in the Cichlids (Cichlidae) and in certain Wrasses (Labridae), the olfactory organs each have only a single external orifice. In some of the Eels (Anguilliformes) the anterior nostril is situated on the upper lip and in many of the Globe-fishes (Tetraodontidae) the apertures are carried at the tips of paired nasal tentacles.

Most of the adult oceanic Ceratioid Angler-fishes with a line and bait have small eyes and normal nostrils [Figs. 21; 91], but in larval forms where the line is undeveloped the eyes and nostrils are more or less enlarged [Fig. 65c], perhaps indicating that they seek their food by smell and sight (cf. p. 244).

There can be little doubt that the sense of smell in fishes is relatively acute, as has been proved by numerous experiments. The large olfactory organs of Sharks are said to enable them to 'scent actively as well as to smell passively,' and it is well known that the smell of flesh or blood, or of a decaying carcase will attract them to it from some distance away. The Piraya (Serrasalmus), a ferocious Characin fish of the rivers of South America (cf. p. 110), is irresistibly attracted by the smell of blood, and woe betide the animal unfortunate enough to be bitten by one of these pests, for hundreds more will rush to the spot with incredible rapidity.

It seems very unlikely that any fishes find their food by smell alone and it is difficult to generalize on the relative importance of the roles played by smell and sight in hunting prey.

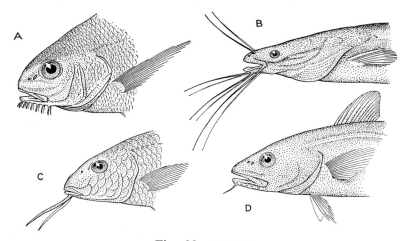

Fig. 66 BARBELS
A. Head of Sciaenid or Drum (Pogonias fasciatus), x ¹/₂; B. Head of African Cat-fish (Clarias lazera), x ¹/₂; C. Head of Red Mullet (Mullus surmuletus), x ¹/₂; D. head of Cod (Gadus morhua), x ¹/₄

Research in America indicates that smell may play an important part in the orientation of Salmon when they return to their natal streams as adult, spawning fishes. This work is still incomplete but the results seem to indicate that young Salmon may become conditioned to a particular and characteristic odour of the stream in which they hatched. They retain a 'memory' of the odour and are able to respond to it when they return as adults to the river system of their birth.

Smell may also be an important element in a fish's warning system. Experiments with Minnows (*Phoxinus phoxinus*) show that an injured fish liberates from its skin an 'alarm substance'. Other fishes in a shoal react to this by a well-marked alarm reaction, the shoal breaks up and the individuals look for cover or flee. Fishes from other genera and families have been tested but not all liberate an 'alarm substance'.

Closely allied to the sense of smell is that of taste. The anatomical bases of these senses are different, especially with regard to the way

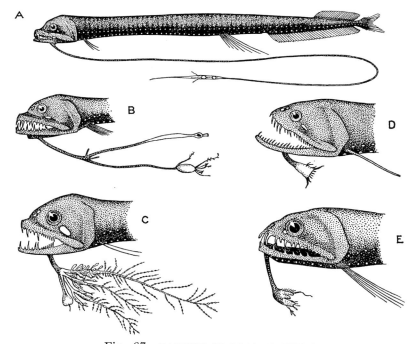

Fig. 67   BARBELS IN OCEANIC FISHES
A. *Eustomias bituberatus*, x ³/₄; B. Head of *Eustomias tenisoni*, x 1¹/₂; C. Head of *Eustomias silvescens*, x 1³/₄; D. Head of *Photonectes intermedius*, x 2; E. Head of *Chirostomias pliopterus*, x 1³/₄; (After Regan and Trewavas)

in which the sensory impulses reach the brain. However, both senses are a response to substances dissolved in the water. Smell can be considered as perception at a distance whilst taste requires more intimate contact. In fishes the sensitive taste-buds (through which the 'taste' is first perceived) are not confined to the mouth and tongue but in many species occur on the outer surface of the head and even on the body (e.g. Carp [*Cyprinus*], Cod [*Gadus*], Mullet [*Mugil*] and the Sturgeon). In others there are concentrations of taste-buds on the barbels which surround the mouth (e.g. many Cyprinids [Carps and their allies] and in all Cat fishes [Siluroidei] see Fig. 66). In those fishes in which the rays of some fins are modified to form elongate feelers (see pp. 36; 48) these are also supplied with numerous taste-buds. The taste-buds are supplied by branches of the VIIth (facial) IXth (glossopharyngeal) and Xth (vagus) nerves. In sharp contrast, the olfactory organs are supplied only by the Ist (olfactory) nerve.

In its general form the eye of a fish is not unlike our own, but it is necessarily somewhat modified for vision under water. The eye, as is well known, acts like a camera, the two essential parts being the sensitive screen or retina at the back, and the lens at the front, which projects an image of the outside world on the screen [Fig. 68]. The lens of a land vertebrate is somewhat flat and convex on both sides, but in the fish it is a spherical body, the extreme convexity being a necessity under water because the substance of the lens is not very much denser than the fluid medium in which the fish lives. The space between lens and retina is filled with a transparent jelly-like substance, the vitreous humour. The transparent outer wall of the eye, the cornea, is somewhat flatter in fishes, and the space between this and the lens is filled by the watery aqueous humour. In land vertebrates the iris of the eye is capable of great contraction, and, acting like the diaphragm of a camera, regulates the amount of light allowed to enter the eye. In Bony Fishes it generally surrounds a rounded pupil, and has comparatively little power of contraction, but in Selachians it is capable of extensive if slow movement. It may be brightly coloured, red, orange, black, blue, or green.

Land vertebrates are able to accommodate the eyes to vision at varying distances (that is to say, to focus the eyes on objects both near and far away) by altering the convexity of the lens through the action of special muscles; in fishes the same end is accomplished by changing the position of the lens with regard to the retina. The retina itself has an elaborate structure, and is made up of numerous sensitive cells; its function is to set up appropriate nervous impulses when acted upon by the rays of light focused upon it by the lens, and thus to convey to the brain an 'impulse picture' of the object which the fish has in view. It may be noted here that as the eyes of most fishes are placed on either side of the head, what is known as monocular vision is the rule. Few fishes are capable of focusing both eyes on the same object at one and the same time (binocular vision).

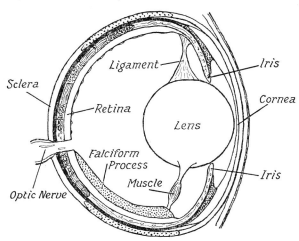

Fig. 68
Section (vertical) through the eye of a Bony Fish; semidiagrammatic.
(After Wall)

Some of the accessory structures associated with the eyes of higher animals are wanting. For example, no lachrymal glands are developed, so that a fish cannot shed a tear, nor is this necessary when the outer surface of the eyeball is kept constantly clean and moist by the surrounding water. No fishes possess true eyelids, the skin of the head simply passing over the eye and becoming transparent as it crosses the orbit. In some fishes, notably some of the Grey Mullets (Mugilidae) and Herrings (Clupeidae), the skin over the eyeball is thickened, and, although still transparent, covers the greater part of its outer surface, leaving a small aperture in the centre. Such forms are said to have an adipose eyelid. Some Sharks (e.g. the Tope, *Eugaleus*) have at the front corner of the eye, a structure, known as the nictitating membrane, which is freely movable and can be pulled down to cover the whole surface. In bottom living-forms like the Rays and Flat-fishes, the upper part of the pupil is covered by a thick dark lobe, often covered with scales, forming an effective curtain to shut off the light from above [Figs. 37B; 31].

A curious modification of the eyes is found in the Four-eyed Fishes (*Anableps*) of the rivers of Central and South America.

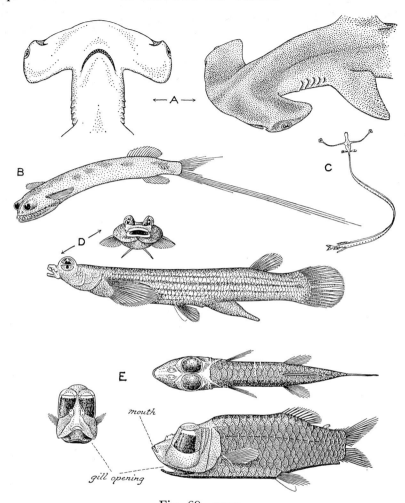

Fig. 69   EYES

A. Head of Hammer-headed Shark (*Sphyrna zygaena*), x ¹/₁₀; B. *Gigantura chuni*, x ¹/₂; C. *Idiacanthus fasciola*, x ¹/₂; D. Four-eyed Fish (*Anableps tetrophthalmus*), x ¹/₂; E. *Opisthoproctus soleatus*, x ¹/₃

Each eye projects well above the top of the head, and is divided into two equal parts by a dark horizontal band: each of these sections is of a different structure, the upper being adapted for vision in the air, the lower for vision under water [Fig. 69D]. These fishes swim about in small shoals at the surface of the water, and the level of the water reaches as far as the bar dividing the eye.

They are thus able to detect not only insects skimming over the surface or actually flying in the air, but also any swimming below the surface.

Some oceanic fishes (e.g. Giganturidae) are provided with curious telescopic eyes, and these generally take the form of short, protruding cylinders, each ending in a very rounded cornea covering a large spherical lens [Fig. 69B]. They may be directed either upwards or forwards, and as they lie parallel to one another, it is possible that these fishes are capable of binocular vision. In the rare and curious oceanic fish *Opisthoproctus* the telescopic eyes are directed upwards, and cannot be turned in any other direction [Fig. 69E].

Tubular eyes are bifocal because, in addition to the main retina at the bottom of the tube, there is a smaller accessory retina situated on the side of the tube immediately below the lens. This retina, being closer to the lens, will be in focus for distant objects whilst the main retina will be in focus for near objects. It is significant that in tubular eyes there is no well-defined mechanism for focusing the lens. Tubular eyes may be associated with the predominance of downwardly directed luminescent organs in fishes. In the young of other oceanic forms (*Idiacanthus*) the eyes are placed at the end of very long stalks growing out from the sides of the head [Fig. 69c]. The Hammer-headed Sharks (*Sphyrna*), with the eyes placed at the extremities of lobe-like lateral outgrowths [Fig. 69A], have already been described in an earlier chapter.

In a large number of Bony Fishes there is a distinct connection between the habitual mode of life and the degree of perfection of the organs of vision. In certain Cat-fishes (Siluroidei) for example, and in other fishes living in more or less turbid water the eyes are much reduced in size and efficiency, and in others (certain Cyprinids, Cat-fishes, Amblyopsids, etc.), which have taken to a life in caves, wells, or subterranean streams, these organs have disappeared altogether, although the young may be born with well-developed and perhaps functional eyes (*cf*. p. 196). In the Hag-fish (*Myxine*), which is in the habit of burrowing into the body of a living fish and devouring its flesh, the eyes are quite vestigial. Among oceanic fishes the eyes vary greatly in size, and biologists have found considerable difficulty in attempting to explain the connection between the size and efficiency of the eyes and the intensity of the light at different depths.

In many deep-sea fishes the eyes show various adaptations for light perception in conditions of very poor illumination. Mere increase in the overall size of an eye does not make it a more efficient organ in these conditions. If the various parts of the eye are enlarged proportionally then the extra amount of light only falls on a larger retinal area and the intensity of this light will be no greater than in a small eye. However, if the pupil and lens are enlarged disproportionately to the rest of the eye then more light will reach the retina. This is just what we find in many deep-sea eyes; in many species the pupil diameter is from a half to three-quarters of the vertical extent of the eye-ball.

Other adaptations are seen in the histological structure of the retina. There is an increase in the number of certain cells (the rods) which respond to faint light.

Species living at various depths down to about 3,000 ft (Lantern fishes, Hatchet fishes and many others) have well-formed eyes with large lenses, wide pupils and highly sensitive retinas. Below this depth (i.e. between 3,000 and 9,000 ft) there is a general tendency for fishes to have small or degenerate eyes, and some are apparently without eyes although the optic nerve is present and it branches in the region of the head where the eyes would normally be situated. In general, this zone is pitch dark and is lit only by the flashes from luminescent creatures. Fishes in this zone probably do not possess sight in the sense that those in the upper regions have; instead their eyes are probably mere receptors of light.

The correlation between eye-development and living-depth in fishes confined to the sea-bottom is not at all obvious. In some cases (the so-called Sea-snails, *Liparis*) there seems to be a relationship. Species living between tide-pool levels and a depth of 900 ft have smaller eyes than the deep-sea species occuring at depths of 600 and 10,000 ft. In many other groups, however, no such correlation exists; the numerous species of Rat-tails (Macrouridae) typify the latter state since, in all but one, the eyes are large.

The position of the eyes departs from the normal in some fishes, and in bottom-living forms, such as the Rays, Anglers, and Star-gazers, instead of being placed on either side of the head, the two eyes lie close together on its upper surface. The Flat-fishes (Pleuronectiformes) are unique in having both the eyes on the same side of the head [Figs. 8B; 31A–C]. In the Mud Skipper (*Periophthalmus*), which is in the habit of leaving the water and walking about on the sand or mud, the eyes are prominent and can be turned in all directions, a modification of obvious advantage [Fig. 24*f*]; the eyes may also be withdrawn and lubricated, an essential procedure for an animal without tear glands if the cornea is not to be damaged and dirtied.

Most Bony Fishes (at least those with a good number of cone cells in the retina) have some form of colour-vision but sensitivity may vary from species to species and also with the age of the individual. Selachians, on the other hand are probably colour-blind.

In describing the brain, mention was made of the pineal gland arising from the roof of the primary forebrain. It is better developed in the Sharks than in the Bony Fishes, but even then it is little more than a nervous enlargement. In the Lampreys and Hag-fishes, however, this structure bears a strong resemblance to an eye, and the external skin covering this region is partially transparent in the adult. In the fossil remains of ancestral Cyclos-tomes there are indications of the presence of one or two such median sense organs on the upper surface of the skull. The pineal body when functional, serves as a light-sensitive organ. There is no evidence to show that it is ever capable of sight.

The auditory organ or inner ear of a fish, the next of the sense organs to be considered, consists of a membranous sac enclosed in a chamber on either side of the hinder part of the skull. Its purpose is twofold, for not only is it the seat of the sense of hearing, but it is also concerned with the maintenance of equilibrium: indeed, the latter function is probably the more important of the two. Com-paring the fish's ear with that of a man or other mammal several important differences are at once apparent. The human ear consists of three parts: the external, middle, and inner ear. In the fish the first two of these are entirely wanting, there being no outer trumpet, no ear-drum, and no Eustachian tube connecting the middle ear with the pharynx, and the inner ear itself is of a much simpler structure. The membranous sac is partially con-stricted into two portions, an upper chamber or utriculus, and a lower or sacculus; a small sac-like outgrowth from the latter, known as the lagena, is all that is developed of the spirally twisted cochlea, the essential seat of hearing in the higher vertebrates [Fig. 70]. Connected with the utriculus are the three semicircular canals, which play an important part in the maintenance of balance, two running in a vertical direction and placed at right angles to one another, the third horizontal. At one end of each of these canals is a swelling, the ampulla. In the Lamprey (*Petro-myzon*) the horizontal canal is wanting, in the Hag-fish (*Myxine*) there is a single canal with an ampulla at each end, but in true fishes all three canals are developed.

In the embryo fish the auditory organ orginates as a hollow bladder, which is simply pushed inwards from the external skin, a mode of development exactly similar to that of the olfactory organs already described. At a later stage this bladder takes on a more complicated structure, and the tube by means of which it communicated with the exterior generally becomes closed up in the adult fish, although in Selachians a small opening on the surface of the skull is retained throughout life.

The inner walls of the utriculus, sacculus, and lagena are provided with patches or ridges of highly sensitive tissue, and the cavities of the chambers are filled with a fluid known as the endo-lymph; a similar fluid, the perilymph, occupies the spaces between these parts and the walls of the containing auditory capsule. In addition to the endolymph, the cavities also contain certain bodies composed of limy matter secreted by their walls. In the Selachians these take the form of small separate particles connected with one another by mucus, but in most Bony Fishes they form large, solid concretions or otoliths, a sagitta in the sacculus, an asteriscus in the lagena, and a lapillus in the utriculus. In nearly all fishes the sagitta is the largest otolith [Fig. 70*a*, *b*] and the lapillus is quite

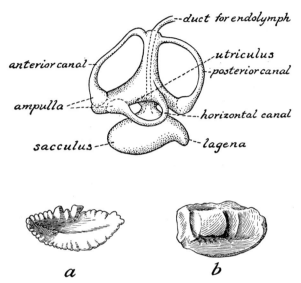

Fig. 70   AUDITORY ORGAN OF A FISH
a. Otolith (Sagitta) of Cod (*Gadus morhua*), x $^2/_3$; *b*. The same of Meagre (*Sciaena aquila*), x $^2/_3$

minute: in some, however, the asteriscus is relatively enormous and the sagitta small. These otoliths or ear-stones are provided with peculiar grooves and markings. They exhibit some variation in shape and size in different fishes, and as the form is fairly constant in any particular species, they are of some use in classification. The otoliths grow by the deposition of lime in layers on the outer surface, and as the rate at which this is laid down varies at different seasons, if one is cut into thin sections and examined under a lens or microscope the layers formed in successive years are clearly visible as a series of alternately light and dark concentric rings, similar to the 'zones' on a scale or the rings on a tree-trunk. Thus by a study of the otoliths it is sometimes possible to ascertain the age of any particular fish. This method of age determination has proved valuable in investigations of life-histories of certain food fishes.   The otoliths of the Sciaenids or Drums (Sciaenidae) are very large, and in ancient times were worn on a string round the neck as a preventive and cure for colic.

During the last twenty-five years an impressive body of evidence has been drawn together concerning sound perception in Bony Fishes.   From all these studies one clear fact has emerged: the Ostariophysine fishes have the best developed sense of hearing particularly with regard to the frequency range of the sound and the discrimination of pitch.   The conclusion is inescapable that hearing has considerable biological significance to these fishes. The ability to hear and to produce sounds (see page 175) also suggests, at least for certain species, that some form of sound communication exists between individuals.

The frequency range over which fishes can detect sound is, in non-Ostariophysine fishes, from 13 to over 3,000 cycles per second and in the Ostariophysi from 16 to 7,000 c.p.s.   It must be stressed that no one species is sensitive to the entire range.   For example, the Cyprinodont *Lebistes reticulatus* has a range of 44–2,068 c.p.s., the Eel one of 36–650 c.p.s. (both are non-Ostariophysine fishes) Amongst the Ostariophysi, the Gold-fish can detect sound at a frequency of 3,480 c.p.s. whilst the Minnow is capable of perceiving sound at 7,000 c.p.s.

The second function of the ear is as an organ of balance.   The semicircular canals and the utriculus are the principal centres of balance (the latter being particularly concerned with responses to gravity).   The lower parts of the ear (sacculus and lagena) play a part in balancing but are also the sole centres of hearing.

As the fish moves, the fluid endolymph in the ear is set in motion and impinges on patches of sensitive cells in the walls of the canals and the sacs, either directly or by pressing against the otoliths. Nervous impulses from these cells are conveyed to the brain through the VIIIth or auditory nerve.   In turn, the brain is able to initiate various muscular responses which serve to adjust and control the position of the fish.

Equilibrium is not controlled by the ear alone, the eyes also play an important role in orientation.

In some Bony Fishes the swimbladder is more or less intimately connected with the internal ear.   In many marine and a few freshwater forms there is an aperture in the hinder wall of the capsule enclosing the auditory organ, and this is closed by a fine membrane.   A tube-like outgrowth from the front end of the swimbladder comes into contact with this membrane on the outer side.   In some of the Herrings (Clupeidae), and in the Mormyrids (Mormyridae), the apertures in the capsule are open, and processes from the swimbladder actually come into contact with protruding outgrowths from the utriculus itself. In the Characins, Gymnotids, Cyprinids (Cyprinoidei), and Cat-fishes (Siluroidei) the connection between the swimbladder and ear is much more elaborate, and these fishes are grouped together under the name of Ostariophysi[1]) derived from two Greek words meaning 'a small bone' and 'inflated'. The connecting apparatus, known as the Weberian ossicles (after its discoverer, Professor Weber), is formed by the modification of the first four vertebrae immediately behind the skull [Fig. 71], certain parts of which have become separated off and form a chain of three or four little bones or ossicles on each side, linking up the swimbladder with the perilymph-filled spaces surrounding the inner ear.

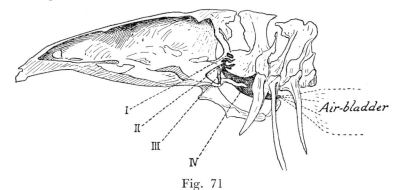

Fig. 71

Section of the skull of Carp (*Cyprinus carpio*), showing the Weberian mechanism, x ¹/₂. I–IV. Weberian ossicles.

The exact function of this remarkable mechanism is not yet fully understood, but it is probably connected with the perception of alterations in pressure, thus serving to accentuate sound waves and acting as an accessory organ of hearing. Of its importance in the life of the fish there can be no doubt, since the elaborate Weberian mechanism is possessed by every member of the dominant group of freshwater fishes living to-day.

The last of the sensory systems to be considered is the lateral line portion of the acoustico-lateralis system. The functions of the acoustic part, the inner ear, have already been outlined.

The basic component of the lateral line system is a sense organ called a neuromast. Each neuromast consists of a group of sensory cells each with a fine hair-like projection. The hairs protrude above the level of the epithelium and are encased in an elongated gelati-

---

[1] Following the classification adopted here, this group should be called the Cypriniformes. However, the term 'Ostariophysi' is so widely used that it is retained as a synonym of Cypriniformes.

nous cupula. The cupula lies free and can be moved by the surrounding water (if the neuromast is exposed) or mucus (if the organ lies in an enclosed canal). There are various modifications to the neuromast and these cells have been given different names. For the purpose of this discussion, however, we can confine ourselves to the neuromasts proper.

The neuromasts are distributed over the body surface along lines whose pattern is remarkably constant in all fishes. The main line runs along the side of the body, and then onto the head where it divides into three main branches, one passing above the eye and ending on the snout, another passing behind the eye and running below it to the snout region, and a third, also passing behind the

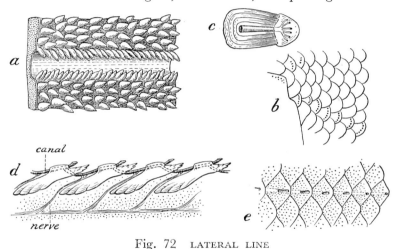

Fig. 72 LATERAL LINE

a. Portion of lateral line of Frilled Shark (*Chlamydoselachus anguineus*), much enlarged; *b.* Scales of the Bow-fin (*Amia calva*), showing apertures of lateral line tubules; *c.* Lateral line scale of Bow-fin (*Amia calva*), greatly enlarged; *d.* Vertical longitudinal section through lateral line of Perch (*Perca fluviatilis*), much enlarged and diagrammatic; *e.* Lateral line scales of Osteoglossid (*Clupisudis niloticus*), x ¹/₂. (*a, b,* and *c* after Bashford Dean.)

eye but proceeding to the lower jaw. The neuromasts of the body are supplied by branches of the vagus (Xth) nerve and those on the head by branches of the facial (VIIth), glossopharyngeal (IXth) and vagus (Xth) nerves.

In the majority of fishes (both Bony and Cartilaginous) the neuromasts are sunk into closed canals which open to the surface through pores [Fig. 72*b–e*]. When discussing scales in Bony Fishes, mention was made of the lateral line scales on the body. These are the scales through which the vertical components of the lateral line canal open. Sometimes these branch canals are themselves subdivided into smaller branches each of which opens in a separate, minute aperture on the scale surface. The canal system has been aptly likened to a tube railway, the external apertures corresponding to the surface stations connected to the deep-lying tube by means of vertical shafts [Fig. 72 d]. In such a closed tube system, the main tubes and the shafts are filled with mucus.

As mentioned earlier, not all fishes have the neuromasts enclosed in tubes. For example, the primitive Frilled Shark (*Chlamydoselachus*) has the sense organs lying in an open grove [Fig. 72a], partially roofed over by bordering denticles; the canals on the body of the Lung-fish (*Protopterus*) are open, although those on the head are tubular, but in the Chimaeras (Holocephali) even the head canals are open [Fig. 73]. Finally, in many deep-sea fishes the neuromasts are freely exposed and may be carried on papillae rising some distance above the skin.

In Bony Fishes the tubes of the head are often deep-lying and the course of the lateral line can only be detected by the distribution of the pores. Some fishes, especially those living at great depths in the sea, have the canals greatly enlarged in certain regions of the head and the surrounding bones are excessively thin and paper-like.

During embryonic development the canals may arise in two ways. Either the superficial organs come to lie in a groove which develops around them and then gradually sinks in and closes over, or, a strip of tissue may become detached from the skin and sink deeper into the dermis. Later these solid strips develop hollow centres in which the neuromasts lie. Both types of development may occur in different parts of the system and neither method can be considered as typical of either Selachians or Bony Fishes.

What is the function of this elaborate sensory system? Various ideas have been put forward, such as a temperature receptor, a form of hearing and even a device for aligning the fish to currents. Experimental evidence lends very little support to these ideas. Instead, it seems that the lateral line serves as a 'distant touch' receptor. As mentioned above, the cupule surrounding the sensory hairs of the neuromast can move freely when the mucus or water surrounding it is set in motion. Now, when a fish moves, and particularly when it changes direction, it sets up pressure waves through the water in all directions. These are detected by the neuromasts of other fishes and serve to indicate the direction and the size of the object producing the waves. Also, as a fish moves through the water it builds up ahead of itself a 'bow-wave' of pressure which is deformed by any solid object it approaches. The lateral line cells respond to the pressure changes and the fish is able to take appropriate avoiding action. By this means, for instance, a fish avoids bumping into the walls of an aquarium.

The response of the lateral line organs of one fish to the swimming vibrations of another has been demonstrated by recording the electrical impulses which pass from the neuromasts down the lateral line nerve. These recordings show that the neuromasts are continuously firing off a steady stream of nerve impulses. When another fish passes there is a sudden burst of intensified nervous activity.

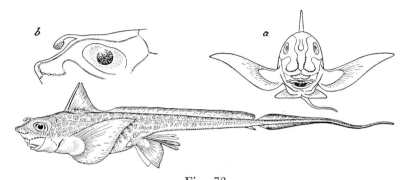

Fig. 73

Male Rabbit-fish (*Chimaera monstrosa*), x ^{1}/$_8$; *a*. Front view; *b*. Upper part of head, showing lateral line canals.

Further evidence comes from experiments carried out with blinded Ruffe (*Acerina cernua*). These fishes have the lateral line system well-developed on the head and a blind Ruffe can detect and snap at a glass rod gently moved in the water. A rod fitted with a disc about half an inch in diameter was located at a distance of two inches, whilst a glass thread only 1 millimeter thick was snapped at when it was brought to within an inch of the fish's head.

As might be expected, many blind or poorly-sighted deep sea fishes show a correlated hyperdevelopment of the lateral line system. It must be stressed, however, that reduction of the eyes and extra development of the lateral line system do not invariably go hand in hand.

In conclusion, the relationship of the ear and the lateral line system may be considered. The two are really only different components of the same system. The inner ear develops in exactly the same way as does a separate sense organ in the lateral line. But, it sinks more deeply into the body and has become especially enlarged and modified to perceive more delicate vibrations than can the neuromasts. In addition, the ear is concerned with the maintenance of balance.

In Selachians (and in one Bony Fish, the tropical marine Catfish *Plotosus anguillaris*) there is a complicated system of jelly-filled canals (the so-called Ampullae of Lorenzini) which open all over the snout region and head.   The canals end in swollen bulbs containing sensory cells which have, according to some authorities, little in common with the sense cells of the lateral line system.   Other authors, however, consider that these cells are closely related to neuromasts; as Lowenstein puts it 'We are here clearly confronted with a dilemma'.   Investigations into the function of the Ampullae of Lorenzini do little to clarify the picture.   Some results suggest that they may serve as temperature receptors whilst others present evidence strongly suggesting that, like the lateral line system, the ampullae serve as pressure receptors.   If the latter interpretation is correct, then the ampullae do not respond as rapidly as do the lateral line organs and they may therefore serve to detect longer lasting pressure stimuli.

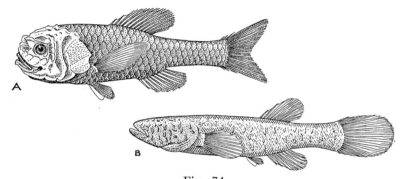

Fig. 74
A. *Melamphaes beanii*, x ¹/₂; B. Kentucky Blind-fish (*Amblyopsis spelaea*),
x ¹/₂

That fishes are highly sensitive to electric currents has long been known, and this knowledge has been turned to practical advantage in recent years by the development of electric fish-screens, used principally in America.   These are designed to keep food-fishes within bounds, and to prevent them from straying into irrigation canals, ditches, mill-races, and other water-courses.   Experiments have also been made to test the feasibility of using electricity for commercial fishing.   As yet, the results are still too scanty to forecast future developments.

The much debated question as to whether or not fishes feel pain may well be considered here.   The angler will always answer it with an indignant denial, and it must be admitted that his experiences with rod and line provide some evidence for his belief. The great difficulty in deciding whether or not under normal conditions fishes feel pain lies in the fact that it is only possible to judge the matter by our own standards. We are quite certain that a barbed hook lodged in our own throat would cause us intense agony, but it is tolerably certain that a fish, with its comparatively lowly organised brain, does not feel anything nearly as acute. At the same time, the fact that all fishes possess an elaborate system of nerves and sense organs suggests that they must at times experience feelings of this nature, although it is impossible to obtain any definite information as to the extent of their sufferings.

It is well known that Trout or Pike, whose mouths have been torn and lacerated by a hook, but which have succeeded in getting away before being brought to the landing net, have returned and taken a tempting bait almost immediately afterwards. There is also the classical story of the Perch hooked in the eye, which necessitated removing the organ from its socket before returning the fish to the water. The angler then baited his hook with the eye, and no sooner did his line reach the water than the bait was swallowed by the identical fish.

It would seem as though some fishes are much less sensitive than others, or at least that they lose their sensitivity to pain under the stress of some emotional excitement. The Greenland Shark (*Somniosus*), when feeding on the carcase of a whale, is said to allow itself to be stabbed repeatedly in the head without abandoning its prey, and two Conger Eels in the act of spawning have been so insensible to other external impressions that they have been lifted together from the water by hand.

Another question frequently raised concerns the habit of sleeping. There can be little doubt that most fishes spend at least a part of the day or night in a state of suspended animation. This has been verified in a number of species, and it has been found possible in many cases to approach a sleeping fish and to remove it from the water with the hand. Aquarium and field studies show that the position adopted by a fish when sleeping varies a good deal, not only in the different groups of fishes, but in closely related species of the same genus. When suddenly disturbed by the flashing of an electric torch, some fishes in tanks were found to be resting in a vertical position on the bottom, others, like the Wrasses (Labridae), were lying at the bottom on their sides, and others were sleeping in a horizontal position but entirely surrounded by water. At night certain Parrotfishes (Scaridae) secrete a loose mucus envelope which surrounds the whole body. The envelope may take as much as half an hour to secrete, and as long to break out of when daylight returns. Not all Parrotfishes form this sleeping cocoon and in those that do, it is only produced under certain conditions the causal factors of which are still unknown.

Fishes which normally sleep when darkness arrives will remain awake and active if hungry, and it is suggested that Trout taking a fly at night are hungry individuals that remain awake owing to the abnormal nocturnal activity of their insect prey. Flat-fishes such as Plaice (*Pleuronectes*) and Dab (*Limanda*) are found just above the bottom of their tanks at night, and the suggestion has been advanced that this is the reason why trawlers make their best hauls of marketable fish at night, since the commercial trawl does not actually drag the bottom, but the lower edge passes a foot or so above this, and in the day-time would miss the fishes lying buried in the sand. Dr. Beebe records that a young Sole (*Achirus*) may leave the bottom and on occasion actually float at the surface of the sea at night. 'It undulated to the surface', he writes, 'curved down to a saucer or cup-shape with the circular fin-rays above the water, and floated until I captured it. The fully expanded fins apparently made such intimate contact with the surface film that, like a vacuum cup, it remained suspended.' Bat-fishes (Ogcocephalidae), which are also normally bottom dwellers, likewise come to the surface in the dark.

Aquarium observations on a number of young Grey Mullet (*Mugil*) are of interest. During the hours of daylight they were observed to swim about in a massed shoal, but at night this broke up, every individual fish going to its own spot on the bottom, the members separating and facing in all directions. If disturbed, however, they rapidly returned to the surface and again adopted the mass formation.

Some indication has been already given as to the manner in which the complex activities of the fish's body are co-ordinated and controlled by the nervous system, and in concluding this chapter the matter may be considered rather more closely. Sensory impressions are received from the outside world by one or more of the organs of sense, and messages in the form of nervous impulses are sent to the appropriate part of the brain, from which motor impulses are promptly transmitted back to muscles, glands, and so on, matters being at once adjusted by an appropriate movement or other activity. It is important to distinguish between two very different types of behaviour, two replies, as it were, to the impressions received from the sense organs. There is the reflex action, which is quite automatic and does not involve any nervous process which could be called thought. A familiar example of this action in human beings is provided by the drawing away of the hand or foot from a source of excessive heat: the movement begins, not as the result of the pain, but before consciousness of any pain has been experienced, and follows almost instantaneously upon the application of the stimulus. In the other type of action memory and consciousness are involved, and this may also be illustrated by an example of human behaviour. A man observes a ripe pear hanging from a tree and moves his arm forward to grasp it, a definitely conscious action following upon the sight of the fruit conveyed to the brain by the eye. At the same time his salivary glands begin to secrete saliva, his stomach to produce digestive juices, and other preparations for the meal are started, all reflexively, as the result of a visual impression.

The two types of action just described have different centres of control in the brain, the conscious action being controlled by the cerebral hemispheres, the seat of mind, and the reflexes by the midbrain and cerebellum. As has been previously pointed out, the cerebral hemispheres are small in fishes, but in higher vertebrates they become progressively larger and take more and more control of the lower centres, until in man they occupy the greater part of the space allotted to the brain. To a large extent, the fish must be looked upon as a reflex machine. That is to say, most of its movements and other activities are the result of reflex actions rather than conscious thought.

There is no doubt that, at least in Bony Fishes, a fish is capable of learning and of developing relatively complex conditioned reflexes, involving the use of memory. But, it is difficult to find any examples of behaviour amongst fishes which can unequivocally be attributed to thought or reason. The field of animal behaviour and psychology is only now being widely developed and our knowledge of fish behaviour has just begun to pass beyond the level of anecdotal natural history. Perhaps future research will cause much of what has been said above to be rewritten.

REFERENCES

BRETT, J. R. (1957). The eye: in, *The Physiology of Fishes*, **2**. Academic Press, New York.

HASLER, A. D. (1957). Olfactory and gustatory senses of fishes: in, *The Physiology of Fishes*, **2**, Academic Press, New York.

HEALEY, E. G. (1957). The nervous system: in, *The Physiology of Fishes*, **2**, Academic Press, New York.

LOWENSTEIN, O. (1957). The acoustico-lateralis system: in, *The Physiology of Fishes*, **2**, Academic Press, New York.

CHAPTER 10

VENOM, ELECTRICITY,
LIGHT, AND SOUND

As HAS BEEN EXPLAINED in an earlier chapter (*cf.* p. 37), the spines arming the gill-covers, or those which support the fins, may form useful weapons of defence, and their effectiveness may be further increased by the development of poison glands in association with them. Such poison organs are more common in fishes than was formerly supposed, but they seem to be used almost entirely for defensive purposes, instead of playing a part in securing food as in the snakes. They are, for the most part, of rather simple structure, often composed merely of strips or bunches of specialised cells, and appear to owe their origin to the modification of certain portions of the epidermal layer of the skin.

Among the Selachians poison organs are found in the Spiny Dog-fishes (*Squalus*), Bull-headed Sharks (*Heterodontus*), Sting Rays (Dasyatidae), Eagle Rays (Myliobatidae) and Chimaeras (Holocephali). Pliny seems to have suspected the presence of venom in Sting Rays. 'Nothing is more terrible,' he writes, ' than the sting that arms the tail of Trygon (the Sting Ray of the Mediterranean), called Pastinaca by the Latins, which is five inches long. When driven into the root of a tree it causes it to wither. It can pierce armour like an arrow, it is as strong as iron, yet possesses venomous properties.' It is now known that in the groove running along either edge of the serrated spine in Sting Rays [Fig. 26*e*] is a tract of glistening white tissue, which may be difficult to detect unless cross-sections of the spine are prepared and examined under the microscope, since the whole spine is sheathed in skin. Similar tissue has been found associated with the dorsal fin-spines of the Spiny Dog-fishes [Fig. 77A], Bull-headed Sharks [Fig. 53B], and Chimaeras [Fig. 73], and the cells of which it is composed secrete a venom capable of causing painful or even dangerous wounds.

Among the Bony Fishes poison glands or cells occur in a number of forms (at least forty species) of which the Cat-fishes, Weevers [Fig. 75A, A'], Scorpion-fishes, and Toad-fishes may be specially mentioned. Several species of Cat-fishes (*Noturus*, *Schilbeodes*, *Heteropneustes*, *Galeichthys*) have the outer ray of each pectoral fin modified to form a stout, flat spine, generally serrated along one or both of its edges, and capable of inflicting nasty jagged wounds. The poison is produced by glandular cells in the epidermal tissue covering the spines. In many of these species the strong spine of the dorsal fin is also venomous.

Fig. 75 POISONOUS FISHES

A, A'. Greater Weever (*Trachinus draco*), x ¹/₈; B. Stone-fish (*Synanceia verrucosa*), x ¹/₄

In the Weevers (*Trachinus*), of which two species occur on our own coasts, the glands are associated with the long, sharp spine with which each gill-cover is armed, as well as with the five or six spines supporting the first dorsal fin [Fig. 76A, A']. The opercular spine is ensheathed by an extension of the skin, only its tip projecting, and is traversed along its upper and lower margins by a deep groove. Along each groove is a pear-shaped mass of glandular tissue, the broad end of which lies towards the base of the spine [Fig. 76A']. There is no canal leading from the gland, and it appears that the venom is set free by the rupture of the cells, and, flowing down the groove, is injected into the wound. It may be noted here that the name Weever is believed to be derived from an Old French word, *wivere*, meaning a viper. Be that as it may, the venom is like that of certain snakes since it produces both neuro- and haemotoxic effects.

The Stone-fishes (Synanceidae), belonging to the order of Scorpion-fishes, are confined to more or less tropical seas, and many of them are as ugly as they are formidable [Fig. 75B]. The glands here lie under the heavy skin at the bases of the dorsal spines, each being continued into a duct situated in the deep groove on either side of the spine [Fig. 76B]. Native fishermen handle these fishes with great care, being well acquainted with their venomous

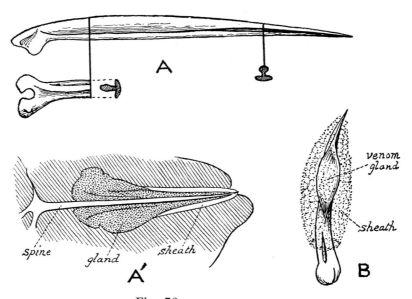

Fig. 76 POISON GLANDS
A. Dorsal fin spine of Weever (After Hasler). A'. Opercular spine of
Greater Weever (*Trachinus draco*) and its poison gland. (After Parker);
B. A dorsal spine with poison sacs of Stone-fish (*Synanceia verrucosa*).
(After Hasler)

nature. It sometimes happens, however, that when wading with
naked feet one will step on a Stone-fish lying buried in the sand:
the erect dorsal fin-spines penetrate the skin, and the venom is
injected into the wound by the pressure of the foot on the bag-like
glands. In the Poison Toad-fishes (*Thalassophryne*) of tropical
America the glands are even more elaborate in structure. As in
the Weevers the opercular spines and the two spines of the first
dorsal fin constitute the venom apparatus. Each of these spines
is hollow and perforated at either end like the venom fang of a
snake. The base of the spine is embedded in the centre of the
poison gland, and the secretion is discharged through the hollow
spine exactly as in a hypodermic needle.

The virulence of the poison seems to vary greatly in the different
fishes or even among individuals of the same species. The Sting
Ray (*Dasyatis*) is particularly venomous, and many are the stories
told of painful and even fatal wounds caused by the tail-spines of
these fishes. The poison of the Spiny Dog-fish (*Squalus*), although
not quite so potent, is nevertheless capable of causing intense pain
and discomfort. The pain has been described as being as severe

as that from a Weever, but of a duller and more numbing character, and there are cases of fishermen who were incapacitated for several days from a wound in the hand. Large quantities of these Dog-fishes are landed by trawlers and find a ready sale, but the two dorsal fins with their offending spines are invariably cut off soon after the fish is caught.

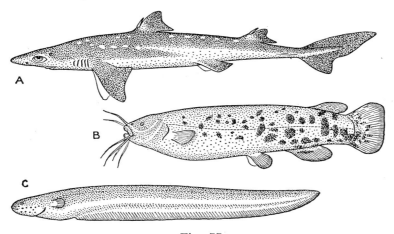

Fig. 77
A. Spiny Dog-fish (*Squalus acanthias*), x $^1/_{10}$; B. Electric Cat-fish (*Malapterurus electricus*), x $^1/_4$; C. Electric Eel (*Electrophorus electricus*), x $^1/_{15}$

The venom of the Weevers (*Trachinus*) is particularly virulent, and a person who has had the misfortune to step on one of these fishes when bathing will not forget his experience in a hurry. On being 'stung' the first symptom is an acute pain of a burning, stabbing character, localized at first but soon spreading through the affected limb. If untreated it will last for several hours or even throughout the day. So acute is the agony that men have been known to attempt to throw themselves overboard in their distress. Among other symptoms which have been noticed in Weever and other fish stings is a tendency to fainting, palpitations, fever, delirium, vomiting, and so on, and in extreme cases heart failure may ensue. As yet, no specific antidote is known for any fish venom. However, first-aid and supportive measures are known which will certainly ease the pain and lessen side effects.

If the venom apparatus has produced a lacerated wound (Sting-ray and some Catfishes) the wound should be washed out as soon as possible. Cold salt water or, better, sterile saline are suitable for this purpose. If the wound is of the puncture variety (Weever fishes) treatment is more difficult. Some doctors recommend soaking the affected part in hot water for half to one hour. The water must be as hot as the victim can tolerate without injury and treatment should be started as soon as possible. If the puncture is on the face or body, hot moist compresses should be used. The shock which follows the stinging responds to the usual supportive treatment. However, certain Sting-ray venoms may produce a secondary shock which results from the action of the poison on the heart. This requires immediate and skilled treatment.

Another form of treatment is gaining popularity. This is the so-called ligature-cryotherapy method. Immediately after being stung the victim puts a ligature (a shoe lace or piece of string is most effective) between the wound and the body, at a point nearest the wound. The hand or foot, including the ligature is then immersed in iced water. After not less than five or more than ten minutes the ligature is removed but the affected part must remain in iced water for a minimum of two hours. There is no danger of frostbite if iced water alone is used.

Besides those fishes with localized poison organs there are a host of others whose flesh must be considered as toxic. The question of poisonous fishes is a complex one because the same species may, under certain conditions, be harmless but in other localities it can prove lethal or at best very unpleasant. Perhaps the commonest reason for a fish becoming poisonous is through feeding on some organism (particularly certain marine plants) which is non-toxic to the fish but capable of producing a poisonous substance in its flesh. Carnivorous fishes may feed on the now poisonous herbivore and become toxic themselves. Man, of course, may feed on either the herbivore or the carnivores.

This type of intoxication, known as ciguatera poisoning, has been attributed to at least 300 different species, mostly tropical marine reef—or shore—species occuring in the Pacific Ocean and the West Indies. Ciguatera poisoning is quite unpredictable and is difficult to control. Past efforts by Governments to list 'dangerous' species have led to all the best food-fishes of an area being damned on the basis of a few individuals' temporary feeding habits.

Besides such poisons produced through food, certain other species may produce toxins in their gonads during the breeding season.

In another group of poisonous fishes the toxins occur in the liver, gonads, intestine or skin, irrespective of the fishes' sexual state or feeding habits. The Puffers and their allies [Figs. 5D; 33G] are such fishes. The flesh is, however, edible and ranks as a great delicacy (fugu) in Japan. Restaurants where fugu is sold employ specially trained cooks and its preparation is carried out with great care. Nevertheless, fugu is still the prime cause of fatal food poisoning in Japan. As Halstead aptly remarks 'At best eating puffer is a game of Russian roulette.' Deaths and illness have been reported after eating sharks and rays. Most such cases occur in tropical regions and particularly when the liver of the shark has been eaten. There are also numerous records of the Greenland Shark (*Somniosus microcephalus*) proving toxic to both men and dogs. The chemical basis of these shark toxins is not known.

Finally, mention may be made of a peculiar poisoning which results from eating stale or inadequately preserved Scombroid fishes (Tuna, Bonito, Mackerel, Skipjack etc.). Here the toxin results from the action of bacteria on a chemical in the flesh of these fishes. This substance is changed by bacterial action into a histamine-like compound which causes an illness resembling a severe allergy. For reasons still unknown, Scombroid fishes seem more likely to become toxic by this means than do other species of fishes. Their flesh can become poisonous if left to stand at room temperature or lying in the sun for a few hours.

Still more remarkable (and unique amongst vertebrates) are the electrical properties of certain fishes. Indeed, about two hundred and fifty species, often unrelated, are known to possess electric organs. Among these special mention may be made of the Torpedoes, Ray-like fishes of tropical and temperate seas [Fig. 78]; the Skates and Rays; the Mormyrids (sometimes called Snout fishes) of Africa, the Electric Eels *Electrophorus* and *Gymnotus* (which are not Eels, but are members of the order Gymnotiformes, related to the Characins and Carps) of South America [Fig. 77c]; the Electric Catfish [Fig. 77b], a freshwater species from Africa; and finally, the marine Star-Gazers [Fig. 47e].

The form and position of the electric organs in these fishes differ greatly but all have a similar microscopic structure. Each organ is made up from a number of regularly arranged, disc-like, multi-nucleate cells (called electroplates) embedded in a jelly-like substance and bound together by connective tissue into an elongate tube. One face of each electroplate is supplied by nerve fibrils, and the jelly-like material is well supplied with blood vessels.

In the Torpedo or Electric ray [Fig. 78] there are two large and two small organs on each side of the head, the small organs lying within the large ones. Each organ is composed of a number of vertical, hexagonal tubes, each tube having the structure described above. The main nerve supplying the organ stems from a special lobe of the brain. It has been demonstrated that the innervated side of each electroplate in a column is negative to the other. In Torpedo the plates are so arranged that the current passes from the upper (positive) side of the fish to the lower (negative) side.

In the Electric Eel (*Electrophorus*) [Fig. 77c], there are three organs on each side, one of which is much larger than the others. The organs form almost half the mass of the body. Unlike those in Torpedo, the electric plates run lengthwise and the nerves supplying them originate from the spinal cord.

The electric organ of the Electric Catfish *Malapterurus* is a much more diffuse affair and envelops the whole trunk as a loose, semi-transparent jacket. Whereas in *Electrophorus* the polarity is from head to tail, that of *Malapterurus* is from tail to head.

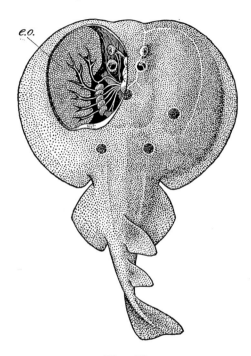

Fig. 78

Electric Ray (*Torpedo*) dissected to show one of the major electric organs with the associated nerve supply. The prismatic areas on the surface of the organ indicate the vertical columns of electric plates, of which there may be 500,000 in each organ. (After Gegenbaur.)

e.o., electric organ.

In the Skates and Rays and in the Mormyridae (Snout fishes) the electric organs are much smaller structures lying on either side of the caudal peduncle. They are of comparatively feeble power. In the Star-gazers (*Uranoscopus*), on the other hand, the organs although relatively small can give a shock of quite painful intensity; they are of a complicated structure and form two oval patches situated behind the eyes.

The way in which the electric discharge is actually produced involves an understanding of complex physiological processes, and cannot be considered here. The force of these discharges has been measured under laboratory conditions. These figures are probably higher than those which might be obtained if they could be measured under natural conditions: Ray (*Raia clavata*) 4 volts: Torpedo, about 40 volts; Electric Eel (*Electrophorus electricus*) 370–550 volts; Electric Catfish (*Malapterurus electricus*) 350–450 volts.

The characteristics of the discharge seem to differ in a way which can be correlated with the power of the organ. In species with large organs (Torpedo and other electric rays, *Electrophorus* [but see below], and *Malapterurus*) the pulses occur in small groups. In fishes with smaller organs (Mormyrids; *Gymnotus carapo* [an electric Eel]) there is a continuous series of small pulses. *Electrophorus* is also capable of a similar discharge which is thought to originate from the smallest of its three electric organs.

These different characteristics are probably related to the different functions of the organs. It seems likely that fishes with powerful organs use them both offensively in their hunt for food and defensively against would-be attackers. Both Torpedo and *Electrophorus* have been seen to stun small fishes before devouring them and there is circumstantial evidence from gut analyses to indicate that Torpedo uses its electricity to capture fishes which would otherwise be too large and swift for it to tackle. Evidence for the Electric Catfish is more equivocal but inclines towards a defensive use of their electrical powers.

The use of weak electrical discharges has only recently been understood and there are still numerous points which require further study. In brief, it appears that fishes like the Mormyrids create an electric field around themselves and that should any object break this field, the fish is immediately made aware of the change. Since the eyes of Mormyrids are poorly developed, and many species live in murky waters, the value of the electric field as a warning device is immediately apparent. It has still to be discovered how the fish detects a break in its field; the extreme development of the cerebellum in Mormyrids may have some connection with this faculty as may have the peculiar cells distributed at the base of the dorsal fin. As was mentioned above, the Electric Eel (*Electrophorus*) also emits continuous pulses and this species may also employ an electrical warning device. Perhaps the small organ in Electric rays (Torpediniformes) serves a like purpose? The function of the small electric organs in other rays (Raiiformes) remains a mystery. Here there is no continuous discharge. In fact the fish can only be stimulated to fire off its organ by vigorously prodding it. The discharge is very weak and it can hardly be an effective deterrent to predators.

How, then, are these complicated electric organs of fishes developed? In order to answer this question it is necessary to study the development of the embryo fish, and it is found that in the Torpedo, for example, each electric plate is nothing more than a transformed muscle fibre. Further, the whole organ has been derived from some of the branchial muscles, which have been relieved from their original duty of moving the gill-arches in order to take on this new function. The organs of the Electric Eel, the Skates, and the Mormyrids are similarly modified muscles, and owe their origin to the transformation of some of the lateral muscles of the tail. In the Electric Catfish the organs develop from certain body muscles; it was previously thought that the electric cells were derived from the skin. In the Star-gazers the electric organs have been shown to be developed from portions of the eye muscles, each of the plates representing a single muscle fibre.

The production of light provides yet another example of transformation, for the luminous organs or photophores owe their origin to the modification of certain gland-cells in the skin. These organs are of varying size and form, ranging from simple aggregations of cells associated with luminous bacteria, to elaborate and powerful structures with lens and reflector. Some fishes seem to have the power of emitting light without possessing any definite light organs, but, in some forms at least, this is due to the presence of luminous bacteria. A member of the Rat-tails or Grenadiers (*Malacocephalus laevis*) has a complicated gland near the anus in which these bacteria are contained [Fig. 79]. When the fish is disturbed it secretes the bacterial mass through a duct.

Certain sharks, most of them inhabitants of deep water and belonging to the family (Squalidae) which includes our own Spiny Dog-fish, have the power of emitting light. This has been described as a vivid and greenish phosphorescent gleam, and has been shown to be due to the presence of numerous tiny light organs of very simple structure scattered over the skin. *Etmopterus* of the Atlantic and Mediterranean, known to fishermen as "Darkie Charlie' has been kept alive in the Naples aquarium and the production of light carefully observed. Another form found near Ceylon was placed on the deck of a ship after capture, and continued to emit a luminous glow until its death three hours later.

Among the Bony Fishes, the members of the great group of Wide-mouths (Stomiatoidei), inhabitants of the open oceans, many of them descending to considerable depths, possess luminous organs which may be of a much more elaborate structure. There are typically two rows of organs, or photophores, on either side of the fish, one on the belly and another parallel to it and near the lower edge of the side, but in some species additional series may be developed above these [Fig. 91]. The rows generally extend

continuously from behind the head to the tail, but may be inter-
ruped in some species and confined to certain regions of the body
and tail.   The arrangement is metameric, that is to say, there
is one set of four organs to each muscle segment or section of the
vertebral column.   The organs may be of a comparatively simple
structure, consisting of little more than a group of gland-cells,
not very different from the ordinary groups of cells in the epidermal
layer of the skin from which the photophores have been derived.
Some of them, however, may be more elaborate in structure,
consisting of a lens set in the opening of a cup which is sunk in the
skin, the walls of the cup being made up of the gland-cells which
manufacture the light-giving substance: the walls may be lined
with black pigment to form a reflector similar to that used in a

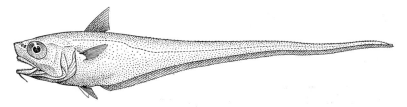

Fig. 79   LUMINOUS FISH
A. Grenadier or Rat-tail (*Malacocephalus laevis*), x ¹/₄

bull's eye lantern, and the outer skin partially projects over the
surface of the lens and functions like the diaphragm or stop of a
camera.   In addition to the body photophores, there are others on
the head and jaws, including a large and sometimes complicated
organ below or just behind each eye.   A still more curious organ is
found in a rare Berycoid fish from the Indian Ocean known as
Anomalops.   This fish has a large light organ below the eye, placed
on a movable flap, so that when light is not wanted it can be
turned inwards and received into a cavity underneath the eye
[Fig. 80c].   Luminosity in this species is due to masses of symbiotic
luminous bacteria living in the cells comprising the organ.
     The function of these lights shining into the eye is still uncertain.
At first sight it would seem to be decidedly disadvantageous to have
a light shining into an eye which is adapted for seeing in very poor
light or even to functioning in total darkness.   However, it has been
suggested that the gentle glow from such an organ may prepare
the eye for what would otherwise be a dazzling burst of light when
the fish 'turns on' the other lights of its body.
     In the Myctophids or Lantern-fishes (Myctophidae) the photo-
phores are fewer in number, but are larger and brighter having the
appearance of glistening jewels or small mother-of-pearl buttons.

Instead of being set out in rows running from the head to the tail they have a complicated arrangement of short rows and groups, which is, nevertheless, perfectly symmetrical [Fig. 80A]. As in the Wide-mouths, the great majority of the photophores occur on the lower parts of the body, rarely on the back or upper parts of the sides. Many species have a special organ above or below the eye, and others possess a very powerful head-lamp covering the greater part of the snout [Fig. 80A]. Certain patches may be developed on the head and body, especially at the bases of the fins, which,

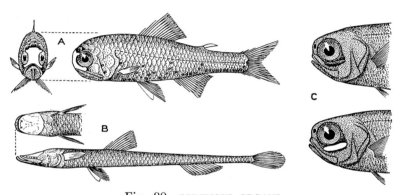

Fig. 80   LUMINOUS ORGANS

A. Lantern-fish (*Diaphus metopoclampus*), x 1; B. *Ipnops murrayi*, x $^1/_2$; c. *Anomalops katoptron*, x $^1/_2$ (in the upper figure the luminous organ is retracted and therefore invisible)

although luminous, lack the specialised structure of the photophores. One or more of these patches may be present on the upper and lower edges of the fleshy part of the tail, where they are described as 'stern-chasers.'

The line and bait of the Angler-fishes, representing the much modified first ray of the dorsal fin, has already been described (*cf*. p. 40). In the deep-sea members of this order (Ceratioidei) the bait is luminous and can probably be 'switched on' at will, serving to attract smaller fishes within reach of the Angler's jaws. In addition to this line and bait certain species possess a much branched tree-like structure below the chin which also has luminous properties and probably acts as a lure [Fig. 21A]. Other deep-sea fishes, in which one or more of the fin-rays may be drawn out to form a fine filament, have these rays tipped with small luminous bulbs. In many species the light may be produced by bacteria.

Another remarkable fish, known as *Ipnops* is blind and has the whole of the upper surface of the flattened head occupied by a pair of large organs lying beneath the transparent superficial bones of the roof of the skull and believed to be luminous [Fig. 80B]. But if this is so their structure is unlike that of any other light organ.

So far only the light organs of fishes inhabiting the open oceanic waters and descending to a fair depth have been mentioned. These structures may also occur, however, in fishes living more or less close to the shore, having been found in the little Cardinal fish (*Sephamia*) and in one of the Toad-fishes (*Porichthys*) of the coast of California. The latter fish, known locally as the Midshipman or Singing-fish, has no less than seven hundred photophores on its head and body, each presenting the appearance of a shining white spot. These organs are developed in connection with the complicated system of lateral lines, and many of them are associated with the sense organs. Each consists of four parts: lens, gland, reflector, and pigment, and, as usual, they are more abundant on the lower parts of the fish.

Although various theories as to the production of luminescence have been advanced, it is now generally agreed that this is due either to the luminous nature of the slime secreted by the gland cells or to the presence of luminous bacteria. The biochemistry of fish luminescence has hardly been studied and little can be said about the way in which the light is produced.

The purpose of the light organs of oceanic fishes is largely a matter for conjecture. The use of the luminous bulbs and barbels of the oceanic Wide-mouths (Stomiatoidei) and Anglers (Ceratioidei) as lures has already been described. In other fishes the emission of light is almost certainly defensive rather than offensive. In the Grenadier just mentioned, for example, it seems probable that a sudden burst of light emitted from the gland between the pelvic fins would tend to confuse an enemy and cover the retreat of the pursued in the same way as does the ink-cloud of the Cuttle-fish. The 'stern-chasers' of the Lantern-fishes (Myctophidae) may serve a similar purpose, a sudden flash from the tail being used to dazzle or even frighten the pursuer. To explain the photophores and other organs on the head and body is rather more difficult. It is generally assumed that they enable fishes living in the depth, of the ocean—the region of eternal night, as one author describes it—to seek for and detect their prey. This may be true in part, but it must be remembered that the same light which illuminates the prey renders its owner equally conspicuous and liable to be hoist by his own petard! Further, an extensive study of the fishes inhabiting the oceans shows that there is no certain connection between the possession of light organs and a life in the abyssal depths. Many fishes spending the greater part of their time at or near the surface have these organs well developed, whilst a number of forms known to live permanently at considerable depths are without them.

In considering the function of luminous organs it is important to bear in mind the following facts. First, the position of the main organs on the sides and belly of the fish, and the presence of special organs in the neighbourhood of the eyes and jaws, provides evidence that they may be used to light up the surrounding water in front of and beneath the fish. Secondly, and this seems to be a fact of some importance, the number and arrangement of the photophores exhibits considerable variation in the different genera and species, but, with the exception of small differences, remains constant in any particular species. Indeed, in the Lantern-fishes (Myctophidae) the number and pattern of the photophores provides a most important character for distinguishing the different species. Finally, there is some evidence that the colour of the emitted light may vary in different fishes. It seems probable, therefore, that the luminous organs may fulfil the same function among the dwellers in darkness or semi-darkness as do the spots and stripes of pigment in many littoral fishes, and that one of the important uses of these structures is to act as recognition marks, enabling their possessor to pick out another individual of its own kind.

There is a widespread and popular belief that fishes do not produce sounds. This is quite untrue, for, although incapable of vocal efforts comparable to those of mammals and birds, a number of Bony Fishes produce sounds of one sort or another, and some forms are provided with special sound-producing organs. These may be associated with the swimbladder, fin-spines, vertebrae, and so on, and provide another example of the assumption of new duties by organs originally employed for a totally different purpose.

The simplest type of sound, for example, is that produced merely by the expulsion of air from the swimbladder through the pneumatic duct, and the grunting or gurgling noises made by some fishes as they are taken from the water may perhaps be ascribed to this cause. The characteristic breathing or murmuring sounds made by the members of the Carp family (Cyprinidae) may be similarly accounted for, but the noises of a like nature made by the Loaches (Cobitidae) are said to be due to the rapid expulsion of air-bubbles through the anus.

In a number of fishes characteristic sounds are made by stridulation; that is to say, by rubbing one surface against another. For example, the Horse Mackerel (*Trachurus*), the Sun-fish (*Mola*), and certain species of Trigger-fishes (*Balistes*) produce harsh noises by grating together the upper and lower pharyngeal teeth. The Bullhead (*Cottus*) uses a portion of the gill-cover for stridulation; the Flying Gurnard (*Dactylopterus*) the hyomanidibula bone; the Trigger-fish (*Balistes*), File-fish (*Monacanthus*), Boar-fish (*Capros*), Surgeon-fish (*Acanthurus*), Stickleback (*Gasterosteus*), and some of the

Cat-fishes (Siluroidei), the spines of the dorsal, anal, pectoral or pelvic fins.

In the 'Drumming' Trigger-fish (*Rhinecanthys aculeatus*) of Mauritius the noise is said to be due to the friction of certain of the bones of the arch supporting the pectoral fin against one another, and since these are more or less intimately associated with the swim-bladder, the latter acts as an amplifier and intensifies the sound vibrations.

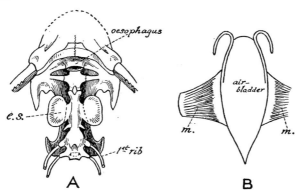

Fig. 81 SOUND PRODUCING ORGANS
A. Elastic spring mechanism of a South American Cat-fish (*Pseudauchen-ipterus nodosus*), showing the oval bony plates (*e.s.*) in which the bony springs terminate; *ca.* x ¹/₂, (After Bridge and Haddon); B. Swimbladder of a Sciaenid (*Micropogon undulatus*), showing the musculo-tendinous extensions (*m*) from the muscles of the body-wall, which partially invest the surface of the bladder, x *ca.* ¹/₂ (After Sörensen.)

In the remaining sound-producing fishes to be discussed, the organs are for the most part of a more elaborate nature, and the noise is produced through the agency of special muscles associated with the swimbladder. In a number of Cat-fishes (Siluroidei) an apparatus known as the elastic spring mechanism occurs, the purpose of which is to cause the walls of the swim-bladder to vibrate. The 'springs' are specially modified portions of the fourth vertebrae and their expanded ends are attached to the front part of the swimbladder [Fig. 81A]. Two strong muscles run from the springs to the hinder portion of the skull, and when these contract the springs, and with them the walls of the bladder, vibrate rapidly and produce a sort of growling or humming noise. Generally, the swimbladder is divided up by internal partitions into a number of chambers all freely communicating with one another, and there can be no doubt that the sound is intensified by the vibratory movements of the gases contained in the bladder across the free edges of the partitions. In the Sciaenids or Drums (Sciaenidae), fishes renowned for their vocal efforts, the sounds are produced by the rapid vibration of special muscles, which are not always attached directly to the bladder, but may run from the abdomen on either side to a central tendon situated above the bladder [Fig. 81B]. The rapid contraction and expansion of the muscle (at the rate of about twenty-four contractions per second) causes the walls of the bladder to vibrate, and since this has a complicated structure, it acts as a sort of resonator and intensifies the sound. An American investigator, has performed a number of experiments on living fish which are of some interest. He found that if the bladder was deflated or removed altogether the drumming entirely ceased, but if he introduced an artificial rubber bladder it again commenced. In the Gurnards or Sea Robins (Triglidae), and in the Toad-fishes (Batrachoidei) the grunting noises are produced by special muscles lying in the walls of the bladder itself, which, when they contract, throw the walls into rapid vibrations. By experiments it has been shown that if either the muscle or the nerve supplying the bladder is artificially stimulated, a perfectly normal sound is produced, even when the bladder has been removed from the fish and placed on the operating table. No sound is produced if the bladder is punctured, but the introduction of a rubber balloon inside the bladder leads to a sound when the muscle is stimulated by electricity.

Similar vibratory swimbladders occur in *Therapon* (Perciformes) and in the Singing Midshipman (*Porichthys*). Certain deep sea Rat-tails (Macrouridae) have swimbladders whose structure suggests that the fishes are capable of sound production, and similar conclusions are drawn from the swimbladder structure in many Gadidae, including the Cod and the Haddock.

The actual noises produced by the different fishes present great diversity, ranging from a more or less melodious vocal effort to a mere grunt. A South American Cat-fish (*Doras*) is said to produce a sound described as a 'deep, growling tone,' distinctly audible at a distance of one hundred feet when the fish is out of the water. There can be little doubt that when in their native element the sounds made by fishes must travel for considerable distances, as water is a much more efficient conductor of sound waves than air. The elastic spring apparatus of the Electric Cat-fish (*Malapterurus*) causes a hissing sound, the Trunk-fishes (Ostraciontidae) and Globe-fishes (Tetraodontidae) are credited with 'growling like dogs,' and the little Sea Horses (*Hippocampus*) are said to utter a 'monotonous sound analogous to that of a tambour, which is characteristic of both sexes, but is more intense and frequent in the breeding season.' An Indian species of Horse Mackerel (*Caranx hippos*) has been described as grunting like a young pig, and a related species from Egypt (*C. rhonchus*) is known to the Arabs as "Chakoura' or 'Snorter'. The sounds made by the Drums (Sciaenidae) have been variously described as creaking, drumming, humming, purring, whistling, etc., and are quite loud enough to be audible to a person standing on the deck of a ship. It has been demonstrated that the noise can be heard when the fish is eighteen metres below the surface of the water and the ear of the listener two metres above the water. In the Malay Peninsula and other tropical countries the native fishermen make use of the sounds to locate shoals of fish, one of their number 'listening in' and instructing his companions where to cast their nets. The Meagre or Weak-fish (*Sciaena aquila*), a species occurring round our own coasts, is abundant in the Mediterranean, and its vocal powers have been the subject of comment and discussion in all ages. It is not improbable that the Greek myth of the song of the Sirens which occurs in the Homeric fable arose from the sounds made by shoals of these fishes. A curious point about the Sciaenids is that some species make no sounds at all, in others only the males make a noise, and in others, again, both sexes are responsible. The drumming seems to take place especially at the breeding season, and is probably a signal for the assembling of the shoals.

In the Gurnards (Triglidae) the sounds are of a somewhat different nature, and have been variously described as grunting, crooning, snoring, etc. Unlike the Drums, these fishes do not make use of rapidly repeated sounds and rolls, but produce short, sharp sounds, repeated at more or less lengthy intervals. The grunts can be imitated, by drawing the forefinger and thumb towards each other over the surface of an inflated rubber balloon.

A recent investigator has concluded that in sound producing fishes of the North Atlantic, the sounds serve for communication and are of especial importance during the breeding season and may be used in keeping together breeding shoals or even to attract the opposite sex. Sounds may also be used to frighten a would-be aggressor invading a breeding territory. It is also suggested, particularly for fishes living over deep water, that the sounds may function rather as an echo-locator and thus help to fix the fish's position in mid-water.

REFERENCES

HALSTEAD, B. W. (1959). *Dangerous Marine Animals*. Cornell Maritime Press, Maryland.

HARVEY, E. N. (1957). Luminous organs of fishes: in, *The Physiology of Fishes* 2, Academic Press, New York.

KEYNES, R. D. (1957). Electric organs: in, *The Physiology of Fishes*, 2. Academic Press, New York.

MARSHALL, N. B. (1954). *Aspects of Deep Sea Biology*. Hutchinson's, London.

CHAPTER 11

COLORATION

WITH THE ADVENT of underwater colour photography, and the increasing popularity of home aquaria, a greater appreciation of fish colours has developed. It is hardly necessary to spend much space in describing some of the beautiful, subtle, weird or even downright garish colours of fishes. A few minutes spent thumbing through any of the books mentioned in the bibliography might convince even the hardest terrestial sceptic that birds do not hold a monopoly in this field. And, a few minutes spent watching Flat-fishes in an aquarium will show that in matters of colour change the chameleon is certainly not unique.

In many species the general coloration, and particularly the characteristic markings in the form of bars, stripes, spots and blotches, are remarkably constant in all the individuals of a particular species, but in others there is a good deal of individual variation; in the Trunk-fishes it is extremely rare to find two specimens exactly alike in the manner in which the bands on the body are arranged. Professor Jordan has described some of the remarkable colour variations found in a species of Sea Perch from the West Indies known as the Vaca (*Hypoplectrus*). Generally, the ground colour is orange, with black marks and blue lines, the fins being chequered with orange and blue. 'In a second form,' he writes, 'the body is violet, barred with black, the head with blue spots and bands. In another form the blue on the head is wanting. In still another the body is yellow and black, with blue on the head only. In others the fins are plain orange, without checks, and the body yellow, with or without blue stripes or spots and sometimes with spots of black or violet. In still others the body may be pink or brown, or violet-black, the fins all yellow, part black or all black. Finally, there are forms deep indigo-blue in colour everywhere, with cross-bands of indigo-black, and these again may have bars of deeper blue on the head or may lack these altogether.'

The apparently meaningless display of colour shades and patterns exhibited by many fishes have for the naturalist a deep, although not always obvious significance, but before dealing with this matter it is important to be quite clear as to the function of coloration. For the most part, the colours of fishes, like those of any other animal, serve to conceal their owners either from their prey or their natural enemies. This is not always the case, however, for in some fishes the colours serve a totally different purpose, and attempts that have been made to explain all types of coloration in terms of concealment sometimes press the matter to the point of absurdity. The fact remains, however, that in a very large number of fishes the particular hues and patterns adopted do tend to render them invisible, or, at least, very inconspicuous in their natural surroundings. A few examples will suffice to illustrate the general principles of these concealing colours.

A Carp (*Cyprinus*) or Roach (*Rutilus*), or almost any other fish to be found in our own rivers, exhibits a gradation of shades from silvery or yellowish-white below to a dark-blue, green, or brown above. This is known as counter shading, and is exactly the opposite of that which would be produced by light thrown upon the fish from above, and the general effect is to destroy the appearance of thickness and make the fish appear as a perfectly flat object. Seen from above against a background of water and the bottom of the stream coloured more or less like itself, the fish is almost indistinguishable at even a short distance, while seen from below the belly bears a close resemblance to the surface of the water and the clear atmosphere above. Many freshwater forms depend entirely on this simple shading to bring about their concealment, but others enhance the obliterative effect by the development of darker markings in the form of bars, stripes, spots and blotches of all kinds. The effect of such markings is twofold: they give the fish a more perfect resemblance to the ground on which it lies or the rocks and weeds among which it lurks; or, by their separate and conflicting patterns, they tend to obliterate the visibility of the form, and to break up the outline of the body against either a pale or dark background, as do the stripes on the body of a Zebra. The beautiful Angel-fish (*Pterophyllum*) of South America, a great favourite with aquarists, provides an excellent example of the value of markings in concealment, its very thin, almost circular body being crossed by several deep black bars, which are continued on to the long filamentous fins [Fig. 8c]. These markings harmonise very closely with the stems of the water plants among which the fish remains suspended almost motionless for hours on end, while the slowly waving fins help to perfect the deception.

In the sea the same general principles apply. Fishes habitually swimming at or near the surface, such as the Herring (*Clupea*), Blue Shark (*Carcharinus*), Mackerel (*Scomber*), or Tunny (*Thunnus*), are coloured silvery or white on the belly and sides, and the back parts are dark green, black or steely blue, sometimes ornamented with black spots or streaks, but as a rule more or less uniform [Fig. 82A]. The water in the sea being generally bluer and clearer than that of the rivers, the olivaceous hues of the freshwater fishes give place to these metallic shades, and seen from above against a background of dark water, or from below against a light sky, the fish is inconspicuous to its enemies, whether they be birds or other fishes. Larval fishes, swimming for the most part at or near the surface, obtain similar protection by the absence of pigments,

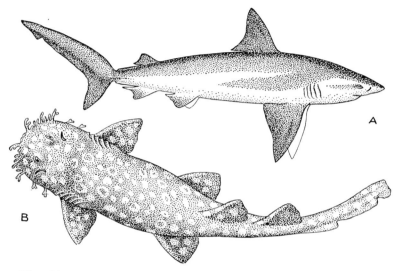

Fig. 82   COLORATION IN PELAGIC AND BOTTOM-LIVING SHARKS
A. Sandbar Shark (*Carcharinus milberti*) x ¹/₂₅; B. Carpet Shark (*Orectolobus barbatus*), x ¹/₁₅

being either transparent and colourless, or with the head and body covered with minute black dots, sometimes locally aggregated to form larger masses, whose purpose is to break up the outline of the moving body. In certain cases larval forms may bear some resemblance to the little bubbles or flecks of foam often to be seen floating on the surface of the sea. A transparent body will also give the larva protection against damage by radiation, particularly from rays in the visible light range.

Below the surface, fishes inhabiting the layers of water from one hundred to five hundred metres are generally of a silvery hue, although a large number of dark brown or velvety black species occur. At greater depths still, five hundred to two thousand metres below the surface, where there is little or no light, the prevailing shades are brown, black or violet-black, generally quite dull, but sometimes with silvery lustres or reflections from the scales. There is also a complete absence of spots, bands, or other distinctive markings such as distinguish the fishes which dwell more or less close to the shore.

On the whole, reddish tints are rare in deep-sea fishes and those species in which these colours occur are mainly centred below the 500 metre level. The significance of the colours in deep-sea fishes is still uncertain and is less easily explained than in shallow water species.

Among the littoral fishes almost every conceivable type of coloration is found, ranging from a simple and uniform grey or brown to the most vivid and bizarre combinations of colours and markings. As a rule, the spots and mottlings, when present, tend to give the fishes a general resemblance to the ground or to the rocks and weeds among which they swim. This protective resemblance is often remarkably exact, and among granite rocks we find fishes with an elaborate series of granite markings; similarly, black species are found among lumps of lava, green ones among the lighter varieties of seaweeds, olive-coloured fishes among the *Fucus*-like weeds, and red ones among the corals of similar shades. Seen apart from their surrroundings some of these fishes are difficult to explain in terms of concealing colours, but studied in their natural haunts many of the puzzling cases immediately become clear. For example, many of the Sea Perches or Groupers (*Epinephelus*) have the head and body covered all over with more or less hexagonal spots of reddish brown, separated from one another by a pale white or blue network—a reticulated pattern recalling that of the Giraffes. Lieut.-Col. Alcock in his book '*A Naturalist in Indian Seas*' records how he was in a boat with a native fisherman who speared one of these fishes, which, when wounded, took shelter in an adjacent clump of coral and lay concealed therein. The red spots bore a most exact resemblance to the coral polyps and the fish refused to leave its shelter.

Judged from this standpoint, the vivid colours of the fishes of tropical reefs are more easily understood. Seen as museum specimens they appear as highly conspicuous objects, but observed against a background of corals and associated forms of animal life, themselves presenting a perfect riot of colour, they attract comparatively little attention. Many of these reef-dwelling forms exhibit an extraordinary variety of darker markings of every description, the pattern, however, being fairly constant in any particular species [Fig. 83]. The purpose of such markings is to break up the outline of the fish and to conceal the shape. Some of the Butterfly-fishes (Chaetodontidae) have the head and eye crossed by a dark band, often bordered with white or blue, while at the hinder end of the body is an eye-like spot or ocellus, sometimes ringed with white or yellow [Fig. 83D]. They are said to be in the habit of swimming for a short distance very slowly tail first, but, if disturbed, they will dart off with great rapidity head first in the opposite direction. It has been suggested that the effect of this curious pattern tends to make a potential enemy regard the tail end of the fish as the head, and it is thus able to save itself by darting off in the direction least expected by its aggressor. When considering the colours of coral-reef fishes, however, it is important to guard against the tendency to look upon all types of coloration as concealing, for in many regions the reefs themselves are dull greyish, and the associated forms of animal life more or less soberly coloured, but the little fishes are as vividly coloured as elsewhere. Under such conditions they cannot be protected by their liveries, and must rely on their exceptional alertness and agility, and on

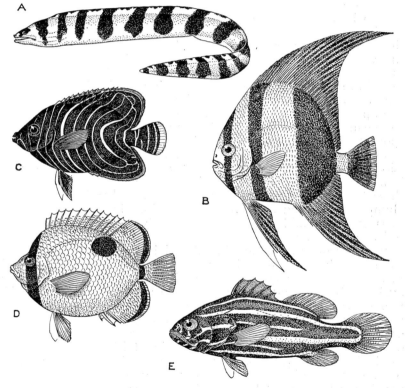

Fig. 83 COLOUR PATTERNS IN TROPICAL MARINE FISHES
A. Muraena or Moray (*Gymnothorax petelli*), x ¹/₈; B. Bat-fish (*Platax orbicularis*), x ¹/₈; C. Butterfly-fish (*Pomacanthodes semicirculatus*), x ¹/₂; D. Butterfly-fish (*Chaetodon unimaculatus*), x ¹/₄; E. Sea Perch (*Grammistes sexlineatus*), x about ¹/₂

their ability to shelter within the clumps of coral or to bury themselves in the coral sand.

Mention may be made of a Butterfly-fish (*Pomacanthodes semicirculatus*), in which the dark ground colour of the head and body is broken up by a series of narrow curved white stripes, the caudal fin being ornamented with markings of a similar nature [Fig. 83c]. In a specimen which made its appearance in the fish-market at Zanzibar these markings on the fin bore a remarkable resemblance to old Arabic characters [Fig. 84], reading on one side of the tail 'Laillaha Illalah' (There is no God but Allah) and on the other side 'Shani-Allah' (A warning sent from Allah). This caused

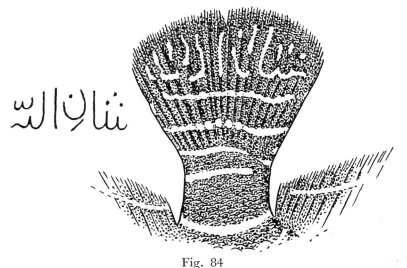

Fig. 84
Tail of a Butterfly-fish (*Pomacanthodes semicirculatus*), with markings resembling Arabic characters

considerable excitement, and the fish, which was originally sold for a few cents, eventually fetched five thousand rupees!

The most perfect examples of protective resemblance are encountered among the shore-dwelling fishes living actually on the sea bottom, and their spotted and mottled liveries imitate the background of sand, mud, pebbles, crushed coral, lava, and so on with remarkable exactitude. The Carpet Shark (*Orectolobus*), for example, has a beautiful, variegated coloration and simulates a weed-covered rock [Fig. 82B], and many of the Rays (*Raia*), Flat-fishes (Pleuronectiformes), Anglers (Lophiidae) and other fishes, have the upper surface coloured in harmony with the ground on which they are lying. Most of the Frog-fishes (Antennariidae) are shore-dwelling forms, but some species of the genus *Histrio* live in the open sea, drifting about with the currents in masses of Sargasso weed. The particular species living in the Sargasso weed of the Atlantic is of a pale yellow colour, with small white spots and irregular brown bands, giving an almost perfect concealment in its natural habitat among the weed [Fig. 85].

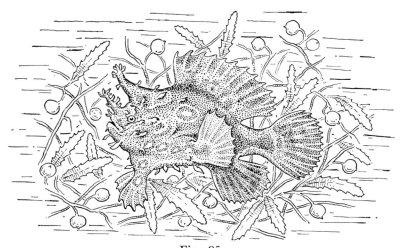

Fig. 85
Frog-fish (*Histrio histrio*) in Sargasso weed. x ½

In some fishes the protective resemblance is carried still further by actual mimicry, both in form and colour, of a particular inanimate object. For example, the Pipe-fishes (Syngnathidae), not only in their shape and colour, but also in their slowly swaying movements, bear a marked resemblance to the fronds of seaweed among which they live. The Florida Pipe-fish when among tufts of eel-grass is said to be dark green in colour, but when placed in an aquarium among pale weeds it becomes light green. Another American form is normally of a muddy brown hue, but examples collected from a tide-pool filled with red seaweeds were brick-red in colour. The grotesque Sea Dragon (*Phycodurus*) of Australian shores has carried mimetic resemblance to perfection, the outline of the body being broken up by the development of numerous spinous or membranous processes: some of these form leaf-like blades, and, when streaming out in the water, give the fish an almost perfect likeness to a piece of seaweed [Fig. 86]. The general appearance of a Carpet Shark (*Orectolobus*) or Angler (*Lophius*), with its series of branched membranous appendages, which tend to give it a general resemblance to a weed-covered rock, has been already described, and there are a number of other bottom-living forms which feed on smaller fishes and rely on their resemblance to ordinary objects to escape detection.

Some of the poisonous Stone-fishes (*Synanceia*), when lying motionless on the bottom and partially buried in the sand, have the appearance of lumps of rock or lava; the Gar Pike (*Lepisosteus*)

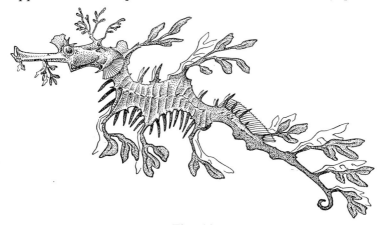

Fig. 86
Sea Dragon (*Phycodurus eques*), x ½

when cautiously drifting towards its prey, bears a strong likeness to a piece of driftwood. Some small fishes found in the mangrove swamps of the islands in the Pacific look exactly like the old leaves of the mangrove trees among which they swim. Another fish (*Monocirrhus*), even more like a dead leaf, has been observed in the Amazon River, and here, not only the colour, but also the shape of the fish imitates the leaf, even to the extent of simulating a short stalk at one end [Fig. 87]. In the Bay of Panama little fishes

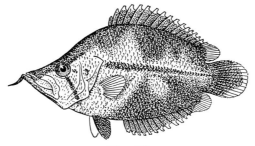

Fig. 87
Monocirrhus polyacanthus, x 1.

have been seen swimming about among pieces of driftwood, and so close was the resemblance that it was almost impossible to pick out the living fishes from the fragments of wood. Young Half-beaks (*Hemirhamphus*) appear very like pieces of seaweed when observed at the surface of the water, and it is said that when a net is passed over the water in their vicinity, or when they are otherwise alarmed, they at once become quite rigid, floating about in any position and apparently in a helpless, inanimate condition. Similar cases of mimicry might be multiplied indefinitely, but one more must suffice. Dr. Beebe has described some Slender Filefishes (*Alutera*) feeding among clumps of eel-grass, and notes that when poised head downwards with the fins gently waving, the general tapering form of the body, together with the undulating fins and mottled green colour, gives them a remarkable resemblance to a frond of seaweed [Fig. 88].

The variation in colour found among individuals of the same species has already been mentioned, and in such a form as the common Brown Trout (*Salmo trutta*) of our own rivers and streams,

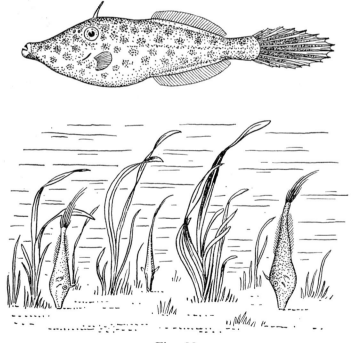

Fig. 88
Filefish (*Alutera scriptus*) among eel-grass. (After Beebe)

the connection between a particular type of coloration and the nature of the surroundings is often striking. Dr. Günther has observed that 'Trout with intense ocellated spots are generally found in clear rapid rivers and in small open Alpine pools; in the large lakes with pebbly bottom the fish are bright silvery, and the ocellated spots are mixed with or replaced by X-shaped black spots; in pools or parts of lakes with muddy or peaty bottom the Trout are of a darker colour generally, and when enclosed in caves or holes they may assume an almost uniform blackish coloration.' Two or three Trout from the Thames sent to the British Museum exhibited all the characteristic silvery and black-spotted appearance of typical Sea Trout, but proved to be merely Brown Trout that had been living in shallow reaches with a light gravelly bottom. In a stream near Ivy Bridge the Trout were observed to have become much lighter in colour after the water had been polluted with white china clay. Dr. Day has described two lochs in Inverness-shire which were both stocked at the same time with Trout from Loch Morar. The larger of the two, with a sandy and weedy bottom, had the effect after a few years of changing the fish into forms with golden sides and covered with numerous red spots, and with white flesh. In the smaller loch, where the water was dark coloured and the bottom rocky, the fish developed nearly black heads, yellowish-olive sides, comparatively few black and red spots on each side, and the flesh became pink. Numerous other cases of a similar nature might be described, but the above should suffice to show that the coloration may undergo a definite change resulting in greater harmony with the surroundings, and that these changes are connected particularly with the amount of light available and the nature of the bottom. Further, there is evidence to suggest that, in some cases at least, the nature of the food may have its effect on the colour of the fish.

Similar changes have been produced under artificial conditions, and Sticklebacks kept in glass dishes with a background of black and white tiles have shown considerable variation in colour, those on the white tiles tending to become partially blanched, while those on the black more or less retained their normal coloration. If only exposed to the white tiles for a few days they tend to regain the original colour when put back on the black, but prolonged exposure extending over a period of weeks seems to make the pale colour more or less permanent. Minnows (*Phoxinus*) kept for experimental purposes in a white porcelain sink will also assume a bleached condition which matches the background, and anglers will sometimes paint the interior of their minnow-can white, so that the bait will assume a lighter colour and thus be more con-spicuous to Pike and Perch in deeper and dark water.

The colour changes in Trout just described are generally slow, but in some fishes they may be practically instantaneous. Most of the tropical Sea Perches (*Epinephelus*), for example, are capable of changing in a moment from black to white, yellow to scarlet, red to dull green or dark brown, and can equally readily switch on, as it were, a series of spots, blotches, bars or stripes. A former director of the New York Aquarium, Dr. Townsend, has made a detailed study of the colour changes undergone by the fishes under his charge, and he has found that fishes from the coral reefs might have anything from two to seven distinct normal colour phases, according to the species. These varied greatly in the different forms, being most marked in the Sea Perches or Groupers (*Epinephelus*), but nearly always included one very pale or even white phase, and another which was exceptionally dark. To describe even a few of these colour phases would be impossible, but Dr. Townsend's description of a species of Sea Perch known as the Nassau Grouper will serve as a typical example. 'Eight phases of coloration are sometimes observed in a tank containing specimens of the Nassau Grouper (*Epinephelus striatus*). In one the fish is uniformly dark; in another creamy white. In a third it is dark above with white under parts. In a fourth the upper part is sharply banded, the lower pure white. A fifth phase shows dark bands, the whole fish taking on a light brown coloration. While in a sixth the fish is pale, with all dark markings tending to disappear. The seventh phase shows a light-coloured fish with the whole body sharply banded and mottled with black. This is instantly assumed by all specimens when they are frightened and seek hiding-places among the rock-work. The banded phase shown here is no more the normal appearance of the fish than the uniformly dark, the uniformly white, or any other phase. Singularly enough, no two photographs of this banded phase are quite alike, the extent of the markings being dependent apparently upon the degree of disturbance to which the fish has been subjected.' Another observer has described a fish of a shining blue colour with three broad vertical bands of brown, which swam into a clump of coral, emerging a few minutes later 'clad in brilliant yellow, thickly covered with black polka-dots.'

It is, however, in the Flat-fishes (Pleuronectiformes) that the capacity for changing the coloration in harmony with the surroundings reaches its height. In the Flounder (*Platichthys*), for example, the colour is generally greyish-olive, often more or less marbled with brown, but this may vary from yellow to almost black, and so perfect is the resemblance to the mud, sand or gravel on which the fish happens to be resting, that unless it moves it is wellnigh invisible. The bright orange-red spots of the Plaice (*Pleuronectes*) will be familiar to all, but when the fish moves on to a piece of ground covered with little white pebbles the red spots are said to become pale to match the altered surroundings. The

a. On Gravel

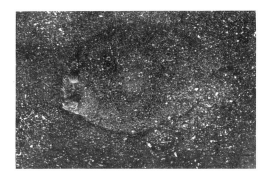

b. On Coarse Sand

c. On Shingle

Colour changes in a MEDITERRANEAN FLAT-FISH (*Bothus podas*)

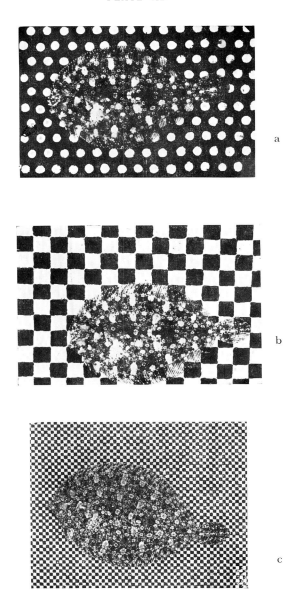

Colour changes in a MEDITERRANEAN FLAT-FISH (*Bothus podas*)
On three different artificial backgrounds

Turbot (*Scophthalmus*) living on dirty mud or sand on the sea bottom is a dull-greyish fish, but in an aquarium tank with sanded floor it is of a pale yellowish hue, and if placed on a background of coarse gravel, yellowish spots are developed over the head and body, separated from one another by a dark network.

Some experiments conducted in the aquarium at Naples on a Mediterranean Flounder (*Bothus*) are of interest (Pl. II). The same individual was successively placed in glass dishes on the bottom of which were painted chessboard backgrounds of black and white squares, black and white circles, and so on, and was induced to imitate the pattern. As the background was an unaccustomed one, the colour change took about half an hour instead of the usual second or so. It was found, however, that with practice a fish was soon able to harmonise with the background more rapidly than at first, but its capacity for colour change was limited to the black, brown, grey and white of its ordinary surroundings. An American investigator, experimenting on Flounders (*Paralichthys*, etc.), carried the matter further, and found that when placed on backgrounds of white, black, grey, brown, blue, green, pink and yellow, they made very good attempts to produce a coloration similar to that on which they were lying. They copied red backgrounds with less accuracy than those of other colours, and whereas yellows and browns were simulated with rapidity, greens and blues took a greater time, and a considerable interval sometimes elapsed before the full effect was obtained.

Very remarkable colour changes often occur after death, and the hues of many fishes a few hours after capture are quite different to those exhibited in life. In Mackerels (*Scomber*), Mullets (Mullidae) and other brightly iridescent forms, the colours appear to be brightest at the time intervening between the capture of the fishes and their death. In Roman times Red Mullet were not infrequently brought alive to the banqueting table, swimming round and round in a glass vessel, so that the guests might gaze on the brilliant display of colour changes afforded in the death struggles of the fish. So esteemed were these fishes for their vivid hues and exquisite flavour that at the height of the Roman Empire fabulous sums were paid for particularly fine specimens. The death colour of Dolphins —in this case the fish *Coryphaena hippurus* and not the mammal— are another classical case, in comparison with which those of the Mackerel (*Scomber*) are more mundane and certainly less spectacular.

There are, of course, other functions of coloration besides concealment. The question of recognition and warning marks has already been touched upon (*cf.* p. 172), and it is difficult to find any other explanation of the sudden switching on, for example, of a row of black or white spots along the side of the body. Many species exhibit peculiar markings which are remarkably constant

in all individuals—a spot below or behind the eye, a stripe from eye
to mouth, a blotch on the gill-cover, a bright red fin, a brilliant
margin to dorsal, anal or caudal fins, a purple or emerald spot
in the axil of the pectoral or pelvic, or a brilliant eye-like spot often
ringed with white or yellow on a particular part of the body or fins.

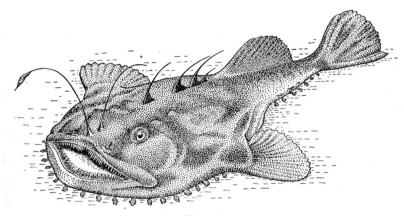

Fig. 89
Anglerfish (*Lophius piscatorius*), x ¹/₈

The young of some species are conspicuously differently coloured
from the adults, and although in some cases this may be shown to go
hand in hand with a corresponding difference in habits or environment, and is undoubtedly protective, in others no such connection
seems to exist.

Although colour changes are generally associated with an
attempt to harmonise more closely with a changed background,
there are other and emotional reasons for the change. Fishes when
frightened, sexually excited or affected by a chemical or physical
change in the water often show a marked change in coloration or
colour patterns.

In many fishes the two sexes exhibit differences in coloration,
particularly in those forms which pair at the breeding season and
indulge in some sort of courtship (*cf*. p. 230). The difference in
colour may be noticeable at all seasons, or may be developed in the
male only and make its appearance as the time of breeding approaches, the colours afterwards vanishing and leaving the two
sexes once more alike. Experiments show that such changes are
often important in reproductive activities, serving as sexual
recognition signs and even to heighten the sexual excitement of one
partner (see p. 234).

Finally, some types of coloration seem to be of the nature of 'warning colours', a signal to would-be enemies that their possessors are dangerous, either by virtue of their poisonous flesh or on account of the possession of venomous spines and the like. The brilliant hues of such poisonous tropical forms as the Trigger-fishes (Balistidae), Trunk-fishes (Ostraciontidae), and Globe-fishes (Tetraodontidae), probably partake of this nature, and act as danger signals to predaceous fishes that have learnt to associate a particular type of coloration with unpalatable qualities, thus operating to the mutual advantage of both species. One or two species of Serpent Eels (Ophichthyidae) of the South Seas have a banded coloration similar to that of the venomous Sea-snakes, for which it would be to their advantage to be mistaken. The Weever-fish (*Trachinus*) may provide another example of warning coloration. The dorsal fin, which is the only part of the fish visible when it is buried in the sand, being intense black in colour, and in contrast with the pale yellow and brown tints of the rest of the fish (and of the surrounding sand) is clearly visible from a considerable distance [Fig. 75A]. Upon provocation this fin is erected and spread out in a conspicuous manner, and it is suggested that this acts as a danger signal to warn predatory fish of the Weever's whereabouts, fish which might otherwise mistake it for a harmless species of similar size and habits. The Common Sole (*Solea*) has a deep black patch on the pectoral fin of the upper side, and, when alarmed, is in the habit of burying itself in the sand, and raising this fin verti-cally like a small flag. It has been suggested that the pectoral fin of the Sole mimics the dorsal fin of the Weever, and the fish is thus left severely alone. In the Star Gazers (Uranoscopidae), and Flat-heads (Platycephalidae), likewise armed with poisonous spines, the dorsal fin is generally black and is the only part visible when the fish is buried in the sand.

It is thought that the bright colours of 'Cleaner fishes' serve as an advertizing signal which, because these species are not attacked by the larger fishes on which they work (see p. 207), also gives them a goodly measure of protection. Perhaps it is significant that several species which are not 'Cleaners' mimic the coloration of the 'Cleaners'. In this way they not only gain a certain immunity from attack but are able themselves to attack the fishes 'recognizing' them as 'Cleaners'.

The colours of a fish are mainly due to the presence in the dermal layer of the skin of numerous pigment-containing cells known as chromatophores [Fig. 90]. Each of these is a much branched, small sac with thin walls. By expansion or contraction the contained pigment granules may be concentrated into a minute spot, or flattened out to form a relatively large and irregular sheet, the cell itself retaining its shape since only the pigments move. The granules of pigment deposited in each of the chromatophores may be either red, orange, yellow or black. Other shades are produced by the blending of two or more of these primary colours. The exquisite green colour on the back of the Mackerel (*Scomber*) is due, not to a green pigment, but to a combination of black and yellow chromatophores in suitable proportions: in the same way, a blending of yellow and black, or of red and black, may give a brownish coloration, and by the appropriate mixing of chromato-

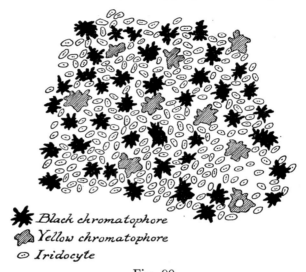

✳ *Black chromatophore*
🌸 *Yellow chromatophore*
◎ *Iridocyte*

Fig. 90
The colour elements in the skin from the upper side of a freshly killed Flounder, seen by transmitted light

phores of different colours almost any shade is produced. A black spot or stripe may be due either to the concentration of the black pigment in certain regions and its comparative absence elsewhere, or to the expansion of black pigment in particular areas as contrasted with its contraction in other parts of the body.

But the colours are not all due to pigment, and the presence of a peculiar reflecting layer composed of structures known as iridocytes also plays an important part. Iridocytes are made up of opaque crystals of a substance called guanin (a waste product of metabolism) whose chief feature is the power of reflecting light. Both the chalky white and the bright silvery appearance of fishes is due to the manner in which light is reflected from iridocytes. By interference these same colour elements are also responsible for the prismatic hues and brilliant iridescence characteristic of so many fishes. The relative abundance of either type of colour agent varies greatly, not only in different species, but in different parts of the same individual, chromatophores being most abundant in the dark back region, whereas, in the pale belly the iridocytes play the chief part.

Thus, the relative abundance of chromatophores and the kind of pigment they contain, the manner in which they are distributed in the skin, as well as the iridescence and the reflecting powers of the iridocytes, all play their part in determining the characteristic colour of a fish. The dark bluish-grey colour of the back of a Whiting (*Micromesistius merlangus*) is due largely to the abundance of black and yellow chromatophores in this region, but these are much less numerous on the sides and absent altogether on the pale belly. The iridescence and silvery appearance of the sides are due to the iridocytes lying above the scales, combined with the reflecting but non-iridescent layer of similar structures below the scales. The dead white of the abdominal region owes its appearance to the different reflecting power of another deep layer of iridocytes in this region known as the argenteum, and to the absence of chromatophores.

The colour changes described in the foregoing pages, whether slow, rapid, or instantaneous, are all due, therefore, to the action of the chromatophores. If their pigment be expanded, the particular shade of colour is intensified: when the pigment is contracted it may shrink to a mere dot and thus diminish the vividness of the colour involved. This latter process may even change the colour, for yellow chromatophores become orange when the pigment contracts, and orange or red appear brown or black. The prevailing hues of the body are altered, not only by the expansion or contraction of the pigment, but also by an increase or decrease in the number of chromatophores, or by an alteration in the manner of their distribution in the skin.

The initial stimuli leading to colour change are undoubtedly received through the eyes, but full details of the physiological mechanisms involved in the movement of pigments within the chromatophores have still to be worked out. It seems that both nervous and hormonal control is involved. Rapid colour changes are probably under nervous control but slower, more stable changes may be effected through the action of hormones.

There is certainly some evidence pointing to the direct action of light on the production of pigment in areas normally unpigmented. Conversely, lack of light can result in a reduction of pigmentation. For example, if the Catfish (*Ameiurus*) or the Flounder (*Paralichthys*) are kept in an aquarium with blackened sides and top but with an illuminated bottom, numerous dark chromatophores appear in areas of the body normally lacking pigments cells; if a blinded

Ameiurus is kept in darkness, reductions in pigmentation take place due to the lack of illumination.

An almost complete absence of pigment is found in blind cave-fishes but even here light may have an effect because blind African Carp (*Caecobarbus*) living in caves with some light have more pigment than those living in darker grottoes. Incidentally, the pale pink colour of many cave-fishes is due to blood in the numerous superficial blood vessels showing through the transparent skin.

Some fishes exhibit a condition known as xanthochromism, sometimes occurring in the wild state, but generally brought about by the artificial conditions associated with domestication. In such individuals the black or brown pigment is entirely wanting and the whole body has a golden coloration, or, if the orange and red are also undeveloped, a uniformly silvery hue. The familiar Gold-fish (*Carassius auratus*) is a native of Eastern Asia, and in its natural habitat has the greenish and brownish colours of the other Cyprinids, only the domesticated varieties exhibiting the golden or silver liveries. Individuals that have escaped from artificial ponds and regained the rivers often revert to the original coloration. Golden Tench (*Tinca*), Golden Orfe (*Idus*), and Golden Trout (*Salmo*) are other well-known varieties produced by fish culturists, but Trout of this type are sometimes found in the wild state, and golden-coloured Eels (*Anguilla*) are by no means rare.

The relation between the incidence of light and the distribution of pigment in the skin has already been mentioned in connection with obliterative shading, and it is interesting to find that in certain species of the African Cat-fish *Synodontis*, which have the remarkable habit of swimming with the belly upwards (*cf.* p. 23) the normal coloration is reversed, the lower parts being dark and the back pale [Fig. 13].

All Flat-fishes (Pleuronectiformes) are, of course, coloured on one side only, the right side in some species, the left in others. The Arabs have a curious legend to account for this, saying that Moses was once engaged in cooking a Flat-fish, and that when this had been broiled until it was brown on one side the oil gave out; this so annoyed him that he threw the fish into the sea, when, although half cooked, it promptly came to life again, and its descendants have preserved this curious colour ever since. Radcliffe has described a Russian legend which states that the Virgin Mary heard the tidings of the Resurrection when engaged in eating a *Scophthalmus* (Turbot or Brill): 'incredulous and as one of little faith she flung the uneaten half of the *Rhombus* [= *Scophthalmus*] into the water, bidding it, if the message be true, come back to life whole! And lo! this it instantly did!' It sometimes happens that a Flat-fish develops pigment on the lower side as well as on the upper. This colouring may take the form of scattered brown or black spots on a white ground, or the hinder part of the lower side may have a complete coloration similar to the upper surface. In the Plaice (*Pleuronectes*), for example, the pigmentation of the blind side may even include the red spots so characteristic of this species. Often the pigment extends over the whole body, only the under side of the head remaining white, and in rare cases even this is coloured. This phenomenon of ambicoloration is of particular interest, for it is known that Flat-fishes are descended from symmetrical fishes, and it has been observed that complete (or nearly complete) pigmentation of the blind side, in whatsoever species it occurs, is almost invariably accompanied by other variations towards this original symmetry. The skin and scales of the lower surface not only assume the colour of those of the upper side, but also resemble them in structure. In a normal Dab (*Limanda*), for example, the scales on the eyed side are spiny, those on the blind side smooth, but in ambicoloured examples they are spiny on both sides. In the Turbot bony tubercles are present on the upper surface but not on the lower, yet in ambicoloured individuals they are nearly equally developed on both sides.

Finally, the occurrence of albino fishes, in which no pigment is developed at all, may be mentioned. The body is white, often tinged with pink, but, as a rule, the albinism is not complete, the fish retaining patches or spots of black or brown, as in the black and silver varieties of the Gold-fish (*Carassius*). Completely albino Flat-fishes (Pleuronectiformes) are caught from time to time, and it is probable that a number of such cases occur in a natural state; but the fish are at such a great disadvantage in the struggle for existence, being visible to their enemies against almost any background, that comparatively few of them survive to reach maturity. Albinism occurs in freshwater fishes (other than the blind cave forms) as well: albino Cat-fishes of the genus *Clarias* have been found in Africa, and albino specimens of the Congo Lung-fish (*Protopterus dolloi*) are known; again, they are not common.

REFERENCES

Cott, H. B. (1940). *Adaptive Coloration in Animals*. Methuen, London.
Danois, E. le (1957). *Fishes of the World*. Harrap, London.
Fox, D. L. (1957). Pigments of fishes: in, *The Physiology of Fishes*, **2**. Academic Press, New York.
Herald, E. S. (1961). *Living Fishes of the World*. Hamish Hamilton, London.
Marshall, N. B. (1954). *Aspects of Deep Sea Biology*. Hutchinson's, London.
Odiome, J. M. (1957). Colour changes: in, *The Physiology of Fishes*, **2**. Academic Press, New York.
Van den Nieuwenhuizen, A. (1960). *Exotische Vissen*. De Bezige Bij, Amsterdam.

CHAPTER 12

CONDITIONS OF LIFE

IN DESCRIBING the various organs of a fish's body, the relation between the environment or conditions of life and the structural modifications has been stressed throughout. Just as competition in terrestrial regions has led to the colonisation of the air by birds, and the return to the sea by the whales and other aquatic mammals, so, under the stress of competition, certain fishes have been compelled to penetrate into regions where it would seem impossible for them to survive, or to adopt some markedly unusual mode of life. In the present chapter some of the more interesting of these specialised forms may be considered and their bodily peculiarities described.

The middle layers and abyssal depths of the oceans provide a number of special conditions, particularly a reduction in available food, which are clearly reflected in the structural modifications of the fishes inhabiting these regions [Fig. 91]. For example, there is a marked reduction in the skeletal and muscular systems, these parts being but feebly developed as compared with the same structures in littoral forms and in related species from lesser depths. The bones are very thin, light, frequently quite flexible, and the ligaments connecting them are fragile and easily torn. The lateral muscles of the trunk and tail, although powerful enough, are often extremely thin, and the connective tissue binding them together loose and feeble. The skin may be little more than a fine membrane, and capable of great distension. Other characteristic modifications involving the light-producing organs, lateral line system, barbels, eyes, teeth, colour, and so on, have been considered in earlier chapters.

In some parts of the world, wells and other subterranean waters are populated by fishes belonging to very different families but all convergently adapted to life in more or less total darkness. These include three Cyprinid fishes allied to the Barbels (*Barbus*), found in wells and subterranean waters in Africa; Cat-fishes of four different families inhabiting caves and wells in Africa, the United States, Trinidad and Brazil; the famous cave-dwelling Amblyopsidae of the United States; and the blind Brotulids of Cuba and Mexico. As might be expected, where the cave-dwelling habit has been

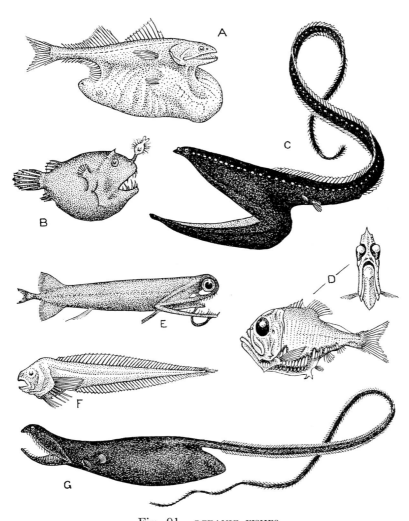

Fig. 91 OCEANIC FISHES
A. 'Great Swallower' (*Chiasmodus niger*), x ¹/₂; B. *Borophryne apogon*, x ¹/₂; C. 'Gulper' (*Eurypharynx pelecanoides*), x 1; D. Hatchet-fish (*Argyropelecus* sp.), x ¹/₂; E. 'Widemouth' (*Malacosteus indicus*), x ¹/₂; F. *Paraliparis* sp., x ¹/₂; G. 'Gulper' (*Saccopharynx ampullaceus*), x ¹/₄

adopted comparatively recently the fishes are not especially modified, but in nearly every case there has been reduction or loss of the eyes, and a complete loss of pigment, sometimes accompanied by the special development of certain sense organs to compensate for the loss of sight (*cf.* p. 155). Some of the African Cyprinid species are fully scaled, but others are naked, and the sensory organs of the skin may be highly developed.

The most interesting of the blind forms belong to the family Amblyopsidae. All are small fishes under four or five inches in length, and occur only in the United States of America. Of the five species included in this family some are cave-dwellers, and some live in the open, but all agree in having reduced eyes, and the vent placed remarkably far forward in the region of the throat. One species (*Chologaster cornutus*) inhabits open streams and springs, being particularly abundant in the swamps and streams of the southern Atlantic coastal plains; it lives amongst stones and bottom debris away from bright light. This fish is normally coloured, and the body is striped with longitudinal bands of black. Another closely related form (*G. agassizii*) is found in the subterranean streams of Tennessee and Kentucky. Both these fishes have small but quite functional eyes, and, in addition, ridges of sense organs developed on the head and body. The remaining genera of the family (*Amblyopsis, Typhlichthys*), including the famous Kentucky Blind-fish (*Amblyopsis spelaea*) first described in 1842 [Fig. 74B], all live permanently in the underground waters of limestone caves. They are translucent and colourless, the eyes are represented in the adults by mere vestiges hidden under the skin, and elaborate ridges of sensitive papillae are present to a varying degree on the head and body.

In the underground streams of Cuba are found the well-known Cuban Blind-fishes (*Lucifuga, Stygicola*) or 'Pez Ciego' [Fig. 92A]. The streams inhabited by these fishes first run above ground, then enter the ground, and finally emerge again near the coast. They are in no place far below the surface, and here and there the roofs of the channels are cracked and broken, forming the entrances to the so-called caves. The two forms and a species from Yucatan, Mexico, represent the only freshwater members of a large and varied family of fishes known as Brotulids (Brotulidae), the majority of which live at considerable depths in the oceans. They grow to a length of about five inches, and the coloration varies from dark blue to pinkish. They are quite blind, the eyes, which are comparatively well formed in the young, degenerate in the adult and become covered with skin [Fig. 92A]. The head, however is provided with numerous minute sensitive barbels.

It seems clear that the adoption of cavernicolous habits inevitably leads to the loss of the body pigments and to the degeneration of the eyes; and further, if this mode of life is extended over a considerable period, the reduction of the visual sense is compensated for by the special development or improvement of some other organ or organs of sense. The ridges of papillae present on the head and body in the Amblyopsidae are regularly arranged, and, as might be expected, are only slightly developed in those species

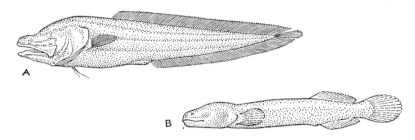

Fig. 92   BLIND FISHES
A. Cuban Blind-fish (*Stygicola dentatus*), x about 1; B. Californian Blind Goby (*Typhlogobius californiensis*), x 1

which possess eyes, but reach their maximum development in the totally blind forms. Their function is almost certainly the same as that of the lateral line (*cf.* p. 154), enabling the fish to perceive movements in the water, and thus to avoid obstacles or to detect the presence of their prey. Further, experiments have shown that the senses of smell, taste and hearing of these fishes are, on the whole, much the same as those of other fishes, and that it is the intensification of the 'lateral line sense' which serves as compensation for the loss of sight.

The suggestion that Blind-fishes were originally carried into the caves by accident, or that individuals without eyes or with relatively feeble eyes arose in the open as mutations or 'sports' and by finding their way into caves were enabled to survive, may be dismissed as highly improbable. In the case of the Cuban forms it seems likely that they developed along with the caves, gradually accustoming themselves to a life in fresh water. In all the other Blind-fishes the penetration of the caves must have been a voluntary matter, and in this connection it must be remembered that nearly all are species of a type which might be described as peculiarly fitted to be blind! The Cat-fishes, for example, live mostly in muddy rivers and streams, and depend more on the sensitive barbels than on the eyes in obtaining food. The blind Amblyopsids must have been descended from eyed forms belonging to the same family; the living eyed forms already inhabit situations in which the eyes are of little use and are much reduced in size. Further, one of these species is habitually found under stones in small rivulets, and another, which has reached the underground streams, has developed ridges of sensory papillae.

On the whole, therefore, it seems probable that fishes which have elsewhere become accustomed to do without light, and have adapted themselves to such conditions, have voluntarily penetrated into caves, colonising them gradually step by step, becoming more and more specialised for a life in darkness as successive generations penetrated deeper and deeper into the recesses. All kinds of fishes abound in the so-called twilight regions near the entrances to caves, and some of these might well be attracted into caves themselves, drawn thither by the presence of food, or to avoid the stress of competition in the outside world. It is well known that fishes living in holes in river banks or under stones tend to have reduced eyes, and it is possible that the ancestors of the existing Blind-fishes spent their lives in such a manner.

The peculiar Blind Goby (*Typhlogobius*) is found on the reefs of the shores of southern California, fastened to the underside of rocks or crawling about in the crevices or in the burrows made by crustaceans. It is about two inches in length, pale pink in colour, with a smooth, naked skin. The eyes are small and functional in the young, but are mere vestiges hidden under the skin in the adult fish. The head is well supplied with sensory organs [Fig. 92B]. The channels excavated by a species of burrowing shrimp are used by at least two other kinds of Goby as well as by the blind form, but these normally live outside the holes and only retire into them when danger threatens, whereas the Blind Goby never leaves the shelter of the burrows. Further, the normal Gobies are found all over the shore in this region, but the blind form is restricted in its distribution to a particular part. There can be little doubt that the Blind Goby is descended from a species which habitually sought the crevices and holes in the rocks, and in which the eyes were already reduced and the sensory papillae more extensively developed than in most members of this order.

Certain other Gobies (*Evermannichthys*, etc.) habitually live inside sponges, the bodies of the little fishes being of an even diameter which allows them to slip in and out of the larger orifices of the sponge's surface. The scales of these forms are mostly either absent or very feebly developed, but along the lower posterior line of the sides there are two series of large, well-separated scales, the edges of which are produced into long spines, while a series of four more is situated in the middle-line behind the anal fin. It is suggested that these specialised structures are used for climbing up the inner surfaces of the sponge cavities.

Another unusual environment to which many fishes have successfully adapted themselves is provided by the torrential streams of hills and mountain ranges. Here again the fishes probably colonised the streams very gradually. Among the more interesting of the hill-stream forms are the naked Cat-fishes (*Astroblepus*), [Fig. 93], found only in the torrential creeks and rivers of the Andes, most of them merely a succession of falls, cascades, pot-holes and short 'riffles'; and the Cyprinids, Loaches, Suckers and Cat-fishes of the hills of Asia, India, and the Malay Archipelago.

Some idea of the difficulties encountered by fishes colonizing hill-streams may be gained if it is borne in mind that huge volumes of water have to be carried away by a number of relatively tiny streams after heavy falls of rain. In the region of the Khasi Hills in India the average rainfall is no less than 458 inches, and so great is the rush of water at times that huge blocks of rock measuring four feet across have been described as rolling along almost as easily as pebbles in an ordinary stream, while the torrent of water is said to be actually turbid with pebbles of some inches in size, suspended in the water like mud.

Thus, the strength of the current is the principal factor influencing the evolution of fishes in torrential streams, but food is also of great importance, for, although quite abundant, this consists largely of algae covering the rocks and stones of the bed of the stream. No other type of vegetation is able to avoid being swept away by the force of the current, and although insect larvae are found in fair numbers in certain regions and form an important article of fish diet, the ultimate source of food is vegetable. Another adverse factor, but one of less importance, is the extraordinary clearness and shallowness of the water, which means that during the day the inhabitants have to endure an intense light. On the credit side of the account may be reckoned the rocky nature of the bottom, with its large boulders and pot-holes, forming ideal hiding-places for small fishes, and the abundance of air dissolved in the water, due to its rapid and constant motion.

The structural modifications resulting from these conditions are of special interest, and involve such diverse parts of the body as the skin, scales, mouth, fins, intestines and swimbladder. Nearly all are connected with the need for providing against the danger of being swept away by the force of the current, but others have been brought about by one or more of the other factors just mentioned.

All hill-stream fishes are necessarily bottom-living forms, and their bodies are generally much flattened from above downwards, sometimes being almost leaf-like [Fig. 25c]. The Loaches (Cobitidae) form an exception, but their small size and narrow cylindrical form are admirably adapted for creeping into holes and crevices beneath stones. The lower surface of the body in other forms is almost invariably flat, and the scaly covering much reduced below, especially in the region of the chest and belly. At the same time, the absence of larger predaceous fishes has obviated the necessity for armour, and thick scales, scutes and spines are normally absent. In the Loricariids, for example, the bony scutes with which the whole head and body are covered in the numerous lowland species are entirely wanting in those of the streams of the Andes. Where the current is rapid, many fishes have developed an elaborate adhesive apparatus. In some Asiatic Cat-fishes (*Glyptosternum, Pseudecheneis*) the skin of the lower surface is puckered up into grooves and ridges, these being generally most prominent on the chest, or on the under side of the outer ray or rays of the pectoral or pelvic fins. These ridges seem to act as a mechanical friction device, serving simply to prevent the fish from slipping, but where the skin is produced into loose folds a more or less effective vacuum may be created by raising or depressing the folds, the apparatus functioning in much the same way as the sucker of a Remora (*cf.* p. 39). In some Cyprinids the skin covering the lower surface of a few of the outer rays of the paired fins is greatly thickened, in places forming cushion-like pads which enable the fish to cling to the surface of a rock. In others, some sort of adhesive disc working on the vacuum principle is developed, generally taking the form of a rounded or oval structure composed of a pad-like central portion surrounded by a membraneous flap. As a rule this lies close behind the mouth, the surrounding membrane being formed by the modification of the lips. In the Loaches (Cobitidae) and Suckers (Gastromyzonidae) it is the mouth itself that forms the disc, the lips being greatly swollen and divided in the middle, so that when pulled outwards away from the mouth they provide a ring-like sucker. Some of the Asiatic Cat-fishes (*Glyptosternum, Exostoma,* etc.) have the lips reflected even more outwards and backwards, these structures being provided with folds, ridges, or papillae on their inner surfaces, and spread continuously round the mouth in the form of a broad, flat sucking disc. The naked Cat-fishes of the Andes (*Astroblepus*) have a similar sucker-like mouth, which, in conjunction with an apparatus formed by the lower surfaces of the pelvic fins, also serves as an organ of locomotion [Fig. 93]. By means of the alternate action of the mouth and of this apparatus the fish is able to creep slowly forward against even a rapid current, and it has been observed to ascend the vertical walls of large pot-holes in the bed of the stream [Fig. 93]. In other hill-stream fishes the paired fins also take part in the formation of an adhesive disc, generally being placed more or less horizontally at the sides of the body, as in the Bornean Sucker (*Gastromyzon*), in which there are as many as twenty-six to twenty-eight rays in each pectoral fin, and twenty to twenty-one in each pelvic [Fig. 25c].

Other modifications of the mouth and associated structures are

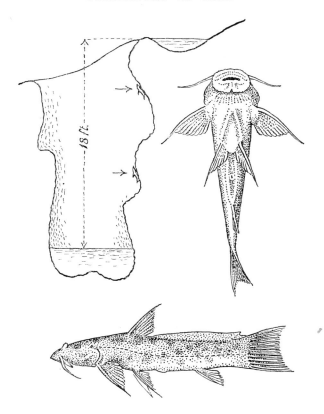

Fig. 93
'Capitane' (*Astroblepus chotae*), x about ¹/₂; Section of a pot-hole 22 **feet** deep in Santa Rita Creek, Colombia, showing the fishes ascending the rocky walls. (After Johnson)

connected with the food and methods of feeding in these waters, and may be directly traced to the habit of stripping vegetable slime from the surface of rocks and stones. The snout is nearly always broad and flat, and the mouth, generally crescentic in outline, lies on the under side of the head. In rapidly flowing water barbels would be a hindrance, and these are reduced to minute proportions or absent altogether. In the toothless Cyprinids the jaws may be sharp and cutting at their edges, and in some species they are covered with a strong horny sheath. In the Cat-fishes of the family Sisoridae the jaws are often armed with broad bands or patches of minute teeth of various shapes, which act after the manner of miniature rasps. A remarkable Cyprinid (*Gyrinocheilus*), found only in the mountain streams of the Malay Peninsula and Archipelago, has taken to feeding solely on mud, and the pharyngeal teeth, so characteristic of other members of this family, have entirely disappeared, the pharyngeal bones themselves being vestigial, and the horny pad at the base of the skull absent. The lips surround the mouth and form a funnel-like sucker, serving not only to scoop up the mud, but also to enable the fish to cling to stones and other objects. The diet has also led to changes in the internal organs, and, since the proportion of nutritive matter in mud is very small, large quantities must be swallowed at a time, and so the intestine has become very much elongated, being about fourteen times the length of the fish itself.

When attached by the mouth to stones in the stream bed, or engaged in feeding, it is obvious that these fishes are often unable to take in water through the mouth for breathing purposes in the usual manner. In the Malay Cyprinid (*Gyrinocheilus*) just mentioned, this difficulty is overcome by having the external gill-opening on each side divided in such a way that the water flows in through the upper part and out through the lower, and a similar arrangement is adopted by some of the Cat-fishes. In other hill-stream forms, however, the method of breathing seems to be normal, but they are capable of suspending their respiratory movements for considerable periods. The relatively high amount of air dissolved in the water of hill-streams, coupled with the low temperature of the water, enabling the fish to exist with a small consumption of oxygen, are other factors which help to make this temporary cessation of breathing possible.

The modifications undergone by the eyes, swimbladder, etc., must be briefly dismissed. With the flattening of the fish the eyes tend to be pushed more and more towards the upper surface and in many species they lie close together on the upper side of the head. They are generally reduced in size, probably on account of the intense light encountered in clear shallow water. In fishes living mainly on the bottom, upward and downward movements are comparatively few, and in rapidly flowing water solidity rather than buoyancy is required. For this reason the swimbladder is always much reduced. Finally, it may be noticed that in hill-stream forms the tail is especially muscular and capable of whip-like movements, by means of which the fish is able to dart rapidly from one stone to another.

The general effects of temperature on the life of a fish may conveniently be considered here, for although extremes of heat and cold do not appear to have led to marked structural modifications, they play an important part in limiting the distribution of certain species. The range of temperature under which different fishes live is very great, the frozen streams of Alaska and Siberia and the hot springs and warm stagnant pools of equatorial swamps are all inhabited by some form of fish life.

As far as the freshwaters are concerned, certain species have pushed very far northwards, being held up only when the water becomes actually frozen. Some, indeed, are able to survive in regions where the water freezes over for several months. The little Black-fish (*Dallia*) of Alaska and Siberia [Fig. 22H], a relative of the Pike (*Esox*), is renowned for its extraordinary vitality, reputedly remaining in solid ice for weeks on end and thawing out in an active condition as the spring approaches. Dr. Gill described how he kept some little Mud Minnows (*Umbra*) in a large glass jar of water, which froze solid during an exceptionally severe spell of weather, the jar being broken. The lump of ice was allowed to melt gradually, and every one of the fishes revived and swam about in a perfectly normal manner. However, if the tissues of a fish should freeze, it will not survive. Marine fishes have also succeeded in adapting themselves to low temperatures, and a number of species are found in Arctic seas, although a mere handful as compared with the number found in tropical and temperate regions. In the Antarctic there is a fairly rich fish fauna, even within the limits of the pack-ice. At certain seasons of the year some of these circumpolar fishes live in water that is at or near to freezing-point. Many oceanic fishes must also endure very low temperatures, the deeper layers of the oceans being at the most three or four degrees Fahrenheit above freezing.

Few, if any, marine fishes are able to endure water of any great heat, but some freshwater forms, and particularly the inhabitants of tropical swamps, are able to live in water which, during certain seasons, becomes considerably heated. The hot-springs of Arabia, many of them containing water which feels hot to the hand, all serve as dwelling-places for swarms of tiny Cyprinodont fishes, apparently unharmed by the high temperature. A small Cichlid (*Tilapia grahami*) found in large numbers in Lake Magadi, in the Rift Valley of Kenya Colony, is especially interesting. This lake is completely isolated, and the temperature varies in different regions, but the fishes seem to thrive equally well in water, or rather soda solution, ranging from 80° F. to 112° F.

Although certain kinds of fishes are able to survive in waters of extreme temperature without apparent hurt, it must not be supposed that this is always the case. Actually the range of temperature which most fishes can tolerate is comparatively limited; about 12° to 15° F. for most species. Some experiments conducted by two French scientists on such well-known forms as the Roach (*Rutilus*), Tench (*Tinca*), Gudgeon (*Gobio*), Bleak (*Alburnus*) and Eel (*Anguilla*) are of interest. They subjected individuals kept in aquaria to varying temperatures, carefully noting their behaviour in every case, and found that, as a general rule, few were able to endure water that was hotter than about 99° F., and that cold was resisted much more easily than heat. The fishes were found to behave in a perfectly normal manner in water at 73° to 75° F., their breathing was affected at 93°, a loss of equilibrium occurred at 99°, coma and convulsions at 106° to 109°, and death supervened when the temperature reached 113° to 116°. In the reverse experiment, the fish were normal until the water reached 64°, breathing movements were exaggerated at 60° to 57°, much affected at 53.5° to 50°, equilibrium was upset at 43° to 39°, convulsions occurred at 37.5° to 35.5°, followed by death before freezing-point was reached. The power of resistance to heat or cold varies considerably in different fishes, but it is a little difficult to explain why some species should be so much more easily affected than others. It is clear that those fishes which are less sensitive to change of temperature are most easily acclimatised in new countries, and for this reason the Carp (*Cyprinus*) and some of its allies, such as the ubiquitous Gold-fish (*Carassius*) thrive equally well in tropical and temperate countries. This is not to say that they can stand a sudden and violent change in the temperature of the water, and ignorance of this fact has led to the death of many a pet Gold-fish, which has met its end through being plunged suddenly into fresh *cold* water from the tap during the process of cleaning the bowl or aquarium. Salmon and Trout (*Salmo*) bear transplantation fairly well so long as the water is clear and rather cold, but the closely related Grayling (*Thymallus*) is highly sensitive to the slightest change in its conditions.

A curious and interesting example of a marine catastrophe, believed to be due to such a climatic cause as a sudden influx of cold water, was provided in 1882 by the Tile-fish (*Lopholatilus*), an inhabitant of the deep water below the Gulf Stream in the Atlantic [Fig. 94B]. This species was unknown in 1879, but in the following year was extremely abundant everywhere off the coast of southern New England at a depth of from seventy-five to two hundred and fifty fathoms. Numerous specimens, varying from ten to fifty pounds in weight were captured, and as the flesh was well flavoured, the Tile-fish became the object of an extensive American fishery with long lines. In March 1882, however, following heavy gales, millions of these fishes were to be seen floating dead at the surface of the water, covering an area of no less than fifteen thousand square miles of the sea. For many years afterwards not a single fish was caught, and the species was believed to be extinct, but some twenty years later it had reappeared in its old haunts. The Scabbard-fish (*Lepidopus*), an oceanic Trichiuroid or Hair-tail [Fig. 94A], is another species that is remarkably sensitive to cold weather. It is found in all warm seas, and in New Zealand it is known as 'Frost-fish', a name which refers to its habit of swimming ashore in thousands on cold nights. The related Cutlass-fish (*Trichiurus*) has been observed in a comatose condition off the coast of Florida while the temperature was still above freezing-point.

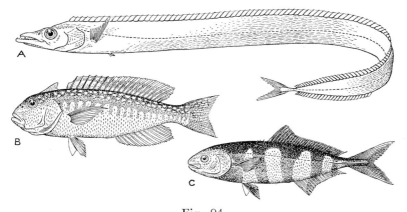

Fig. 94

A. Frost-fish (*Lepidopus caudatus*), x about ¹/₂₀; B. Tile-fish (*Lopholatilus chamaeleonticeps*), x about ¹/₂₀; C. Pilot-fish (*Naucrates ductor*), x about ¹/₂₀

A few fishes solve the problem of severe weather by 'hibernating'. This condition is gradually induced by the fall in temperature as winter approaches, and is sustained until the mercury once again rises in the spring. They do not seem to fall into a complete unconsciousness like the reptiles or such mammals as the dormouse, but simply cease to feed, seek shelter among weeds or stones, and become more or less torpid. Carp (*Cyprinus*), for example, always move into deeper water, and are reported to spend the winter in groups, some of which may contain fifty to a hundred individuals, clustered together in circles with their heads together. Respiration is so much slowed down that the movements of the gill-covers are scarcely apparent. The Tench (*Tinca*) spends the winter actually buried in the mud, and individuals which were dug up and placed on the bank of a river showed no sign of life until struck smartly with a stick. Fresh-water Eels (*Anguilla*) generally seek deep water and lie buried in the mud in a torpid condition. It is recorded that in 1841 large numbers of these fishes were killed in parts of Ireland owing to the protracted hard frosts with severe easterly winds. Among marine fishes hibernation is practially unknown, but there is reason to believe that young Plaice (*Pleuronectes*) remain in shallow water, and pass the cold period in a quiescent state buried in the sand.

Aestivation or summer-sleep does not occur among the inhabitants of the sea, but among a few freshwater fishes, and particularly among those that inhabit equatorial swamps which are liable to dry up for weeks or months at a time, this is by no means an uncommon reaction.

Certain Lung-fishes (Dipneusti) make elaborate preparations to avoid death during the dry seasons. The West African species, *Protopterus annectens*, is the best studied, and with the Congo species, (*P. dolloi*) are the only African Lung-fishes known to aestivate regularly. The East African species, *P. aethiopicus*, is able to aestivate but, probably because of different environmental conditions, is rarely found aestivating in nature.

Protopterus annectens inhabits swamps and small streams which may be completely dried out for several months each year. At the onset of the dry season the fish burrows down into the still soft mud, using both its mouth and body. The fish widens the lower end of the tube thus formed so that it may turn within the tube. When the water table falls below the upper end of the tube the fish curls itself up in the lower chamber and begins to secrete copious quantities of mucus which, on hardening, forms a cocoon around the fish, perforated only above the fish's mouth. The upper end of the tube is closed by a porous mud lid through which air can percolate. Thus, able to breathe air and protected from desiccation by the tight-fitting mucus cocoon, the fish is able to survive the dry season. During aestivation, the metabolic rate of the fish is greatly reduced and it is able to obtain sufficient energy by utilizing its body tissues, particularly the muscles.

With the return of the rains the fish again becomes active and, as the cocoon is softened, it breaks out and leaves the sleeping nest. In nature, the dormant period only lasts for a few months but aestivating Lung-fishes in their cocoons have been dug out and kept for over four years before being freed by artificial flooding. The fishes were greatly emaciated, somewhat rumpled, and swam awkwardly, but soon resumed normal feeding and behaviour.

The South American Lung-fish (*Lepidosiren*) also aestivates but its sleeping chamber is less elaborate than that of the African species in that no cocoon is produced. The Australian Lung-fish (*Neoceratodus*), on the other hand, is incapable of surviving drought and ultimately dies if removed from the water for any length of time.

To eat and to avoid being eaten by others are two important factors in the daily life of a fish. Certain species, in order to further these ends, have formed associations with other animals, including other fishes. Such association is termed symbiosis, (literally 'living together'). It is often possible to recognise a subdivision of

PLATE III

Cocoon of African Lung-fish (*Protopterus annectens*) embedded in mud. From a specimen in the British Museum (Natural History)

symbiosis, commensalism, in which the association is of benefit to both partners. But, in the present state of our knowledge about fish behaviour in nature it is perhaps best not to draw far-reaching conclusions from scanty data. Thus, excepting clear-cut cases of parasitism, it seems advisable to consider cases of association amongst fishes under the general term of symbiosis.

On of the best known cases is found among tropical coral fishes (Damsel-fishes) of the family Pomacentridae. Five species of Pomacentrid fishes live in association with species of large sea-anemones. The relationship is an intimate one and the fishes will remain within the anemone when it closes its tentacles. Clearly these habits afford them a great measure of protection from predators. Indeed, although the anemone can exist without its fishes, the fishes are soon devoured if their 'home' is removed. Newly hatched Damsel-fishes live at the surface, feeding on plankton, but soon leave this habitat for that of the anemone. Two questions still remain unanswered: are the stinging cells of the anemone lethal to fishes other than the symbiont species? If this is so, how are the Damsel-fishes protected? Views on this subject are varied but the most recent research suggests that the toxin of the stinging cells is of a mild type and that the fish's mucus covering provides complete protection.

Be this as it may, other fishes certainly associate with toxic animals and seem to be immune to their poisons. The classic case is found among members of the Stromateidae or Rudder-fishes. The young of certain species often shelter in the tentacles of Jelly-fishes. One of these fishes (*Nomeus*) is sometimes called the Portugese Man-of-War fish on account of its constant association with the large and curiously shaped siphonophore *Physalia* or Portugese Man-of-War. Other juvenile fishes of several families including some Stromateidae, certain Cods (Gadidae) and some Horse Mackerels (Carangidae) shelter amongst the stinging tentacles of Jelly-fishes. Again, we know little about the way in which the fishes are protected from the stings of their 'shelters' but their mucus coats seem to provide the most likely explanation.

The Rudder-fish (*Lirus*), another Stromateid, has the curious habit of accompanying floating logs or planks, or of taking up station within barrels or broken boxes, a habit which has earned the species the name of 'Wreck fish'. In this association the fish not only gains shelter but also feeds on the barnacles and other forms of life with which flotsam is almost invariably covered.

Even more extraordinary are the Cleaner or Barber fishes whose diet is mainly the parasitic organisms living on the bodies and gills of fishes. Cleaner species are found in many marine families and are especially abundant in tropical regions. To date no freshwater Cleaners are known. All the species, even though distantly related, show convergent adaptations for their specialized feeding habits; pointed snouts and tweezer-like teeth are a common feature. Also, in tropical seas the Cleaners are generally brightly coloured and patterned in sharp contrast to their surroundings. In fact, they could be considered as advertising their presence. Some species are Cleaners only when young but others fulfil this role throughout life.

The association of Cleaner and 'customer' is not permanent. Fishes willing to be cleaned congregate in certain areas of the sea bottom and then behave according to a stereotyped pattern which the Cleaners recognise as an invitation to action. The 'customers' will allow the Cleaners to swarm over their bodies and work in such sensitive areas as the mouth and eyes. The cleaners are even permitted to swim into the branchial cavity and remove parasites (usually Crustacea) from the gill surfaces. The Cleaners enjoy an undoubted immunity, not only when on the job, but also at other times. Many of the 'customers' habitually feed on fishes of the same size and proportions as the Cleaners, yet the latter are rarely eaten. The definite coloration of the Cleaners may play an important part in establishing this immunity. In fact, at least two unrelated species mimic the colours and behaviour of certain Cleaners and are thus able to approach large and unsuspecting fishes. However, their intentions are unlike those of the Cleaners, because once near the large fish they bite at its fins or skin and do not remove ectoparasites.

Cleaner fishes play an important role in the ecology of the sea, as experiments have shown. Not only do they help to maintain the well-being of the other fishes but their very presence exerts considerable influence on the distribution of the larger fishes.

The famous Shark Sucker or Remora (*Remora*) is also a cleaner, and one which has formed a particular association with Sharks (although it is also found with other large fishes and turtles). It is probable that between bouts of cleaning, the Remora attaches itself to the host, thus ensuring a continuous supply of food as well as a passage at reduced rates of energy expenditure.

Equally well-known are the so-called Pilot-fishes (*Naucrates*) often found swimming alongside Sharks and Rays [Fig. 94c]. It was once believed that the Pilot-fishes guided Sharks towards suitable prey, receiving in return protection from enemies because of their proximity to a formidable companion. Unfortunately this neat tale must be discarded in the light of more precise and less sentimentally inclined observations. In reality both fishes are in search of food, the Pilot often benefitting from the efforts of its larger companion, but never leading the foray. As for protection, it may certainly gain some because of its proximity to the Shark but it is perhaps significant that Pilots do not swim close to the Shark's jaws, although they may take refuge in the mouth of non-piscivorous Rays with which they are travelling!

A little eel-shaped fish, related to the Blennies, without pelvic fins and with the anal fin extending forward nearly to the head, is in the habit of sheltering within the bodies of marine animals known as Holothurians or Sea Cucumbers, allies of the Star-fishes and Sea Urchins. This fish, *Carapus*, has a transparent body with a number of scattered dots of pigment in the skin. When entering a Holothurian the fish searches for the anus with its head, and then

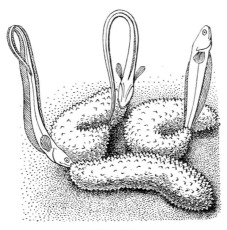

Fig. 95
Carapus acus and Holothurians, x about ⅓. (After Emery)

bends the tail round, inserts it into the opening, and straightening its body, wriggles backwards until completely housed within the body of its host [Fig. 95]. More than one fish can occupy the same 'dwelling', and no fewer than seven have been observed to enter a Sea Cucumber, one after another. By this habit the *Carapus* obtains shelter during the day, and at night sallies forth in search of the small crustaceans on which it feeds. The unfortunate holothurian gets no return for its services and its internal organs may even suffer damage through the presence of its uninvited guest. A Japanese species has been found inside a Star-fish, and on the coast of North America it is not uncommon to find these fishes living inside the Pearl Oysters. This association may be fatal to the fish, however, for it is sometimes imprisoned by the Oyster and its body sealed up in a layer of mother-of-pearl.

Quite recently a little Cardinal-fish (*Apogonichthys*) has been discovered on the coast of Florida, which habitually shelters within the mantle cavity of a large Sea Snail or Conch, leaving its host at intervals to search for food. Other related species are equally at home within the cavities of sponges (*cf.* p. 198). A little Goby (*Gobius*) has been found living inside the gill-chamber of a Shad (*Alosa*), lying curled up quite comfortably beneath the operculum of its host, and a similar association between small Eels and Devil-fishes (Mobulidae) has also been described. Small Eels are said occasionally to find their way into the body cavities of larger fishes, generally with fatal results as far as the Eel is concerned.

We may now consider a case which might be regarded as an example of commensalism. In the seas of India there is a little Scorpion-fish (*Minous*), and practically all the individuals of this species are more or less covered with a thick colony of hydroid polyps. Many examples of this fish have been captured, but very few indeed are without the polyps, and the hydroid itself has never been found living apart from the fish. The benefits derived from this association are mutual, the encrusting polyp growth concealing the fish from watchful enemies by giving it the appearance of a weed-covered stone, while the hydroid colony is carried about constantly by the fish and thus obtains fresh feeding-grounds without effort.

Finally, there is the type of association known as parasitism, where one animal lives on or inside another, nourishing itself at the expense of the living tissues of its host. In man, the louse provides a good example of an ectoparasite, while the tape-worm is a well-known endoparasite. As might be expected, such a mode of life is nearly always accompanied by some degree of degeneration on the part of the tenant, and throughout the whole of the animal kingdom internal parasites are, with few exceptions, degenerate creatures, and in extreme cases only the reproductive organs retain any semblance of their original perfection. Cases of true parasitism among fishes are very rare, although the Lampreys (Petromyzo-nidae) and Hag-fishes (Myxinidae) may be regarded as extreme ectoparasites. Certain members of a family of South American Cat-fishes (Pygidiidae) are in the habit of attaching themselves to any kind of fish or animal, piercing the skin and gorging themselves on the blood of the living victim. Others, known to the natives as 'Candiru' or 'Carnero' (*Branchioica*), habitually live within the gill-cavities of large Cat-fishes (*Sorubim*, *Platystoma*, etc.), and other freshwater fishes, their slender form enabling them to penetrate between the gills, the sharp teeth and opercular spines being used to start a flow of blood from the host, which is sucked up by the mouth [Fig. 96]. The patches of spines on the gill-covers also serve to assist the fish to wriggle between the gill-lamellae, and to retain their hold when once established. In some parts of Brazil another species of Candiru (*Vandellia*) is very much dreaded by the natives, owing to its unpleasant habit of entering the urethra of persons bathing in the rivers, and both men and women are in the habit of wearing special sheaths made of palm fibres to protect the external genitalia, when obliged to enter the water. The little fish appears to penetrate into

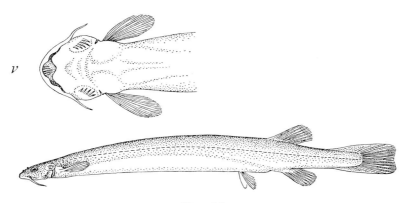

Fig. 96

Candiru (*Vandellia cirrhosa*), x 1¹/₂; *v*. Lower view of head, x 3

the urethra especially, if not always, during micturition, and it has been suggested that it is definitely attracted by urine. It seems more probable, however, that the flow of urine is merely mistaken by the fish for the respiratory current coming from the gill-opening of a fish. An accident of this nature may have serious consequences, for once the fish has entered it cannot always be pulled out on account of the erectile opercular spines, and a prompt surgical operation is necessary to prevent it from reaching the bladder and causing death from inflammation.

The only case of true parasitism occurs among the oceanic Angler-fishes (Ceratioidei), and will be considered in detail in a subsequent chapter (*cf*. p. 244). Here the dwarf male is a parasite on the female, spending the greater part of his life as a mere appendage attached to the body of his mate, and deriving nourishment from her blood.

REFERENCES

JOHNELS, A. G. and SVENSSON, G. S. O. (1954). On the biology of *Protopterus annectens* (Owen) *Ark. Zool.* **7**, 131–164.
LIMBAUGH, C. (1961). Cleaning Symbiosis. *Scientific American*, **205**, No. 2, 42–49.

MARSHALL, N. B. (1954). *Aspects of Deep Sea Biology*. Hutchinson's, London.
MYERS, G. S. (1952). Annual Fishes. *Aquarium J.*, **23**, No. 7.
OMMANNEY, F. D. (1961). *The Ocean*. Oxford University Press, London.
THINES, G. (1955). Les Poissons Aveugles (I). *Ann. Soc. Roy. Zool. Belg.*, **86**, 1–128.

CHAPTER 13

BREEDING

THE REPRODUCTIVE organs or gonads of fishes are of two kinds, ovaries in the female and testes in the male, the former being popularly known as hard roes, the latter as soft roes. In most fishes these are elongate in shape, paired, and more or less intimately associated with the kidneys. The ovaries are pinkish or yellow in colour, granular in texture, and usually lie just below and behind the swimbladder when this is present [Fig. 97]. As the breeding season approaches, the ovaries become much enlarged, fill a considerable part of the body cavity, and the separate eggs are plainly visible. The eggs may pass from the ovary to the exterior by way of a passage known as the oviduct, opening either by a special aperture or by one which it shares with the excretory duct; in some fishes no continuous oviducts are developed, and the eggs drop into the main body cavity, passing out through short, separate ducts. The testes have much the same position as the ovaries, but are much smaller, paler in colour, and to the naked eye have a creamy rather than granular texture. A narrow duct leads from each testis to the genital aperture. Occasionally, individuals are found in which both male and female organs are fully developed, this condition having been recorded in such well-known species as the Cod (*Gadus*), Herring (*Clupea*), and Mackerel (*Scomber*). Such individuals are abnormal, but certain species of perch-like marine fishes (Serranidae) are invariably hermaphrodite, and, further, are capable of self-fertilisation. Sex reversal occurs in several Percomorph and Cyprinodont families; usually the fish starts life as a female, but protandrous species are known.

The act of reproduction, by which a new life is brought into being, will be associated by most people with such activities as courtship and pairing of male and female individuals, and with physical union of the two sexes. In fishes, however, such pairing is the exception rather than the rule, and in the majority of Bony Fishes the relations of the sexes at the breeding season are quite promiscuous. This is especially the case in those fishes like the Herring (*Clupea harengus*) and Cod (*Gadus morhua*) which congregate in dense shoals at certain seasons for the purpose of spawning. The actual reproductive act is, of course, essentially similar to that of all the higher vertebrates, and consists in the fusion of two kinds of gametes, the eggs or ova of the female and the spermatozoa or sperms of the male (sometimes referred to as the milt). The difference lies in the manner in which the fusion, or fertilisation, as it is called, takes place. In mammals it occurs within the body of the female as the result of copulation between the sexes, and the fertilised egg develops within a special chamber in her body. In the majority of fishes however, the ova and sperms are merely shed into the water, where fertilisation takes place.

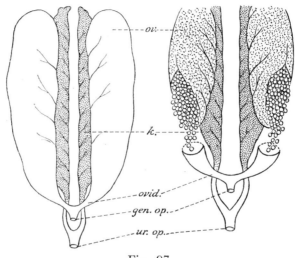

Fig. 97

Reproductive and excretory organs of a typical Bony Fish (female); left, with oviducts continuous with the ovaries; right with oviducts separated from the ovaries. (After Rey)

The time at which spawning takes place varies somewhat in different species, and naturally occurs at different seasons in various parts of the world. As far as our northern food-fishes are concerned, the majority breed in the first half of the year, the spawning season of the Plaice (*Pleuronectes*) extending from January to April, that of the Cod (*Gadus morhua*) in the North Sea from February to May, and of the Sole (*Solea*) from April to July. As is pointed out in another chapter, each race of Atlantic Herring (*Clupea harengus*) has its own spawning season, and some deposit their eggs close to the shore in winter or spring, others in deeper water during the summer or autumn. By the spawning period or breeding season of a particular species or race is meant that period during which most individuals may be found to possess ripe ova or sperms, and this may last only a few days or extend over as many weeks or even months.

As the time for spawning approaches the fishes congregate in huge shoals in suitable localities, and on some grounds they may be very closely packed together at this season. Analysis of these shoals generally shows the females to be in greater numbers than the males, but this is by no means always the case. Here the individuals of both sexes simply discharge their ova and sperm into the water and the fertilised eggs are subsequently abandoned by the parents and left to the mercy of physical conditions. The actual rate at which the eggs are extruded varies a good deal in the different species, in some cases all or a large proportion of the ova being ripe for fertilisation at more or less the same time, while in others the process is comparatively slow and only a certain number ripen and are extruded at one time.

In the Cod and Plaice, indeed in all our food-fishes with the exception of the Herring and Shad (*Alosa*), the eggs are minute and buoyant, and float at or near to the surface of the sea. Under such conditions the haphazard mode of reproduction must inevitably lead to a great waste of sex-cells, but this is diminished to a certain extent by the fact that the fishes are closely congregated and that both eggs and sperm will float roughly at the same rate and in the same direction. Drifting about in the sea at the mercy of the wind and currents, many of the eggs serve as food for other fishes, many are killed by changes of temperature and other physical catastrophes, and many more are cast on the shore by adverse currents. These enormous risks of destruction to which the larval fishes as well as the eggs are subjected, coupled with the difficulty of ensuring that every egg is fertilised after extrusion, are associated with the production of huge numbers of eggs by fishes of this type. A single Ling (*Molva*), 61 inches long and weighing 54 lbs. was found to have 28,361,000 eggs in the ovaries, a Turbot (*Scophthalmus*) of 17 lbs. weight more than 9,000,000, and a Cod (*Gadus*) weighing 21½ lbs., 6,652,000; a Flounder (*Platichthys*), however, produces a mere million ova on the average, and a Sole (*Solea*) only 570,000. So great is the destruction of eggs and fry that it has been estimated that in the case of the Cod less than one egg in every million liberated ever becomes an adult fish.

The eggs of the Herring (*Clupea harengus*) are heavier than sea water and are deposited in sticky clumps on shingly banks on the sea-floor. They thus escape many of the dangers to which the floating ova are subjected, but are still exposed to the depredations of hungry fishes of all kinds. The number of eggs produced by a single female is relatively small as compared with the fishes already mentioned, varying from 21,000 to 47,000.

Many marine fishes migrate to the quieter and shallower inshore regions to deposit their eggs, and others leave the sea altogether and spawn in rivers. These anadromous fishes include such well-known forms as the Sea Lamprey (*Petromyzon*), Sturgeon (*Acipenser*), Shad (*Alosa*), Salmon and Sea Trout (*Salmo*). Most of them leave the eggs and larvae quite uncared for, and exposed to attacks by predaceous fishes and enemies of all kinds. Again the ova are produced in large numbers thus compensating for the risks to which they are subjected. A mature female Salmon, for example, produces from 600 to 700 ova for every pound of her weight, so that a fish of 20 lbs. will have about 14,000 eggs. The breeding season of our own Atlantic Salmon (*Salmo salar*) extends from September to February, but these fishes approach the coasts and enter suitable rivers in almost every month of the year; spawning takes place mainly during November and December. While in the estuaries their ascent may be helped by the tide, but higher up they have to make their way unassisted, and so great is the urge for reproduction that they will display immense perseverance in negotiating obstacles such as falls or weirs lying in their path. Once in fresh water, active feeding is almost entirely given up, and as a result there is a gradual decrease in the weight of the fishes after they leave the sea. When first entering the rivers fresh from a lengthy stay in the sea, with its rich and abundant food supply, the Salmon are in fine condition, and exhibit the graceful form and familiar silvery coloration so characteristic of the species. With the approach of the spawning time they undergo very marked changes, particularly in their external appearance. The silver livery is replaced by one of a dull reddish-brown tint, and in the males the front teeth become enlarged, the snout and lower jaw are drawn out, and the latter is turned upwards at the tip to form a prominent hook or 'kype' [Fig. 98]. Further, the skin of the back becomes thick and spongy, so that the scales are embedded in it, the body becomes spotted and mottled with red and orange, and large black spots edged with white are also developed. Such male breeding Salmon are known as 'Red-fish', and the ripe females, which are darker in colour, as 'Black-fish'. Another important change is in the character of the flesh. In a freshly run fish, that is to say, in a Salmon which has just left the sea, the muscles are firm and red, with a good store of fat in the tissues, but as the time for spawning draws near this fat is used up and the flesh itself becomes pale and watery.

Gravelly shallows where the stream runs fairly rapidly are selected as the spawning grounds, and on arrival the Salmon more or less segregate into pairs, the female setting to work to scoop out a shallow saucer-like depression, about 6 inches deep, by means of vigorous flapping movements of her body and tail. This may take several days. When finished, the female assumes a characteristic 'crouching' position and spawning takes place. The fertilized eggs sink and being somewhat sticky externally they adhere to the bottom. The female then loosely covers the eggs with fine gravel, through which they can be properly aerated by the swiftly flowing water of the stream. The whole process is repeated at intervals of a few minutes, the fish moving gradually farther up stream at each spawning, until at the end of a period of one or two weeks all the eggs have been extruded and fertilised. The spawning beds or

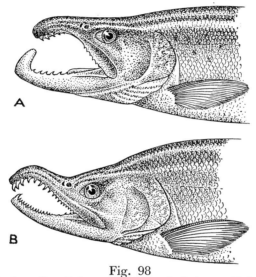

Fig. 98

Heads of male breeding Salmon. A. Atlantic Salmon (*Salmo salar*), x $\frac{1}{4}$; B. Pacific Sockeye Salmon (*Oncorhynchus nerka*), x $\frac{1}{6}$

troughs are known as 'redds' and that of a single pair of fish may be several feet long. During the spawning period the males are generally very fierce, driving away intruders with great pugnacity and vigour or engaging in formalised combats with other males. They do not always succeed, however, in keeping away the precociously ripe male parr which attend the female Salmon on the spawning grounds, and these take any opportunity to spawn with her.

The spawning process is a very exhausting one, particularly to the male fish, and few of the latter survive to breed a second time. The spent fish, which are known by the name of 'kelts' or 'slats', may be recognised by their large heads and general lean appearance. They are in a very enfeebled condition, and if the return journey to the sea be at all long or arduous many succumb to disease, injuries or starvation, or fall an easy prey to poachers, otters, or other enemies. Many females, however, succeed in regaining the sea, where regular feeding and abundant food soon restores them to their normal condition, the silver livery being again assumed. A Salmon which survives to spawn more than once does not necessarily do so at regular intervals, and whereas some may actually spawn in successive seasons, spending only a few months in the sea to recover their condition, others miss a year or even allow two or more years to elapse before the call of reproduction once more urges them to enter fresh water. Few Salmon live beyond eight or nine years, and it is exceedingly rare for any individual to spawn more than three times in its life. It is of interest to note that with few exceptions Salmon always return to the same rivers from which they originally came, but this powerful homing instinct often receives a check nowadays owing to the poisonous chemical effluents poured into some of our Salmon rivers by factories. In former times the Thames was a famous Salmon river, but pollution of its lower reaches made the ascent impossible, and the last fish was captured here in about 1833. Every year, however, a few Salmon make their appearance at the mouth of the Thames, and there can be little doubt that were the river to become miraculously purified these fish would run up once more and spawn in the upper reaches.

The Salmon of the Pacific coast of North America, a natural group (genus *Oncorhynchus*) of six species which includes the famous Quinnat or King Salmon (*O. tschawtyscha*) have somewhat similar breeding habits, although many of the features of their spawning cycle are more accentuated. The Quinnat has its spawning run in late spring or early summer at the age of about four years and at an average weight of 22 lbs. Those individuals which run first have the greatest distance to travel, and in the Yukon the spawning grounds are situated near Caribou Crossing and Lake Bennett, a distance of no less than 2250 miles from the sea. The Sock-eye Salmon or Red-Fish (*O. nerka*) also runs in the spring, ascending the rivers for 1500 miles or more, but the remaining species—the Silver Salmon (*O. kisutch*), Dog Salmon (*O. keta*), Humpback Salmon (*O. gorbuscha*), and Masu (*O. masou*)—all ascend the rivers in the autumn and do not make such long journeys, the longest (Humpback) being about 200 miles. The differences between the sexes in the breeding season are more marked than in our own species, the males of the Sock-eye or Red-fish being hump-backed, with sunken scales, much enlarged, hooked, bent or twisted jaws, and huge dog-like teeth [Fig. 98B]. The reproductive act seems to be more exhausting to these fishes, for after spawning the male and female drift helplessly downstream tail foremost, and no fish, either male or female, succeeds in regaining the sea. If the spawning grounds lie far inland the bodies of the fish may be covered with bruises even before they reach them, and on these injuries patches of deadly fungus are developed; the fins may be mutilated, the eyes injured or destroyed, the gills heavily infested with parasitic worms, and the flesh white from loss of oil. Thus, as soon as the reproductive act is accomplished, sometimes even before, all of them die, and in some rivers the corpses of spent fish may be observed lining the banks for miles, piled, in some cases, to the height of several feet.

The Sea Lamprey (*Petromyzon*) will serve as another example of an anadromous animal whose spawning habits are of special interest. They ascend the rivers in spring or early summer, in the British Isles running up our southern rivers from February to May and those of Scotland from May or June to July. They not infrequently facilitate their journey by stealing a ride on some large fish bound in the same direction, attaching themselves to the unfortunate victims with their sucker-like mouths and feeding on their flesh *en route*. As in the case of the Salmon, the Lampreys undergo considerable changes in colour at this time, and the two sexes differ markedly in appearance. They make their way to clear, shallow streams, where the bottom is sandy and strewn with pebbles and the current fairly rapid. Here a space is cleared in the bed by moving the stones a little way downstream. This so-called nest is usually oval or roughly circular in form, two or three feet in diameter, and slightly hollowed out, with a pile of stones just below it. Often the males are the first to arrive, and these commence nest-building on their own account; soon, however, each male is joined by a female who assists him in the operations. They move the stones by attaching themselves to them with their suctorial mouths, loosening them by powerful tugs and shakes, and finally dragging them to the pile below the nest. In rare cases a second female has been observed to assist the pair in this work, and the male has subsequently mated with both indiscriminately. The mating act is interesting, and takes place in the following manner. The female hangs on by her mouth to a large stone near the upper end of the nest, and the male seizes her by the top of the head in the same way, winding himself partly round her, the bodies of the two fishes being arranged so as to form an ellipse. They then vibrate the hinder parts of their bodies with great vigour, stirring up the fine sand in the process, and the ova and sperms are simultaneously extruded. The eggs are covered with a sticky substance to which particles of sand adhere, and they sink to the bottom of the nest. The adults now separate, and both at once commence to remove stones from above the nest and to place them on the pile below it, thus loosening a good deal of sand which is carried down by the stream and covers the fertilised eggs. The whole process is then repeated at short intervals until all the eggs have been extruded, when the parents leave the nest. They are by this time so exhausted that they fall an easy prey to enemies of all kinds, including other Lampreys, the wounds inflicted upon one another during mating are attacked by fungus, which invades and ultimately destroys the tissues, and indeed they are so completely debilitated that recovery is out of the question and every one dies.

The Common or Freshwater Eel (*Anguilla*) is another fish which may undertake a very extensive journey for spawning purposes, from which it never returns, but here the migration is in the opposite direction. Until quite recently the breeding habits of this species were a complete mystery, and some of the older naturalists were driven to advance the most extraordinary and unscientific theories as to the manner in which the Eels bred. So great was the interest in this matter that, from Aristotle onwards, almost every zoologist propounded his view as to when and where these fishes breed. Aristotle, pointed out that Eels had never been found with ripe milt or ova and seemed to possess no generative organs,[1]) and argued that they must be derived out of 'the bowels of the earth', presumably by some kind of spontaneous generation, a view which held favour with the great Izaak Walton. Oppian had somewhat more acceptable views on the subject, but these probably refer to the Lamprey.

> 'Strange the formation of the eely race
> That know no sex, yet love the close embrace.
> Their folded lengths around each other twine,
> Twist amorous knots, and slimy bodies joyn;
> Till the close strife brings off a frothy juice,
> The seed that must the wriggling kind produce,
> Regardless they their future offspring leave,
> But porous sands the spumy drops receive.
> That genial bed impregnates all the heap,
> And little eelets soon begin to creep.'

Pliny, asserting that the Eel has no sex, either masculine or feminine, suggests that, having lived their day, they rub themselves against rocks, and the pieces scraped off their bodies come to life. According to him, 'they have no other mode of procreation'. Other authors attributed the birth of Eels to the dews of May mornings, or to the transformation of hairs of horses which fell into the water, and others, again, decided that they sprang from the gills of other fishes. Still more extraordinary is the theory of a certain Mr. Cairncross, which appeared in 1862, this author being convinced that the 'progenitor of the Silver Eel is a small beetle'. Even sixty years ago the matter still remained a mystery, and all that was known was that large numbers of adult Eels made their way to the sea every autumn, and that in the spring shoals of elvers or little

---

[1]) The ovaries were first discovered in 1777, and the testes in 1874.

Eels, about two and a half inches in length, entered the rivers and made their way upstream. It was very naturally assumed that these elvers were the progeny of those adults that had descended to the sea a few months previously, and that breeding took place in the estuarine waters, a theory shown to be quite incorrect by subsequent discoveries. The first substantial hypothesis resulted from the patient and elaborate investigations of a Danish biologist, Dr. Johannes Schmidt, whose discoveries have provided one of the important biological events of this century. The life-history of the European Eel (*A. anguilla*), as elucidated by Dr. Schmidt, may be briefly described here, although consideration of the development and metamorphosis of the curious leaf-like larvae or Leptocephali will be deferred until a later chapter (*cf.* p. 262).

Two distinct kinds of Eels may be recognised: Yellow Eels, representing individuals in their ordinary feeding and growing coloration, and Silver Eels, which are those in their special breeding livery. Yellow Eels are found in both salt and fresh water, inhabiting the regions among rocks and weeds close to the shore, in harbours, estuaries, rivers, lakes, small brooks and even isolated ponds. They vary in length from a few inches to five feet or more, and the females grow to a much larger size than the males. Towards the autumn a certain number of Yellow Eels assume their breeding livery and prepare to undertake the journey to the spawning grounds. Of these, the males are generally about eight to ten years old, the females ten to eighteen years. They cease to feed, the eyes become enlarged and structurally take on the characters of those of deep-sea fishes, the lips become thinner, the snout sharper, the pectoral fins more pointed and blackish in colour, and the yellowish or greenish coloration is replaced by a metallic silvery sheen on the sides with a deep blackish back [Fig. 99]. All these characters become more and more accentuated as the time for breeding approaches, and internally the Silver Eel may be recognised by the developing reproductive organs and the shrunken alimentary tract. They make their way down to the rivers in the late summer and autumn. So powerful is the reproductive drive that even those individuals isolated in ponds and lakes will make an effort to reach the sea if a river be fairly near at hand, wriggling across stretches of meadow at night when the dew lies on the grass. Once in the sea knowledge of their activities is more conjectural, but it is believed that they migrate across the Atlantic Ocean to their breeding-ground which lies in the Western Atlantic, south of Bermuda. This stupendous journey may be as much as three thousand or even four thousand miles. It was formerly thought that the Eels from the countries bordering the Mediterranean spawned in the depths of that sea, but it is now known that this is not so. It is believed that the Eels spawn at a depth of about four hundred metres below the surface, and that a fairly high temperature (16–17° C.) is required for the proper development of the eggs, as well as water of a certain salinity. Spawning completed the parents die.

The eggs float for a time, and the young, when hatched out, feed and grow at a depth of 60–150 ft, and gradually move in an easterly direction, approaching the coasts of Western Europe when they are about three inches long and a little more than two years old. They now undergo a metamorphosis and turn into elvers or glass eels, about two and a half inches in length. These move inshore and commence the ascent of the rivers when about three years of age.

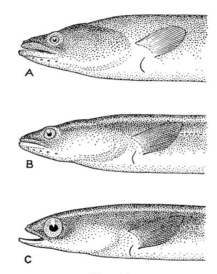

Fig. 99
Heads of Common Eel (*Anguilla anguilla*), x ¹/₃; A. Yellow eel; B. Silver eel; C. Mature eel.

The number of elvers passing up a river during these migrations or 'Eel-fares' is enormous; upwards of three tons are said to have been captured in a single day in the Gloucester district in 1886, and it has been estimated that more than fourteen thousand individuals go to make a pound weight. Few obstacles seem too great to be overcome by the elvers in their ascent, and they will wriggle over weirs etc., and even travel overland if the ground be wet in order to reach a suitable resting-place. Here they will feed and grow for some years until the time arrives for them to set off on their own breeding migration.

On the coasts and in the rivers of the Atlantic slope of North

America is another closely related species of Eel (*A. rostrata*), distinguished from its European ally by the smaller number of vertebrae in its backbone (but see p. 224). The breeding area of this species overlaps that of the European Eel, although its centre lies rather more to the south-west [Fig. 100]. In the Western Atlantic, however, larvae of both species are found living together. How is it, then, that these larvae sort themselves out, one kind going to America, the other migrating across the Atlantic to Europe? The explanation according to Schmidt lies in the fact that the American Eel grows more rapidly, and the development from egg to fully metamorphosed elver occupies only one year, as against

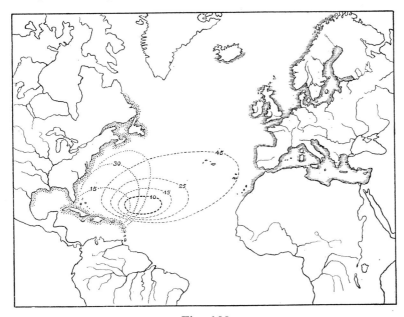

Fig. 100

Breeding-grounds and distribution of the European Freshwater Eel (*Anguilla anguilla*) and the American Eel (*Anguilla rostrata*). The continuous curved dotted lines show the limits of occurrence of the larvae (the European species represented thus - - - - -, the American species thus . . . . .). In the case of the European Eel, that marked 10 embraces an area that must include the actual spawning places of the species, for within it larvae less than 10 millimetres in length have been captured in large numbers, but never outside it. The numbers on the other curves denote the length of the larvae in millimetres captured therein. The adults of the European species occur in the countries outlined with short horizontal lines, those of the American species in the regions shown by dots outside the coast line. (Based on Schmidt's data; see text)

three years in the case of the European species. Thus, if the larva
of the European Eel travels in a westerly instead of an easterly
direction it will reach the coast of America long before it is ready
to change into an elver; and conversely, if the larva of the American
Eel migrates in an easterly direction it will undergo its metamorphosis in the middle of the Atlantic. In other words, the larval
life in each case is geared to the distance to be travelled, and the
length of that of the European species is to be regarded as a special
adaptation related to the great distance of the breeding-ground
from the coasts.

In 1959, a British zoologist, Dr. Denys Tucker, put forward
alternative ideas to explain the breeding habits of the Common
Eel. In essence, Tucker's hypothesis considers that the American
Eel (*Anguilla rostrata*) and the European Eel (*A. anguilla*) are really
one and the same species. The differences used to separate the
'species' (particularly the number of vertebrae, 103–111 for the
American and 110–119 for the European Eel) are due to environmental effects (especially a temperature 'shock') on the developing
embryo. He also considers that European Eels are physiologically
in no fit state to survive the presumed 3,500 mile journey from
Europe to the Sargasso sea. American Eels, on the other hand, are
in a condition to make the shorter journey from America to the
spawning grounds. Thus, Tucker considers that the European Eel
does not return to the ancestral spawning grounds and that the
populations of so-called European Eels are really derived from
American parents; the actual spawning sites determine whether the
developing embryos, and later the larvae, will be carried by currents
to Europe or America and also (because of the temperature conditions which the embryos will encounter in their ascent from the
deep-water spawning sites) whether they will show the 'American'
or 'European' characters of vertebral numbers and the age at
which they will be able to respond to the environmental changes
triggering-off metamorphosis.

Tucker's hypothesis is based on many carefully considered data
(some not available to Johannes Schmidt) and can at least claim
parity, as a hypothesis, with Schmidt's classical ideas. There the
matter must rest pending more field and experimental studies.
The discovery of sexually mature European Eels on the spawning
grounds would, of course, invalidate Tucker's ideas, whilst experimental work on the effects of temperature and vertebral numbers
in *Anguilla* would also help to clarify the position.

Among true freshwater fishes, members of the large and varied
Carp family (Cyprinidae) produce ova which adhere to weeds,
stones, and other objects. After spawning no further care of the
offspring is taken by the parents. A female Carp (*Cyprinus*) of four
pounds weight has about four hundred thousand eggs, one of

sixteen and a half pounds more than two million. The relations between the sexes in the breeding season may be described as polyandrous, for, although in certain species pairing may take place, in the majority each female is attended by two, three, or even more males, all of which take part in the fertilisation of the eggs when extruded. In many Cyprinid species the males develop hard, wart-like, nuptial tubercles at this season, which may be confined to the head or extend on to the skin of the back and sides. These excrescences, which sometimes disappear as soon as spawning has been completed, are of unknown function, but may be used in the battles between rival males, in nest building, or for a variety of purposes, including that of assisting to hold the female and to facilitate the extrusion of the ova by pressure on her body. All the European Carps and their allies breed in spring or early summer, and even the most sluggish become intensely active under the stress of sexual excitement, swimming at the surface and sometimes leaping clean out of the water. As the time for spawning approaches they congregate into shoals, and usually move into quiet, weedy shallows near the banks of rivers or in tributary streams. Roach (*Rutilus*) are said to mass so closely together that by their movements against one another they produce a kind of gentle hissing noise. In Norfolk they have been described as crowding together among the rushes that fringe the banks, in such dense multitudes 'that every instant one may see small ones raised half out of the water by the passage of larger fish.'

The breeding habits of other common British freshwater fishes are varied. Two (Stickleback and Miller's Thumb) are nest-builders and are dealt with in the next chapter. The Pike scatters its numerous eggs amongst aquatic plants but the Perch (*Perca fluviatilis*) lays its eggs in long gelatinous strings which become attached to the stems of plants or to other submerged objects. The Pope or Ruffe (*Acerina cernua*), a relative of the Perch, does not produce egg strings; the eggs adhere singly to sunken branches, plants or stones. Little is known about the breeding biology of the two Loaches (Cobitidae) occurring in Britain. The Stone Loach (*Nemachilus barbatula*) was once recorded as laying its eggs amongst the submerged roots of an old willow tree.

Finally, we may consider two of the most unusual types of breeding biology, a species that spawns out of water and a group of species which produce embryos capable of surviving in dried-up places. *Copeina arnoldi* (Characinoidei) the so-called Splashing Tetra spawns on the underside of leaves overhanging the water surface. The male and female jump together and rest for a moment on the lower surface of the leaf. At this point the adhesive eggs are shed and fertilized. The parents fall back into the water but the male remains near the leaf splashing drops of water on to it with his tail.

After two to three days the eggs hatch and the larvae fall into the water. *Copeina arnoldi* is found in the Brazilian Amazon and in Venezuela; it is the only species of the genus with this type of spawning behaviour.

In Tropical Africa and South America there are a number of small Cyprinodont fishes which produce eggs capable of surviving for some time amongst the bottom detritus of dried-up streams and ponds. These are the 'Annual Fishes' whose adult life is usually confined to a single year. Spawning takes place just before the onset of the dry season. The fertilized eggs are buried in the bottom deposits and embryonic development continues until the water of the stream or pond has evaporated, a rapid process in a tropical dry season. Naturally the parent fishes are killed but the now dormant embryos are protected by the drought resistant egg membrane and are probably protected from complete desiccation by the small quantities of moisture trapped between the particles of soil and humus. Embryonic development is resumed with the return of the waters, the eggs hatching shortly after the floods and the young growing to spawn and die within that year. Aquarium observations suggest that even if there is no drought the adults die within a year of hatching, the whole biology of the species being geared to an annual life cycle. Although Annual Fishes have been known for more than thirty years we are still extremely ignorant about many aspects of their biology, especially from the view point of studies made in nature. So far most of our information has come from aquarium studies. In South America four genera (*Rachovia, Austrofundulus, Cynolebias* and *Pterolebias*) comprising some twenty-four species are known to be 'Annuals'; in Africa two genera (*Nothobranchius* and *Aphyosemion*) comprising at least eight species are 'Annuals' and doubtless many more species will be discovered.

REFERENCES

BERTIN, L. (1956). *Eels*. Cleaver-Hume Press, London.
FRASER, J. (1962). *Nature Adrift*, G. T. Foulis, London.
JONES, J. W. (1959). *The Salmon*. Collins, London.
MENZIES, W. J. M. (1931). *The Salmon*, Wm. Blackwood, Edinburgh and London.
TCHERNAVIN, V. (1938). Absorption of bones in the skull of Salmon, during their migration to rivers. *Fisheries, Scotland. Salmon. Fish.*, No. 6.
TUCKER, D. W. (1959). A new solution to the Atlantic Eel problem. *Nature*, **183**, 495–501.

CHAPTER 14

PAIRING, COURTSHIP AND PARENTAL CARE

Those fishes in which there is a definite courtship very often show marked differences in the two sexes. These may be of two kinds; (1) structural peculiarities directly concerned with the fertilisation of the ova, generally taking the form of special male organs for introducing the milt into the body of the female; and (2) structural differences, peculiarities of colour etc., having no connection with sexual union but concerned more with courtship and display, or with the battles which take place between rival males. The so-called "claspers" of a Shark are examples of the first type, the bright colours of male Sticklebacks at spawning time of the second.

In all Selachians the fertilisation of the ova takes place within the female's body, and there is consequently a definite sexual union. The mature males are provided with special organs, the 'claspers' or mixopterygia, appendages of the pelvic fins [Fig. 101]. Each has an internal cartilaginous skeleton, and along the whole length runs a groove or canal, leading from a glandular sac at its base. During copulation the two grooves or canals are placed close together, both the claspers are thrust into the cloacal aperture of the female, and the seminal fluid is introduced into the oviducts. In addition to the mixopterygia which they possess in common with the Sharks and Rays, the Chimaeras (Holocephali) are provided with other claspers: the front portion of each pelvic fin is modified and separated off to form an organ provided with two large dermal denticles, which can be withdrawn into a shallow glandular pouch in front of the fin; the head is surmounted by a curious clublike appendage, the frontal or cephalic clasper, armed with a group of curved spines, and this can be lowered into a depression in the skin when not required [Fig. 73]. Distinct marks and scratches that have been observed on the skin of female Chimaeras at the base of the dorsal fin are believed to have been caused by the frontal claspers of the males, who probably make use of these organs to retain their hold when curling their bodies round those of their mates during coition.

Apart from the mixopterygia, sexual differences are rare in Selachians, but in many of the Rays the males are provided with a

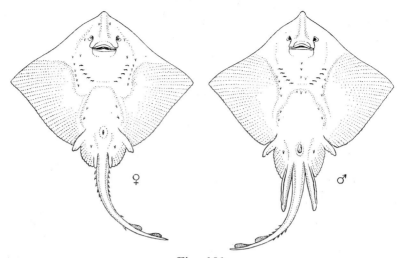

Fig. 101
Thornback Ray (*Raia clavata*), x ¹/₈. Ventral views of male and female.

patch of sharp spines on the upper surface of each pectoral fin, and
this is entirely wanting in the other sex.   These spines probably
help to hold the female when the male embraces her with his
'wings' during copulation. In some species the form and arrangement of the spines on the body and tail differs in the two sexes,
and in the Thornback Ray (*Raia clavata*) the teeth of the male are
quite unlike those of the female, although alike in immature
individuals of both sexes (*cf.* p. 108).

    Among Bony Fishes intromittent organs (*i.e.* organs for introducing
the spermatozoa into the body of the female) naturally occur only
in those fishes in which fertilisation of the eggs is internal. A simple
organ of this nature is provided by the prolongation or the genital
or urino-genital orifice to form a conical papilla or a more or less
lengthy tube.   In some of the Toothed Carps or Cyprinodonts
the duct from the male reproductive organ is produced as a tube
to the end of the anterior rays of the anal fin, and in the Four-
eyed Fish (*Anableps*) this tube is covered with scales [Fig. 69D]. The
genital aperture of the female Four-eyed Fish is covered by a
special scale, the foricula, which is free on one side but not on
the other. In some individuals the opening beneath the scale is on
the right side, in others on the left, while among the males some
have the intromittent organ turned towards the right, some towards
the opposite side. Thus, in order to transfer the milt to the genital
duct of the female, copulation takes place sideways.   In many
South American and Central American Cyprinodonts (subfamily

Poeciliinae) the males are provided with complicated intromittent organs developed from modified anal fin rays [Fig. 102A].   The third, fourth and fifth rays of the fin are enlarged and produced forming the margin of a groove or closed tube into which the genital duct opens.   The rays may end in curved hooks, spines, or barbs, the function of which at least in some species seems to be connected with keeping the organ in position during copulation. The whole organ is freely movable, and is supported internally by bony processes. The genital aperture is placed just in front of the base of the anal fin, and may be covered by the pelvic fins, which take part in conveying the seminal fluid into the groove. Another type of Cyprinodont (*Phallostethus*), ranging from the Malay Peninsula to the Philippines, is remarkable for the possession by the male of a large fleshy appendage known as the priapium, which is situated below the head and chest.   This appendage has a complicated internal skeleton of its own, and contains not only the ducts from the kidneys and reproductive organs, but also the terminal parts and opening of the intestine. In addition, there are external movable bony appendages which may serve to grasp the female during intercourse, the priapium serving as an intromittent organ.   As in the case of the intromittent organ of the Four-eyed fish, the priapium is placed either to the right or to the left, but is never symmetrical in position.

All Cyprinodonts with complicated intromittent organs retain the fertilised ova within their bodies, and the young are born in a relatively advanced stage of development.   There are, however, a number of forms in which eggs are extruded and fertilisation takes place externally.   Here the differences between the sexes are concerned merely with the coloration or with the shape of the fins [Fig. 102B], but there is a definite pairing of male and female,

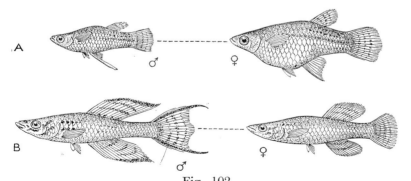

Fig. 102
Sexual differences in Toothcarps (Cyprinodonts). A. Male and female Gambusia (*Gambusia* sp.), x 1; B. Male and female *Aphyosemion* sp., x 1

usually an elaborate courtship, and spawning takes place in the following manner. The two fishes lie side by side, the heads looking in the same direction, and the male clasps his partner by folding his dorsal and anal fins across her body, while the paired fins also may interlock. The ova and sperms are then extruded simultaneously in such close proximity that fertilisation of the vast majority of the eggs is certain.

The second type of difference between the sexes, the secondary sexual characters, which have no connection with actual union between male and female, may be present during the whole of adult life, but are frequently developed only as the spawning season approaches, and are lost as soon as this is over. The difference in the size of the two sexes is worthy of notice. In the great majority of Bony Fishes the females are larger than the males, and in some Cyprinids she may be as much as six times as large as her mate, whilst in certain Cyprinodonts the disparity in bulk is even more marked. In some fishes, however, of which the Cod, Haddock, and Angler (*Lophius*) may be mentioned, the males are slightly the larger. One of the commonest of the secondary sexual differences in fishes is concerned with the coloration of the body and fins, the males almost always having a brighter livery than their mates. This is the case in nearly all the Cyprinodonts, Cichlids, Labyrinth-fishes, many Damsel-fishes (Pomacentridae), Wrasses (Labridae) and so on (*cf.* p. 187). Blue, red, green, black and silvery-white pigments are specially characteristic of the males, whereas the females generally exhibit dull, olivaceous, or variously mottled hues. In some fishes, notably in some of the Wrasses (Labridae) and in the Dragonets (Callionymidae), not only are the colours different, but also the characteristic markings. In our own Cuckoo Wrasse (*Labrus mixtus*), to mention only one example, the male is yellow or orange tinged with red, with five or six blue bands radiating backwards from the eye; the fins are yellow or orange with a large blue blotch on the front part of the dorsal fin. The female is reddish, there are no blue bands, but two or three large black spots are present on the back, below the hinder part of the dorsal fin. In many of the Cyprinids the males become much brighter during the spawning season, chiefly through the development of bright red or blue pigment, especially in the lower parts of the body, and these colours may become very much intensified during the actual courtship, with its attendant emotional excitement. In the little Three-spined Stickleback (*Gasterosteus aculeatus*) both sexes change their colours in the breeding season, the dark greenish colour of the back extending on to the sides in the form of vertical bars, whilst the lower parts change from a silvery white to pale yellowish in the female and a brilliant red in the male. In the Ten-spined Stickleback (*G. pungitius*) the males change from a greenish-olive powdered with small black dots to a dark brownish. Among other changes in livery, that of the breeding Salmon (*Salmo*) has already been described (*cf.* p. 216) and there are other examples too numerous and varied to be mentioned in detail here. The male Bow-fin (*Amia*) of North America may be recognised quite readily by his smaller size and by the presence of a deep black spot ringed with white at the base of the caudal fin, which although present throughout the life of the fish, becomes much more intense as the spawning season draws near.

Differences in the form of the fins are nearly as common among fishes which indulge in pairing or courtship as differences in coloration, those of the male always being larger and more brightly

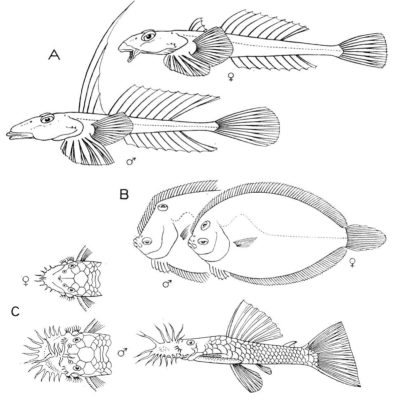

Fig. 103   SECONDARY SEXUAL CHARACTERS
A. Male and female of the Common Dragonet (*Callionymus lyra*);
B. Female, and head of male of *Bothus podas*; C. Male, and heads of male and female of Mailed Cat-fish (*Xenocara occidentalis*). All x *ca* 1/3

marked. In many Cichlids and Cyprinodonts some of the rays of the dorsal and anal fins may be prolonged to form fine streamers, and the membrane provided with eye-like spots of red, blue or yellow. In some of the Mailed Cat-fishes (Loricariidae) the sexual differences are even more marked, affecting the shape of the snout, the form of the mouth and lips, the development of bristles on the head and fins, or of fleshy tentacles on the snout [Fig. 103c]. In the Scald-fish (*Arnoglossus*), and in some other Flat-fishes, the first few rays of the dorsal fin, as well as some of the rays of the pelvics, are prolonged to form more or less lengthy filaments in the male; in the closely related genus *Bothus* the males are provided with spines on the snout and have the eyes much wider apart than the females, while the upper rays of the pectoral fin of the coloured side are frequently very elongate [Fig. 103b]. The Sword-tailed Minnow (*Xiphophorus*) from Mexico and Central America, a favourite Cyprinodont for the aquarium, has the lower lobe of the caudal fin drawn out to form a long blade-like filament in the male, and in another species of the same family (*Mollienesia*) the dorsal fin is enlarged in the male to form a relatively huge, sail-like structure marked with brilliant ocelli.

Among the characteristic peculiarities of the males, developed only as the breeding season approaches, the horny tubercles on the head and body of many Cyprinids, and the hooked jaws and enlarged teeth of the Salmon have already been described (*cf.* p. 225). Some male Cichlids (Cichlidae) Sparids, Scarids and Labrids develop a huge fleshy hump on the forehead, which is gradually resorbed after spawning in some species and retained throughout life in others. A few Cichlids have a much branched structure in the region of the vent, brilliantly coloured, generally with orange. It has been supposed that this is used for brushing the milt on to the ova, but recent studies show that it serves to attract the female, who by mouthing at it draws sperms into her mouth, there to fertilize the eggs (see p. 238) she has just laid and picked up. In the male of the South American Lung-fish (*Lepidosiren*) the pelvic fins are covered during the breeding season with bright scarlet processes, richly supplied with blood-vessels (*cf.* p. 236).

Sexual differences in the dentition are also known. In some Gobies and Blennies the males have enlarged anterior (canine) teeth, resembling small scimitars. More remarkable is the case of the Ray (*Raia clavata*) where the male has pointed teeth and females and juveniles have flattened and molar-like teeth.

The courtship of the female by the male may consist merely in swimming round and round in her vicinity, betraying a varying degree of sexual excitement, or may take the form of a most elaborate display comparable to the nuptial antics of some birds.

The relationship, however, only appears to last for the period of pairing or, at the most, for one breeding season, and there is nothing that can be described as personal affection between the two fishes. The courtship habits of the little Fighting-fish (*Betta*) of Siam are worthy of special mention [Fig. 104]. The brilliantly coloured male swims round and round his mate, his beautiful fins

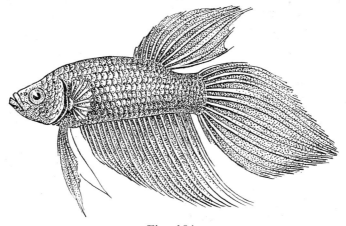

Fig. 104

Siamese Fighting-fish (*Betta splendens*), x 1¹/₄. (From a photograph)

extended to their utmost, his mouth wide open, the branchiostegal membranes protruded and the bright-red gills visible beneath. During these preliminary movements the already vivid hues become even more intensified and his body and fins have been described as 'resplendent with iridescent colours and quivering with excitement'. Should the female not respond, as sometimes happens, the grace of his movements is soon lost and he attacks the female with slaps and bites. To quote Bertin: 'la parade nuptiale resemble plus alors à un combat qu'à un jeu d'amour'.

Among marine fishes courtship is apparently rare, but the Common Dragonet (*Callionymus*) of our own coasts indulges in elaborate nuptial displays, yet afterwards abandons the eggs to float about in the sea, showing no concern whatsoever for the fate of the offspring. The male is about twelve inches in length, yellowish or orange, with two blue stripes along each side of the body and a row of light-blue or green spots above; the head is marked with spots or stripes of violet or blue, and the fins, which are larger than those of the female, the first dorsal being greatly prolonged, are variously spotted and banded with yellow, green and blue [Fig. 103A]. The mature female is about eight inches long, dull yellowish-brown passing into white beneath, ornamented with greenish spots enclosed in dark-brown rings. So different are the two sexes that they were originally regarded as distinct species, and known as the Gemmeous and Sordid Dragonet respectively. At the time of courting the male rushes about in a state of great excitement, swimming round the female, erecting all his fins, and displaying his highly intensified colours. Finally, this display stimulates the female and she signals her readiness to mate. The male lifts his mate by placing his pelvic fin beneath hers, and at first the two fishes swim obliquely towards the surface of the water side by side. Then their positions change somewhat, the ascent becomes vertical and the anal fins of the two fishes are brought together forming a gutter into which the eggs and sperm are shed. The fertilized eggs float freely to the surface where development continues.

In many species (but particularly those in which a nest is made or a spawning territory is established) the males become very pugnacious during the breeding period. However, this pugnacity rarely leads to bloodshed and the combats are generally stylized displays of threat. Reports of such fights ending mortally, with one participant ripped open or torn to pieces, are either due to faulty observation or the observation of the rare case when severe physical damage is done.

Perhaps the most pugnacious fishes are the little Siamese fighters (*Betta*). Certainly, under artificial conditions the males of this species do inflict considerable damage on one another. Thus, males are pitted against one another by the natives for sport, after the manner of fighting-cocks. Considerable sums of money, to say nothing of their own persons and families, were wagered on the results of the combats. In a state of quiet the colours of the fish are rather dull, but if two be placed in the same aquarium, or if one sees its own image in a looking-glass, the fins and whole body shine with dazzling, metallic hues, and it will make repeated darts at its real or fancied antagonist.

The males of many of the Gobies (Gobiidae) also engage in hectic fights, rushing at each other and biting viciously, the victor afterwards spreading his fins and showing off his colours to the female. Some of the male Klip-fishes (*Clinus*) of South Africa seem to fight according to well-defined rules, the preliminary position adopted being side by side or face to face; in the latter case the mouth is wide open and the gill-covers raised, so that the opercular spots look like a pair of eyes. They may engage in several 'rounds' with short intervals of rest, but finally one of them backs away and leaves the field to his conqueror.

Courtship displays and territorial boundary fights are no haphazard affairs and the procedures involved are clearly defined displays of colour and body position which are recognised by the participants. Fish behaviour studies are now a well established research field in animal psychology.

As a general rule, in those fishes in which courtship and pairing takes place at the breeding season the number of eggs produced by a single female is small or moderate, and these are cared for to a greater or lesser extent by one or other of the parents. This parental care may take the form of constructing some sort of nest for the reception of the fertilized eggs (varying from a simple hollow scooped out in the gravelly bed of a stream to a beautiful and elaborate structure), or of some other precautions tending to ensure the safety of the eggs or offspring until they are old enough to take care of themselves.

The Darters (*Etheostoma*), pretty little fishes of the family Percidae, found in the rivers of eastern North America, congregate together in gravelly shallows at the spawning season, the larger males each selecting a suitable place which they regard as their own domain, repelling with vigour any attempt by a rival male to dispute their claim. Any female entering the territory is allowed to remain, and she constructs a kind of trough with her body into which she sinks as the eggs are extruded. These are promptly fertilised by the male, and being covered with a sticky substance, they adhere to the stones. The extent to which the Salmon and Trout care for their offspring is almost equally primitive, and has been described already. Many of the North American Cyprinids, known as Chubs and Shiners, construct somewhat more elaborate nests composed of large heaps of stones, some of which may weigh nearly eight ounces, but the eggs are here again left to the mercy of physical conditions, to say nothing of predaceous fishes.

The freshwater Sun-fishes (Centrarchidae) scoop out a shallow basin-like nest, from the bottom of which all pebbles are carefully removed, leaving a layer of fine sand or gravel to which the fertilised eggs adhere. The work is carried out entirely by the male, who remains to guard the eggs until the young are hatched.

Males of Cichlids (Cichlidae) also construct relatively simple nests, either as a scooped-out hollow or as a hollow on top of a mound. The shape and form of the nest is, of course, partly determined by the nature of the bottom but is nevertheless often characteristic of the species. In mouth-brooding species (see p. 238) the nest serves merely as a spawning site, but in non-mouth brooding species the ova are left in the nest and guarded by both parents. More than one nest may be dug and the eggs transported, in the mouth of a parent, from one nest to another.

Other freshwater fishes make a nest by clearing a space among aquatic vegetation. That of the African Osteoglossid (*Clupisudis*) is built in about two feet of water, is as much as four feet across, and the walls, which are several inches thick, are made up of the stems of grasses removed by the fish from the centre, the floor being formed by the smooth, bare ground of the swamp. One of the Mormyrids (*Gymnarchus*) constructs a floating nest of large size, the walls projecting several inches above the surface of the water at two sides and one end, the opposite end, forming the entrance, being some six inches below the water.

Two species of African Lung-fish (*Protopterus annectens* and *P. aethiopicus*) prepare a simple but often deep pit or hole, usually in swampy places, along river banks, lake shores, or in true swamps. It seems that the male alone is responsible for preparing the nest, but that he may spawn with two or three females. After spawning, the male remains in the nest, aerating the water by his body movements and even stirring the surface by slow slapping movements of his tail. He also protects the young by snapping at any creature that may attempt to enter the nest from above or below. But, despite this assiduous protection against predators, some manage to slip in and catch the young as they surface to breathe. Perhaps the most successful predator is a species of water spider which is able to station itself without disturbing the water and thus arousing the watchful male.

A third species (*Protopterus dolloi*) prepares a more elaborate nest in the form of a closed burrow in swamp soil. The form of this nest rather closely resembles that of the South American Lung-fish (*Lepidosiren paradoxa*). Unlike the related African species, the breeding male of the South American form develops highly vascularized filaments on the pelvic fins. The function of these gill-like structures is still debated. Some suggest that they may serve to secrete oxygen from the fish's blood into the water and thus increase the oxygen content of the water which is low and rapidly depleted by the developing eggs. Other workers suggest that the filaments act as gills and that the male obtains oxygen from the water, thus reducing the necessity of his making frequent trips to the surface in order to gulp air. Surprisingly, very little research and experiment has been done to elucidate this intriguing question.

The male Bow-fin of North America (*Amia*) constructs a crude, circular nest, usually placed at the swampy end of a lake where there is an abundance of aquatic herbage, and when this is completed he is attended by one or more females, the fertilised eggs adhering to the leaves and roots at the bottom of the hollow. They are guarded henceforward by the male, who remains constantly either on the nest itself or in a passage through the reeds leading to it. After the young are hatched they are said to leave the nest in a body, still under the protection of the watchful male, who keeps them together in a compact mass by circling slowly around them. Many of the Cat-fishes (Amiuridae) of North

America excavate a crude nest in the mud, a labour in which both parents share, and which may mean two or three days of incessant work. Sometimes this nest is placed in crevices in the river banks, beneath logs, stones, or even in pails or other receptacles lying in the water.

The Three-spined Stickleback (*Gasterosteus aculeatus*) constructs a much more elaborate nest, and as the breeding habits of this fish are of special interest, they may be described in some detail. The construction of the nest is undertaken entirely by the male, who sets about his duty before courtship is begun, selecting a suitable site, such as one among the stems of aquatic plants where the water flows regularly but not too swiftly, in quiet shallows, or in rock-pools which are only reached by the sea at high tides.

Next, the male collects nest material (usually algae or other aquatic plants) and presses them into a small pit he has made in the cleared area. At intervals, the fish swims across the plant-mass, secreting a sticky substance produced by the kidneys. This secretion sticks the pieces of plant together. When a small pile of plant material has been assembled, the male burrows his way through the centre, thereby making a small tunnel into which he will eventually coax a ripe female, and where she will lay the eggs.

Once the eggs are fertilized, the female departs and all parental care devolves upon the male. At first he 'fans' the developing embryos, sending a constant stream of water through the nest. When the eggs hatch and the young larvae become active (seven or eight days after fertilization) the male stops his fanning activities and starts to guard the brood. If a young fish should stray from the shoal, the male chases after it and sucks it into his mouth. The truant is then spat back among the brood. During the next fourteen days or so, the young Sticklebacks become more active and stray further from the nest site. At first the male actively keeps the brood together, but gradually his parental drive wanes until he finally abandons the young altogether.

The Fifteen-spined Stickleback (*Spinachia*), an exclusively marine form, builds an elaborate nest from a suitable branch of seaweed, binding the fronds of weed with the sticky secretion from the kidneys. The threads are passed round and round the fronds until they are finally bound together into a rough pear-shaped structure about the size of a man's clenched fist.

Many of the Labyrinth-fishes (Anabantoidei) make a most unusual type of nest, the male blowing bubbles of air and sticky mucus, which adhere together to form a floating mass of foam, dome-shaped or more or less flat on the upper surface. In the case of the little Fighting-fish (*Betta*), the elaborate courtship (see p. 233) is followed by the surrender of the female, who approaches her mate and suddenly assumes a vertical position; he then curves and tightens his body around her, and turns her upside down, but in a few moments and after the milt is extruded the pressure is relaxed and the male takes up position below the female. The eggs are extruded, and after being held for a few moments by the female to ensure fertilisation, are allowed to drop. Being heavier than water, they sink downward towards the waiting male. He catches the eggs in his mouth, and swims upwards, gives them a coating of mucus, and sticks them to the under side of the mass of foam. From three to seven ova are extruded at a time, and the process is repeated until some one hundred and fifty or two hundred are produced. They are then guarded by the male. The larvae remain adherent to the foamy nest for some time after hatching, and if any of them should begin to sink, they are caught and replaced by the watchful male, until they finally drop off when old enough to find food for themselves. The related Paradise-fish (*Macropodus*) has very similar breeding habits, but here the eggs are lighter than the water, and thus rise to the mass of bubbles without the intervention of the male. The female is completely inverted while the eggs are extruded, and any which fail to adhere to the nest are collected by one or both of the parents and placed in position.

The Bitterling (*Rhodeus*), a small Cyprinid found in the rivers of Central Europe, takes remarkable precautions to ensure the safety of its offspring [Fig. 105]. When the female is ready to spawn the oviduct is drawn out to form a long tube, acting as an ovipositor, by means of which the eggs are deposited within the valves of fresh-water pond mussels, where they are out of reach of enemies. The male fertilises the eggs after they have been extruded. In this situation they undergo their development, the respiratory current of water produced by the mussel serving to aerate the ova. The fry finally leave their temporary host about a month after the deposition of the eggs. It is interesting to note that the mussel's breeding season coincides with that of the Bitterling, and it is in the habit of throwing off its own embryos into the water, where they become attached to the gills of the Bitterling and there undergo their early stages of development.

Many of the Cichlids (Cichlidae) protect their eggs by carrying them in their mouths, thus ensuring their safety and perfect aeration at one and the same time. This duty is nearly always undertaken by the female, and even after hatching the young fry do not leave the shelter of her mouth. Later, they swim about in the water, keeping always within easy reach of her head, and should danger threaten they return to their refuge with extraordinary rapidity. Most of the Sea Cat-fishes (Ariidae) found on the coasts and in the rivers of North and South America have similar habits, but here it is always the male who undertakes the

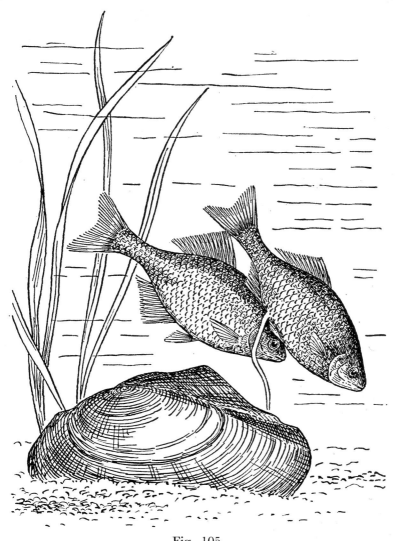

Fig. 105

Male and female Bitterling (*Rhodeus amarus*) with freshwater Pond
Mussel, x ²/₃. The female is about to deposit eggs. (From a photograph)

care of the eggs. These are produced in small numbers, and are of remarkable size, measuring as much as seventeen or eighteen millimetres in diameter in a species growing to a length of three or four feet. The eggs are carried about until hatched, and the male does not appear to take any food during this period. Mouth, or rather branchial brooding also occurs in the blind cave fishes of the family Amblyopsidae.

A unique form of parental care is shown by the South American Cichlid *Symphysodon discus* (the Discus or Pompadour fish). In addition to caring for the developing embryos, the parents allow the newly hatched larvae to feed on the mucus covering their bodies. Both parents share feeding duties, flicking the brood from one to the other. In aquarium-raised fishes this supply of food is utilized by the larvae for at least five weeks, even though other sources of food are available.

Apart from the Sticklebacks, nest building is the exception rather than the rule among marine fishes, and any sort of parental care is very rare. Some of the Wrasses (Labridae) are said to construct crude nests of seaweed, shells or stones, an operation in which both sexes take part. Many of the Gobies (Gobiidae), Blennies (Blenniidae), Bull-heads or Sculpins (Cottidae), and Cling-fishes (Gobiesocidae) nearly all of them inhabitants of rock-pools between tide-marks or in the case of the freshwater Miller's Thumb (*Cottus gobio*), of swift streams, provide for the safety of their eggs by depositing them in the dead shells of mussels, oysters etc., in crevices in the rocks, on the under sides of stones, on fronds of seaweed, or even within the broken 'bulbs' of the familiar Bladder-wrack. The male usually mounts guard, and in the case of some of the Sculpins (Cottidae) may actually 'brood' over them, clasping the egg-masses with his pectoral and pelvic fins, the inner surfaces of which are provided with asperities or hooks to enable him to obtain a firmer grip. Aeration of the eggs is another duty falling upon the male and is generally accomplished by fanning the surrounding water with the pectoral fins. The Common or Sand Goby (*Gobius minutus*) of our own shores makes a more elaborate shelter, the male first seeking a suitable shell, generally a cockle or small scallop, which he turns over so that the concave side is downwards. He then gets underneath it, clearing away the sand with his tail, until a little chamber has been constructed, communicating with the exterior by a single tunnel-like opening. Finally, he covers the whole structure with fine loose sand, and sets off in search of a suitable mate.

The Lump-sucker or 'Cock and Hen Paddle' (*Cyclopterus*) generally deposits its spawn in crevices in the rocks above the level of low water at spring tides. The large masses, containing anything from 80,000 or 136,000 eggs, vary in colour from dark brown to red, pink or pale yellow. For a portion of each tide the eggs are, of course, uncovered, and are preyed upon by numerous enemies in the shape of starlings, rooks, seagulls, and rats, whilst at high water they may be devoured by various fishes. It is doubtful, however, whether there are many better cases of parental devotion than that of the male Lump-sucker. For several weeks he devotes himself to the care of the eggs, rarely leaving his post, from time to time pressing his head into the clump of spawn to allow the water to

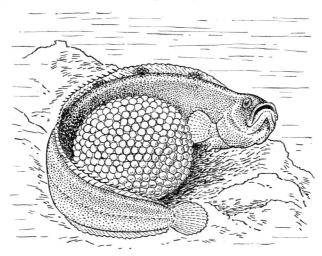

Fig. 106
Gunnel or Butterfish (*Pholis gunnellus*) with a mass of spawn, x ¹/₂

penetrate to the centre, and thus ensuring the proper aeration of the eggs, a process which he further helps by fanning them with his pectoral fins. He removes any animals such as crabs, star-fishes, and molluscs which may crawl on to the spawn, and defends it with intense vigour against predators both large and small.

The Gunnel or Butter-fish (*Pholis*) an elongate Blenny-like fish, some ten inches in length, is in the habit of rolling its mass of spawn into a ball, about the size of a Brazil nut, an operation in which both parents may assist. Afterwards, one of them remains on guard, coiled round the eggs, but it is not certain whether this is the male or the female, or whether both take their turn. Often the mass of eggs, accompanied by the parent fish may be found between the valves of empty oyster shells, or in the holes made by boring molluscs in the rocks. [Fig. 106].

In the Indo-Pacific genus *Kurtus* (Kurtoidei, Perciformes), the male is provided with a bony hook projecting from the forehead, supported by a special process of the skull. On extrusion the eggs are formed into two bunches by filamentous processes from the egg membranes. This egg mass becomes attached to the hook in such a manner that one bunch of eggs lies on either side of the male as he swims about in the water.

A Cat-fish (*Platystacus*), of the rivers of Brazil and the Guianas, exhibits a different method of caring for the eggs, but here the female is entirely responsible for their safety. During the breeding season the skin of the lower surface of her body becomes very swollen and tender, assuming a soft spongy condition. As soon as the eggs have been extruded and fertilised, she lies on them, presses them into this soft tissue, and each egg becomes attached to the skin by a small, stalked cup, remaining thus fixed until hatched. Each cup is well supplied with blood-vessels and may assist in nourishing the embryo.

In Pipe-fishes (Syngnathidae) the care of the eggs and fry is always undertaken by the male fish, who carries them about until hatched, either lodged within a simple groove lined with soft skin in the lower surface of the abdomen, or in a special pouch closed by flaps of skin and situated on the under side of the trunk or tail. [Fig. 107*d*]. In the Florida Pipe-fish (*Syngnathus*), in which the whole process has been observed, mating is preceded by an elaborate courtship. The two fishes swim round in nearly vertical positions,

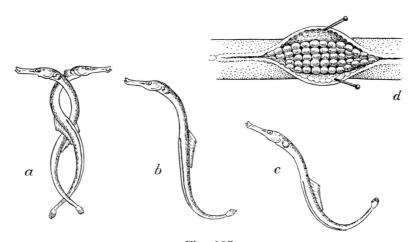

Fig. 107
Breeding habits of the Florida Pipe-fish (*Syngnathus floridae*). *a*. Position of fishes during transfer of eggs; *b*. Attitude assumed by male while moving eggs backward in the pouch; *c*. Position of male during period of rest following several egg transfers, x *ca* ¹/₄. (After Gudger); *d*. Portion of pouch opened to show eggs.

but with the head and shoulder region bent forward. They then swim slowly past one another, their bodies come into contact, the male bending his body around the female, frequently caressing his mate with his snout. Just before the actual transfer of ova takes place, the male becomes violently excited, wriggles his body about in corkscrew fashion, and rubs the belly of the female with his snout. This demonstration is repeated several times, the fishes becoming more and more excited, until finally the transfer [Fig. 107a] occurs, after which the fishes separate, to commence the process again after an interval of a few minutes. During the embrace, when the bodies of the two fishes are intertwined, the protruding oviduct of the female is rapidly thrust into the small opening at the front end of the male's pouch, and the eggs are thus transferred. By a series of contortions the male then succeeds in moving the eggs to the hinder end of the pouch [Fig. 107b], and then the whole process is repeated until the pouch is full, after which the male appears to be very exhausted and is quiescent for some time [Fig. 107c].

The eggs remain in the pouch until hatched, but even after this event the fry may occupy it for some time, and, when they are able to swim freely in the sea, will still return to its shelter when danger threatens.

It is of interest to note that something of the habits of the Pipe-fish (the *Belone* of the Greeks and the *Acus* of the Romans) was known to Aristotle, although his interpretation of the facts may have been rather wide of the mark. 'That fish which is called *Belone*' he states, 'at the season of reproduction, bursts asunder, and in this way the ova escape; for the fish has a division beneath the stomach and bowels like the serpents called typhlinae. When it has produced its ova it survives and the wound heals up again'.

In a related family (Solenostomidae) the female takes care of the eggs, keeping them in a pouch formed by the pelvic fins, the inside of the chamber being provided with numerous long filamentous processes, which serve to assist in retaining the eggs in position. In the Sea Horses (*Hippocampus*), as in the Pipe-fishes, it is the male who looks after the eggs and young, the former being received into the brood-pouch beneath the tail, where they remain until hatched. At the breeding season this pouch becomes thickened and well supplied with blood-vessels, thus being prepared for the reception of the eggs. At the same time the flesh around the opening of the genital ducts in the female becomes somewhat extended to form a genital papilla, which acts as a kind of intro-mittent organ for the transfer of her ova to the male. The final extrusion of the young fish from the pouch is a much more protracted affair than in the Pipe-fishes, and may occupy several hours, only five or six individuals being set free at a time. The small aperture

of the sac-like pouch makes it impossible for the young to return
to its shelter, and it is probable that they are retained for a longer
period than in the case of the Pipe-fishes.

Finally, mention must be made of the remarkable sex relationships in the deep-sea Ceratioid Angler-fishes [Fig. 108]. So far,
the only adult males to be found have been virtually parasitic
on females. The males are mere dwarfs and are firmly attached to
the body of the female. There is almost complete fusion between
the skin around the jaws of the male and the body skin of the female,
although on each side there is a small aperture through which the
male draws in water for respiration. The male apparently does not
depend on the female for oxygen, but as there is a placenta-like
contact between the blood-vessels of the two fishes it seems that
the female provides the male with nourishment. The male's body
and sensory organs are also poorly developed and in fact he is
little more than an attached testis.

Free living but sexually immature males are known. They have
well-developed eyes and fins, but lack the characteristic angling
device, and the alimentary tract is little developed.

The life history of one Ceratioid Angler, *Ceratias holboeli*, is fairly
well known. Spawning is restricted to the summer months and
probably takes place in deep water. The fertilized eggs float to
the surface waters and here further development takes place and
the young hatch. Even in the larvae the sexes can be distinguished
since the females show the beginnings of the angling device.

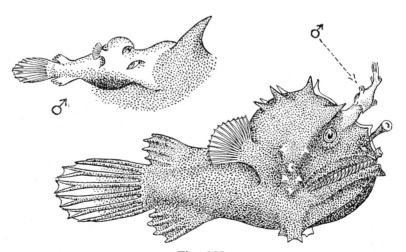

Fig. 108

A ceratioid Angler-fish (*Photocorynus spiniceps*): female with parasitic
male, x 1¹/₂ (Male x 3)

When the larvae are about a third of an inch long, metamorphosis takes place, the sexual differences become more pronounced and the small fishes sink to depths of 3,000 and more feet, where metamorphosis is completed. At this stage, the male is characterized by its long, slender body and the development of larger, gripping denticles around its mouth. The female develops a spiny skin and the rod and light become more clearly developed. We do not know at what stage the adolescent males seek out their females, but it does seem likely that they attach themselves at about this period in their development.

When both fishes are mature, the size discrepancy between the sexes is outstanding. For example, the largest known male is little more than six inches long and is attached to a female of more than three feet. More than one male may fuse with a female and the point of attachment to her body varies. Sometimes the male fuses with the belly of the female, sometimes to the sides of the head or in the region of the gill-openings.

The fate of males which do not find a mate is unknown but we can infer (since no free swimming adults have been found) that death is the most likely alternative.

This unusual mode of life probably evolved in response to the habits and environment of the fishes. Living in the comparative darkness of the ocean's middle layers and sluggish in their habits, the chances of a mature fish finding a mate of its own species would be greatly reduced. The answer seems to have been provided by this form of irrevocable 'child-marriage' contracted at the one time when the individuals occur together in some numbers.

References

BAERENDS, G. P. and BAERENDS–VAN ROON. (1950). An introduction to the study of the ethology of cichlid fishes. *Supplement 1 to Behaviour.* E. J. Brill, Leiden.

GREENWOOD, P. H. (1958). Reproduction in the East African Lung-fish *Protopterus aethiopicus* Heckel. *Proc. zool. Soc. Lond.* **130**, 547–567.

CHAPTER 15

DEVELOPMENT

BY THE TERM development is understood all those changes that take place in the egg or ovum from the moment it is fertilised until the fish reaches maturity. As has been already pointed out, the process of fertilisation consists in the union of the two kinds of sex-cells or gametes, the ovum of the female and the sperm of the male. The early history of these gametes cannot be detailed here, and it must suffice to point out that they are at first similar to the ordinary body-cells, and only later become specialised for their reproductive functions. Each gamete is a single cell, consisting of a ground substance or cytoplasm with its contained nucleus. The ovum is large, being distended with yolk, and is immobile. The sperm on the other hand, has no such food reserve, and is consequently very much smaller. It consists of a head (which may be globular, elliptical, wavy, or rod-like in shape) composed largely of nuclear material and a propelling, whip-like tail [Fig. 109]. The ovum is generally provided with a minute aperture or micropyle in its surrounding membrane, situated at one of the poles, through which the head of the sperm makes its entry, the tail, having played its part in bringing the two together, being left outside to die. The nuclei of egg and sperm then fuse and the single cell thus formed divides into two. This first division initiates a long series of cell divisions which form the foundations and materials from which the new individual will develop.

The eggs of fishes present great diversity, not only in size and shape, but in the manner in which they are protected [Fig. 110]. In the Cyclostomes there is a very striking difference in the characters of the eggs in the two families. In the Lampreys (Petromyzonidae) they are minute, spherical, and enclosed in delicate membranes, the average size being about one millimetre (one-twenty-fifth of an inch) in diameter. In the Hag-fishes (Myxinidae) on the other hand, they are large, roughly spindle-shaped, and enclosed in tough horny capsules, measuring up to thirty millimetres in length and ten millimetres in width [Fig. 110E]. At each end of the capsule is a tuft of horny processes, each of which ends in a tiny anchor-like hook, and in the middle of one of the tufts is the micropyle. The whole of this end of the capsule is thrown off like a cap at the time of hatching, thus allowing the young Hag-fish to make its escape. The eggs are extruded one at a time, but are afterwards linked together by means of the hook-like processes to form long strings or bunches, usually attached to pieces of seaweed at the bottom of the sea. Like all other large eggs, those of the Hag-fish consist almost entirely of yolk, the essential portion containing the nucleus being represented by a small hillock at the end nearest to the micropyle.

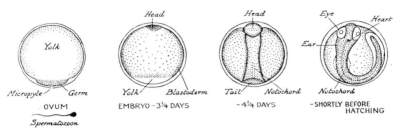

Fig. 109
Development of egg of Flounder (*Platichthys flesus*). Greatly enlarged. (After Johnstone.)

The Selachians may be oviparous or viviparous: that is to say, they either produce eggs which are extruded shortly after fertilisation and left to develop in the sea, or this development takes place in the oviduct of the female, the young being born in an advanced stage of development. The former is without doubt the more primitive method, for in many, if not in all, viviparous Sharks and Rays a rudimentary capsule is at first formed round the egg, this being later resorbed. The eggs are large and filled with yolk, and fertilisation takes place in the upper part of the oviduct, the nidimentary gland. In the oviparous forms, the eggs, as they pass through this gland, are enclosed in a shell or envelope of horny texture, tough but not brittle, and of a flattened, oblong shape, which besides the egg, contains a certain amount of semi-fluid, albuminous material. The capsule is formed by a special gland peculiar to Selachians, and it varies somewhat in pattern according to the species. In Sharks (Pleurotremata), the outer surface may be quite smooth, or delicately ribbed [Fig. 110A], and the four corners are usually drawn out into long tendrils, which become coiled round pieces of seaweed, rocks, stones, and other fixed objects, and serve to anchor the egg during development. They may also assist the extrusion of the capsules themselves, for as these project from the oviducts through the cloaca of the female fish, the tendrils become entangled with objects on the sea-floor and thus help to pull the eggs out. As might be expected where

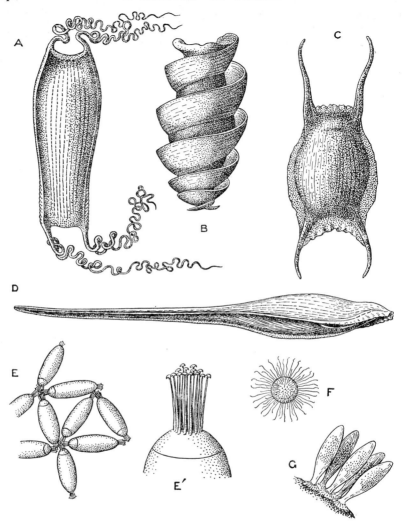

Fig. 110 EGGS AND EGG-CAPSULES

A. Egg-capsule of Spotted Dog-fish (*Scyliorhinus* sp.), x $^1/_2$; B. Of Port Jackson Shark (*Heterodontus phillippi*), x $^1/_2$; C. Of Ray (*Raia* sp.), x $^1/_2$; D. Of Chimaera (*Chimaera phantasma*), x $^1/_2$; E. Eggs of Californian Hag-fish (*Polistotrema stouti*), x *ca.* 5; E'. Animal pole of a single egg, greatly enlarged; F. Egg of Garfish (*Belone belone*), x *ca.* 2$^1/_2$; G. Eggs of Black Goby (*Gobius niger*), x *ca.* 10.

such elaborate precautions for the safety of the embryos are taken, the eggs are always few in number, and are deposited one or two at a time over a long period. The Bull-headed Sharks (Heterodontidae) of the Pacific produce eggs of unique shape, these being of relatively large size, and protected by an elongate cone-shaped capsule with very thick walls, provided with two broad flat flanges twisted spirally round it, and two long, coiled filaments at the pointed end [Fig. 110B]. The Greenland or Sleeper Shark (*Somniosus*), alone among Selachians, produces small eggs, and these are deposited in the sea quite unprotected by a horny envelope.

The oblong capsules of the Skates and Rays (Raiidae) are basically similar to those of the Sharks, but instead of the coiled tendrils, the corners are produced to form more or less stiff, pointed horns [Fig. 110C]. These are known variously as 'skate barrows', 'sailors' purses', 'mermaids' purses', and 'mermaids' pin-boxes', and may frequently be picked up on the shore after storms. The horns of the capsule are hollow and provided with small slits, through which a current of water passes to the contained embryo. The period of incubation lasts from four and a half to nearly fifteen months, and the little fish finally makes its escape through a slit in one end of the capsule, as in the Sharks. The capsules vary in shape and size in the different species, the largest being one hundred and eighty millimetres in length and about one hundred and forty millimetres in width, the smallest sixty-three millimetres and thirty-seven millimetres respectively. They are generally deposited on muddy or sandy flats, and the more convex surface is provided with a sticky substance, to which small pieces of stone, shell, seaweed etc. adhere, and thus help to anchor the capsule.

The capsules of the Chimaeras (Holocephali) are essentially similar to the above, but of somewhat different form, being spindle-shaped in outline and bordered by a broad fringe [Fig. 110D]. In the Californian Chimaera or Spook-fish (*Hydrolagus*) they are about six inches long, and one end is produced into a lengthy 'tail', which sticks into the mud of the sea-floor when the egg is deposited. The shape of the Chimaeroid capsule is adapted, not to the egg as it exists when the capsule is formed, but to the later developed embryo, and the interior cavity may be divided into three distinct chambers, each of which corresponds in shape and size to a definite portion of the embryo fish. There is a row of small slits along each side of the envelope, closed by a membrane when the egg is first extruded, but by a process of gradual decay these become open at a later stage of development, thus allowing currents of water to flow through the case and provide the growing embryo with the necessary oxygen. The upper and lower halves of the capsule are at first united by a membrane, but at the time of hatching they separate at one end, leaving an opening through which the fish can make its escape.

The eggs of Bony Fishes are enclosed only in a vitelline membrane varying from a tough and almost leathery structure to a very fine and fragile skin. As a rule, the shape of the egg is spherical, and although always provided with some yolk, the eggs are never as large as those of the Selachians. Two main types of eggs may be recognised, according to their structure and the manner in which they undergo development: pelagic eggs, which are buoyant and generally provided with a thin and non-adhesive membrane; and demersal eggs, which are heavy and sink to the bottom, and have a hard and smooth or adhesive membrane. Marine fishes may produce eggs of one type or the other, but with very few exceptions, the eggs of freshwater fishes are demersal. Most of our well-known food-fishes have pelagic eggs, only the Herring (*Clupea harengus*), Wolf-fish (*Anarrhichas*), Sand Eel (*Ammodytes*), and a few others depositing their spawn on the sea-floor. No evident connection seems to exist between the habits of a particular species and the nature of its eggs, for whereas the pelagic, plankton-feeding Herring (*Clupea harengus*) produces demersal eggs that are deposited in adhesive masses among gravel and shingle on the sea-bottom, the closely related Sprat (*Clupea sprattus*), with exactly the same habitat, as well as the Pilchard (*Sardina*) and the Anchovy (*Engraulis*), have typical pelagic eggs which float separately near the surface. The Angler (*Lophius*), a typical bottom dwelling form, has pelagic eggs, but the Wolf-fish (*Anarrhichas*), also living on or close to the bottom, has large demersal eggs.

Pelagic eggs are very much smaller than those of the demersal type, and it is their small size and glassy transparency when in the sea that helps to render them inconspicuous to other fishes. Those of the Plaice (*Pleuronectes*) which are to be regarded as giants of their kind, never exceed two millimetres in diameter. Eggs of this type when developing in the ovaries are pinkish, opaque objects, but as they mature they become quite translucent. A conspicuous feature of many pelagic eggs is the presence of a single large oil-globule, forming a glistening object moving about freely on the surface of the yolk. In others the yolk itself may be partially or completely broken up into small masses, giving the egg a characteristic appearance. For the most part, they are non-adhesive, floating freely and separately at or near the surface of the sea, but those of the Angler (*Lophius*) are invested by a gelatinous outer coat and unite together to form a transparent mass, which may be as much as one hundred feet square in area. The little fish known as *Carapus* also has adhesive floating eggs, forming a mass of cylindrical shape, two or three inches in length.

Of the fishes with demersal eggs, those breeding in fresh water have, as a general rule, larger eggs than those spawning in the sea. Among the largest are those of *Gymnarchus* of Africa, which measure about ten millimetres in diameter, and those of some of the Sea Cat-fishes (Ariidae), occasionally exceeding fifteen millimetres. Among marine fishes, those of the Lump-sucker (*Cyclopterus*) are about two and a half millimetres in diameter, and of the Wolf-fish (*Anarrhichas*) about six millimetres. Demersal eggs may also be quite free and separate, as in the Salmon (*Salmo*), Shad (*Alosa*), and other anadromous fishes, in which case they are usually provided with fairly tough and smooth outer membranes; more usually, however, they have adhesive surfaces, and stick to one another as well as to fixed objects. The spawn of the Smelt (*Osmerus*), which adheres to the gravel bottom in estuaries, or to the piles of harbours and piers, is peculiar in its manner of attachment. After extrusion, a portion of the surrounding membrane of the egg breaks away and becomes turned back, remaining attached to the egg at one point, and it is by this piece of membrane that the egg is fixed. In some of the Gobies (Gobiidae), Blennies (Blenniidae) and other shore-dwelling fishes the eggs may be oval or pear-shaped, and attached to rocks, stones, pieces of seaweed, shells and the like by one end, and this end may be provided with a bunch of adhesive filaments [Fig. 110G]. The eggs of the Skippers (Scombresocidae), Gar-fishes (Belonidae), and Flying-fishes (Exocoetidae) have sticky threads developed from opposite points on their surfaces, which either serve to anchor them to foreign objects or become entangled with those of other eggs of the same species [Fig. 116F]. The eggs of many freshwater fishes are adhesive, being attached to rocks or stones on the river bed or to the leaves or stems of aquatic plants.

It will be impossible to follow in detail the manifold and complex series of changes by which the fertilised egg is transformed into a mature fish. A beautifully written and well-illustrated account of early embryonic development may be found in Balinsky's text-book '*An Introduction to Embryology*'.

The early stages of development may conveniently be termed embryonic, in contrast to the post-embryonic or larval development which takes place after the egg has hatched. Such a division of development into two stages, is, of course, arbitrary, and the whole process from the fertilised egg to the mature fish goes on without a break. In a large number of fishes the development may be almost entirely embryonic, the young fish, when hatched, being a replica of its parents, except in size and its sexual immaturity. In others, on the other hand, the young fish leaves the shelter of the egg membrane before it has reached this stage, and has to undergo a further series of changes, constituting the larval development, before its bodily structure is that of a mature fish. There is an important relation between the size of the egg and the condition of the young fish on hatching. As a general rule, in those fishes producing large eggs the young are hatched in a fully developed condition, and have little, if any, larval development. In those with small eggs, on the other hand, the post-embryonic or larval stage is more or less prolonged. This relation is clearly connected with the amount of yolk present in the egg. In the case of the oviparous Selachians, with their large and heavily yolked eggs, the abundance of food enables the embryo to remain within the egg for a long period, and when hatched it has reached an advanced stage of development. Thus, a Black-mouthed Dog-fish (*Pristiurus*) hatches out about nine months after fertilisation, a Spotted Dog-fish (*Scyliorhinus*) about seven months. In the case of small pelagic ova, the amount of yolk available for the nutrition of the embryos is comparatively small, and consequently only suffices to support embryonic development for a short time.

In viviparous fishes the development is necessarily almost wholly 'embryonic'. The majority of Selachians produce their young alive, and in Rays (Hypotremata) only the true Skates and Rays (Raiidae) and a few allied forms are oviparous. The number of young produced at birth varies. Thus, the Spiny Dog-fish (*Squalus*) produces only 7 or 8, the Monk-fish (*Squatina*) 25, and as many as 32 have been counted in a single Tope (*Eugaleus*). In nearly all viviparous Selachians some sort of connection is established between the growing embryo and its mother, serving to aid its respiration and nutrition, and in its more elaborate forms recalling the complicated placenta developed in mammals. During the early stages of development the embryo is nourished by the yolky portion of the ovum, which, after a time, comes to lie in a flask-like bag or yolk-sac, attached to the under surface of the body of the embryo by a long and narrow neck [Fig. 111A]. When first formed the contents of the yolk-sac pass directly into the alimentary canal, but at a later stage the connection between the two is interrupted and the last remains of the yolk are absorbed by the blood-vessels alone.

Even after birth young Sharks may carry, for some time, the pendent yolk-sac, and continue to derive some nourishment from that source [Fig. 111A, III). In many Selachians the walls of the lower part of the oviduct (*i.e.* the uterus), in which the embryos develop, throw out long filamentous processes known as uterine villi or trophonemata. These are richly supplied with tiny blood-vessels and secrete a nutritive fluid, which is either absorbed by the blood-vessels of the embryonic yolk-sac, and thus passed to the embryo itself, or is taken up in a more direct manner. In some of the tropical Sting Rays and Eagle Rays the fluid seems to be taken into the alimentary canal of the embryo directly through the mouth or spiracles. In the Butterfly Rays (*Pteroplatea*) the villi from the walls of the uterus are particularly long, and these are gathered into two bundles which pass through the very large spiracles into the pharynx of the embryos. It is probable that the secretion is first digested in the alimentary canal and afterwards taken up in the embryonic blood-vessels. In a few Sharks such as certain of the Smooth Hounds (*Mustelus canis* for example) another type of connection is established between embryo and parent when the food material in the yolk-sac is nearly used up. The walls of the yolk-sac are abundantly supplied with blood-vessels, and special folds or processes of these walls closely interdigitate with the walls of the uterus, which are similarly highly vascular. Through this intimate vascular association the embryo both receives food and respires.

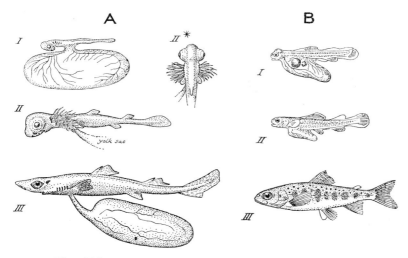

Fig. 111   DEVELOPMENT OF SHARK AND BONY FISH
A. Three stages in the development of the Spiny Dogfish (*Squalus acanthias*). I and II nat. size, III *ca* x 1/2 (I after Balfour). B. Three stages in the development of Salmon. I and II Alevins, nat. size; III Parr, x 1/2.

The actual extrusion of the young in Sharks and Rays has rarely been observed, so that the observations made by Mr. Coles on the birth of a Devil-fish (*Manta*) off the coast of Florida are of particular interest. 'Almost immediately after being struck by the harpoon' he writes, 'the Manta made the sideways revolution alongside the boat, and just before the tail had reached the perpendicular an embryo was violently ejected to a distance of about four feet. The embryo appeared tail first, folded in cylindrical form, but it instantly unfolded, and its pectorals, moving in bird manner, retarded its descent until the mother fish had disappeared below the surface.

I was almost in the act of securing this embryo when it was swept below by the pectoral of the large male mate which was near the big female. The embryo was well advanced, with a width of more than three feet and a tail approximating eight feet in length.' It must be borne in mind that this extrusion took place after the severe wounding of the mother fish, and may not represent the normal process of birth.

The embryos of Saw-fishes (*Pristis*) are generally produced in fairly large numbers, as many as twenty-three having been taken from a female fifteen and a half feet in length caught off the coast of Ceylon. The saw seems to remain more or less soft and flexible until after birth, and the process of parturition is assisted by the fact that the teeth along the margin of the saw scarcely project through the membrane enveloping them.

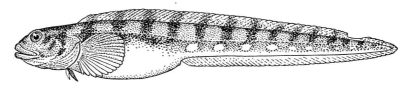

Fig. 112
Viviparous Blenny or Eel Pout (*Zoarces viviparus*), x ³/₈

Amongst viviparous Bony Fishes the number of young produced at a single birth varies considerably. In the Surf-fishes (Embiotocidae) it varies from three to forty or fifty; in most of the Cyprinodonts from fifteen to twenty-five, although the Four-eyed Fish (*Anableps*) may have only four or five; in the Viviparous Blenny or Eel Pout (*Zoarces*) of our own shores [Fig. 112] a female of seven or eight inches in length produces twenty to forty young, one from eight to ten inches, from fifty to one hundred and fifty, while larger specimens have been found to contain more than three hundred. The eggs of the Eel Pout hatch in about twenty days, but the young do not leave the body of the mother until some four months after fertilisation: they are then about one and a half inches in length, and externally at least, closely resemble their parents.

As in Selachians, a variety of maternal-embryonic connections occur which cater for the nourishment and respiration of the embryo. These range from a condition not far removed from oviparity (e.g. *Lebistes*) to the formation of a pseudoplacenta (*e.g.* in the Four-eyed Fish, [*Anableps*]).

The accompanying figures [Fig. 111A] have been selected to show three of the main stages through which the developing embryo passes in a typical Selachian, and to a large extent explain themselves. As in any other vertebrate, the head of the early embryo is very large in proportion to the body, and is bent downwards at an angle, forming the cranial or cephalic flexure (I). As development proceeds, this angle becomes less and less marked (II). The median fins appear at an early stage, and take the form of a continuous membranous fold surrounding the trunk, only later differentiating into dorsal, anal and caudal fins. (*cf.* p. 21). Concurrently with this differentiation of the median fins, the first rudiments of the pectoral fins make their appearance, and soon afterwards the pelvics also appear. At the same time, the head commences to take on the form of that of the adult, accompanied by marked changes in the form of the mouth and gills, and the lateral line appears. An interesting feature of Selachian embryos is the presence of the so-called external gills (*cf.* p. 15), long filamentous processes developing from the walls of the branchial clefts and protruding through the external gill-openings (II). Their function appears to be twofold: they assist the embryo to breathe, and may also aid in the absorption of nutriment in viviparous forms. Having served their purpose, they completely disappear. The last figure shows a final larval stage, in which all the external features of the adult fish are recognisable, and only the pendent yolk-sac remains as a legacy from the embryonic life (III).

Turning to the Bony Fishes, it will be found that in its essential details the development follows much the same course as in the Selachians, but, as the amount of yolk available is considerably less, the larva hatches out in a much less advanced condition. The Salmon (*Salmo*) will serve to illustrate the development of a Bony Fish with fairly large and well-yolked demersal ova [Fig. 111B]. As compared with that of a pelagic egg, the period of embryonic life is long, and varies from five weeks to more than five months, being very much slower when the temperature of the surrounding water is low. In this connection it may be mentioned that the successful introduction of Salmon and Trout into such distant countries as Australia and New Zealand before the days of air-transport was made possible by the fact that the development of the fertilised ova may be artificially prolonged by reducing the temperature. Normally, however, the eggs of the Salmon hatch out at the end of winter, and the fry or alevins, about sixteen millimetres in length, remain for some time hidden away in the spaces between the stones on the spawning bed. They are weighed down at this stage by the large yolk-sac, which is relatively smaller than that of the embryo Shark, and is packed away beneath the body instead of being pendent (I, II). This provides the fry with nutriment during the early part of their lives, but at the end of a month or two all the yolk has been absorbed and they have to fend for themselves. By this time they have grown to about twenty-six millimetres in length, but hereafter growth is rapid, and they normally grow three or four inches in a year, and five or six inches in two years. During the first two years of their life, when they live in fresh water, feeding on small crustaceans, insects etc., they are known as Parr (III). The Parr are especially distinguished by the bluish or purplish colour of the back, and by the presence of seven to eleven oblong or oval spots of the same hue, the 'parr-marks', along the middle of each side. At the end of the two years, or a little later, another change occurs, and the Parr becomes transformed into a Smolt. A bright silver livery is assumed, the parr-marks are obscured, and the smolts drop down the rivers and migrate rapidly out to the open sea, where they soon assume all the characters of the adult fishes.

In those fishes with small pelagic eggs, the period of embryonic life although varying considerably in the different species, is always very much shorter. As far as our own food-fishes are concerned, this period rarely exceeds two weeks, and the Anchovy (*Engraulis*) and Sprat (*Clupea sprattus*) actually hatch out from two to four days after fertilisation. In both pelagic and demersal eggs, a low temperature delays hatching. For instance it has been found that the eggs of the Herring (*Clupea harengus*) will hatch in eight or nine days in water kept at a temperature of 52° to 58° F., but will take forty-seven days in water of 32° F. As might be expected, the newly hatched pelagic larvae are very small, sometimes only three millimetres in length, and are at an early stage of development. At the same time, the remainder of the development is sometimes crowded into an incredibly short space of time, and the three-millimetre larva hatched on the fourth day may have assumed the essential features of the all but mature fish before a month has elapsed, and before it is much more than ten millimetres in length.

As a general rule, the larva hatched from a pelagic egg is transparent, with the pectoral fins developed to a greater or lesser extent, and with a continuous median fin-fold along the back, round the tail, and along the lower edge of the body as far forward as the vent or even farther: this fold has the form of a simple membrane, and is not yet supported by rays. The mouth is frequently not yet formed, the blood is quite colourless, and even the gill-clefts may still be wanting. In this condition nourishment is provided by the remains of the yolk, but as this is used up the mouth is developed and the larva begins to feed on the minute organisms of various kinds found near the surface of the sea. At a later stage the continuous median fin becomes split up into its definitive components, and the pelvics make their appearance. By degrees, the form, proportions, and structure of the adult fish are assumed, and, as a rule, all the essential organs, including the bony internal skeleton, are developed before the fish is much more than an inch in length. It may be noted here that the fins vary a good deal in their development in different species, the dorsal appearing before the anal in some, the anal before the dorsal in others.

Frequently special larval organs are developed, which disappear when the more permanent organs have been acquired. Such structures are for the most part concerned with feeding, respiration, or locomotion, and may give the larva an appearance so unlike that of the mature fish that it has sometimes been mistaken for a distinct species.

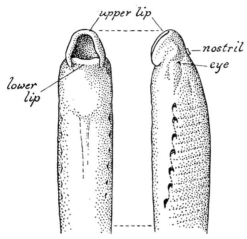

Fig. 113
Two views of the head of the larval Lamprey or Pride, x 4

In the Lampreys (Petromyzonidae), for example, the newly hatched larva is so unlike the parents that it has received distinct generic and specific names (*Ammocoetes branchialis*), and is popularly known as a Pride or Niner. It is curiously worm-like in form, and differs from the adult in having rudimentary eyes buried beneath the skin, a horse-shoe shaped mouth, with a small transverse lower lip and a hood-like upper lip, and no teeth [Fig. 113]; the entrance to the mouth is surrounded by a number of fringed barbels forming a perfect strainer. The small external gill-openings lie in a marked groove. The Prides are hatched some ten to fifteen days after fertilisation of the eggs, and remain in the nest for about thirty days. They then wander down the stream, and having selected a suitable spot, burrow in the sand or mud. They live buried in tubes for three or four years, quite blind, and feeding on minute organisms or on organic matter contained in the mud. In their mode of life, and particularly in the manner in which they obtain their food, these larvae bear a marked resemblance to the little sand-dwelling Hemichordate, the Lancelet *Branchiostoma*. The minute particles comprising the food are carried through the mouth into the pharynx by currents of water produced by the action of special ciliated cells working in unison. The particles become entangled in strings of mucus secreted in a groove, the endostyle (which, in the adult Lamprey, becomes the thyroid gland), in the floor of the pharynx and are swept into the stomach by bands of cilia.

At the end of three to five years a metamorphosis occurs, and in the course of about two months the larva assumes the characters of the adult. First the eyes appear, the mouth is contracted and takes on the suctorial disc-like form, so characteristic of the Lampreys, the tongue and horny teeth are developed, and the branchial groove disappears. At the same time important changes take place in the form of the skeleton, gill-pouches, alimentary canal, kidneys etc..

Among other examples of larval or provisional organs, adhesive or cement organs and external gills may be mentioned. In the Lung-fishes (Dipneusti) the newly hatched larva is not unlike the tadpole larva of the amphibian; there is no pendent yolk-sac, the small amount of food-material still present being distributed over the lower region of the body. The resemblance is further strengthened in the African (*Protopterus*) and South American (*Lepidosiren*) species by the presence of four pairs of feathery external gills, projecting freely from above the gill-arches, and of a glandular adhesive organ situated behind the mouth. The gills disappear during the metamorphosis [Fig. 41A] being functionally replaced by the internal gills and lungs. In certain African species vestiges of the external gills are retained throughout life. In the larval Bichir (*Polypterus*) there is a single pair of fringed pinnate external gills [Fig. 41B] which generally disappear completely during the metamorphosis, but occasionally one or both are retained for a longer period. Some of the more primitive Bony Fishes have been described as possessing larval external gills (Mormyridae, Osteoglossidae, Cobitidae etc.), but these are merely the ordinary gill-filaments which are excessively long and project to the exterior. The development of these structures is always correlated with life in poorly oxygenated waters, and there can be little doubt that they assist the respiration of the larvae until the permanent breathing organs are developed. The larval Bow-fins (*Amia*) and Gar Pikes (*Lepisosteus*), hatched in the more temperate climate of North America, and in better aerated water, do not possess external gills. They are, however, provided with cement organs, but instead of being placed behind the mouth, these are situated at the end of the snout.

Traces of an adhesive disc are to be found in the larval Sturgeon (*Acipenser*), in the form of a shallow pigmented groove in front of the mouth. Such structures enable the larvae to attach themselves to weeds and other fixed objects when at rest, and it has been found that artificially hatched Gar Pikes and Lung-fishes will adhere by their discs to the sides of a glass jar.

Some pelagic larvae and young fishes also possess curious structures that disappear during later development, and the larvae may be so different from the adults that they have been described as distinct species or even genera. In the oceanic Sun-fishes

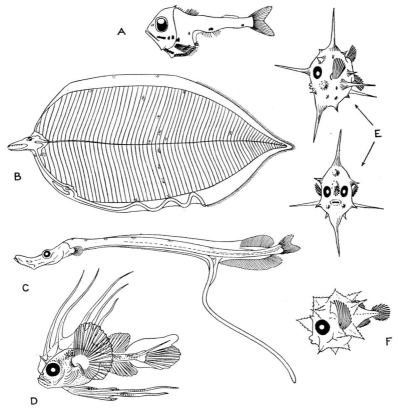

Fig. 114   LARVAL FISHES

A. *Argyropelecus* sp. x 4. (After Brauer); B. Eel leptocephalus x 1¹/₂ (after Roule); C. *Idiacanthus* sp., x 2¹/₂. (After Regan); D. Anglerfish (*Lophius piscatorius*) x 2¹/₂ (After Tåning); E. Sunfish (*Masturus lanceolatus*) x 2¹/₂, (After Schmidt); F. Truncated Sunfish (*Ranzania laevis*), x 8. (After Schmidt)

(Molidae) for example, the newly hatched larva is quite normal, but soon loses its caudal fin and acquires a regular armour of strong spines projecting in every direction all over the body, which serve to protect it during a period of helplessness [Fig. 114E, F]. Five of these spines afterwards grow out into long 'horns' one of which projects from the middle of the back, one from the snout, one from the chest, and one from each side of the body [Fig. 114E]. A little later the fish undergoes a remarkable change in shape, the body actually becoming deeper than long; the spines shorten, and a new tail-fin develops which connects the abbreviated dorsal and anal. The fish is now about half an inch in length, and from this stage onwards it gradually assumes the form of the adult.

The young of the Deal-fish (*Trachypterus*) is remarkable for the extraordinary development of the fin-rays, those of the front part of the dorsal, of the pelvics, and of the lower lobe of the caudal being produced into very long filaments, which may be many times longer than the body and are ornamented with lappet-like membranous processes [Fig. 115B]. As the fish grows these filaments get progressively shorter and the lower lobe of the caudal fin disappears. The Deal-fish is an oceanic species, and it seems probable that the young live at some considerable depth where the water would be fairly calm, for the currents prevailing at or near the surface of the sea would soon damage such delicate structures. These filamentous or spinous processes, by increasing the surface area of the larva, may act as floatation devices.

The Sword-fishes (Xiphiidae) and their allies, the Sail-fishes and Spear-fishes (Istiophoridae) are distinguished by having the snout prolonged to form a long flat or rounded spear or sword, and the changes undergone by these fishes during development are very striking. The young of the Sail-fish (*Istiophorus*) have been beautifully illustrated by Dr. Günther, whose figures are produced here. In the first stage [Fig. 115AI], an individual nine millimetres in length, both jaws are equally produced and armed with pointed teeth; the edge of the head above the eye is provided with a series of short bristles; from the back of the head project, above and below, long pointed spines. The dorsal fin is a long low fringe, the pectoral is large and truncated, and the pelvics are represented by a pair of short buds. In the next stage [AII], a fish fourteen millimetres long, the dorsal has increased enormously in size, the pelvics have grown out into long filaments, and the pectorals have changed their shape. The spines on the head are still prominent, but the bristles above the eyes have disappeared, and the upper jaw has grown a little longer than the lower. At the third stage [AIII], when the fish has grown to a length of sixty millimetres, even more marked changes have occurred. The dorsal fin has become differentiated into an anterior portion of great size and a

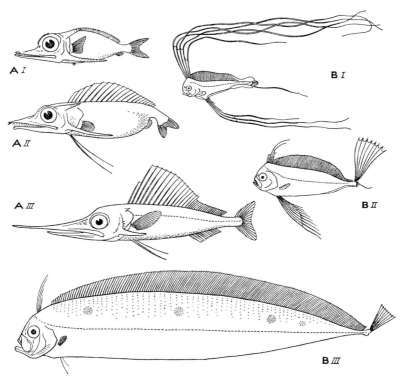

Fig. 115   DEVELOPMENT OF SAILFISH AND DEALFISH
A. Three stages in the development of a Sailfish (*Istiophorus* sp.) (After Günther) I. 9 mm. x $3^{1}/_{2}$; II. 14 mm. x $3^{1}/_{2}$; III. 60 mm. nat. size. A full grown specimen is shown in Fig. 6A; B. Three stages in the development of the Dealfish (*Trachypterus arcticus*) (After Emery and Smitt) I. 16 mm. x $1^{1}/_{4}$; II. 100 mm. x $^{1}/_{4}$; III. 1,000 mm. x $^{1}/_{10}$

smaller posterior part; the upper jaw has grown out still farther and now projects considerably beyond the lower, and the teeth have all but disappeared; the long spines from the back of the head have been reduced to comparatively minute proportions, and the fila-mentous pelvic fins are much smaller. It will be observed that the eye is relatively smaller at each stage.   The young Sword-fish (*Xiphias*) undergoes a very similar series of changes, but the body is covered with small, rough warts arranged in regular lengthwise rows, these still being apparent after the individual has assumed all the other features of the adult fish.

The Gar-fishes (Belonidae) also possess long beak-like jaws, but a study of the development of these fishes reveals the fact that it is the lower jaw which is first prolonged and the upper afterwards grows out to equal it. Thus during its development the Gar-fish passes through a temporary stage in which, as far as the jaws are concerned, it is exactly like the adult Half-beak (*Hemirhamphus*). It might be assumed that the Half-beaks are ancestral to the Gar-fishes, but it is more probable that the unequal jaws of the larval Gar-fish are associated with some specialised feeding habit, and that this condition was later retained by some of the primitive Half-beaks in the adult stage.

In the Ten-pounders (*Elops*), Lady-fishes (*Albula*), and in the Eels (Anguilliformes), the larvae are of a peculiar, transparent leaf-like form, quite unlike the mature fishes, and the period of larval life is greatly prolonged; further, in Eels, these larvae may grow to a relatively large size, in certain species reaching a length of several feet. This type of larva is known as a *Leptocephalus* (thin head), and the first specimen of its kind was discovered in 1777 by a naturalist called Scopoli, but he regarded it as representing a distinct group of fishes. The first British *Leptocephalus* was discovered in 1763 by one William Morris near Holyhead, but this was not described until 1788, when Gmelin named it after the finder *Leptocephalus morrisii*. It was not until 1861 that Carus first recognised that these creatures were larval forms, but he was mistaken in regarding them as young Ribbon-fishes. In 1864 Gill expressed the view that they were larval Eels, and established the fact that *Leptocephalus morrisii* was the young stage of the Conger Eel (*Conger*). Günther (1880) accepted this explanation but held that they were abnormally developed forms, 'arrested in their development at a very early period of their life . . . and perishing without having attained the character of the perfect animal'. This view was soon disposed of when a French scientist, Yves Delage, succeeded in keeping a specimen of the Conger larva alive in an aquarium for seven months, and watched the whole process of transformation into the adult state. The next step in the solution of what came to be known as the 'Eel question', occurred when an Italian naturalist, Raffaele, described the eggs of five species of Eels, which he succeeded in hatching and kept the larvae alive for about two weeks. Next (1893–6) two other Italian investigators, Grassi and Calundruccio, made a thorough study of the Leptocephali of the Straits of Messina, and were able to trace the transformation of several kinds of larvae into their respective species of Eels. They showed beyond any doubt that the larva which had been named by Kaup (1856) *Leptocephalus brevirostris*, was the young of the Common or European Freshwater Eel, (*Anguilla anguilla*), thus establishing that freshwater as well as marine forms pass through the same larval history. They concluded that the European Eel bred in deep water near the coast, and that the larvae lived at considerable depths, being

PLATE IV

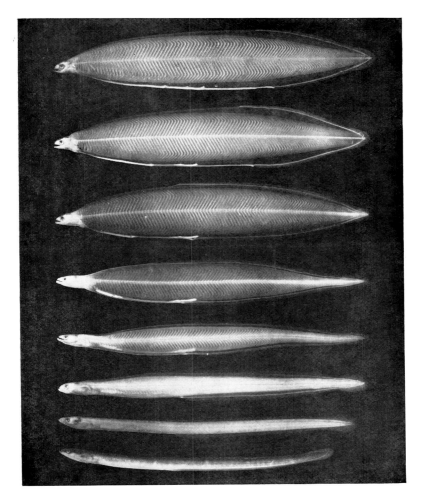

Stages in the metamorphosis of the larval European Eel
(*Anguilla anguilla*)

brought to the surface in the Straits by the agency of the strong currents and whirlpools prevailing there. This explanation was ingenious, and not surprising in view of the data at their disposal, but, as has been already pointed out (*cf.* p. 221), was still far from the truth. Finally, the life-history of the European Eel was elucidated by Dr. Johannes Schmidt (see also p. 221) who traced the larvae on their long journey across the Atlantic, and examined them at almost every stage of their development. He has also paid considerable attention to the American Eel (*Anguilla rostrata*). Eggs of the European Eel have yet to be described, but an American expedition to the Atlantic procured five eggs which were hatched out in the laboratory, and these are believed to be those of the American species (but see p. 224).

The larval history and metamorphosis of the European Eel may be briefly summarised. The breeding-grounds lie in the Western Atlantic, south-east of Bermuda (*cf.* p. 223) and the eggs hatch out some time in the spring. The larvae or Leptocephali, living in the upper layers of the ocean, are provided with curious long, needle-like teeth, which may assist them to seize the minute organisms believed to form their food. They at once commence the long homeward journey, the majority travelling north-eastward with the Gulf Stream, floating at a depth of about one hundred fathoms, in water of a temperature of about 68° F. They grow rapidly during the first few months, averaging about twenty-five millimetres in length in their first summer, and are to be found at this time in the Western Atlantic west of 50° longitude. From now onwards they inhabit the upper strata of the sea, sometimes being found actually at the surface; by the second summer most of them have reached the Middle Atlantic, and have grown to fifty or fifty-five millimetres. They finally arrive off the coasts of Europe when fully grown, about three inches in length, and a little over two years old. They are now ready to undergo metamorphosis, and this takes place in the autumn. The larvae cease to feed, the needle-like teeth are lost, and a progressive shrinking takes place both in length and depth, until they assume a cylindrical, although still perfectly transparent form, about two and a half inches long. These Elvers or Glass Eels at once acquire a fresh set of teeth, small and conical and quite unlike those of the larvae, and are ready to commence the ascent of the rivers. Considering this account of the larval history with that of the breeding of the adults given on page 221 it will be seen that the remarkable life-story of the Eel may be divided into four chapters. These are: (1) a pelagic larval stage—a period of active growth and passive migration; (2) the metamorphosis into the Elver; (3) the growth of the ordinary Yellow Eel; and (4) the change into the breeding Silver Eel, and seaward migration which ends in death.

The true Flat-fishes (Pleuronectiformes) are distinguished from all other fishes by having both eyes on the same side of the head: the upper or eyed side only is coloured, the lower or blind side being white but ambicolored individuals are recorded. The larval history and metamorphosis of these fishes is remarkable, and throws considerable light on the evolutionary history of the group (Plate V). The eggs are pelagic and hatch in a very few days. The newly hatched larvae are quite symmetrical, with an eye on each side of the head as in any other fish, and they swim at or near the surface of the sea. After a time, when the larvae have grown to half an inch or more in length, one eye moves round to the upper edge of the head and finally round to the opposite side, where it comes to lie close to its fellow; at the same time, the dorsal fin is prolonged forward, and as soon as the eye has moved round the fin extends along the edge of the head above it. In some species the migration of the eye is delayed until the dorsal fin has grown forward on to the head, and the eye is then obliged to push its way through between the base of the fin and the margin of the head. While these important changes are taking place the little fish sinks to the bottom of the sea, and thereafter lies or swims at or near the bottom with the eyed side uppermost. The twisting of both eyes to the one side of the head leads to radical changes in the symmetry of the skull. The skull is at first cartilaginous as in any other larva, and there is a curved bar of cartilage above each eye: long before the young fish settles on the bottom, the bar above the eye destined to migrate is resorbed, so that there is no obstacle in its path. Associated with the migration of the eye is one involving the nostril of the same side, and a twisting of the mouth. It is probable that the anatomical aspects of metamorphosis take place rather rapidly.

In concluding a chapter on development, it may be convenient to mention very briefly the question of hybrids, that is to say, of individuals that have sprung from an ovum fertilised by a sperm of another, usually related species. Such cases are comparatively rare in marine fishes, as far as our knowledge goes, but are not uncommon between the various members of the Salmon family (Salmonidae), as well as among Carps (Cyprinidae), and Cyprinodonts. The best-known crosses occurring in a state of nature in the former group are Salmon and Trout and Trout and Char, and these are easily made by artificial fertilisation. It has been shown experimentally that the hybrid offspring of Salmon and Trout are deficient in vitality, and seldom—in the case of males never—come to maturity. Dr. Day remarks, concerning the handsome Zebra hybrid of the Trout (*Salmo trutta*) and the American Brook Trout (*Salvelinus fontinalis*) that the developing eggs show a very high mortality, and that the resulting offspring are frequently deformed in one way or another. In the Cyprinidae hybrids have

PLATE V

Stages in the metamorphosis of the PLAICE
(*Pleuronectes platessa*)

been described between Bleak and Chub, Bleak and Dace, Bleak and Roach, Bleak and Rudd, Bleak and White Bream, Bream and Roach, Bream and Rudd, Carp and Crucian Carp, Roach and Rudd, White Bream and Roach, and White Bream and Rudd in the British Isles alone. In these cases the resulting offspring seem to be quite viable and, as in the case of the Salmon and Trout, generally exhibit more or less equally the characters of both parent species. In most fishes where hybrids are known the characters of the hybrids also appear intermediate between the parental types. However, there is often an imbalance in the ratio of the sexes, with fewer males amongst the offspring than is the case in intra-specific crosses.

REFERENCES

BALINSKY, B. I. (1960). *An Introduction to Embryology*, Saunders, Philadelphia and London.
BERTIN, L. (1956). *Eels*. Cleaver-Hume Press, London.

CHAPTER 16

DISTRIBUTION

ZOOGEOGRAPHY or the geographical distribution of animals presents many fascinating problems to the biologist, who has to consider a variety of factors in order to understand the almost cosmopolitan range of some species and the extremely restricted range of others. In the case of terrestrial vertebrates, the presence of such physical barriers as mountain ranges, arid deserts, large stretches of water, and dense forests is generally sufficient to explain the localisation of faunas into their own particular regions. Similar physical factors probably serve to limit the wanderings of many freshwater fishes, but with all the great oceans connected with one another, the dispersal of marine fishes must be restricted by barriers of another kind.

The understanding of these involves the study of such diverse factors as the temperature and salinity of the water, its chemical properties, the nature and strength of the ocean currents, the configuration of the coast-line, the presence of submarine ridges and deeps, as well as the all-important subject of the available food supply and its distribution. Nor is it sufficient to consider only the barriers existing to-day, for the present geographical range of many species has resulted from conditions which exerted their influence in the more or less remote past, when the disposition of the great land masses was quite different [Fig. 116]. A number of cases of apparently meaningless and anomalous distribution became clear when considered in relation to past history as unfolded by the geologist.

The first and most obvious distinction which suggests itself is between the seas on the one hand and the freshwaters on the other, the conditions in the two regions being, for the most part, of a very different nature. Certain fishes, like some of the Sharks (*Carcharinus*), Saw-fishes (Pristidae), and Sting Rays (Dasyatidae), ascend rivers for considerable distances, and others like the Flounder (*Platichthys*) and Stickleback (*Gasterosteus*) are equally at home in either salt or fresh water. They are unable to survive a sudden change from fresh to saline water, but can pass quite rapidly from the sea to the brackish estuary, and from thence to the fresh water proper, and *vice versa*. Others such as the Salmon (*Salmo*) and Shad

(*Alosa*) migrate annually from the sea to the rivers for spawning purposes, and others, again, like the Common Eel (*Anguilla*) leave the fresh water for the sea as the breeding time approaches.

Two main categories of marine fishes may be conveniently distinguished: oceanic and coastal or littoral. In the open oceans, from the surface down to about one hundred and fifty metres, large, swift, predaceous fishes such as the Tunny (*Thunnus*) and Sword-fish (*Xiphias*) are found, together with swarms of smaller forms such as the Lantern-fishes (Myctophidae); the region from one hundred and fifty to five hundred metres is mostly occupied by

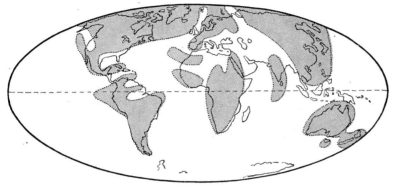

Fig. 116
Land distribution in Eocene times. (After Gregory)

small silvery fishes of various kinds, the majority with large eyes. Below this the bathypelagic fishes occur—Wide-mouths (Stomiatidae), Ceratioid Angler-fishes, and so on—mostly blackish in colour with comparatively small eyes; and finally, there are the abyssal fishes such as the Grenadiers (Macrouridae) which spend their lives in the ocean depths and live on or near to the sea bottom. The pelagic fishes, and those dwelling in the upper layers of the ocean, are mostly found in the warm tropical and temperate regions, few penetrating into the colder waters of the Arctic and Antarctic. As far as the bathypelagic and abyssal forms are concerned, knowledge of their distribution is still incomplete, but there can be little doubt that their supposed world-wide range has been overestimated although some do occur in two or three oceans. Many bathypelagic species seem to have a wide vertical range, spending part of their time, usually during darkness, comparatively close to the surface and part, the day, in the deeper layers of water. The contour of the ocean bed may play an important part in restricting the horizontal range of abyssal forms.

Underwater basins provide particularly interesting examples of the way in which abyssal fishes may encounter inimical conditions which limit their distribution. The Mediterranean and Red Sea are such basins, each with a fairly high sill lying near the entrance. Owing to various physical processes the basin waters below the sill have fairly uniform features and are demarcated from the overlying water masses. The water below 600 fathoms in the Mediterranean has a temperature between 13° C and 14° C, whilst at equal depths in the Atlantic the temperature falls from 14° C to 2.5° C. In the Red Sea, the waters below the sill (50–1000 fathoms) have a temperature of about 23° C. In the Indian Ocean beyond the sill, temperatures at comparable depths drop from 20° C to 2.5° C. Such differences in salinity and temperature provide an impassable barrier for many species, particularly deeper-living fishes (for example the Ceratioid Angler-fishes).

For the Red Sea and Mediterranean in general it may be said that the deeper-living fishes found there are species which have a wide distribution and occur in two or three oceans.

Coastal fishes may be described as those forms that live comparatively near to the shore, dwelling either at or near the surface like the Herring (*Clupea*) and Mackerel (*Scomber*), or close to the sea-floor like the Gurnard (*Trigla*) or Plaice (*Pleuronectes*), the latter being found both in the shallow inshore waters and on the Continental Shelf. This plateau or shelf, varying greatly in width in the different regions, surrounds all the great land masses or continents, and is formed either by the erosion of the land by the waves or by the extension into the sea of deposits of mud or silt carried down from the land by rivers. This Continental Shelf slopes gradually downwards, its outer edge being about two hundred metres below the surface of the sea. Beyond this edge is the Continental Slope, with a much steeper declivity, extending to a depth of nearly two thousand metres. Below this is the true abyssal region. The coastal fishes generally present a far greater abundance and diversity in the shallower waters of the shelf, and as the abyssal depths are approached the number of species and of individuals becomes progressively less and less.

This point is well illustrated by the following table, compiled by Sir John Murray to show the average yield of bottom dwelling animals at different depths. The data were derived from various stations collected by H.M.S. *Challenger*.

Depth in metres	No. of stations	Average yield per station	
		Species	Individuals
180– 900	40	47	150
900–1,800	23	27	87
1,800–2,700	25	20	80
2,700–3,600	32	12	39
3,600–4,500	32	8	26
4,500	25	6	24

The factors influencing the decline in the number of species and individuals are complex and include decreasing light and temperature which in turn decrease the availability of food and increase inter- and intraspecific competition. Marshall, in his book '*Aspects of Deep Sea Biology*' (1954), gives a full treatment of these various factors, illustrating the problems with many examples from deep-sea fishes.

The relative abundance of fishes on the Continental Shelf and upper part of the Continental Slope is an important factor in the development of the sea fisheries, the prominence of the Atlantic and North Sea industries being due to the presence of large areas of sea-floor at a depth of five hundred metres or less in these regions.

By far the most important factor limiting the geographical range of coastal fishes is the temperature of the sea. This naturally shows some variation in different regions, as well as at different seasons of the year, but it is possible to construct a map to show the average annual temperature in various parts of the world. Such a temperature chart of the oceans is crossed by a series of wavy and irregular lines, running from east to west, and know as isotherms, or to give them their full title, mean annual surface isotherms, lines drawn through points of equal temperature [Fig. 117]. In other words, the isotherm of 6° C. is a line connecting all the localities in which the average annual surface temperature of the sea is 6° C. The distribution of many pelagic and coastal fishes corresponds remarkably closely with the temperature of the water, and it is possible to divide the world into a number of zones of distribution, encircling the globe like a series of horizontal bands, each lying between two of these isotherms. In the centre is the broad Tropical Zone, limited by the isotherm of 20° C.; above and below are North and South Temperate Zones, extending to the isotherms of 6° C. in the north and south, each of which may be further subdivided by the isotherm of 12° C. into subtropical and subarctic and subantarctic zones; finally, beyond the isotherms of 6° C. are the Arctic and Antarctic Zones, encircling the North and South Poles of the Earth [Fig. 117].

The Tropical Zone contains by far the greatest number and diversity of genera and species, although as far as actual numbers of individuals are concerned some of the more northerly species like the Cod (*Gadus*) and the Herring (*Clupea*) probably surpass any of those in tropical regions. Among the characteristic oceanic forms inhabiting this region are the Tunnies, Bonitoes, and Albacores (Scombridae), 'Sword-fishes' (Xiphiidae, Istiophoridae), Flying-fishes (Exocoetidae), and so on, and as all the coral reefs of the world are included within its limits, such typical reef-dwelling forms as the Butterfly-fishes (Chaetodontidae), Pomacentrids (Pomacentridae), Wrasses (Labridae), Parrot-fishes (Scaridae), File-fishes

(Monacanthidae), Trunk-fishes (Ostraciontidae), etc., are largely confined to this zone. The vast majority of the marine Perch-like fishes (Perciformes)—Groupers, Grunts, Drums, Carangids, and the like—are inhabitants of the Tropical Zone, which also includes many diverse members of the Herring family (Clupeidae) as well as numerous kinds of Flat-fishes (Pleuronectiformes).

As far as the coastal fishes are concerned, two main divisions or regions of the Tropical Zone may be recognised: Indo-Pacific and Atlantic. The same genera may occur in both regions, but are nearly always represented by distinct species. A careful examination of the fishes living on either side of the continent of America, and particularly of those in the neighbourhood of the narrow isthmus connecting North and South America, reveals the fact that those of the Atlantic bear a marked resemblance to those of the Pacific. Indeed, in the Panama region many of the species can be arranged in pairs, one being found on the Atlantic side and its nearest relative on the Pacific, the two being frequently so alike that they can only be distinguished with difficulty. How has this similarity of the two faunas been brought about? The artificially constructed Panama Canal, with its series of locks, may be dismissed as a connecting passage, and it is equally impossible for any mixing to have taken place *via* the cold waters of the Arctic and Antarctic Oceans. It is known, however, that in the geological period known as the Eocene the present isthmus of Panama was submerged beneath the sea and the Atlantic and Pacific Ocean were continuous [Fig. 116]. The same types of fishes could thus be distributed on both sides of the continent. But the subsequent formation of the isthmus provided a definite physical barrier, and the effects of isolation continued over a long period of time has led to the evolution of distinct species in the two oceans.

The vast Indo-Pacific region extends from the Red Sea and the coast of Africa eastwards through the Indian Ocean and Archipelago to Northern Australia and the islands of Polynesia. It includes a far greater number of genera and species than the American region. The long and almost unbroken coast-line provided by the huge continent of Asia has enabled shore-dwelling forms to extend their ranges slowly and gradually, and as a result of this gradual extension the geographical range of some species includes both the Red Sea and the islands of the South Seas. On the coast of West Africa the state of affairs is very different to that of the Indo-Pacific, and in place of the teeming and diverse fish-life of the latter region there is a comparatively poor fauna. A certain number of species are the same as those occurring on the Atlantic coast of America and must have been able to cross the ocean at some period of their history, others are identical with those found in the Mediterranean, while many others exhibit a definite affinity to those of the Indo-Pacific. As far as the pelagic and deep-sea fishes are concerned, the Cape of Good Hope offers no barrier to their dispersal, but since the isotherm of 20° C., the southern limit of the Tropical Zone, cuts off the south-western part of the African continent, the change of temperature provides an adequate barrier to the mixing of coastal species of the two faunas *via* the Cape [Fig. 117]. Here again, the configuration of the land masses in Eocene times explains to some extent the distribution of the existing forms, for during this period the Mediterranean extended much farther eastwards and opened into the Pacific [Fig. 116]. Further, a study of the fossil fishes dug up in Southern Europe reveals the presence during this period of many typically Indo-Pacific genera and there was nothing to prevent these from ranging in the other direction to West Africa. Later this connection closed up, but the West African fauna remains as an indication of its former existence. At the present time the fish fauna of the Red Sea is totally different to that of the Mediterranean, but unlike the canal across the isthmus of Panama, the present Suez Canal, opened in the middle of the last century, probably provides a passage from one sea to the other for certain species. The canal is only about one hundred miles in length and there are no locks along its course. The only physical barrier to fishes is the high degree of salinity of the Bitter Lakes which lie in its southern half. It seems that these lakes may be effective in preventing the passage of certain species, but not others. The Lakes themselves possess quite a rich fish fauna including species from both the Red Sea and the Mediterranean. Only one or two Mediterranean species have, however, succeeded in reaching the Gulf of Suez at the northern end of the Red Sea, and have not penetrated far from the neighbourhood of the canal entrance. On the other hand, no less than sixteen species of Indo-Pacific fishes from the Red Sea have penetrated into the Mediterranean and are now well established there. One species (*Siganus rivulatus*) has reached Cyprus and another, a little Sand Smelt (*Hepsetia pinguis*), has been caught about two hundred miles to the west of Alexandria.

What is it that apparently makes the Suez Canal such a differential barrier, allowing an East to West flow but severely restricting movement in the opposite way? In earlier editions of this book it was suggested that the presence of rapid tidal currents in the lower part of the canal would tend to sweep floating eggs and larvae into the Bitter Lakes. Also suggested was the fact that in the northern half of the canal there is a slow, constant streaming to the north for ten months in the year. These factors must have some influence, especially over eggs and larvae, but might be less effective against adult individuals. In conversation with the present reviser,

Mr. N. B. Marshall (who has studied the area and its fishes) put forward another idea. Namely, that there is less competition in the eastern Mediterranean and the habitats there do not demand such a high degree of ecological specialization as those in the Red Sea (for example the coral reefs).

Turning to the Southern Hemisphere, it may be noticed that south of the Tropical Zone the currents are not deflected by the land masses to nearly the same extent as in the north, and the zones of distribution are easier to define and the isotherms more nearly parallel. As far as the subtropical region of the South Temperate

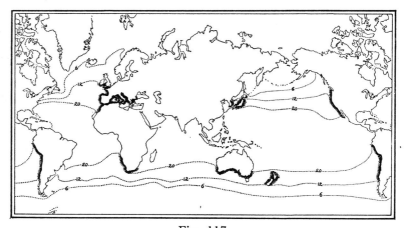

Fig. 117

Distribution of the genera *Sardina* and *Sardinops*. The mean annual surface isotherms of 6°, 12° and 20° C. are shown

Zone is concerned, it is not unusual to find genera common to this region and that of the North Temperate Zone, the Cape fauna having many points in common with that of the Mediterranean. In the accompanying map [Fig. 117] the dotted areas illustrate the distribution of the genera of Pilchards or Sardines (*Sardina* and *Sardinops*). It will be observed how closely their geographical range corresponds to the subtropical regions of the Temperate Zones.

The Common Pilchard (*Sardina pilchardus*) occurs in the seas of Western Europe and is represented in the Mediterranean by a closely related subspecies (*S. pilchardus sardina*). A closely related genus (*Sardinops*) is found on the coasts of Chile and Peru (*Sardinops sagax sagax*), South Africa (*S. s. ocellatus*), Japan (*S. s. melanosticta*) and the southern half of Australia and in New Zealand waters (*S. s. neopilchardus*). A second species, *Sardinops caerulea*, is found off the Pacific coast of the United States and Lower California. The absence of Pilchards on the Atlantic coast of America is difficult to understand, but this may be due to the sudden transition from subarctic to almost tropical conditions in the western North Atlantic, where the cold Labrador Current meets the warm Gulf Stream. It would be comparatively easy for a South American species to reach South Africa or New Zealand, but it would be quite another matter to cross the Tropical Zone. The Hakes (*Merluccius*) represent another genus largely confined to these subtropical regions, but also extending into subarctic and subantarctic waters.

A remarkable illustration of the part played by temperature and currents in determining the distribution of fishes is provided by certain forms found round the small islands of Tristan da Cunha and St. Paul, both of which lie in the subtropical region of the South Temperate Zone. Although about four thousand miles apart, the two islands lie roughly on the same isotherm, and the current known as the Westwind Drift runs direct from one to the other. As a result of these physical factors, there are species of fish common to both islands, but found nowhere else in the world. A similar case of wide geographical range occurs in the subantarctic half of the same zone, a few species being common to southern New Zealand and the Magellan-Falkland Island area, but found nowhere else.

In the true Antarctic Zone, bounded on the north by the isotherm of 6° C, there is a peculiar and diverse fauna which must have taken a considerable period of time to evolve. The importance of temperature as a factor in distribution is again illustrated by the great similarity between fishes of South Georgia and Grahamland, which are, however, quite unlike those of the Magellan-Falkland plateau. The great bulk of the Antarctic fauna is made up of fishes known as Notothenids (Notccheniidae); some of these forms occur in the subantarctic region, but nearly always belong to distinct species. The Antarctic Zone may be conveniently divided into a glacial region, including the Antarctic continent and South Georgia, and a periglacial region, outside the limits of the pack-ice, including Kerguelen and Macquarie Islands.

In the Northern Hemisphere the seasonal variations in the temperature of the sea are very much greater, and the zones of distribution are not so easy to define, although on the whole the same isotherms may be regarded as giving fairly satisfactory boundaries. Whereas in the south the isotherms are roughly parallel with each other, in the northern seas the spreading of the great ocean currents produces the effect of crowding together in the west, but wide separation in the east. This is particularly marked in the North Atlantic, and on the coast of North America the meeting of the cold Labrador Current with the warm water of the Gulf Stream produces a very abrupt change from ice-cold to almost tropical conditions, with a corresponding change in the characteristic fishes. The isotherm of 6° C. runs for a space almost directly north and south off the coasts of Labrador and Newfoundland, then turns in a north-easterly direction towards Iceland, curves to the south of that island, runs still further north-eastwards, and finally bends southwards to meet the Norwegian coast: starting from about 45° N. latitude on the coast of America, this isotherm ends at about 68° N. on the coast of Norway, a difference of latitude of more than one thousand two hundred sea miles [Fig. 117]. The reasons for these irregularities of temperature cannot be detailed here, and it must suffice to point out that the principal factors involved are the Gulf Stream or North Atlantic Drift, which carries warm water to the shores of Western Europe, and the Labrador Current, which brings ice-cold water, with icebergs and pack-ice, southwards during the early part of the year.

A glance at the accompanying map [Fig. 117] shows that the isotherm of 12° C., marking the boundary between the subtropical and subarctic regions of the North Temperate Zone, runs roughly to the mouth of the English Channel, and it is in this region that the characteristic fish-fauna shows a definite change. It is, so to speak, the meeting ground of two great areas, and the Pilchard (*Sardina*), Anchovy (*Engraulis*), Red Mullet (*Mullus*), and other lovers of warm water, give place to the typically northern forms like the Herring (*Clupea*), Cod (*Gadus*), and Plaice (*Pleuronectes*). Many Mediterranean species have their northern limit at about this latitude, which also marks the southerly limit of the Salmon and Trout (*Salmo*) as marine fishes. The isotherm of 6° C., marking the northern boundary of the Temperate Zone, is not so satisfactory as a limit of distribution, but it is fairly close to the northern limit of many of our own fishes, and marks the southern limit of the typically Arctic Char (*Salvelinus*) as a sea fish.

In the North Pacific the isotherms, although less irregular than in the North Atlantic, have the same general arrangement, being close together in the west and farther apart in the east. Again, there seems to be a fairly close correspondence between the temperature and the range of the fishes, and such regions as the Bering Sea, and northern Japanese Sea, each have their characteristic faunas. Certain subarctic fishes are common to both Atlantic and Pacific, and in other cases the genera are the same, but there is one species in one ocean and a very closely related species in the other. The species common to both do not generally extend, however, along the northern coasts of Europe and Asia, but it is certain that they had such a continuous range in the Arctic Ocean in fairly remote times, when the climatic conditions are know to have been considerably milder than they are to-day.

After the Eocene period there was a land connection between Alaska and Siberia, but in order to explain the similarity between the fish-faunas of the Atlantic and Pacific it is necessary to assume that this was subsequently broken, and there is evidence to suggest that this happened more than once. The Pacific Herring (*Clupea pallasia*) provides an interesting example of what is known as discontinuous distribution. This fish is related to our own Herring (*C. harengus*), and both species extend into the Arctic Zone. The Pacific species has an isolated colony in the White Sea, but outside on the coasts of Northern Europe and Asia, both to the east and to the west, the Atlantic species occurs.

The last of the zones, the Arctic, has a very poor fish-fauna. A certain number of Bull-heads (Cottidae) are common here and some of the Cods (Gadidae) and Flat-fishes (Pleuronectidae), a few of which seem to have a very wide range right round the North Pole, are found only within the limits of this zone. One family (Zoarcidae) found in this zone also occurs in the Antarctic, but is represented by quite distinct genera in the two regions.

So much for the general distribution of marine fishes. Although a given species has a definite geographical range in the sea, within limits of this area individual shoals, or even individual fishes themselves, are more or less constantly on the move, and may undertake extensive journeys from one locality to another. Such movements, or migrations, are rarely sporadic, but generally occur with regularity at certain seasons of the year. They are nearly always undertaken for one of two purposes—reproduction or food—and are consequently known as spawning or feeding migrations respectively. In the case of the Tunny (*Thunnus*), for example, shoals of these gigantic fish may make their appearance in a given locality, and after a stay varying from a few weeks to several months, disappear for the remainder of the year. The movements of this species are still imperfectly understood, but there is little doubt that they are connected with both the movements of the shoals of fishes on which the Tunny habitually preys as well as with spawning migrations. Tunnies enter the Mediterranean in huge numbers in the earlier summer and the fishermen, being conversant with this habit, set special nets, sometimes miles in length, that serve to intercept the fish and to guide them into a very strong net, where they are surrounded, speared or clubbed, loaded on to the boats, and finally landed to be cut up and tinned. Mackerel (*Scomber*), which are essentially warm water fish, keep to the open water during the winter, but in summer, when the inshore waters become warmer, they approach the coasts on both sides of the North Atlantic, and in our own waters travel up the Channel into the North Sea. During May and June they spawn close to the coast, and then move into the bays and estuaries, drawn thither by the presence of shoals of larval and young fishes. During this period the Mackerel can be caught by means of seine-nets drawn on to the beach, but from November to the following May none are to be found in the North Sea. The Anchovy (*Engraulis*) is another species passing up the Channel in the spring, but here the spawning takes place in the estuary of the River Scheld. The Pilchard (*Sardina*) approaches the coast of Cornwall, the northernmost limit of its range, from July to November or December, but always retires to warmer regions on the approach of winter. It is of interest to note that only the adults appear to travel so far north, and the young or Sardines are never found in any abundance on the Cornish coast. In this species the migration is entirely connected with the movements of the food supply, for as has been already mentioned, spawning takes place in the open sea, well away from land. The Scad or Horse Mackerel (*Trachurus*) feeds almost entirely on the fry of Herring, Pilchard, and other fishes, and sometimes appears quite suddenly off our coasts in incredible numbers at certain seasons, and then equally suddenly disappears. Yarrell, a nineteenth century naturalist, described a shoal of these fishes seen on the coast of Glamorganshire in 1834, which passed the particular locality for a whole week in such vast numbers that the sea, looked on from above appeared 'one dark mass of fish'. They were pursuing the fry of the Herring, and feeding-time was observed to be morning and evening.

On account of its great economic importance and because of its sporadic occurrence, the migrations of the Herring (*Clupea*) are of special interest. The seasonal movements of the shoals have been studied extensively by scientists of several European countries, but although our knowledge of this intricate problem has been enormously increased, much has still to be learned. At some seasons Herrings may be found in huge numbers in a given locality, at others they will disappear almost entirely; in other places they may be caught all the year round, but the numbers captured on a given ground may exhibit an immense amount of variation from one season to another. These annual fluctuations in the yield of Herrings have attracted the attention of naturalists for many years.

Some of the earlier accounts credited the Herring with very extensive wanderings, but this was due mainly to the confusion of the different races now known to exist. It has been discovered that the species may be divided into a large number of races, each with its own range of distribution and its own season of spawning. Thus it is possible to recognise North Sea, Baltic, Norwegian, Icelandic Herring, and so on, and each of these may include forms spawning at various times of the year. Off the British coasts there is scarcely any month in which spawning is not taking place on one or other of the recognised grounds, and a broad distinction may be made between winter-spawning Herrings shedding their eggs close to the shore, and summer Herrings spawning in deeper water. The migrations undertaken by the different races, concerned either with reproduction or with food, vary greatly in extent, and the Norwegian Spring Herring may move from the south-west coasts of Norway as far north as the Barents Sea and back again, whereas some of the races spawning in the Kattegat and the Belt Sea do not leave these waters. The movements of the shoals between the spawning seasons are less understood, but there is reason to suppose that the fish do not move far away from the coast. It is clear that the times when they congregate in dense shoals are those when they may be most easily caught by the drift-nets of the fishermen, and as a general rule, Herrings may be said to collect together at four periods of their life: as young fish, as mature fish just before spawning, as spawning fish, and as spent fish soon after spawning has occured.

It is impossible to enter into the heated discussions on whether fishes evolved in freshwater or marine conditions. To-day almost every order of fishes includes a greater or lesser number of freshwater representatives, and at least one order (the Cypriniformes or Ostariophysi) has evolved entirely in freshwater, only a few of its members being secondarily marine.

Freshwater fishes may be conveniently divided into two main categories: (1) those spending part of their life in the sea; (2) those living permanently in fresh water. Among the members of the first group are the Grey Mullets (Mugilidae), which inhabit estuaries and may penetrate for considerable distances up rivers, as well as fishes like the Flounder (*Platichthys*) and Stickleback (*Gasterosteus*), equally at home in salt or fresh water. The Three-spined Stickleback (*G. aculeatus*) has a very wide range, being found on the coasts and in the rivers of the arctic and temperate regions of the Northern Hemisphere, extending as far north as Greenland, Alaska, and Kamchatka and as far south as Japan, California, New Jersey and Spain. In northern regions it is essentially a marine fish; in the British Isles it is equally common on the coasts and in the rivers; and in Spain and Italy it is almost entirely confined to freshwater.

Also belonging to the first category are the catadromous fishes, forms which feed and grow in freshwater, but return to the sea to breed. The Common Eel (*Anguilla anguilla*) is the best known of these fishes, and its distribution in Europe is of special interest when considered in relation to its life history, and particularly to its breeding habits. These were described in an earlier chapter (*cf.* p. 221), but it may be noted here that the adult Eels spawn in deep water to the south of Bermuda, the larvae subsequently making their way slowly in an easterly direction, reaching the coasts of Europe when about two and a half years of age. Here they become transformed into elvers, which are about three years old when they enter the rivers of the British Isles. A glance at the map [Fig. 100] shows that the distribution of the species in fresh water is a wide one, extending from Iceland and northern Norway to Morocco, and throughout the countries bordering the Mediterranean. Now these are just the coasts that the larvae reach at a time when they are ready to become elvers, or the further regions to which the elvers or young eels are subsequently able to make their way.

Among other, at least partly catadromous forms mention may be made of a family of small fishes allied to our own Salmon and Trout that are found in the Southern Hemisphere. These Galaxids (Galaxiidae) are for the most part confined to the rivers of the southern extremity of South America, the Falkland Islands, the Cape of Good Hope, Southern Australia and New Zealand, but one species (*Galaxias attenuatus*) from Patagonia, Australia, and New Zealand reverses the habit of its northern relatives and returns to its original home in the sea to spawn.

Anadromous fishes are also to be included among those which spend part of their life in the sea, for such fishes feed and grow in this habitat, merely ascending the rivers at more or less regular intervals to spawn. The best know examples of fishes of this type are the Sea Lamprey (*Petromyzon*), Sturgeon (*Acipenser*), Shad (*Alosa*), Salmon, Trout (*Salmo*), and Char (*Salvelinus*). The members of the Salmon family (Salmonidae) include marine fishes of arctic and northern seas and a large number of species which have become permanently established in the freshwaters of Europe, Northern Asia, and North America. The various Salmon and Trout comprise two genera represented by about ten species in the North Atlantic and North Pacific: those from the Atlantic form a natural group (*Salmo*) distinct from those of the Pacific, the latter being placed in a separate genus (*Oncorhynchus*). Our own Salmon and Trout are to be regarded as two very closely related species. They are found in the sea from Iceland and the northern part of Norway southwards to the Bay of Biscay. The Salmon (*S. salar*) has succeeded in crossing the ocean and is found on the Atlantic coast of North America, but the Trout (*S. trutta*), which is thought not to go nearly so far out to sea, is absent from America. In some of the larger lakes and rivers of Quebec, New Brunswick, and Maine there are Salmon (*S. salar sebago* and *S. salar ouananiche*) which never go to the sea, having become permanent residents in fresh water. In Europe, where it occurs alongside the Trout, the Salmon does not generally form freshwater colonies in this way, but Lake Väner in Sweden, now completely isolated from the sea by inaccessible falls, possesses a stock of land-locked and non-migratory

Salmon. The Trout forms freshwater colonies in practically every suitable lake and river which it enters, and many of these permanent residents have become so much modified in the course of time that they present an extraordinary diversity of form, size, coloration, and so on, some of the freshwater races being so different from their migratory ancestors that they have been regarded as distinct species. This erroneous conclusion is understandable when one compares the lordly Trout of a deep lake, scaling as much as fifty pounds, with the small fishes of three or four ounces inhabiting the mountain streams of Wales, or the silvery Sea Trout with the non-migratory Brown Trout.

It has been already stated that the range of both *Salmo* species in the sea extends southwards only as far as the Bay of Biscay, and it is of interest to find that there are freshwater colonies of Trout in the Atlas Mountains of North Africa, in the islands of Corsica and Sardinia, and in the countries north of the Mediterranean as far east as the Adriatic Sea. There can be little doubt that the present marine distribution of the Salmon and Trout is limited mainly by temperature, and it is this factor which prevents them from entering the Mediterranean to-day. It may be assumed, however, that if the climatic conditions in Europe were colder, as they were known to be during the Ice Ages, the limit of their range would be farther south. It is certain that during the glacial periods of the Pleistocene period both Salmon and Trout occurred in the Mediterranean and ran up suitable rivers to spawn, and that, when the migratory fish once more retreated northwards on the return of milder climatic conditions in Europe, freshwater colonies were left behind in some of the rivers. The presence of a fluviatile race of Three-spined Sticklebacks (*Gasterosteus aculeatus*) in Algeria may be explained on the same hypothesis.

The freshwater colonies or races of White-fish (*Coregonus*) and Char (*Salvelinus*) probably originated in much the same way. The Char are primarily marine fishes, inhabiting the Arctic Ocean, and running up the rivers to spawn. They have at some time formed permanent freshwater colonies in various lakes of Scandinavia, Switzerland, Scotland, Ireland, and the Lake District of England, but, as they only thrive in deep cold water, have not colonised rivers, like the Trout has done. In the same way the White-fish of our lakes, such as the Pollan (*Coregonus pollan pollan*), Vendace (*C. vandesius vandesius*), Gwyniad (*C. clupeoides pennanti*), etc., are probably descended from a northern migratory species which was in the habit of ascending rivers to spawn, as do certain Arctic species to-day. There is little doubt that the Char and White-fish reached the lakes that they now inhabit from the sea during the glacial period, when the climate was considerably colder and the range of migratory Salmonids extended much farther south. When these again retreated northwards, isolated colonies remained behind in the lakes, and these have continued to evolve in various directions according to the nature of the local conditions, many being now so distinct from their migratory ancestors that they have been regarded as separate species.

The fishes of the second category, spending their whole lives in freshwater, include fluviatile species of genera otherwise marine in habitat, or of genera normally anadromous, freshwater genera of marine families and even suborders which include only freshwater fishes. The Bull-heads (*Cottus*), for example, represent a typically marine genus, but the little Miller's Thumb (*C. gobio*) of Europe, a species common in the rivers and streams of England and Wales, is entirely confined to freshwater. The Grayling (*Thymallus*) belongs to the family Salmonidae but the genus is strictly fluviatile and contains no anadromous species. The family Brotulidae includes many diverse genera found at great depths in the oceans, but the Cuban and Mexican Blind-fishes (*cf.* p. 196) are the only freshwater members. The Cods and their allies (Gadidae) represent another big marine family, which includes a single freshwater genus and species, the Burbot (*Lota lota*). The Atherines or Sand Smelts (Atherinidae) are little silvery fishes frequenting bays and estuaries, many of them entering the rivers. In countries where true fresh-water fishes are scarce or absent species of Sand Smelts have become permanently resident in fresh water, and there is a distinct subfamily of these little fishes in the rivers of Australia and New Guinea, while other forms occur in Madagascar. In the lakes of the Valley of Mexico there are several species of Atherines, most of which grow to a fair size and are valued as food by the Mexicans, who know them as 'Pescados blancos'. These must have entered the lakes (which lie at the southern end of the Mexican plateau) from the Pacific Ocean in remote times, before they had been cut off from the sea by inaccessible falls. The only other fishes in the lakes are a few Cyprinids which have found their way down from the rivers of North America.

The primary freshwater fishes, that is to say, fishes which have evolved in the rivers and lakes and have a narrow salinity tolerance, may form distinct families, such as the Sun-fishes (Centrarchidae) of North America and the Perches (Percidae) of the Old and New World, or even whole suborders such as that which includes the Pikes, Mud-fishes, and Black-fishes (Esocoidei). To such fishes the sea may be looked upon as constituting a definite and generally impassable barrier and their distribution is limited by factors which are rather different to those governing the geographical range of marine fishes. The distribution of the Ostariophysi, (which includes the majority of the freshwater fishes of the world), is full of interest. There is good reason to believe that their evolution has taken place in freshwater, and that their dispersal, necessarily slow as compared with that of land animals, has been very gradually effected by hydrographical changes, among which the capture by one big river of the tributaries of another, the union of two or more rivers due to the elevation of the land, or the joining of two river-systems, the head-waters of which may be separated by only a few miles of swampy land, during abnormal floods, are probably the more important. It is sometimes suggested that a species may have become established in a river system from which it was previously absent through the spawn being carried considerable distances by aquatic birds, through the agency of water-spouts, and by other accidental methods, but there is no evidence of such transferences having occurred. It seems more than probable that the present intercontinental distribution of these fishes was accomplished mainly at the beginning of the geological epoch known as the Tertiary, and that the subsequent land connections and interchanges which had such important effects on the movements of the mammals and reptiles did little to influence the distribution of the freshwater fishes.

In considering the distribution of the primary freshwater fishes, and particularly those of the order Ostariophysi, the land masses of the globe may be conveniently divided into a number of zoo-geographical regions. These are: (1) an Australian region including Australia, New Guinea, and all the islands of the Indo-Australian Archipelago lying east of a line running between Borneo and Celebes, plus the islands of Bali and Lombok; (2) Madagascar; (3) a Neotropical region including Central and South America; (4) an African or Ethiopian region but excluding the northern tip; (5) an Oriental region, including India, South-eastern Asia, and the islands of Java, Sumatra and Borneo; (6) a Palaearctic region, including Europe and Asia as far south as the Himalayas and the River Yangtse-Kiang; and (7) a Nearctic region, which includes Canada, the United States, and the greater part of Mexico.

The Australian region presents features of particular interest since here there is an almost complete absence of true freshwater fishes. In this region there are a number of freshwater genera and species closely allied to marine forms, such as Gobies, Sea Perches, Herrings, Grey Mullets, Sand Smelts, etc., but there are no peculiar fluviatile families. The only true freshwater species are two in number, and both belong to archaic and once widespread groups one of which, the Lung-fishes, dates back at least to the Devonian period. The Australian Lung-fish (*Neoceratodus*) is found to-day only in portions of the Burnett and Mary Rivers of northern Queensland, and the other members of this ancient group occur in tropical Africa and South America [Fig. 118]. The second archaic freshwater fish is a species of Osteoglossid found in northern

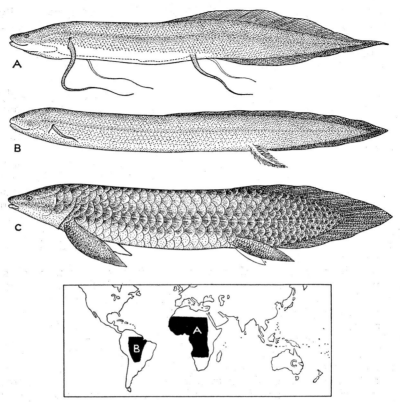

Fig. 118   LIVING LUNGFISHES AND THEIR DISTRIBUTION
A. African Lungfish (*Protopterus aethiopicus*), x about ¹/₈; B. South American
Lungfish (*Lepidosiren paradoxa*) a breeding male with vascularized pelvic
fins, x *ca* ¹/₈; C. Australian Lungfish (*Neoceratodus forsteri*), x *ca* ¹/₁₀.
In the map the black area marked A represents the distribution of the
genus *Protopterus*, that marked B of *Lepidosiren*, and that marked C of
Neoceratodus; the area of C if shown to scale, would be little more than
a pin-prick

Australia and New Guinea which belongs to a genus (*Scleropages*)
containing one other species found in Siam, Sumatra and Borneo.
The Osteoglossids are an old family of which the remaining extant
members occur in Africa and South America [Fig. 119] but Eocene
fossils are found in North America and Britain.   The almost
complete absence of fishes of the order Ostariophysi is remarkable,
and a comparison of the fauna of Borneo with that of the neigh-
bouring island of Celebes produces striking results: in the former

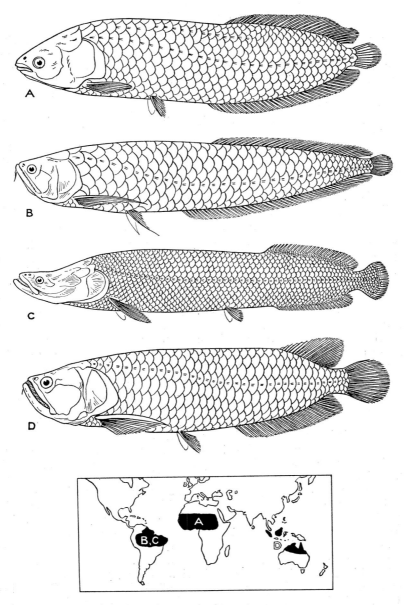

Fig. 119 OSTEOGLOSSIDS (OSTEOGLOSSIDAE) AND THEIR DISTRIBUTION
A. *Clupisudis niloticus*, x $^1/_8$; B. *Osteoglossum bicirrhosum*, x $^1/_4$; C. *Arapaima gigas*, x $^1/_{15}$; D. *Scleropages leichardti*, x $^1/_4$. In the map the black area marked A represents the distribution of the genus *Clupisudis*, that marked B and C, of *Osteoglossum* and *Arapaima*, and that marked D of *Scleropages*.

there are numerous species of Cyprinids, Loaches, Suckers, Cat-fishes, Labyrinth-fishes, etc., peculiar to the island or common to the Malay Peninsula and Archipelago whereas, in Celebes, there is not a single indigenous primary freshwater fish. It is true that there are certain widely distributed Indian species in Celebes, as well as in Australia and New Guinea, but these are either estuarine fishes capable of crossing the sea, or air-breathing forms which can be carried about alive in jars, and may well have been transported from one island to another by man. The only fishes of the order Ostariophysi in the Australian region are certain freshwater genera and species of Cat-fishes. These belong to two families (Ariidae; Plotosidae) which are thought to have assumed a marine habitat, reached Australia by sea, and have there again formed freshwater species.

In most respects Madagascar resembles the Australian region, being characterised by the complete absence of Ostariophysi, with the sole exception of a species of a marine family of Cat-fishes (Ariidae). The characteristic African families of Carps (Cyprinidae), Characins (Characidae and Citharinidae) Cat-fishes (Clariidae, Mochocidae, Amphiliidae etc.), and so on, are all absent and only the Perch-like Cichlids (Cichlidae) are common to the two regions. But the Cichlids are not entirely confined to fresh water, certain species being known to thrive in brackish or even salt water, and all those found in Madagascar are of the estuarine type. It may be concluded, therefore, that Madagascar has been isolated from Africa for a very long time, and that any freshwater fishes found there to-day have reached the island subsequently from the sea.

In the Neotropical (Central and South America) region the characteristic fishes might be expected to be somewhat similar to those of North America, but in point of fact, the faunas of the two regions of the New World are of a totally different nature. South America may be said to be inhabited by two distinct freshwater fish-faunas. The Patagonian fauna occupying the region south of a line drawn from Valparaiso to Bahia Blanca, is very poor in species, and consists mainly of immigrants from the sea which are more or less permanently established in the rivers, plus a few stragglers (Characins and Cat-fishes) from the north. On the other hand the region from La Plata River northwards to Central America is inhabited by a fauna extremely rich in genera and species, and bears a marked similarity to that of Africa. The Characins (Characoidei) are found in the African and Neotropical regions and nowhere else, and of the six families, one (Characidae), is found in both continents [Fig. 120], four are exclusively South American, and one occurs only in Africa. The family common to the Old and New World presents a much greater diversity and

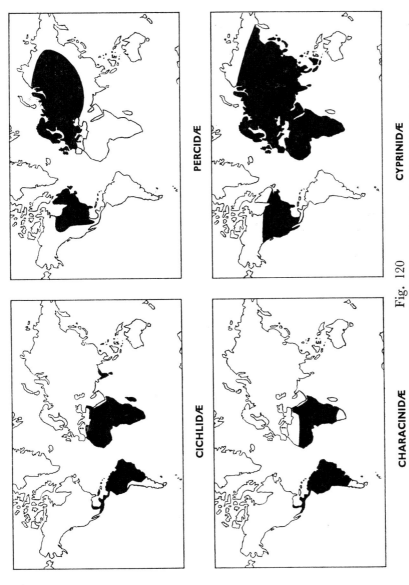

Fig. 120

Sketch maps showing the distribution of four major families of freshwater fishes. (After Regan)

number of genera and species in South America, and although there are no genera common to both, *Alestes* in Africa is very closely related to *Brycon* of South America. The peculiar Eel-like Gymnotids (Gymnotoidei) are confined to the Neotropical region, and there are no Carps, Loaches, Suckers, or Labyrinth-fishes. Of the Cat-fishes there are nine families in the Neotropical region all of them peculiar to this part of the world. The Cichlids (Cichlidae) are for the most part confined to Africa and Central and South America [Fig. 120]. Cyprinodonts are likewise found in both continents, but, like the Cichlids, they are able to live in brackish-water lagoons, and cannot be regarded as strictly freshwater fishes. Finally, the Lung-fishes are represented by one endemic genus of the same family in each of the two continents.

The very distinct Nearctic (North American) and Neotropical fish faunas scarcely meet, much less overlap. A few typically Neotropical forms, such as some of the Characins and Cat-fishes, have pushed as far north as the southern part of Mexico, but none has succeeded in reaching the great Mexican plateau [Fig. 120]. In the other direction a species of Gar Pike (*Lepisosteus tropicus*) has extended as far as Costa Rica, but although a few other Nearctic fishes have reach Central America, none has penetrated to South America.

The fish faunas of the Ethiopian and Oriental regions show certain affinities and share several families including three families of Cat-fishes, the Carps (Cyprinidae), Spiny-eels (Mastacembelidae), Cichlids (Cichlidae), the so-called Climbing Perches (Anabantidae) and the Featherbacks (Notopteridae). Within narrower limits the resemblance extends to shared genera in the Cyprinidae, Notopteridae and the Cat-fishes, but no species is common to both regions. In contrast there are, in the Ethiopian region, several families found only in Africa; for example the Snout-fishes (Mormyridae), Moon-fishes (Citharinidae) and the Bichirs (Polypteridae). Indeed, the Mormyridae form an order (Mormyriformes) and the Polypteridae a subclass (Brachiopterygii) found only in Africa, either as living fishes or as fossils. Apart from some highly specialized families of Cat-fishes there are few endemic families in the Oriental region although there are numerous endemic genera.

So much for the resemblances, but what of the differences? These are perhaps even more significant, particularly when compared with the relatively slight differences between the Ethiopian and Neotropical regions. To start with there are no Lung-fishes in the Oriental region, the Characoidei are totally unrepresented and whereas the African Cichlidae are abundant and much differentiated, in the Orient they are represented by a single endemic genus of three species, confined to Ceylon and peninsular India. The Oriental Cyprinidae, on the other hand, are more highly differentiated than those of Africa, and include numerous specialized genera.

When the South American, Ethiopian and Oriental regions are compared we find a certain pattern of familial and ordinal distribution which may provide a clue to the past distribution of the fishes. South America and Africa share a single family of Lungfishes, the two continents have a well-developed array of Characin and Cichlid fishes (the former absent from the Orient, the latter poorly represented), South America lacks Cyprinids but the Oriental and African regions share the family and even certain genera; Cat-fishes are present in all three regions but those from South America are the most diverse. It is impossible to treat the subject in any detail here, especially with regard to the evolutionary relationships of the fishes concerned. It must suffice to state dogmatically that, at a fundamental level, the fish fauna of South America is more closely related to that of Africa than the fauna of either is to that of the Oriental region; the fauna of Africa is more 'archaic' than that of the Oriental region and even that of South America; and lastly, the most primitive living Cyprinids occur in the Oriental region. These are important considerations in the story of past intercontinental distribution, a subject which has intrigued zoologists for over half a century.

For many years, the concept of 'Continental Drift' seemed the most favoured basis for explaining the relationships of the African, South American and Oriental fishes (see previous editions of this book); in all these theories, the emphasis was on relationships and less attention was paid to the all-important differences between the faunas. The geological evidence for continental drift is still vigourously disputed and, if drift occurred, it seems that it would have happened too early in geological history to account for the distribution of modern fishes.

If the three continents were not once part of a single land mass, one must assume several things in order to account for the present picture, amongst others a fairly uniformly distributed and circumtropical archaic fauna for certain groups, local (i.e. continental) differentiation within these groups and local changes in the relative dominance of the various families so evolved; finally, there is the need for temporary intercontinental landbridge connections between Europe and North America (perhaps across the Bering Straits) and possibly between South America and Africa. Despite their number and the apparent magnitude of these assumptions, most receive support from other fields and from other animal groups.

With these points in mind, we can return to a more detailed consideration of the fishes. First, we must differentiate between primary freshwater fishes (those with a limited salinity tolerance) and those, like the Cichlids and Cyprinodonts which are known to have a high salinity tolerance and can live and spawn in brackish or even salt water. The primary freshwater fishes which feature in this argument are the Ostariophysi, that is, the Carps, Cat-fishes and Characins. The Cat-fishes are a very distinct subgroup of the Ostariophysi but comparative anatomical work suggests a relatively close relationship between the Carps and the Characins, the latter probably being ancestral to the former.

In order to explain the distribution of the Ostariophysi, one theory assumes that the group evolved, sometime in the Cretaceous period, in the freshwaters of the Old World tropics and that its first division was into Cat-fishes and Characins. Part of this basic Ostario-physian fauna spread from the Old World to South America, either by way of Eurasia and North America (*via* a Bering land bridge) or more directly from Africa across a South Atlantic bridge (for which, at present, there is no evidence from other animals or from geology). If the Characins and Cat-fishes spread to South America from an evolutionary centre in either tropical Asia or Africa *via* Europe and North America, they have left no trace of their passage in these continents. A possible explanation for this is the essentially tropical nature of these fishes. To-day, Characins are only found in tropical or subtropical zones and the Cat-fishes are very poorly represented (and not by genera closely related to tropical forms) in North America. Likewise in the Palaearctic region, Cat-fishes are sparsely represented by genera which are probably recent invaders from tropical Asia. Clearly then, at least the Cat-fishes could invade temperate regions but would be an unstable element in the fauna, an element likely to be exterminated by climatic changes away from temperate conditions. There is no evidence of Characins in present-day temperate regions so we must assume that these fishes were able to pass through the present Palaearctic and Nearctic regions presumably during periods when the climate there was more suited to their requirements.

The alternative route, by means of landbridges from Africa to South America has the advantage of not requiring the postulated extermination of Characins in North America and Europe, nor does it demand the adaptation of these fishes to temperate climates in order to migrate from an evolutionary centre in the Tropics.

Temporally, the next step in this story is the evolution of Carps (Cyprinidae). Again, evidence suggests an origin, probably from a Characin stem, in tropical South East Asia. Here the early Cyprinids underwent a period of explosive evolutionary radiation which led to their becoming the dominant freshwater fishes in the area. A presumed consequence of this dominance in Asia was the displace-ment of the older, less adaptable fishes, in particular the Characins, and a spread of Cyprinids into Eurasia (Palaearctic region), North America (again *via* a Bering landbridge) and Africa. In

Africa the Characins were apparently able to compete against the Cyprinid invaders and the two groups evolved side by side. At this period in geological history (probably early in the Eocene) South America was isolated from North America; only in comparatively recent times have the two continents been connected by the Central American landbridge. This area has proved an important biological filter (see above, page 286) since it has held back several families of primary freshwater fishes, including the wide-ranging and successful Cyprinids, which were thus prevented from invading South America.

It must now be self-evident that we still require a lot more biological, palaeontological and geological evidence before more definite ideas are forthcoming on the zoogeography of tropical freshwater fishes. The evidence to date is elegantly and objectively reviewed in P. J. Darlington's excellent book '*Zoogeography*', which should be consulted to clothe and activate the bare bones offered here.

The fish faunas of the Palaearctic (Eurasian) and Nearctic (North American) regions also exhibit definite resemblances, such important freshwater families as the Carps (Cyprinidae), Pikes (Esocidae) Mud-fishes (Umbridae), and Perches (Percidae) being common to both [Fig. 120] although a number of characteristic North American families are absent in the Old World. The Ostariophysi of the Palaearctic region are represented by comparatively few Cat-fishes, all of which belong to genera also occurring in Asia, and a large number of Carps and Loaches. These must have spread northwards from their original headquarters, penetrating first into temperate Asia and later invading Europe. A fair number of Carps occur in Europe, a few Loaches, and two Cat-fishes, the Wels or Glanis (*Silurus*), found only in the rivers east of the Rhine and an endemic species of the Asian genus *Parasilurus* isolated in Greece.

In Britain about twenty-two species of true freshwater fishes may be recognised, of which fourteen belong to the order Ostariophysi. All of these are also found in continental Europe, and a number extend eastwards into Asia. The importance of the Pyrenees mountains as a barrier is emphasised by the fact that only one of these fishes occurs in the Iberian Peninsula although about half of them have succeeded in penetrating into Italy. Two species, the Burbot (*Lota*) and the Pike (*Esox*), occur also in North America. It is of interest to note that all the twenty-two species occur in Yorkshire, and nearly all in the Trent, the Ouse, and in Norfolk, but there are parts of the British Isles where the freshwater fauna is a very poor one. In Ireland there are only ten species, and in Britain there is a marked diminution in the number of species from south to north, culminating in a complete absence of true indigenous freshwater fishes in the northern highlands of Scotland.

A similar decrease in number of species is noticeable from east to west, and quite a number are absent from Wales west of the Severn system.   The reasons for the very dissimilar distribution in the British Isles of certain species with a very wide and essentially similar distribution on the continent of Europe and Asia are to be found in the former connection of the islands with one another and with the mainland.   The whole question of the origin and distribution of British freshwater fishes has been dealt with in full by Dr. Regan in his book on 'British Fresh-water Fishes,' to which reference may be made for further details.   He points out that the British Isles must have been connected with each other and with continental Europe comparatively recently, 'when our eastern, and probably our southern, streams were tributaries of continental rivers and received from them the fishes which they contained; only nine or ten of these had reached Ireland before it became a separate island, and the distribution of the rest in Britain at varying rates, according to circumstances has not yet proceeded long enough to spread them all over the island.'   The accompanying map [Fig. 121] will give some idea of the manner in which the freshwater fishes reached Britain, and the main routes along which they must have travelled.

In addition to the families common to the temperate regions of the Old and New Worlds (Esocidae, Umbridae, Cyprinidae, Percidae, etc.) the Nearctic region possesses a number of families occurring nowhere else.   They include the archaic Gar Pikes (Lepisosteidae) and Bow-fins (Amiidae), the Moon-eyes (Hiodont-

Fig. 121
Restoration of the Pleistocene geography of the British Isles, showing the coast-line coincident with the 80 fathom contour. (After Jukes-Browne)

idae), Blind Cave-fishes (Amblyopsidae), Trout Perches (Percopsidae), and Sun-fishes (Centrarchidae). The Ostariophysi are represented in this region by a large number of genera and species of Cyprinidae, all of a similar type to those found in the Palaearctic region; the family of Suckers (Catostomidae), which, with the exception of one species found in China and one common to North America and East Siberia is confined to North America; and the family of Cat-fishes (Amiuridae) variously known as Amiurids, Horned Pouts, Stone Cats, Channel Cats, Mad Toms, etc., of which only a single species is found outside North America. The Suckers and Cat-fishes have been established in this region for some time, as fossil remains of genera and species not very unlike the existing ones occur in Oligocene and Miocene strata.

With the increased interest now shown in fish as a source of food and sport, the old zoogeographical barriers are gradually being broached. Non-native food and game fishes are now widely transplanted, even between continents. European trout (*Salmo trutta*) have been successfully introduced into many parts of North America, whilst the American Rainbow trout (*S. gairdneri*) has been imported into Britain. The King Salmon (*Oncorhynchus tshawytscha*) was introduced into New Zealand waters where it is well established. The Pink Salmon (*O. gorbuscha*) whose range is from Northern Japan to Alaska and south to La Jolla, California, has recently appeared in some British rivers. The species was introduced into the Baltic and has successfully made its way across the North Sea; it remains to be seen whether it will establish populations around the British Isles. Perhaps the most widespread introductions, and in the shortest time, are those of the African Cichlid *Tilapia mossambica*. The first extra-territorial appearance of the species was in Java[+], and no explanation has been provided for its arrival in that country. This happened just before the 1939–45 war and since then it has spread (often with the aid of world authorities but also unofficially in a soldier's kit-bag) to Sumatra, Bali, Lombok, Celebes, the Malayan mainland[+], Thailand[+], the Philippines[+], Taiwan[+] (where it has become a dominant element of the local fauna), Ceylon[+] and South Korea[+]. In the western hemisphere it has arrived in St Lucia[+] (British West Indies), Trinidad, Haiti and, most recently, in Texas. The localities marked[+] are those in which the species has escaped from fish ponds and has formed 'wild' populations.

All these cases are, fortunately, well documented. Far more troublesome to the zoologist are incompletely documented transfers of endemic species from one basin or river system to another where the species is not native. This is particularly so in Africa where we had not yet acquired a full knowledge of natural distributions before man interfered. Species of *Tilapia* have been carried all over

Central and Eastern Africa and many have escaped into local river systems. To cite but one example: in Lake Victoria there were two endemic *Tilapia* species only; now, there are at least three other species. Beside the known introductions there is always the risk of other species being introduced at the same time, especially if fry are being used. In Africa this has happened more than once; in certain areas it is now impossible to carry out zoogeographical studies with any degree of certainty and we may never be able to work out the evolution and distribution of many species.

REFERENCES

BERG, L. S. (1932). Übersicht der Verbreitung der Süsserwasserfische Europas. *Zoogeographica*, **1**, No. 2, 107–208.

BERTIN, L. (1956). *Eels*. Cleaver-Hume Press, London.

DARLINGTON, P. J. (1957). *Zoogeography*. Wiley, New York.

MARSHALL, N. B. (1954). *Aspects of Deep Sea Biology*. Hutchinson's London.

REGAN, C. T. (1911). *The Fresh-Water Fishes of the British Isles*. Methuen, London.

SCHINDLER, O. (1957). *Guide to Freshwater Fishes*. Thames and Hudson. London.

CHAPTER 17

FOSSILS AND PEDIGREES

An IMPORTANT branch of Zoology is that known as taxonomy, which is concerned with arranging or classifying the multitude of diverse forms of animal life. A century and a half ago any scheme of classification was mainly artificial, being constructed in the belief that the world had come into existence quite suddenly, and that the different kinds of animals inhabiting it were separately created in the beginning and have remained unchanged ever since. Such a view has now been proved untenable, and slowly and steadily a mass of evidence has been accumulated which shows beyond any shadow of doubt that the existing species of animals have all been produced from earlier and simpler types by a process of gradual evolution. It has been demonstrated that the birds and mammals arose from the cold-blooded reptiles, the reptiles from the amphibians, the amphibians from some of the primitive fishes, while the fishes themselves have arisen from some even more primitive type of vertebrate, itself presumably derived from an invertebrate stock. The same evidence also shows that the fishes living to-day, multitudinous and diverse as they are, represent but a proportion of the total number of fishes that have, at various times, lived in the seas and freshwaters. The existing forms may be compared to the topmost branches and twigs of the fish 'family tree'; they are the forms that have succeeded in adapting themselves to present-day conditions, and have accordingly gained a temporary triumph in the struggle for existence. There are innumerable other branches, some short and simple, others long and further branched, representing forms that flourished for a time but finally died out. Of these, some failed to adapt themselves to changed conditions and so perished, others became variously changed and modified, to give rise to new and perhaps more successful types.

The term phylogeny is applied to the pedigrees of animals, as opposed to ontogeny, which is concerned with the development of the individual from the egg to the mature animal: the one deals with the history of the group, the other with the history of the individual. The business of the systematic ichthyologist is to study and compare the existing fishes, in an endeavour to make out their affinities one to the other, and to discover the lines of descent that connect the various branches of the 'tree' upon which his classification is based. A perfect taxonomy would express all the known facts in the evolution and development of the various forms. The evidence upon which it would be based would be drawn mainly from three sources: comparative anatomy, embryology, and palaeontology. Palaeontology is concerned with the remains of extinct animals and plants preserved in the rocks, and no scheme of classification, nor any phylogenetic tree that may be composed to illustrate the lines of descent of a particular group of animals, is worthy of serious consideration until it has been tested by a study of the record provided by the rocks. It is reasonable to suppose that if evolution is an established theory and not a mere hypothesis, the series of fossils studied by the palaeontologist should provide some evidence of this process, and that it should be possible to reconstruct from these remains, if not the ancestral types at least some of their near relations. To give any sort of detailed account of the large number of fossil fishes that have now been described would be altogether beyond the scope of this book, and it will be possible only to survey very briefly some of the more interesting forms, and to consider their affinities with living fishes.

As the result of many years of study of the organic remains contained in the fossil-bearing rocks of the world, most of these rocks have now been assigned to their correct place in the geological record, and the history of the earth has been split up into a series of divisions of various grades, which may be likened to the chapters, sections, and paragraphs of a book. The names given to the different kinds of rock by the geologist, such as the Chalk, Cambridge Greensand, Oolite, Red Sandstone, London Clay, etc., may be ignored here, but the main divisions and subdivisions into which geological time has been split up are of greater importance, and it will be necessary to mention these by name in the course of this chapter. The main divisions are known as eras, each era being subdivided into several periods, which may be further split up into epochs. Just as it is customary to speak of ancient, mediaeval, and modern history of the human race, so do geologists refer to the Palaeozoic, Mesozoic, and Tertiary (or Caenozoic) eras in the history of the earth. In the accompanying diagram [Fig. 122] the earliest era, the Archaean or Pre-Cambrian, need not concern us, for although it may represent more than half of geological time, this time was passed before there were many living organisms with structures sufficiently hard to form fossils. The other eras from the Cambrian to the present day are all fossiliferous, and the sizes of the spaces in the diagram represent very approximately the relative lengths of the periods in geological time. Some idea of the time-scale may be gained from the fact that it has been estimated

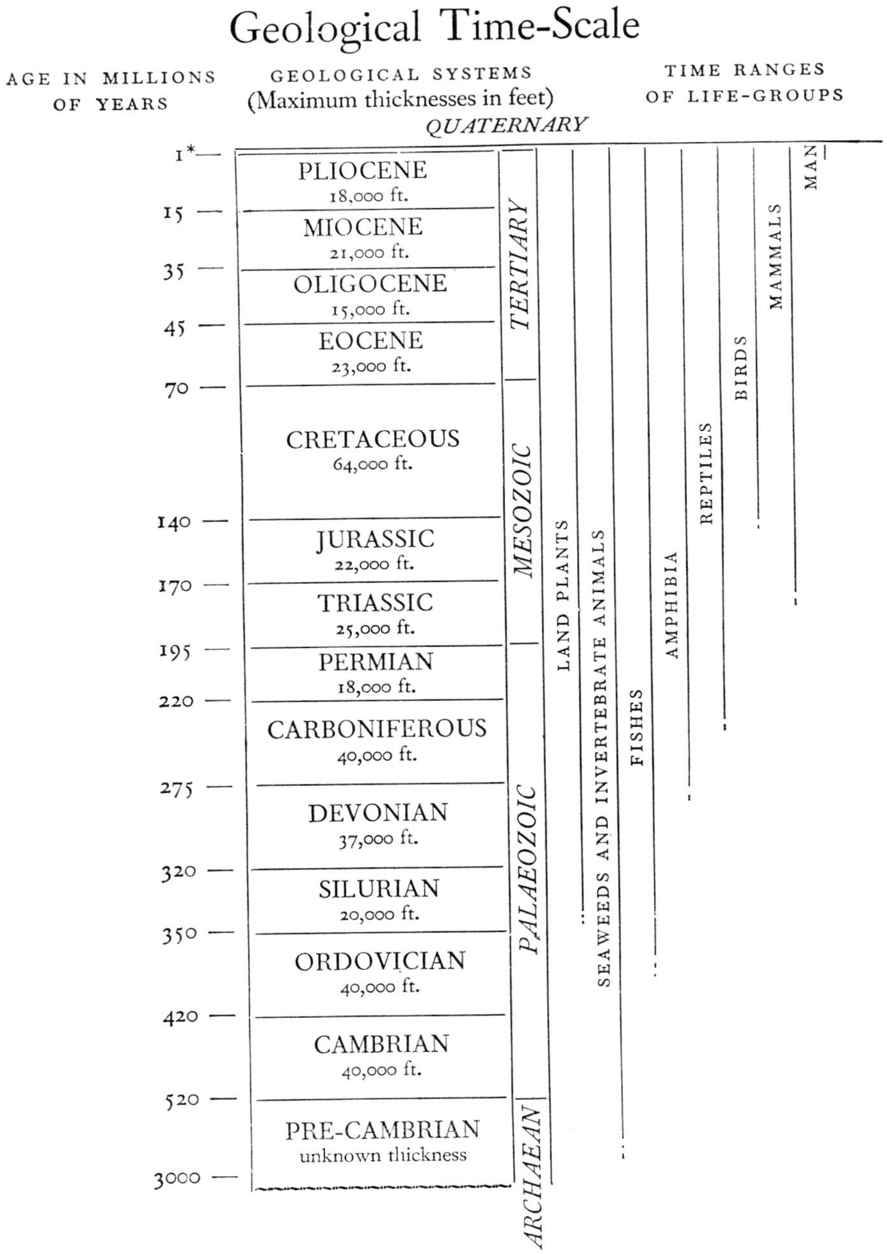

Geological Time-Scale

AGE IN MILLIONS
OF YEARS
GEOLOGICAL SYSTEMS
(Maximum thicknesses in feet)
TIME RANGES
OF LIFE-GROUPS

QUATERNARY

AGE IN MILLIONS OF YEARS	GEOLOGICAL SYSTEMS		TIME RANGES OF LIFE-GROUPS
1*—	PLIOCENE 18,000 ft.		MAN
15 —	MIOCENE 21,000 ft.	*TERTIARY*	MAMMALS
35 —	OLIGOCENE 15,000 ft.		
45 —	EOCENE 23,000 ft.		BIRDS
70 —	CRETACEOUS 64,000 ft.	*MESOZOIC*	REPTILES
140 —	JURASSIC 22,000 ft.		
170 —	TRIASSIC 25,000 ft.		AMPHIBIA
195 —	PERMIAN 18,000 ft.		LAND PLANTS / SEAWEEDS AND INVERTEBRATE ANIMALS
220 —	CARBONIFEROUS 40,000 ft.		FISHES
275 —	DEVONIAN 37,000 ft.	*PALAEOZOIC*	
320 —	SILURIAN 20,000 ft.		
350 —	ORDOVICIAN 40,000 ft.		
420 —	CAMBRIAN 40,000 ft.		
520 —	PRE-CAMBRIAN unknown thickness	*ARCHAEAN*	
3000 —			

* Quaternary (Pleistocene and Holocene) 4,000 feet.

Fig. 122 Geological time-scale (after de Beer; from various sources)

that the lower layers of the Triassic period, during which mammals first made their appearance on earth, were deposited somewhere in the neighbourhood of 195,000,000 years ago. Fish-like vertebrates first made their appearance during the Ordovician period, and became very abundant during Devonian and Carboniferous times, when they were the dominant form of animal life and had already produced a large number of diverse types.

It must not be supposed that the fossil-bearing strata always have the regular arrangement depicted in the diagram, or that the record of the rocks provides a continuous story in which the history of all the main groups of animals and their lines of descent may be deciphered with the aid of a complete series of well-preserved fossil remains. Quite often the proper arrangement of the layers has been much disturbed, the rocks being variously tilted, buckled, twisted, broken, or even turned wrong way up. The reading of the story of the earth's history may be likened to the reading of a book, but a book which has been extensively damaged by fire, water, and decay, so that many of its pages are altogether missing, while others are variously torn, dogeared, crumpled, and their contents rendered illegible. The following passage emphasising the imperfection of the geological record was written in 1898 by Sir Arthur Smith Woodward, then one of the leading authorities on fossil fishes. In spite of many discoveries made since that date, its substance remains fundamentally true to-day. 'We may, in fact, without exaggeration declare that every item of knowledge we possess concerning extinct plants and animals depends upon a chapter of accidents. Firstly, the organism must find its way into water where sediment is being deposited and there escape all the dangers of being eaten; or it must be accidentally entombed in blown sand or a volcanic accumulation on land. Secondly, this sediment, if it eventually happens to enter into the composition of a land area, must escape the all-prevalent denudation (or destruction or removal by atmospheric or aqueous agencies) continually in progress. Thirdly, the skeleton, of the buried organism must resist the solvent action of any waters which may percolate through a rock. Lastly, man must accidentally excavate at the precise spot where entombment took place, and someone must be at hand, capable of appreciating the fossil, and preserving it for study when discovered.'

The geological record has so far provided no evidence as to the origin of the fishes, and shortly after the time when fish-like fossils first made their appearance in the rocks the Cyclostomes, Selachians, and Bony Fishes are not only already differentiated from each other and firmly established, but are represented by a number of diverse and often specialised types, a fact suggesting that each of the classes had already enjoyed a respectable antiquity. It will be convenient, therefore, to consider the fossil history of each sepa-

PLATE VI

Slab of chalk (Sussex) with remains of *Hoplopteryx superbus*. From a specimen
in the British Museum (Natural History)

rately, commencing with the Cyclostomes as being admittedly the most primitive.

In Cyclostomes the gills are contained in a series of separate muscular pouches, which expand and contract during respiration, and are quite unlike those of any other fishes (*cf.* p. 72). This character, coupled with the complete absence of jaws and of gill-arches, serves to distinguish them from both Selachians and Bony Fishes. It had formerly been supposed that these characters represented secondary modifications brought about by the highly specialised, semi-parasitic habits of the existing Cyclostomes, but the past history of the group effectually disposes of this view, and shows beyond all doubt that the differences between the Cyclostomes and other vertebrates in the structure of the mouth and gills are truly fundamental. It must be understood, of course, that the fossil remains furnished by the Silurian and Lower Devonian rocks provide only a few clues as to the lines of descent of the existing forms. The archaic forms are quite as specialised in many respects as are their descendants living to-day. At the same time, however, they are of very great interest, and show in their anatomy undoubted evidence of descent from the same stock.

The fossil CYCLOSTOMI are, according to Stensiö, a Swedish authority, divisible into three subclasses, the *Cephalaspidomorphi*, the *Pteraspidomorphi* and the *Thelodonti*. This author places the living Cyclostomes in two superorders, the Petromyzontidea and the Myxinoidea, contained respectively in the Cephalaspidomorphi and Pteraspidormorphi. Such an arrangement does not meet with universal approval or acceptance, the living Cyclostomes then being considered as comprising a fourth subclass derived from the Cephalaspids.

The fossil *Cephalaspidomorphi* are divided into two superorders, the Osteostraci and the Anaspida. The Osteostraci range in time from the Upper Silurian to the Lower Devonian. Remains of these fishes from deposits in Spitzbergen are so perfectly preserved that it is possible to work out their internal anatomy almost as accurately as if fresh specimens were available for dissection. This fact, coupled with the immense skill and patience displayed by Professor Stensiö and his school of Swedish Palaeozoologists, make the Osteostraci the best known group of fossil fish-like vertebrates.

The Osteostraci are of small size, few exceeding a foot in length. The head is flattened and covered by a large bony shield, rounded in front and with the hinder corners generally produced into pointed 'horns' [Fig. 123c]. The body is sheathed in numerous bony plates arranged in regular rows, those on the sides being high and narrow. Beneath the head shield is an internal skeleton at least partly composed of bony tissue. All the blood-vessels and nerves penetrating or lying in contact with this tissue have left an impression and it has proved possible to work out the arrangement of the nervous and vascular systems. According to Stensiö, these bear a marked resemblance to those of living Cyclostomes. Peculiar patches of hexagonal plates on the head shield are supplied by large nerves which run upwards and outwards from the hinder part of the brain. These may represent either electric organs or sense organs of an unknown function. On the lower surface of the shield is a series of separate gill-openings on each side; from impressions left on the inner aspect of the shield it seems that the gills themselves were contained in pouches. An important feature is the position of the first pair of pouches. These lie in advance of the position occupied by the jaws in other vertebrates. The significance of this becomes clear when we remember that in the Chondrichthyes and Bony Fishes the modification of one pair of gill arches into biting jaws has resulted in the disappearance of the gills in front of them. It follows, therefore, that the Osteostraci cannot have had true jaws, nor can they have been descended from animals with such jaws. There is a single nostril in the middle of the upper surface of the head shield and in the auditory region there are only two semi-circular canals (as in the living Lampreys), the horizontal one being undeveloped. A study of the development of the Lamprey indicates still more evidence of its relationship with these Palaeozoic forms, for the plate of so-called mucous cartilage which arises in the head region of the larva is suggestive, both in form and position, of the head shield in Osteostraci. In general, the cranial nerves also resemble those of the Lampreys, the differences that exist being attributable to the respective specializations of the two groups.

The Osteostraci were probably sluggish creatures that lived on the bottom. In their dorso-ventrally flattened shape they bear much the same relationship to the other Cephalaspidomorph superorder, the Anaspida, as the modern Rays do to the Sharks. In mid-Devonian deposits, the Osteostraci gradually decrease in abundance, become comparatively rare in deposits from the latter half of the Devonian and finally disappear from the record before the beginning of the Carboniferous period. The causes which led to their extinction must remain conjectural, but several similar cases are found in other groups of fishes. The story is the same; elaborate, clumsy, heavily armoured creatures die out and give place to less specialized and less protected but more active forms.

Members of the second superorder (Anaspida) are quite unlike the Osteostraci in appearance. Typically they have a slender, fusiform body covered with series of small, scale-like bony plates, the head being armoured with numerous plates of a similar nature but irregularly arranged [Fig. 123A]. Immediately behind the head on either side is a row of pores, thought to be gill openings. Posterior to these, small plates and spines are believed to represent

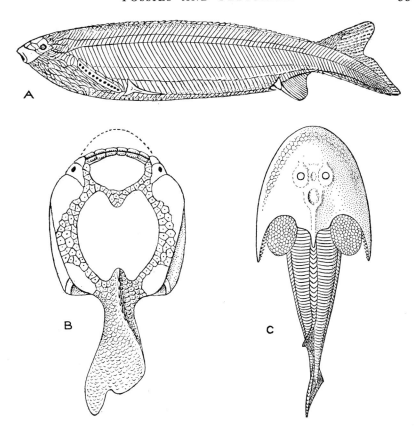

Fig. 123 RESTORATIONS OF SILURIAN AND DEVONIAN CYCLOSTOMI
A. An Anaspid (Cephalaspidomorphi), *Pharyngolepis oblongus*, lateral view, x 1; B. A Drepanaspid (Pteraspidomorphi), *Drepanaspis gemuendensis*, dorsal view, x 1/5; C. An Osteostracian (Cephalaspidomorphi), *'Cephalaspis' lyelli*, dorsal view, x 1/2. (A after Stensiö; B after Stensiö and Obrutscher; C after Traquir)

the pectoral appendages. Like the Osteostraci, the Anaspida do not bear even a superficial resemblance to Lampreys. But, closer study again shows several points of resemblance. In both Lampreys and Anaspids there is a pineal organ between the eyes and a single unpaired nostril in front of it [Fig. 124]. The form of the mouth cannot easily be determined in the fossils but it seems possible, however, that it was a small, elliptical and terminal slit not unlike that in the ammocoete larva of modern Cyclostomes. The tail of the Anaspida, a reversed heterocercal or hypocercal type, is

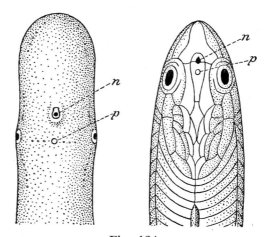

Fig. 124
Head of *Rhyncholepsis* (right) compared with that of a Lamprey (*Lampetra*);
n., nostril; *p.*, pineal organ. (After Kiaer)

unusual but such a tail does occur as a transitory structure in the ammocoete larva.

The flexible body and fusiform shape suggest that the Anaspida were relatively good swimmers, whilst the mouth form indicates that they fed on small organisms sucked up from bottom mud.

Before leaving the Anaspida we must mention a peculiar Anaspid-like fossil, *Jamoytius kerwoodi* from upper Silurian sediments of Lanarkshire [Fig. 125]. Authorities have differed in their opinions of just what this animal really was. Some think it a conservative form of the main stock from which the various groups of higher chordates arose, and possibly an ancestor of the living acraniate

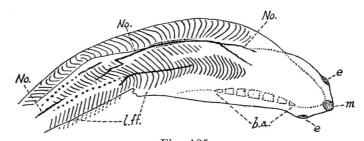

Fig. 125
Jamoytius kerwoodi, x *ca.* ³/₄. *b.a.*, branchial apparatus (or apertures); *e.*, eye; *l.ff.*, lateral fin-fold; *m.*, mouth; *No.*, notochord. (Simplified after White and Ritchie)

Branchiostoma. More probably it is an aberrant member of the Anaspida. For our purpose, its most interesting feature is the presence of paired lateral fin folds (see p. 27) and the fact that of all the fossil Cyclostomi it seems closest to the living forms (see Ritchie).

The second, and chronologically oldest, subclass is the *Pteraspido-morphi* [Figs. 123B; 126]. These first occur in Ordovician strata and die out in late Devonian times (unless one accepts Stensiö's contention that the living Hagfishes (Myxinoids) are members of the group). The Pteraspids have the head and trunk enclosed in bony plates, those on the hinder part of the body are small and have the general appearance of scales. The best known genus is

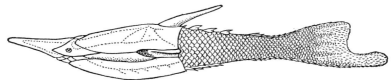

Fig. 126
A Pteraspid (*Pteraspis rostrata*), x *ca* ¹/₃. (After White)

Pteraspis [Fig. 126]. The mouth is a transverse slit on the lower surface of the head, surrounded by bony plates bearing minute denticles but with no trace of any structures that might be interpreted as true jaws. Unlike the Cephalaspidomorphi, the gills open to the exterior by a single aperture on either side (as in the living Hagfishes) and the nostrils are paired and open on the lower side of the head. Several curious types of Pteraspids have been described, some of them box-like with broad rounded snouts and short thick bodies. Others have the head shield prolonged to form a pointed rostrum. The generally flattened form, rigid head and trunk of the Pteraspids suggest sluggish habits and, like the Osteostraci, they probably lived at or close to the bottom.

The third subclass, the *Thelodonti*, are the least known fossil Cyclostomes; their time range is from the Silurian to the middle Devonian. Little is known of their internal skeleton, but the body and head are covered with placoid denticles. The body is flattened, the mouth ventral and terminal, and there are traces of about seven branchial supports, whose arrangement is of the living Cyclostome type.

Before passing to the class CHONDRICHTHYES (Sharks and Rays) proper we must consider a group of extinct, shark-like fishes. Their remains occur in Silurian, Devonian and lower Carboniferous strata and their anatomy has been carefully studied by the Swedes. Once thought to be primitive Bony Fishes, the two classes, ACANTHODII and PLACODERMI, are now thought to represent an independent offshoot from the main stem of primitive Chondrichthyes.

The ACANTHODII occur in strata from the upper Silurian to the lower Permian; complete or well-preserved remains are comparatively rare. The fins of these creatures, both paired and unpaired, have a strong spine at the anterior edge; in the genus *Climatius* (lower Devonian of Forfarshire) there is a row of spines on each side of the body between those supporting the pectoral and pelvic fins. The body is encased in an elaborate armour, the denticles being modified to form a mosaic of minute, diamond-shaped ganoid scales. In the region of the head, some of these scales have fused to form a series of separate bony plates for the protection of the skull. The teeth (where known) are more or less large and many-cusped. The known fossils are all of small size and none shows the development of that truly Chondrichthyean character, 'claspers' on the pelvic fins. These shark-like fishes cannot be regarded as ancestral to any existing shark group. Rather, they are a highly specialized branch springing from near the base of the Chondrichthyean 'tree'.

The PLACODERMII (comprising the subclasses *Antiarchi* and *Arthrodiri*), [Fig. 127], have a stout exoskeleton of bony plates, but the underlying skull is essentially Shark-like. The armour of these fishes is concentrated into an anterior box-like structure, the cephalothorax; the hinder part of the body is covered by small scales or is even naked. The head portion of the cephalothorax is hinged to the box-like armour of the thoracic region.

Coccosteus is perhaps the most familiar Arthrodire. It is a comparatively small fish, occurring in Europe and is particularly abundant in the Old Red Sandstone of Scotland [Fig. 127A]. Members of this genus range in size from about twelve to eighteen inches long. Certain Arthrodires (*Dinichthys*, *Titanichthys*) from North America rival some of the largest living sharks, attaining lengths of twenty or more feet. The great variation in the form and dentition of the Arthrodires suggests that their habits were equally varied. The group includes fusiform (?pelagic) types such as *Coccosteus*, flattened ray-like forms with expanded pectoral fins (*Gemuendina*, [Fig. 127C]), and others [Fig. 127B] remarkably similar to the living Rabbit-fishes (superorder Holocephali of the Bradyodonti).

Members of the subclass *Antiarchi* are also remarkable looking creatures; *Pterichthyodes* [Fig. 127E] from the Old Red Sandstone of Scotland and *Bothriolepis* [Fig. 127D] of North America may be taken as typical genera. The mouth is small, the eyes small and placed close together on the upper surface of the head, there are no pelvic fins and anteriorly there is a pair of curious, two-jointed and freely movable appendages. These fins, not unlike the limbs of Crustacea in appearance, are entirely without parallel in verte-

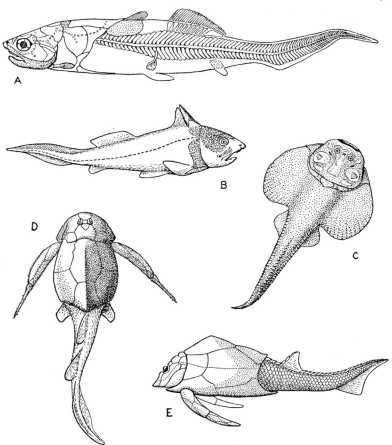

Fig. 127 VARIOUS PLACODERMS (SUBCLASSES ANTIARCHI AND ARTHRODIRI)
A. *Coccosteus*, an Arthrodire, x ¹/₆; B. *Rhamphodopsis*, a Ptyctodont
Arthrodire, x ¹/₃; C. *Gemuendina*, a ray-like Arthrodire, x *ca* ¹/₆; D. *Bothriolepsis*, an Antiarch, x ¹/₇; E. *Pterichthyodes*, an Antiarch, x ¹/₃. (A, B, and
E after Stensiö; C, after Broili; D, modified after Patten)

brate animals [Fig. 127D, E]. Each is hollow and is made up from a
number of bony plates; their function remains problematical but
there is little doubt that they are homologous with the pectoral
fins in the *Arthrodiri* and with the pectorals of higher fishes.

The grotesque *Antiarchi* must be regarded as being in the nature
of evolutionary experiments which flourished for a time but were
doomed to extinction under the stress of competition with later and
evolutionarily more flexible types.

The origin of the CHONDRICHTHYES is obscure, and our knowledge of the early history of this class is based largely on fragmentary remains and a few well-preserved skeletons. The earliest traces of these fishes take the form of isolated spines, teeth, dermal denticles and the like, from the Upper Silurian and Lower Devonian rocks, interesting enough in themselves, but giving no clue to the structural features of their owners. Their diversity, however, is evidence that there must have existed, even at this period, a wealth of genera and species, and that the CHONDRICHTHYES had already been in existence for a long time. The late Professor Bashford Dean suggests that they probably reached the zenith of their differentiation in the Carboniferous period, 'when specialised sharks existed whose varied structures are paralleled only by those of existing bony fishes—sharks fitted to the most special environment; some minute and delicate; others enormous, heavy, and sluggish, with stout head and fin spines, and elaborate types of dentition.'

Recent classifications divide the class CHONDRICHTHYES into two subclasses, the *Selachii* (Sharks and Rays) and the *Bradyodonti* (Chimaeras and their allies). The Selachii is composed of two superorders one of which, the Protoselachii, contains only extinct forms. The best known Protoselachian is *Cladoselache* (order **Cladoselachiformes**); it is found in upper Devonian strata of Ohio. This shark is by far the most primitive yet discovered and could be regarded as ancestral to many later types. It varies in length from two to six feet, and in shape and general appearance is not very unlike a modern Shark; the mouth, however, is terminal. The paired fins are little more than balancers and have broad bases. The internal structure of these fins is primitive [Fig. 16A], the basal elements of the pelvics being quite separate and the pectorals are scarcely more advanced in structure. These broad-based, pointed fins and the strongly heterocercal tail suggest that *Cladoselache* was a pelagic shark. In no fossil has there been found any trace of 'claspers' on the pelvic fins.

The second order of Protoselachians, the **Pleuracanthiformes** is characterized by its members having a diphycercal caudal fin

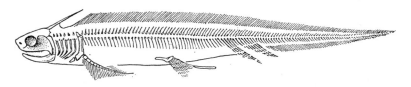

Fig. 128
Pleuracanthus sessilis, a Protoselachian (order Pleuracanthiformes), x *ca* 1/7. (After Jaekel)

and the pelvic fins modified to form 'claspers' (a feature of all modern Sharks). *Pleuracanthus* is the best known genus and well preserved skeletons have been found in Carboniferous and Permian rocks of Europe, Australia and North America [Fig. 128]. Its paired fins are unique amongst Sharks, being paddle-shaped, the supporting basals forming a jointed central axis with the radials symmetrically arranged on either side. Dermal denticles as such do not appear to be present. There are no dermal ossifications in the head region but the brain-case is calcified. The mouth is terminal and the teeth shark-like. A curious feature is the presence of a long median spine projecting from the back of the head. *Pleuracanthus* is known to have reached a length of six feet. The form of the fins suggest that it was a slow swimmer and lived at or close to the bottom.

The third order (**Hybodontiformes**) is related to certain living sharks (*e.g. Heterodontus*, [Fig. 53B, *b*]) and to one of the earliest known Euselachians, coexisting with it in Jurassic times.

The subclass *Bradyodonti* also dates from the Devonian; it reached its zenith during the Cretaceous and Eocene. The comparatively few living Bradyodonti (superorder Holocephali) are first known from Cretaceous deposits and may be looked upon as the descendants of an important group, the members of which were once numerous and diverse. The extinct Bradyodonti are known principally from their teeth. The range and diversity of tooth form is fantastic [see Fig. 129]. Whereas the living Chimaeras rarely exceed a length of three or four feet, the extinct Bradyodont *Edaphodon* attained relatively gigantic proportions.

No remains that can definitely be ascribed to the members of the superorder Euselachii have yet been discovered in rocks earlier than those of the Jurassic period, but fragments of teeth and spines from Permian strata may have belonged to such Sharks. All the

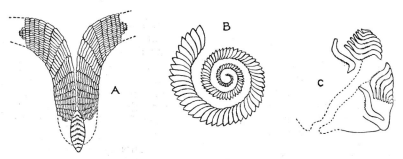

Fig. 129 TEETH OF SOME EXTINCT BRADYODONTI
A. *Agassizodus* sp.; B. *Helicoprion bessonowi*; C. *Janassa bituminosa*. (From Moy-Thomas). All reduced.

families of existing Selachians, with the sole exception of the Blue
Sharks and their allies (Carcharinidae) and the Sting Rays
(Dasyatidae), include genera which have been found as fossils in
Cretaceous rocks, and such specialised forms as the Monk-fish
(*Squatina*) and Guitar-fish (*Rhinobatus*), as well as the Comb-
toothed Sharks (Hexanchidae), Bull-headed Sharks (Heterodontidae), and some of the Dog-fishes (Scyliorhinidae), date back to
the Jurassic period. Indeed, so little have some of these changed in
the course of time, that well-preserved remains of *Squatina* or *Rhinobatus* from the Cretaceous are almost indistinguishable from their
descendants of the present day. The curious Elfin Shark (*Mitsukurina*; Scapanorhynchidae) was first found in a living condition in
deep water off Japan in 1898, but a related genus (*Scapanorhynchus*)
had long been known from fossil remains in the Cretaceous rocks.

As in the case of the Chondrichthyes, little is known of the actual
beginnings of the Bony Fishes (class OSTEICHTHYES); probably
they arose as an offshoot from the early vertebrate stock at some time
during the Silurian period or perhaps even earlier. The Bony
Fishes can be divided into three main groups or subclasses: *Actinopterygii* (ray-fins), *Crossopterygii* (fringe-fins) and *Dipneusti* (lung-
fishes). The differences between the subclasses are of a technical
nature, involving the skeleton, the scales and the structure of the
fins. As far as the living representatives are concerned, the sizes
of the three groups differ vastly. The Crossopterygii and Dipneusti
together include only four living genera with seven species all told,
whereas the Actinopterygii contains some fifty orders and many
thousand genera. In the past, however, before the modern
Actinopterygii (superorder Teleostei) had come into existence, the
other subclasses were spread all over the world and were represented
by a large number of orders, genera and species. The fact that
during the Devonian period these groups were already represented
by several diverse forms, suggests that the Bony Fishes had had a
long history even at this early time.

The earliest members of the *Actinopterygii* were an order of fishes
known as **Palaeonisciformes**, which had their beginnings in the
Lower Devonian, attained their maximum development during the
Carboniferous and Permian periods, and finally became extinct
towards the end of the Jurassic. They ranged over the major part
of the globe, fossil remains having been found in the British Isles,
various parts of Europe, South Africa, Australia and North America.
The Palaeonisciformes exhibit such a combination of primitive
features that they may be looked upon as the ancestors of many
other orders of Bony Fishes. They are mostly elongate fishes,
fusiform in shape, with a large heterocercal tail and a single dorsal
fin [Fig. 130A]. The body is ensheathed in a complete armour
of small, closely fitting, diamond-shaped palaeoniscoid scales

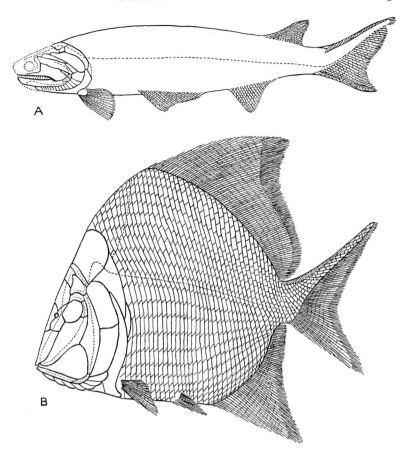

Fig. 130 PALAEONISCIFORM FISHES
A. An upper Devonian Palaeoniscid, *Cheirolepis canadensis* (Suborder Palaeoniscoidei) x ¹/₄. (After Lehman). B. A Triassic Platysomoid, *Platysomus superbus* (Suborder Platysomoidei) x ca ¹/₃. (After Moy-Thomas and Bradley Dyne)

(see p. 56), the shining surfaces of which are often elaborately sculptured; the head is protected by a series of bony plates. The mouth is rather large, and usually armed with sharp, pointed teeth, while above it projects a short and blunt snout. From their general build there can be little doubt that some Palaeonisciforms were fast-swimming, predaceous fishes.

During the Carboniferous period a branch of the Palaeoniscids gave rise to the Platysomoidei which flourished, together with the other Palaeonisciforms until late Permian times. The Platysomoids are of a very different shape, with a deep, compressed body [Fig. 130B], larger dorsal fin, smaller mouth and blunt, crushing teeth; the scales however, are of a typical palaeoniscoid type. These fishes held their own for a long period of time but their record is shorter than that of the parent stock (Palaeoniscoidei) from which they arose; they do not appear to have given rise to any later forms.

Another primitive order is the **Perleidiformes**, first found in Triassic formations of Europe, North America, Africa and Australia. The same ganoid armour still persists but the upturned portion of the tail fin is very much shorter; that is, the structure is more nearly homocercal.

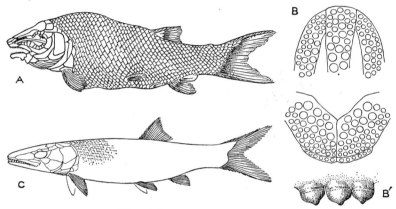

Fig. 131   HOLOSTEAN FISHES

A. *Lepidotus notopterus* (Order Semionotiformes), from the upper Jurassic (After Thiollière and Saint-Seine), x *ca* $^1/_7$. B. Dentition of *Lepidotus mantelli*; B′, three teeth enlarged. C. *Eugnathus orthostomus* (Order Amiiformes) from the lower Lias (After Woodward), x $^1/_8$. The scales have been largely omitted in figure C

At present, besides the orders mentioned above, fifteen others are recognised. Together, the seventeen orders are grouped in the superorder Chondrostei. Only one order, the **Acipenseriformes** (Sturgeons, Spoonbills, etc.) has survived until the present time. The Sturgeons were probably derived from the Palaeoniscid stock during the Triassic. A group of fishes, the **Chondrosteiformes,** which lived during the Lias seem to bridge the gap between the Palaeonisciformes and the Acipenseriformes. In the Chondrosteiformes, the thick palaeoniscoid scales are greatly reduced and, apart from the presence of a series of branchiostegal rays and a few other minor characters, the genus *Chondrosteus* and its allies are not very unlike their extant descendants.

The Bichirs (*Polypterus*), and their eel-like relative *Calamoichthys*, which are confined to the rivers and swamps of tropical Africa are probably also derived from Palaeonisciform ancestors. They differ, however, in numerous characters and are now placed in a subclass of their own (*Brachiopterygii*).

A more highly developed division of the *Actinopterygii* had its origin in Permian times and includes the supposed ancestors of the vast majority of living Bony Fishes. These are the superorder Holostei. The earliest Holosteans are the **Semionotiformes** [Fig. 131A, B, B'] which lived from Permian to Cretaceous times. They seem to have evolved from a Palaeonisciform stem; the principal changes involve the freeing of certain upper jaw elements from their union with the cheek bones, and the simplification of the palaeoniscoid type scale (through the loss of the cosmine layer) to a type known as lepisostoid (see page 57). The caudal fin is heterocercal, but there is a reduction in the number of rays in the dorsal and anal fins so that they correspond numerically with the internal supports, the radials. The Semionotiforms were probably slow swimmers, feeding at the bottom on plants or molluscs. In all, the mouth is small and the teeth either fine and bristle-like or stout and hemispherical [Fig. 131, B']. The order includes a number of diverse genera from such widely separated localities as England, Europe, South Africa, India, Australia and North America. Some had a fusiform shape but others, like the family Pycnodontidae, were deep-bodied and bore a superficial resemblance to the modern File-fishes. The second order of Holostei, the **Amiiformes**, is typified by the family Eugnathidae. These were large-mouthed predaceous forms which first appeared during the Triassic and flourished throughout the Jurassic. They have a fusiform body, forked tail-fin and strong jaws armed with sharp teeth [Fig. 131c]. Within this order there evolved the Amiidae, a family dating back to the Jurassic and still persisting. The Amiidae differ from the Eugnathidae in having a long dorsal fin and rounded caudal fin, besides other less obvious characters. The sole living representatives of this family, the Bowfins (*Amia*) are today confined to the freshwaters of North America. But, a closely related species has been found in European deposits as late as the Eocene.

The Pachycormidae, another Amiiform family, was also apparently derived from the Eugnathids. They are large-mouthed predaceous fishes not unlike the modern Mackerels in appearance; one genus, *Protosphyraena*, of the Cretaceous had the snout developed into a veritable rostrum, analogous with that of the modern Swordfish (*Xiphias*).

Finally, there is the other group of extant Holosteans, namely the Gar Pikes (*Lepisoteus*) which constitute the Amiiform family Lepisosteidae. The Lepisostids were apparently derived inde-

pendently from the Semionotiform stem, probably during the
Jurassic. Gar Pikes were abundant in Europe during Eocene and
Miocene times but today are confined to North America where they
made their appearance during the Cretaceous.

During the Triassic period an offshoot of Herring-like fishes, the
Pholidophoriformes (superorder Halecostomi) arose, probably
from the Semionotiform stem, and evolved contemporaneously
with the Holostei. In their general form and fin shape these fishes
bear a marked resemblance to the modern Clupeiform (Herring-
like) fishes. However, in other, deeper-lying characters they bear
the Holostean imprint. Their time span was short (Triassic to
Jurassic) but before their extinction they gave rise to another order,
the **Leptolepiformes**, the most advanced Holosteans and the
first Bony Fishes with a homocercal tail. Indeed, the Leptolepi-
forms bridge the gap between the Holostei and the Teleostei and
are considered by some authorities to belong to the latter superorder.
The Leptolepiformes, as represented by the family Leptolepidae,
show several characters which apparently link them with the
Teleost family Dussumeridae, a group of herring-like fishes (order
Clupeiformes). The Leptolepids also share several characters
with the Elopidae (Tarpons and allies), perhaps the most primitive
of all the living Clupeiformes, forms of which are known from
Cretaceous deposits.

The Leptolepids, then, can be considered as one of the stems
from which the first of the great orders (**Clupeiformes**) of modern
Bony Fishes (Teleostei) arose. The Clupeiformes include all the
Herrings, Salmon, Trout and their allies, as well as the Osteoglossids, Mormyrids and other related forms (see page 328). During the
Cretaceous period the Clupeiforms underwent considerable evolution and several important offshoots made their appearance,
amongst which were the first spiny-rayed fishes, the **Beryciformes**
(see page 330), ancestors in turn of that multititudinous order of
Perch-like fishes, the **Perciformes**.

No true Perch-like fishes appear until towards the end of the
Cretaceous but from then onwards their evolution was very rapid.
It will be impossible to follow the history of modern Teleosts
further here. The geological record for the group is still incomplete
but it is known that many families originated sometime before the
early Eocene, for remains of Scorpion-fishes, Sucker-fishes, File-
fishes, Mackerels, Sword-fishes and Angler-fishes have been found
in rocks of that period.

We must now return to the two other subclasses of Bony Fishes,
the *Crossopterygii* and *Dipneusti*. It will be recalled that both are
poorly represented by living forms, but their geological record is a
rich one. They first appeared in Devonian times, flourished during
the Palaeozoic, but during the Mesozoic nearly all the orders

became extinct. Today, the Crossopterygii are represented only by the Coelacanth *Latimeria* (Indian Ocean), and the Dipneusti by three genera of Lung-fishes, one from Australia, one from South America and one from Africa.

Two superorders of Crossopterygii are recognised, the Rhipidistia and the Actinistia. Representatives of the former were already in existence by the middle Devonian and were contemporaneous with the earlier Palaeonisciformes.

The Rhipidistia survived until the Carboniferous period and are of particular interest because they are the most probable ancestors of the four-footed terrestrial vertebrates. Furthermore, these are the only fishes with true internal nostrils. The paired fins are either short and rounded with a broad muscular lobe (order **Osteolepiformes**) or slender and leaf-like (order **Porolepi-formes**). The body is covered with cosmoid scales and the teeth are either simple, with an involuted base (Osteolepiformes) or strongly involuted over their complete height (Porolepiformes). Like all Crossopterygii the skull is in two parts, moveably jointed. The anterior part of the skull carries the olfactory organs and the posterior part the brain and auditory organs. The functional significance of this arrangement is obscure but it is suggested that it would serve as a shock-absorber when the fish snapped at its prey. In certain details, the bone arrangement in the skull resembles that of the earliest amphibians, as does the complicated structure of the teeth in certain genera. It is not difficult to see how the paired fins

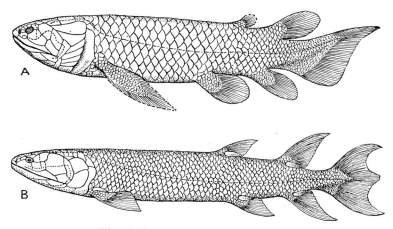

Fig. 132 CROSSOPTERYGIAN FISHES
A. *Holoptychius*, an upper Devonian Porolepiform. x ¹/₈. B. *Eusthenopteron*, an upper Devonian Osteolepiform, x ¹/₆. (Both after Jarvik)

of these fishes provide the basic structure from which the primitive tetrapod limb could develop.

The characteristic Osteolepiform family, the Osteolepidae occurs in the Old Red Sandstone of Scotland, and other members are found in North America, Antarctica, Asia and Europe. The Rhizodontidae are a closely allied family, but they have a somewhat more complicated tooth structure and thinner, cycloid scales. The genus *Eusthenopteron* [Fig. 132B] shows many Amphibian-like characters and its anatomy is the best known of the whole group.

The **Porolepiformes** [Fig. 132A] differ principally in their elongate, so-called archipterygial, pectoral fins and strongly folded enamel of the teeth. Some authorites believe (on anatomical grounds) that the ancestry of the Urodele Amphibians (Newts) stems from the Porolepiformes whilst the Anuran Amphibians (Frogs, etc.) arose from Osteolepiform stocks.

The second superorder of Crossopterygii, the Actinistia, includes a number of specialized fishes but is an evolutionary blind alley. It contains only one order and two suborders (**Coelacanthiformes**), but has a most remarkable time range from the Carboniferous to the present day. Unlike the extant Dipneusti, however, the living Coelacanth differs far less from its fossil representatives [see Figs. 133; 134]. The characters in which the Actinistia differ from other Crossopterygians are rather technical, but we may note that the head skeleton shows several reductions including the loss of a bony element in the upper jaw, there are no internal nostrils and the teeth are of a very simple kind. In some fossil Coelacanths there is a large structure interpreted as a swim-

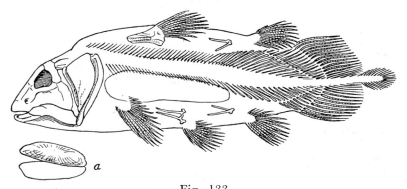

Fig. 133
Undina penicillata (x $\frac{1}{4}$), an upper Jurassic Coelacanth. The large, ossified 'swimbladder' is clearly visible below the vertebral column; also note the well-defined epichordal lobe of the tail fin. *a*, the gular plates which lie between the halves of the lower jaw.

bladder; the bladder walls are apparently calcified, a development not seen in any other fishes and one hardly consistent with any known function of a swimbladder (see page 133).

The first living Coelacanth (*Latimeria chalumnae*; [Fig. 134A, A']) was caught near East London, South Africa in December 1938. It was a large fish, five feet long and was trawled at a depth of

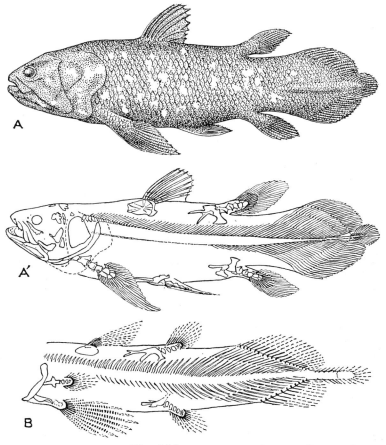

Fig. 134 COELACANTHS

A. *Latimeria chalumnae*, the only species of extant Coelacanth, x $^1/_{12}$.
A', the axial skeleton of *L. chalumnae*; note the nature of the fin supports and the large notochord quite unconstricted by vertebral centra. B, part of the skeleton of a Jurassic Coelacanth (*Laugia*) x *ca* $^1/_2$; in this genus the pelvic fins are anterior in position and associated with the pectoral girdle. In other respects, however, the axial skeleton agrees closely with that of *Latimeria*. (All after Jarvik)

about 40 fathoms.   Unfortunately it was some time before the
fish could be preserved and much of its soft anatomy was destroyed.
The recognition of this fish as a Coelacanth, a group reputedly
extinct for some 70 million years, reflects great credit on Professor
J. L. B. Smith.   At that time Professor Smith was a chemist by
profession and an ichthyologist in his spare time.   The discovery of
this 'living fossil' aroused much excitement since it provided an
opportunity to learn about the soft parts of animals otherwise
known only from their skeletons.   But, by the time Smith got to the
body it was little more than a well-preserved fossil.   Then followed a
period of fourteen years during which Professor Smith carried out a
well-organised campaign of search and advertisement aimed at
getting another specimen.   In 1952 a second fish was caught, this
time in the Comoro Islands near Madagascar.   Again, delays and
bacteria did their worst and the specimen was badly damaged
before Professor Smith reached it.   An easily read, downright
exciting account of Professor Smith's adventures, written by himself, was published recently as '*Old Four Legs*'.

From this point, the story passes to the French in whose territorial
waters the second specimen was caught.   Under the direction of
Professor J. Millot a vigorous campaign has produced some twelve
specimens and a flow of detailed papers describing the anatomy and
histology of these ultraconservative survivors of an age long before
our own group, the Mammals, had made their tentative appearance
in a world dominated by Reptiles.

Millot's researches are still far from complete but already we
have learned of several surprising features in the anatomy of the
Coelacanths.   For example, the heart is of a very simple structure
even when compared with the hearts of other fishes and is like the
hypothetical structure postulated by comparative anatomists when
considering the evolution of that organ.   The kidneys, unlike those
of all other vertebrates are *ventral* in position and fused over part
of their length; the stomach is a large bag and the intestine is
provided with a complex spiral valve (see page 129).   There are no
vertebral centra, the only longitudinal support coming from the
large and tough notochord.   The skeleton of the fins differs little
from the fossils but it was very surprising to find that the pectoral
fins have a considerable degree of mobility; they can be turned
through an arc of 180°.   The swimbladder of *Latimeria*, unlike that
of certain fossils, is slender and fat-filled; certainly it cannot
function as either a lung or hydrostatic organ.   An organ of unknown
function has been found in the snout.   This is the median rostral
organ, which communicates with the exterior by three tubes on
each side of the snout.   The rostral organ is unconnected with the
olfactory organs and is filled with a gelatinous substance.   As was
expected, the skull is in two hinged parts but it was of interest to

learn that the notochord extends forwards below the posterior part of the skull and is attached to the front part, thus providing a supple joint between the two parts of the skull. Flanking the notochord below is a pair of large muscles which unite the two parts of the skull base.

For a further and more detailed account of Coelacanth anatomy, the reader is referred to Dr. Ethelwynn Trewavas' article 'The Coelacanth Yields its Secrets' in 'Discovery' for May, 1958.

The *Dipneusti* (Lung-fishes) are readily distinguished from the *Crossopterygii* by the nature of their teeth, as well as by several differences in the skeleton. The teeth consist of paired upper and lower plates which form an efficient cutting and crushing mechanism [Fig. 135].

Like the *Crossopterygii*, the *Dipneusti* first appear in Devonian deposits, reach their peak during the Palaeozoic and begin to dwindle during the Triassic, from whence they are represented by forms not unlike the extant Australian Lung-fish *Neoceratodus*. Although the modern Lung-fishes are restricted to Africa, Australia

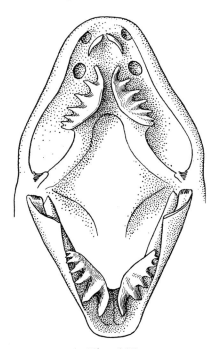

Fig. 135
Upper and lower jaws of the Australian Lung-fish, (*Neoceratodus forsteri*) to show the tooth plates and nostrils; x ¹/₂

and South America, the Palaeozoic forms had a much wider distribution. Fossils have been found in England, Europe, Africa, India and North America. Even as late as the Triassic, certain types had an almost world-wide distribution.

The evolutionary trend of the *Dipneusti* is clearly one of reduction. The earliest members (e.g. *Dipterus*, see [Fig. 136A]) had bony skeletons, heterocercal tails and a substantial armour of cosmoid scales (see p. 56). Gradually there was a reduction in armour (including a simplification of the complex of bones in the skull),

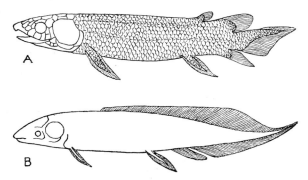

Fig. 136   FOSSIL LUNGFISHES (DIPNEUSTI)
A. *Dipterus* (Devonian) x ¹/₆. B. *Phaneropleuron* (upper Devonian) x ¹/₅
(Both from Jarvik)

a reduction in the number of median fins and the loss of the heterocercal tail. In the later *Dipneusti* and in the living forms the caudal fin may be a pseudocaudal formed by the union of the dorsal and anal fins [see p. 31 and Figs. 136; 118]. The living Australian species (*Neoceratodus forsteri*) retains more of the primitive characteristics (particularly the structure of the paired fins) than do the African (*Protopterus*) and South American (*Lepidosiren*) forms. But, all three living genera must be looked upon as specialised, albeit degenerate, derivatives of the Devonian stocks.

Older authors considered that the *Crossopterygii* and *Dipneusti* were closely related, but recent and more detailed research indicates that even at their first appearance in the fossil record the two groups were quite distinct. There are certain suggestive resemblances between the modern Lung-fishes and the Urodele Amphibians which have led workers to suggest that the *Dipneusti* were perhaps ancestral to at least certain Tetrapod groups. But again, detailed researches have shown the unlikelihood of this arrangement. What resemblances there are, are doubtless due to convergent evolution as a result of adaptations to similar environments.

REFERENCES

HEINTZ, A. (1958). The head of the Anaspid *Birkenia elegans*, Traq.: in, *Studies on Fossil Vertebrates*. Athlone Press, University of London.

JARVIK, E. (1959). *Théories de l'Evolution des Vertébrés*. Masson et Cie, Paris.

PARRINGTON, F. R. (1958). On the nature of the Anaspida: in, *Studies on Fossil Vertebrates*. Athlone Press, University of London.

RAYNER, D. H. (1958). The geological environment of fossil fishes: in, *Studies on Fossil Vertebrates*. Athlone Press, University of London.

RITCHIE, A. (1960). A new interpretation of *Jamoytius kerwoodi* White. *Nature*, **88**, 647–9.

SMITH, J. L. B. (1956). *Old Four-Legs*. Longmans, London.

TREWAVAS, E. (1958). The Coelacanth yields its secrets. *Discovery*, **19**, No. 5, 196–206.

WHITE, E. I. (1958). Original environment of the craniates: in, *Studies on Fossil Vertebrates*. Athlone Press, University of London.

CLASSIFICATION

CLASSIFICATION is the sorting of different kinds of individuals into groups. The classifications of most older naturalists were necessarily of an artificial nature. They were well aware of the existence of natural affinities, and of the fact that individuals fall naturally into groups, which in turn may be linked together into larger categories, and so on, but the units of classification which they used remained convenient pigeon-holes and little more. The acceptance of evolution as a process has changed all this, and the modern systematist endeavours to arrange his animals into groups which are in accord with their natural relationships. Such a classification may be visualised as a dense bush. The roots of such a genealogical or phylogenetic tree are deeply buried far back in geological time, and in each succeeding period of the earth's history its branches have become more and more ramified. The existing fishes are represented by the topmost and youngest twigs and branches of the fish 'bush'. In spite of the knowledge of the past provided by a study of fossils, most of the branches connecting the living twigs with the lower parts are unknown, having died out and left little, if any, trace of their former existence. It is this dying away of the older parts of the bush, the connecting links, as it were, that makes it possible to sort the living fishes into groups, for if it were possible to examine at one time all the individuals, both past and present, existing and extinct, each would be found to be linked up with the others by a complete series of small gradations. In the accompanying diagram of a hypothetical evolutionary 'tree' the continuous black lines represent existing species, the dotted lines extinct stems and branches [Fig. 137*a*]. The branches marked A and B are totally extinct, while that marked C is moderately successful and represented at the present day by a few species. The remaining branches, D and E, have been most successful, and the topmost twigs show an abundance of closely allied living species. The second diagram [Fig. 137*b*] represents a part of one of these end branches in greater detail, and illustrates the manner in which species may become more 'distinctive' as the result of connecting links dying out. Here the dark lines represent the separate individuals, and the enclosed areas are the limits of existing species. All the individuals within each of these areas, although differing from one another in minor characters, are fundamentally alike, and the three groups of individuals shown in the diagram have become well differentiated by the dying away of the branches from which they sprang. Further, the two on the right, marked A and B, may be seen to diverge from a common stem at a point not very far down the tree, whereas that

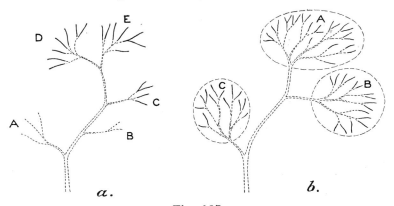

Fig. 137

Diagrams of portions of supposed phyletic trees. (For explanation see text)

marked C joins the same branch at a point nearer to the base. The species A and B, therefore, might reasonably be expected to resemble each other more closely than either resembles C, and in this example they may be regarded as representing one genus, while C forms another.

The lowest unit in any classification is, of course, the individual, and these must first of all be grouped into larger units or species. The Latin word *species* means literally a particular kind, and the average observer familiar only with the better known fishes will perhaps say that he experiences little difficulty in arranging these into more or less well-defined groups. He will be able to distinguish, say, a Roach from a Bream, Chub, or Barbel, and something in the general appearance of these fishes will suggest that they are fairly closely related to one another, but widely separated from a Salmon or Perch. The task of the systematist, studying every kind of fish from all parts of the world, is by no means as easy as this, however, and he may experience considerable difficulty in distinguishing the species in some groups of fishes, besides constantly coming across apparently intermediate forms connecting two species.

A great deal has been written, not only on the subject of what does and what does not constitute a species, but also on the vexed problem of the way in which new species first come into being. It is beyond the scope of this work to enter into such controversial matters in any detail, but since the term species has been used fairly frequently, some sort of explanation of its meaning seems necessary.

That we are able to recognise different 'kinds' of animals implies that each 'kind' breeds true and does not grade into another 'kind'. Since most characters can only be transferred by inter-breeding the very existence of different kinds of animals demands that there must be some form of reproductive isolation between them. Thus, the species in nature (biospecies) is an objective unit and can be defined as follows: 'Species are groups of actually or potentially interbreeding populations which are reproductively isolated from other such groups' (Mayr). It must be stressed that this reproductive isolation applies to animals living under natural conditions. In captivity or under artificially altered conditions in nature the barriers may break down and interspecific hybrids result.

Now, the systematist usually has to define the species he studies from dead specimens, often without the aid of many data on the way the animals behaved when alive. He must of necessity choose permanent characters which other workers can study and evaluate. In many cases these characters would mean nothing to the animal itself as far as recognising other members of its own species are concerned. The systematist's species is merely an attempt to recognise and define the real or biospecies as it occurs in nature. It is often referred to as a morphospecies because it is based primarily on morphological characters. Despite the limitations within which the systematist must work, the correspondence between the bio-species (the objective species) and the morphospecies (the human attempt to define the biospecies) is often remarkably close and becomes even more exact when the systematist is able to use bio-logical as well as morphological characters. The often quoted definition of a species given by Regan (at the 1925 meeting of the British Association) is very much that of a morphospecies and is an accurate reflection of the way in which a museum worker must proceed. 'A species' Regan said, 'is a community or a number of related communities, whose distinctive morphological characters are, in the opinion of a competent systematist, sufficiently definite to entitle it, or them to a specific name.' By the term community is meant a collection of individuals such as occurs in nature, with similar habits, which live together in a certain area and breed freely with one another.

It is one of the fundamental characteristics of living organisms that no two are ever exactly alike, and it follows that even within the limits of a species, and quite apart from differences due to age, sex, and so on, there will be a greater or lesser degree of individual variation. Ignorance of the wide range of variation exhibited by some species often leads systematists to describe as distinct species what are in reality nothing more than extreme variations of a single form, and it is only when a more complete series of specimens is studied and intermediate forms come to light that such errors can be rectified. In the case of the European Trout, to quote a characteristic example, specific names have been given to the Brown Trout (*Salmo trutta*), the Phinock or Eastern Sea Trout (*Salmo albus*), the Sewen or Western Sea Trout (*S. cambricus*), the Great Lake Trout (*S. ferox*), the Loch Leven Trout (*S. levenensis*), the Brook Trout (*S. fario*), the Gillaroo of Ireland (*S. stomachius*), and the Welsh Black-finned Trout (*S. nigripinnis*), among others, but in spite of the differences in size, form, colour, number of caecal appendages, nature of the vomerine teeth, etc., a complete series of transitional forms has now been traced between all these 'species', and most modern authorities are agreed in regarding all the Trout found in the British Isles as belonging to a single very variable species, *Salmo trutta*. In the same way, most anthropologists regard all living races of mankind as representing one species of *Homo*, to which the name *Homo sapiens* is given. But, supposing that all the races were to die out, with the exception of the European and the Bushman, these two types would undoubtedly be placed in distinct species.

A species is not, and never can be, a fixed, immutable unit, and no systematist living is able to lay down any rule as to the amount of difference required to recognise a species. He must inevitably be guided by the circumstances of the particular case that he happens to be studying. As Dr. Regan put it: 'In practice it often happens that geographical forms, representing each other in different areas, are given only sub-specific rank, even when they are well defined, and that closely related forms, not easily distinguished, are given specific rank when they inhabit the same area but keep apart.' Moreover, the value of a particular morphological character, whether it be the form of the fins, the arrangement of the scales, or the colour pattern, differs enormously in different families or orders, and a character which serves to distinguish two species of, say, Cyprinids, may be sufficiently trenchant to separate two genera of Cichlids. In spite of the huge collections preserved in some of the great national museums of the world, many of the species known to science have been described on the basis of one or two specimens, sometimes young, sometimes poorly preserved. It is not until every species is represented by a large series of examples illustrating its geographical range, variation, growth, seasonal changes, sexual differences, and so on (a highly Utopian and improbable state of affairs), that any sort of finality is to be expected. As it is, almost every new species discovered modifies in some way our conception of the relationships of the species already known, and it not infrequently happens that the discovery of one or two new forms leads to the complete reclassification of the genus, or even of the family to which it belongs.

Yet another unit of classification is the subspecies. It represents a community or group of related communities, whose distinguishing features (biological and morphological) are not of sufficient importance to entitle them to rank as a true species, but which, nevertheless, enable an expert to separate them from other nearly related communities. The different forms of Char (*Salvelinus*) found in the lakes of Switzerland, Scandinavia, and the British Isles, are probably to be looked upon as subspecies of the widely distributed Alpine Char (*S. alpinus*), which is a migratory fish in the Arctic Ocean. Here again, however, it must be remembered that some systematists would regard many of the lacustrine Char as distinct species. To turn to another example, recent research has shown that several important food-fishes, such as the Herring (*Clupea harengus*) and Plaice (*Pleuronectes platessa*) can each be split into a number of races, each with its own slight morphological peculiarities, area of distribution, and time and place of breeding. The different forms can only be distinguished when a large number of specimens is examined. Such races have not yet received subspecific names, but they are of exactly the same nature as the lacustrine Char, and it may be concluded that in general the terms 'race' and 'subspecies' mean one and the same thing.

It sometimes happens that certain individuals of a species differ from the normal or mode to a greater or lesser extent, but such differences are not found among a particular community, nor are they related in any definite way to the habits of the fish or to its environment. For example, among the individuals of a species characterised by its uniform coloration there may be some which exhibit a black spot on the head or a series of dark bars on the sides of the body. The name varieties may be given to such individuals, although this term has been used by some authors in a totally different sense (as subspecies). Well-known examples of varieties are the Gold-fish, Golden Carp, Mirror Carp, Leather Carp, Golden Trout, and so on.

So much for the lower units of classification. It is not sufficient, however, to group the individuals together into species, but the species must in their turn be arranged to form genera. Again, there can be no hard and fast rule as to the morphological differences necessary to distinguish one genus from another, it being entirely a matter of individual opinion; and it will sometimes happen that one worker will split up into a number of genera a group of species which another systematist would assign to a single genus.

Genera are, in their turn, grouped into families, separated from one another by morphological features of more fundamental importance. The Salmon and Trout (*Salmo*), the Char (*Salvelinus*), the White-fishes (*Coregonus, Leucichthys, Argyrosomus*), the Grayling (*Thymallus*), etc., constitute the family Salmonidae. Families are grouped into suborders and orders, orders into subclasses and classes, classes into subkingdoms and kingdoms. There are only two kingdoms, animals and plants, but even here no sharp line of distinction can be drawn, for there are certain lowly forms of life which might equally well be described as animal or vegetable. The accompanying diagram [Fig. 138] illustrates these divisions, and represents a mere fragment of the taxonomic tree of living organisms

KINGDOM	**ANIMALIA**
PHYLUM	**CHORDATA**
SUBPHYLUM	VERTEBRATA
CLASS	*OSTEICHTHYES*
SUBCLASS	ACTINOPTERYGII
ORDER	CLUPEIFORMES
SUBORDER	CLUPEOIDEI
FAMILY	*CLUPEIDAE*
GENUS	*Clupea*
SPECIES	*Clupea harengus*

Fig. 138
The systematic position of the Herring, illustrating the main divisions used in a classification

by showing the systematic position of a single fish, the Herring (*Clupea harengus*).

The question of nomenclature is an important one, and unfortunately there is still considerable diversity of opinion as to the correct scientific name to be applied even to our commonest food-fishes. It may well be asked why it should be necessary to give scientific names at all. The reason is that vernacular or common names, although convenient, are by no means precise, and are frequently used in a very loose manner. The same name may be given to two or more totally different fishes in different parts of the country or in various regions of the world; or, as is even more common, the same species may be known by quite different names in various localities. The name 'whiting,' for example, is not only applied to the well-known food-fish of the Cod family (*Micromesistius merlangus*), but also to various kinds of freshwater fishes. Conversely, the following names, among others, are all used for the Sea Trout (*Salmo trutta*) in various parts of the British Isles, while the non-migratory members of this very variable species have received as many vernacular names again: Orange Fin, Black Tail, Phinock, Salmon Trout, Truff, Scurf, Sewen, Bull Trout, Grey Trout, and Round Tail. The names of Peal and Bull Trout are used in some parts of the country for the Trout (*S. trutta*), but in others for the Salmon *S. salar*. Another good reason for the use of scientific names is the fact that of the twenty-five thousand species of fish known to-day probably less than half have a common name in any language. There are over a hundred species of Cichlids in Lake Tanganyika alone, but very few of them are distinguished by the natives under a particular name, and the same species will perhaps be given one name by one tribe and a totally different one by another. It is agreed, therefore, that, in order to obtain precision and to avoid confusion, it is necessary to give every species of fish a scientific name. In the words of Dr. Regan, the name of an animal 'is a clue to all that is known or that has been recorded in literature about its structure, habits, economic importance or anything else; without the correct name we are in the dark and the conclusions we arrive at may be founded on erroneous grounds.' It not infrequently happens that two workers have published conflicting statements about the habits or anatomy of a particular animal, but it has subsequently turned out that they were really dealing with different species, their specimens having been incorrectly named. In just the same way, it is of real importance for the economic entomologist to know the correct name of the insect pest which is ravaging the crops of cotton or tobacco. Closely related species in insects may have very different life-histories, and unless the correct name of the species is known it is impossible to be sure as to the right method of attack.

The first and one of the greatest of modern systematists was the Swedish naturalist Linnaeus, who was born in 1707 and died in 1778. He was the first to adopt the system of what is known as binominal nomenclature, that is to say, of referring to every species by two names, its generic as well as its trivial name. This method was consistently applied by him for the first time in the tenth edition of his famous *Systema Naturae*, published in 1758, and by common consent systematists throughout the world have agreed to regard this year as marking the commencement of the scientific naming of animals. No account is taken of any names given before this year for, except by accident, these were never binominal. It has been already pointed out that the same species has often received two or more different names, and the question naturally arises as to how the correct scientific name of a species or genus is to be fixed, so that a particular animal shall be known by the same name throughout the world. A code of rules has been drawn up by an International Commission on nomenclature for the guidance of systematic workers, so as to secure as far as possible uniformity of method. Among other rules, this lays down that generic and trivial names should be given either in Latin or in Latinised Greek, and that above all, strict attention must always be paid to the law of priority, the name first given taking precedence over any other that may be proposed at a subsequent date. Further, no generic name may be used twice among animals, and no trivial name twice in the same genus. Thus, if a fish and a bird have inadvertently been given the same generic name, that which was proposed first would stand and the other must receive a new designation. In theory these rules would seem to be quite straightforward, but in actual practice a certain amount of confusion has arisen with regard to the names of some animals, which is due to a number of reasons. Two different systematists, perhaps in ignorance of each other's work, or with an erroneous conception of the limits of a variable species, may have successively described the same fish and each given it a different name, or may have given distinct names to what are mere variations of the same species. In such cases that name which was first published takes precedence, even should the later one be eminently suitable and perhaps provide a better description of the fish in question; this second name becomes what is known as a synonym of the first name. It sometimes happens that the second or later name for a species or genus has been in use among zoologists throughout the world for generations, and it is only later discovered that another name has priority; the question then arises as to whether it is more fitting to apply the strict law of priority and to revive some long buried and little known name to supplant one which is familiar to all and has been in constant use. It is in such cases that the greatest divergence of opinion exists, some workers using one name, some the other. Other factors which tend to lead to confusion are the description of different fishes under the same name, or the inclusion of two or more distinct forms in a description which purports to be that of a single genus or species, but such debatable points cannot be considered here.

As a general rule, the Greek form is used for generic names the Latin adjectives being more commonly used for the names of species. The most satisfactory generic names are those giving some sort of description of the main features of the group in question, or drawing attention to the morphological character or characters that separate the group from its nearest allies. *Ostracion* (a little box) for the Trunk-fishes, *Catostomus* (inferior mouth) for a genus of Suckers, and *Alepocephalus* (scaleless head) for a genus of Smooth-heads, are examples of such names. Others have been given in honour of some scientific man, such as *Copeina* or *Copeichthys* (literally, Cope's fish) after Dr. Cope, or *Valenciennellus* after the French ichthyologist,

Valenciennes. Some workers have been a little whimsical in their methods, constructing names by drawing letters out of a hat, or, as in the case of one systematist, by anagrams on his wife's name, Caroline (e.g. *Cirolana, Conilera, Nerocila*). The trivial name may be descriptive, such as *brachycephalus* (short-headed), *macrognathus* (large-jawed), *maculatus* (spotted), *fasciatus* (barred), and so on; it may be in honour of a person, often the traveller who discovered the species, such as *livingstoni, shackeltoni, forbesi*, etc., or it may refer to the place at which the fish was first found, such as *japonicus, hispanicus, nigeriensis, brasiliensis*, etc. The code of rules lays it down that a name is nothing more than a name, and cannot be ignored because of its unclassical form or its unsuitability, or for any other reason except the existence of a prior name. Generally speaking, it is customary in books on systematic zoology to give, not only the full scientific name, but to add the name of the author who first described the species and gave it the name. Thus, '*Clupea harengus* Linnaeus' means that the common Atlantic Herring was first named and described by Linnaeus; the use of brackets around the author's name, as in '*Alosa fallax* (Lacépéde)' means that the trivial name *fallax* was first given by Lacépéde to the Twaite Shad, but he placed it in a different genus, in this case the Linnean genus *Clupea*, from which it was removed by a later authority and placed in the genus *Alosa*.

Of the five classes constituting the 'Fishes', the Cyclostomi, Acanthodi and Placodermi have been dealt with in some detail in the previous chapter and need not be discussed further here. The two latter are extinct, and the few living Cyclostomes are divided into two families, the Petromyzonidae or Lampreys and the Myxinidae or Hag-fishes. The arrangement of the subclasses, orders, suborders, etc., of the other two classes may be very briefly outlined, but this will consist of little more than a list of their scientific names: however, it should serve to give some idea of the manner in which modern authorities classify the Cartilaginous and Bony Fishes.

The class CHONDRICHTHYES, or cartilaginous fishes, may be divided into two subclasses, the *Selachii* (Sharks and Rays) and the *Bradyodonti* (Chimaeras and their allies). The Selachii in turn are divisible into two superorders of which the first, the Protoselachii, is made up entirely of extinct forms (families Cladoselachidae, Pleuracanthidae, Hybodontidae) and the second, the Euselachii, contains all the living (and some extinct) Sharks and Rays. Within the Euselachii two divisions are recognised: the Pleurotremata (Sharks) in which the front margin of each pectoral fin is free and the external gill clefts lie on the sides of the head; and the Hypotremata (Rays) which have the front margin of each pectoral fin continuous with the head, and the gill openings placed on the lower surface of the head.

The Pleurotremata, in turn, are subdivided into four orders. Of these the **Hexanchiformes** are amongst the most primitive living sharks: the gill clefts number six or seven, the vertebral column is of a simple form and there is only one dorsal fin. This order includes the relatively rare Frilled Shark (*Chlamydoselachus*) and the Comb-tooth sharks (family Hexanchidae). The order **Galeiformes** contains two suborders and the majority of fishes which we call to mind on meeting the word 'shark'. Galeiform sharks have five gill clefts, two dorsal and one anal fin, the former not armed with spines. Included in this order are the Sand shark (*Carcharias*) of the family Carchariidae and the Elfin shark (*Mitsukurina*) of the Scapanorhynchidae; the Mackerel shark (*Lamna*), Porbeagles (*Isurus*), the so-called Man-eaters (*Carcharodon*) and the Thresher shark (*Alopias*) all of the family Isuridae; the unique Basking shark (*Cetorhinus*) of the family Cetorhinidae; the large and varied family (Orectolobidae) of Carpet sharks (*Orectolobus*) and the Nurse shark (*Ginglymostoma*); the Dogfishes of the family Scyliorhinidae; the family Carcharinidae, represented by the Blue sharks (*Carcharinus*), Topes (*Eugaleus*) Smooth-hounds (*Mustelus*) and Tiger sharks (*Galeocerdo*); and finally the Hammerhead sharks, forming the family Sphyrinidae.

The third order of sharks, the **Squaliformes**, contains two suborders, the Squaloidei (Piked-dogfishes, Bramble sharks, Saw sharks, etc.) and the Squatinoidei (Angel or Monk fishes). The Squaloids have two dorsal fins, each usually preceded by a spine, and no anal fin. The Squatinoids are an unusual group, probably derived from the Squaloids but having a flattened body with enlarged, wing-like pectorals and somewhat ventrally displaced gill clefts. This resemblance to the Rays is, however, superficial and a good example of convergent evolution.

The fourth and final order, **Heterodontiformes**, is sometimes included with the Squaloidei. It contains but a single family of rather primitive sharks closely related to certain members of the now extinct Protoselachian family, the Hybodontidae. The **Heterodontiformes** are small, mollusc crushing species at present confined to the Pacific and Indian Oceans and include the Port Jackson shark. The fossil genus *Palaeospinax* from Jurassic deposits can be considered as the first known Euselachian.

The Rays or Hypotremata are divided into two orders, the **Raiiformes** (Skates and Rays) and the **Torpediniformes** (Electric rays or Torpedoes). The former order is made up of three suborders, the Rhinobatoidei (the Guitar-fish *Rhinobatis* and Saw fish *Pristis*), the Raioidei (Rays and Skates) and the Dasyatoidei or Sting rays, which include *Dasyatis* (the sting ray or *Trygon* of the ancients) the Eagle rays (*Myliobatis*) and the Mantas or Devil rays (*Manta* and *Mobula*).

The second subclass of cartilaginous fishes, the *Bradyodonti* is nowadays represented only by the Chimaeras, but it contains a host of extinct forms. Members of this group are readily recognised by having the primary upper jaw (palatoquadrate cartilage) fused with the neurocranium [see Fig. 56] and by the gill clefts opening into a chamber with a single external opening. The dentition of the Bradyodonti is also characteristic; some of the extinct forms (e.g. *Helicoprion*, [Fig. 129B]) possessed a fantastic dental apparatus.

The class of Bony Fishes (OSTEICHTHYES) is much larger and the forms more diverse than in the Chondrichthyes. Consequently there is a considerable diversity of opinion as to the limits of the subclasses and orders, and the relationships of the various divisions one to the other. The scheme outlined here is based principally on the classification of Berg.

Four subclasses are recognised, *Dipneusti*, *Crossopterygii*, *Brachiopterygii* and *Actinopterygii*. The three latter subclasses are defined by the nature of their scales, fins and skulls and the *Dipneusti* (Lungfishes) by the structure of the skull, the dentition and the possession of lungs.

The *Dipneusti* and *Crossopterygii* contain very few extant forms and have been considered in some detail in the previous chapter. The subclass *Brachiopterygii* was created for two aberrant African genera, *Polypterus* and *Calamoichthys*, of apparently archaic form but not showing the characteristics of other archaic fishes living or extinct.

The *Actinopterygii* includes the vast majority of living Bony Fishes; it is subdivided into four superorders and some fifty orders of varying sizes. The archaic forms, most of which are extinct, are grouped into the superorders Chondrostei, Holostei and Halecostomi (see p. 308f.). The Sturgeons and Spoonbills (Acipenseridae and Polyodontidae) are the only living members of the first superorder, the Bowfins (*Amia*) and the Gar or Alligator Pikes (family Lepisosteidae) of North America are the sole survivors of the Holostei, whilst no living representatives are known of the Halecostomi, which died out in the Cretaceous period.

The **Clupeiformes**, the first of the orders of modern Bony Fishes (superorder Teleostei) is an important group including a vast assemblage of families, genera and species, all of which agree in having the swimbladder connected with the oesophagus by a pneumatic duct, and in having the pelvic fins abdominal in position and not associated with the pectoral girdle. The **Clupeiformes** are split into nineteen suborders, of which the most important are the Clupeoidei, including the Tarpons (Elopidae), Lady fishes (Albulidae), Herrings (Clupeidae), Smooth-heads (Alepocephalidae), Milk fishes (Chanidae) etc; the Stomiatoidei, oceanic fishes with well-developed luminous organs, and the

Salmonoidei, which include the Salmon, Trout and their allies (Salmonidae), and the Smelts (Osmeridae). The remaining suborders of importance are: the Osteoglossoidei, Notopteroidei (Feather backs), Mormyroidei (Elephant Snout fishes) and Gonorhynchoidei.

From the generalized **Clupeiformes** have been evolved a number of more specialized orders and suborders. These include the Esocoidei, containing the Pikes (*Esox*), Mud-fishes (*Umbra*), and the Black-fish (*Dallia*), and the Myctophoidei, including many deep sea forms, the Lantern-fishes (Myctophidae) and the Lizard-fishes (Synodontidae).

Amongst the more specialized Clupeiform derivatives may be mentioned the eels (**Anguilliformes**) and the vast order **Cypriniformes** (or **Ostariophysi**) which includes the majority of the world's freshwater fishes. The **Cypriniformes** are characterized by the presence of Weberian ossicles, a chain of small bones linking the inner ear with the swimbladder (p. 152). The four suborders of Cypriniform fishes are: the Characoidei (or Characins, including such well-known species as the Tiger-fishes of Africa and many aquarium fishes from South America), the Gymnotoidei or Electric eels of South America, the Cyprinoidei (Carps, Barbs and Suckers) and the Siluroidei or Cat-fishes. Another fairly important and certainly interesting order is the **Beloniformes**, a group which includes the Gar-fishes (Belonidae), Half-beaks (Hemirhamphidae) and the marine Flying-fishes (Exocoetidae).

The **Cyprinodontiformes** (Tooth Carps) are a large and varied order of small fishes, well known to aquarists and ichthyologists but still of uncertain relationships to other orders, but possibly related to the Grey Mullets (below, p. 331).

Four other orders, whose systematic position is also obscure are: the **Tetraodontiformes**, which include the Trunk-fishes (suborder Ostracionoidei), the Puffer-fishes (suborder Tetraodontoidei) and the Ocean Sun-fishes (Moloidei); the **Aulostomiformes** containing the tube-mouthed fishes such as the Trumpet-fishes (Fistulariidae), Shrimp and Snipe-fishes (Macrorhamphosidae); the order **Syngnathiformes** or Pipefishes, and finally, the **Gadiformes**, an important order which contains the Cods and allied forms (Gadidae) and the Rattails or Grenadiers (Macrouridae). The **Tetraodontiformes** are sometimes considered (probably rightly) as related to the **Perciformes** (see below).

To conclude this brief synopsis of the so-called soft finned fishes, we may consider the rather isolated order **Lampridiformes**. This is an assemblage of curious and diverse fishes which all have in common a protractile mouth of peculiar structure and worked by a mechanism different to that of all other fishes (p. 100). The order includes the large oceanic Opah or Moon-fish (*Lampris*), the Deal and Ribbon-fishes (Trachypteridae) and the remarkable deep-sea *Stylephorus*.

All fishes in the orders listed so far have (with few exceptions like some Cat-fishes) soft-rayed fins. With the **Beryciformes** we begin a brief survey of the spiny-rayed orders, the Acanthopterygii of older classifications. In these fishes the rays of the anterior parts of the dorsal and anal fins are generally modified into stiff, pointed spines (but there are soft-rayed exceptions) and the pelvic fins are placed well forward, the pelvic girdle is attached to that of the pectoral fins and the first pelvic ray is spinous.

The **Beryciformes** are usually regarded as the most primitive of the spiny-rayed fishes. The order reached its climax during the Cretaceous period and comparatively few genera are found living today (Squirrel or Soldier-fishes).

Allied to the Beryciformes is the order **Zeiformes**, in which are placed, among others, the John Dories (Zeidae) and the Boar-fishes (Caproidae). Further up the main evolutionary stem is the huge order of Perch-like fishes, the **Perciformes**. The suborder Percoidei includes all the more typical families of the group: Sea Perches (Serranidae), Sunfishes (Centrarchidae) Cichlids (Cichlidae), Perches (Percidae), Snappers (Lutjanidae), Drums (Sciaenidae), Horse Mackerels (Carangidae), Red Mullets (Mullidae), Sea Breams (Sparidae), etc.

Of the other Perciform suborders the more important include: the Acanthuroidei (Surgeon-fishes); Balistoidei (Trigger-fishes); Labroidei (Wrasses [Labridae], Damsel fishes [Pomacentridae], and the viviparous Surf-Perches [Embiotocidae]) Trichiuroidei, Hairtails and Cutlass-fishes (Trichiuridae); the Scombroidei, the Mackerels, Tunnies and their allies, and the Swordfishes, Spear-fishes and Sailfins; the Gobioidei and Blennioidei comprising the well-known Gobies and Blennies of coastal shores, as well as the Wolf-fishes (Anarhichadidae) and the Kelp or Klip-fishes (Clinidae); the Stromateoidei or Butter-fishes, Rudder-fishes and Square-tails; and the Anabantoidei, a suborder containing all the fishes with labyrinthic accessory air-breathing organs, such as the Climbing perch *Anabas*, the Siamese fighting-fish *Betta*, and the Gouramies, *Macropodus*.

The Mail-cheeked fishes, forming the suborder Scorpaenoidei, are a large and varied group the more generalized members of which are closely related to some of the Perciformes. All differ from the Perciformes in having a bony stay or process running from a bone below the eye towards the operculum. Typical members of this suborder are the Scorpion-fishes (Scorpaenidae) Rock or Poison-fishes (Synanceidae) and the Gurnards (Triglidae). Closely allied to the Scorpaenids are three other suborders, the Cottoidei comprising the Sculpins and Bullheads (Cottidae) and the Lump-suckers (Cyclopteridae); the Dactylopteroidei or Flying Gurnards; and thirdly, the peculiar and grotesque little Dragon-fishes (*Pegasus*) of the suborder Pegasoidei.

Also derived from the Percoids are the peculiar little Cling-fishes (e.g. *Lepadogaster*) with their complex adhesive organs formed partly from the pelvic fins. These fishes constitute the suborder Gobiesocoidei.

The Grey Mullets (Mugilidae), the Barracudas (Sphyraenidae), and Silversides (Atherinidae) are grouped together, but the suborder or order which they comprise is of uncertain relationships. Some authors consider them to be a suborder of the **Perciformes** (Mugiloidei) whilst others give the group ordinal status (**Mugiliformes**) and place it amongst the soft-rayed orders.

The Flatfishes (**Pleuronectiformes**), however, have clearly been derived from the Perciform stock. The order is divided into three suborders, the Psettodoidei which includes the most primitive genus *Psettodes*; the Pleuronectoidei with the Halibut (*Hippoglossus*), Plaice (*Pleuronectes*) and Turbot (*Scophthalmus*) etc., and the Soleoidei, with the Soles (Soleidae) and Tongue Soles (Cynoglossidae).

Finally we may consider the order **Lophiiformes** which includes the common Angler-fishes (Lophiidae), the bizarre Frog-fishes (Antennaridae) and Bat-fishes (Ogcocephalidae), and the various families of deep sea Angler-fishes, usually placed in a distinct suborder the Ceratioidei. All these fishes differ from their Percoid ancestors in having the first ray of the dorsal fin placed on the head and modified into a lure or angling device, and in having the pectoral fin carried on an arm-like pedicel.

This classification is essentially that of L. Berg (1947). Another widely used system, and the one adopted by the British Museum of Natural History, is that of C. Tate Regan (1929). The parts of Regan's classification relevant to those of Berg's are tabled below. Opposite each of Regan's divisions are given (in brackets) the equivalent divisions of the Berg classification. Divisions containing only extinct fishes are marked thus +.

Class *Selachii*	(Class Chondrichthyes)
Subclass Pleuropterygii +	(Superorder Protoselachii in part)
Acanthodii +	(Class Acanthodii)
Ichthyotomi +	(Superorder Protoselachii in part)
Euselachii	(Subclass Selachii)
Order Pleurotremata	(Division Pleurotremata)
Suborder Notidanoidea	(Order Hexanchiformes)
Galeoidea	(Order Galeiformes)
Squaloidea	(Order Squaliformes)

Order Hypotremata	(Division Hypotremata)
Suborder Narcobatoidea	(Order Torpediniformes)
Batoidea	(Order Raiiformes)
Subclass Holocephali	(Sublcass Bradyodonti)
Class *Pisces*	(Class Osteichthyes)
Subclass Palaeopterygii	
Order Archistia +	(Superorder Chondrostei in part)
Belonorhynchii +	(Order Saurichthyformes of above)
Chondrostei	(Superorder Chondrostei)
Cladistia	(Subclass Brachiopterygii)
Subclass Neopterygii	(Subclass Actinopterygii)
Order Protospondyli	(Superorder Holostei in part)
Ginglymodi	(Holostei in part, family Lepisosteidae)
Halecostomi +	(Superorder Halecostomi)
Isospondyli	(Order Clupeiformes)
Suborder Clupeoidea	(Suborder Clupeoidei)
Stomiatoidea	(Suborder Stomiatoidei)
Salmonoidea	(Suborder Salmonoidei)
Osteoglossoidea	(Suborder Osteoglossoidei)
Notopteroidea	(Suborder Notopteroidei)
Order Haplomi	(Suborder Esocoidei, of Clupeiformes)
Iniomi	(Suborder Myctophoidei, of Clupeiformes)
Ostariophysi	(Order Cypriniformes)
Apodes	(Order Anguilliformes)
Synentognathi	(Order Beloniformes)
Microcyprini	(Order Cyprinodontiformes)
Solenichthyes	(Order Syngnathiformes)
	(Order Aulostomiformes)
Anacanthini	(Order Gadiformes)
Allotriognathi	(Order Lampridiformes)
Berycomorphi	(Order Beryciformes)
Zeomorphi	(Order Zeiformes)
Percomorphi	(Order Perciformes)
Suborder Percoidea	(Suborder Percoidei)
Teuthidoidea	(Suborder Acanthuroidei)
Trichiuroidea	(Suborder Trichiuroidei)
Scombroidea	(Suborder Scombroidei)
Gobioidea	(Suborder Gobioidei)
Blennioidea	(Suborder Blennioidei)
Stromateoidea	(Suborder Stromateoidei)

Suborder Anabantoidea	(Suborder Anabantoidei)
Mugiloidea	(Order Mugiliformes)
Order Scleroparei	(The following Perciform sub-
Suborder Scorpaenoidea	orders: Scorpaenoidei
Dactylopteroidea	Cottoidei
Gasterostoidea	Dactylopteroidei
	+
	Order Gasterosteiformes)
Order Hypostomides	(Pegasoidei, a suborder of the Perciformes)
Heterosomata	(Order Pleuronectiformes)
Plectognathi	(Order Tetraodontiformes, and the Perciform suborder Balistoidei)
Xenopterygii	(Suborder Gobiesocoidei of the Perciformes)
Haplodoci	(Suborder Batrachoidei of the Perciformes)
Pediculati	(Order Lophiiformes)
Subclass Crossopterygii	(Subclass Crossopterygii, which excludes the Dipneusti)
Order Actinistia	(Superorder Actinistia)
Rhipidistia	(Superorder Rhipidistia)
Dipneusti	(Subclass Dipneusti)

This list does not, of course, include all the orders and suborders recognised by Regan, but only those of the commoner fishes and particularly those mentioned in the text of this book. Regan's 'Class Pisces' contains three subclasses, forty orders and thirty-nine suborders (of which fifteen are in the order Percomorphi).

References

BERG, L. (1947). *Classification of Fishes both Recent and Fossil*. J. W. Edwards, Ann Arbor.

BERTIN, L. and ARAMBOURG, C. (1958). Super-ordre des Téléostéens: in, *Traité de Zoologie* (Ed. Grassé) **12**, fasc. 3. Masson et Cie, Paris.

CAIN, A. J. (1954). *Animal Species and their Evolution*. Hutchinson's, London.

REGAN, C. T. (1929). Articles on Fishes, Selachians, etc.: in, *Encyclopaedia Britannica*. (14th ed.) London and New York.

CHAPTER 19

FISHES AND MANKIND

A S A STAPLE ARTICLE of food, fish must have found favour
with man at a very early stage of his history, and there
can be very few races living to-day who do not include
this valuable protein food in their ordinary diet. Whether
eaten raw, as in Japan and the Hawaiian Islands, cooked, salted,
smoked, or preserved in one way or another, the popularity of
fish-flesh is world-wide. Apart from certain species whose flesh is
watery, dry and tasteless, full of small bones, or heavily charged
with rank oils, the flesh of fishes is generally white and flaky, and
has an agreeable flavour. In the ease with which its contained
proteins and fats are digested by the human body it compares very
favourably with beef or other meats, and it has been shown that
man is able to digest completely as much as 93.2 per cent of the
protein content of tinned Salmon, and 93.1 per cent of that of
fresh Mackerel, and can make use of 93.7 per cent and 95.2 per cent
respectively of the fatty content of the same fishes.

The muscular tissue or flesh of a fish is made up of 60 to 82
per cent water, about 13 per cent to 20 per cent proteins, and a
greater or lesser amount of fat. The following table illustrates the
percentages of these substances in the flesh of some of our commoner
food-fishes, and the figures in the fourth column represent the
'energy value' or 'fuel value' expressed in calories. Calories are
nothing more than measurements of heat, and provide a simple
means of comparing one article of food with another in terms of
its energy value, which may be briefly defined as 'the number of
calories of heat equivalent to the energy which it is assumed the body
would be able to obtain from one pound of given food material,
provided the nutrients of the latter are fully digested.'

It will be observed that the fat content varies considerably, and
this is true, not only of different kinds of fishes, but of individuals
of the same species taken at different seasons and in various
conditions. Herring, Salmon and Mackerel are to be looked upon
as fatty fishes at all seasons, but Mackerel caught in the late autumn
or winter are usually much fatter than those caught in spring or
summer, and the percentage of fat in a spawning or spent Herring
is considerably less than that in a fish taken at any other time.

Name	Water	Protein	Fats	Fuel Value per lb. (Calories)
Herring	72.5	19.5	7.1	660
Salmon	61.4	17.5	17.8	1080
Cod	82.6	16.5	0.4	325
Haddock	81.7	17.2	0.3	335
Mackerel	73.4	18.7	7.1	645
Halibut	75.4	18.6	5.2	565
Loin of Beef	61.3	19.0	19.1	1155
Leg of Mutton	67.4	19.8	12.4	890
Chicken	63.7	19.3	16.3	1045

This variation in the fat content is shown in the next table. Such fishes as the Cod, Haddock, Plaice and Sole are to be regarded as lean fishes at all seasons.

Name	Protein	Fats	Fuel value per lb. (Calories)
Herring —			
Shetland Matties	21.10	16.68	1095
Small immature autumn	18.65	14.25	951
Spawning	18.91	2.02	430
Spent	18.05	0.68	360
Eel —			
Fat autumn.	13.40	32.90	1635
Lean average	17.60	7.90	660
Mackerel —			
Fat autumn	18.21	16.30	1025
Average	18.77	8.21	695

In addition, the flesh of a fish contains relatively large amounts of vitamins, substances indispensable to an adequate and properly balanced diet. The vitamins present in the bodies of fatty fishes and in the livers of almost all fishes are derived directly from the plankton, that host of minute organisms which directly or indirectly provides the source of food for all fishes.

Although in many countries, and more particularly in those situated in the tropics, freshwater fishes provide a valuable source of food supply, it is the marine fishes that form the bulk of the food of mankind. In America, however, the fisheries of the Great Lakes are of considerable economic importance, the more valuable kinds of fish including the White-fish (Ciscoes and Lake Herrings), Pike-Perch and Carp; and the river fisheries may be of some local importance. As far as the British Isles are concerned, apart from the Salmon and Eel, which are not exclusively freshwater, the fishes of the lakes and rivers are quite unimportant as a source of food supply. The freshwater area of England and Wales is only about three hundred and forty square miles, and the annual production of fish has been estimated as two thousand tons, a very small figure when compared with the yield of the sea-fisheries, or that of a tropical lake such as Lake Victoria where the yield in 1958 was 70,418 tons.

There exists a regular market for freshwater fishes in London and other large cities, but this amounts to only a few hundred tons each year. It is maintained chiefly by the importation of fishes from Holland, where, as in other parts of Europe, the cultivation of Carp and other coarse fishes for the table is a flourishing and well-organised industry. The supplies marketed in this country are bought largely by the foreign population and the Jewish community, and there seems to be a deep-rooted prejudice among the British against the use of these freshwater fishes as food. The chief objection lies in the muddy or weedy flavour which often permeates the whole flesh, but experiments have shown that this is readily overcome by special methods of cooking. As far as nutritive value and digestibility are concerned, they do not differ overmuch from marine fishes, as illustrated by the following table, and the popularity of the latter must be entirely a matter of custom and palatability.

Name	Water	Protein	Fats	Fuel Value per lb. (Calories)
Carp	78.9	15.79	4.77	495
Bream	78.7	16.19	4.09	473
Pike	79.5	18.76	0.66	377
Perch	78.8	18.45	1.40	402
Trout	80.5	17.96	0.74	365

The number of different kinds of fishes eaten in some countries is comparatively small. In Great Britain, for example, the number of species that may be regarded as fairly common in the sea is about one hundred and sixty, yet the official returns and annual reports of the Ministry of Agriculture and Fisheries for England and Wales enumerate only thirty-four edible kinds, including Whitebait. This last is not a single species, as is sometimes supposed, but is composed of young Herrings or Sprats, and may occasionally include young Gobies, Sand Eels, Blennies and other species. The fish trade classifies these thirty-four fishes into two main categories, round and flat, the last including the Skates and Rays as well as the true Flat-fishes. A fair amount of what is known as unclassified fish is also landed, and, with the fishing-vessels making extensive voyages, comparatively rare species make their way into the markets from time to time. The average housewife is probably familiar with less than half of the thirty-four fishes enumerated by the trade, and attempts have been made to overcome a deep-rooted conservatism or even actual prejudice, and to educate the British public to make use of several excellent food-fishes to which they were previously unaccustomed. The case of the much despised Dog-fish is a particularly interesting one, for the modern industry concerned with this fish in England, Canada and the United States, arose almost entirely as the result of an attempt to exterminate what was a serious pest to the existing fisheries. It was found almost impossible to do away with these fishes, or even to reduce their numbers to any appreciable extent, and it was finally found preferable to convert what was previously a useless and actually injurious creature into a valuable asset. The first step towards overcoming popular prejudice to the Dog-fish as food was to give it a more pleasing name, and it was marketed in England as 'Flake', in Canada and the United States as 'Grey-fish', and in Germany as 'See-Aal' (Sea Eel). Chemical analysis of the flesh has shown that it is highly nutritious and easily digested, but so far its use has been limited largely to establishments supplying fried-fish dinners. In this country Dog-fish is eaten fresh, but abroad there are considerable tinning and preserving industries. Another fish which has come in for a good deal of unfair unpopularity is the Cat-fish or Wolf-fish (*Anarrhichas*), chiefly on account of its tough skin and ugly head. Here, again, it has been found convenient to market this perfectly wholesome fish under a more pleasing name, and, deprived of its head and skin, it is sold as 'Rock Salmon', or, in Scotland, 'Rock Turbot'.

The sea fisheries of the world may be roughly divided into deep-sea and inshore fisheries, the former being very much more valuable. The deep-sea fisheries of the continental shelves and the banks of the great oceans lie almost entirely within the limit of a depth of two hundred fathoms, and the majority within one hundred fathoms. The principal fisheries of the world lie in the North Temperate Zone, for the most part between the latitudes of 40° and 70° N., regions in which there are great areas of water less than two hundred fathoms in depth, forming the grounds inhabited by the valuable demersal or bottom-living fishes on which the trawling industries depend. As an example of this concentration of the fisheries in northern seas it may be mentioned that those of Great Britain, France, Spain, Norway, Russia, Canada, the United States and Japan together represent no less than 70 per cent of the total yield of the fisheries of the world. A visit to any fish market in the tropics will reveal the fact that in warmer seas the number of commercial species of fish is far greater than in the northern latitudes, but there are, as a rule, fewer great concentrations of individuals of any one species, and, at the same time, the areas of water of a depth of less than two hundred fathoms are of far less extent. In certain provinces of India sea fisheries are being actively developed and these are exploited in Ceylon and

Malaya, but it is the inland fisheries which are of greatest economic importance in these countries.

Quite apart from their economic value, the sea fisheries in historical times have played an important part in the destinies of nations. Fishing was one of the earliest forms of hunting, and since men were almost certainly hunters before they were cultivators, it follows that fishing is the oldest industry in the world. Even in Tudor times our fishermen were at work, not only in the North Sea and other home waters, but also off the coasts of Lapland and Iceland, and from this time onwards the part played by the fisheries in the development of sea trade, in giving an impetus to the building of ships, and so on, was a very important one. As a further example of the importance of the sea-fisheries to the lives of nations, it may be mentioned that in their pursuit of the Cod the French fishermen were led further and further out into the Atlantic Ocean, and in due course this resulted in the discovery of Canada; it is by no means unusual for the location of an important town or port to be settled with reference to its relation to the fishing industry. According to a Scandinavian authority, wherever a shoal of Herrings touches the coast of Norway, there a village springs up, and the same is true in Scotland, Newfoundland, Japan, Alaska and Siberia.

The literature concerning the numerous and diverse methods of catching fish is voluminous, and it is no part of this work to more than touch briefly on some of the more interesting methods in use to-day. Leaving out of account such curious practices of oriental countries as fishing with a tame otter, with the Remora or Sucking-fish, and with a cormorant (a method used in Japan for catching the *Ayu*, a kind of dwarf Salmon), fishes may be said to be caught in four ways: by spears, by traps, by nets, and by baited hooks. The spear and the trap were almost certainly the earliest weapons to be employed and are still in use to-day in many parts of the world. From primitive traps were evolved the more efficient fish-weir or dam, a snare which worked on the principle of allowing fishes to enter on the flood-tide and retaining them on the ebb. Such weirs are still in use on parts of the coast of Great Britain and in many other countries, and led on to the development of more elaborate structures composed of wattle fencing, and from these, by a process of gradual evolution, to fixed nets. Baited hooks must also have been used at a very early stage in man's history, the first probably being somewhat similar to the thorn hooks once employed in parts of Wales and in the Thames estuary. Finally, instead of waiting for the fish to enter the snare, attempts were made to bring the net to the fish, and the first trawls or seines worked from boats or from the shore were invented.

Four principal methods are used by the commercial fisheries

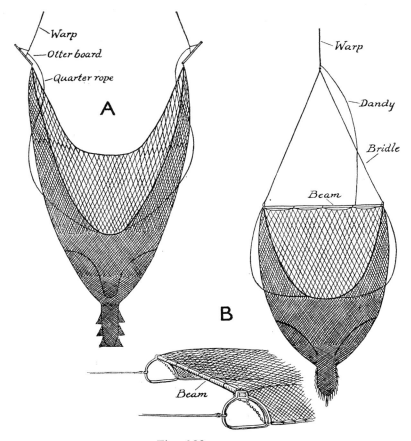

Fig. 139   TRAWLS
A. Otter Trawl, viewed from above; B. Beam trawl, viewed from above
and an oblique side view of the mouth

of the present day, namely, trawling, seining, drifting, and lining,
each method involving the use of a particular kind of gear and
designed to catch particular kinds of fish. The trawlers, seiners, and
liners take chiefly demersal fish such as the Cod, Haddock, Hake,
Halibut, Plaice and Sole, known to the trade as 'white fish', while
the drifters capture pelagic fish like the Herring, Pilchard and
Mackerel.

The trawl [Figs. 139; 141B] is a net of flattened conical shape,
sometimes as much as one hundred feet in length, with a wide
mouth at one end and tapering at the other to the 'purse' or 'cod-

end'. This great bag is dragged slowly along the sea bottom by means of strong 'warps' attached to a powerful winch on the ship, and the fish, once they are in the net, are prevented from swimming out again by special valve-like devices. The 'foot-rope', forming the lower edge of the mouth of the net, may play an important part in stirring up the fish, particularly those like the Flat-fishes, which lie buried in the sand. In the 'beam trawl' [Fig. 139B], now used only for research purposes, the upper edge of the mouth-opening is formed by a stout wooden beam, anything from forty to fifty feet in length, at either end of which are D-shaped iron runners, the 'shoes' or 'trawl-heads', to which the towing warps are attached. The 'otter trawl'' [Fig. 139A] has no such frame round the mouth of the net, which is here kept open by two large 'doors' or 'otterboards', constructed of heavy, iron-bound wood, from eight to nine feet in length and four or five feet high.

As the net is towed slowly along the sea-floor, the resistance of

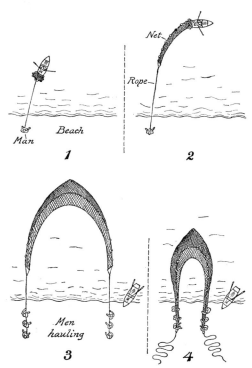

Fig. 140 SEINE NET
Diagrams illustrating the stages in laying and hauling a beach-operated seine.

the water causes the two doors to pull away from one another, each door with its attached warp acting after the manner of a boy's kite. An important and widely adopted modification of the otter trawl is known as the 'Vigneron-Dahl Trawl'. In this net the wings are longer than in the ordinary trawl, giving a greater mouth opening or 'fishing spread', and the ground warps being in close contact with the sea-floor tend to scare the fish towards the track of the net.

Several types of seine net are in use in various countries, but cannot be described in detail here. Briefly, seining consists in surrounding a shoal of fish with a long net, suitably buoyed, and gradually drawing this closer until the imprisoned fish can be readily removed. The net is usually paid out by a boat sailing or rowed round the shoal in a circle or half-circle, and this is finally hauled into the boat by the use of a special winch or is towed ashore [Fig. 140]. In the days when the Pilchard industry flourished on the Cornish coast, deep seine nets were used to surround the shoals, which were paid out by rowing-boats and drawn slowly to the shore. The shoals were sighted by men known as 'huers' or 'balkers', who raised the cry of 'Hev-ah, hev-ah!' when the fish were seen, and who received about three pounds a month and a share of the fish caught. The Purse Seine is a net extensively used in America for catching the valuable Menhaden.

The Danish Seine or 'Snurrevaad' is another important type of net, the use of which has been much developed by British fisheries in recent years. In many respects it lies midway between the trawl and the seine. Over a mile of warp is attached to each wing of the net, which may have a span of one hundred and sixty feet or more, and a large bag of some fifty to sixty feet in length. It is not hauled ashore, but is worked from a boat in offshore waters.

Drift nets are worked on a very different principle to the trawls and seines, and are not actually approached to the fish. At the same time, they differ from fixed nets and traps in that they are attached either to a slowly drifting ship (hence the name) or to a floating buoy, and move with the ship or buoy under the influence of the tide and wind [Fig. 141A]. The types of fish caught with the drift nets are those which spend their time swimming in the layers of water above the sea-floor, keeping, as a rule, fairly deep down during the day, but approaching the surface at night. Each drift net is a simple stretch of strong netting, about fifty or sixty yards in length and about fourteen yards deep, the upper edge of which is buoyed with corks and the lower edge weighted with lead. As night approaches the drifters start to shoot their nets with the tide, 'fleets' of as many as eighty-five nets being used at one time from a single vessel, so that a complete wall of netting, perhaps three miles in length, is hanging vertically in the water, either at the surface or a few fathoms down. The ship, with one end of the wall of netting attached, then drifts for several hours with the tide. The mesh of the net is so constructed that the fish is able to push its head through but not its body; once the gill-covers are through it is impossible for the fish to release its head, and in the dark vast numbers of fish swim into the nets and are securely held.

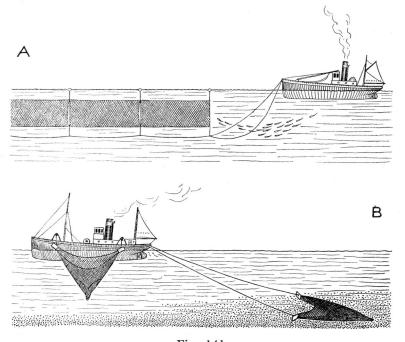

Fig. 141

A. Steam drifter fishing. B. Trawler fishing with an Otter Trawl (astern) and with net hauled into the ship's side. This drawing combines two phases, (fishing and bringing in the gear) of one operation.

At dawn the nets are hauled in to the ship and the catch shaken out of their meshes.

Lining is a method of fishing used to catch such demersal fish as the Cod and Halibut, the Cod fisheries once carried out in this way on the Newfoundland banks were world famous. The old hand-line is now of little commercial importance and has been superseded by the long line, which may be more than four thousand yards in length, with hooks attached at regular intervals to short 'snoods' two to six feet long. On a large motor liner the number of hooks on a single line may be anything from one thousand to five thousand five hundred. The bait varies considerably, including whelks, mussels, squid, and herrings. The lines may be shot in the morning or afternoon, and, unlike the hand lines, are left quite unattended for several hours before being hauled in.

The flesh of fishes, as might be expected, is a highly perishable commodity, and very soon after death begins to undergo certain changes, at first not undesirable, but which, if allowed to continue, render it unfit for human consumption. Modern developments in the techniques of 'deep-freezing' have largely overcome the difficulties of transporting fresh fish, and to a certain extent, of its storage for moderately protracted periods. In the early days of civilisation the heavy curing of many kinds of fish was almost essential, but the tendency nowadays is for the harder cures to be replaced either by fresh fish or by lightly cured preparations.

Four principal methods of curing fish are still in use, namely, salting or pickling in brine, smoking, drying and canning, the former being perhaps the method in most general use throughout the world. The dry salting of Cod was an important industry in both Europe and America. Sometimes the whole process is carried out ashore, but more generally the fish are decapitated, split, cleaned and salted almost as soon as they are caught, and after being washed are stacked in the fish-hold with heavy layers of salt between them. After being landed, the fish are removed to 'cod farms', where the curing is completed by drying, and they are finally packed in barrels for export. Salt Cod, known as 'klip-fish' are split and spread out on rocks to dry, whereas 'stock-fish' are hung up to dry without being split in any way. Salt Cod has played an important part in the economy of European nations for several centuries, and formed the Lenten fare of Catholic Europe in the Middle Ages.

The smoking of fish consists of a combination of salting and drying, and it is upon the degree to which either of these processes is used that the characteristic flavour depends. Smoking is employed largely for Herrings, but Whiting, Cod, Ling, Saithe, Haddock, Cat-fish and Mackerel are also preserved in this manner. Primitive man smoked his fish by hanging them over open camp fires, just as many native races do to-day, but as the commerical fishing industry grew up, more efficient methods were required, and in a modern smoke-house thousands of fish can be cured at one time. The type of wood used for the fires is of special importance, hard woods such as oak, hickory and mahogany being preferred, as these contain less oils and resins which might impart a taste to the fish. The smoke is produced, not by burning the wood itself, but by burning sawdust, which smoulders gently and gives off dense clouds of smoke.

The three principal types of smoked Herring are Red Herring,

Bloater and Kipper. Red Herrings and Bloaters are both cured without splitting, only being cut open sufficiently for cleaning. The Red Herring is much more strongly salted, being buried in salt for at least five days and then smoked for ten days, whereas the Bloater is less heavily salted, and is smoked only long enough to dry the fish but not to cure it. The Red Herring can, therefore, be exported for considerable distances, but the Bloater, like the Kipper, is a perishable product, and cannot be kept for more than a few days at ordinary temperatures. A Kipper is a Herring which has been split down the back from head to tail, immersed in brine for a period varying from fifteen to sixty minutes, slightly dried, and finally smoked for several hours. In recent years many Kippers have been cured by immersion in chemical mixtures, but these are much inferior in taste, and may even prove injurious as food.

The smoking of Haddock dates back to the middle of the eighteenth century, and originated at Findon in Scotland, the smoked fish being known as Findon Haddocks, a name which was later abbreviated to Findon Haddies and finally to Finnan Haddies. The fresh fish is decapitated and split down the back, gutted, and an extra cut made part of the way down the back from the right-hand side in order to facilitate the curing of the thick muscles of the back. It is then washed, salted for a short time in strong brine, dried, and then spread open on sticks to be smoked for a period of five or six hours over a fire burning a mixture of peat and sawdust.

Drying is a method of curing which is used mainly in tropical countries, where the heat of the sun's rays is sufficiently powerful. It is the favourite method of preservation in Africa, India, Malay, the Philippines, China and Japan, where dried fish is an important article of food. Generally the fish are simply cut open, gutted and laid in the sun to dry, but sometimes they are first salted to some extent. The well-known 'Bombay Duck' [Fig. 142], that indispensable adjunct to an Indian curry, consists of the dried and salted bodies of the Bummalow (*Harpodon*), a fish which is particularly abundant in the estuaries of Bengal and Burma.

Canning is a comparatively modern method of preservation, and has many obvious advantages over the others. In America it has become a very important industry, particularly the canning of Pacific Salmon, carried on from Alaska to California. In Europe, Herrings, Sprats, Sardines, Anchovies, Mackerel and Tunnies are all tinned, the Sardine industry of France, Spain and Portugal being of great commercial importance to these nations. The Sardine is not, as is often supposed, a distinct species of fish, but the young stage of the Pilchard (*Sardina pilchardus*). The method of curing consists in removing the head and viscera, sprinkling lightly with salt, immersing for a short time in brine, washing, drying and then frying for about two minutes in olive oil. The fish are then packed in olive oil in tins, which are hermetically sealed, other ingredients such as oil of lemon, cloves, bay, truffles, or pickles being sometimes used to give added flavour. A similar trade is carried on to a large extent in Norway, but here the fish used is the Sprat (Brisling) (*Clupea sprattus*) or the young of the Herring (*Clupea harengus*).

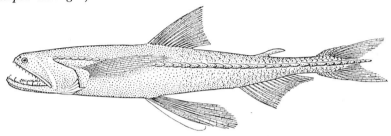

Fig. 142 'BOMBAY DUCK'
The Bummalow (*Harpodon nehereus*) which is dried and salted to produce 'Bombay Duck'.

In some countries fish are pickled in vinegar or cured in one or two other unusual ways, while among the other food products which are derived from the flesh of fish may be mentioned fish sausages, rissoles, anchovy paste, fish cake of Japan and caviare. This last is prepared from the roes of the Sturgeons, the great caviare industries being carried on round the Black Sea and Caspian Sea, where these fishes are numerous. At one of the fishing stations in this region it has been estimated that as many as fifteen thousand Sturgeons have been caught in a single day. In Great Britain the Sturgeon is a 'Royal Fish', for by an unrepealed law of Edward II it is enacted that 'the King shall have the wreck of the sea throughout the realm, whales and great sturgeons . . . except in certain places privileged by the King.' In parts of the Orient, notably in China and the Philippine Islands, there is a considerable trade in shark fins, which are used for making soup. After being cut from the body, the fins are well salted or dusted with lime, and then dried in the sun. The Japanese prepare a tasty dish from the flesh of Sharks and Dog-fishes, which is known by the name of 'Shark-flesh paste.'

In addition to providing man with food, most fishes yield a number of by-products, which may be of some commercial importance. Chief among these are the oils of various grades, ranging from the crude oils used in certain manufacturing processes to medicinal cod-liver oil. In fishes like the Herring, Sardine, Menhaden, Salmon, and Mackerel, the bulk of the oil is found in the body, and furnishes what is known to the trade as 'fish-oil', a product used in the manufacture of paints. In the Cod and many other fishes, the oil is contained mainly in the liver, and yields a product which in the crude state is used by the tanning industry, being particularly valuable in the manufacture of 'chamois' leather, for tempering steel, and in the preparation of lower-grade soaps, while, after refining, it provides the well-known medicinal oil.

Fish meals and fish fertilisers are products of some economic importance, and succeed in using up all the waste parts of the fish. The former is used to feed poultry, pigs, and cattle, and is particularly reliable for chickens and young animals, as it contains protein in a readily digestible form, as well as a high percentage of calcium phosphate. It is of interest to note that the Greek historian Herodotus, writing in about the fourth century B.C., mentions a tribe living in pile-dwellings round Lake Prasias that 'feed their horses and other beasts on fish, which abound in the lake in such a degree that a man has only to open his trap-door, and let down a basket by a rope into the water, and then wait a very short time, when he draws it up quite full of fish' (Rawlinson's translation).

Fish glue is a product obtained mainly from such fishes as the Cod, Haddock, Pollack and Hake. Most of it is derived from the skin of the fish, but waste glue and fish-head glue are also manufactured. Isinglass is a pure gelatinous substance obtained from the inner lining of the swimbladder of certain fishes, and is principally used for the clarification of wines and beer, for making jellies, etc., and in the preparation of certain cements. It is made in various parts of the world from the swimbladders or 'sounds' as they are known to the trade, of such diverse fishes as the Sturgeons, Carps, Cat-fishes, Cod, Ling, Hake, Squeteagues, Drums, and Thread Fins. The Russian isinglass, marketed as 'leaf', 'pipe,' and 'cake,' is perhaps best known and of the finest quality, being manufactured entirely from the sounds of various species of Sturgeon.

The skins of some fishes, and particularly those of the Sharks and Rays, are sometimes of use to mankind. With the bony dermal denticles *in situ*, the crude skins of Sharks and Dog-fishes are used by carpenters and cabinet-makers for smoothing and polishing, as well as by metal-workers; suitably prepared and dyed skins provide the shagreen used for covering card cases, jewel boxes, sword scabbards, and for ornamental work of all kinds. After being specially tanned, and having had the dermal denticles removed, the skins of most Sharks and Rays provide a strong and highly durable leather. Recently, experiments have been made with the skins of some of the Bony Fishes, the Wolf-fish (known to the trade as 'Sea Leopard'), Cod, Bream, Corvina, and Sole being most popular, but they lack the durability of shark leather. In certain of the

Islands of the South Seas the natives made use of the dried and
spiny skins of the Globe-fishes or Porcupine-fishes for war helmets,
and in Japan it is a common practice to make lanterns out of the
inflated and dried skins of Puffers, by cutting out the back and
suspending the fish by a wire. A candle being placed inside, the
light shines as brightly through the stretched skin of the fish as
through a piece of oiled paper.

Finally, the silvery scales of the Bleak (*Alburnus*), a Cyprinid fish
found all over Europe north of the Pyrenees and Alps, were
used extensively in the manufacture of artificial pearls, especially
in France, where the industry dates from the middle of the seventeenth century. A pigment, obtained by scraping the scales, is
coated on the inside of hollow glass beads and these are then filled
with wax.

Speaking in 1883 Professor T. H. Huxley said: 'I believe that
the cod fishery, the herring fishery, the pilchard fishery, the
mackerel fishery, and probably all the great sea-fisheries are
inexhaustible; that is to say that nothing we do seriously affects
the numbers of fish.' In those days of trawling and lining from
sailing vessels this statement was probably true enough, but with
the advent of steam-trawling, and with the enormous growth in
the volume of fishing that followed, coupled with a great increase
in the destructiveness of fishing gear, conditions were altogether
changed, and apprehensions have arisen as to whether the operations of mankind are not depleting the stocks of fishes in the sea.
Many authors have described this great international asset as the
'harvest of the sea,' but it must be remembered that the harvest
gathered by the fisherman is one that he has never sown, and that,
although he may take large quantities of fish from the sea, he does
nothing towards increasing or conserving the supply. As has often
been pointed out (but as often unheeded), the present generation
is the trustee for future generations in the matter of preserving our
species of fish and of maintaining a reasonable supply of fish for
food, and it is, therefore, of great importance that this problem
should constantly receive the attention of scientific men before
irreparable damage is done to the stocks. Much has been written
concerning the application of various branches of science to the
fishing industry, and in the following pages a brief account of some
of the problems awaiting solution and of the methods employed
by fishery investigators will be given.

It was the pressing need for a scientific investigation of the
alleged decline in the numbers of fish, due to over-fishing, coupled
with the increased interest taken in the science of oceanography,
which had received a marked stimulus from the *Challenger* expedition
in 1872 to 1876, that led to the establishment of fishery research
towards the close of the nineteenth century. The Fishery Board

for Scotland led the way in the 'eighties, but with the foundation
of the now famous Marine Biological Association at Plymouth in
1884, similar investigations were soon undertaken in England.
The greatest advance took place in 1899, when, realising the
international character of the great sea-fisheries, the King of
Sweden invited representatives of all the interested maritime
powers to a conference at Stockholm 'to elaborate a plan for the
joint exploration in the interests of the sea fisheries of the hydrographical and biological conditions of the Arctic Ocean and the
North and Baltic Seas.' The response was general, and as a result
of this conference and another similar gathering held in Copenhagen
in 1902, the 'International Council for the Exploration of the Sea'
came into being, with permanent headquarters at Copenhagen
and a central laboratory at Oslo. Included in the Council are
representatives of all the countries of Northern Europe, with
important fishing interests, as well as those of Spain, Portugal and
Italy. Its object is to see that the natural resources of the sea
are exploited in a rational manner, and to this end to co-ordinate
the researches of the various countries involved, each being allotted
a certain area of the sea for special investigation, in addition to
carrying out general work on a more extensive scale with the
approval of the Council. The central bureau publishes a number
of monographs, papers and notes of all kinds, mostly of a technical
nature and written in various languages, dealing with the fish and
fishery investigations, and in addition each country publishes its
own reports, often of a voluminous nature, of investigations undertaken by its own specialists in the different branches of fishery
research. In this way a great deal of overlapping is avoided, and
a vast amount of valuable information has been placed on permanent
record.

Considerations of space will not allow even a brief account of the
many and varied branches of fishery research, and it must suffice
to indicate a few of the more important problems that present
themselves and the method adopted for their solution. Mention
has been made of the comparatively recent science of oceanography,
and it is clear that no hard and fast line can be drawn between
this and fishery research. Practically all the work carried out by
the oceanographer, whether of a biological or hydrographical
nature, will be found to have some bearing, direct or indirect,
on the lives of the food-fishes. Even when in its infancy the practical
value of marine biological work to the welfare of the fisheries
was amply demonstrated when a controversy arose in the latter
part of the last century as to the possible harmful effects of the
introduction of steam trawling. It was suggested that the heavy
trawl dragged over the sea-floor would destroy large quantities
of fish eggs, but on the matter being referred to the scientific

advisers, they were able to say at once that such fears were without foundation. The development of the more important food-fishes had already been studied, and it was pointed out that, with the sole exception of the Herring, whose eggs are deposited in adhesive masses on grounds generally so rough that trawling would be almost impossible, the eggs of all our food-fishes are of the pelagic, drifting kind.

To obtain a complete and intimate knowledge of the life-history and habits of each species is one of the most important branches of research. This involves a study of the spawning habits, the location of the spawning grounds, the recognition of the eggs and larvae and a knowledge of their development, the rate at which the fish grow, and the relation between this growth-rate and the available food supply, as well as an investigation of the migrations of the shoals of adult and young fish, and so on. Further, in order to study the life-history of a particular fish, it is necessary to study its environment, and fishery research must include the study of the plankton food of the pelagic fishes, as well as the bottom-living invertebrates forming the food of the demersal fishes. This in turn involves the study of the minute vegetable and inorganic constituents in the diet of the plankton and the invertebrates of the sea bottom, and the lines of research must be further broadened out to include a study of the physical nature of the sea-floor, the movements of the tides, the currents, the temperature and salinity of the water; in fact, the general physics and chemistry of the sea. In addition to biological and hydrographical investigations, the collection of statistics forms another important branch of inquiry. Records of the quantities and sizes of the different species landed at various ports by vessels employing different kinds of fishing gear must be accurately kept over long periods, and numerous measurements of individual fishes made at sea, for it is only by methods of this nature that it is possible to obtain some idea of the stocks of fish in the sea and the reasons for the fluctuations in their composition.

While at sea the fishery investigator is kept constantly employed in measuring fish, obtaining otoliths and scales from selected specimens in order that their age may be ascertained, marking fish with metal discs for the purpose of studying their movements, collecting samples of the sea bottom and of the surface plankton, making observations of the temperature and salinity, and of the chemical constituents of the water at various depths, collecting eggs and larvae, and releasing special drift bottles, which, when subsequently recovered, serve to measure the movements of the water under the influence of tides and currents. Back in the laboratory, the water samples are analysed, the physical and chemical data tabulated, the plankton and bottom samples studied, the scales and otoliths read, and the thousand and one tasks connected with fishery research are constantly being carried out. Each specialist working on his own particular subject contributes his quota to the solution of the general problems involved. 'What, then, are these general problems?' wrote Dr. Russell in an account of the work of the fisheries research laboratory at Lowestoft. 'Apart from the general acquisition of knowledge, which has a remarkable way of turning out in the long run to be of practical use, the main problems whose solution we seek may be said to be two — the rational and economical exploitation of the fisheries, and the prognostication of good and bad years.' As far as the second of these problems is concerned, science has for some time been able to form a pretty good idea of the probable success or failure of a particular fishery during the next year or two, and a stage has now been reached when actual and accurate prophecy is possible. That stocks of fish do vary considerably from year to year, quite independent of the amount of fishing, has been known for some time, and it will clearly be of the greatest practical importance to the industry when the factors that govern these fluctuations are thoroughly understood. Finally, there is room for a good deal of research on the types of gear used in fishing, and on such subsidiary branches of the industry as the handling of fish, refrigeration, preservation, packing, etc.

The maintenance or improvement of the stocks of certain species of edible fish by some form of pisciculture is a very ancient practice, and it is known that in classical times the Greeks and Romans made a habit of cultivating fishes in captivity for the table, and of stocking their lakes and ponds with ova or young fish obtained from other localities. Two main types of modern pisciculture may be recognised: (1) the rearing of fishes in confinement until they are large enough to be eaten, and (2) the stocking of waters with eggs or fry obtained from fishes breeding in captivity. The ancient Romans certainly carried on the first method, and were in the habit of admitting young fishes from the sea into special enclosures or *vivaria* by means of sluices, and then fattening them up for the table. Exactly similar cultivation of marine fishes is carried out at the present day in the lagoons of the Adriatic and the salt, marshes of various parts of France. The number of different kinds of fish which can be successfully reared from the egg to maturity in captivity is rather small. The Carp, Crucian Carp, Tench, Orfe, Ide, Bream, Roach, Dace, Trout, Pike, Eel and Perch are all cultivated to a greater or lesser extent by fish culturists of Europe, but of these only the Carp lends itself to domestication to an extent which makes it a commercial proposition. This is one of the principal fishes used in pond culture throughout the world, and in Central and Southern Europe, as well as in China and other oriental countries, Carp culture forms a flourishing industry, but it has long died out in England. The Carp is a very hardy fish, can be bred and reared to maturity under all kinds of conditions, requires no costly food, consuming refuse and other natural products which are otherwise useless, grows rapidly, and, if properly cooked, has a delicate flavour. Rapid growth to a marketable size is essential to a profitable industry, and modern growers have succeeded in producing races that grow to an average weight of two and a half pounds at the end of their third summer, and in some tropical countries the rapid growth is even more striking.

The second type of pisciculture, namely, the artificial propagation of fishes for stocking purposes, is carried on extensively in various parts of Europe, America, the Far East and Africa. Trout lend themselves particularly well to this form of cultivation, and can by profitably hatched in special receptacles. In our own country great advances have been made in this industry with the marked growth which has taken place in the volume of angling, and every Trout stream of any value or note is restocked from time to time as a matter of course. In the United States the Brook Trout, Black Bass, and to a lesser extent some of the Sun-fishes, are cultivated in huge numbers, the Brook Trout also being reared to a fair size in ponds. By feeding these fishes on a diet of slaughter-house offal, in addition to the natural food in the ponds, they can be made to grow two or three times as fast as in the wild state. The actual process of artificial fertilisation is very simple, the ripe female fish generally being 'stripped', the eggs being pressed from the body into a vessel into which a little of the milt of the male is introduced. When fertilised, the eggs are either distributed at once to the waters which have to be stocked, or they are placed in special receptacles provided with a suitable stream of water until the fry are hatched. These may be planted at once, but do not always flourish, and it is advisable to stock the waters either with unhatched eggs or with fry which have been reared for a period in the hatcheries until they are active and hardy.

The ease with which the natural development of the ova can be retarded by storing them in ice made it possible to introduce certain species of fish into new countries or even into fresh continents. Trout were taken into New Zealand from England as early as the eighteen-sixties, and this country now boasts the finest Trout fishing in the world. American Trout of various kinds have been introduced into England from time to time, and our own Brown Trout introduced into the United States. The only foreign species at all well-known in Great Britain is the Rainbow Trout. This has been used extensively for stocking sporting waters. Comparatively recently, Trout have been introduced with great success into Tasmania, Ceylon, Kashmir, South Africa and Kenya, in every case for sporting ends. However much such introductions of foreign species may benefit the sportsman, they are to be wholly deprecated by the biologist, who wishes to study the indigenous fauna of a country under normal conditions, and it has been found necessary to enter a strong protest against these interferences with natural conditions. It is well known that the introduction of new elements into a fauna may upset the established balance and produce quite unexpected results. In consequence the new species may even become a serious pest and defy all efforts to exterminate it. It is said that the Carp in North America and the Goldfish in Madagascar have spread and done considerable damage to the existing fisheries for other and better fish.

As far as the British Isles are concerned, it has already been pointed out that, apart from migratory species such as the Eel and the Salmon, the freshwater fishes are of very little value as a potential source of food supply. If the strictly freshwater fishes are commercially unimportant, the same cannot be said of the migratory forms such as the Salmon, Sea Trout, and Eel, and it behoves us to make every effort to maintain or even increase the numbers of these fishes. It is held by some people that artificial hatching of Salmon will provide an easy and infallible remedy for any amount of over-fishing, but so far there is no definite evidence that the yield of any river has been maintained or improved by this method of cultivation. It seems far more likely that a careful regulation of the fisheries, coupled with a thorough knowledge of the life histories of the fishes concerned, will do more towards improving the stocks than any amount of hatching and stocking. To improve the fisheries it is sometimes necessary to regulate the netting, so as to allow the passage of a reasonable number of adult fish to propagate their kind and to satisfy the angler; the journey of the fish to the spawning grounds in the upper waters must be facilitated as far as possible; and finally, the fish must be protected while engaged in spawning. As far as netting is concerned, a good deal has already been carried out, and serious over-fishing virtually controlled. The removal of obstructions of all kinds, whether natural or artificial, lying between the fish and the spawning beds, is of the greatest importance, and it is in this direction that action is urgently required on many rivers. Such natural obstacles as waterfalls may provide a complete barrier to the ascent of Salmon or Sea Trout, and those of the artificial kind, such as dams, dykes, and weirs, are even more numerous. The remedy often lies in the provision of some type of Salmon pass, ladder or lift, to facilitate the passage of the fish over or round the obstacle, but the expense incurred has prevented this from being done in many cases.

The most serious obstacle of all to the welfare of freshwater fishes, and one which provides an all too effective barrier to the ascent of Salmon and Sea Trout, is the wholesale pollution of the rivers which has been going on practically unchecked for a long time. The development of certain industries has reduced the water in some rivers to a terrible state, and crude, untreated sewage, the poisonous effluents of steel and iron works, factories, chemical works, collieries, mines, and the like, are being poured into our rivers and streams in ever-increasing quantities to poison or asphyxiate vast numbers of fishes and other forms of animal life. Fortunately, the outlook is not hopeless, and a vast amount of research and inquiry is now being carried out as to the best methods of dealing with this menace. Another form of commercial under-taking that provides a menace to the fisheries for Salmon and Trout is the development of hydro-electric schemes, which means the building of large dams, the alteration of water-courses, and changes in the volume of water, to say nothing of the damage done to the spawning grounds. The Salmon rivers of the Pacific coast of North America have been particularly affected by such under-takings for a number of years.

Among other contributory causes to the decline in the stocks of fish, mention may be made of the depredations of otters and fish-eating birds, and of human poachers, but in most cases these are unimportant in comparison with those dealt with above.

The subject of fish diseases is worthy of some consideration, for there are certain contagious maladies that play havoc with the stocks of freshwater fish and constitute a serious menace to fish culturists. It is among the freshwater forms, and more particularly among those living under artificial conditions, that predisposition to serious infections is most marked. These may be due to bacterial infection, to animal or plant parasites, to bad feeding, to pollution of the water, and to physical causes of many kinds.

Among the more serious epidemic diseases is that known as Furunculosis or 'Ulcer Disease', and the damage caused by this illness to the stocks of Salmon and Sea Trout has sometimes reached alarming dimensions. It is due to a specific bacterium, *Bacillus salmonicida*, which invades the blood-stream and is thus distributed through every organ of the body. It is highly infectious, being spread by the contact of infected with healthy fish, or by the discharge of the bacteria from the body of a diseased fish into the water; there is also reason to believe that perfectly healthy fish may act as carriers without themselves developing the disease. So far, it has been possible to do very little in the matter of treatment, but the prompt notification of outbreaks, and the quick removal and burial of dead fish from infected waters, may do much towards preventing the spread of the disease. The 'Salmon Disease', so-called because it is most prevalent in Salmon and Sea Trout, is likewise caused by a bacillus (*B. salmonispestis*), and this invades the tissues of the fish, gaining entrance through an abrasion or ulceration of the skin, multiplies rapidly, and forms areas of dead flesh which form an ideal substratum for the growth of a deadly fungus (see below). In 'Tail-rot' and 'Fin-rot', particularly rife among Goldfish and other cultivated species, bacteria of one kind or another are again the causative factors. The tail or fins become gradually frayed and stringy, finally disintegrating and dropping off. *Ichthyophthiriasis* or 'White-spot Disease' is another very common fish disease, the victim being covered with white specks, each of which represents a minute pit eaten through the scale pigment by a Protozoan parasite. Such an attack is not necessarily fatal in itself, but the resulting sores are nearly always attacked by fungus which eventually kills the fish. The parasitic protozoa, known as Myxosporidia often cause epidemic diseases of a serious nature, the epidermis of the gills, the fins, and certain internal organs, developing creamy white, wart-like growths or tumours in which bacteria develop and multiply rapidly. When these tumours burst, the parasites are disseminated in the water, and the resulting ulcers are attacked by fungus.

The fungus mentioned above (*Saprolegnia*) is not in itself a specific disease, but only makes its appearance on individuals weakened by other maladies, or those whose vitality has been lowered by unhealthy conditions, pollution, or by the strain of reproduction; it nearly always attacks fish with bruises, wounds, or abrased surfaces, on which the spores floating in the water are able to obtain a hold. Once established, the fungus penetrates into the living tissues of the victim, and commencing with a small infection on the site of an injury, it spreads over the whole body, fins, eyes, gills, and other parts, until death supervenes. It attacks young and old fish alike, and the spores may lodge on dead or unfertilised ova, and from thence spread to healthy eggs. Examined under a powerful lens, the fungus may be observed to have the form of numerous fine filaments projecting from the surface of the skin, while to the naked eye the growth has the appearance of fine cotton-wool. It is particularly prevalent among fishes kept in small ponds and aquaria, but also attacks those living in a wild state.

Nearly all fishes are infested to a greater or lesser extent by animal parasites of various kinds, some of them causing serious discomfort or injury, others apparently harmless. Two kinds may be recognised: (1) those that live on the external surface of the host (ectoparasites), and (2) those that live inside the host (endoparasites). The first category includes the Leeches and parasitic Crustaceans, the second the Protozoa and worms of various kinds. Leeches are frequently found attached to freshwater fishes, but, although they suck the blood of their hosts, they do little harm unless present in large numbers. Among the Crustacean parasites

are included the Sea Lice and Gill Maggots. Fresh-run Salmon
and Sea Trout are generally infested with Sea Lice (*Lepeophtheirus*),
belonging to the group of Crustacea known as Copepods, but
differing from their free-swimming relatives in having fewer
segments and limbs, and in having their organs modified in various
ways to fit them for their peculiar mode of life [Fig. 143]. They
become firmly attached to the body of the fish, living entirely on
the nourishment obtained from its blood. They are unable to live

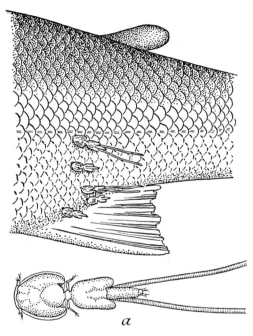

a

Fig. 143
Sea Lice (*Lepeophtheirus salmonis*) on Salmon. *a*. Single specimen. x 3

for any length of time in fresh water, so that their presence is a sure
indication that the fish has recently left the sea. Females are much
more numerous than males, and are considerably larger, measuring
about three-quarters of an inch in length. Other forms of parasitic
Copepods occur in both marine and freshwater fishes, and many of
them are so much modified for a parasitic life that their Crustacean
affinities are scarcely recognisable, and it is only when their whole
life history is know that their place in the system can be determined.
Generally, the conspicuous egg-sacs draw attention to the presence

of the parasite, whose head and anterior parts may be buried in the tissues of the host.

The so-called 'maggots' (*Salmincola*) infesting the gills of Salmon and other fish are more remarkable, and are much less Crustacean-like in appearance. One pair of limbs has been modified into long arms, uniting at the tip to form a sucker, by means of which the animal adheres to the gills. At the other end of the shapeless, fleshy body is a pair of long egg-sacs, each containing several series of eggs [Fig. 144]. The males of this genus are little known, but are dwarfed, and sometimes to be found attached to the females, which grow to a length of a little more than a quarter of an inch.

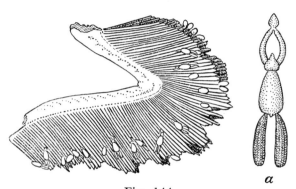

a

Fig. 144

Gill Maggots (*Salmincola salmonea*) on gills of Salmon. *a*. Single specimen, x 3

Mention may also be made of the so-called Carp Louse (*Argulus*), another Crustacean parasite. This creature has a broad, flat and very transparent body, about three-sixteenths of an inch in length, and attaches itself to different species of freshwater fishes by means of a pair of large round suckers on the under side of the head. It is only a temporary parasite, and is frequently found swimming free in ponds and rivers. It sucks the blood of the fish, but does little harm except in the ponds of hatcheries, where the fish are crowded together.

Internal parasitic worms of one kind or another often occur in most marine and freshwater fishes, and include Trematodes or Flukes, Tape Worms, Round or Thread Worms, and Thorn-headed Worms. Flukes (Trematoda) are most common in river and lake fishes, some occurring in the adult form, either as ectoparasites on the gills or skin, or as endoparasites in the alimentary canal, while others in the pre-adult stage become encysted in the tissues or in the body cavity. Thus, sometimes the fish is the final host of the fluke, but in other cases it is only a temporary or intermediate host, and the development of the parasite is completed within some fish-eating vertebrate. Roach, Dace, Bream, and other coarse fish are sometimes found with the body covered in small black spots. When examined under a microscope each of these spots is seen to consist of a mass of pigment surrounding a larval Trematode.

As with the Flukes, so with the Tape Worms (Cestoda), the fish is sometimes the final host, the worm passing the earlier stages of its development in some smaller animal preyed upon by the fish, and sometimes only the intermediate host. Two genera, of which one (Ligula) occurs in various freshwater fishes, and the other (Schistocephalus) is very common in the Sticklebacks, grow to a very large size as larval forms in the body cavity of the fish, and become adult in the intestine of various fish-eating birds. In certain seasons nearly all the Sticklebacks living in a given locality have been found to be infected with this parasite, which fills the abdominal cavity to such a degree that the host appears unusually plump or is even swollen like a miniature balloon. In North America, Tape Worms forty centimetres in length, attributed to the genus Ligula, have been taken from Suckers (Catostomidae) only ten centimetres long, the weight of the parasite being more than one-quarter that of the fish. The worms lie quite free in the body cavity, and although they do not move about and have no suckers or hooks to cause definite injury, they do considerable damage by crowding the organs of the fish into unnatural positions, as well as by absorbing the serous fluid. It is of some interest to note that Ligula is considered a delicacy in Italy and the south of France, where it is known as 'Maccaroni piatti' and 'Ver blanc' respectively. A Tape Worm known as Diphyllobothrium latum passes the last larval stage of its development in fishes, the larvae occurring in large numbers in the viscera and muscles of the Pike and other freshwater species, which become infected by swallowing the small 'water-fleas' in which the earlier stages occur. Cooking destroys them, but in parts of Eastern and Central Europe, as well as in North America and Japan, the fish are eaten raw, smoked, or inadequately cooked and the worm continues its life-cycle in the intestine of its human host. The larvae (plerocercoids) may grow to a length of twenty to thirty feet, and are sometimes responsible for a severe type of anaemia. Man is not the only host, the same worm occurring in wild and domesticated carnivorous mammals.

Round Worms or Thread Worms (Nematoda) of various kinds occur in the adult form in almost all fishes, generally in the alimentary canal, while larval Nematodes may be found in the connective tissue, body cavity, or muscles. These parasites rarely do much harm unless very abundant. Small Nematodes are frequently to be seen encysted or free in the tissues surrounding the abdominal cavity of such food-fishes as the Cod, Hake and Haddock, and many people hesitate to eat the fish on this account. Such fears are quite groundless, however, for not only are the worms destroyed by cooking, but they are not of the type likely to flourish in a human host. Thorn-headed Worms (Acanthocephala) may occur in large numbers in the intestines of fishes, where they may sometimes

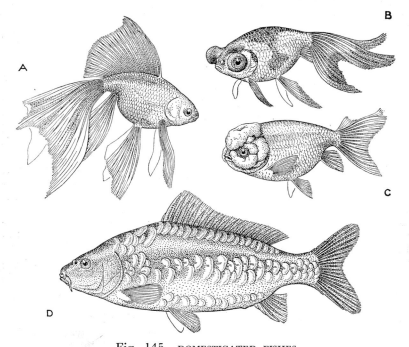

Fig. 145 DOMESTICATED FISHES
A. Veil-tailed variety of Goldfish (*Carassius auratus*); B. Telescopic-eyed variety; C. Lion-headed variety. All x *ca.* $^1/_3$; D. Mirror or King Carp, a cultivated mutant form of the Common Carp. x *ca.* $^1/_6$

cause intense irritation and gastric disturbance. The larval stages are passed in some smaller animal, forming part of the normal diet of the fish.

Monstrosities are comparatively rare in a state of nature, and cannot be considered in any detail. 'Bulldog-nosed' or 'Pug-headed' Trout, Pike, etc., in which the snout is abnormally shortened so that the lower jaw projects, are captured from time to time, and hump-backed or hog-backed specimens, with the vertebral column shortened, curved, or otherwise malformed, also occur among marine and freshwater fishes. Such individuals are not necessarily handicapped in the struggle for existence, often attaining a fair age, and generally appearing well-nourished. Abnormalities of the fins also occur in a wild state, extra fins being developed in unusual situations, or normal ones reduced in size or absent altogether, as well as variations in scaling, coloration, and so on. Among domesticated fishes monstrosities are much more common, and, in the case of the Goldfish (*Carassius*), abnormal types originally appearing as mutations have been perpetuated by the Japanese breeders to become distinct true-breeding varieties. The grotesque 'Pop-eye', the 'Veil-Tail', and the remarkable 'Lion-head' are familiar objects in aquaria [Fig. 145A–c], and represent monstrosities that have bred true to type. Double-headed fry, or young fishes abnormally united or incompletely divided, frequently occur in fish hatcheries, but very rarely live beyond the stage at which the yolk-sac is absorbed. These and other abnormalities of a like nature are generally congenital in origin, but some may be due to accidents to the young or adult fish. Fishes in general have little power to regenerate lost parts, beyond reproducing the tips of the fins and other superficial structures which may be injured or broken. Many fishes that have had their tails bitten off will survive the injury, the wound will heal, and rudimentary fin-rays may be developed in the region of the scars.

In considering the relations between fishes and mankind, the keeping of living examples in aquaria and the exhibition of dead specimens in museums will naturally come to mind. Where it is impossible to observe fishes in their natural surroundings, much may be learned of their habits by studying them in captivity. Aquarium-keeping undertaken in an intelligent manner will be found to provide a fascinating hobby at a comparatively small cost, and will prove a source of infinite amusement and instruction. Many rare and interesting tropical fishes are nowadays imported by dealers. The formation and maintenance of marine and freshwater aquaria is a subject too vast to be dealt with here, and, moreover, is one which has been treated by experts in books especially devoted to the matter. The subject of museum exhibitions is likewise worthy of a chapter to itself, but considerations of space will make it necessary to give only a few lines on the collection of fishes in the Natural History Museum at South Kensington.

A visitor to the fish gallery at the Natural History Museum often goes away under the impression that the series of some two or three thousand coloured plaster casts and models, stuffed and painted skins, preparations in alcohol, skeletons, etc., represent the whole of the collection, and some have expressed disappointment at the absence of representatives of certain species from the cases. Actually, the exhibits represent a carefully selected series of specimens, displayed and labelled in such a manner as to interest visitors and to give a general impression of some of the more interesting members of the fish world, as well as to illustrate their relationships one to the other. In addition, special cases are devoted to breeding, development, coloration, sexual differences, and so on, while others are designed to give an idea of the anatomy of the fish's body as described in these pages. But this is by no means the only collection in the museum, and there is a very much more important series of specimens which is not exhibited to the public. Some of these consist of dried skins, stuffed examples, and skeletons, but the vast bulk of them are preserved in alcohol in glass bottles. These bottles are clearly labelled with the correct name of the species, and are all catalogued and arranged in cupboards according to their natural relationships. This study collection contains more than two hundred thousand specimens, and although there are naturally a number of gaps still to be filled, it includes representatives of over half of the thirty-thousand species known to science. This vast series of fishes is available to recognised students, and ichthyologists from all over the world come to the museum to work on the specimens. Every year more new examples are added to the existing collection, and it is one of the duties of the curators to see that these are correctly named and incorporated with the others. Many are obtained through the medium of large expeditions sent out to various regions of the world, but even more owe their existence in the museum to the interest and energy of explorers, travellers, and others resident in foreign countries, who have spent their spare time in capturing fishes in little known parts of the world to enrich the collections of the museum.

REFERENCES

AXELROD, H. R., & VORDERWINKLER, W. (1957). *Encyclopedia of Tropical Fishes.* T. F. H. Publications, New Jersey.

CUTTING, C. L. (1955). *Fish Saving. A History of Fish Processing.* London.

FRIDRIKSSON, A. (1962). International Council for the Exploration of the Sea. *Fish. News Internat.*, **1** No. 5, 35–37.

GRAHAM, M. (1943). *The Fish Gate.* Faber and Faber, London.

HICKLING, C. F. (1961). *Tropical Inland Fisheries.* Longmans, London.

MORGAN, R. (1956). *World Sea Fisheries.* London.

OMMANNEY, F. D. (1961). *The Ocean.* Oxford University Press, London.

RUSSEL, E. S. (1942). *The Overfishing Problem.* Cambridge University Press, Cambridge.

SCHAPERCLAUS, P. W. (1954). *Fisch-Krankheit.* Berlin.

STERBA, G. (1959). *Süsserwasserfische aus aller Welt.* Verlag Zimmer & Herzog. Berchtesgaden.

VAN DUIJN, C. (1956). *Diseases of Fishes.* Water Life. London.

CHAPTER 20

MYTHS AND LEGENDS

MYTHS AND LEGENDS concerning fishes are both numerous and diverse, but since it is impossible to include a fraction of them within the space of a single chapter, it must suffice to select a few of the more interesting for consideration here.

Legends concerning fish of abnormal size and weight are all too common, and incredible tales have appeared in print of monstrous specimens that have just escaped the fisherman's net or the angler's hook, to say nothing of those 'fish stories' never actually published. Certain fishes do, of course, grow to a large size, and as far as the sea is concerned, pride of place, must be given to the Whale Shark (*Rhincodon*), which reaches a total length of fifty feet or more and a weight of several tons [Fig. 146]. The Basking Shark (*Cetorhinus*), with a length of some thirty-five to forty feet, comes a good second, with some of the Blue Sharks (Carcharinidae) not very far behind. Certain species of Flat-fishes (Pleuronectiformes) grow to a comparatively large size, the classical example being the Adriatic Turbot (*Scophthalmus*) mentioned by Juvenal in his Fourth Satire. This particular fish is described as being so enormous that the fisherman promptly took it as a present to the Emperor Nero, who summoned his senators to view this monster, for which there was no dish of sufficient size. A touch of comedy is given to the scene by the description of the blind Catullus Messalinus, who was profuse in his wonder and admiration of the fish, although turning in the direction exactly opposite to that in which it lay! The Halibut (*Hippoglossus*) reaches an even greater bulk, specimens of seven or eight feet in length and weighing three hundred or four hundred pounds being by no means rare, and much larger examples have been recorded. Among strictly freshwater fishes the record for size is held by the Arapaima or Pirarucu (*Arapaima gigas*) of the rivers of Brazil and the Guianas, with a length of about fifteen feet and a weight of four hundred pounds. [Fig. 119c].

At the other end of the scale is a tiny Goby (*Mistichthys luzonensis*) found only in one of the lakes of Luzon in the Philippine Islands, which enjoys the distinction of being the smallest of all known vertebrates, fully mature individuals measuring only half an inch

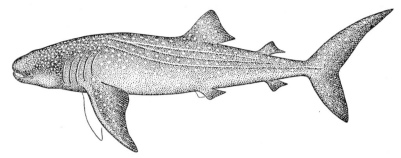

Fig. 146 THE LARGEST FISH
Whale Shark (*Rhincodon typicus*), x *ca.* ¹/₁₄₀. (After Gudger)

in total length [Fig. 147]. This fish is very abundant, and in spite of its small size forms an important article of food. Some of the Gobies found in the coral-reef pools of Samoa and other islands of the Pacific are nearly as small, and certain Tooth-Carps or Cyprinodonts of the New World are less than an inch long when fully grown.

There is a widespread and popular belief that certain species of fish live to a vast age, and stories of Carp of one hundred or one hundred and fifty years of age, and of hoary Pike more than two hundred years old, occur in some of the works on natural history published during the eighteenth and nineteenth centuries. As Dr. Regan has pointed out, the statements concerning most of the very old Carp 'rest on very unreliable evidence', and although there is good reason for believing that under artificial conditions this fish may attain an age of fifty years, it is doubtful whether it exceeds fifteen years in a wild state. Satisfactory proofs of the alleged great age of Pike are likewise difficult to find, but the same author remarks that 'it is probable that fish of sixty or seventy pounds weight are at least as many years old.' The story of the so-called 'Emperor's Pike' makes amusing reading, and is one that was a great favourite with all writers on fishes since it was first printed by Gesner in 1558. The fish was said to have been captured in a

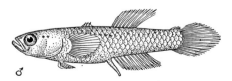

Fig. 147 ONE OF THE SMALLEST FISHES
Mistichthys luzonensis, x 4. (After H. M. Smith)

lake in Württemburg in the year 1497, and was found to have a copper ring encircling the gill region bearing an inscription to the effect that the Pike had been placed in the lake by the Emperor Frederick II in the year 1230, no less than two hundred and sixty-seven years before its final capture. Unfortunately, the accounts given by other authors reveal a number of discrepancies, and they cannot agree as to which of the Fredericks was responsible for marking the fish, or as to the exact locality at which it was finally recaptured. Its length has been stated to be nineteen feet, and its weight five hundred and fifty pounds, and an oil painting of it is said to be preserved at the castle of Lautern in Swabia; what appears to be a contemporary copy of this painting is in the Natural History Museum at South Kensington. The actual skeleton of the monster is reputed to be preserved in the cathedral at Mannheim, but this was studied by a celebrated German anatomist during the last century, who found that the vertebrae in the back-bone were too numerous to belong to a single individual—in other words, the skeleton had been lengthened to fit the story.

One of the shortest-lived fishes would appear to be the Trans-parent or White Goby (*Latrunculus pellucidus*), the course of whose life is run in a single year, although other annual fishes are known from the rivers of Tropical South America and Africa.

A curious myth has arisen concerning the alleged healing powers of the Tench, and it has long been believed that sick or wounded fish were cured by the touch of this fish. It is true that other fishes have been observed to rub themselves against the Tench's body, but the idea that the slime acts as a kind of balsam is now generally discredited. According to Izaak Walton the Tench is the particular physician of the Pike, who 'forbears to devour him though he be never so hungry.' As a matter of actual fact, a small Tench is regarded by many anglers as an excellent bait for Pike in certain localities. Its healing powers were also supposed to extend to man: applied to the hands or feet of a sick person it cured him of fever, and jaundice, headache, toothache, and other complaints were treated in a similar manner. In ancient times fish played an impor-tant part in the pharmacopoeia of the physician. Radcliffe in his book, '*Fishing from the Earliest Times*,' tells us that, in one book alone of Pliny, fish are recommended as remedies, internal or external, no less than (according to his reckoning) three hundred and forty-two times. Among other medicinal uses of fish at the present time, mention may be made of cod-liver oil and the flesh of the Escolar or Castor-oil-fish (*Ruvettus*), which acts as a purgative. In certain parts of the world the otoliths or ear-stones of fishes are used as a prevention or cure of colic, as well as a talisman to avert the evil eye.

There is an extremely ancient legend concerning the Remora or

Shark-sucker (*Remora*) to the effect that it is able to impede the progress of sailing vessels or even to stop them altogether, It occurs repeatedly in classical and mediaeval literature, and is illustrated on Greek and Roman vases and other pottery. Pliny tells us that the death of the Emperor Caligula was due to his great galley being held up by a Remora while the remainder of the fleet escaped. The earliest known published figure of this fish in the act of staying the progress of a ship is to be found in J. von Cube's *Hortus sanitatis*, a curious work published in 1479. The method of fishing for turtles with the Remora, witnessed by Christopher Columbus in 1494 and described by his son, Ferdinand Columbus, has been noted with in a previous chapter (*cf*. p. 338). The scientific name of the fish, *Remora*, signifies 'holding back,' and the older writers consequently refer to it as the *Reversus* or 'Ship-holder.' The name *Reversus* was also applied to the Porcupine-fish (*Diodon*), a species which seems to have been confused with the Remora, one author, Aldrovandi, describing and figuring it as the spinous variety of the *Reversus*. It has been suggested that this name was applied to the Porcupine-fish on account of its curious antics when hooked.

Among the grotesque and entirely mythical fishes described during the Middle Ages mention may be made of the 'Monk-fish' and 'Bishop-fish', both of which are illustrated in Rondelet's '*Histoire Entière des Poissons*', published in 1558. Rondelet remarks that his picture of the 'Monk-fish' was given to him by the very illustrious lady, Margaret de Valois, Queen of Navarre, who received it from a gentleman, who gave a similar one to the Emperor Charles V, then in Spain. This gentleman affirmed that he had actually seen the monster portrayed cast on to the shore in Norway during a violent storm.

The mermaid, half-maiden, half-fish, represents a particularly tenacious myth. In certain cases Dugongs and Sea Lions, with their somewhat human heads and fish-like bodies, have been mistaken for mermaids, but the persistence of the belief is due largely to the dried specimens once brought home by travellers in the Orient. On close examination these are found to consist of the head and shoulders of a monkey cleverly united by wires to the tail-end of fish. Mermaids were manufactured in some numbers by the Egyptians and Chinese, who sold them at a handsome profit to credulous tourists, together with documents purporting to be signed by witnesses of the capture of these creatures in the sea. It is said that the great Linnaeus was once forced to leave a town in Holland for questioning the genuineness of one of these mermaids, the property of some high official.

Another persistent myth, but one which may any day be transferred from the realm of legend to that of actual scientific

PLATE VII

A downpour of Fishes in Scandinavia. From Olaus Magnus'
Historia de Gentibus Septentrionalibus, 1555

a

Fishing with Remora. From Conrad Gesner's *Historiae Animalium*
Lib. iv., 1558

b

The great Sea Serpent. From Conrad Gesner's *Historiae Animalium*,
Lib. iv., 1558 (After Olaus Magnus, 1555)

c

fact, is that of the great Sea Serpent. There are, of course, the poisonous Sea Snakes of tropical seas, some of which grow to a length of ten or twelve feet, but these, although certainly 'serpents,' are not the Sea Serpents of legends. The great Sea Serpent, descriptions of which have appeared in almost every language of civilised peoples, has unfortunately not yet come under the observation of zoologists and it is to be feared that many records of its occurrence are to be put down to seamen's yarns, perhaps aided by strange tricks of light on waves, the power of suggestion, or to cases of mistaken identity. The Sea Serpents of Aristotle, Pliny, and other classical authors seem to have been nothing more than gigantic eels. The monster described as having the head of a horse with a flaming red mane is the Oar-fish or Ribbon-fish (*cf.* p. 34), a species which probably grows to more than fifty feet in length, and may sometimes be seen swimming with undulating movements at the surface of the sea. The famous Sea Serpent, measuring fifty-six feet in length, that was cast up on the shore of Orkney in 1808 was almost certainly this fish. Other reputed Sea Serpents are believed to be giant Squids or Cuttle-fishes, many of the oceanic species attaining an immense size, and although normally living in the abyssal depths they are known to come to the surface on occasions or to be stranded on the shore after a violent storm. Very little is known of these monsters of the deep, and some of the species have been described only from the semi-digested remains that have been taken from the stomachs of Sperm Whales. It will be recalled that many of the tales of the Sea Serpent describe it as battling with a whale, and the long and sinuous tentacles or arms of these molluscs, coupled with their habit of sometimes spouting water, account for the so-called 'spouting head and writhing tail.' Other objects that might conceivably be mistaken for a serpent by an untrained observer include a school of porpoises swimming in line, their curved bodies suggesting the sinuous coils of an eel-like body; two large Basking Sharks, swimming one behind the other, as is sometimes their habit; a fragment of wreckage, or even a long string of seaweed. Dr. Oudemans has published a most valuable book on the subject, in which nearly all the records are discussed at some length, and the available evidence carefully sifted. He concludes that, although many of the accounts may be disposed of in one of the ways mentioned above, there remains a number which display a certain amount of general agreement and appear to describe something for which none of these theories will really suffice. What this 'something' may be can only be guessed, but Dr. Oudemans believes it to be a large mammal allied to the Seals and Sea Lions. Finally, mention may be made of a remarkable creature that was observed off the coast of Brazil in 1905 by two competent naturalists,

and described in the *Proceedings of the Zoological Society of London.*
'At first', they write, 'all that could be seen was a dorsal fin about
four feet long, sticking up about two feet from the water; this fin
was of a brownish-black colour and much resembled a gigantic
piece of ribbon seaweed . . . Suddenly an eel-like neck about six
feet long and of the thickness of a man's thigh, having a head
shaped like that of a turtle, appeared in front of the fin.' The
creature soon disappeared from view, before it was possible for
them to make out the shape or size of its body, and it is still doubtful
whether it was mammal, reptile or fish.

The following news item appeared in the *Northern Whig and
Belfast Post* on 30th May 1928 and caused considerable interest:

> 'Dozens of tiny red fish were found on the roof of a bungalow
> on the farm of Mr. James McMaster, Drumhirk, near Comber,
> and on the ground in the vicinity yesterday morning, and the
> extraordinary occurrence caused considerable speculation. In the
> course of enquiries it was ascertained that just before the discovery
> of the fish there had been an exceptionally violent thunderstorm
> with heavy rain. There is no river in the neighbourhood, the nearest
> sheet of water being Strangford Lough, two miles distant, and the
> theory advanced by an expert was that the fish had been lifted
> from the sea in a waterspout.'

Occurrences of this nature are rare, but by no means unknown,
more than fifty accounts of these 'rains of fishes' having been
recorded from various parts of the world. The first mention of the
phenomenon is to be found in the *Deipnosophistae* of Athanaeus,
who lived at the end of the second and the beginning of the third
century A.D. In an English translation, under the heading
'*De pluvia piscium*,' occurs the following:

> 'I know also that it has rained fishes. At all events Phoenias,
> in the second book of his Eresian Magistrates, says that in the
> Chersonesos it once rained fishes uninterruptedly for three days,
> and Phylarchus, in his fourth book, says the people had often seen
> it raining fish.'

Several explanations have been put forward to account for the
sudden appearance of fishes from the clouds, but there seems to be
little doubt that the suggestion of Eglini in 1771, that the falls are
due to the action of heavy winds, whirlwinds and waterspouts is
the correct one. The 'rains' have nearly always been described
as being accompanied by violent thunderstorms and heavy rain,
and moreover they are usually confined to restricted areas, and the
fishes are found in a comparatively straight path over a wide
stretch of country. It appears that the action of a waterspout
passing over shallow coastal water, or of a tornado over shallow
inland pools and lakes, may be sufficient to lift small fishes to a

considerable height, and to transport them and deposit them at some distance from the locality at which they were picked up. Waterspouts and tornadoes are physically similar phenomena, the former occurring over stretches of water or over the ocean, the latter over dry land. In some cases it is believed that the fishes are not only carried up into the rapidly rotating vortex of air that forms the body of the waterspout or tornado, but even right up into the thunderstorm cloud itself. There is a case on record in which a hailstone as large as a hen's egg was observed to fall during a heavy storm at Essen in 1806, containing a frozen Crucian Carp (*Carassius*) about forty millimetres in length, indicating that the fish must not only have entered the cloud but have been lifted to the very considerable height necessary for the formation of hail. Occasionally, the fish involved are of larger size, and at Jelapur, in India, a specimen has been described as falling with others, which was about 'one cubit in length and weighed more than six pounds.' Falls in Europe have included Herrings, Sprats, Trout, Smelts, Pike, Minnows, Perch, Sand Eels, and Sticklebacks; the small red fishes mentioned in the Irish account quoted above were probably of the latter species.

The Biblical story of the Miraculous Draught, to be found in the twenty-first chaper of the Gospel according to St. John, will be familiar to all, and an American ichthyologist, E. W. Gudger, has quite recently pointed out that this seemingly miraculous phenomenon is capable of a perfectly rational explanation in the light of modern research on the habits of the fishes to be found in the Lake of Tiberias or Galilee. These fishes are chiefly of the family Cichlidae, and occur in huge numbers in the lake, swimming at or near the surface of the water. Writing on the habits of the commonest species (*Tilapia galilaea*), Canon Tristram observes: 'I have seen them in shoals of over an acre in extent, so closely packed that it seemed impossible for them to move, and with their dorsal fins above the water, giving at a distance the appearance of a tremendous shower pattering on one spot of the surface of the glassy lake. They are taken both in boats and from the shore by nets run deftly round, and enclosing what one may call a solid mass at one swoop, and very often the net breaks.' Now the procedure of the lake fishermen at the present day, as described by Dr. Masterman in his account of the inland fisheries of Galilee, is as follows:—a man is stationed on the high ground on shore, whose duty it is to detect the presence of a shoal of Cichlids and to direct the movements of those in the boats who proceed at once to the point indicated and surround the fish with a net. The bottom of the lake is said to be covered with large stones, and it is frequently necessary for one or more of the fishermen to leap overboard to free the net and to prevent it from breaking.

When young, the *Tilapia* found in the Lake of Galilee, have a dark spot on each side of the dorsal fin, and this is locally reputed to represent the mark of St. Peter's thumb, made when he took a piece of money from the fish's mouth. The Cichlids compete for the honour of bearing this mark with the John Dory (*Zeus*), which, however, has a round black spot on the side. This fish is known in Germany as the 'Petersfisch,' and our own name John Dory is believed to be the equivalent of the Italian 'Janitore,' meaning a doorkeeper. All this despite the fact that Peter could not have encountered this fish in freshwater.

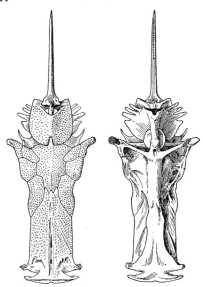

Fig. 148 'CRUCIFIX FISH'
Upper and lower views of the skull from a marine Cat-fish (*Arius* sp.) x ¹/₃

Travellers in South America and the West Indies often return with tales of the so-called 'Crucifix-fish,' which is said to be held in great esteem and even veneration by the natives of these parts, who look upon it as a kind of fetish or charm against danger or sickness. These are nothing more than the prepared skeletons of certain Cat-fishes that abound on the coasts and in the rivers of Central and South America. The skulls of many of these fishes exhibit on their lower surfaces a rough but readily recognisable resemblance to a crucifix [Fig. 148], while the small bones known as the Weberian ossicles (*cf.* p. 152) form a halo. The upper surface of the skull, with its rugose bones, has been described as resembling 'a hooded monk with outstretched arms,' or 'the breastplate of a

Roman soldier,'; the dorsal spine is said to represent the spear; and the otoliths, which rattle when the skull is shaken, are the 'dice with which the soldiers cast lots for the garments of our Lord'! Another account published in 1789 states that 'when the bones of the head are separated, each represents some one of the instruments of the passion of our Redeemer, forming the spear, cross, nails, etc.' Such crucifix skulls may be seen frequently in the Orinoco district, and in the Guianas, and are familiar objects in the curio shops of the West Indies as well as in Georgetown, British Guiana, some of the specimens being fancifully painted and decorated.

Many other interesting matters more or less remotely connected with fishes must be omitted for considerations of space, or because they lie somewhat outside the scope of this book. They include the Fish Gods, of which Ebisu of Japan is perhaps best known; the reverencing of certain species by the ancient Egyptians; the preparation of fish mummies; and the part played by fishes in the myths and legends of various lands, or in pagan and Christian symbols. Many of these matters are dealt with in Radcliffe's valuable book, 'Fishing from the Earliest Times,' the only work of its kind, and a monument of painstaking research.

REFERENCES

MYERS, G. S. (1952). Annual fishes. *Aquarium J.*, **23**, No. 7.

NORMAN, J. R. and FRASER, F. C. (1948). *Giant Fishes, Whales and Dolphins*. Putnam, London.

OUDEMANS (1892). *The Great Sea-Serpent*. Leiden and London.

RADCLIFFE, W. (1921). *Fishing from the Earliest Times*. London.

LIST OF BOOKS

The following list is not an exhaustive bibliography of even the more important works on fishes and related subjects. It is intended as a list of books, more or less easily obtained, which give a synoptic treatment of their subjects. It includes some of the older books on fishes; in certain respects these are out of date but in others they still provide the fundamental information on anatomy and osteology. The most recent work on fishes (and the most comprehensive) are the three fascicles of Grassé's *Traité de Zoologie* (volume 12, Agnathes et Poissons) published in 1958. The bibliographies in that work cover the most important papers in general ichthyology. For more recent works the reader is referred, as always, to the *'Pisces'* section of the *Zoological Record*.

Atlantic Ocean Fisheries. London. 1961.
BOULENGER, G. A. and BRIDGE, T. W., *Fishes*. Volume VII of the Cambridge Natural History. London, 1910.
DANIEL, J. F. *The Elasmobranch Fishes*. California, 1928.
DAY, F., *The Fishes of Great Britain and Ireland*. Two volumes. London, 1880–1884.
DAY, F., *British and Irish Salmonidae*. London 1887.
Fish in Nutrition; F.A.O. Washington Conference. London, 1962.
DEAN, B. *Fishes Living and Fossil*. New York and London, 1895.
FRIES, B. EKSTRÖM, C. U., and SUNDEVALL, C., *A History of Scandinavian Fishes*. Second Edition. Revised and completed by F. A. Smitt. Stockholm and London. 1893.
GOODRICH, E. S. *Cyclostomes and Fishes*. Part IX, fascicle I, of 'A Treatise on Zoology.' Edited by Sir R. Lankester. London, 1909.
GÜNTHER, A. C. L. G., *An Introduction to the Study of Fishes*. Edinburgh, 1880.
MARSHALL, N. B. *Aspects of Deep Sea Biology*. London 1954.
NORMAN, J. R. and FRASER, F. C., *Giant Fishes, Whales and Dolphins*. London, 1948.
RADCLIFFE, W. *Fishing from the Earliest Times*. London 1921.
REGAN, C. T., *The Fresh-Water Fishes of the British Isles*. London, 1911.
REGAN, C. T., Articles on Fishes, Selachians, etc., in the Fourteenth Edition of the *Encyclopaedia Britannica*, London and New York, 1929.
TREWAVAS, E., The coelacanth yields its secrets. *Discovery*, **19**, No. 5., 1958.

INDEX

Words in italics are names of genera or species; figures in bold type refer to an illustration; f. = in following page or pages.

Abdominal vertebrae, **123**
Abducens nerve, 140
Abnormalities, **358**
Abramis, see Bream
Abyssal fishes, 267; eyes, 148; factors influencing distribution, 267 f.
Acanthenchelys, 34
Acanthocephala, see Thorn-headed Worm
Acanthodii, 301 f.
Acanthopterygians, 34; 330
Accessory respiratory organs, 79 f.
Accommodation, of eye, 144, 147
Acipenser, see Sturgeon
Acipenseriformes, 308
Actinistia, 311, 312 f., 333
Actinopterygii, 306, 328
Acus, 243
Adhesive organs, 39, 200, 258
Adipose eyelid, 145
Adipose fin, 38
Aeoliscus, see Shrimp-fish
Aestivation, 206
Aetobatis, see Spotted Eagle Ray
Africa, freshwater fishes of, 286 f.
African Cat-fishes (*Clarias*; *Heterobranchus*), **142**; accessory breathing organs, **81**, 83
African Lung-fish (*Protopterus*), **282**, 315; aestivation, 206; breeding, 236; larvae, 40; systematic position, 315 f., 328
African region, 281, 286 f.
Agassizodus, 305
Age, 67 f., 362
Age determination, 67 f.
Agonus, see Pogge
Agriopus, see Horse-fish
Air-breathing, 79 f.
Albacore (*Germo*), blood, 131
Albinos, 193
Albula, see Lady-fish
Albulidae, 328

Alburnus, see Bleak
Alepidosaurus, see Lancet-fish
Alepocephalidae, 328
Alestes, 286
Alevin, 255, **253**
Alimentary canal, 126 f.
Alligator Gar Pike (*Lepisosteus*), feeding, 96
Allis Shad (*Alosa alosa*), **42**; gill-rakers, food, **76**; 79
Allotriognathi, 332
Alopias, see Fox Shark, Thresher Shark
Alosa, see Shad; *A. alosa*, see Allis Shad; *A. fallax*, see Twaite Shad
Alpine Char (*Salvelinus alpinus*), 280, 322
Alveoli, 86
Ambicoloration, 193
Amblyopsidae, 196 f.
Amblyopsis, 196; see also Kentucky Blind-fish
American Brook Trout (*Salvelinus fontinalis*), 264, 351
American Eel, breeding, 223 f.; development, 223, 263
American Flounder, **66**; colour changes, 187
Amia, see Bow-fin
Amiidae, 309
Amiiformes, 309 f.
Amiurids, distribution, 291
Ammocoetes branchialis, 257
Ammodytes, see Sand Eel
Ammonia, excretion of, 78
Amphibians, origin of, 312
Amphiliidae, 284
Amphipnous, see Cuchia
Amphistylic jaws, 91
Ampulla, of Lorenzini, 155; of semicircular canal, 149, **150**
Anabantoidea, 333; see also Anabantoidei, 330
Anabas, see Climbing Perch

373

Anableps, see Four-eyed Fish
Anacanthini, 332
Anadromous fishes, 132, 218 f., 278 f.
Anal fin, in locomotion, 19 f; structure, 28 f.; form and function, 41 f.; as intromittent organ, 229
Anarrhichadidae, 330
Anarrhichas, see Wolf-fish
Anaspida, 297, 298 f.
Anchovy (*Engraulis*), migrations, 276; distribution, 274; eggs, 250; incubation period, 256; canning, 344
Anemone, association with fish, 207
Angel-fish (*Pterophyllum*), **12**; shape, 12; colours, 177
Angler-fish(es), **41**, **188**, **195**; form of body, 12; line and bait, 40 f., 170; teeth, 110; feeding, 41, 118; larva, **141**, 245; eye, 142; colours, 181; distribution, 268; parasitic males, **244** f.; eggs, 244, 250; systematic position, 331; antiquity, 310
Anguilla, see Eel, Fresh-water Eel; *A. anguilla*, see European Eel, Common Eel; *A. rostrata*, see American Eel
Anguilliformes, 329, 332
Annual fishes, 226, 363
Anomalops, luminous organ, 169; *A. katopron*, **170**
Antarctic fishes, 273
Antarctic Zone, 269, 273
Antennariidae, 331; see also Frog-fish
Antennarius, see Frog-fish
Antiarchi, 302, **303**
Anus, 130
Aortic bulb, 131
Aphyosemion, **229**; breeding, 226
Apodes, 332; see also Eel and Anguilliformes
Apogon, see Cardinal-fish
Apogonichthys, 209
Aqueous humour, 144
Arabic characters on tail, **181**
Arapaima, **283**; distribution, 283; size, 361
Archaean period, 294
Archer-fish (*Toxotes*), 114, **115**
Archistia, 332
Arctic fishes, 275
Arctic Zone, 275
Argenteum, 191
Argulus, see Carp Louse
Argyropelecus, **195**; larva, **259**
Ariidae, 238; 284; see also Sea Cat-fish
Arius, see Cat-fish; 'Crucifix fish'

Armoured Bull-head, see Pogge
Arnoglossus, see Scald fish
Artery, 131
Arthrodiri, 302
Artificial propagation, 350 f.
Assimilation, 128
Associations, 206 f.
Asteriscus, 150
Astroblepus, armour loss 62; adipose dorsal, 38; adaptations to torrential streams, 200; *A. chotae*, **201**
Atherines, fresh-water forms, 280
Atherinidae, 280
Atlantic region, 270 f.
Atlantic Salmon, 216 f., 278
Atlantic Trout, 278
Atrium, 131
Auditory capsule, 120, 122
Auditory nerve, 140, 151
Auditory organ, 149; connection with swimbladder, 151; for equilibrium, 151; and lateral line, 155
Aulostomiformes, 329
Auricle, 131
Australian Lung-fish (*Neoceratodus forsteri*), **282**; 206; lung, **85**; pectoral fin, **30**; 46; distribution, 281; 282; jaws and teeth, **315**; ancestry, 315 f.
Australian region, 281 f.
Austrofundulus, breeding, 226
Autostylic jaw suspension, 91
Axillary scale, 65
Ayu, fishing for, 338

Bacillus salmonicida, *B. salmonispestis*, 353
Backbone, see vertebral column
Bacteria, luminous, 168, 169, 170, 171
Balancing, 151
Balao, see Half-beak
Balistes, see Trigger-fish
Balistoidei, 330
Balkers, 341
Baltic Herring, 276
Barbels, **142**, **143**, 144
Barber fishes, see Cleaners
Barracuda (*Sphyraena*), **111**; teeth, food, 112; systematic position, 331
Basals, **28**, 29
Basking Shark (*Cetorhinus*), gill-clefts, 71; gill-rakers, food, **76**, 79; systematic position, 327; size, 361
Bass (*Morone*), pelvic fin, 49; scales, 58; teeth, 109
Bat-fish (Ogcocephalidae), **60**; form of

body, 12; line and bait, 40; pectoral fin, 47; tubercles, **60**, 64; at surface, 158; systematic position, 331
Bathypelagic fishes, 267; swimbladder in, 134 f.; luminous organs, 168 f.; eyes, 147 f.
Batoidea, 332; see also Raiiformes, 327
Beam-trawl, **339**, 340
Becune, see Picuda,
Belone, 243; see also Gar-fish
Belonidae, 329
Belonorhynchii, 332
Beryciformes, 310, 330
Berycomorphi, 332; see also Beryciformes
Betta, see Fighting-fish
Bichir, (*Polypterus*), **35**; caudal fin, 31; dorsal fin, **35**, 39; swimbladder, **85**, 86; scales, **56**, 57; external gills 75, 76, **77**; skull, 120; spiral valve, 130; ancestry, 309; systematic position, 328, 332
Bifocal eyes, 147
Binocular vision, 145, 147
Binominal nomenclature, 324 f.
Bird's feet, in fish distribution, 281
Bishop-fish (mythical), 364
Bitter Lakes, 271
Bitterling (*Rhodeus*), **239**; breeding, 238
Black Bass (*Micropterus*), cultivation and introduction, 351
Black-finned Trout, 321
Black-fish (*Dallia*), **42**, 203; effects of cold, 203; Salmon, name for, 216
Black Goby, **50**; pelvic fins, **50**; eggs, **248**, 251
Black-mouthed Dog-fish (*Pristiurus*), incubation period, 252
Black Sea Turbot (*Scophthalmus maeoticus*), **60**; tubercles, 59
Black-tail, 324
Bleak (*Alburnus*), effects of heat and cold, 203 f.; scales, use of, 347
Blennioidea, 332
Blenioidei, 330, 332
Blenny, 330; pelvic fins, 49; canine teeth, 113; care of eggs, 240; eggs, 251; viviparous (*Zoarces*), **254**
Blind-fishes, 194 f.
Blind Goby (*Typhlogobius*), **197**, 198
Bloater, 344
Blood, 69, 131
Blue-fish (*Pomatomus*), **111** f.
Blue Shark (*Carcharinus*), form of body, 10; feeding, 11; fossils, 306; colours, 177, systematic position, 327

Boar-fish (*Capros*), sounds, 172; systematic position, 330
Bombay Duck (*Harpodon*), 344, **345**
Bone, 120
Bonito (*Katsuwonus*), **7**; form of body, 8; caudal fin, 19; finlets, 39
Bony Fish, 4, 120, 306; gills, 73 f.; scales, 56 f.; jaws, **91**, 92 f.; mouth, 92 f.; teeth, 109 f.; skull, 120 f.; brain, 137 f.; optic nerves, 140; nasal organs, 141 f.; pineal gland, 149; hearing, 151; lateral line, 153f.; eggs, **248**; 250; origin, fossil forms, 306 f.; classification, 328 f.
Bornean Sucker (*Gastromyzon*), **50**; paired fins, 49; adhesive disc, 200
Borophryne apogon, (Deep-sea angler), **195**
Bothriolepis, 302, **303**
Bothus, colour changes, 187, Plate II; secondary sexual characters, **231**, 232
Bow-fin (*Amia*), **20**, **35**; locomotion, **20**; swimbladder, **85**, 86; caudal fin, 31; scales, 57; pharyngeals, **110**; spiral valve, 130; colour of male, 231; parental care, 236; larval cement organs, 258; ancestry, 309; systematic position, 309, 328
Box-fish, see Trunk-fish
Brachiopterygii, 286, 309, 328, 332
Bradyodonti, 302, 304, 305, 326, 328; teeth of extinct forms, **305**
Brain, 136 f., 158
Bramble Shark (*Echinorhinus*), dermal denticles, **53**, 54; systematic position, 327
Branchial arch (gill arch), 72 f.
Branchial basket, 73
Branchial chamber, 73
Branchial lamellae (gill filaments), 70 f., 79
Branchioica, 210
Branchiostoma, 258, 301
Bream (*Abramis*), **66**; lateral line, **66**, 67; mouth, 100; value as food, 336
Breathing, see respiration
Breeding, 213 f., 227 f.
Breeding ground of Eel, 221 f.
Bregmaceros, see Dwarf Cod-fish
Brevoortia, see Menhaden
Brill (*Scophthalmus rhombus*), scales, 59
Brine salting, 343
Brisling (*Clupea sprattus*), 345
British freshwater fishes, distribution, 289 f.
Brook Trout (*Salmo fario*), 321; Brook

Trout, American, (*Salvelinus fontinalis*), 351
Brotulid, Cuban blind forms; Mexican blind forms, 196
Brotulidae, 280
Brown Trout (*Salmo trutta*), 184, 278, 279, 321; introduction, 351
Brycon, 286
Buccal incubation, 238
Buckler, **53,** 54
Bulldog-nosed Trout, 358
Bull-head (*Cottus*), sound production, 172; distribution, 280; care of eggs, 225, 240; systematic position, 330
Bull-headed Shark (*Heterodontus*), **106;** fin-spines, 33; suspension of jaws, 91; teeth, **106,** 108; poison, 160; egg-capsules, **248,** 249; antiquity, 305, 306; systematic position, 305, 327
Bull Trout (*Salmo trutta*), 324
Bummalow (*Harpodon nehereus*), **345;** as food, 344
Burbot (*Lota*), brain size, 139; distribution, 280, 289
Burrowing, 25
Butter-fish, 330; see also Stromateoidei, Gunnel
Butterfly-fish, form of body, 12, **180;** mouth, **94;** colours, 179, **180;** see also Chisel-jaw
Butterfly Ray (*Pteroplatea*), nutrition of embryo, 252
By-products, 345 f.

Caecobarbus, coloration, 192
Caenozoic era, 294, **295**
Calamoichthys, 309
Californian Blind Goby (*Typhlogobius*), **197,** 198
Californian Chimaera (*Hydrolagus*), egg-capsule, 249
Californian Hag-fish (*Polistotrema*), egg-capsule, **248**
Callionymus, see Dragonet
Cambrian period, 294, **295**
Campostoma, see Stone Roller
Candiru (*Vandellia*) 210 f., **221**
Canning, 344
Capitane, see *Astroblepus*
Caproidae, 330
Capros, see Boar-fish
Carangidae, 330; association with jelly-fishes, 207; see also Pampano
Caranx, see Pampano
Carapus, habits, **209;** caudal fin, 44; eggs, 250

Carassius, see Gold-fish, Crucian Carp
Carchariidae, 327
Carcharinidae, 306, 327
Carcharinus, see Blue Shark
Carcharodon, see Great White Shark
Cardinal-fish, dorsal fin, **35,** 37; association with mollusc, 210
Care of eggs and young, 227 f.
Caribe (*Serrasalmus*), 110, **112,** 142
Carnero, see Candiru
Carpet Shark (*Orectolobus*), **178;** form of body, 10 f.; colours, 181; systematic position, 327
Carp (*Cyprinus carpio*), fins, 36, 38, 43, 48; scales, 58, **65;** domesticated forms, **358,** 60; lateral line, 66; lower pharyngeals, **110,** 117; food, 117, 351; sense of hearing, 151; Weberian mechanism, **152;** taste buds, 144; colours, 177; hibernation, 205; breeding, 244; as food, 335, 336; culture, 350; introduction, 350, 351; longevity, 362
Carp Louse, 356
Cartilage, 119
Cartilage bones, 92, 120
Cascadura, see Hassar
Castor-oil Fish (*Ruvettus*), 363
Catadromous fishes, 133, 227 f.
Cat-fish, distribution 284 f.; swimming upside-down, 23, 24, 192; accessory breathing organs, 80, **81,** 83; adipose fin, 38; fin-spines, 36, **37,** 46; skin, 52, 62; dermal denticles, 55; scutes, **61,** 62, **63;** poison glands, 46, 161; electric organ, 166 f.; sound-production, **173** f.; eyes, 147; barbels, **142,** 144; Weberian mechanism, 152; marine forms, 284; nests, 236; breeding habits, 236, 238
Caudal fin, 9, **11,** 16 f., 29 f., **42,** 43, **44;** types of, 29 f., 42, 43, **44, 312, 313;** shape and speed, 19; in locomotion, 16 f.; structure, 29 f., **312, 313**
Caudal peduncle, 19
Caudal vertebrae, **123**
Cave-fishes, 194 f.
Caviare, 345
Cement organs, 258
Centrarchidae, 330; see also Freshwater Sun-fish
Centriscus, see Shrimp-fish
Centrum, **123**
Cephalaspidomorphi, 297 f.
'*Cephalaspis*' *lyelli*, **299**
Cephalic clasper, **155,** 227

Cephalic fins, 90
Cephalic flexure, 255
Ceratioid (Deepsea Anglers), line and bait, 40, **41**, 170; mouth, 95; feeding, 41, 118; tubercles, 64; teeth, 110; nostrils, **141**, 142; life history 244; parasitic males, **244** f.; systematic position, 331, 333; see also Angler-fish
Ceratotrichia, 28
Cerebellum, **137**, 138, 167
Cerebral hemispheres, **137**, 159
Cerebrum, 137
Cestoda, see Tape Worm
Cetacean, and fish compared, 2 f.
Cetorhinus, see Basking Shark
Chaetodon, see Butterfly-fish
Chakoura (*Caranx rhonchus*), 175
Chanidae (Milk fishes), 328
Channel Cat, 291
Char, distribution, 279; subspecies, 322
Characidae, 284; distribution, **285**; see also Characins
Characins (Characidae), Weberian mechanism, 152; teeth, 109; distribution, 284 f., 288 f.; systematic position, 329, 332
Characoidei, 329
Chauliodus, **111**; teeth, food, 113; jaws, 100; skull, first vertebra, 124, **125**
Chaunacidae, see Sea Toad
Cheirolepis canadensis, **307**
Chelmo, **94**; see Butterfly-fish
Chiasmodus, 95, **195**; see also Great Swallower
Chilomycterus, **8**; see Globe-fish
Chimaera, gills, respiration, 74, 75; dermal denticles, 55; jaws, 91, **112**; tooth plates, food, 108 f., **305**; poison glands, 160; lateral line, 154, **155**; clasper, **155**, 227; egg-capsule, **248**, 249; fossil forms, 305; systematic position, 305, 328, 332; see also Rabbit-fish.
Chimaera phantasma, egg-capsule, **248**
China-fishes (Ophiocephalidae), 82
Chinese Sturgeon (*Psephurus*), anal fin, **28**
Chirostomias pliopterus, **143**
Chisel-jaw (*Pantodon*) flight, 47
Chlamydoselachus, see Frilled Shark
Chologaster, (Cave fish), 196
Chondrichthyes, 304 f., 326 f., 331
Chondrostei, 308, 328, 332
Chondrosteiformes, 308
Chromatophores, 189 f.

Cichlasoma, **94**; see Thick-lipped Mojarra
Cichlid, lips, 93, **94**; teeth and jaws, 114; nostrils, 142; colours (of Angel fish), **12**, 177; of soda lakes, 203; in brackish water, 284, 286; in Madagascar, 284; secondary sexual characters, 230, 232; parental care, 235, 238, 240; of Lake Galilee, 367
Cichlidae, distribution, 284 f.; by man, 291 f.
Ciguatera poisoning, 164
Ciliated scales, 58
Circulatory system, see vascular system
Cirrhitid (*Paracirrhites*), **45**; pectoral fin, 48
Ciscoe, 335
Citharinidae, 284
Cladistia, (see also Brachiopterygii), 332
Cladoselache, 304; fins, **30**; systematic position, 304
Cladoselachiformes, 304
Clarias, (see also Cat-fish) air-breathing organs, **81**, 83
Clariidae, 284
Claspers, 51, 55, 227 f., 305
Class, **323**
Classification, 318 f.
Cleaner fishes, 207 f.; coloration, 189
Climbing Perch, accessory respiratory organs, **81** f.; locomotion, 82
Cling-fish (Gobiesocoidei), **50**; pelvic fins, **50**; sucker, **50**; care of eggs, 240; systematic position, 331
Clinidae, 330
Cloaca, 130
Clupea harengus, see Herring; *C. pallasii*, see Pacific Herring; *C. sprattus*, see Sprat
Clupeidae, 328; see also Herring
Clupeiformes, 310, 328, 332
Clupeoidei, 328, 332
Clupisudis, see Osteoglossid; *C. niloticus*, **283**
Coastal fishes, distribution, 268 f.
Cobitidae, see Loach
Cobitis, see Loach
Coccosteus, 302, **303**
"Cock and Hen Paddle", see Lump-sucker
Cod (*Gadus morhua*), **35**; number of individuals, 5; tail, 31; dorsal and anal fins, **35**, 36, 43; pelvic fins, 49; pectoral fin, **30**; teeth, 109; food, 109, 118; vertebrae, **123**; brain, **137**; barbel, **142**, 144; otolith, **150**; spawning, 213, 214, 215; herma-

phrodite, 213; eggs, 215; systematic position, 329, 332; as food, 335; fishery for, 342; salting, 343

Cod liver oil, 346

Coelacanth, see *Latimeria*

Coelacanthiformes, 312 f.

Coffer-fish, see Trunk-fish

Cold, effects of, 203 f.

Collection of fish in British Museum (Natural History), 359

Coloration, 176 f.; in two sexes, 230

Colour changes, 185 f.

Colour perception, 148

Comb-toothed Sharks (Hexanchidae), gill-clefts, 71; suspension of jaws, 91; teeth, 104, **105**; vertebrae, **123**; antiquity, 306; systematic position, 327, 331

Commensalism, 207

Common Eel, see Freshwater Eel

Common Goby (*Gobius minutus*), nest, 240

Communities, 320

Compressed body, 12 f.

Concealing colours, 176 f.

Conditions of life, 194 f.

Conger eel, larva, 262

Connective tissue, 119

Consumption of fish by man, 334 f.

Continental Drift, 287

Continental Shelf, Slope, 268

Copepods, 355 f.

Coprolites, 129

Copulation, 227 f.

Coral reef fishes, colours, 179 f.; see also Reef fishes

Coregonus, see White-fish; *C. pennantii*, see Gwyniad; *C. pollan*, see Pollan; *C. vandesius*, see Vendace

Cormorant, fishing with, 338

Cornea, 144, **145**

Cosmine, 56

Cosmoid scales, 56 f.

Cottidae, 330

Cottus, see Bull-head; *C. gobio*, see Miller's Thumb

Counter currents, 70

Counter shading, 177

Courtship, 232 f.

Cow-fish, see Trunk-fish

Cow Shark, see Comb-toothed Shark

Cranial nerves, **137**, 140, 298

Crenulated scales, 58

Cretaceous period, **122**, 306, 310

Crossopterygii, 310 f., 328, 333

Crucian Carp, in hailstone, 367

Crucifix-fish, **368**

Crustacean parasites, 354 f.

Ctenoid scales, **56**, 58

Cuban Blind-fishes, 196, **197**

Cuchia (*Amphipnous*), **83**; accessory respiratory organs, 83 f.

Cuckold, see Trunk-fish

Cuckoo Wrasse (*Labrus mixtus*), secondary sexual characters, 230

Cultivation, 350 f.

Curing, 343 f.

Cutaneous respiration, 80

Cutlass-fish (Trichiuridae), form of body, 14, **205**; effect of cold on, 205; systematic position, 330; see also Scabbard-fish

Cycloid scales, 58, **56**

Cyclopteridae, 331

Cyclopterus, see Lump-sucker

Cyclostome, 4, **35**; fins, 27; skin, 52; gills, 72, **74**; respiration, 77; mouth, 88, **89**; 'teeth', 102; skeleton, 122; alimentary canal, 126; spiral valve, 129; brain, 136, 138; optic nerves, 140; nostril, **141**; ear, 149; pineal gland, 149; spawning, 219 f.; eggs, 219, 246, **248**; development, **257** f.; systematic position, classification, fossils, 296 f., 326

Cyclostomi, 297 f., see also Cyclostome

Cynodon, teeth, 113; *C. scomberoides*, **111**

Cynoglossidae, 331; see also Tongue Sole

Cynoglossus, see Tongue Sole

Cynolebias, breeding, 226

Cyprinid (Carps), pharyngeals, **110**, 117; sound, 172; hearing, 151; Weberian mechanism, **152**; taste, 144; blind forms, 194; hill-stream forms, 200, 202; distribution, 284 f., 288 f.; breeding, 224 f.; secondary sexual characters, 225; hybrids, 265; origin of, 288

Cyprinidae, distribution, 284 f., **285**; systematic position, 329; see also Cyprinid

Cypriniformes, 329, 332; see also Ostariophysi

Cyprinodont (Tooth Carps), **229**, **146**; anal fin, 43, 228 f.; lateral line, 67; of hot springs, 203; in brackish water, 286; intromittent organ, 43, 228 f.; breeding, 226, 229; secondary sexual characters, 228, 229, 232; viviparous forms, 229, 254; size, 362

Cyprinodontiformes, 329

Cyprinoidei, 329

Dab (*Limanda*), scales, 58, 59; mouth, 101; nocturnal activity, 158; ambicoloration, 193
Dactylopteroidei, 331, 333; see also Flying Gurnard
Dallia, see Black-fish
Damsel-fish (Pomacentridae), locomotion, 21; association with anemone, 207
Dangerous fishes, see Man
Danish Seine, 341
Darkie Charlie (*Etmopterus*), luminous organs, 168
Darter (*Etheostoma*), breeding, 235
Dasyatidae, 306
Dasyatis, see Sting Ray
Dasyatoidei, 327
Deal-fish, see Ribbon-fishes
Death, colour changes at, 187
Deciduous scales, 59
Deep-sea-fishes, see Oceanic fishes
Delphinus, see Dolphin (Mammal)
Demersal eggs, 250
Denticles, 52 f.
Dentine, 53
Depletion of stocks, 347, 353
Depressed body, 11 f.
Depressible teeth, 110
Dermal bones, 120
Dermal denticles, 52 f.
Dermis, 52
Development, 246 f.; of fins, 27, 29; of dermal denticles, 53, **54**; of brain, 136; of auditory organ, 149; of lateral line, 154
Devil-fish (*Manta, Mobula*), **24**; leaping, 25; birth of young, 253; systematic position, 327
Diamond Flounder (*Platichthys stellatus*), **60**; tubercles, 59
Diaphus, see Lantern-fish
Digestion, 128
Dinichthys, 302
Diodon, **63**; see Porcupine-fish
Diphyllobothrium, 357
Dipneusti, 315 f., 328, 333; see also Lung-fish
Dipterus, **316**
Discocephali, see Remora
Discontinuous distribution, 275
Discus fish, see Pompadour
Diseases, 353 f.
Distribution, 266 f.
Dog-fish, **45**; gills, **71, 73**; dermal denticles, **53**, 54; skull, 90 f.; teeth, 103; eggs, **248**; development, 252, 254; systematic position, 327; as food,

337; see also Spotted Dog-fish, Spiny Dog-fish
Dog Salmon (*Oncorhynchus keta*), 218
Dolphin (Fish, *Coryphaena hippurus*), colours, 187
Dolphin (Mammal, *Delphinus*), compared with fish, **2**; paddle **3**; compared with aquatic reptile, **4**
Domesticated fishes, 350 f., **358**
Doras, **45**; noises, 174; pectoral girdle, **37**; pectoral spines and locomotion, 46; see also South American Cat-fish
Dorosoma, see Hickory Shad
Dorsal aorta, 131
Dorsal fin, 9, **11**; use in locomotion, **20**, 21, 33; variation in form, 33 f.; in function, 40 f.; structure, **28** f.; position, 38, **35**
Double-headed fry, 359
Dragon-fishes (Pegasoidei), 331, 333; see also Scorpion- or Lionfish (*Pterois*).
Dragonet (*Callionymus lyra*), courtship, sexual differences, **231, 233** f.
Drepanaspis gemuendenensis, **299**
Drift nets, 341 f.
Drifter, **342**
Drinking, 132
Drum (Sciaenidae), barbels, **142**; sound production, **173**, 174, 175; systematic position, 330; see also Sciaenid
Drumming Trigger-fish (*Rhinecanthys aculeatus*), 173
Drying, 343, 344
Dwarf Cod-fish (*Bregmaceros*), pelvic fins, 49
Dwarf male, **244**

Eagle Ray, **45**; median fins, 33; teeth, **104**, 108; poison glands, 160; nutrition of embryo, 252; systematic position, 327
Ear, see auditory organ
Ear-stone, see otolith
Eastern Sea Trout, see Phinock
Ebisu (Fish God), 369
Echeneis, see *Remora*, Shark-sucker
Echinorhinus, see Bramble Shark
Echo-location, 175
Ectoparasites, 354 f.
Edaphodon, 305
Eel, form of body, **8**, 14, **42**; fins, 31, 34, 43, 46, 49; locomotion, 17, **18**; scales, 59; food, 117; vertebrae, 123, 224; position of heart, 131; nostrils,

142; golden variety, 192; effects of heat and cold, 204; in gill-cavities of Devil-fishes, 210; eggs, larvae, 222 f., 262 f.; systematic position, 329, 332; as food, 335; see also Freshwater Eel, Conger, etc.
Eel-fare, 222
Eel Pout, see Viviparous Blenny
Egg, 213 f., 246 f.; number produced, 215, 216, 240; of Sea Cat-fishes, 240, 251; size, 250, 251; artificial fertilisation, 351
Egg-pouch in Pipe-fishes, etc., **242**, 243
Elasmobranch, 72; see also Selachii
Elastic spring mechanism, **173**
Electric Cat-fish (*Malapterurus*), **163**; electric organs, 166 f.; noises, 174
Electric discharge, 167
Electric Eel, **20**, **163**, 165; systematic position, 165, 329; locomotion, 20; fins, 34; electric organs, 165 f.; vent, 130
Electric organs, 165 f.; of Cephalaspids, 298
Electric Ray, **166**; see also *Torpedo*
Electricity, fishes sensitive to, 156, 167
Elephant-fish, see Chimaera
Elephant-snout Mormyrid, **94**; mouth, 98
Elfin Shark (Scapanorhynchidae), 105, **106**; teeth, **106**; ancestry, 105, 306; systematic position, 306, 327
Elopidae, 328
Elops, see Ten-pounder
Elver, 222, 263
Embiotocidae, see Surf-fish
Embryology, 251
Embryos, 246 f.
Emperor's Pike, 262 f.
Enamel, 53, 56 f., 102
Endolymph, 149
Endoparasites, 354, 356 f.
Endoskeleton, 119 f.
Endostyle in Ammocoete larva, 258
Engraulis, see Anchovy
Engyprosopon, see Flat-fish
Environment, effects of, 194 f.
Eocene period, 122
Epibulus, skull, **99**; mouth, **99**, 100
Epidermis, 52 f.
Epinephelus, **35**; see Sea Perch
Epiphysis, see pineal gland
Equilibrium, 151
Escolar, 363
Esox, see Pike
Etheostoma, see Darter
Ethiopian region, 281, 286 f.

Etmopterus, luminesence 168
Eugaleus, see Tope
Eugnathidae, 309
Eugnathus orthostomus, **308**
European Eel, see Fresh-water Eel
Eurypharynx, see Gulper
Euselachii, 305, 326 f., 331
Eusthenopteron, **311**, 312
Eustomias, vertebral column, 124, **125**; E. bituberatus, **143**; E. silvescens, **143**; E. tenisoni, **143**
Evermannichthys, commensalism with sponge, 198
Evolution, 293 f., 318 f., 281 f.; of fins, 27 f.; of electric organs 167 f.; of cave-fishes, 197 f.
Excretion, 78, 132; through gills, 78; and osmoregulation, 132
Exocoetidae, 329; see also Flying-fish
Exoskeleton, 119, 52 f.
Exostoma, 200
External gills, 75 f., **77**, 258
Extinct fishes, 293 f.
Extrusion of eggs, 215, 247
Euryhaline, 132
Eye, 144 f.; of hill-stream fishes, 202
Eyelid, 145

Facial nerve, **137**, 140, 144, 153
Family, 323
Fats, 334 f.
Feather-back (*Notopterus*), dorsal fin, 36
Feeding migrations, 275 f.
Feeler, see Barbel
Fertilisation, 214, 246
Fertiliser, 346
Fertility, of species, 320
Fifteen-spined Stickleback (*Spinachia*), nest, 237
Fighting-fish (*Betta*), **233**; respiration, 81; courtship, 233; breeding, 234, 237
Filamentous rays, 48
File-fishes (Monacanthidae), **20**, **184**; locomotion, 20; pelvic fins, 49; scales, 64; teeth, 109; sound-production, 172; mimicry, **184**; antiquity 310
Filiform body, 14, 42
Fin, 9, **11**, 27 f.; function, 32 f.; different kinds, 27 f.; origin and evolution, 27 f., 31; development, 27; structure, 28 f.; abnormalities, **358**, 359

Finlets, 39

Fin movements in swimming, 18, 19 f., 314

Finnan Haddie, 344

Fin-rays, 28 f., 33 f.

Fin-rot, 354

Fin-spines, see Fin-rays

Firm-fin, see Cirrhitid

Fish, definition, 1 f.; systematic position, 4; classification of, 318 f.; poisoning, 164; fights, 234; as food, 334 f.; hooks, traps, weirs, 338; curing, 343 f.; cake, rissoles, sausages, 345; fertiliser, 346; oil, meal, glue, leather, 346; gallery at British Museum (Natural History), 359; gods, mummies, 369; myths and legends, 361 f.

Fisheries, 337

Fishery Board for Scotland, 347

Fishery investigations, 347 f.

Fishing-frog, see Angler-fish, Angler, Common Angler

Fishing grounds, 269, 337

Fishing methods, 338 f.

Fistularia, see Flute-mouth

Fistulariidae, 329

Flake, 337

Flat-fishes (Pleuronectiformes), form of body, 13; locomotion, 21; dorsal fin, **35**, 37; pelvic fins, 50; lateral line, **66**, 67; mouth, 101; teeth, 114; pyloric caeca, 127; eyes, 145; colours, 176, 186; ambicoloration, 192; albinos, 193; development, 264; systematic position, 331; trade term, 336

Flat-head (Platycephalidae), 189

Flesh, 334 f.; poisonous properties, 164 f.; see also muscles

Flight, 46 f.

Florida Pipe-fish (*Syngnathus floridae*), breeding, **242** f.

Flounder, **12**; caudal fin, 43; tubercles, 59, **60**; teeth, food, 114; colour changes, 186, 191; in salt and fresh water, 132, 266, 277; eggs, 215, **247**; development of eggs, **247**

Fluctuations in numbers, 350

Fluke, 356 f.

Flute-mouth (*Fistularia*), **99**

Flying Characins (Gasteropelecidae), 47

Flying-fish, **45**; pectoral fins, 46; flight, 47; eggs, 251; systematic position, 329, 332

Flying Gurnard (Dactylopteridae),

pectoral fins, flight, 47, 48; sound-production, 172; systematic position, 331, 333

Focusing, of eye, 144, 147

Food, 102 f.; absorption, 128; of hill-stream fishes, 201; of parasitic Cat fishes, 210

Food-fishes, 334 f.

Food value of fish, 335, 336

Fore-brain, 136, **137**

Foricula, 228

Form, 7 f.; of hill-stream fishes, 199 f.

Fossil-fishes, 293 f.

Four-eyed Fish (*Anableps*), **146**; eye, 145, **146**; intromittent organ (foricula), 228; number of young, 254; pseudoplacenta, 254

Four Legs, see *Latimeria*

Fox Shark (*Alopias*), **42**; caudal fin, 43; feeding, 106

Freezing, 343

Fresh-run Salmon, 216

Freshwater Eel (*Anguilla*), **8**; tenacity of life, 80; scales, 59; food, 117; lymph heart, 131; effects of temperature on, 204; hibernation, 205; distribution, 277; breeding, 220 f.; development, 262 f.

Freshwater fisheries, 335 f.; 352 f.

Freshwater fishes, distribution, 277 f.; as food, 336

Freshwater Sun-fish (Centrarchidae), **45**; dorsal fin, 37; parental care, 235; distribution, 291

Frilled Shark (*Chlamydoselachus*), **42**; gill-clefts, 71; lateral line, **153**, 154; systematic position, 306, 327, 331

Frog-fish (*Histrio*), **182**; line and bait, 40; pectoral fins, 47; systematic position, 331

Frontal clasper, 227, **155**

Frost-fish (*Lepidopus*), **205**

Fry, see larva

Fungus, 354

Furunculosis, 353

Fusiform body, 9

Gadidae, dorsal fins, **35**, 36

Gadiformes, 329, 332; see also Cod

Gadus, see Cod

Galaxiid, distribution, 278

Galeiformes, 327, 331

Galeocerdo, see Tiger Shark

Gall-bladder, 128

Gambusia, **229**

Gametes, 213, 246

Ganoid scales, see Cosmoid and Lepisostoid scales
Ganoine, 56 f.
Gar-fish (Belonidae), **94**; jaws, 95, 97; feeding 96, 13; green bones, 124; eggs, **248**, 251; development, 97, 261; systematic position, 329, 332
Gar Pike (*Lepisosteus*), **96**; dorsal and anal fins, **28**, 38; swimbladder, **85**, 86; caudal fin, 31; scales, **56**, 57; food and jaws, 96; vertebrae, 123; mimicry, 96; distribution, 286, 290; larval cement organs, 258; ancestry, 310; systematic position, 310, 328, 332
Gas, of swimbladder, 134
Gasteropelecus, flight, 47
Gasterosteus, see Stickleback; *G. aculeatus*, see Three-spined Stickleback
Gasterostoidea, 333
Gastric glands, 127
Gastromyzon, see Bornean Sucker
Gemmeous Dragonet, 234
Gemuendina, 302, **303**
Genus, 322
Geographical races, 322
Geological record, **295**, 296
Gephyrocercal tail, 44, **32**
Germo, see Albacore
Giant Loach (*Cobitis*), respiration, 80
Gigantura chuni, **146**
Giganturidae, eyes, 147
Gill-arches, 70, **71**, 72, **75**, 90; -clefts, **71**, **73**; -cover, 74, **121**; -filaments, 70, 72; -pouches, 71 f.; -rakers, **76**, 78 f.; -maggots, **356**
Gillaroo, 128, 321
Gills, 69 f.; and excretion, 78; and osmoregulation, 78; of fossil Cyclostomes, 298, 301
Ginglymodi, 332 (see also Gar Pike)
Ginglymostoma, 107; see also Nurse Shark
Gizzard, 128
Glacial region, 273
Glanis, see Wels
Glass Eel, see Elver
Globe-fish (Tetraodontidae), **8**; form of body, **8**, 13; inflation, 13; locomotion, 21; spines, 64; teeth, 116; noises, 174; spinal cord, 139; nostrils, 142; poisonous flesh, 164; colours, 189; systematic position, 329, 333; helmets from skin, 347
Glossopharyngeal nerve, 140, **137**, 153
Glottis, 85
Glue, 346

Glyptosternum, 200
Gnathonemus, see Elephant Mormyrid
Gobiesocidae, see Cling-fish
Gobiesocoidei, 331
Gobiidae, see Goby
Gobio, see Gudgeon
Gobioidei, 330, 332
Gobius, see Goby; *G. minutus*, see Common Goby; *G. niger*, see Black Goby
Goblin Shark, see Elfin Shark
Goby, caudal fin, 43; pelvic fins, 49, **50**; lateral line, 67; canine teeth, 113; in sponges, 198; blind, 198; in gill-cavities of Shad, 210; pugnacity of male, 234; care of eggs, 240; eggs, **248**, 251; systematic position, 330, 332; size, 261, **262**
Golden Ide, 192
Golden Orfe, 192
Golden Tench, 192
Golden Trout, 192, 322
Gold-fish (*Carassius auratus*), **358**, 359; feeding, 117; sense of hearing, 151; coloration, 192, 193; effects of temperature on, 204; introduction, 204, 352; varieties, **358**, 359
Gonads, 213, **214**
Gonorhynchoidei, 329
Gourami (*Osphronemus*), respiration, 81; pelvic fins, 49
Grammistes, see Sea Perch
Grayling (*Thymallus*), 204, 280
Great Lake Trout, 321
Great Swallower (*Chiasmodus*), 95, **195**
Great White Shark (*Carcharodon*), teeth, 104, **105**; food, 105, 106
Greater Weever (*Trachinus draco*), **161**; poison gland, 161, **162**; venom and its effects, 163; warning coloration, 189
Greenland Shark (*Somniosus*), feeling, 157; toxicity of, 165; eggs, 249
Greenling (Hexagrammidae), lateral lines, **66**, 67
Grenadier (Macrouridae), **169**; tail, 31; luminous organs, 168; eyes, 148; sound production, 174; distribution, 267; systematic position, 329, 332
Grey-fish, 337
Grey Mullet (Mugilidae), **24**; leaping, 25; mouth, teeth, food, **112**, 116, 126; stomach, intestine, 126; adipose eyelid, 145; habits of shoal, 158; salt tolerance, 132; distribution, 277; systematic position, 331, 333
Grey Trout, 324

Grouper, see Sea Perch
Guanin, 190
Gudgeon (*Gobio*), effects of heat and cold, 203 f.
Guitar-fish, teeth, **104**, 108; antiquity, 306; systematic position, 327, 332
Gulf Stream, 273 f.
Gullet, 71, 84, 117
Gulper, **195**; mouth, 95, **99**; teeth, 110
Gunnel (*Pholis*), **241**; care of eggs, 241
Gurnard (Triglidae), **45**; pectoral fins, 48, 144 (taste buds); scutes, 61; sound production, 174, 175; systematic position, 330, 333
Gwyniad, 279
Gymnarchus, nest, 236; eggs, 251
Gymnothorax, see Muraena
Gymnotids, fins, **20**, 34, 41, **163**; snout, 98; vent, 130; Weberian ossicles, 152; distribution, 286
Gymnotoidei, 329
Gyrinocheilus, 202

Haddock (*Melanogrammus*), caudal fin, **32**; dorsal fins, 36; sound production, 174; as food, 335; smoked, 344
Haemal arch, **123**
Haemal spine, **123**
Haemoglobin, 69
Hag-fish, fins, 27; gills, 72 f., **74**; respiration, 70; mucus, 52; mouth, 88; tongue, 102; cerebellum, 138; nostril, 141; eyes, 147; ear, 149; pineal gland, 149; way of life, 210; eggs, 246, 248; systematic position, 297, 301
Hair-tail (Trichiuridae), **205**, 330, 332
Hake (*Merluccius*), dorsal fins, 36; distribution, 273
Halecostomi, 310
Half-beak, **94**; leaping, 46; jaws, **94**, 96 f., 262; food, 96; mimicry, 184; systematic position, 329, 332
Halibut (*Hippoglossus*), mouth, 101; as food, 335; size, 361
Hammer-headed Shark, head, **146**; food, 105, 106; eyes, 147; spiral valve, 129; systematic position, 327
Hand-lines, 342
Haplodoci, 333
Haplostomias, see Wide-mouth
Hard roes, 213
Harpodon, see Bummalow
Hassar (*Hoplosternum*), 62, **63**
Hatcheries, 350 f.
Hatchet-fish, see *Argyropelecus*

Head-fish, see Sun-fish
Hearing, 149 f.
Heart, 130 f., 314
Heat, effects of, 203 f.
Hebrews, food-fishes permitted to, 59
Helicoprion bessonowi, teeth of, **305**
Hemirhamphidae, 329
Hemirhamphus, see Half-beak
Hepsetia, see Sand Smelt
Heptranchias, see Comb-toothed Shark
Hermaphrodites, 213
Herring (*Clupea harengus*), number of individuals, 5; gill-rakers, 78 f.; dorsal fin, 36, 38; caudal fin, 43; pelvic fins, 48; scales, 58, 59, 68; "hybrid" with Pilchard, 65; teeth, food, 78, 115 f.; nasal organ, **141**; swimbladder and auditory organ, 151; colours, 177; migrations, 276 f.; races, 276; spawning, 213, 250; hermaphrodites, 213; eggs, 215, 250; incubation period, 256; fossil relatives, 310; nomenclature, **323**; systematic position, 328; as food, 335; curing, 343 f.; fishery, 338, 339
Heterocercal tail, 29 f., **32**; properties of, 32
Heterobranchus, 83
Heterodontidae (Heterodontiformes), 306, 327; see also Bull-headed Shark
Heterodontiformes, 327
Heterodontus, see Bull-headed Shark, Port Jackson Shark
Heteropneustes, **81**, 83
Heterosomata, 333; see also Flat-fish, Pleuronectiformes
Heterostraci, see Pteraspidomorphi
Hexagrammidae, see Greenling
Hexanchidae, 306, 327, 331; see also Comb-toothed Shark
Hexanchiformes, 327
Hexanchus, see Comb-toothed Shark
Hibernation, 205
Hickory Shad (*Dorosoma*), food, 116; gizzard, 128
Hill-stream fishes, 199 f.
Hind-brain, **137**, 138
Hiodontidae, see Moon Eye
Hippocampus, see Sea Horse
Hippoglossus, see Halibut
Histrio, **182**; colours, 182
Hog-backed-fishes, 358
Holacanthus, see Butterfly-fish
Holocentrum, see Soldier-fish
Holocephali, 305, 328, 332; see also *Chimaera*
Holoptychius, **311**

Holostei, 309, 328
Homocercal tail, 29, 30, **32**
Hoplopteryx, Plate VI
Hoplosternum, see Hassar
Horned Pout, 291
Horny fin-rays, 28
Horny tubercles, in Cyprinids, 232
Horse-fish (*Agriopus*), casting skin, 52
Horse Mackerel (*Trachurus*), anal fin, 43; scutes, 61; sound-production, 172; migrations, 276; systematic position, 330; see also Scad
Hound (*Mustelus*), teeth, 103, 107; systematic position, 327, 331
Huer, 341
Hump-backed Salmon (*Oncorhynchus gorbuscha*), breeding, 218; occurence in British waters, 291
Hybodontiformes, 305
Hybrids, 264 f.
Hydro-electric schemes, effects of on fishes, 353
Hydrolagus, see Californian Chimaera
Hyoid arch, 90
Hyomandibula, 91 f.
Hyostylic jaw suspension, 91
Hypocercal tail, 299
Hypoplectrus, see Vaca
Hyporhamphus, **94**; see Half-beak
Hypostomides, 333; see also Pegasoidei, 331
Hypotremata, 326, 327, 332
Hypural, 30
Hysterocarpus, see Viviparous Perch

Icelandic Herring, 276
Ichthyology, 5
Ichthyophthiriasis, 354
Ichthyosaur, 3, **4**
Ichthyotomi, 331; see Pleuracanthiformes, 304
Idiacanthus, **146**, **259**; eyes, 147
Idus, see Golden Orfe,
Incubation period, in Rays, 249; in Black-mouthed Dog-fish, 252; in Spotted Dog-fish, 252; in Herring, 256; in Lampreys, 257; in Bitterling, 238; Stickleback, 237
Indian Cat-fish, (*Heteropneustes*), accessory respiratory organs, **81**, 83
Indo-Pacific region, 270 f.
Infrahaemal bones, 123
Infundibulum, 138
Iniomi, 332 (see Myctophoidei, 329)
Inner ear, 149 f.
Interbranchial septa, 71, 74, **75**

Internal organs, 119 f., 136 f.
International Commission on nomenclature, 325
International Council for the Exploration of the Sea, 348
Interspinous bones, 29
Intestine, 128 f.; respiration with, 80
Introductions, 291 f.; of Salmon and Trout, 291, 351
Intromittent organs, 227 f.; see also mixopterygia
Ipnops, luminous organs, 170; *I. murrayi*, **170**
Ireland, fresh-water fishes, 289
Iridescence, 190
Iridocytes, 190
Iris, 144
Isinglass, 346
Isocercal tail, 31
Isospondyli, 332 (see Clupeiformes, 310, 328)
Isotherms, 269, **272**
Istiophoridae, see Scombroidei, 330; also Sail-fish, Spear-fish
Istiophorus, see Sail-fish
Isuridae, 327
Isurus, see Mackerel Shark

Jamoytius kerwoodi, **300**; fin fold, 28, 301; systematic position, 300
Janassa bituminosa, **305**
Janitore, 368
Japan, fisheries, 337
Jaws, 88 f.
Jet propulsion, 21 f.
John Dory (*Zeus*), anal fin, 43; mouth, feeding, **99**, 100; systematic position, 330, 332; "thumb-mark" on side, 368
Juvenal's Turbot, 361

Kelp-fish (Clinidae), 330; fighting, 234
Kelt, 217
Kentucky Blind-fish (*Amblyopsis*), **156**, 196
Kidneys, 132; secretion of in Stickleback, 237
King Salmon, see Quinnat; introduced in New Zealand, 291
Kipper, 343 f.
Klip-fish, see Kelp-fish; also 343
Kurtus, care of eggs, 241

Labial nostrils, 142
Labrador Current, 273

Labridae, 330; see also Wrasse
Labrus, see Wrasse; *L. mixtus*, see
Cuckoo Wrasse
Labyrinth Fishes, air-breathing
organs, **81** f.; breeding, 233 (*Betta*),
237 f.; systematic position, 330, 333
Lactophrys, see Trunk-fish
Lady-fish (*Albula*), larva, 262;
systematic position, 328
Lagena, 149 f.
Lake Herring, 335
Lake Nicaragua Shark (*Carcharinus
nicaraguensis*), 106
Lake Väner Salmon, 278
Lake Victoria, fisheries of, 336;
introduced species, 292
Lamprey (*Petromyzon*), gills, branchial
basket, 72 f.; respiration, 77; mouth,
88, **89**; tongue, 102; "teeth", 102,
89; skull, 119; vertebral column,
122; cerebral hemispheres, 137;
cerebellum, 138; nostril, **141**; pineal
gland, 149; semi-circular canal, 149;
eggs, 246; development, **257** f.;
endostyle, 258
Lampridiformes, 329, 332
Lampris, see Opah
Lancelet (*Branchiostoma*), 258, 301
Lancet-fish (*Alepisaurus*), head, **112**;
teeth, food, 112
Landlocked Salmon, 278
Lantern-fish (Myctophidae), **170**; eyes,
148; luminous organs, 169 f., 171;
systematic position, 329, 332; see
also Scald-fish
Lapillus, 150
Large intestine, 129
Large-mouthed Wrasse, see *Epibulus*
Largest fish, 361, **362**
Larva, 241 f.; coloration, 178
Larval organs, 258; cutaneous respira-
tion in, 80
Lasiognathus, **41**; line and bait, 40
Lateral line, **66**, 152 f.
Lates, see Nile Perch
Latimeria, **313** f.; caudal fin, 29; scales,
56; systematic position, 312 f., 333
Latin names, see nomenclature
Latrunculus, see Transparent Goby
Laugia, **313**
Leaping, 23 f.; of Tarpon, 25
Learning, 138, 159
Leather, from fish skins, 346
Leather Carp, 60, 322
Leatherjacket, see File-fish
Leather-mouth, 117
Lederkarpfen, see Leather Carp

Leech, 354
Legends, 361
Lens, 144 f.
Lepadogaster, see Cling-fish
Lepeophtheirus, see Sea Louse
Lepidopus, see Frost-fish
Lepidosiren, see Lung-fish, South
American Lung-fish
Lepidotrichia, 29
Lepidotus mantelli, dentition, **308**;
L. notopterus, **308**
Lepisosteidae, 310, 332
Lepisosteus, see Gar Pike; *L. tropicus*, 286
Lepisostoid scale, 57
Lepomis, see Freshwater Sun-fish
Leptocephalus, of Eel, 262 f.; of *Elops*
and Lady-fish, 262; *Leptocephalus
morrisii*, 262; *L. brevirostris*, 262
Leptocercal tail, 31
Leptolepiformes, 310
Light, production of, 171
Ligula, 357
Limanda, see Dab
Ling (*Molva*), dorsal fin, 36; number
of eggs, 215
Lingual teeth, 102, 109
Lining, 342
Linnean system of nomenclature, 324
Linophryne arborifer, **41**; *L. macrorhinus*,
141
Lion-fish, see Scorpion-fish
Lion-head Gold-fish, **358**, 359
Lip, 93, **94**; of hill-stream fishes, 200 f.;
of Ammocoete larva, **257**
Liparis, see Sea-snail
Lirus, see Rudder-fish
Littoral fishes, 267; colours, 179 f.
Liver, 128, **127**; oil, 345 f.
Lizard-fish, 329
Loach, respiration, 80; sound-produc-
tion, 172
Loch Leven Trout, 321
Locomotion, 15 f.
Long lines, 342
Longevity, 362 f.
Long-nosed Gar Pike, **96**
Lophiidae, 331
Lophius, see Angler, Common Angler
Lophobranchs, 75
Lopholatilus, see Tile-fish
Lorenzini's ampullae, 155 f.
Loricaria, see Mailed Cat-fish
Lota, see Burbot
Lower pharyngeals, 116 f.; **110**
Lucifuga, see Cuban Blind-fish
Luminescence, 168 f.
Luminous organs, 168 f.

Lump-sucker, **50**; pelvic fins, 50; tubercles, 60; eggs, 240, 251; parental care, 240; systematic position, 331, 333
Lung, 69 f., 84 f.
Lung-fish (Dipneusti), **282,316**; nostrils, 141; caudal fin, 31; external gills, 75 f., 258; pectoral fin, **30**, 46; teeth, **315**; swimbladder, 84 f.; scales, 56; notochord, 122; vertebrae, 123; spiral valve, 130; heart, 131; cerebral hemispheres, 137; optic lobes, 138; lateral line, 154; aestivation, 206; distribution, **282**; parental care, 236; larvae, 75, **77**, 258; ancestry, 315 f.; systematic position, 316, 328, 333
Lutjanidae, 330; see also Snapper
Lymphatic system, 131

'Maccaroni piatti,' 357
Mackerel (*Scomber scombrus*), **8**; form of body, 9; locomotion, 9; dorsal and anal fins, 9, 37, 39; caudal fin, 43; pelvic fins, 49; scales, 59; flesh, 126; pyloric caeca, 127; colours, 177; migrations, 275; hermaphrodites, 213; systematic position, 330, 332; as food, 335
Mackerel Shark (*Isurus oxyrhynchus*), **2**; dorsal fin, **28**; systematic position, 327 (Isuridae)
Macropodus, see Paradise-fish
Macrorhamphosidae (Snipe-fishes), 329
Macrorhamphosus, see Snipe-fish
Macrouridae, 329; see also Grenadier
Mad Tom, 46, 291; see also Stone Cat
Madagascar, 281, 284
Mahseer, scales, 59
Mail-cheeked fishes, (Scorpaenoidei), systematic position, 330, 333
Mailed Cat-fish, **42**, **63**; respiration, 80; adipose fin, 38; scutes, 62; mouth, **89**, 93; intestine, 128; secondary sexual characters, **231**, 232
Malacocephalus, see Grenadier
Malacopterygians, 34
Malacosteus indicus, **195**
Malapterurus, see Electric Cat-fish
Malformations, 358 f.
Man, attacked by fishes, 106 f., 110 f., 113, 211; fishes dangerous to, see *above*, and 96, 160 f.
Mandibular arch, 90

'Man-eater', see Great White Shark
'Man-eaters', 106
Manta, see Devil-fish, Sea Devil
Marine Biological Association, 348
Marine fishes, 267 f.
Mastacembelidae, see Spiny Eel
Masu (*Oncorhynchus masou*), 218
Maxilla, 92, **91**
Meagre (*Sciaena aquila*), otolith, **150**; sounds, 175
Meal, 346
Meckel's cartilage, 90, **91**, 92
Median fins, 9, **11**
Medicinal uses of fish, 363
Mediterranean fishes, 271 f.
Medulla oblongata, 138, **137**
Medullary canal, 136
Megalodoras, see South American Cat-fish
Megalops, see Tarpon
Melamphaes beanii, **156**
Melanocetus johnsoni, **41**
Membrane bones, 92, 120
Memory, 159
Menhaden (*Brevoortia*), 112
Mental appendage, 98
Merluccius, see Hake
Mermaid, 364; mermaid's purse, pin-box, **248**, 249
Mesozoic era, 294, **295**
Metamorphosis, of Eel, 262 f.; of Lamprey, 258; of Plaice, 264
Microcyprini, see Cyprinodontiformes
Micropogon, see Sciaenid
Micropyle, 246, **247**
Mid-brain, 138
Midshipman (*Porichthys*), 171, 174
Migrations, 216, 218, 219, 221, 275 f.
Milk-fish (*Chanos*), 328
Miller's Thumb (*Cottus gobio*), 225, 240, 280
Milt, 214; see also testis
Mimicry, 182 f., 208
Minnow (*Phoxinus phoxinus*), alarm substance, 143; sensitivity of hearing, 151; colour variation, 185; systematic position, see Cypriniformes
Minous, association with hydroids, 210
Miraculous draught, 367
Mirror Carp, 60, 322, **358**
Mistichthys luzonensis, 361, **362**
Mitsukurina, see Elfin Shark
Mixopterygia, 227
Mobula, see Sea Devil, Smaller Devil-fish
Mochocidae, 284
Mola, see Sun-fish

Mollienesia, 232
Molva, see Ling
Monacanthidae, see File-fish
Monacanthus, see File-fish
Monk-fish (*Squatina*), number of young, 252; antiquity, 306; mythical, 364
Monocentrus, see Pine-cone Fish
Monocirrhus, mimicry, **183**
Monstrosities, 358 f.
Moon-eye (Hiodontidae), 290
Moorish Idol (*Zanclus canescens*), **35**
Moray, see Muraena
Mormyridae, electric organs, 165, 166, 167; size of brain, 139; swimbladder and auditory organ, 151; 'external gills', 258; distribution, 286
Mormyroidei, 329
Morone, see Bass
Motella, see Rockling
Motor nerves, 140
Mouth, 88 f.; of hill-stream fishes, 200 f.; of Ammocoete larva, 257; of fossil Cyclostomes, **299**, 301
Mouth-breeding, 238 f.
Movable teeth, 110
Mucus, 52
Mucous cartilage, 298
Mud-fish (*Protopterus*), **282**; aestivation, 206; parental care, 236; systematic position, 315 f., 328; see also African Lung-fish, Lung-fish
Mud Minnow (*Umbra*), burrowing, 25; effects of cold, 203
Mudskipper (*Periophthalmus*), **45**; respiration, 80; walking, jumping, swimming, 47 f.; eyes, 148
Mugil, see Grey Mullet
Mugiliformes, 331
Mugiloidea, 333; see also Mugiliformes, 331
Mullidae, 330; see also Red Mullet
Muraena, **180**; fins, 34
Muscles, 15, 124 f.; of gill-arches, 72; of abyssal fishes, 194
Muscular swimming movements, 16 f.
Museums, 359 f.
Mustelus, see Hound, Smooth Hound
Myctophid, luminous organs, 169 f., 171 f.
Myctophidae, 329
Myliobatis, see Eagle Ray
Myocommata, 126
Myomeres, 15
Myotomes, 126
Myths, 361 f.; 181
Myxine, see Hag-fish
Myxosporidia, 354

Names, see nomenclature
Narcobatoidea, 332; see also Torpediniformes, 327
Naseus, see Unicorn-fish
Nassau Grouper (*Epinephalus striatus*), colour phases, 186
Natural History Museum, 359
Naucrates, see Pilot-fish
Nearctic region, 281, 289
Needle-fish, see Shrimp-fish
Nematoda, see Round Worms
Nemichthys, see Snipe Eel
Neoceratodus, see Australian Lung-fish, Lung-fish
Neopterygii, 332; see also Actinopterygii, 306, 328
Neotropical region, 281, 284
Nerves, 139 f., **137**
Nervous system, 136 f.
Nests, 235 f.
Neural arch, **123**
Neural spine, **123**
Neurocranium, 119 f.
Neuromast, 152 f.
Nictitating membrane, 145
Nile Perch (*Lates niloticus*), skeleton, **121**
Niner, see Pride
Nomenclature, 323 f.
Nomeus, see Portugese Man-of-war-fish
North Atlantic fishes, 273
North Pacific fishes, 274
North Sea Herring, 276
North Temperate Zone, 269, 274
Norwegian Herring, 276
Nostril, 141 f.; true internal, 311
Nothobranchius, breeding, 226
Notidanoidea, 331; see also Hexanchiformes, 327
Notochord, 122
Notopteroidea, 332
Notopteroidei, 329
Notopterus, see Feather-back
Notothenids, 273
Noturus, see Mad Tom, Stone Cat
Nucleus, 246
Number of species, 5
Nuptial colours, 230
Nuptial tubercles, 225
Nurse Shark (*Ginglymostoma*), teeth, **104**, 107; systematic position, 327, 331
Nutrition, of embryo, 252 f.

Oar-fish (*Regalecus*), dorsal fin, 34; pelvic fin, 49; as Sea Serpent, 365; see also Ribbon-fish

Ocean Bonito, see Bonito
Oceanic fishes, eyes, 147 f.; colour, 176 f.; modifications, 194, **195**; habitat, 267 f.; distribution, 267 f.
Oceanography, 348
Oculomotor nerve, 140
Odontoid, see dermal denticle
Oesophagus, see gullet
Ogcocephalidae, 331
Ogcocephalus, see Bat-fish
Oil globule, 250
Oils, 345
Olfactory lobe, 136 f.
Olfactory nerve, 140
Olfactory organ, 140 f.
Oligocene period, 295
Oncorhynchus, 218; see also Pacific Salmon
Opah, (*Lampris*), mouth, 100; systematic position, 329, 332
Opercular spine, 161, **162**
Operculum, 73
Ophichthyidae, see Serpent Eel
Ophiocephalus, see Snake-head
Opisthoproctus, **146**
Optic lobe, 138, **137**
Optic nerve, 140
Optic vesicle, 137
Orange Fin, 324
Orbit, 120
Order, 323
Orectolobidae, 327
Orectolobus, see Carpet Shark
Origin of species, 320 f.
Oro-nasal grooves, 141
Osmeridae, 329
Osmerus, see Smelt
Osmoregulation, 132
Osphronemus, see Gourami
Ossicles, 152
Ostariophysi, Weberian mechanism, **152**; sensitivity to sounds 151; origin and distribution, 288 f.; systematic position, 329, 332
Osteichthyes, 306, 328
Osteoglossidae, **283**; swimbladder and respiration, 86; lateral line scales, 153; distribution, 282, **283**; nest, 235; 'external gills', 258
Osteoglossoidea, 332
Osteoglossoidei, 329
Osteoglossum bicirrhosum, **283**
Osteolepidae, 312
Osteolepiformes, 311
Osteostraci, 297 f.
Ostracion, see Trunk-fish
Ostracionoidei, 329

Osteostraci, 297 f.; **299**
Otolith, **150**
Otter, fishing with, 338
Otter trawl, **339**, 340
Ouananiche (*Salmo salar ouananiche*), 278
Oval, 133
Ovary, 213 f.
Over-fishing, 347
Oviduct, 213
Oviparous fishes, 247 f.
Ovum, 346; see also egg
Oxygen, consumption of, 69, 77; in swimbladder, 134

Pachycormidae, 309
Pacific Herring (*Clupea pallasia*), distribution, 275
Pacific Salmon (*Oncorhynchus*), 218; head of male, **217**, 218; spawning, 218; canning, 344
Paddle-fish (*Polyodon*), **94**; mouth, 93, **94**; scales, 56; systematic position, 308, 328
Pain, 156 f.
Paired fins, 9, **11**, 27 f., 44 f., 302 f., 304, 314; origin of, 27 f.
Pairing, 213, 216, 219, 227 f.
Palaearctic region, 281, 289 f.
Palaeonisciformes, 306 f.; scales, 56
Palaeoniscoid scales, 56, **57**
Palaeontology, 293 f.
Palaeopterygii, 332
Palaeospinax, 327
Palaeozoic era, **295**
Palatability of fishes, 126
Palate, **91**, 92
Palatine bone, 92
Palatine teeth, 109
Pampano (Carangidae), 61; scutes, 61
Panama Canal, 270
Pancreas, 128
Pantodon, see Chisel-jaw
Parachordal, 122
Paracirrhites, see Cirrhitid
Paradise-fish (*Macropodus*), respiration, 81; breeding, 238
Paralichthys, colour changes, 187, 191; see American Flounder
Paraliparis, **195**
Parasiluris, 289
Parasites, 354 f.
Parasitic males, 244 f.
Parasitism, 210 f.
Parental care, 235 f.
Parr, **253**, 68, 256
Parrot-fish (Scaridae), **66**; lateral line,

67, **66**; jaws, **112**; teeth, food, **112**, 116; sleeping habits, 157
Parrot Wrasse, see Parrot-fish
Pastinaca, 160
Patagonian fishes, 284
Peal, 324
Pearl-fish (*Carapus*), **209**; tail, 44; habits, 209
Pearls, from scales of Bleak, 347
Pectoral fin, **30**, 31 f., 44 f.
Pediculati, 333; see also Lophiiformes, 331
Pegasidae, see Dragon-fish
Pelagic eggs, 215, 250
Pelagic fishes, 267 f.; body form of, 9
Pelvic fin, 48 f.; of South American Lung-fish, 236
Perca, see Perch
Perch (*Perca*), gill-rakers, **76**; caudal fin, 43; pelvic fin, 48; scales, 58; lateral line, 67, **153**; teeth, 109; internal organs, **127**; caught with own eye, 157; distribution, 289, 290; eggs, 225; systematic position, 330, 332; as food, 336
Perch-like fishes, origin, 310
Perciformes, 310, 330
Percidae, distribution, 289, 290
Percoidea, 332; see also Percoidei, 330
Percopsidae, 291
Pericardium, 130
Periglacial region, 273
Perilymph, 149
Periophthalmus, see Mudskipper
Peristedion, see Sea Robin
Perleidiformes, 308
'Pescados blancos', 280
Petersfisch, 368
Petromyzon, see Lamprey
Pez Ciego, 196, **197**
Phallostethus, 229
Phaneropleuron, **316**
Pharyngeal openings, 71, 73
Pharyngeals, 109, **110**, 114, 116, 117
Pharyngolepis oblongus, **299**
Pharynx, **71**, 126; of Ammocoete larva in Cyclostomes, 258
Phinock, 321, 324
Pholidophoriformes, 310
Pholis, see Gunnel
Photocorynus spiniceps, **244**
Photonectes intermedius, **143**
Photophores, 168 f.
Phoxinus, see Minnow
Phycodurus eques, **183**, 182
Phylogenetic tree, 318 f.
Phylogeny, 318 f.

Physoclistous fishes, 133
Physostomatous fishes, 133
Pickling, 345
Picuda, 113
Pigment cell, see chromatophore
Pigmentation, effect of light on, 191 f.
Pike (*Esox*), gill-rakers, 78; dorsal and anal fins, 38; skull, **91**; premaxilla, 92; teeth, 109; feeding, 110; size of brain, 138; distribution, 289, 290; systematic position, 329; as food, 336; longevity, 362 f.
Pilchard (*Sardina pilchardus*), scales, 59; "hybrid" with Herring, 65; distribution, **272** f.; migrations, 276; eggs, 250; fishery, 341; as Sardines, 344
Pilot-fish (*Naucrates*), **205**; association with Sharks, 208
Pine-cone Fish (*Monocentrus*), **63**; dorsal fin, 38; pelvic fin, 49; scales, 64
Pineal gland, 148
Pink Salmon (*Oncorhynchus gorbuscha*), 218; in British waters, 291
Pipe-fish (Syngnathidae), **42**; locomotion, 21; gills, 75; bony rings, 63; mouth, feeding, 98; colours, mimicry, 182; egg-pouch, **242** f.; systematic position, 329, 332
Piranha, see Caribe
Pirarucu, see *Arapaima*
Piraya, see Caribe
Pisces, see Bony Fish
Pisciculture, 350 f.
Pituitary gland, 138
'Placenta', 253, 254
Placodermi, 302 f.
Placoid scale, see dermal denticle
Plaice (*Pleuronectes*), scales, 59; mouth, 101; teeth, food, 114; palatability, 126; nocturnal activity, 158; colour changes, 186; ambicoloration, 193; hibernation, 205; spawning, 214, 250; eggs, 250; races, 322; systematic position, 331
Plankton-feeders, 115
Plasma, 69
Platax, see Bat-fish
Platichthys, see Flounder
Platysomoidei, **307** f.
Platysomus superbus, **307**
Platystacus, care of eggs, 242
Plecostomus, see Mailed Cat-fish
Plectognathi, 333; see also Tetraodontiformes, 329
Pleuracanthiformes, 304 f.
Pleuracanthus, **304**, 305; pectoral fin, **30**

Pleural ribs, 123
Pleuronectiformes, 331, 333
Pleuronectes, see Plaice
Pleuronectoidei, 331
Pleuropterygii, 331
Pleurotremata, 326 f., 331
Pliotrema, see Saw Shark
Plotosidae, 284; Ampullae of Loren-
zini in, 155
Pneumatic duct, 85, 133
Poeciliinae, 229
Pogge (*Agonus*), 63; shields, 62
Poison-fish (*Synanceia verrucosa*), 161;
dorsal fin, 38; poison gland, 161,
162; mimicry, 183; systematic
position, 330
Poison glands, 160 f.
Poisonous fishes, 160 f.
Poison Toad-fish (*Thalassophryne*), 162
Polistotrema, see Californian Hag-fish
Pollack (*Pollachius pollachius*), dorsal
fins, 36
Pollan (*Coregonus pollan pollan*), 279
Pollution, 353
Polynemus, see Thread Fin
Polyodon, see Paddle-fish, Spoon-bill
Polypterus, see Bichir
Pomacentrid, associating with ane-
mone, 207; see also Damsel-fish
Pomatomus, see Blue-fish
Pompadour fish (*Symphysodon discus*),
parental care, 240
Pop-eye Gold-fish, 358, 359
Pope, see Ruffe
Porbeagle, 327
Porcupine-fish,(Diodontidae),63;form
of body, 13; habits, 13; locomotion,
21; spines, 63, 64; teeth, 116;
systematic position, 329, 333;
helmets from skins, 347
Pores, of lateral line, 153 f.
Porichthys, see Toad-fish
Porolepiformes, 311, 312
Port Jackson Shark (*Heterodontus*), 106;
teeth, 106, 108; venomous tissue;
160; egg-capsule, 248, 249; anti-
quity, 305, 306; systematic position,
305, 327; see also Bull-headed
Sharks.
Portuguese Man-of-war fish (*Nomeus*),
207
Premaxilla, 92, 91, 100
Pre-Cambrian period, 294, 295
Priapium, 229
Pride, 257 f.
Primary vesicles, 136
Prionotus, see Sea Robin

Priority, in nomenclature, 325
Pristiophorus, see Saw-Shark
Pristis, see Saw-fish
Pristidae, 55
Pristiurus, see Black-mouthed Dog-fish
Procurrent rays, 43
Protandry, 213
Protective colours, 176 f.
Protein, 334 f.
Protocercal tail, 29, 31
Protopterus, see African Lung-fish,
Lungfish, Mud-fish
Protosphyraena, 309
Protospondyli, 332
Protractile mouth, 99, 100
Psephurus, see Chinese Sturgeon
Psettodes, dorsal fin, 37; mouth, 101;
systematic position, 331
Psettodoidei, 331
Pseudauchenipterus, elastic spring
mechanism, 173
Pseudecheneis, 200
Pseudobranch, 74
Pseudoplacenta, of *Anableps*, 254
Pseudoscarus, see Parrot-fish
Pteraspidomorphi, 297, 301
Pteraspis, 301
Pterichthyodes, 302, 303
Pterois, see Scorpion-fish
Pterolebias, breeding, 226
Pterophyllum, see Angel-fish
Pteroplatea, see Butterfly Ray
Pterygoid bones, 92
Pterygoid teeth, 109
Pterygoquadrate, 90, 91, 92
Ptyctodont, 303
Puffer (Tetraodontidae), spines, 64;
poisonous flesh, 164; systematic po-
sition, 329, 333; see also Globe-fish
Pug-headed Trout, 358
Pugnacity, of breeding males, 234
Pulp cavity, 53, 102
Pupil, 144
Purse Seine, 341
Pycnodontidae, 309
Pygidiidae, 210 f.
Pyloric caeca, 127 f.
Pyloric sphincter, 128

Quinnat (*Oncorhynchus tschawtyscha*),
spawning, 218

Raad, see Electric Cat-fish
Rabbit-fish (*Chimaera*), 73, 155; skull,
91, 112
Races, 276, 279, 322

Rachovia, breeding, 226
Radial, **28** f.
Raia, see Ray, Skate
Raiiformes, 327
Rainbow Trout (*Salmo gairdneri*),
   introduction, 291, 351
Rains of fishes, 366
Raioidei, 327
Ranzania, see Truncated Sun-fish
Rat-tail, see Grenadier
Rate of breathing, 77
Ray, **12**, **20**, **228**; form of body, 10 f.;
   locomotion, **20**, 21; respiration, 72,
   78; median fins, 33; caudal fin, 43;
   pectoral fin, 44 f.; dermal denticles,
   53, 54; mouth, 90; feeding, 90; teeth,
   108; electric organs, 165, 166, 167;
   intestine, **129**; spiral valve, **129**;
   brain, **137**; eyes, 145; colours, 181;
   secondary sexual characters, 227,
   228; eggs, **248**, 249, 252; classification, 327, 332
Recognition marks, 172, 187 f., 189,
   230 f.
Rectum, 130
Red body, 133
Red corpuscles, 69
Red-fish, breeding phase of Salmon,
   216; see also Sockeye Salmon
Red Herring, 344
Red Mullet (*Mullus surmuletus*), head,
   142; colour changes, 187; system-
   atic position, 330
Red Sea fishes, 270 f.
Redd, 217
Reef fishes, coloration of, 179 f.; body
   form, 12; symbiosis, 207; distribu-
   tion, 269 f.
Reflex action, 158 f.
Regalecus, see Oar-fish, Ribbon-fish
Regeneration, 68, 359
Remora (*Remora*), **40**; sucker, 39;
   habits, 39, 208; fishing with, 338;
   myth of ship-holder, 364
Replacement, of scales, 54, 68; of teeth,
   102, 109
Reproductive organs, **127**, 133, 213 f.
Respiration, 69 f.; in hill-stream fishes,
   202
Resting, position adopted, 157 f.
Retina, 144, 147, 148
Reversal of coloration, 192 f.
Reversus, 364
Rhamphodopsis, **303**
Rhina, see Guitar-fish
Rhincodon, see Whale Shark
Rhinobatoidei, 327

Rhinobatus, antiquity, 306; see also
   Guitar-fish
Rhipidistia, 311 f.
Rhodeus, see Bitterling
Rhombosolea, pelvic fin, 51
Rhynchobatus, teeth, 108
Rib, 123
Ribbon-fishes (Trachypteridae), also
   Deal-fishes, dorsal fin, 34; caudal
   fin, 44; swimming, 17; mouth, 100;
   larva, 260, **261**; systematic position,
   329; see also Oar-Fish
Roach (*Rutilus*), scales, 58; lateral line,
   67; colours, 177; effects of heat and
   cold, 203 f.; breeding, 225; hybridi-
   zation, 265
'Rock Salmon', 337
'Rock Turbot', 337
Rockling (*Motella*), dorsal fin, 36
Roe, 213; poisonous property of, 164
Rostral organ, of Coelacanths, 314
Round fish, 336
Round-tail, 324
Round-tailed Sun-fish (*Mola*), **8**, 13,
   116, 139
Round Worms, 357
Rudder-fish (*Lirus*), association with
   jelly-fish, 207; systematic position,
   330, 332
Ruffe (*Acerina cernua*), lateral line
   system, 155; breeding, 225
Rutilus, see Roach
Ruvettus, see Escolar

Saccopharynx, **195**; head and jaws, **99**;
   mouth, feeding, 95; see also Gulper
Sacculus, 149 f.
Sagitta, **150**
Sail-bearer (*Velifer*), **35**, 36
Sail-fish (*Istiophorus*), **10**; dorsal fin, 39;
   jaws, 97; ramming ships, 97; verte-
   brae, 124, **125**; larvae, 260, **261**;
   systematic position, 330
Sailor's purse, 249
St. Paul Island, fishes, 273
Saithe, see Coal-fish
Salmincola, see Gill Maggot
Salmo, see Salmon, Trout; *S. albus*, see
   Phinock; *S. cambricus*, see Sewen; *S.
   fario*, see Brook Trout; *S. ferox*, see
   Great Lake Trout; *S. levenensis*, see
   Loch Leven Trout; *S. nigripinnis*, see
   Black-finned Trout; *S. stomachius*,
   see Gillaroo
Salmon, **24**; head of adult male, **217**;
   speed, 22; leaping, 23, gills, 73;

adipose dorsal fin, 38; pelvic fin, 48; scales, 58, 67; axillary scale, 66; scale reading, 67 f.; development of skull, 122; flesh, 126; pyloric caeca, 127; salinity tolerance 133; migrations, 278; distribution, 278; spawning, 216 f.; eggs, 216, 251; development, **253**, 255 f.; fry, 255; hybrids, 264; systematic position, 329, 332; as food, 334 f.; fisheries, 352; diseases, 353; parasites, 355 f.

Salmon disease, 353

Salmon Trout, 324

Salmonidae, distribution, 278; hybrids, 264; systematic position, 329, 332; introduction, 291, 351

Salmonoidei, 329

Salting, 343

Salvelinus, see Char

Sand Eel (*Ammodytes*), pyloric caeca, 127; eggs, 250

Sand or Common Goby (*Gobius minutus*), nest, 240

Sand Shark (*Carcharias taurus*), feeding, 106; as man-eater, 106; teeth, **103**, **105**; systematic position, 327

Sand Smelt (*Hepsetia pinguis*), passing Suez Canal, 271

Saprolegnia, 354

Sardina (Pilchard), distribution, **272** f.; *S. pilchardus*, 272

Sardine, 344 f.; see also Pilchard

Sardinops (Pilchard), distribution, **272** f.

Sargasso Weed Fish (*Histrio histrio*), **182**

Saury, jaws, 96

Saw-fish (*Pristis*), **55**; rostrum, 55; teeth, 55, 108; in fresh water, 266; embryo, 254; systematic position, 327

Saw Shark (*Pliotrema*), gill-clefts, 71; systematic position, etc., 327

Scabbard-fish (*Lepidopus*), effects of cold, 204 f.

Scad (*Trachurus*), scutes, 61; migrations, 276

Scald-fish (*Arnoglossus*), pelvic fin, 50; secondary sexual characters, 232

Scales, 52 f.; counts, 64; **65**; reading, 67; of lateral line, **66**; **153**; of sponge-living Goby, 198; of hill-stream fishes, 200

Scapanorhynchidae, 105, 306, 327

Scapanorhynchus, 306

Scardinius, see Rudd

Scaridae, see Parrot-fish

Scarus, 116; see also Parrot-fish

Schilbeodes, see Mad Tom, Stone Cat

Schistocephalus, 351

Sciaenidae, sound-production, 174 f.; otoliths, **150**, 151; barbels, **142**; systematic position, 330

Scientific names, see nomenclature

Scleropages, distribution, 282, **283**; *S. leichardti*, **283**

Scleroparei, 333; see also Mail-cheeked fish

Scomber, see Mackerel

Scombresocidae, 251

Scombresox, see Saury, Skipper

Scombroidea, 332

Scombroidei, 330; toxicity of, 165

Scophthalmus (Turbot), legends, 192 f.; see also Brill, Turbot

Scorpaenidae, 330

Scorpaenoidei, 330; antiquity, 310

Scorpion-fish (*Pterois*), **45**; (*Minous*), with symbiotic hydroids, 210; systematic position, 330

Sculpin, 240, 330; see also Bull-head

Scurf, 324

Scutes, **61** f.

Scyliorhinidae, 327; antiquity of, 306

Scyliorhinus, see Spotted Dog-fish

Sea Bream (Sparidae), teeth, food, 114; systematic position, 330

Sea Cat-fishes, parental care, 238; eggs, 240, 251

Sea Cucumbers inhabited by fishes, **209**

Sea Devil (*Manta*), leaping, 25; mouth, cephalic fins, feeding, 90; teeth, 108; birth of young, 253

Sea Dragon (*Phycodurus*), 182, **183**

Sea fisheries, 337 f.

Sea Horse (*Hippocampus*), **8**; form of body, 14; locomotion, 19, 21, 22; gills, 75; tail, 43, 14; rings and plates, 63; feeding, 98 f.; noises 174; breeding, 243; systematic position (Syngnathiformes), 329

Sea Lamprey (*Petromyzon*), **35**, **141**; mouth, 88, **89**; breeding, 219 f.

'Sea Leopard', 346

Sea Louse, 355

Sea Perch, **35**, **180**; dorsal fin, 36; scales, 58; teeth, 113; colours, 176, 179, 186; systematic position, 330

Sea Robin (*Prionotus*, *Peristedion*), pectoral fin, 48; shields, 62; see also Gurnard

Sea Serpent, 365 f.

Sea Snail (*Liparis*), pelvic fins, 50; eye, 148

Sea Snake, 189, 365
Sea Squirt, see Ascidian
Sea Toad (Chaunacidae), pectoral fin, 47
Sea Trout (*Salmo trutta*), 185, 279, 321, 324; fisheries, 352; diseases, 353; parasites, 355
Sebago Salmon (*Salmo salar sebago*), 278
Sebastes, see Norway Haddock
Secondary sexual characters, 230 f.
'See-Aal', 337
Seine, **340**, 341.
Selachii, 304 f., 326 f.; fins, **28**, 29 f., 33, 43, 44, 51; gills, **71** f.; gill rakers, 79, **76**; external gills, 75, pelvic fins, 51; dermal denticles, 52 f.; mouth, **89** f.; jaws, 90 f.; teeth, 102 f.; skull, 119 f.; vertebral column, **123**; spiral valve, **129**; heart, 131; brain, 136 f.; optic nerves, 140; olfactory organs, 141; eye, 144 f.; lateral line, **153** f.; claspers, 51, 227; electric organs, 165 f.; eggs, 247 f.; origin, fossil forms, 304 f.; classification, 304 f., 326 f., 331 f.
Semicircular canal, 149, **150**, 151
Semionotiformes, 309, **308**
Sense organs, 136 f.
Sensory nerve fibres, 139
Sensory nerves, 140
Sephamia, light organs, 171
Serpent Eel (Ophichthyidae), colours, 189
Serranidae, 330; see also Sea Perch
Serrasalmus, see Caribe
Sewage, effects of, 353
Sewen, 321
Sex reversal, 213
Sexual differences, 213 f., 227 f.
Shad (*Alosa*), gill-rakers, **76**, 79; scales, 59; eggs, 215, 251; migrations, 267
Shagreen, 346
Shape, of body, 7 f.
Shark, gills, 71 f.; dorsal and anal fins, 33 f.; caudal fin, 29 f., 32, **42**, 43; pectoral fin, 32 f., 44; swimming, **18**; dermal denticles, 52 f.; leather from skin, 346; lateral line, 153 f.; mouth, 89 f.; teeth, 102 f.; feeding, 105 f.; attacking man, 106 f.; intestine, 129; spiral valve, 129; brain, 136 f.; sense of smell, 142; eye, 144 f.; pineal gland, 148; in fresh water, 266; claspers, 51, 227; eggs, 247 f.; fossil forms, 304 f.; classification, 304 f., 326 f., 331 f.

Shark-fins, as food, 345
Shark-flesh paste, 345
Shark-sucker (*Remora*), habits, 39, 208; see also Remora
Sheat-fish, see Wels
Shiner, nest, 235
Ship-holder, myth, 364
Ships, and fish, 7; rammed by, 97 f.
Shoulder girdle, **3**, **37**
Shrimp-fish (*Aeoliscus*), **23**, **63**; swimming position, **23**; fins, 38; cuirass, 62 f.; systematic position, 329, 332
Siganid (*Siganus rivulatus*), passing Suez Canal, 271
Silurian period, **295**
Siluroidei, 329; see also Cat-fish
Silurus, see Wels
Silver Eel, 221, **222**, 263
Silver Salmon (*Oncorhynchus kisutch*), 218
Singing-fish (*Porichthys*), 171, 174
Sinus venosus, 131
Sisoridae, 201
Size, 361 f.; of brain, 138 f.; of eye, 147 f.; of eggs, 246 f.; 240, 250
Skate, respiration, 72, 78; electric organ, 165, 168; systematic position, 327; see also Ray
Skate barrow, 249
Skeleton, 90 f., 119 f.; of oceanic fishes, 135, 194
Skin, 52 f.; respiration through, 80; sense organs of, 144; as leather, 346
Skipper (*Scomberesox*), leaping, 46; green bones, 124; eggs, 251
Skull, 119 f., 311, 314 f.
Slat, see Kelt
Sleep, 157 f.
Sleeper Shark, see Greenland Shark
Slender File-fish (*Alutera scriptus*), mimicry, **184**
Smaller Devil-fish (*Mobula*), feeding, 90
Smallest fish, 361, **362**
Smell, sense of, 142 f.
Smelt (*Osmerus*), eggs, 251; systematic position, 329
Smoking, 343 f.
Smolt, 256
Smooth Hound (*Mustelus canis*), placenta, 253
Snake-head (*Ophiocephalus*), **83**; respiration, 83 f.
Snapper (Lutjanidae), 330
Snipe Eel (*Nemichthys*), **42**; form of body, 14; jaws, 97

Snipe-fish (*Macrorhamphosus*), scales, 62; systematic position, 329, 332
Snorter (*Caranx rhonchus*), 175
Snurrevaad, 341
Sockeye Salmon (*Oncorhynchus nerka*), 218
Soft-rays, 29, 34
Soft roe, 213
Soldier-fish (Berycidae), fins, 38; scale, 56; systematic position, 330, 332
Sole, fins, 38; sensory papillae, 60; mouth, feeding, 101; palatability, 126; nocturnal activity, 101, 158; mimicry, 189; spawning, 214; number of eggs, 215; systematic position, 331, 333
Solea, see Sole
Soleidae, 331; see Sole
Solenichthyes, 332; see Tube-mouth, Aulostomiformes
Solenostomidae, egg-pouch, 243
Soleoidei, 331
Somniosus, see Greenland Shark
Sordid Dragonet, 234
Sound (swimbladder), 133 f., 346
Sound-production, 172 f.
South American Cat-fish, **42**, **45**, 61; pectoral fin, 46, **37**; parental care, 242
South American fishes, 284 f.
South American Lung-fish (*Lepidosiren paradoxa*), **282**; external gills, 75, **77**, 258; lungs, **85** f.; aestivation, 206; breeding, 236; pelvic fins, 236; see also Lung-fish
South Temperate Zone, 272 f.
Sparidae, 330; see also Sea Bream
Spawning, 213 f.; mark, 68; migrations, 215 f., 275; times, 214
Spear, fishing with, 338
Spear-fish (*Makaira*), **10**; jaws, 97; vertebrae, 124; systematic position, 330, 332
Species, 319 f., number of, 5
Speed, 22
Spent Salmon, see Kelt
Spermatozoa, 213, 246, **247**
Sphyraena, see Barracuda
Sphyraenidae, 331, 333
Sphyrna, see Hammer-headed Shark
Spiegelkarpfen, see Mirror Carp
Spinachia, see Fifteen-spined Stickleback
Spinal cord, 138 f.
Spinal nerves, 140
Spines, 33 f.
Spiny Dog-fish (*Squalus*), 163; fin-

spines, 34; poison gland, 160; venom, 162; number of young, 252; development, **253**, 254 f.; systematic position, 327
Spiny Eels (Mastacembelidae), 286
Spiracle, **71**, 72, **73**
Spiral valve, **129** f., 314
Splashing Tetra (*Copeina arnoldi*), breeding habits, 225
Spleen, 128
Sponge-inhabiting Goby (*Evermannichthys*), 198
Spook-fish, see Californian Chimaera
Spoon-bill (*Polyodon*), scales, 56; snout, 93, **94**; ancestry, 308; see also Paddle-fish
Spotted Dog-fish (*Scyliorhinus*), **45**, **73**; gills, **71**; dermal denticles, **53**; mouth, **89**; jaws, 90 f.; skull, 90 f, 119 f.; embryonic teeth, **103**; incubation period, 252; egg-capsule, **248**
Spotted Eagle Ray (*Aetobatis*), teeth, 108; venom, 160
Sprat (*Clupea sprattus*), scales, 59; eggs, 250; incubation period, 256; canning, 345
Squalidae, fin-spines, 34; systematic position, 327
Squaliformes, 327
Squaloidei, 327, 331
Squalus, see Spiny Dog-fish
Square-tail (*Tetragonurus*), teeth, 117; systematic position, 330, 332
Squatina, Cretaceous form, 306; see Monk-fish
Squatinoidei, 327
Stalked eye, **146**, 147
Star-gazer (*Uranoscopus*), head, **94**; mouth, feeding, 94 f.; electric organs, 165, 166, 168; eyes, 148
Steering, 32 f.
Stenohaline, 132
Sterility, 264, 320
Stern-chaser, 170, 171
Stickleback, **35**, **61**; fin-spines, **35**, 49, 173; pelvic fin, 49; scutes, 61; food, 112; sound-production, 172; colour variation, 185; in salt and fresh water, 61 f, 132, 277; secondary sexual characters, 230; distribution, 277; breeding, 237; parasites, 357; 'rains' of, 367
Sting Ray (Dasyatidae), **42**; median fins, 33, 43; tail, 43; tail-spine, **53**, 54 f., 160; teeth, 108; poison gland, 160; venom, 162; in fresh water,

266; nutrition of embryo, 252; systematic position, 327
Stock-fish, 343
Stomach, 127
Stomiatoidei, 110; see also Wide-mouth
Stone Cat, 291; poison gland, 160; see also Mad Tom
Stone fish, see Poison fish
Stone Roller (*Campostoma*), intestine, 128
Streamline form, 7 f., 97
Stridulation, 172
Stromateidae, see Rudder-fish
Stromateoidei, teeth, 117; systematic position, 330, 332
Sturgeon (*Acipenser*), **61**; fins, 29, 30, **32**; scutes, scales, **56**; mouth, 93, **89**, 100; barbels, 93; skull, 120; vertebrae, 123; spiral valve, 130; larva, 259; ancestry, 308, 328; roe, 345; as royal fish, 345
Stygicola, see Cuban Blind-fish
Stylephorus, vertebrae, 124, **125**; mouth and feeding, 124
Suborder, **323**
Subspecies, 322
Succession of teeth, in Selachians, 102 f., in Bony Fishes, 109
Sucker, 39f., 49f.; of hill-stream fishes, 200
Sucker (Catostomidae), distribution, 291; systematic position, 329; parasites, 357
Sucking-fish, see Remora
Suez Canal, 271 f.
Sun-fish (Freshwater); see Freshwater Sun-fish
Sun-fish (Marine), **8**; form of body, **8**, 13 f.; skin, 14, 52; caudal fin, **32**, 44; teeth, 116; sound-production, 172; spinal cord, 139; distribution, 13; relationships, 13, 329; larva, **259** f.; systematic position, 329
Supramaxillary, 92
Supraneural, 123
Suprarenal bodies, 132
Surf-fish, (Embiotocidae), young, 254
Surgeon-fish (Teuthidae), spine, 64; sound-production, 172; systematic position, 330;
Swimbladder, functions, 133; gases, 134; development, 133; as a lung, 84 f.; and fin form, 33; origin and evolution, 86; as sound-producing organ, 173 f.; as hydrostatic organ, 133 f.; connection with ear, 151 f.;

in hill-stream fishes, 134, 202; in bathypelagic fishes, 135; isinglass, 346
Swimming, see locomotion
Sword-fish (*Xiphias*), **10**; speed, 22; denticles on sword, 56; jaws, 97; feeding, attacks on vessels, 22, 97 f.; vertebrae, 124; blood, 131; young, 261; antiquity, 310; systematic position, 330
Sword-tailed Minnow (*Xiphophorus*), 232
Symbiosis, 206 f.
Synanceia, **161**; see Poison-fish
Synanceidae, 330
Synaptura, see Sole
Synbranchoid, Eel, **83**, 14; see also Cuchia
Synentognathi, 332, see also Beloniformes, 329
Syngnathiformes, 329; see also Pipe-fish
Syngnathus, see Pipe-fish
Synodontis, reversed colours, **24**, 192
Synonym, 325
Systema Naturae, 324

Tail, shape and speed, 19; supposed breathing with, 80; of hill-stream fishes, 202; of Anaspids, 299 f.; see also caudal fin
Tail-rot, 354
Tail-spine, **53**, 54 f.
Tape Worm, 357
Tarpon (*Megalops*), **24**; leaping, 25; dorsal fin, 36; scales, **56**, 58
Taste, 143 f.
Taxonomy, 293, 318 f.
Teeth, 102 f.; of Crossopterygii, 311
Teleostei, 306, 310, 328
Telescopic eye, 147
Temperature, of blood, 131; effects of, 202 f.; on distribution, 267, 269 f.; on development, 255, 256
Ten-pounder (*Elops*), caudal fin, **32**; skull, **91**; larva, 262; ancestry, 310; systematic position, 310, 328
Ten-spined Stickleback (*Gasterosteus pungitius*), 250
Tench (*Tinca tinca*), effects of heat and cold, 203 f.; hibernation, 205; alleged healing powers, 363
Tertiary era, 295
Testis, **127**, 213
Tetragonurus, see Square-tail
Tetraodon, see Globe-fish, Puffer

Tetraodontidae, 329
Tetrapod, 312, 316
Teuthidae, see Surgeon-fish
Teuthidoidea, 332
Thalassophryne, see Poison Toad-fish
Thames, as a Salmon river, 218
Thelodonti, 297, 301
Thick-lipped Mojarra (*Cichlasoma lobochilus*), **94**
Third eye, 148 f.
Thorn hook, 338
Thornback Ray (*Raia clavata*), **12, 73, 228**; bucklers, **53**, 54; teeth, 108; sexual differences, 228
Thorn-headed Worm, 358
Thought, 159
Thread-fin (*Polynemus*), **45**; pectoral fin, 48;
Thread Worm, see Round Worm
Three-spined Stickleback (*Gasterosteus aculeatus*), **35, 61**; distribution, 61 f., 277; bony plates, 61 f.; secondary sexual characters, 230; breeding, 237; see also Stickleback
Thresher Shark (*Alopias*), **42**; feeding, 43, 106; systematic position, 327; see also Fox Shark
Thunder-fish, see Electric Cat-fish
Thunnus, 131; finlets, 39; see also Tunny
Thymallus, see Grayling
Thyroid, 132, 258
Tiddler, see Stickleback
Tiger Shark (*Galeocerdo*), teeth, 104, **105**; food, 105, 106; systematic position, 327
Tilapia grahami, salt and temperature tolerance, 203; *Tilapia* of Lake Galilee, 367 f.; in Lake Victoria, 292; *T. mossambica*, distribution, 291; see also Cichlid
Tile-fish (*Lopholatilus*), 204, **205**
Tinca, see Tench, Golden Tench
Tinning, see Canning
Titanichthys, 302
Toad-fish (*Porichthys*), luminous organs, 171; sound-production, 174; also called Singing Fish, and Singing Midshipman
Tobacco-pipe Fish, see Flute-mouth
Tongue, 88, 90, 127
Tongue Sole (*Cynoglossidae*), **66**; median fins, 38; sensory papillae, 60; lateral line, 67; mouth, 101; systematic position, 331
Tooth, see teeth
Top Minnow, see Cyprinodont
Tooth Carp, see Cyprinodont

Tope (*Eugaleus*), nictitating membrane, 145; number of young, 252; systematic position, 327
Topography, of fins, **11**
Tornado, in fish distribution, 366
Torpediniformes, 327
Torpedo (*Torpedo*), electric organ of, 165, **166** f.; systematic position, 327
Toxotes, see Archer-fish
Trabecula, 122
Trachinus, see Weever-fish; *T. draco*, see Greater Weever
Trachurus, see Horse Mackerel, Scad
Trachypteridae, 330; see also Ribbon-fish
Trachypterus, see Deal-fish
Transparent Goby (*Latrunculus pellucidus*), length of life, 363
Trawl, **339** f.
Trawler, **342**
Treatment of fish stings, 163 f.
Trematoda, see Fluke
Triassic period, **295**
Trichiuridae, see Cutlass-fish
Trichiuroidea, 332, see also Trichiuroidei, 330
Trichiurus, see Cutlass-fish, Hair-tail
Trigeminal nerve, 140
Trigger-fish (Balistidae), **63**; orgin of name, 39; dorsal fin, **37**, 39; pelvic fin, 49; scales, 64; teeth, 109, 116; sound-production, 172; colours, 189; systematic position, 330
Trigla, see Gurnard
Triglidae, 330
Tristan da Cunha, fishes, 273
Tritor, 109, **112**
Trivial name, 325
Trochlear nerve, 140
Trophonemata, 252
Tropical Zone, 269 f.
Trout (*Salmo trutta*), **73**; caudal fin, 43; scales, 66; lateral line, 66; swimming analysed, 16; nocturnal activity, 157 f.; colours, 184 f.; distribution, 278 f.; hybrids, 264; 'species,' 321; common names, 324; systematic position, 329; as food, 336; artificial propagation, 351; monstrosities, 358
Trout Perch (Percopsidae), 291
Truff, 324
Trumpet-fish (Fistularidae), teeth, 98; food and mouth, 98; systematic position, 329, 332
Trumpeter (*Latris*), pectoral fin, 48
Truncated Sun-fish (*Ranzania laevis*), larva, **259** f.

Trunk-fish (Ostraciontidae), **8**, **65**; form of body, 13; swimming, 18; scales, 64; noises, 174; colours, 189; systematic position, 329, 333
Trygon, see Sting Ray
Tube-mouth, 62, 98, 329
Tubercles, 59 f.; in Cyprinids, 225
Tunny (*Thunnus*), **45**; finlets, 39; caudal fin, 43; scales, 59; respiration, 77; flesh, 126; blood, 131; colours, 177; distribution, 267, 269; migrations, 275; fishery, 275; systematic position, 330, 332; canning, 344
Turbot (*Scophthalmus*), caudal fin, 43; tubercles, 59, **60**; pyloric caeca, 127; colours, 187; ambicoloration, 192; number of eggs, 215; size, 361
Twaite Shad (*Alosa fallax*), gill-rakers, **76**, 79; nomenclature, 326
Tylosurus, **94**; see Gar-fish
Typhlichthys, 196
Typhlogobius, see Californian Blind Goby

Ulcer disease, 353
Umbra, see Mud Minnow
Undina, calcified 'swimbladder', 313; tail fin, **312**; *U. penicillata*, **312**
Unicorn-fish, **61**
Upper pharyngeals, 109, **110**
Uranoscopus, see Star-gazer
Urenchelys, fins, 49
Urinary duct, 132
Urine, 132
Uterine villi, 252
Uterus, 252 f.
Utriculus, 149 f.

Vaca (*Hypoplectrus*), colour variation, 176
Vagus nerve, 140, 144
Vandellia, see Candiru
Variation, 320 f., 322
Variety, 322
Vascular system, **130** f.
Veil-tail Goldfish, **358**, 359
Vein, 131
Velifer, dorsal fin, **35**, 36; see also Sailbearer
Vendace (*Coregonus vandesius*), 279
Venom, 160 f.
Vent, 126, 130
Ventral aorta, 131
Ventral fin, see pelvic fin
Ventricle, of heart, 131; of brain, 136
'Ver blanc', 357

Vernacular names, 323 f.
Vertebral column, 122 f., **125**, **127**
Vesicle, of brain, 136
Vigneron-Dahl Trawl, 341
Visceral arches, 90, 119
Vision, 144 f., colour, 148
Vitamins, 335
Vitelline membrane, 250
Vitreous humour, 144
Vitrodentine, 53
Viviparous Blenny (*Zoarces viviparus*), **254**; dorsal fin, 34; number of young, 254;
Viviparous fishes, 247, 252 f.
Viviparous Perch (*Hysterocarpus traski*), **66**
'Voltage', of electric fishes, 167

Warning colour, 189
Water balance, 132
Waterspouts, in fish distribution, 281, 366
Weak-fish, see Meagre
Weberian mechanism, **152**
Weever (*Trachinus*), **161**; dorsal fin, 38; mouth, 94; poison gland, venom, 161, **162**; warning colours, 189
Wels (*Siluris*), **35**; dorsal fin, 96; food, 117 f; distribution, 289
West Africa, Marine fish fauna, 270 f.
Western Sea Trout, see Sewen
Westwind drift, 273
Whale, 2 f.
Whale Shark (*Rhincodon*), **262**; gill-rakers, 79; size, 361
Whitebait, 336
White-fish (*Coregonus*), distribution, 279 f.
White Goby, see Transparent Goby
White-spot disease, 354
Whiting (*Micromesistius merlangus*), 323; dorsal fin, 36; pyloric caeca, 127; colours, 191
Wide-mouth (Stomiatoidei), **195**; head, **112**, **143**; jaws, 95, 100 f.; teeth, 110; vertebrae, 124, **125**; luminous organs, 168; barbel, **143**
Winter sleep, see hibernation
Wolf-fish (*Anarrhichas*), teeth, food, 114; eggs, 250, 251; systematic position, 330; as food, 337
Wrasse (Labridae), locomotion, 21; mouth, 93, **99**, 100; pharyngeals, **110**; teeth, 113; nostrils, 142; sleeping, 157; nests, 240; systematic position, 330

Xanthochromism, 192
Xenocara occidentalis, **231**
Xenopterygii, 333, see also Gobieso-
coidei, 331
Xiphias, see Sword-fish
Xiphophorus, see Sword-tailed Minnow

Yellow Eel, 221, **222**, 263
Yolk, 246 f., 250, 252 f., 256
Yolk-sac, 252, **253**, 255
Young, colours, 178, 188

Zanclus, see Moorish Idol
Zebra hybrid of Trout, 264
Zeidae, 330
Zeiformes, 330
Zeomorphi, 332
Zeus, see John Dory
Zoarces, see Viviparous Blenny
Zoarcidae, distribution, 275
Zones, of distribution, 269 f.
Zoogeography, 266 f.

THIS BOOK TO BE RETURNED BY:

Printed by
Drukkerij Holland n.v., Amsterdam